W9-BYK-194

PRINCIPLES OF FRAUD EXAMINATION

PRINCIPLES OF FRAUD EXAMINATION

THIRD EDITION

JOSEPH T. WELLS, CFE, CPA

WILEY

JOHN WILEY & SONS, INC.

VICE PRESIDENT AND PUBLISHER   George Hoffman

ACQUISITIONS EDITOR   Michael McDonald

PROJECT EDITOR   Brian Kamins

EDITORIAL ASSISTANT   Jacqueline Kepping

MARKETING MANAGER   Ramona Sherman

SENIOR PRODUCTION MANAGER   Janis Soo

ASSISTANT PRODUCTION EDITOR   Annabelle Ang-Bok

DESIGNER   Wendy Lai

COVER PHOTO   ©Ian McKinnell/Getty Images, Inc.

This book was set in 10/12 Times Roman by LaserWords, Inc. and printed and bound by The Hamilton Printing Company. The cover was printed by The Hamilton Printing Company.

This book is printed on acid free paper.

Founded in 1807, John Wiley & Sons, Inc. has been a valued source of knowledge and understanding for more than 200 years, helping people around the world meet their needs and fulfill their aspirations. Our company is built on a foundation of principles that include responsibility to the communities we serve and where we live and work. In 2008, we launched a Corporate Citizenship Initiative, a global effort to address the environmental, social, economic, and ethical challenges we face in our business. Among the issues we are addressing are carbon impact, paper specifications and procurement, ethical conduct within our business and among our vendors, and community and charitable support. For more information, please visit our website: www.wiley.com/go/citizenship.

To order books or for customer service, please call 1-800-CALL WILEY (225-5945).

Library of Congress Cataloging-in-Publication Data

Wells, Joseph T.
   Principles of fraud examination / Joseph T. Wells. – 3rd ed.
      p. cm.
   Includes bibliographical references and index.
   ISBN 978-0-470-64629-8 (hardback)
1. Fraud. 2. Fraud investigation. 3. Fraud–Prevention. 4. Auditing, Internal. I. Title.
   HV6691.W46 2010
   657′.458–dc22

                                                     2010043301

Printed in the United States of America

10 9 8 7 6 5 4

To the memory of my father,
Coyle A. Wells (1906–1962),
and my mother,
Vola D. Wells (1910–1990).

FOREWORD

It is a pleasure to write the foreword for *Principles of Fraud Examination*, a book authored by my friend, Dr. Joseph T. Wells. I have known Joe for over twenty years. Most students, practitioners, and academics know him as the founder and chairman of the Association of Certified Fraud Examiners, but I know Joe as a friend, as one who has influenced my thinking, knowledge, and research about fraud, and as a person who is one of the most thorough, ambitious, and thoughtful fraud researchers I have ever met. And as you will see from reading this book, Dr. Wells is an excellent communicator who can make numerous fraud theories and schemes easy to understand.

Joe is a prolific writer. For several years, he authored a fraud-related article in nearly every issue of the *Journal of Accountancy*, and he has written many other books and articles. He has also written and produced more than a dozen fraud-related videos that are an integral part of nearly every accounting, auditing, and fraud curriculum in the United States. Dr. Wells' work has won numerous awards.

I believe that Joseph T. Wells has made a greater contribution to the prevention, detection, and investigation of fraud than any person in the world. Because of his work in fraud education and research and his vision in organizing the ACFE, tens of thousands of people have a better understanding of fraud and are working to reduce its cost and occurrence.

Principles of Fraud Examination provides an excellent description of the behavioral and social factors that motivate occupational offenders. It also provides an analysis and taxonomy of various kinds of frauds and cases that illustrate and help readers understand each type of fraud. The concepts described in the book are sound, based on the most extensive empirical research ever conducted on the subject. This book is a must-read for any student interested in the study of fraud.

Reading *Principles of Fraud Examination* will help you better understand the various ways that fraud and occupational abuse occur, thus helping you identify exposures to loss and appropriate prevention, detection, and investigation approaches. And, as you will see, the book is written in a way that will capture and hold your attention. The numerous fraud stories and personal insights provided by Joe will have you believing you are reading for enjoyment even as you are learning from one of the true master educators. I believe this book is destined to become one of the classic, definitive works on the subject of fraud.

W. Steve Albrecht, Ph.D.
Brigham Young University

PREFACE

The headline-grabbing accounting scandals of the past decade—Enron, WorldCom, Adelphia, Tyco, HealthSouth, and Satyam Computer Services, among others—would be reason enough to study the serious issue of fraud. But these methods are not new; they are merely variations of tried-and-true scams. Pliny the Elder first wrote of fraud over two thousand years ago when he described the adulteration of wine by crooked merchants in Rome. Since that time, fraud has become an increasingly serious issue; in the new millennium, it threatens the very underpinnings of our economy.

Accountants have historically had an important role in the detection and deterrence of fraud. But fraud, as you will read in the following pages, is much more than numbers. It involves complex human behaviors such as greed and deception, factors that are difficult to identify and quantify. In short, books and records don't commit fraud—people do.

Understanding why and how "ordinary" people engage in fraudulent behavior has been my life's work. Like many readers of this book, I began my professional career as an accountant. But after two years toiling in the ledgers of one of the large international accounting firms, I realized that auditing was not my forte. In search of adventure, I became a real-life, gun-toting FBI agent.

The truth is that I was more often armed with my Sharp QS-2130 calculator than my trusty Smith & Wesson Model 60 five-shot stainless-steel revolver. Sure, there were the occasional gun battles. But most of the time I was waging war against corporate titans and crooked politicians. In the decade I spent with the FBI, I learned a difficult and humbling lesson: my accounting education and training had not adequately prepared me to fight fraud.

But antifraud education has begun to change, little by little. To assist today's accounting students, *Principles of Fraud Examination* is written to provide a broad understanding of fraud—what it is and how it is committed, prevented, and resolved.

Understanding how fraud is committed is paramount to preventing and detecting it. I've learned that in the nearly thirty years since I carried a badge and gun. Beginning in the early 1980s, I offered fraud investigation services to major corporations. In 1988, I became the chairman of the Association of Certified Fraud Examiners, the world's largest antifraud organization—a position I still hold. In that capacity, I write, educate, and research fraud issues.

This work has its genesis in my fifth book, *Occupational Fraud and Abuse*, first published in 1997. At the time, I was intrigued by the definition of *fraud* as classically set forth in *Black's Law Dictionary*:

> *All multifarious means which human ingenuity can devise, and which are resorted to by one individual to get an advantage over another by false suggestions or suppression of the truth. It includes all surprise, trick, cunning or dissembling, and any unfair way which another is cheated.*

The definition implied to me that there was an almost unlimited number of ways people could think up to cheat one another. But my experience told me something else: after investigating and researching thousands of frauds, they seemed to fall into definite patterns. Determining what those patterns were, and in what frequency they occurred, would aid greatly in understanding and ultimately preventing fraud. And because so much fraud occurs in the workplace, this particular area would be the starting point.

So I began a research project with the aid of more than 2,000 Certified Fraud Examiners. CFEs typically work for organizations in which they are responsible for aspects of fraud detection and deterrence. Each CFE provided details on exactly how his organization was being victimized from within. That information was subsequently summarized in a document made available for public consumption, the *Report to the Nation on Occupational Fraud and Abuse*. The first *Report to the Nation* was issued in 1996. Since then, it has been updated five times, most recently in 2010.

Rather than an unlimited number of schemes, these reports have concluded that occupational fraud and abuse can be divided into three main categories: asset misappropriation, corruption, and fraudulent statements. From the three main categories, several distinct schemes were identified and classified; they are covered in detail herein.

Principles of Fraud Examination begins by providing an understanding of fraud examination methodology. Thereafter, it sets forth the schemes used by executives, managers, and employees to commit fraud against their organizations. Chapters are organized similarly. The major schemes are illustrated and detailed. Statistics are provided, and schemes flowcharted. Case studies are provided for each chapter. Prevention, detection, and investigation strategies are outlined. And lists of essential terms, review questions, and discussion issues help you understand and retain the material you have learned.

Today, commerce—and life—without the use of computers is nearly unimaginable. But regardless of our dependence on technology in the business world, computers are hardly necessary for carrying out occupational frauds; fictitious billing schemes committed through the use of accounting software could just as easily be accomplished using a manual bookkeeping system. As a result, the emphasis on computers in the following pages is in how they can be used to detect various frauds, not on how they can be used to commit them.

Writing this book is not a solo venture (though I accept responsibility for every word—right or wrong). I am deeply indebted to John Warren, JD, CFE; without his assistance, this undertaking would have been a nearly impossible task. John is responsible for major areas, including the statistical information and analysis, writing, and editing. Special thanks are also due to several key ACFE staffers who assisted me: John Gill, Andi McNeal, Dawn Taylor, Jeanette LeVie, Jim Ratley, and Jenny Rutherford. And for their assistance in helping prepare learning objectives, chapter summaries, essential terms, review questions, and discussion issues, I am indebted to Linda Chase, Scarlett Farr, Kristy Holtfreter, Robert Holtfreter, Bonita Peterson, Zabiollah Rezaee, Nazik Roufaiel, and Matthew Samuelson. Additionally, Mary-Jo Kranacher provided invaluable assistance through her work on Chapters 10, 11, 12, and 16.

Finally, I must thank my wife, Judy. During the time I have spent authoring what now total sixteen books, she has learned well that this endeavor is a solitary pursuit. Without her unconditional love, encouragement, and patience, these pages could not have been written.

Joseph T. Wells
Austin, Texas
July 2010

BRIEF CONTENTS

CONTENTS

PRINCIPLES OF FRAUD EXAMINATION

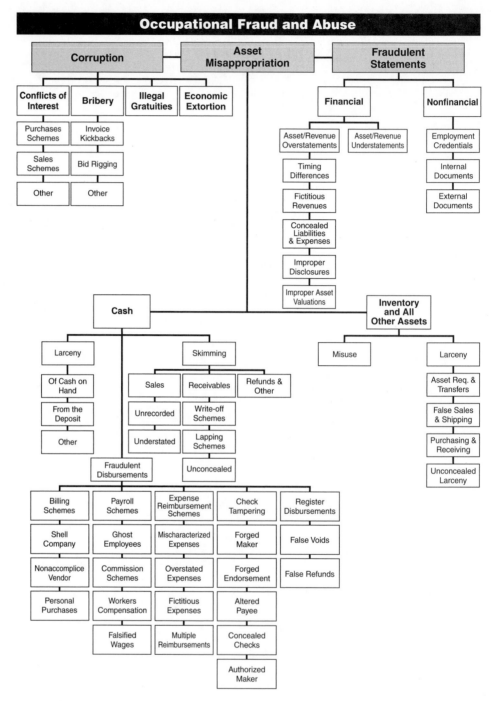

EXHIBIT 1-1

CHAPTER 1

INTRODUCTION

LEARNING OBJECTIVES

After studying this chapter, you should be able to:

1-1   Define fraud examination and differentiate it from auditing

1-2   Understand the fraud theory approach

1-3   Define occupational fraud

1-4   Define fraud

1-5   Define abuse

1-6   Know the difference between fraud and abuse

1-7   Describe the criminological contributions of Edwin H. Sutherland

1-8   Understand Donald Cressey's hypothesis

1-9   Give examples of nonshareable problems that contribute to fraud

1-10 Understand how perceived opportunity and rationalization contribute to fraud

1-11 Explain W. Steve Albrecht's "fraud scale"

1-12 Summarize the conclusions of the Hollinger-Clark study

1-13 Summarize the findings in the *2010 Report to the Nations on Occupational Fraud and Abuse*

Assume that you are an auditor for Bailey Books Corporation of St. Augustine, Florida. With $226 million in annual sales, Bailey Books is one of the country's leading producers of textbooks for the college and university market and of technical manuals for the medical and dental professions.

On January 28, you received a telephone call. The caller advised that he did not wish to disclose his identity. However, he claimed to have been a long-term supplier of paper products to Bailey Books. The caller said that since Linda Reed Collins took over as purchasing manager for Bailey Books several years ago, he was systematically squeezed out of doing business with the company. He hinted that he thought Collins was up to something illegal. You queried the caller for additional information, but he hung up. What do you do now?

This case is fictional, but the situation is a common one in the world of commerce. Organizations incur costs in order to produce and sell their products or services. And such costs run the gamut: labor, taxes, advertising, occupancy, raw materials, research and development—and yes, fraud and abuse. The last cost, however, is fundamentally different from the others—the true expense of fraud and abuse is hidden, even if it is reflected in the profit-and-loss figures. Sometimes these offenses can constitute multi-billion-dollar accounting misstatements, but much more frequently, they involve asset misappropriations or corruption, such as the fraud alluded to by the caller in the example above.

Resolving allegations of fraud—whether from tips, complaints, or accounting clues—is the discipline of *fraud examination*. It involves obtaining documentary evidence, interviewing witnesses and potential suspects, writing investigative reports, testifying to findings, and assisting in the general detection and prevention of fraud. Fraud examination has similarities to the field of *forensic accounting*, but the two terms are not precisely equivalent. Forensic accounting is the use of any accounting knowledge or skill for courtroom purposes, and can therefore involve not only fraud, but also bankruptcy, business valuations and disputes, divorce, and a host of other litigation support services. On the other hand, though fraud examinations are typically performed by accountants, they can also be conducted by professionals in other fields, such as law enforcement officials, corporate security specialists, or private investigators.

Similarly, fraud examination and auditing are related, but are not identical. Because most occupational frauds are financial crimes, a certain degree of auditing is necessarily involved. But a fraud examination encompasses much more than just the review of financial data; it also involves techniques such as interviews, statement analyses, public records searches, and forensic document examination. Furthermore, there are significant differences between the two disciplines in terms of their scopes, objectives, and underlying presumptions. The following table summarizes the differences between the two disciplines.

Auditing vs. Fraud Examination

Issue	Auditing	Fraud examination
Timing	**Recurring** Audits are conducted on a regular, recurring basis.	**Nonrecurring** Fraud examinations are nonrecurring. They are conducted only with sufficient predication.
Scope	**General** The audit is a general examination of financial data.	**Specific** Fraud examinations are conducted to resolve specific allegations.
Objective	**Opinion** An audit is generally conducted to express an opinion on financial statements or related information.	**Affix blame** The fraud examination determines whether fraud has occurred, and if so, who is responsible.
Relationship	**Nonadversarial** The audit process does not seek to affix blame.	**Adversarial** Fraud examinations involve efforts to affix blame.
Methodology	**Audit techniques** Audits are conducted primarily by examining financial data.	**Fraud examination techniques** Fraud examinations are conducted by (1) document examination, (2) review of outside data such as public records, and (3) interviews.
Presumption	**Professional skepticism** Auditors are required to approach audits with professional skepticism.	**Proof** Fraud examiners approach the resolution of a fraud by attempting to establish sufficient proof to support or refute an allegation of fraud.

FRAUD EXAMINATION METHODOLOGY

Fraud examination methodology requires that all fraud allegations be handled in a uniform, legal fashion, and that they be resolved in a timely manner. Assuming there is sufficient reason (predication) to conduct a fraud examination, specific steps are employed in a logical progression that is designed to narrow the focus of the inquiry from the general to the specific, eventually centering on a final conclusion. The fraud examiner begins by developing a hypothesis to explain how the alleged fraud was committed, and by whom. As each step of the fraud examination process uncovers more evidence, that hypothesis is amended and refined.

Predication

Predication is the totality of circumstances that would lead a reasonable, professionally trained, prudent individual to believe that a fraud has occurred, is occurring, or will occur. All fraud examinations must be based on proper predication; without it, a fraud examination should not be commenced. An anonymous tip or complaint, as in the Linda Reed Collins example cited earlier, is a common method for uncovering fraud; such a tip is generally considered sufficient predication. However, mere suspicion, without any underlying circumstantial evidence, is not a sufficient basis for conducting a fraud examination.

Fraud Theory Approach

In most occupational fraud cases, it is unlikely that there will be direct evidence of the crime. There are rarely eyewitnesses to a fraud, and—at least at the outset of an investigation—it is unlikely that the perpetrator will come right out and confess. Thus a successful fraud examination takes various sources of incomplete circumstantial evidence and assembles them into a solid, coherent structure that either proves or disproves the existence of the fraud.

To solve a fraud without complete evidence, the fraud examiner must make certain assumptions, not unlike a scientist who postulates a theory based on observation and then tests it. When investigating complex frauds, the fraud theory approach is almost indispensable. Fraud theory begins with an assumption, based on the known facts, of what might have occurred. That assumption is then tested to determine whether it can be proven. The fraud theory approach involves the following sequence of steps:

1. Analyze available data
2. Create a hypothesis
3. Test the hypothesis
4. Refine and amend the hypothesis

Let us illustrate using the Linda Reed Collins scenario. When you received the telephone call from a person purporting to be a vendor, you had no idea whether the information was legitimate. There could have been many reasons why a vendor would feel unfairly treated. Perhaps he just lost Bailey's business because another supplier provided inventory at a lower cost. Under the fraud theory approach, you must analyze the available data before developing a preliminary hypothesis about what may have occurred.

Analyzing Available Data If an audit of the entire purchasing function was deemed appropriate, it would be conducted at this time, and would specifically focus on the possibility of fraud resulting from the anonymous allegation. For example, a fraud examiner would look at how contracts are awarded and at the distribution of contracts among Bailey Books' suppliers.

Creating a Hypothesis Based on the caller's accusations, you would develop a hypothesis to focus your efforts. The hypothesis is invariably a "worst-case" scenario. That is, with the limited information you possess, what is the worst possible outcome? In this case, for Bailey Books, it would probably be that its purchasing manager was accepting kickbacks to steer business to a particular vendor. A hypothesis can be created for any specific allegation, such as a bribery or kickback scheme, embezzlement, a conflict of interest, or financial statement fraud.

Testing the Hypothesis After the hypothesis has been developed, it must be tested. This involves developing a "what-if" scenario and gathering evidence to either prove or disprove the proposition. For example, if a purchasing manager like Linda Reed Collins were being bribed, a fraud examiner likely would find some or all of the following:

- A personal relationship between Collins and a vendor
- Ability of Collins to steer business toward a favored vendor
- Higher prices or lower quality for the product or service being purchased
- Excessive personal spending by Collins

In the hypothetical case of Linda Reed Collins, you—using Bailey Books' own records—can readily establish whether one vendor is receiving a proportionally larger share of the business than other vendors. You can ascertain whether Bailey Books was paying too much for a particular product, such as paper, simply by calling other vendors and determining competitive pricing. Furthermore, purchasing managers don't usually accept offers of kickbacks from total strangers; a personal relationship between a suspected vendor and the buyer could be confirmed by discreet observation or inquiry. And whether Collins has the ability to steer business toward a favored vendor could be determined by reviewing the company's internal controls to ascertain who is involved in the decision-making process. Finally, the proceeds of illegal income are not normally hoarded; such money is typically spent. Collins's lifestyle and spending habits could be determined through examination of public documents such as real estate records and automobile liens.

Refining and Amending the Hypothesis In testing the hypothesis, a fraud examiner might find that the facts do not fit a particular scenario. If this is the case, the hypothesis should be revised and retested. Gradually, as the process is repeated and the hypotheses is continually revised, the examiner works toward the most likely and supportable conclusion. The goal is not to "pin" the crime on a particular individual, but rather to determine, through the methodical process of testing and revision, whether a crime has been committed—and if so, how.

Tools Used in Fraud Examinations

Three tools are available regardless of the nature of a fraud examination. First, the fraud examiner must be skilled in the examination of financial statements, books and records, and supporting documents. In many cases, these will provide the indicia of fraud upon which a complete investigation is based. The fraud examiner must also know the legal ramifications of evidence, and how to maintain the chain of custody over documents. For example, if it is determined that Linda Reed Collins was taking payoffs from a supplier, checks and other financial records to prove the case must be lawfully obtained and analyzed, and legally supportable conclusions must be drawn.

The second tool used by fraud examiners is the interview, which is the process of obtaining relevant information about the matter from those who have knowledge of it. For example, in developing information about Linda Reed Collins, it might be necessary to interview her coworkers, superiors, and subordinates.

In a fraud examination, evidence is usually gathered in a manner that moves from the general to the specific (see Exhibit 1-2). That rule applies both to gathering documentary evidence and to taking witness statements. Thus, a fraud examiner would most likely start by interviewing neutral third-party witnesses, persons who may have some knowledge about the fraud but who are not involved in the offense. Next, the fraud examiner would interview corroborative witnesses—those people who are not directly involved in the offense, but who may be able to corroborate specific facts related to the offense.

If, after interviewing neutral third-party witnesses and corroborative witnesses, it appears that further investigation is warranted, the fraud examiner proceeds by interviewing suspected co-conspirators in the alleged offense. These people are generally interviewed in a particular order, starting with those thought to be least culpable and proceeding to those thought to be most culpable. Only after suspected co-conspirators have been interviewed is the person who is suspected of committing the fraud confronted. By arranging interviews in order of probable culpability, the fraud examiner is in a position to have as much information as possible by the time the prime suspect is interviewed. The methodology for conducting interviews will be discussed in Chapter 15.

The third tool that must be used in a fraud examination is observation. Fraud examiners are often placed in a position in which they must observe behavior, search for displays of wealth, and, in some instances, observe specific offenses. For example, a fraud examiner might recommend a video surveillance if it is discovered that Linda Reed Collins has a meeting scheduled with a person suspected of making payoffs.

EXHIBIT 1-2 Evidence-Gathering Order in Fraud Examinations

Fraud examination methodology can be applied to virtually any type of fraud investigation. Although suspected frauds can be categorized by a number of different methods, they are usually referred to as "internal frauds" or "external frauds." The latter refers to offenses committed by individuals against other individuals (e.g., con schemes), by individuals against organizations (e.g., insurance fraud), or by organizations against individuals (e.g., consumer frauds), but the former refers to offenses committed by the people who work for organizations; these are the most costly and the most common frauds. A more descriptive term for these crimes, as we shall see, is *occupational fraud and abuse*. This book will concentrate exclusively on occupational fraud and abuse: how it is committed, how it is prevented, and how it is investigated.

DEFINING OCCUPATIONAL FRAUD AND ABUSE

For purposes of this book, *occupational fraud and abuse* is defined as

> *The use of one's occupation for personal enrichment through the deliberate misuse or misapplication of the employing organization's resources or assets.*[1]

This definition's breadth means that occupational fraud and abuse involves a wide variety of conduct by executives, employees, managers, and principals of organizations, ranging from sophisticated investment swindles to petty theft. Common violations include asset misappropriation, fraudulent statements, corruption, pilferage and petty theft, false over-time, use of company property for personal benefit, and payroll and sick time abuses. Four elements common to these schemes were first identified by the Association of Certified Fraud Examiners in its *1996 Report to the Nation on Occupational Fraud and Abuse*, which stated: "The key is that the activity (1) is clandestine, (2) violates the employee's fiduciary duties to the organization, (3) is committed for the purpose of direct or indirect financial benefit to the employee, and (4) costs the employing organization assets, revenues, or reserves."[2]

An "employee," in the context of this definition, is any person who receives regular and periodic compensation from an organization for his labor. The employee moniker is not restricted to the rank-and-file, but specifically includes corporate executives, company presidents, top and middle managers, and other workers.

Defining Fraud

In the broadest sense, fraud can encompass any crime for gain that uses deception as its principal modus operandi. Of the three ways to illegally relieve a victim of money—force, trickery, or larceny—all offenses that employ trickery are frauds. Since deception is the linchpin of fraud, we will include *Merriam-Webster's* synonyms: "'Deceive' implies imposing a false idea or belief that causes ignorance, bewilderment, or helplessness; 'mislead' implies a leading astray that may or may not be intentional; 'delude' implies deceiving so thoroughly as to obscure the truth; 'beguile' stresses the use of charm and persuasion in deceiving."[3]

Although all frauds involve some form of deception, not all deceptions are necessarily frauds. Under common law, four general elements that must be present for a fraud to exist:

1. A material false statement
2. Knowledge that the statement was false when it was uttered

3. Reliance of the victim on the false statement

4. Damages resulting from the victim's reliance on the false statement

The legal definition of fraud is the same whether the offense is criminal or civil; the difference is that criminal cases must meet a higher burden of proof.

Let's assume an employee who worked in the warehouse of a computer manufacturer stole valuable computer chips while no one was looking and resold them to a competitor. This conduct is certainly illegal, but what law has the employee broken? Has he committed fraud? The answer, of course, is that it depends. Let us briefly review the legal ramifications of the theft.

The legal term for stealing is *larceny*, which is defined as "felonious stealing, taking and carrying, leading, riding, or driving away with another's personal property, with the intent to convert it or to deprive the owner thereof."[4] In order to prove that a person has committed larceny, we would need to prove the following four elements: (1) There was a taking or carrying away (2) of the money or property of another (3) without the consent of the owner and (4) with the intent to deprive the owner of its use or possession. In our example, the employee definitely "carried away" his employer's property, and we can safely assume that this was done without the employer's consent. Furthermore, by taking the computer chips from the warehouse and selling them to a third party, the employee clearly demonstrated intent to deprive his employer of the ability to possess and use those chips. Therefore, the employee has committed larceny.

The employee might also be accused of having committed a tort known as *conversion*.[5] Conversion, in the legal sense, is "an unauthorized assumption and exercise of the right of ownership over goods or personal chattels belonging to another, to the alteration of their condition or the exclusion of the owner's rights."[6] A person commits a conversion when he takes possession of property that does not belong to him and thereby deprives the true owner of the property for any length of time. The employee in our example took possession of the computer chips when he stole them, and by selling them he has deprived his employer of that property. Therefore, the employee has also engaged in conversion of the company's property.

Furthermore, the act of stealing the computer chips also makes the employee an embezzler. According to *Black's Law Dictionary*, to *embezzle* means "willfully to take, or convert to one's own use, another's money or property of which the wrongdoer acquired possession lawfully, by reason of some office or employment or position of trust."[7] The key words in that definition are "acquired possession lawfully." In order for an embezzlement to occur, the person who stole the property must have been entitled to possession of the property at the time of the theft. Remember, "possession" is not the same thing as "ownership." In our example, the employee might be entitled to possess the company's computer chips (to assemble them, pack them, store them, etc.), but clearly the chips belong to the employer, not the employee. When the employee steals the chips, he has committed embezzlement.

We might also observe that some employees have a recognized fiduciary relationship with their employers under the law. The term *fiduciary*, according to *Black's Law Dictionary*, is of Roman origin and means:

> *a person holding a character analogous to a trustee, in respect to the trust and confidence involved in it and the scrupulous good faith and candor which it requires. A person is said to act in a 'fiduciary capacity' when the business which he transacts, or the money or property which he handles, is not for his own benefit, but for another person, as to whom he stands in a relation implying and necessitating great confidence and trust on the one part and a high degree of good faith on the other part.*[8]

In short, a fiduciary is someone who acts for the benefit of another.

A fiduciary has a duty to act in the best interests of the person whom he represents. When he violates this duty he can be liable under the tort of *breach of fiduciary duty*. The elements of this cause of action vary among jurisdictions, but in general they consist of the following: (1) a fiduciary relationship between the plaintiff and the defendant, (2) breach of the defendant's (fiduciary's) duty to the plaintiff, and (3) harm to the plaintiff or benefit to the fiduciary resulting from the breach. A fiduciary duty is a very high standard of conduct that is not lightly imposed on a person. The duty depends on the existence of a fiduciary relationship between the two parties. In an employment scenario, a fiduciary relationship will usually be found to exist only when the employee is "highly trusted" and enjoys a confidential or special relationship with the employer. Practically speaking, the law will generally recognize a fiduciary duty only for officers and directors of a company, not for ordinary employees. (In some cases a quasi-fiduciary duty may exist for employees who are in possession of trade secrets; they have a duty not to disclose that confidential information.) The upshot is that the employee in our example most likely would not owe a fiduciary duty to his employer, and therefore would not be liable for breach of fiduciary duty. However, if the example were changed so that an officer of the company stole a trade secret, then that tort would most likely apply.

But what about fraud? Recall that fraud always involves some form of deceit. If the employee in question simply walked out of the warehouse with a box of computer chips under his coat, this would not be fraud because there is no "deceit" involved. (Although many would consider this a deceitful act, what we're really talking about when we say *deceit*, as reflected in the elements of the offense, is some sort of material false statement upon which the victim relies.)

Suppose, however, that before he put the box of computer chips under his coat and walked out of the warehouse, the employee tried to cover his trail by falsifying the company's inventory records. Now the character of the crime has changed. Those records are a statement of the company's inventory levels, and the employee has knowingly falsified them. The records are certainly material because they are used to track the amount of inventory in the warehouse, and the company relies on them to determine how much inventory it has on hand, when it needs to order new inventory, and so forth. Furthermore, the company has suffered harm as a result of the falsehood, as it now has an inventory shortage of which it is unaware.

Thus, all the elements of fraud have now been satisfied: The employee has made a *material false statement;* the employee had *knowledge* that the statement was false, the company *relied* on the statement, and the company has suffered *damages*.

As a matter of law, the employee in question could be charged with a wide range of criminal and civil conduct: fraud, larceny, embezzlement, conversion, or breach of fiduciary duty. As a practical matter, he will probably be charged only with larceny. The point, however, is that occupational fraud always involves deceit, and acts that look like other forms of misconduct such as larceny may indeed involve some sort of fraud. Throughout this book we will study not only schemes that have been labeled "fraud" by courts and legislatures, but any acts of deceit by employees that fit our broader definition of occupational fraud and abuse.

Defining Abuse

Obviously, not all misconduct in the workplace amounts to fraud. There is a litany of abusive practices that plague organizations, causing lost dollars or resources but not actually constituting fraud. As any employer knows, it is hardly out of the ordinary for employees to:

- Use equipment belonging to the organization
- Surf the Internet while at work
- Attend to personal business during working hours
- Take a long lunch or break without approval
- Come to work late or leave early
- Use sick leave when not sick
- Do slow or sloppy work
- Use employee discounts to purchase goods for friends and relatives
- Work under the influence of alcohol or drugs

The term *abuse* has taken on a largely amorphous meaning over the years, frequently being used to describe any misconduct that does not fall into a clearly defined category of wrongdoing. *Merriam-Webster's* states that the word *abuse* comes from the Latin word *abusus*—to consume—and that it means "1. A corrupt practice or custom; 2. Improper or excessive use or treatment: misuse; 3. A deceitful act: deception."[9]

Given the commonality of the language describing both fraud and abuse, what are the key differences? An example illustrates: Suppose a teller was employed by a bank and stole $100 from his cash drawer. We would define that broadly as fraud. But if the teller earns $500 a week and falsely calls in sick one day, we might call that abuse—even though each has the exact same economic impact to the company—in this case, $100.

And of course, each offense requires a dishonest intent on the part of the employee to victimize the company. Look at the way each is typically handled within an organization, though: In the case of the embezzlement, the employee gets fired; there is also a possibility (albeit remote) that he will be prosecuted. But in the case in which the employee misuses sick time, the person perhaps gets reprimanded, or his pay might be docked for the day. In many instances there would be no repercussions at all.

But we can also change the "abuse" example slightly. Let's say the employee works for a governmental agency instead of in the private sector. Sick leave abuse—in its strictest interpretation—could be a fraud against the government. After all, the employee has made a false statement (about his ability to work) for financial gain (to keep from getting docked). Government agencies can and have prosecuted flagrant instances of sick leave abuse. Misuse of public money in any form can end up being a serious matter, and the prosecutorial thresholds can be surprisingly low.

Here is one real example: Many years ago I was a rookie FBI agent assigned to El Paso, Texas. That division covered the Fort Bliss military reservation, a sprawling desert complex. There were rumors that civilian employees of the military commissary were stealing inventory and selling it out the back door. The rumors turned out to be true, albeit slightly overstated. But we didn't know that at the time.

So around Thanksgiving, the FBI spent a day surveying the commissary's back entrance. We had made provisions for all contingencies—lots of personnel, secret vans, long-range cameras—the works. But the day produced only one measly illegal sale out the back door: several frozen turkeys and a large bag of yams. The purchaser of the stolen goods tipped his buddy $10 for merchandise valued at about $60. The offense occurred late in the day. We were bored and irritated, and we pounced on the purchaser as he exited the base, following him out the gate in a caravan of unmarked cars with red lights. The poor guy was shaking so badly that he wet his pants. I guess he knew better than we did what was at stake.

Because he did the wrong thing in the wrong place at the wrong time, our criminal paid dearly: He pled guilty to a charge of petty theft. So did his buddy at the commissary. The employee was fired. But the thief, it turned out, was a retired military colonel with a civilian job on the base—a person commonly known as a "double dipper." He was let go from a high-paying civilian job and now has a criminal record. But most expensively, he lost several hundred thousand dollars in potential government retirement benefits. Would the same person be prosecuted for petty theft today? It depends entirely on the circumstances. But it could, and does, happen.

The point here is that abuse is often a way to describe a variety of petty crimes and other counterproductive behavior that have become common, even silently condoned, in the workplace. The reasons employees engage in these abuses are varied and highly complex. Do abusive employees eventually turn into out-and-out thieves and criminals? In some instances, yes. We'll discuss that later. But next, we turn to some classic research into why so-called "good" employees turn bad. Although some of these studies are decades old, they are landmarks in the antifraud field.

RESEARCH IN OCCUPATIONAL FRAUD AND ABUSE

Edwin H. Sutherland

Considering its enormous impact, relatively little research has been done on the subject of occupational fraud and abuse. Much of the current literature is based on the early works of Edwin H. Sutherland (1883–1950), a criminologist at Indiana University. Sutherland was particularly interested in fraud committed by the elite upper-world business executive, whether against shareholders or against the public. As Gilbert Geis noted, Sutherland said, "General Motors does not have an inferiority complex, United States Steel does not suffer from an unresolved Oedipus problem, and the DuPonts do not desire to return to the womb. The assumption that an offender may have such pathological distortion of the intellect or the emotions seems to me absurd, and if it is absurd regarding the crimes of businessmen, it is equally absurd regarding the crimes of persons in the economic lower classes."[10]

For the uninitiated, Sutherland is to the world of white-collar criminality what Freud is to psychology. Indeed, it was Sutherland who coined the term *white-collar crime*, in 1939. He intended the definition to mean criminal acts of corporations and individuals acting in their corporate capacity, but since that time the term has come to mean almost any financial or economic crime, from the mailroom to the boardroom.

Many criminologists, myself included, believe that Sutherland's most important contribution to criminal literature lay elsewhere. Later in his career, Sutherland developed the "theory of differential association," which is now the most widely accepted theory of criminal behavior. Until Sutherland's landmark work in the 1930s, most criminologists and sociologists held the view that crime was genetically based: that criminals beget criminal offspring.

Although this argument may seem naive today, it was based largely on the observation of non-white-collar offenders—the murderers, rapists, sadists, and hooligans who plagued society. Numerous subsequent studies have indeed established a genetic base for "street" crime, which must be tempered by environmental considerations. (For a thorough explanation of the genetic base for criminality, see *Crime and Punishment* by Wilson and Herrnstein.) Sutherland was able to explain crime's environmental considerations through the theory of differential association. The theory's basic tenet is that crime is learned, much as are math, English, and guitar playing.[11]

Sutherland believed that learning of criminal behavior occurred with other persons in a process of communication. Therefore, he reasoned, criminality cannot occur without the assistance of other people. Sutherland further theorized that the learning of criminal activity usually occurred within intimate personal groups. This explains, in his view, how a dysfunctional parent is more likely to produce dysfunctional offspring. Sutherland believed that the learning process involved two specific areas: the techniques for committing crime and the attitudes, drives, rationalizations, and motives of the criminal mind. You can see how Sutherland's differential association theory fits with occupational offenders: dishonest employees will eventually infect a portion of honest ones, but honest employees will also eventually have an influence on some dishonest ones.

Donald R. Cressey

One of Sutherland's brightest students at Indiana University during the 1940s was Donald R. Cressey (1919–1987). Although much of Sutherland's research concentrated on upper-world criminality, Cressey took his own studies in a different direction. Working on his Ph.D. in criminology, he decided his dissertation would concentrate on embezzlers. To serve as a basis for his research, Cressey interviewed about 200 incarcerated inmates at prisons in the Midwest.

Cressey's Hypothesis Embezzlers, whom he called "trust violators," intrigued Cressey. He was especially interested in the circumstances that led them to be overcome by temptation. For that reason, he excluded from his research those employees who took their jobs for the purpose of stealing—a relatively minor number of offenders at that time. Upon completion of his interviews, he developed what still remains as the classic model for the occupational offender. His research was published in *Other People's Money: A Study in the Social Psychology of Embezzlement*.

Cressey's final hypothesis was:

> *Trusted persons become trust violators when they conceive of themselves as having a financial problem which is non-shareable, are aware this problem can be secretly resolved by violation of the position of financial trust, and are able to apply to their own conduct in that situation verbalizations which enable them to adjust their conceptions of themselves as trusted persons with their conceptions of themselves as users of the entrusted funds or property.*[12]

Over the years, the hypothesis has become better known as the "fraud triangle" (see Exhibit 1-3). The first leg of the triangle represents a *perceived nonshareable financial need*, the second leg represents *perceived opportunity*, and the third leg stands for *rationalization*.

Nonshareable Financial Problems The role of the nonshareable problem is important. As Cressey said, "When the trust violators were asked to explain why they refrained from violation of other positions of trust they might have held at previous times, or why they had not violated the subject position at an earlier time, those who had an opinion expressed the equivalent of one or more of the following quotations: (a) 'There was no need for it like there was this time.' (b) 'The idea never entered my head.' (c) 'I thought it was dishonest then, but this time it did not seem dishonest at first.'"[13]

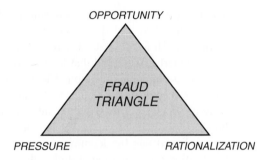

EXHIBIT 1-3 The Fraud Triangle

"In all cases of trust violation encountered, the violator considered that a financial problem which confronted him could not be shared with persons who, from a more objective point of view, probably could have aided in the solution of the problem."[14]

What is considered nonshareable is, of course, wholly in the eyes of the potential occupational offender, Cressey noted:

> *Thus a man could lose considerable money at the race track daily but the loss, even if it construed a problem for the individual, might not constitute a non-shareable problem for him. Another man might define the problem as one that must be kept secret and private, that is, as one which is non-shareable. Similarly, a failing bank or business might be considered by one person as presenting problems which must be shared with business associates and members of the community, while another person might conceive these problems as non-shareable.*[15]

In addition to being nonshareable, the problem that drives the fraudster is described as "financial" because these are the types of problems that generally can be solved by the theft of cash or other assets. A person saddled with large gambling debts, for instance, would need cash to pay those debts. Cressey noted, however, that some nonfinancial problems could be solved by misappropriating funds through a violation of trust. For example, a person who embezzles in order to get revenge on his employer for perceived "unfair" treatment uses financial means to solve what is essentially a nonfinancial problem.[16]

Through his research, Cressey also found that the nonshareable problems encountered by the people he interviewed arose from situations that fell into six basic categories:

1. Violation of ascribed obligations
2. Problems resulting from personal failure
3. Business reversals
4. Physical isolation
5. Status-gaining
6. Employer-employee relations

All of these situations dealt in some way with status-seeking or status-maintaining activities by the subjects.[17] In other words, the nonshareable problems threatened the status of the subjects, or threatened to prevent them from achieving a higher status than the one they occupied at the time of their violation.

Violation of Ascribed Obligations Violation of ascribed obligations has historically proved a strong motivator of financial crimes:

Financial problems incurred through non-financial violations of positions of trust often are considered as non-shareable by trusted persons since they represent a threat to the status which holding the position entails. Most individuals in positions of financial trust, and most employers of such individuals, consider that incumbency in such a position necessarily implies that, in addition to being honest, they should behave in certain ways and should refrain from participation in some other kinds of behavior.[18]

In other words, the mere fact that a person holds a trusted position carries with it the implied duty to act in a manner becoming that status. Persons in trusted positions may feel they are expected to avoid conduct such as gambling, drinking, drug use, or other activities that are considered seamy and undignified.

When these persons then fall into debt or incur large financial obligations as a result of conduct that is "beneath" them, they feel unable to share the problem with their peers, because this would require admitting that they have engaged in the dishonorable conduct that lies at the heart of their financial difficulties. By admitting that they had lost money through some disreputable act, they would be admitting—at least in their own minds—that they are unworthy to hold their trusted positions.

Problems Resulting from Personal Failure   Problems resulting from personal failure, Cressey writes, are those that a trusted person feels he caused through bad judgment, and for which he therefore feels personally responsible. Cressey cites one case in which an attorney lost his life's savings in a secret business venture. The business had been set up to compete with some of the attorney's clients, and though he thought his clients probably would have offered him help if they had known what dire straits he was in, he could not bring himself to tell them that he had secretly tried to compete with them. He also was unable to tell his wife that he'd squandered their savings. Instead, he sought to alleviate the problem by embezzling funds to cover his losses.[19]

While some pressing financial problems may be considered as having resulted from "economic conditions," "fate," or some other impersonal force, others are considered to have been created by the misguided or poorly planned activities of the individual trusted person. Because he fears a loss of status, the individual is afraid to admit to anyone who could alleviate the situation the fact that he has a problem which is a consequence of his "own bad judgment" or "own fault" or "own stupidity."[20]

In short, pride goeth before the fall. If a potential offender has a choice between covering his poor investment choices through a violation of trust or admitting that he is an unsophisticated investor, it is easy to see how some prideful people's judgment could be clouded.

Business Reversals   Business reversals were the third type of situation Cressey identified as leading to the perception of nonshareable financial problems. This category differs from the class of "personal failure" described above, because here the trust violators tend to see their problems as arising from conditions beyond their control: inflation, high interest rates, economic downturns, and so on. In other words, these problems are not caused by the subject's own failings, but rather by outside forces.

Cressey quoted the remarks of one businessman who borrowed money from a bank using fictitious collateral:

Case 36. "There are very few people who are able to walk away from a failing business. When the bridge is falling, almost everyone will run for a piece of timber. In business there is this eternal optimism that things will get better tomorrow. We get to working on the business, keeping it going, and we almost get mesmerized by it... Most of us don't know when to quit, when to say, 'This one has me licked. Here's one for the opposition.'"[21]

It is interesting to note that even in situations where the problem is perceived to be out of the trusted person's control, the issue of status still plays a big role in that person's decision to keep the problem a secret. The subject of Case 36 continued, "If I'd have walked away and let them all say, 'Well, he wasn't a success as a manager, he was a failure,' and took a job as a bookkeeper, or gone on the farm, I would have been all right. But I didn't want to do that."[22] The desire to maintain the appearance of success was a common theme in the cases involving business reversals.

Physical Isolation   The fourth category Cressey identified consisted of problems resulting from physical isolation. In these situations, the trusted person simply has no one to whom to turn. It's not that the person is afraid to share his problem, it's that he has no one with whom to share the problem. He is in a situation in which he has no access to trusted friends or associates who would otherwise be able to help. Cressey cited the subject of Case 106: a man who found himself in financial trouble after his wife had died. In her absence, he had no one to whom to go for help, and he wound up trying to solve his problem through an embezzlement scheme.[23]

Status Gaining   The fifth category involves problems relating to status-gaining, which is a sort of extreme example of "keeping up with the Joneses." In the categories previously discussed, the offenders were generally concerned with maintaining their status (i.e., with not admitting to failure, or with keeping up an appearance of trustworthiness), but here the offenders are motivated by a desire to *improve* their status. The motive for this type of conduct is often referred to as "living beyond one's means" or "lavish spending," but Cressey felt that these explanations did not get to the heart of the matter. The question was: What made the desire to improve one's status nonshareable? He noted:

> *The structuring of status ambitions as being non-shareable is not uncommon in our culture, and it again must be emphasized that the structuring of a situation as non-shareable is not alone the cause of trust violation. More specifically, in this type of case a problem appears when the individual realizes that he does not have the financial means necessary for continued association with persons on a desired status level, and this problem becomes non-shareable when he feels that he can neither renounce his aspirations for membership in the desired group nor obtain prestige symbols necessary to such membership.*[24]

In other words, it is not the desire for a better lifestyle that creates the nonshareable problem (we all want a better lifestyle); rather, it is the inability to obtain the finer things through legitimate means, and, at the same time, an unwillingness to settle for a lower status, that creates the motivation for trust violation.

Employer-Employee Relations   Finally, Cressey described problems resulting from employer-employee relationships. The most common situation, he stated, was that of an employed person who resents his status within the organization in which he is trusted, yet who at the same time feels that he has no choice but to continue working for the organization. The resentment can come from perceived economic inequities, such as inadequate pay, or from feeling overworked or underappreciated. Cressey said that this problem becomes nonshareable when the individual believes that making suggestions to alleviate his perceived maltreatment will possibly threaten his status in the organization.[25] There is also a strong motivator for the perceived employee to want to "get even" when he feels ill-treated.

The Importance of Solving the Problem in Secret   Cressey's study was done in the early 1950s, when the workforce was obviously different from that of today. But the employee faced with an immediate, nonshareable financial need hasn't changed much over the years. That employee is still placed in the position of having to find a way to relieve the pressure that bears down upon him. But simply stealing money is not enough; Cressey found that it was crucial that the employee be able to resolve the financial problem in secret. As we have seen, the nonshareable financial problems identified by Cressey all dealt in some way with questions of status; trust violators were afraid of losing the approval of those around them and thus were unable to tell others about the financial problems they encountered. If they could not share that they were under financial pressure, they would not be able to share the fact that they were resorting to illegal means to relieve that pressure. To do so would be to admit that the problems existed in the first place.

The interesting thing to note is that it is not the embezzlement itself that creates the need for secrecy in the perpetrator's mind, but the circumstances that led to the embezzlement (e.g., a violation of ascribed obligation, a business reversal). Cressey pointed out, "In all cases [in the study] there was a distinct feeling that, *because of activity prior to the defalcation*, the approval of groups important to the trusted person had been lost, or a distinct feeling that present group approval would be lost if certain activity were revealed [the nonshareable financial problem], with the result that the trusted person was effectively isolated from persons who could assist him in solving problems arising from that activity"[26] (emphasis added).

Perceived Opportunity   According to the fraud triangle model, the presence of a nonshareable financial problem will not by itself lead an employee to commit fraud. The key to understanding Cressey's theory is to remember that all three elements must be present for a trust violation to occur. The nonshareable financial problem creates the motive for the crime to be committed, but the employee must also perceive that he has an opportunity to commit the crime without being caught. This *perceived opportunity* constitutes the second element.

In Cressey's view, there were two components of the perceived opportunity to commit a trust violation: general information and technical skill. *General information* is simply the knowledge that the employee's position of trust could be violated. Such knowledge might come from hearing of other embezzlements, from seeing the dishonest behavior of other employees, or just from generally being aware of the fact that the employee is in a position in which he could take advantage of the employer's faith in him. *Technical skill* refers to the abilities needed to commit the violation. These are usually the same abilities that allowed the employee to obtain—and that allow him to keep—his position in the first place. Cressey noted that most embezzlers adhere to their occupational routines (and their job skills) in order to perpetrate their crimes.[27] In essence, the perpetrator's job will tend to define the type of fraud he will commit: "Accountants use checks which they have been entrusted to dispose of, sales clerks withhold receipts, bankers manipulate seldom-used accounts or withhold deposits, real estate men use deposits entrusted to them, and so on."[28]

Obviously, the general information and technical skill that Cressey identified are not unique to occupational offenders; most if not all employees have these same characteristics. But because trusted persons possess this information and skill, when they face a nonshareable financial problem they see it as something that they have the power to correct. They apply their understanding of the *possibility* for trust violation to the specific crises that face them. Cressey observed, "It is the next step which is significant to violation: the application of the general information to the specific situation, and conjointly, the perception of the fact that in addition to having general possibilities for violation, a specific position of trust can be used for the specific purpose of solving a non-shareable problem."[29]

Rationalizations The third and final factor in the fraud triangle is the *rationalization*. Cressey pointed out that the rationalization is not an *ex post facto* means of justifying a theft that has already occurred. Significantly, the rationalization is a necessary component of the crime *before* it takes place; in fact, it is a part of the motivation for the crime. Because the embezzler does not view himself as a criminal, he must justify the misdeeds before he ever commits them. The rationalization is necessary so that the perpetrator can make his illegal behavior intelligible to himself and maintain his concept of himself as a trusted person.[30]

After the criminal act has taken place, the rationalization will often be abandoned. This reflects the nature of us all: The first time we do something contrary to our morals, it bothers us. As we repeat the act, it becomes easier. One hallmark of occupational fraud and abuse offenders is that once the line is crossed, the illegal acts become more or less continuous. So an occupational fraudster might begin stealing with the thought, "I'll pay the money back," but after the initial theft is successful, he will usually continue to steal until there is no longer any realistic possibility of repaying the stolen funds.

Cressey found that the embezzlers he studied generally rationalized their crimes by viewing them (1) as essentially noncriminal, (2) as justified, or (3) as part of a general irresponsibility for which they were not completely accountable.[31] He also found that the rationalizations used by trust violators tended to be linked to their positions, and to the manner in which they committed their violations. He examined this by dividing the subjects of his study into three categories: *independent businessmen, long-term violators*, and *absconders*. He discovered that each group had its own types of rationalizations.

Independent Businessmen The *independent businessmen* in Cressey's study were persons in business for themselves who converted "deposits" that had been entrusted to them.[32] Perpetrators in this category tended to use one of two common excuses: (1) they were "borrowing" the money they converted, or (2) the funds entrusted to them were really theirs—and you can't *steal* from yourself. Cressey found the "borrowing" rationalization to be the one most frequently used. Such perpetrators also tended to espouse the idea that "everyone" in business misdirects deposits in some way, a fact that they considered would make their own misconduct less wrong than "stealing."[33] Also, the independent businessmen almost universally felt that their illegal actions were predicated by an "unusual situation" that Cressey perceived to actually be a nonshareable financial problem.

Long-Term Violators Cressey defined *long-term violators* as individuals who converted their employer's funds, or funds belonging to their employer's clients, by taking relatively small amounts over some duration of time.[34] Similar to independent businessmen, the long-term violators also generally preferred the "borrowing" rationalization. Other rationalizations of long-term violators were noted, too, but they almost always were used in connection with the "borrowing" theme: (1) they were embezzling to keep their families from shame, disgrace, or poverty, (2) theirs was a case of "necessity"—their employers were cheating them financially, or (3) their employers were dishonest toward others and deserved to be fleeced. Some even pointed out that it was more difficult to return the funds than to steal them in the first place, and claimed that they did not pay back their "borrowings" because they feared that would lead to detection of their thefts. A few in the study actually kept track of their thefts, but most did so only at the outset. Later, as the embezzlements escalated, it is assumed that the offender would rather not know the extent of his "borrowing."

All the long-term violators in the study expressed a feeling that they would like to eventually "clean the slate" and repay their debt. This feeling usually arose even before the perpetrators perceived that they might be caught. Cressey pointed out that at this point, whatever fear the perpetrators felt in relation to their crimes was related to losing their social position by the exposure of their nonshareable problem, not the exposure of the theft itself or the possibility of punishment or imprisonment; this was because their rationalizations still prevented them from perceiving their misconduct as criminal. "The trust violator cannot fear the treatment usually accorded criminals until he comes to look upon himself as a criminal."[35]

Eventually, most of the long-term violators finally realized they were "in too deep." It is at this point that an embezzler faces a crisis. While maintaining the borrowing rationalization (or whatever other rationalizations), the trust violator is able to maintain his self-image as a law-abiding citizen; but when the level of theft escalates to a certain point, the perpetrator is confronted with the idea that he is behaving in a criminal manner. This is contrary to his personal values, and to the values of the social groups to which he belongs. This conflict creates a great deal of anxiety for the perpetrator. A number of offenders described themselves as extremely nervous and upset, tense, and unhappy.[36]

Without the rationalization that they are borrowing, long-term offenders in the study found it difficult to reconcile stealing money with seeing themselves as honest and trustworthy. In such a situation, long-term offenders have two options: (1) they can readopt the attitudes of the (law-abiding) social group with which they identified with before the thefts began; or (2) they can adopt the attitudes of the new category of persons (criminals) with whom they now identify.[37] From his study, Cressey was able to cite examples of each type of behavior. Those who sought to readopt the attitudes of their law-abiding social groups "may report their behavior to the police or to their employer, quit taking funds or resolve to quit taking funds, speculate or gamble wildly in order to regain the amounts taken, or 'leave the field' by absconding or committing suicide."[38] On the other hand, those who adopt the attitudes of the group of criminals to which they now belong "may become reckless in their defalcations, taking larger amounts than formerly with less attempt to avoid detection and with no notion of repayment."[39]

Absconders   The third group of offenders Cressey discussed was *absconders*—people who take the money and run. Cressey found that the nonshareable problems for absconders usually resulted from physical isolation. He observed that these people "usually are unmarried or separated from their spouses, live in hotels or rooming houses, have few primary group associations of any sort, and own little property. Only one of the absconders interviewed had held a higher status position of trust, such as an accountant, business executive, or bookkeeper."[40] Cressey also found that the absconders tended to have lower occupational and socioeconomic status than the members of the other two categories.

Because absconders tended to lack strong social ties, Cressey found that almost any financial problem could be defined as nonshareable for these persons, and also that rationalizations were easily adopted because the persons had to sever only a minimum of social ties when they absconded.[41] The absconders rationalized their conduct by noting that their attempts to live honest lives had been futile (hence their low status). They also adopted an apathetic attitude about what happened to them, as well as a belief that they could not help themselves because they were predisposed to criminal behavior. The latter two rationalizations, which were adopted by every absconder in Cressey's study, allowed them to remove almost all personal accountability from their conduct.[42]

In the 1950s, when Cressey gathered this data, "embezzlers" were considered persons of higher socioeconomic status who took funds over a limited period of time because of some personal problem such as drinking or gambling, whereas "thieves" were considered persons of lower status who took whatever funds were at hand. Cressey noted,

"Since most absconders identify with the lower status group, they look upon themselves as belonging to a special class of thieves rather than trust violators. Just as long-term violators and independent businessmen do not at first consider the possibility of absconding with the funds, absconders do not consider the possibility of taking relatively small amounts of money over a period of time."[43]

Conjuncture of Events   One of the most fundamental observations of the Cressey study was that it took all three elements—perceived nonshareable financial problem, perceived opportunity, and the ability to rationalize—for the trust violation to occur. If any of the three elements were missing, trust violation did not occur.

> [A] trust violation takes place when the position of trust is viewed by the trusted person according to culturally provided knowledge about and rationalizations for using the entrusted funds for solving a non-shareable problem, and that the absence of any of these events will preclude violation. The three events make up the conditions under which trust violation occurs and the term "cause" may be applied to their conjuncture since trust violation is dependent on that conjuncture. Whenever the conjuncture of events occurs, trust violation results, and if the conjuncture does not take place there is no trust violation.[44]

Conclusion   Cressey's classic fraud triangle helps explain the nature of many—but not all—occupational offenders. For example, although academicians have tested his model, it still has not fully found its way into practice in terms of developing fraud prevention programs. Our sense tells us that one model—even Cressey's—will not fit all situations. Furthermore, the study is nearly half a century old; there has been considerable social change during the interim. Now, many antifraud professionals believe there is a new breed of occupational offender—one who simply lacks a conscience sufficient to overcome temptation (even Cressey saw the trend later in his life).

After his landmark study in embezzlement, Cressey went on to a distinguished academic career, eventually writing thirteen books as well as nearly 300 articles on criminology. He rose to the position of Professor Emeritus in Criminology at the University of California, Santa Barbara.

I was honored to know Cressey personally. Indeed, he and I collaborated extensively before he died in 1987, and his influence on my own antifraud theories has been significant. Our families are acquainted; we stayed in each other's homes, we traveled together—he was my friend. In a way, we made the odd couple: he the academic, me the businessman; he the theoretical, me the practical.

I met him as the result of an assignment, in about 1983, when a *Fortune* 500 company hired me on an investigative and consulting matter. They had a rather messy case of a high-level vice president who was put in charge of a large construction project for a new company plant. But the $75 million budget for which he was responsible proved too much of a temptation. Construction companies wined and dined the vice president, and eventually provided him with tempting and illegal bait: drugs and women. He bit.

From there, the vice president succumbed to full kickbacks. By the time the dust settled, he had secretly pocketed about $3.5 million. After completing the internal investigation for the company, assembling documentation and interviews, I worked with prosecutors, at the company's request, to put the perpetrator in prison. Then the company came to me with a very simple question: "Why did he do it?" As a former FBI agent with hundreds of fraud cases under my belt, I must admit I had not thought much about the motives of occupational offenders. To my mind, they committed these crimes simply because they were crooks. But the company—certainly progressive on the antifraud front for the time—wanted me to invest the resources required to find out why and how employees go bad, so that the company could do something to prevent it. This quest took me to the vast libraries of the University of Texas at Austin, which led me to Cressey's early research. After reading Cressey's book, I realized that he had described to a T the embezzlers I had encountered. I wanted to meet him.

Finding Cressey was easy enough. I made two phone calls and found that he was still alive, well, and teaching in Santa Barbara. He was in the telephone book—I called him. Immediately, he agreed to meet me the next time I came to California. That began what became a very close relationship between us that lasted until his untimely death in 1987. It was he who recognized the real value of combining the theorist with the practitioner; he used to proclaim that he learned as much from me as I from him. And in addition to Cressey's brilliance, he was one of the most gracious people I have ever met. Although we worked together professionally for only four years, we covered a lot of ground. Cressey was convinced there was a need for an organization devoted exclusively to fraud detection and deterrence. The Association of Certified Fraud Examiners, started about a year after his death, is in existence in large measure because of his vision. Moreover, although he didn't know it at the time, he created the concept of what eventually became the certified fraud examiner. Cressey theorized that it was time for a new type of "corporate cop"—one trained in detecting and deterring the crime of fraud. Cressey pointed out that the traditional policeman was ill equipped to deal with sophisticated financial crimes—as were traditional accountants. A hybrid professional was needed, someone trained not only in accounting, but also in investigation methods: someone as comfortable interviewing a suspect as reading a balance sheet. Thus was the certified fraud examiner program born.

Dr. W. Steve Albrecht

Another pioneer researcher in occupational fraud and abuse—and another person instrumental in the creation of the certified fraud examiner program—was Dr. Steve Albrecht of Brigham Young University. Unlike Cressey, Albrecht was educated as an accountant. Albrecht agreed with Cressey's vision: traditional accountants, he said, were poorly equipped to deal with complex financial crimes.

Albrecht's research contributions in fraud have been enormous. He and two of his colleagues, Keith Howe and Marshall Romney, conducted an analysis of 212 frauds in the early 1980s under a grant from the Institute of Internal Auditors Research Foundation, leading to their book *Deterring Fraud: The Internal Auditor's Perspective*.[45] The study's methodology involved obtaining demographics and background information on the frauds through the use of extensive questionnaires. The participants in the survey were internal auditors of companies that had experienced frauds.

Albrecht and his colleagues believed that taken as a group, occupational fraud perpetrators are hard to profile, and that fraud is difficult to predict. His research included an examination of comprehensive data sources to assemble a complete list of pressure, opportunity, and integrity variables, resulting in a list of fifty possible red flags or indicators of occupational fraud and abuse. These variables fell into two principle categories: perpetrator characteristics and organizational environment. The purpose of the study was to determine which of the red flags were most important to the commission (and thus to the detection and prevention) of fraud. The red flags ranged from unusually high personal debts and belief that one's job is in jeopardy to a lack of separation of asset custodial procedures and inadequate checking of potential employees' backgrounds.[46] Following is the complete list of occupational fraud red flags that Albrecht identified:[47]

Personal characteristics	Organizational environment
1. Unusually high personal debts	26. A department that lacks competent personnel
2. Severe personal financial losses	27. A department that does not enforce clear lines of authority and responsibility
3. Living beyond one's means	
4. Extensive involvement in speculative investments	28. A department that does not enforce proper procedures for authorization of transactions
5. Excessive gambling habits	
6. Alcohol problems	29. A department that lacks adequate documents and records
7. Drug problems	
8. Undue family or peer pressure to succeed	30. A department that is not frequently reviewed by internal auditors
9. Feeling of being underpaid	31. Lack of independent checks (other than internal auditor)
10. Dissatisfaction or frustration with job	
11. Feeling of insufficient recognition for job performance	32. No separation of custody of assets from the accounting for those assets
12. Continuous threats to quit	33. No separation of authorization of transactions from the custody of related assets
13. Overwhelming desire for personal gain	
14. Belief that job is in jeopardy	34. No separation of duties between accounting functions
15. Close associations with suppliers	
16. Close associations with customers	35. Inadequate physical security in the employee's department such as locks, safes, fences, gates, guards, etc.
17. Poor credit rating	
18. Consistent rationalization of poor performance	36. No explicit and uniform personnel policies
19. Wheeler-dealer attitude	37. Failure to maintain accurate personnel records of disciplinary actions
20. Lack of personal stability such as frequent job changes, changes in residence, etc.	
	38. Inadequate disclosures of personal investments and incomes
21. Intellectual challenge to "beat the system"	39. Operating on a crisis basis
22. Unreliable communications and reports	40. Inadequate attention to details
	41. Not operating under a budget
23. Criminal record	42. Lack of budget review or justification
24. Defendant in a civil suit (other than divorce)	43. Placing too much trust in key employees
25. Not taking vacations of more than two or three days	44. Unrealistic productivity expectations
	45. Pay levels not commensurate with the level of responsibility assigned
	46. Inadequate staffing
	47. Failure to discipline violators of company policy
	48. Not adequately informing employees about rules of discipline or codes of conduct within the firm
	49. Not requiring employees to complete conflict-of-interest questionnaires
	50. Not adequately checking background before employment

The researchers also gave participants both sets of twenty-five motivating factors and asked which factors were present in the frauds with which they had dealt. Participants were asked to rank these factors on a seven-point scale indicating the degree to which each factor existed in their specific frauds. The ten most highly ranked factors from the list of personal characteristics, based on this study, were:[48]

1. Living beyond their means
2. An overwhelming desire for personal gain
3. High personal debt
4. A close association with customers
5. Feeling pay was not commensurate with responsibility
6. A wheeler-dealer attitude
7. Strong challenge to beat the system
8. Excessive gambling habits
9. Undue family or peer pressure
10. No recognition for job performance

As you can see from the list, these motivators are very similar to the nonshareable financial problems Cressey identified.

Additionally, the ten most highly ranked factors from the list dealing with organizational environment were:[49]

1. Placing too much trust in key employees
2. Lack of proper procedures for authorization of transactions
3. Inadequate disclosures of personal investments and incomes
4. No separation of authorization of transactions from the custody of related assets
5. Lack of independent checks on performance
6. Inadequate attention to details
7. No separation of custody of assets from the accounting for those assets
8. No separation of duties between accounting functions
9. Lack of clear lines of authority and responsibility
10. Department that is not frequently reviewed by internal auditors

All the factors on this list affect employees' opportunity to commit fraud without being caught. Opportunity, as you will recall, was the second factor identified in Cressey's fraud triangle. In many ways, the study by Albrecht et al. supported Cressey's model. Like Cressey's study, the Albrecht study suggests that there are three factors involved in occupational frauds:

> *[I]t appears that three elements must be present for a fraud to be committed: a situational pressure (non-shareable financial pressure), a perceived opportunity to commit and conceal the dishonest act (a way to secretly resolve the dishonest act or the lack of deterrence by management), and some way to rationalize (verbalize) the act as either being inconsistent with one's personal level of integrity or justifiable.*[50]

The Fraud Scale   To illustrate this concept, Albrecht developed the "Fraud Scale," which included the components of: *situational pressures, perceived opportunities*, and *personal integrity*.[51] When situational pressures and perceived opportunities are high

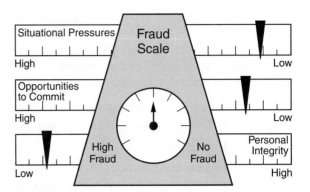

EXHIBIT 1-4   The Fraud Scale

and personal integrity is low, occupational fraud is much more likely to occur than when the opposite is true[52] (see Exhibit 1-4).

Albrecht described situational pressures as "the immediate problems individuals experience within their environments, the most overwhelming of which are probably high personal debts or financial losses."[53] Opportunities to commit fraud, Albrecht says, may be created by individuals, or by deficient or missing internal controls. Personal integrity "refers to the personal code of ethical behavior each person adopts. While this factor appears to be a straightforward determination of whether the person is honest or dishonest, moral development research indicates that the issue is more complex."[54]

In addition to its findings on motivating factors of occupational fraud, the Albrecht study also disclosed several interesting relationships between the perpetrators and the frauds they committed. For example, perpetrators of large frauds used the proceeds to purchase new homes, expensive automobiles, recreation property, and expensive vacations, to support extramarital relationships, and to make speculative investments. Those committing small frauds did not.[55]

There were other observations: Perpetrators who were interested primarily in "beating the system" committed larger frauds. However, perpetrators who believed their pay was not adequate committed primarily small frauds. Lack of segregation of responsibilities, placing undeserved trust in key employees, imposing unrealistic goals, and operating on a crisis basis were all pressures or weaknesses associated with large frauds. College graduates were less likely to spend the proceeds of their loot to take extravagant vacations, purchase recreational property, support extramarital relationships, and buy expensive automobiles. Finally, those with lower salaries were more likely to have a prior criminal record.[56]

Richard C. Hollinger

The Hollinger-Clark Study   In 1983, Richard C. Hollinger of Purdue University and John P. Clark of the University of Minnesota published federally funded research involving surveys of nearly 10,000 American workers. In their book, *Theft by Employees*, the two researchers reached a different conclusion than Cressey: They found that employees steal primarily as a result of workplace conditions. They also concluded that the true costs of employee theft are vastly understated: "In sum, when we take into consideration the incalculable social costs . . . the grand total paid for theft in the workplace is no doubt grossly underestimated by the available financial estimates."[57]

Hypotheses of Employee Theft   In reviewing the literature on employee theft, Hollinger and Clark noted that experts had developed five separate but interrelated sets of hypotheses to explain employee theft. The first was that external economic pressures, such as the "non-shareable financial problem" that Cressey described, motivated theft. The second hypothesis was that contemporary employees, specifically young ones, are not as hard-working and honest as those in past generations. The third theory, advocated primarily by those with years of experience in the security and investigative industry, was that every employee can be tempted to steal from his employer; this theory assumes that people are greedy and dishonest by nature. The fourth theory was that job dissatisfaction is the primary cause of employee theft, and the fifth was that theft occurs because of the broadly shared formal and informal structure of organizations: that is, over time, the group norms—good or bad—become the standard of conduct. The sum of Hollinger and Clark's research led them to conclude that the fourth hypothesis was correct—that employee deviance is primarily caused by job dissatisfaction.

Employee Deviance   Employee theft is at one extreme of employee deviance, which can be defined as conduct detrimental to the organization and to the employee. At the other extreme is counterproductive employee behavior, such as goldbricking and abuse of sick leave. Hollinger and Clark defined two basic categories of deviant behavior by employees: (1) acts by employees against property, and (2) violations of the norms regulating acceptable levels of production. The former includes misuse and theft of company property, such as of cash or inventory; the latter involves acts of employee deviance that affect productivity.

Hollinger and Clark developed a written questionnaire that was sent to employees in three different sectors: retail, hospital, and manufacturing. The employees were presented with lists of category 1 and category 2 offenses and were asked which offenses they had been involved in, and with what frequency. The researchers eventually received 9,175 valid employee questionnaires, representing about 54 percent of those sampled. Below are the results of the questionnaires. The first table represents category 1 offenses—acts against property.[58] Hollinger and Clark found that approximately one-third of employees in each sector admitted to committing some form of property deviance.

Combined Phase I and Phase II Property-Deviance Items and Percentage of Reported Involvement, by Sector

Items	Involvement				
	Almost daily	About once a week	Four to twelve times a year	One to three times a year	Total
Retail Sector (N = 3,567)					
Misuse the discount privilege	0.6	2.4	11	14.9	28.9
Take store merchandise	0.2	0.5	1.3	4.6	6.6
Get paid for more hours than were worked	0.2	0.4	1.2	4	5.8
Purposely under-ring a purchase	0.1	0.3	1.1	1.7	3.2
Borrow or take money from employer without approval	0.1	0.1	0.5	2	2.7
Be reimbursed for more money than spent on business expenses	0.1	0.2	0.5	1.3	2.1
Damage merchandise to buy it on discount	0	0.1	0.2	1	1.3
Total involved in property deviance					35.1

(*Continued*)

(*Continued*)

Items	Involvement				
	Almost daily	About once a week	Four to twelve times a year	One to three times a year	Total
Hospital Sector (N = 4,111)					
Take hospital supplies (e.g., linens, bandages)	0.2	0.8	8.4	17.9	27.3
Take or use medication intended for patients	0.1	0.3	1.9	5.5	7.8
Get paid for more hours than were worked	0.2	0.5	1.6	3.8	6.1
Take hospital equipment or tools	0.1	0.1	0.4	4.1	4.7
Be reimbursed for more money than spent on business expenses	0.1	0	0.2	0.8	1.1
Total involved in property deviance					33.3
Manufacturing Sector (N = 1,497)					
Take raw materials used in production	0.1	0.3	3.5	10.4	14.3
Get paid for more hours than were worked	0.2	0.5	2.9	5.6	9.2
Take company tools or equipment	0	0.1	1.1	7.5	8.7
Be reimbursed for more money than spent on business expenses	0.1	0.6	1.4	5.6	7.7
Take finished products	0	0	0.4	2.7	3.1
Take precious metals (e.g., platinum, gold)	0.1	0.1	0.5	1.1	1.8
Total involved in property deviance					28.4

Adapted from Richard C. Hollinger, John P. Clark, *Theft by Employees*, Lexington, MA: Lexington Books, 1983, p. 42.

Following is a summary of the Hollinger and Clark research with respect to production deviance. Not surprisingly, they found that this form of employee misconduct was two to three times more common than property violations.[59]

Combined Phase I and Phase II Property-Deviance Items and Percentage of Reported Involvement, by Sector

Items	Involvement				
	Almost daily	About once a week	Four to twelve times a year	One to three times a year	Total
Retail Sector (N = 3,567)					
Take a long lunch or break without approval	6.9	13.3	15.5	20.3	56
Come to work late or leave early	0.9	3.4	10.8	17.2	32.3
Use sick leave when not sick	0.1	0.1	3.5	13.4	17.1
Do slow or sloppy work	0.3	1.5	4.1	9.8	15.7
Work under the influence of alcohol or drugs	0.5	0.8	1.6	4.6	7.5
Total involved in production deviance					65.4

Hospital Sector (N = 4,111)					
Take a long lunch or break without approval	8.5	13.5	17.4	17.8	57.2
Come to work late or leave early	1	3.5	9.6	14.9	29
Use sick leave when not sick	0	0.2	5.7	26.9	32.8
Do slow or sloppy work	0.2	0.8	4.1	5.9	11
Work under the influence of alcohol or drugs	0.1	0.3	0.6	2.2	3.2
Total involved in production deviance					69.2
Manufacturing Sector (N = 1,497)					
Take a long lunch or break without approval	18	23.5	22	8.5	72
Use sick leave when not sick	0	0.2	9.6	28.6	38.4
Do slow or sloppy work	0.5	1.3	5.7	5	12.5
Work under the influence of alcohol or drugs	1.1	1.3	3.1	7.3	12.8
Come to work late or leave early	1.9	9	19.4	13.8	44.1
Total involved in production deviance					82.2

Adapted from Richard C. Hollinger, John P. Clark, *Theft by Employees*, Lexington, MA: Lexington Books, 1983, p. 45.

Income and Theft In order to empirically test whether economics had an effect on the level of theft, the researchers sorted their data by household income, under the theory that lower levels of income might produce higher levels of theft. However, they were unable to confirm such a statistical relationship. This would tend to indicate—at least in this study—that absolute income is not a predictor of employee theft.

Despite this finding, Hollinger and Clark were able to identify a statistical relationship between employees' *concern* over their financial situation and the level of theft. They presented the employees with a list of eight major concerns, ranging from personal health to education issues to financial problems. They noted, "Being concerned about finances and being under financial pressure are not necessarily the same. However, if a respondent considered his finances as one of the most important issues, that concern could be partially due to 'unshareable [*sic*] economic problems,' or it could also be that current realities are not matching one's financial aspirations regardless of the income presently being realized."[60] The researchers concluded, "In each industry, the results are significant, with higher theft individuals more likely to be concerned about their finances, particularly those who ranked finances as the first or second most important issue."[61]

Age and Theft Hollinger and Clark found in their research a direct correlation between age and the level of theft. "Few other variables... have exhibited such a strong relationship to theft as the age of the employee."[62] The reason, they concluded, was that the younger employee generally has less tenure with his organization and therefore has a lower level of commitment to it than the typical older employee. In addition, there is a long history of connection between youth and many forms of crime. Sociologists have suggested that the central process of control is determined by a person's "commitment to conformity." Under this model—assuming employees are all subject to the same deviant motives and opportunities—the probability of deviant involvement depends on the stakes that one has in conformity. Since younger employees tend to be less committed to the idea of conforming to established social rules and structures, it follows that they would be more likely to engage in illegal conduct that runs contrary to organizational and societal expectations.

The researchers suggested that the policy implications from the commitment to conformity theory are that rather than subjecting employees to draconian security measures, "companies should afford younger workers many of the same rights, fringes, and privileges of the tenured, older employees. In fact, by signaling to the younger employee that he is temporary or expendable, the organization inadvertently may be encouraging its own victimization by the very group of employees that is already least committed to the expressed goals and objectives of the owners and managers."[63] Although this may indeed affect the level of employee dissatisfaction, its policy implications may not be practical, for non-fraud-related reasons.

Position and Theft Hollinger and Clark were able to confirm a direct relationship between an employee's position and the level of the theft, with thefts being highest in jobs affording greater access to the things of value in the organization. Although they found obvious connections between opportunity and theft (for example, retail cashiers with daily access to cash had the highest incidence), the researchers believed opportunity to be "only a secondary factor that constrains the manner in which the deviance is manifested."[64] Their research indicated that job satisfaction was the primary motivator of employee theft; the employee's position affects the method and amount of the theft only *after* the decision to steal has already been made.

Job Satisfaction and Deviance The research of Hollinger and Clark strongly suggests that employees who are dissatisfied with their jobs—across all age groups, but especially younger workers—are the most likely to seek redress through counterproductive or illegal behavior in order to right the perceived "inequity." Other writers, notably anthropologist Gerald Mars and researcher David Altheide, have commented on this connection. Mars observed that among both hotel dining room employees and dock workers it was believed that pilferage was not theft; rather, it was "seen as a morally justified addition to wages; indeed, as an entitlement due from exploiting employers."[65] Altheide also documented that theft is often perceived by employees as a "way of getting back at the boss or supervisor."[66] Jason Ditton documented a pattern in U.S. industries called "wages in kind," in which employees "situated in structurally disadvantaged parts [of the organization] receive large segments of their wages invisibly."[67]

Organizational Controls and Deviance Hollinger and Clark were unable to document a strong relationship between control and deviance in their research. They examined five different control mechanisms: company policy, selection of personnel, inventory control, security, and punishment.

Company policy can be an effective control. Hollinger and Clark pointed out that companies with a strong policy against absenteeism have a lesser problem with it. As a result, they would expect policies governing employee theft to have the same impact. Similarly, they believed that employee education as an organizational policy has a deterrent effect. Control through selection of personnel is exerted by hiring persons who will conform to organizational expectations. Inventory control is required not only for theft, but for procedures to detect errors, avoid waste, and ensure that a proper amount of inventory is maintained. Security controls involve proactive and reactive measures, surveillance, internal investigations, and others. Control through punishment is designed to deter the specific individual, as well as others who might be tempted to act illegally.

Hollinger and Clark interviewed numerous employees in an attempt to determine their attitudes toward control. With respect to policy, they concluded, "The issue of theft by employees is a sensitive one in organizations and must be handled with some discretion. A concern for theft must be expressed without creating an atmosphere of distrust and paranoia. If an organization places too much stress on the topic, honest employees may feel unfairly suspected, resulting in lowered morale and higher turnover."[68]

Employees in the study also perceived, in general, that computerized inventory records added security and made theft more difficult. With respect to security control, the researchers discovered that the employees regarded the purpose of a security division as taking care of outside—rather than inside—security. Few of the employees were aware that security departments investigate employee theft, and most such departments had a poor image among the workers. With respect to punishment, the employees who were interviewed felt that theft would result in job termination in a worst-case scenario. They perceived that minor thefts would be handled only by reprimands.

Hollinger and Clark concluded that formal organizational controls provide both good and bad news. "The good news is that employee theft does seem to be susceptible to control efforts... Our data also indicate, however, that the impact of organizational controls is neither uniform nor very strong. In sum, formal organizational controls do negatively influence theft prevalence, but these effects must be understood in combination with the other factors influencing this phenomenon."[69]

Employee Perception of Control The researchers also examined the perception—not necessarily the reality—of employees who believed they would be caught if they committed theft: "We find that perceived certainty of detection is inversely related to employee theft for respondents in all three industry sectors—that is, the stronger the perception that theft would be detected, the less the likelihood that the employee would engage in deviant behavior."[70]

This finding is significant, and is consistent with other research. It suggests that increasing the perception of detection may be the best way to deter employee theft, whereas increasing the sanctions that are imposed on occupational fraudsters will have a limited effect. Recall that under Cressey's model, embezzlers are motivated to commit illegal acts because they face some financial problem that they cannot share with others because it would threaten their status. It follows that the greatest threat to the perpetrator would be that he might be caught in the act of stealing, which would bring his nonshareable problem out into the open; the possibility of sanctions is only a secondary concern. The perpetrator engages in the illegal conduct only because he perceives an opportunity to fix his financial problem *without getting caught*. Thus, if an organization can increase in its employees' minds the perception that illegal acts will be detected, it can significantly deter occupational fraud. Put simply, occupational fraudsters are not deterred by the threat of sanctions because they do not plan on getting caught.

Control in the workplace, according to Hollinger and Clark, consists of both formal and informal social controls. Formal controls can be described as external pressures that are applied through both positive and negative sanctions; informal controls consist of the internalization by the employee of the group norms of the organization. These researchers, along with a host of others, have concluded that—as a general proposition—informal social controls provide the best deterrent. "These data clearly indicate that the loss of respect among one's acquaintances was the single most effective variable in predicting future deviant involvement." Furthermore, "in general, the probability of suffering informal sanction is far more important than fear of formal sanctions in deterring deviant activity."[71] Again, this supports the notion that the greatest deterrent to the fraudster is the idea that he will be caught—not the threat of punishment by his employer.

Other Conclusions   Hollinger and Clark reached several other conclusions based on their work. First, they found that "substantially increasing the internal security presence does not seem to be appropriate, given the prevalence of the problem. In fact, doing so may make things worse."[72] Second, they concluded that the same kinds of employees who engage in other workplace deviance are also principally the ones who engage in employee theft. They found persuasive evidence that slow or sloppy workmanship, sick leave abuses, long coffee breaks, alcohol and drug use at work, late arrival, and early departure were more likely to be present in the employee-thief.

Third, the researchers hypothesized that if efforts are made to reduce employee theft without reducing its underlying causes (e.g., employee dissatisfaction, lack of ethics), the result could create a "hydraulic effect" whereby tightening controls over property deviance may create more detrimental acts affecting the productivity of the organization—for example, pushing down employee theft may push up goldbricking. Fourth, they asserted that increased management sensitivity to its employees would reduce all forms of workplace deviance. Fifth, they concluded that special attention should be afforded young employees, the ones statistically most likely to steal. However, it must be pointed out that although the incidence of theft is higher among younger employees, the losses associated with those thefts are typically lower than the losses caused by more senior employees, who have greater financial authority.

Hollinger and Clark asserted that management must pay attention to four aspects of policy development: (1) clearly understanding theft behavior, (2) continuously disseminating positive information reflective of the company's policies, (3) enforcing sanctions, and (4) publicizing sanctions.

The researchers summed up their observations by saying, "perhaps the most important overall policy implication that can be drawn . . . is that theft and workplace deviance are in large part a reflection of how management at all levels of the organization is perceived by the employee. Specifically, if the employee is permitted to conclude that his contribution to the workplace is not appreciated or that the organization does not seem to care about the theft of its property, we expect to find greater involvement. In conclusion, a lowered prevalence of employee theft may be one valuable consequence of a management team that is responsive to the current perceptions and attitudes of its workforce."[73]

The 2010 Report to the Nations on Occupational Fraud and Abuse

In 1993, the Association of Certified Fraud Examiners (ACFE) began a major study of occupational fraud cases with the goal of classifying occupational frauds and abuses by the methods used to commit them. There were other objectives, too. One was to get an idea of how the professionals—the certified fraud examiners (CFEs)—view the fraud problems faced by their own companies. After all, they deal with fraud and abuse on a daily basis. Another goal was to gather demographics on the perpetrators: How old are they? How well educated? What percentage of offenders are men? Were there any correlations that we could identify with respect to the offenders? What about the victim companies: How large were they? What industries did they cover? For good measure, the ACFE also decided to ask the CFEs to take an educated guess—based upon their experience—of the extent of fraud and abuse within their own organizations.

Beginning in 1993, the ACFE distributed a detailed four-page questionnaire to about 10,000 CFEs, asking them to report the details of one fraud case they had investigated. By early 1995, 2,608 surveys had been returned for analysis, including 1,509 usable cases of occupational fraud. Although the survey design was not perfect, the sheer number of responses made it—to the ACFE's knowledge—the largest such study on this subject at the time. Of the cases analyzed, the total loss caused by fraud was about $15 billion, ranging from a low of $22 to a high of $2.5 billion. From that survey, the ACFE developed in 1996 the first *Report to the Nation on Occupational Fraud and Abuse*. Association President Gil Geis decided that the name *Report to the Nation on Occupational Fraud and Abuse* was a bit long, so he alternatively titled it *The Wells Report*.

Since 1996, the ACFE has released five updated editions of the *Report*—in 2002, 2004, 2006, 2008, and the most recent version in 2010. Each edition has been based on detailed case information provided by CFEs and has built on the findings of its predecessors.

The ACFE's most recent survey was conducted in late 2009 and resulted in the *2010 Report to the Nations on Occupational Fraud and Abuse*, the first ACFE *Report* to include cases from countries outside the U.S. The current edition of the *Report* is based on 1,843 actual cases of occupational fraud that were investigated worldwide between January 2008 and December 2009. The CFEs who participated were asked to provide information on the single largest case they investigated during this time period; from this information, researchers were able to observe trends in and draw conclusions about how fraud is committed, how it can be classified, and how it affects business across the globe.

The majority of statistical data pertaining to the ACFE's research on occupational fraud that is cited in this book is derived from the results of the *2009 Global Fraud Survey*, as reported in the *2010 Report to the Nations on Occupational Fraud and Abuse*.

Measuring the Costs of Occupational Fraud   Participants in the *2009 Global Fraud Survey* were asked what percent of gross revenues they believe—based on their personal experience and general knowledge—the typical organization loses to fraud and abuse. The median response was 5 percent, a slight decrease from the 6 and 7 percent estimates provided by respondents in previous editions of the survey. Optimistically, this reduction could be viewed as progress in the war against fraud.

However, because the responses provided were only estimates, the data should not be read as a literal representation of the true rate of fraud in organizations throughout the world. Nevertheless, even at a rate of 5 percent, this estimate of the cost of fraud is astounding. Applying this figure to the Gross World Product—which, for 2009, was estimated to be $58.07 trillion[74]—results in a projected total global fraud loss of $2.9 trillion annually. It is a staggering sum, to say the least.

But what does the figure really mean? It is simply the collective opinions of those who work in the antifraud field. Unfortunately, finding the actual cost of fraud may not be possible by any method. One obvious approach would be to take a scientific poll of the workforce and ask them the tough questions: Have you stolen or committed fraud against your organization? If so, how? How much was the value of the fraud or abuse you committed? But the unlikelihood of people answering such questions candidly would make any results obtained by this method unreliable at best.

Another approach to finding the cost of fraud would be to do a scientific poll of a representative sample of organizations. Even assuming the respondents answered the poll correctly, there would still be an obvious flaw in the data: Organizations typically don't know when they are being victimized. And, of course, there is the definitional issue which plagues all the methods: Where do we draw the line on what constitutes occupational fraud and abuse? So asking the experts—the approach used here—may be as reliable as anything else. But the reader must be cautioned that, by any method of estimation, the numbers on fraud and abuse are soft and subject to various interpretations.

Whatever the actual costs, organizations are unwittingly paying them already as a part of their total operating expenses. Such is the insidious nature of fraud, and what to do? How can we possibly detect something we don't know about in the first place? It's as if a secret "fraud tax" has been levied on organizations. Interestingly, many organizations may silently condone fraud and abuse, which is committed from the top down. Indeed, some sociologists see abuse as an informal employment benefit and have even suggested that chronic pilferage and certain other abuses might actually have a positive effect on morale and therefore increase productivity.[75]

The Perpetrators of Fraud By definition, the perpetrators of occupational fraud are employed by the organization they defraud. Participants in the 2009 survey provided information on the perpetrators' position, gender, age, education, department, tenure, and criminal histories. In cases where there was more than one perpetrator, respondents were asked to provide data on the *principal perpetrator*, which was defined as the person who worked for the victim organization and who was the primary culprit.

The Effect of the Perpetrator's Position

Personal data gathered about the perpetrators indicated that most of the frauds in this study were committed by either employees (42 percent) or managers (41 percent). Owners/executives made up less than one-fifth of the perpetrators (see Exhibit 1-5).

Although the highest percentage of schemes was committed by employees, these frauds had the lowest median loss, at $80,000 per incident. Frauds committed by managers caused median losses of $200,000 per incident, while the median loss in schemes committed by owner/executives was $723,000—more than nine times higher than the typical loss in employee schemes. The differences in the loss amounts were most likely a result of the degree of financial control exercised at each level: Those with the highest positions also have the greatest access to company funds and assets (see Exhibit 1-6).

The Effect of Gender

The results of the *2009 Global Fraud Survey* showed that male employees caused median losses more than twice as large as those of female employees; the median loss in a scheme caused by a male employee was $232,000, while the median loss caused by a female employee was $100,000 (see Exhibit 1-7). The

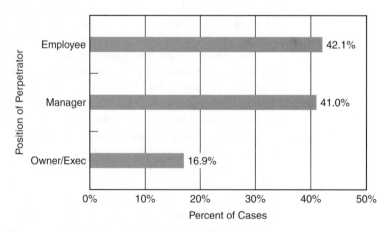

EXHIBIT 1-5 *2009 Global Fraud Survey*: Percent of Cases by Position

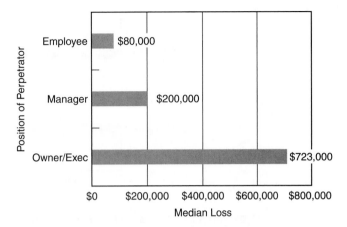

EXHIBIT 1-6 *2009 Global Fraud Survey*: Median Loss by Position

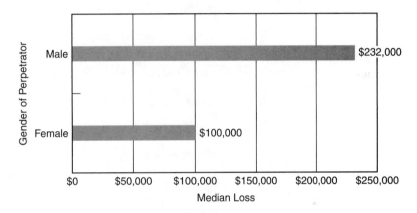

EXHIBIT 1-7 *2009 Global Fraud Survey*: Median Loss by Gender

most logical explanation for this disparity seems to be the "glass ceiling" phenomenon: generally, men occupy higher-paying positions than their female counterparts, and, as we have seen, there is a direct correlation between median loss and position.

According to survey data, males are also the principal perpetrator in a majority of cases, accounting for 67 percent of frauds in the study versus the 33 percent in which a female was the primary culprit (see Exhibit 1-8).

The Effect of Age The ACFE *Reports* continually reveal a direct and linear correlation between the perpetrator's age and median loss. The reason for the trend, ACFE researchers believe, is that those in an organization who are older generally tend to occupy higher-ranking positions with greater access to revenues, assets, and resources. In other words, researchers believe age to be only a secondary factor to that of position as a predictor of relative fraud losses.

As illustrated in Exhibit 1-9, those in the oldest age group were responsible for median losses almost sixty-five times higher than the youngest perpetrators. Furthermore, although some studies, including Hollinger-Clark, have suggested that younger employees are more likely to commit occupational crime, only 5 percent of the frauds in the study were committed by individuals below the age of twenty-six, while nearly half the frauds were committed by persons over the age of forty (see Exhibit 1-10).

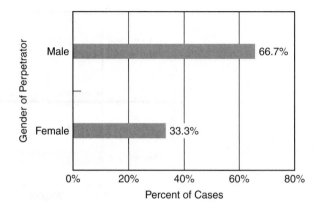

EXHIBIT 1-8   *2009 Global Fraud Survey*: Percent of Cases by Gender

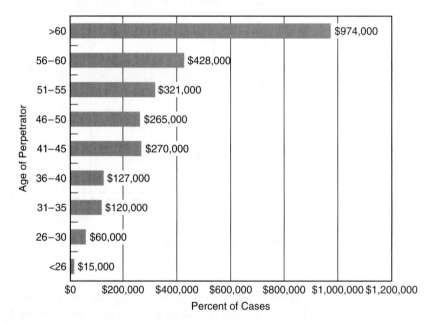

EXHIBIT 1-9   *2009 Global Fraud Survey*: Median Loss by Age

The Effect of Education   In general, those with higher education levels would be expected to occupy higher positions in an organization, and to have greater access to organizational assets. Therefore, researchers expected a fairly linear correlation between education and median loss. This was evident in the study, as shown in Exhibit 1-11. Fraudsters with only a high school education caused median losses of $100,000, but that figure more than doubled for perpetrators who had a college degree. The median loss caused by those with postgraduate degrees was $300,000 (see Exhibit 1-12).

The Effect of Collusion   It was not surprising to see that in cases involving more than one perpetrator, fraud losses rose substantially. The majority of survey cases (57 percent) only involved a single perpetrator, but when two or more persons conspired, the median loss more than tripled (see Exhibits 1-13 and 1-14).

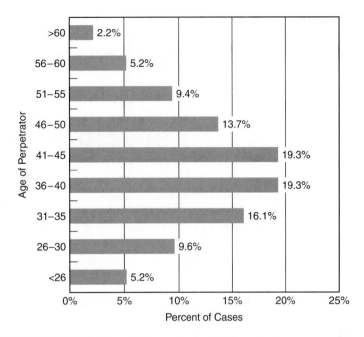

EXHIBIT 1-10   *2009 Global Fraud Survey*: Percent of Cases by Age

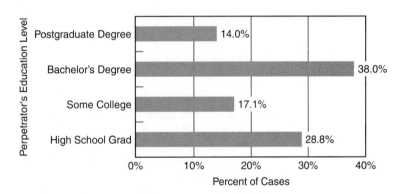

EXHIBIT 1-11   *2009 Global Fraud Survey*: Percent of Cases by Education

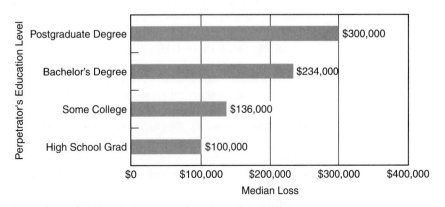

EXHIBIT 1-12   *2009 Global Fraud Survey*: Median Loss by Education

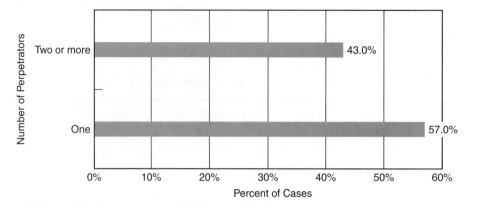

EXHIBIT 1-13 *2009 Global Fraud Survey*: Percent of Cases by Number of Perpetrators

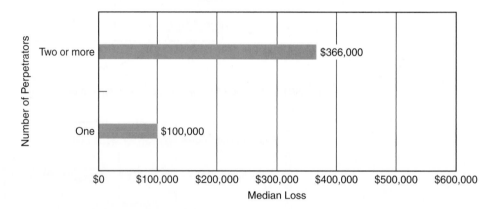

EXHIBIT 1-14 *2009 Global Fraud Survey*: Median Loss by Number of Perpetrators

The Perpetrator's Department Of the fraud cases studied, 22 percent were perpetrated by an employee in the accounting department. Further, 80 percent of all the frauds were committed by employees in six departments: accounting, operations, sales, executive/upper management, customer service, and purchasing (see Exhibit 1-15). The perpetrators holding the highest levels of autonomy and authority within the organization—those in executive/upper management roles and those on the board—caused the greatest losses to the victim organizations, at $829,000 and $800,000, respectively (see Exhibit 1-16).

The Effect of Tenure The results of the 2009 survey revealed a direct correlation between the length of time an employee had been employed by a victim organization and the size of the loss in the case. Employees who had been with the victim for ten years or more caused median losses of $289,000, whereas employees who had been with their employers for one year or less caused median losses of $47,000 (see Exhibit 1-17). Interestingly, Exhibit 1-18 shows that employees with tenure of one to five years were involved in the greatest percentage of fraud cases.

Criminal History of the Perpetrators Only approximately 7 percent of the perpetrators identified in the 2009 study were known to have been convicted of a previous

EXHIBIT 1-15   *2009 Global Fraud Survey*: Percent of Cases by Department of Perpetrator

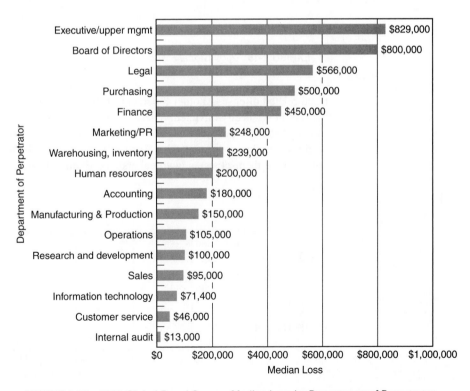

EXHIBIT 1-16   *2009 Global Fraud Survey*: Median Loss by Department of Perpetrator

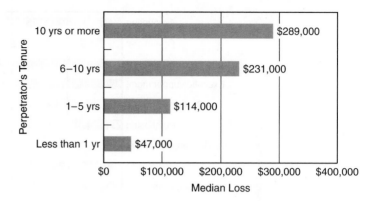

EXHIBIT 1-17 *2009 Global Fraud Survey*: Median Loss by Years of Tenure

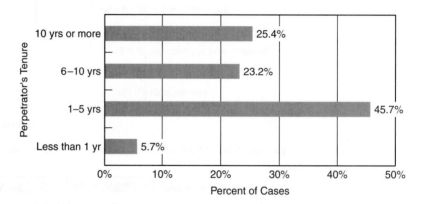

EXHIBIT 1-18 *2009 Global Fraud Survey*: Percent of Cases by Years of Tenure

fraud-related offense. Another 8 percent of the perpetrators had previously been charged, but had never been convicted. These figures are consistent with other studies that have shown that most people who commit occupational fraud are first-time offenders. The findings are also consistent with Cressey's model, in which occupational offenders do not perceive themselves as lawbreakers (see Exhibit 1-19).

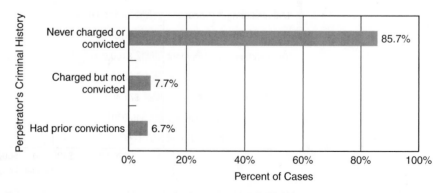

EXHIBIT 1-19 *2009 Global Fraud Survey*: Percent of Cases by Criminal History

The Victims The victims of occupational fraud are organizations who are defrauded by those they employ. The 2009 survey asked respondents to provide information on, among other things, the size and type of organizations that were victimized and the antifraud measures those organizations had in place at the time of the frauds.

Type of the Victim Organization Most of the cases reported in the *2009 Global Fraud Survey* involved victims that were privately held companies (42 percent), whereas not-for-profit organizations had the lowest representation (10 percent) (see Exhibit 1-20). It should be noted that researchers made no effort to obtain a random sample of business organizations. The *Report* was based on a survey of CFEs throughout the world; consequently, the demographics of the victim organizations in the study depended in large measure upon the organizations that retain CFEs.

The study revealed that privately held and publicly traded companies were not only the most heavily represented organization types, but they also suffered the largest losses, at $231,000 and $200,000, respectively. In comparison, losses in government ($100,000) and not-for-profit organizations ($90,000) were about half as much (see Exhibit 1-21).

Size of the Victim Organization Exhibit 1-22 shows the breakdown of victim organizations in our study based on their size (as measured by the number of employees). Over 30 percent of the cases in the study occurred in small organizations—those with fewer than 100 employees.

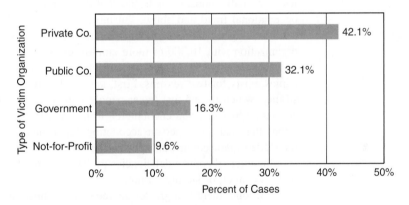

EXHIBIT 1-20 *2009 Global Fraud Survey*: Percent of Cases by Organization Type

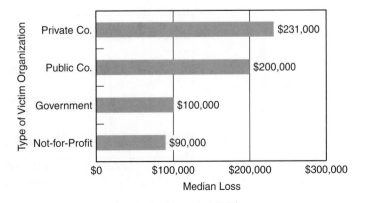

EXHIBIT 1-21 *2009 Global Fraud Survey*: Median Loss by Organization Type

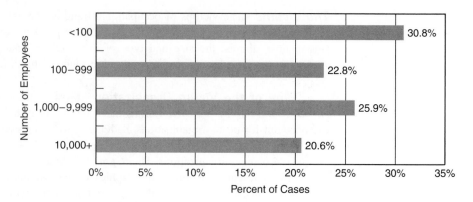

EXHIBIT 1-22 *2009 Global Fraud Survey*: Percent of Cases by Number of Employees

Organizations with 100 to 999 employees experienced the largest median loss ($200,000), whereas organizations employing 1,000 to 9,999 had the lowest median loss ($139,000). Interestingly, the organizations on either end of the size spectrum—those with fewer than 100 employees and those with 10,000 or more employees—had losses in the middle, at $155,000 and $164,000 respectively. Although the smallest organizations did not experience the largest median loss in absolute terms, the relative size of the median loss for small companies indicates that these entities are disproportionately vulnerable to occupational fraud and abuse. Put more simply, absorbing a $155,000 loss is typically a much bigger burden on a small company than absorbing a $164,000 loss is on an organization with 10,000 or more employees (see Exhibit 1-23).

Researchers theorize that the disproportionate nature of fraud losses at small companies exists for two reasons. First, smaller businesses have fewer divisions of responsibility, which means that fewer people must perform more functions. One of the most common types of fraud encountered in the ACFE studies involved small business operations that had a one-person accounting department—a single employee wrote checks, reconciled the accounts, and posted the books. An entry-level accounting student could spot the internal control deficiencies in that scenario, but apparently many small business owners cannot, or simply do not.

Second, there is a greater degree of trust inherent in a situation in which everyone knows each other by name and face. Who of us would like to think our coworkers

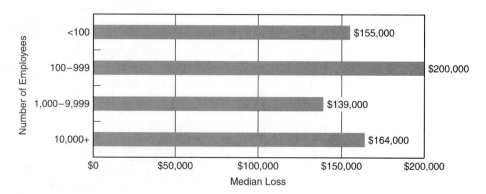

EXHIBIT 1-23 *2009 Global Fraud Survey*: Median Loss per Number of Employees

would, or do, commit these offenses? As a result, our defenses are naturally relaxed. There, again, is the dichotomy of fraud: It cannot occur without trust, but neither can commerce. Trust is an essential ingredient at all levels of business—we can and do make handshake deals every day. Transactions in capitalism simply cannot occur without trust. The key is seeking the right balance between too much trust and too little.

Antifraud Measures at the Victim Organization   CFEs who participated in the *2009 Global Fraud Survey* were asked to identify which, if any, of fifteen common antifraud measures were utilized by the victim organizations at the time the reported frauds occurred. More than three-quarters of the victim organizations had their financial statements audited by external auditors, whereas two-thirds had dedicated internal audit or fraud examination departments, and almost 60 percent had independent audits of their internal controls over financial reporting. Additionally, nearly 70 percent of the organizations had a formal code of conduct in place at the time of the fraud, though only 39 percent extended that to include a formal antifraud policy (see Exhibit 1-24).

To examine the effectiveness of these common antifraud controls, researchers also compared by those organizations that had a particular antifraud control in place against the median loss for those organizations without that control at the time of the fraud (excluding all other factors). The results indicate that hotlines, employee support programs, and surprise audits were the mechanisms most associated with a reduced cost of fraud. Organizations without these mechanisms in place reported frauds that cost more than twice as much as those in organizations that had any one of these mechanisms in place at the time of the fraud. Conversely, external audits—the most common antifraud measure utilized by victim organizations—showed the second lowest impact on median losses in the ACFE study (see Exhibit 1-25).

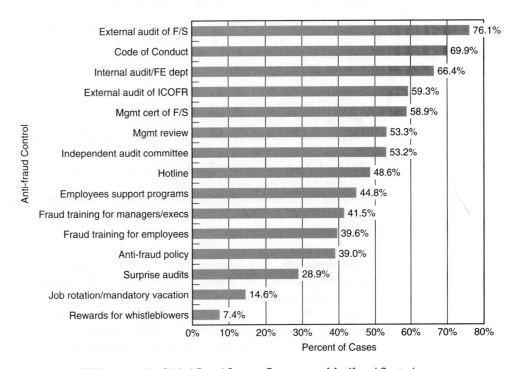

EXHIBIT 1-24   *2009 Global Fraud Survey*: Frequency of Antifraud Controls

	% of cases implemented	Yes	No	% Reduction
Hotline	48.6%	$100,000	$245,000	59.2%
Employee support programs	44.8%	$100,000	$244,000	59.0%
Surprise audits	28.9%	$ 97,000	$200,000	51.5%
Fraud training for employees	39.6%	$100,000	$200,000	50.0%
Fraud training for managers/ executives	41.5%	$100,000	$200,000	50.0%
Job rotation/mandatory vacation	14.6%	$100,000	$188,000	46.8%
Code of conduct	69.9%	$140,000	$262,000	46.6%
Antifraud policy	39.0%	$120,000	$200,000	40.0%
Management review	53.3%	$120,000	$200,000	40.0%
External audit of ICOFR	59.3%	$140,000	$215,000	34.9%
Internal audit/FE department	66.4%	$145,000	$209,000	30.6%
Independent audit committee	53.2%	$140,000	$200,000	30.0%
Management certification of F/S	58.9%	$150,000	$200,000	25.0%
External audit of F/S	76.1%	$150,000	$200,000	25.0%
Rewards for whistleblowers	7.4%	$119,000	$155,000	23.2%

EXHIBIT 1-25   *2009 Global Fraud Survey*: Impact of Antifraud Measures on Median Loss

Detecting and Preventing Occupational Fraud

Initial Detection of Frauds   The obvious question in a study of occupational fraud is: What can be done about it? Given that the ACFE study was based on actual fraud cases that had been investigated, researchers thought it would be instructional to ask how these frauds were initially detected by the victim organizations. Perhaps by studying how the victim organizations had uncovered fraud, researchers would be able to provide guidance to other organizations on how to tailor their fraud-detection efforts. Respondents were given a list of common detection methods and were asked how the frauds they investigated were initially detected. As illustrated in Exhibit 1-26, the frauds in the study were most commonly detected by tip (40 percent). Unfortunately, as shown earlier, in Exhibit 1-24, the majority of fraud victims did not have established reporting structures in place at the time they were defrauded. It is also interesting—and rather disconcerting—to note that accident was the fourth-most common detection method, accounting for 8 percent of the fraud cases in the survey, while external audits detected less than 5 percent of the reported frauds.

The Methods   The principal goal of the first *Report to the Nation* was to classify occupational frauds and abuses by the methods used to commit them. As a result of the 1996 study, researchers were able to develop a classification system known informally as the *fraud tree* (see page 2, Exhibit 1-1) that accounts for most, if not all, of the most common occupational fraud and abuse schemes. Researchers tested the structure of the fraud tree against the cases in all subsequent ACFE surveys to make sure that

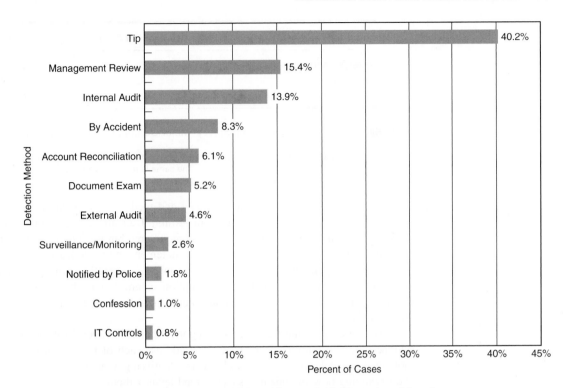

EXHIBIT 1-26 *2009 Global Fraud Survey*: Initial Detection of Frauds

the classification system accounted for every scheme that was reported. Among the six studies, ACFE researchers have applied the fraud tree classification system to more than 6,400 cases of fraud and have found that it has covered them all.

By classifying and categorizing occupational frauds, the researchers are able to study these crimes in more detail. Instead of lumping every case under the general heading of "fraud," researchers observe discrete groups of frauds with similar characteristics in order to learn what methods are most commonly used to commit occupational fraud and what schemes tend to cause the biggest losses. Also, by comparing schemes in well-defined categories, researchers can identify common methods used by the perpetrators as well as common vulnerabilities in the victim organizations that allow such frauds to succeed. This, in turn, should help in the development of better, more efficient antifraud tools.

According to the fraud tree, there are three major categories of occupational fraud:

1. *Asset misappropriations*, which involve the theft or misuse of an organization's assets. (Common examples include skimming revenues, stealing inventory, and payroll fraud.)

2. *Corruption*, in which fraudsters wrongfully use their influence in a business transaction in order to procure some benefit for themselves or another person, contrary to their duty to their employer or the rights of another. (Common examples include accepting kickbacks and entering into conflicts of interest.)

3. *Fraudulent statements*, which involve purposeful misreporting of financial information about the organization with the intent to mislead those who rely on it. (Common examples include overstating revenues and understating liabilities or expenses.)

	Percent of Cases[a]	Median Cost
Asset Misappropriations	86.3	$135,000
Corruption Schemes	32.8	$250,000
Fraudulent Statements	4.8	$4,100,000

EXHIBIT 1-27   *2009 Global Fraud Survey*: Major Occupational Fraud Categories

[a]The sum of percentages listed in this column exceeds 100 percent because some cases involved fraud schemes that fell into more than one category. The same is true for every scheme classification chart in this book that is based on the *2009 Global Fraud Survey*.

The data from the study on frequency and median loss for the three major occupational fraud categories are presented in Exhibit 1-27 above. Asset misappropriations made up more than 85 percent of the cases encountered but were by far the least costly in terms of median loss. Meanwhile, fraudulent statements were the least common, accounting for only 5 percent of cases, but they caused far greater harm, on average, than schemes in the other two categories. Corruption schemes were the "middle children" of the study; they were more common than fraudulent statements and more costly than asset misappropriations.

Within each of the three major categories there are several subcategories of fraud scheme types. In coming chapters we will address each of these subcategories in turn, looking at research on their costs and effects, identifying how the schemes are committed, and discussing how organizations can defend against them.

SUMMARY

This chapter defines the field of fraud examination, gives an overview of fraud and abuse, and points out the differences between the two terms. It also describes various criminological theories as to why "ordinary" people engage in these illegal behaviors. Included are Sutherland's *theory of differential association*, which argues that criminal behavior and attitudes toward crime are learned from family and peers; Cressey's *fraud triangle*, which explains fraud as a result of the conjunction of a nonshareable financial problem, perceived opportunity, and rationalization; Albrecht's *fraud scale*, which contends that committing fraud is the interaction of situational pressures, opportunities, and personal integrity; and the *Hollinger-Clark Study*, which hypothesizes that occupational fraud is primarily caused by workplace dissatisfaction. The chapter concludes by providing the resulting data from the Association of Certified Fraud Examiners' *2009 Global Fraud Survey*, which demonstrates that losses from fraud are affected by such factors as the perpetrator's position and tenure, the size of the victim organization, and the antifraud controls that the victim had in place at the time of the fraud.

ESSENTIAL TERMS

Fraud examination A process of resolving allegations of fraud from inception to disposition. It involves not only financial analysis, but also taking statements, interviewing witnesses, writing reports, testifying to findings, and assisting in the detection and prevention of fraud.

Fraud theory approach The methodology used to investigate allegations of fraud. It involves developing a theory based on a worst-case scenario of what fraud scheme could have occurred, then testing the theory to see if it is correct.

Occupational fraud and abuse The use of one's occupation for personal enrichment through the deliberate misuse or misapplication of the employing organization's resources or assets.

Fraud Any crime for gain that uses deception as its principal modus operandi. There are four legal elements that must be present: (1) a material false statement, (2) knowledge that the statement was false when it was uttered, (3) reliance on the false statement by the victim, and (4) damages as a result.

Abuse Petty crimes committed against organizations, such as taking excessively long lunch hours or breaks, coming to work late or leaving early, using sick time when not sick, and pilfering supplies or products.

Fiduciary relationship In business, the trusting relationship that the employee is expected to hold toward the employer, requiring the employee's scrupulous good faith to act in the employer's best interests.

Conversion The unauthorized assumption of a right of ownership over the goods of another to the exclusion of the owner's rights. When an employee steals company assets, he is converting the use of them.

Larceny The unlawful taking and carrying away of property of another with the intent to convert it to one's own use.

White-collar crime Coined by Edwin Sutherland, originally defined as criminal acts only of corporations and of individuals acting in their corporate capacity (e.g., management fraud or crime), but now used to define almost any financial or economic crime.

Fraud triangle A model developed to explain the research of Cressey, who noted that most occupational frauds were caused by a combination of three elements: nonshareable financial problems, perceived opportunity, and the ability to rationalize conduct.

Nonshareable problems Financial difficulties that would be hard for a potential occupational offender to disclose to outsiders, such as excessive debt, gambling, drug use, business reversals, or extramarital affairs.

Rationalization The thought process by which an occupational fraudster explains and justifies his illegal conduct. Examples include: "I was only borrowing the money," "the company doesn't treat me fairly," and "I must commit financial statement fraud because otherwise, employees will lose their jobs."

Employee deviance Conduct by employees that is detrimental to both employer and employee, such as goldbricking, work slowdown, and industrial sabotage.

Organizational controls Deterrence mechanisms used by organizations to discourage employee deviance and fraud; includes company policies, selection of personnel, inventory control, security, and punishment.

Social controls Informal deterrence mechanisms that help discourage employee deviance and fraud, such as loss of prestige, and embarrassment of friends and family.

REVIEW QUESTIONS

1-1 (Learning objective 1-1) What is fraud examination?

1-2 (Learning objective 1-2) What is the fraud theory approach?

1-3 (Learning objective 1-3) Occupational fraud and abuse includes any personal enrichment that results from misuse or misapplication of the employing organization's resources or assets. There are four key elements to this activity. What are they?

1-4 (Learning objective 1-4) Under the common law, fraud generally consists of four elements, all of which must be present. List them.

1-5 (Learning objectives 1-4 and 1-5) What is the difference between occupational fraud and occupational abuse? Give examples.

1-6 (Learning objective 1-7) Edwin H. Sutherland, a criminologist, coined the phrase "white-collar crime." What did he mean by this term? How has the meaning of this phrase changed over time?

1-7 (Learning objective 1-7) Sutherland developed what is known as the "theory of differential association." What is the principal tenet of his theory?

1-8 (Learning objective 1-8) Cressey interviewed nearly 200 embezzlers in order to develop his theory on the causation of fraud. As a result of his research, what was Cressey's final hypothesis?

1-9 (Learning objective 1-9) Cressey believed that nonshareable problems provide the motivation for employees to commit occupational fraud. What did he mean by "nonshareable"?

1-10 (Learning objective 1-9) Cressey divided the nonshareable problems of the subjects in his research into six different subtypes. What are they?

1-11 (Learning objective 1-11) Albrecht concluded that three factors that lead to occupational fraud. What are they?

1-12 (Learning objective 1-12) What factor did Hollinger and Clark identify as the primary cause of employee deviance?

1-13 (Learning objective 1-13) The *2009 Global Fraud Survey* covered a number of factors that are related to occupational fraud. List these factors.

DISCUSSION ISSUES

1-1 (Learning objective 1-1) How does "fraud examination" differ from "forensic accounting"?

1-2 (Learning objective 1-2) There are several steps involved in the fraud theory approach. What are they?

1-3 (Learning objectives 1-3 through 1-6) How does occupational fraud and abuse differ from other kinds of fraud? Give examples of other fraud types.

1-4 (Learning objectives 1-7 and 1-8) How does the study of criminology relate to the detection or deterrence of fraud? How does it differ from the study of accounting or auditing?

1-5 (Learning objective 1-7) Sutherland's contribution to criminology, in addition to giving us the term "white-collar crime," involved developing the theory of differential association. What are the implications of this theory with respect to occupational fraud?

1-6 (Learning objective 1-8) Cressey's "fraud triangle" states that three factors—nonshareable financial need, perceived opportunity, and rationalization—are present in cases of occupational fraud. Which of these three factors, if any, is most important in causing executives, managers, and employees to commit occupational fraud?

1-7 (Learning objectives 1-8 and 1-9) Cressey described a number of nonshareable financial problems that he uncovered during his research. Which of these, if any, apply to modern-day executives who are responsible for large financial statement frauds? In the fifty-plus years since Cressey did his study, are the factors he described still valid? Why, or why not?

1-8 (Learning objectives 1-8 through 1-11) Albrecht, in his research, developed the "fraud scale" and furnished a list of the reasons employees and executives commit occupational fraud. How are Albrecht's conclusions similar to Cressey's? How are they different?

1-9 (Learning objective 1-13) The ACFE's *2009 Global Fraud Survey* found, among other things, that the frauds committed by women resulted in smaller median losses than those committed by men. What are some possible reasons for this finding?

ENDNOTES

1. The Association of Certified Fraud Examiners, *Report to the Nation on Occupational Fraud and Abuse* (Austin, TX: ACFE, p. 4. 1996).
2. The Association of Certified Fraud Examiners, p. 9.
3. Henry Campbell Black, *Black's Law Dictionary*, 5th ed. (St. Paul, MN: West Publishing, 1979), p. 792.
4. *Merriam-Webster's Collegiate Dictionary*, 11th ed. (Merriam-Webster, Incorporated, 2008), p. 321.
5. A tort is a civil injury or wrongdoing. Torts are not crimes; they are causes of action brought by private individuals in civil courts. Instead of seeking to have the perpetrator incarcerated or fined, as would happen in a criminal case, the plaintiff in a tort case generally seeks to have the defendant pay monetary damages to repair the harm he has caused.
6. *Black's*, p. 300.
7. *Black's*, p. 468.
8. *Black's*, 6th ed., p. 563.
9. Gilbert Geis, *On White Collar Crime* (Lexington: Lexington Books, 1982).
10. *Merriam-Webster's*, p. 6.
11. Larry J. Siegel, *Criminology*, 3rd ed. (New York: West Publishing, 1989), p. 193.
12. Donald R. Cressey, *Other People's Money* (Montclair: Patterson Smith, 1973), p. 30.
13. Cressey, p. 33.
14. Cressey, p. 34.
15. Cressey, p. 34.
16. Cressey, p. 35.
17. Cressey, p. 36.
18. Cressey, p. 36.
19. Cressey, p. 42.
20. Cressey, p. 42.
21. Cressey, p. 47.
22. Cressey, p. 48.
23. Cressey, pp. 52–53.
24. Cressey, p. 54.
25. Cressey, p. 57.
26. Cressey, p. 66.
27. Cressey, p. 84.
28. Cressey, p. 84.
29. Cressey, p. 85
30. Cressey, pp. 94–95.
31. Cressey, p. 93.
32. Cressey, pp. 101–102.
33. Cressey, p. 102.
34. Cressey, p. 102.
35. Cressey, pp. 120–121.
36. Cressey, p. 121.
37. Cressey, p. 122.
38. Cressey, p. 121.
39. Cressey, p. 122.

40. Cressey, p. 128.
41. Cressey, p. 129.
42. Cressey, pp. 128–129.
43. Cressey, p. 133.
44. Cressey, p. 139.
45. W. Steve Albrecht, Keith R. Howe, and Marshall B. Romney, *Deterring Fraud: The Internal Auditor's Perspective* (Altamonte Springs: The Institute of Internal Auditor's Research Foundation, 1984).
46. Although such red flags may be present in many occupational fraud cases, Albrecht's caution must be reemphasized: perpetrators are hard to profile, and fraud is difficult to predict. To underscore this point, Albrecht's research does not address—nor does any current research—whether nonoffenders have many of the same characteristics. If so, then the list may not be discriminating enough to be useful. In short, though one should be mindful of potential red flags, they should not receive undue attention in the absence of other compelling circumstances.
47. Albrecht, pp. 13–14.
48. Albrecht, p. 32.
49. Albrecht, p. 39
50. Albrecht, p. 5.
51. Albrecht, p. 6.
52. Albrecht, p. 5.
53. Albrecht, p. 5.
54. Albrecht, p. 6.
55. Albrecht, p. 42.
56. Albrecht, p. xv.
57. Richard C. Hollinger and John P. Clark, *Theft by Employees* (Lexington: Lexington Books, 1983), p. 6.
58. Hollinger and Clark, p. 42.
59. Hollinger and Clark, p. 57.
60. Hollinger and Clark, p. 57.
61. Hollinger and Clark, p. 57.
62. Hollinger and Clark, p. 63.
63. Hollinger and Clark, p. 68.
64. Hollinger and Clark, p. 77.
65. Hollinger and Clark, p. 86.
66. Hollinger and Clark, p. 86.
67. Hollinger and Clark, p. 86.
68. Hollinger and Clark, p. 106.
69. Hollinger and Clark, p. 117.
70. Hollinger and Clark, p. 120.
71. Hollinger and Clark, p. 121.
72. Hollinger and Clark, p. 144.
73. Hollinger and Clark, p. 146.
74. United States Central Intelligence Agency, *The World Factbook* (https://www.cia.gov/library/publications/the-world-factbook/geos/xx.html)
75. Albrecht, p. 5.

Skimming Schemes

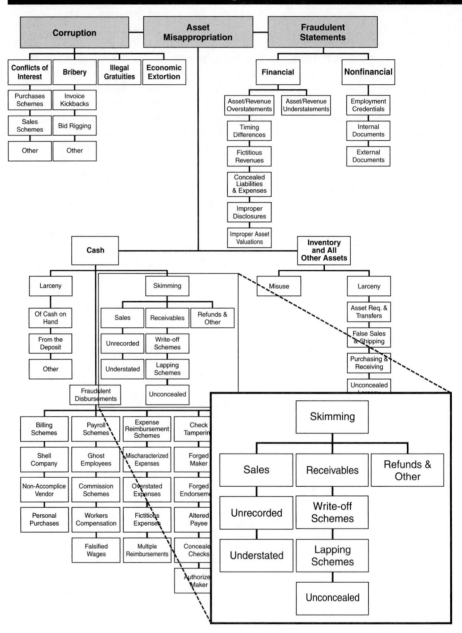

EXHIBIT 2-1

CHAPTER 2

SKIMMING

LEARNING OBJECTIVES

After studying this chapter, you should be able to:

2-1 Define skimming

2-2 List and understand the two principal categories of skimming schemes

2-3 Understand how sales skimming is committed and concealed

2-4 Understand schemes involving understated sales

2-5 Understand how cash register manipulations are used to skim currency

2-6 Be familiar with how sales are skimmed during nonbusiness hours

2-7 Understand the techniques discussed for preventing and detecting sales skimming

2-8 List and be able to explain the six methods typically used by fraudsters to conceal receivables skimming

2-9 Understand what "lapping" is and how it is used to hide skimming schemes

2-10 Be familiar with how fraudsters use fraudulent write-offs or discounts to conceal skimming

2-11 Understand the techniques discussed for preventing and detecting receivables skimming

2-12 Be familiar with proactive audit tests that can be used to detect skimming

CASE STUDY: SHY DOC GAVE GOOD FACE[1]

Brian Lee excelled as a plastic surgeon. His patients touted Lee's skill and artistry when privately confiding the secret of their improved appearance to their closest friends. Exuding a serious, gentle manner, the forty-two-year-old bachelor took quiet pride in his beautification efforts—mainly nose jobs, face lifts, tummy tucks, and breast enhancements.

Lee practiced out of a large physician-owned clinic of assorted specialties, housed in several facilities scattered throughout a growing suburb in the Southwest. As its top producer, Lee billed more than $1 million annually and took home $300,000 to $800,000 a year in salary and bonus. But during one four-year stretch, Lee also kept his own secret stash of unaccounted revenue—possibly hundreds of thousands of dollars.

[1]Several names and details have been changed to preserve anonymity.

Once Lee's dishonesty came to light, the clinic's board of directors (made up of fellow physician-shareholders) demanded an exact accounting. The clinic's big-city law firm hired Doug Leclaire, a certified fraud examiner (CFE) based in Flower Mound, Texas, who had worked well with the lawyers earlier that year on an unrelated case, to conduct a private investigation.

"The doctors wanted an independent person to root around and document how much money was missing," recalled Leclaire. "They also wanted to see how deep this scam ran. As far as I could determine, no one else was involved." Lee's secretary and nurse knew that Lee was performing the surgeries, but they were unaware that the doctor was withholding patient payments from the clinic. Leclaire marveled at the simplicity of the fraud. He said Lee's ill-gotten gains came easily, given the discreet nature of his business.

Leclaire first familiarized himself with both clinic and office policies. (Doctors ran their offices as autonomous units.) During a confidential, free consultation, Lee would examine the patient and explain various options, the expected results, and his total fee. The doctor or his secretary would then discuss payment requirements.

According to Leclaire, "If the patient planned on filing an insurance claim for covered procedures—such as nonemergency, reconstructive surgery for a car crash victim whose nose smashed into a windshield—the patient must pay the deductible beforehand." For pure cosmetic surgery such as liposuction, which is not covered by insurance, patients had to pay the entire amount by cash or check prior to the procedure. Like many plastic surgeons, Lee accepted no credit cards, presumably to guard against economic reprisals from "buyer's remorse." The one-time payment included all post-op visits as well.

Once a patient decided to go under the knife, Lee or his secretary would schedule another appointment or review the doctor's master surgery log to schedule a mutually agreeable date and time. Lee performed the surgeries at the clinic or an affiliated hospital. In theory, a patient would check in at the reception area for a scheduled procedure and pay the secretary, who would immediately attach the payment along with an accompanying receipt to the appropriate procedure form and record the transaction on a daily report. The secretary kept all payments, receipts, and forms in a small lockbox for temporary safekeeping.

"At the end of the day, either the doctor, his nurse, or his receptionist would submit all paperwork and payments—easily totaling tens of thousands of dollars—to the clinic cashier across the hall," explained Leclaire. "If it was late in the day, the doctor would sometimes lock the box in his desk drawer until the following day." For procedures performed at an affiliated hospital, the patient paid in advance, and the clinic relied on someone from the doctor's office to submit the completed paperwork to the head cashier, allowing the clinic to declare its cut.

But even the best-laid plans often fail in their execution, noted Leclaire. The case that finally nailed the plastic surgeon was that of Rita Mae Givens, a rhinoplasty patient. The clinic offices were arranged so that when a patient stepped off the elevator, they could turn right and enter the clinic's main reception area, or turn left and walk down the hall to enter Lee's office reception area. Getting off the elevator on to the fifth floor, Givens proceeded to her left as Lee had earlier instructed. Givens gained admittance via Lee's private office door, bypassing the clinic secretary and receptionist down the hall on the right. As planned, the unsuspecting clinic staff never knew that Lee made the appointment with Givens, nor that he performed surgery to correct her deviated septum and trim her proboscis. Givens had paid the doctor by check.

During her recovery, Givens reviewed her insurance policy, which stated that rhinoplasty may be covered under certain circumstances, or at least may count toward meeting the yearly deductible. She decided to file an insurance claim. But Givens realized she had never received a billing statement to attach to her claim form, which was mandated by her carrier. So Givens made an unplanned call to the clinic's office to request a copy of her bill, which then set off a series of spontaneous reactions. Lee's clinic's cashier located the patient's file, but it showed no charges for the procedure performed. The cashier thought this quite odd. Givens assured the cashier that the procedure had been performed and that she had paid for the surgery with a personal check.

The cashier in turn checked with the office manager of the clinic for the corresponding record of Givens's payment. Of course the office manager failed to find the record and called the clinic administrator in on the search. Knowing that doctors sometimes forgot to immediately reconcile procedures performed at other facilities, the clinic administrator suggested they look at the doctor's surgery log, under the time and date that Givens had provided, for any clues. Meanwhile, the office manager asked the patient to provide a copy of her canceled check, which they later discovered had been endorsed and deposited in the doctor's personal bank account.

The clinic administrator verified that Lee had performed the surgery but had never submitted the payment to the head cashier. When confronted, the doctor admitted his wrongdoing. The administrator alerted the board, which then hired Leclaire to investigate.

The private eye interviewed Lee several times over the course of the investigation. Leclaire described Lee as very apologetic and helpful in reviewing his misdeeds. The doctor only stole payments from elective surgery patients, he explained, so as not to alert any insurance providers who may have requested additional documentation from the clinic. Sometimes Lee helped himself to payments in his secretary's lockbox before turning it in to the head cashier. Sometimes he swiped a payment directly from a patient with a surreptitious appointment. He preferred cash, but often took checks made payable to "Dr. Lee." The doctor often held checks in his desk drawer for a few weeks before depositing them into his personal bank account or cashing the checks. Lee simply destroyed the receipts that were to accompany payments, he told Leclaire. Out of a sense of professional duty, Lee scrupulously maintained all patient medical files, though.

Because the perpetrator cooperated so fully, Leclaire called this case "fun and easy." The doctor kept meticulous records of all his actions, whether or not they were legitimate. With Lee's help, Leclaire compared the doctor's detailed "Day Timer" personal organizer against the clinic's records and readily identified the missing payments. Lee even turned over his bank statements so Leclaire could match the deposits to the booty. Lee also opened up his investment portfolio to Leclaire to quash any doubts over additional unreported revenue.

"The doctor didn't try to hide anything," said Leclaire, who has spent twenty years conducting criminal investigations. "I was able to document everything." In all his talks with the doctor, "Everything he told us was pretty much on the up and up."

After spending so much time with the doctor, Leclaire finally asked Lee the one question that everyone puzzled over—Why? Greed, he said. With all his money, he still craved more. Driven like his father and brother, who are also successful, Lee had little time to enjoy sports and recreation. Wealth was the family obsession, one-upmanship the family game. "It grew to be a serious competition," said Leclaire. "Who could amass the most? Who had the best car?"

To win the game, Lee resorted to grand larceny, which carried an enormous risk of punishment should the fraud be detected. "I kind of felt sorry for the doctor. A guy in that position could have lost everything," Leclaire said.

After weeks of work, the law firm and its private investigator brought their findings to the board and made recommendations as requested. He prefaced his report with lessons that were learned from this case. "Weak internal controls tempt all employees, even those earning over $100,000. If given the opportunity, means, and a very slim chance for detection, there are employees who will justify the commission of a fraud in their own minds."

Leclaire suggested they revamp their entire payment system, setting up a central billing area, posting signs to educate the patients, and assigning and spreading out distinct tasks to several office workers during the payment process. "They had no oversight," said the investigator. He told them they needed to reconcile all steps along the way and perform routine internal audits.

This fraud escaped detection for more than four years, Leclaire told his attentive audience. The bottom line? By his audit, Lee had embezzled about $200,000.

Much discussion and a question-and-answer period followed. Some board members insisted Lee be terminated immediately. "Others showed real sympathy for one of their brethren," said Leclaire.

"Their biggest concern was the clinic's income tax liability." Leclaire, who had been a special agent with the IRS's criminal investigations department for nine years, assured them the clinic held no liability for uncollected income. No one wanted an IRS audit, given the clinic's history of scant oversight and the doctors' uncertainty over their own culpability, said Leclaire. They feared federal agents would snoop around and perhaps find other instances of unreported income or questionable activity. He warned that taxes would definitely be due upon restitution, however.

"The doctors had worked out an agreement among themselves." They decided not to prosecute or terminate Lee. Of course the doctors expected Lee to make immediate and full restitution of $200,000, plus interest. (For the first installment, Leclaire picked up $15,000 in cash the doctor had lying around his modest abode.) They also insisted that Lee place another $200,000 in escrow to cover any contingencies. And naturally, the doctor would foot the bill for both the lawyers and the private investigator involved in the case.

His fellow physicians agreed to let their top moneymaker continue to practice at the clinic provided Lee went for professional counseling to correct his aberration. They would help him any way they could, they said. Encouraged to show Lee there were other things in life besides work, from then on the doctors invited him along on their fishing and hunting trips. On the advice of his psychiatrist, Lee eagerly accepted. The reformed loner even enjoyed himself.

To curb temptations, the clinic immediately instituted new policies on payment procedures. Good thing, said Leclaire: the good doctor later told him that if given a chance, "I would probably do it again."

OVERVIEW

Skimming, as illustrated in the previous case, is the theft of cash from a victim entity prior to its entry in an accounting system. Because the cash is stolen before it has been recorded in the victim company's books, skimming schemes are known as "off-book" frauds, and since the missing money is never recorded, skimming schemes leave no direct audit trail. Consequently, it may be very difficult to detect that the money has been stolen. This is the principal advantage of a skimming scheme to the fraudster.

Skimming can occur at any point where funds enter a business, so almost anyone who deals with the process of receiving cash may be in a position to skim money. This includes salespeople, tellers, waitstaff, and others who receive cash directly from customers. In addition, employees whose duties include receiving and logging payments made by customers through the mail perpetrate many skimming schemes. These employees are able to slip checks out of the incoming mail for their own use rather than posting the checks to the proper revenue or customer accounts. Those who deal directly with customers or who handle customer payments are, clearly, the most likely candidates to skim funds.

Skimming Data from the ACFE *2009 Global Fraud Survey*

In Chapter 1, we learned that there are three major categories of occupational fraud: asset misappropriations, corruption, and fraudulent statements. We further learned that asset misappropriation schemes are the most common of these categories; of the 1,843 cases in the study, 1,590, or over 85 percent, involved some form of asset misappropriation.

As the fraud tree the ACFE (Exhibit 2-1) illustrates, asset misappropriations can in turn be subdivided into two categories: cash schemes and noncash schemes. Exhibit 2-2 shows the percentage of asset misappropriation cases and median losses for each of these two subcategories. As we see, cash schemes were much more common than noncash schemes in the ACFE's *2009 Global Fraud Survey* and also tended to have a higher median cost.

It is important to note that because fraudsters often utilize a variety of tactics to pilfer the victim's money, many fraud schemes involve multiple methods of fraud. Thus, ACFE researchers asked respondents to the survey to identify both the total loss caused by the fraud and the amount of the loss directly attributable to each specific type of asset misappropriation scheme. This subdivision provides a more accurate picture of the effects of asset misappropriation schemes than previously obtained. Consequently, the median loss amounts reported throughout this text reflect just that portion of the fraud loss attributable to the specific scheme being discussed.

Again returning to the fraud tree, cash schemes are subdivided into three distinct categories: skimming, cash larceny, and fraudulent disbursements. Among these subcategories, fraudulent disbursement schemes were the most common, occurring in more than two-thirds of the cash misappropriation cases included in the study. These schemes also caused the highest median loss ($150,000) of the three cash scheme categories. In contrast, skimming schemes were a part of 20 percent of the cash misappropriation cases and caused the lowest median loss of the three categories ($60,000) (see Exhibits 2-3 and 2-4).

SKIMMING SCHEMES

Skimming schemes all follow the same basic pattern: an employee steals incoming funds before they are recorded in the victim organization's books. Within this broad whole, skimming schemes can be subdivided based on whether they target *sales* or *receivables*. The character of the incoming funds has an effect on how the frauds are concealed, and concealment is the crucial element of most occupational fraud schemes.

Scheme Type	Percent of Asset Misappropriation Cases[a]	Median Cost
Cash Misappropriations (1,361 cases)	85.6%	$120,000
Noncash Misappropriations (322 cases)	20.3%	$ 90,000

EXHIBIT 2-2   *2009 Global Fraud Survey*: Cash versus Noncash Schemes

[a]As was stated in Chapter 1, the sum of percentages in this table, as in several tables and charts throughout this book, exceeds 100 percent because some cases involved multiple fraud schemes that fell into more than one category.

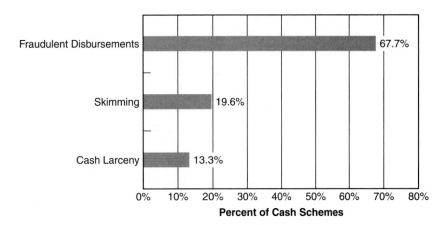

EXHIBIT 2-3 *2009 Global Fraud Survey*: Frequency of Cash Misappropriations

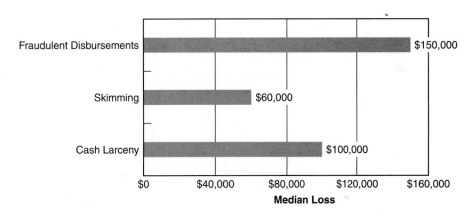

EXHIBIT 2-4 *2009 Global Fraud Survey*: Median Loss of Cash Misappropriations

Sales Skimming

The most basic skimming scheme occurs when an employee makes a sale of goods or services to a customer, collects the customer's payment at the point of sale, but makes no record of the transaction. The employee pockets the money received from the customer instead of turning it over to his employer (see Exhibit 2-5). This was the method used by Dr. Brian Lee in the case study discussed previously. He was performing work and collecting money that his partners knew nothing about. As a result he was able to take approximately $200,000 without leaving any indications of his wrongdoings on the books. Had a patient not made an unexpected call for a copy of a billing statement, Lee's crime could have gone on indefinitely. The case of Dr. Lee illustrates why unrecorded sales schemes are perhaps the most dangerous of all skimming frauds.

In order to discuss sales skimming schemes more completely, let us consider one of the simplest and most common sales transactions, a sale of goods at the cash register. In a normal transaction, a customer purchases an item—such as a pair of shoes—and an employee enters the sale on the cash register. The register tape reflects that the sale has been made and shows that a certain amount of cash (the purchase price of the item) should have been placed in the register. By comparing the register tape to the amount of money on hand, it may be possible to detect thefts. For instance, if $500 in sales is

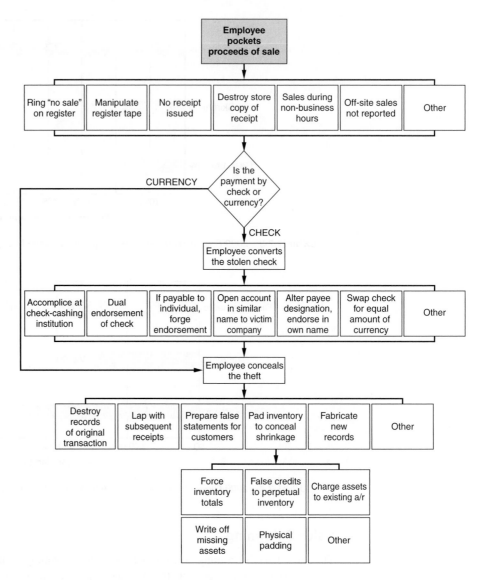

EXHIBIT 2-5 Unrecorded Sales

recorded on a particular register on a given day, but only $400 cash is in the register, someone has obviously stolen $100 (assuming no beginning cash balance).

When an employee skims money by making off-book sales of merchandise, however, the theft cannot be detected by comparing the register tape to the cash drawer, because the sale was never recorded on the register. Think of the example in the preceding paragraph: Assume a fraudster wants to make off with $100, and there are $500 worth of sales at that employee's cash register through the course of the day. Also assume that one sale involves a $100 pair of shoes. When the $100 sale is made, the employee does not record the transaction on his register. The customer pays $100 and takes the shoes home, but instead of placing $100 in the cash drawer, the employee pockets it. Since the employee did not record the sale, at the end of the day the register tape will reflect only $400 in sales. There will be $400 on hand in the register ($500 in total sales minus the

$100 that the employee stole), so the register will balance. By not recording the sale, the employee was able to steal money without the missing funds appearing on the books.

Cash Register Manipulation The most difficult part in a skimming scheme at the cash register is that the employee must commit the overt act of taking money. If the employee takes the customer's money and shoves it into his pocket without entering the transaction on the register, the customer may suspect that something is wrong and report the conduct to another employee or manager. It is also possible that a manager, a fellow employee, or a surveillance camera will spot the illegal conduct.

In order to conceal their thefts, some employees might ring a "no sale" or other noncash transaction on their cash registers to mask the theft of sales. The false transaction is entered on the register so that it appears a sale is being rung up when in fact the employee is stealing the customer's payment. To the casual observer, it looks as though the sale is being properly recorded.

In other cases, employees have rigged their cash registers so that sales are not recorded on their register tapes. As we have stated, the amount of cash on hand in a register may be compared to the amount showing on the register tape in order to detect employee theft. It is thus not important to the fraudster what is keyed into the register, but rather what shows up on the tape. If an employee can rig the register so that sales do not print, he can enter a sale that he intends to skim, yet ensure that the sale never appears on the books. Anyone observing the employee will see the sale entered, see the cash drawer open, and so forth, yet the register tape will not reflect the transaction. How is this accomplished? In Case 1740,[1] a service station employee hid stolen gasoline sales by simply lifting the ribbon from the printer. He then collected and pocketed the sales that were not recorded on the register tape. The fraudster would then roll back the tape to the point where the next transaction should appear and replace the ribbon. The next transaction would be printed without leaving any blank space on the tape, apparently leaving no trace of the fraud. However, the fraudster in this case overlooked the fact that the transactions on his register were prenumbered. Even though he was careful in replacing the register tape, he failed to realize that he was creating a break in the sequence of transactions. For instance, if the perpetrator skimmed sale #155, then the register tape would show only transactions #153, #154, #156, #157, and so on. The missing transaction numbers, omitted because the ribbon was lifted when they took place, indicated fraud.

Special circumstances can lead to more creative methods for skimming at the register. In Case 2230, for instance, a movie theater manager figured out a way around the theater's automatic ticket dispenser. In order to reduce payroll hours, this manager sometimes worked as a cashier selling tickets. He made sure that at these times there was no one checking patrons' tickets outside the theaters. When a sale was made, the ticket dispenser would feed out the appropriate number of tickets, but the manager withheld tickets from some patrons and allowed them to enter the theater without them. When the next customer made a purchase, the manager sold the person one of the excess tickets instead of using the automatic dispenser. Thus, portions of the ticket sales were not recorded. At the end of the night, there was a surplus of cash, which the manager removed and kept for himself. Although the actual loss was impossible to measure, it was estimated that this manager stole over $30,000 from his employer.

After Hours Sales Another way to skim unrecorded sales is to conduct sales during nonbusiness hours. For instance, some employees have been caught running their employers' stores on weekends or after hours without the knowledge of the owners. They were able to pocket the proceeds of these sales because the owners had no idea that their stores were even open. One manager of a retail facility in Case 2103 went to work two hours early every day, opening his store at 8:00 a.m. instead of 10:00 a.m., and pocketed all the sales made during these two hours. Talk about dedication! He rang up sales on the register as if it was business as usual, but then removed the register tape and all the cash he had accumulated. The manager then started from scratch at 10:00 as if the store was just opening. The tape was destroyed, so there was no record of the before-hours revenue.

Skimming by Off-Site Employees Though we have discussed skimming so far in the context of cash register transactions, skimming does not have to occur at a register, or even to involve hard currency. Employees who work at remote locations or without close supervision perpetrate some of the most costly skimming schemes. This can include independent salespersons who operate off-site and employees who work at branches or satellite offices; these employees have a high level of autonomy in their jobs, which often translates into poor supervision, and that, in turn, to fraud.

Several cases reported as part of the ACFE studies involved the skimming of sales by off-site employees. Some of the best examples of this type of fraud occurred in the apartment rental industry, where apartment managers handle the day-to-day operations without much oversight. A common scheme, as evidenced by a bookkeeper in Case 250, is for the perpetrator to identify the tenants who pay in currency and remove them from the books. This causes a particular apartment to appear as vacant on the records when, in fact, it is occupied. Once the currency-paying tenants are removed from the records, the manager can skim their rental payments without late notices being sent to the tenants. As long as no one physically checks the apartment, the fraudster can continue skimming indefinitely.

Another rental-skimming scheme occurs when apartments are rented out but no lease is signed. On the books, the apartment will still appear to be vacant, even though there are rent-paying tenants on the premises. The fraudster can then steal the rent payments, which will not be missed. Sometimes the employees in these schemes work in conjunction with the renters and give a "special rate" to these people. In return, the renter's payments are made directly to the employee and any complaints or maintenance requests are directed only to that employee so the renter's presence remains hidden.

Instead of skimming rent, the property manager in Case 1381 skimmed payments made by tenants for application fees and late fees. Revenue sources such as these are less predictable than rental payments, and their absence may therefore be harder to detect. The central office in Case 1381, for instance, knew when rent was due and how many apartments were occupied, but had no control in place to track the number of people who filled out rental applications or how many tenants paid their rent a day or two late. Stealing only these nickel-and-dime payments, the property manager in this case was able to make off with approximately $10,000 of her employer's money.

A similar revenue source that is unpredictable, and therefore difficult to account for, is parking lot collection revenue. In Case 2045, a parking lot attendant skimmed approximately $20,000 from his employer simply by not preparing tickets for customers who entered the lot. He would take the customers' money and wave them into the lot, but because no receipts were prepared by the fraudster, there was no way for the victim company to compare tickets sold to actual customers at this remote location. Revenue sources that are hard to monitor and predict, such as late fees and parking fees in the examples above, are prime targets for skimming schemes.

Another off-site person in a good position to skim sales is the independent salesperson. A prime example is the insurance agent who sells policies but does not file them with the carrier. Most customers do not want to file claims on a policy, especially early in the term, for fear that their premiums will rise. Knowing this, the agent keeps all documentation on the policies instead of turning it in to the carrier. The agent can then collect and keep the payments made on the policy because the carrier does not know the policy exists. The customer continues to make his payments, thinking that he is insured, when in fact the policy is a ruse. Should the customer eventually file a claim, some agents are able to backdate the false policies and submit them to the carrier, then file the claim so that the fraud will remain hidden.

Poor Collection Procedures Poor collection and recording procedures can make it easy for an employee to skim sales or receivables. In Case 1679, for instance, a governmental authority that dealt with public housing was victimized because it failed to itemize daily receipts. This agency received payments from several public housing tenants, but at the end of the day, "money" received from tenants was listed as a whole. Receipt numbers were not used to itemize the payments made by tenants, so there was no way to pinpoint which tenant had paid how much. Consequently, the employee in charge of collecting money from tenants was able to skim a portion of their payments. She simply did not record the receipt of over $10,000. Her actions caused certain accounts receivable to be overstated where tenant payments were not properly recorded.

Understated Sales The cases discussed above dealt with purely off-book sales. Understated sales work differently in that the transaction is posted to the books, but for a lower amount than the perpetrator collected from the customer (see Exhibit 2-6). For instance, in Case 2210 an employee wrote receipts to customers for their purchases, but she removed the carbon-paper backing on the receipts so that they did not produce a company copy. The employee then used a pencil to prepare company copies that showed lower purchase prices. For example, if the customer had paid $100, the company copy might reflect a payment of $80. The employee skimmed the difference between the actual amount of revenue and the amount reflected on the fraudulent receipt. This can also be accomplished at the register when the fraudster underrings a sale, entering a sales total that is lower than the amount actually paid by the customer. The employee skims the difference between the actual purchase price of the item and the sales figure recorded on the register. Rather than reduce the price of an item, an employee might record the sale of fewer items. If 100 units are sold, for instance, a fraudster might only record the sale of 50 units and skim the excess receipts.

Check-for-Currency Substitutions Another common skimming scheme is to take unrecorded checks that the perpetrator has stolen and substitute them for receipted currency. This type of scheme is especially common when the fraudster has access to incoming funds from an unusual source, such as refunds or rebates that have not been accounted for by the victim organization. The benefit of substituting checks for cash, from the fraudster's perspective, is that stolen checks payable to the victim organization may be difficult to convert. They also leave an audit trail showing where the stolen check was deposited. Currency, on the other hand, disappears into the economy once it has been spent.

An example of a check-for-currency substitution was found in Case 1120, where an employee responsible for receipting ticket and fine payments on behalf of a municipality abused her position and stole incoming revenues for nearly two years. When this individual received payments in currency, she issued receipts, but when checks were received she did not. The check payments were therefore unrecorded revenues—ripe for skimming. These unrecorded checks were then placed in the days' receipts and an equal amount of cash was removed. The receipts matched the amount of money on hand except that payments in currency had been replaced with checks.

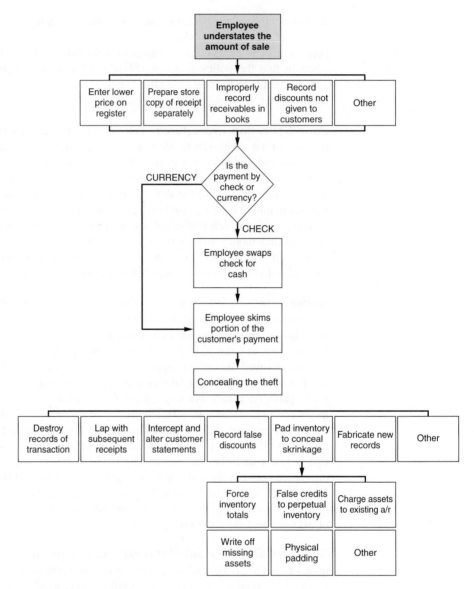

EXHIBIT 2-6 Understated Sales

Theft in the Mail Room—Incoming Checks Another common form of skimming occurs in the mailroom, where employees charged with opening the daily mail simply take incoming checks instead of processing them. The stolen payments are not posted to the customer accounts, and from the victim organization's perspective it is as if the check had never arrived (see Exhibit 2-7). When the task of receiving and recording incoming payments is left to a single person, it is all too easy for that employee to slip an occasional check into his pocket.

An example of a check theft scheme occurred in Case 2052, in which a mailroom employee stole over $2 million in government checks arriving through the mail. This employee simply identified and removed envelopes delivered from a government agency that was known to send checks to the company. Using a group of accomplices acting

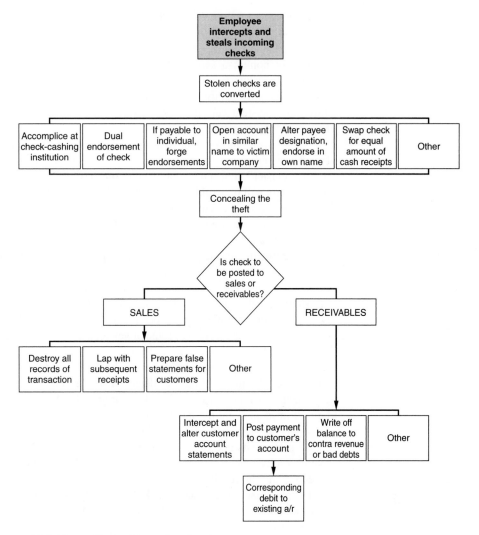

EXHIBIT 2-7 Theft of Incoming Checks

under the names of fictitious persons and companies, this individual was able to launder the checks and divide the proceeds with his cronies.

Preventing and Detecting Sales Skimming   Perhaps the biggest key to preventing skimming of any kind is to maintain a viable oversight presence at any point where cash enters an organization. Recall that the second leg of Cressey's fraud triangle involved a *perceived opportunity* to commit the fraud and get away with it. When an organization establishes an effective oversight presence, it diminishes the perception among employees that they would be able to steal without getting caught. In other words, employees are less likely to try to steal.

Therefore, it is important to have a visible management presence at all cash entry points, including cash registers and the mailroom. This is not to say that a manager must hover over cashiers and mailroom clerks at all times—too much oversight can actually produce a negative effect on employees, causing them to feel mistrusted, possibly making them resentful of management. But managers should routinely check on all cash entry points, not just to look for fraud but also to ensure proper customer service, to monitor productivity, and so forth.

Instead of a physical management presence, video cameras can be installed at cash entry points to serve essentially the same purpose. The principal benefit to the use of video cameras is not that it might detect theft (which it might), but that it might dissuade employees from attempting to steal. Incidentally, a twenty-four-hour video monitoring system can also deter any off-hours sales of the kind that were discussed earlier in this chapter.

Organizations do not have to rely solely on management to oversee cash collections. In retail organizations that utilize several cash registers, the registers are frequently placed in one "cluster" area rather than spread out through the store. One reason for this is so that cashiers will be working in full view of other employees as well as customers. Again, this serves to deter attempts at skimming.

Customers can also be utilized in the monitoring function. Have you ever seen a sign at a retail establishment offering a discount to any customer who does not get a receipt at the time of his purchase? The purpose for these programs is to force employees to ring up sales, thereby making it more difficult to commit an unrecorded sales scheme. In addition, customer complaints and tips are a frequent source of detection for all types of occupational fraud, including skimming. Calls from customers for whom there is no record, for example, are a clear red flag of unrecorded sales. In addition, customer complaints should be received and investigated by employees who are independent of the sales staff.

All cash registers should record the log-in and log-out time of each user. This simple measure makes it easy to detect off-hours sales by comparing log-in times to the organization's hours of operation. In addition, should a theft occur, the user log will be helpful in identifying the potential culprit.

Off-site sales personnel should also be required to maintain activity logs accounting for all sales visits and other business-related activities. These logs should include information such as the customer's name, address and phone number, the date and time of the meeting, and the result of the meeting (e.g., was a sale made?). Employees independent of the sales function can spot-check the veracity of the entries by making "customer satisfaction calls" in which the customer would be asked to verify the information recorded in the activity log.

In addition to monitoring, organizations can take other steps to reduce employees' perceived opportunity to steal. For example, it is advisable, particularly in busy retail establishments, to maintain a secure area where cashiers are required to store coats, hats, purses, and so on. The idea is to eliminate potential hiding places for stolen money.

In the mailroom, employees who open incoming mail should do so in a clear, open area free from blind spots. Preferably there should be a supervisory presence or video monitoring in place when mail is opened, in order to deter thefts. At least two employees should be involved with opening the organization's mail and logging incoming payments, so that one will not be able to steal incoming checks without the other noticing.

Receivables Skimming

Skimming receivables is more difficult than skimming sales. Incoming receivables payments are *expected*, so the victim organization is likely to notice if these payments are not received and logged into the accounting system. As receivables become past due, the victim organization will send notices of nonpayment to its customers. Customers will complain when they receive a second bill for a payment that has already been made. In addition, the customer's cashed check will serve as evidence that the payment was made.

CASE STUDY: BEVERAGE MAN TAKES THE PLUNGE[2]

For most people, Florida shines brightly from postcards and televisions, as brilliant as it must have seemed to the first Europeans who hoped to find the Fountain of Youth there. The contemporary image is a little gaudier than ancient myth, but still going strong. And when most people go to Florida, the vacation schedule and the tourist industry can make it seem as if the postcard image lives and breathes.

There really is something for the entire family: a tropical paradise for Mom and Dad, lots of noise and colors for the kiddies. But televisions switch off, and tourists go home. The land remains a place where people work, where they live and breathe and raise their families. This is the story of one of those people.

Stefan Winkler worked for a beverage company in Pompano Beach, Florida. As director of accounting and controller, Stefan touched the flow of money into and out of the company at every point, though he was particularly focused on how money came in. The beverage company—call it Mogel's, Inc.—collected from customers in two ways: either the delivery drivers brought in cash or checks from their route customers, or credit customers sent checks in the mail.

The cash and checks from drivers were counted and put in the bank as route deposits; the checks arriving by mail from credit customers were filed as office deposits. Drivers gave their daily collections to a cashier who made out the route deposit slip and sent it to Stefan Winkler. Any checks from office mail came directly to Winkler, who verified the money according to the payment schedule—thirty days for some customers, sixty for others, and so on. Winkler's job was to combine office deposits and route deposits for the final accounting before bank deposit. Theoretically, then, Mogel's had two revenue streams, both of which converged at Winkler's desk and poured smoothly into the bank.

But Winkler had other plans. He siphoned off the cash from the route deposits through a lapping operation, covering the money he lifted from one account with funds from another. Winkler took large amounts of cash from the route deposits and replaced each cash amount with checks from the credit customers. He might filch $3,000 in cash from the transportation bags and put in $3,000 worth of checks from the mail. That way, the route deposit total matched the amount listed by the cashier on the deposit slip. There was no gap in office deposits, because he never listed the check as received. Instead, he would extend the customer's payment schedule outward, sometimes indefinitely. He occasionally covered the amount later with other embezzlements. Like a kiting operation, lapping takes a continual replenishment of

2Some names have been changed to preserve anonymity.

money, forcing the perpetrator to extend the circles of deception wider if the scheme is to continue to produce. And like kiting, lapping is destined to crumble, unless the person can find a way to replace the original funds and casually walk away. Winkler probably told himself he'd replace the money sometime, preferably sooner than later. Maybe he figured he'd make a killing in the stock market or win big at the track and set everything right again. Only he knows what he was thinking; he never admitted to taking anything. Acting as his own lawyer, he announced at trial, "There are other people besides me who could have taken that money." The prosecution, then, had to prove that Winkler, and not those other people, had actually stolen the money. How that happened is, as they say, the rest of the story. Mogel's operated in Pompano Beach as a subsidiary of a larger company from Delaware. Oversight was casual; auditors generally prepared their reports by dispatches from the local office. This gave Winkler as accounting director lots of room to maneuver. But perhaps there was too much room.

Over the course of a year and a half, Winkler's superiors became increasingly dissatisfied with his performance. Winkler was, fatefully enough, fired on the Friday morning before auditors were to arrive the following Monday. He didn't have the money to replace what he'd stolen, so he used the time to rearrange what he could of his misdealing and throw the rest into disarray. He took cash receipts journals, copies of customer checks, deposit slips, and other financial records from the office and removed his personnel file. He altered electronic files, too, backdating accounts receivable lines to make them current and increasing customer discounts. Examiners would eventually discover "an extremely unusual general ledger adjustment of $303,970.25" made just before Winkler was fired. As the prosecuting attorney, Tony Carriuolo, puts it, "He attempted, through computers and other manipulations, to alter history."

When the auditors arrived on Monday, they started the long haul of reconstructing what had actually happened. This was, as Carriuolo and certified fraud examiner Don Stine put it, "the fun part, even though it was exhausting, of piecing together what happened and who did it, with documents missing and nothing that we could use to point directly at Winkler and say, 'There it is, he did it.'" Auditors for Mogel's set about evaluating the mess Winkler had left behind, working through bank statements, total deposit schedules, accounting records, and reports from delivery drivers.

They caught on to Winkler's method during the first efforts to reconstruct the previous two years' activity. An auditor found two checks totaling $60,000 on a route deposit slip, but no entry in the accounts receivable brought forward for that month. (This was for July, a little over a month before

Winkler was fired.) The deposit slip, someone pointed out, was not in the cashier's handwriting but Winkler's.

Still, making the case would not be as simple as locating route deposits with checks in them. Some customers paid with checks, and the company's cashier routinely used route money to cash employees' paychecks. Thus, deposits regularly contained checks as well as cash. Examiners would have to cover each deposit and its constituent parts, and compare this against what actually hit the bank and the accounts receivable entries in the office deposits. Carriuolo says, "I can't tell you how many times we had to compare the deposit slips from the cashier—some of which we had, and some we didn't—with the actual composition going to the bank." Because Winkler had removed so much from the office, sometimes the only way to verify what had come through the mail was to go to customers and reconstruct payments based on their records.

Once the auditors had gone through the material, they hired Don Stine to confirm their findings and help Carriuolo make the case against Winkler. Reviewing their work, Stine agreed that approximately $350,000 had been taken, and that Winkler was the man. Mogel's left themselves wide open for this hit because they had no controls covering what happened with the checks that came in the mail, in effect giving Winkler "total authority" to manipulate the accounts. Stine says that the situation at Mogel's is all too common, with managers and employees not recognizing a financial crime in progress until it's too late. "There are plenty of things to alert people—missing deposit slips, cash and credit reconciliations between a company and a customer that don't match. There are signs, but it doesn't hit them in the head, and then when something comes out, they say, 'How did this happen?'" Auditors did ask by phone why customers were paying later and later, but they took Winkler's word for it when he put the delays down to computer systems and reorganizations inside the companies.

First contacts with Winkler didn't pan out. He skipped meetings, stonewalled, and acted sullen and defiant. "I didn't do it," he said. "Trust me. Other people had access, they could have done it, too." But Stine and Carriuolo were ready for this. Winkler admitted that several clerks and cashiers had worked at Mogel's during a two-year period, but that losses had occurred continually. Unless the company was consistently hiring crooks in those positions, Carriuolo argued, the answer lay elsewhere. Besides, the manipulations required someone with accounting skills above the level of the average clerk. The one constant, it turns out, was Stefan Winkler. Two other workers had actually been there during the entire time period, but they had neither the access nor the skills necessary to redirect cash flow on the scale that had occurred.

And there was the physical evidence. When he came to Mogel's, Winkler was in a bind. He had lost his house, and his finances were a mess. But his tenure at the beverage company brought a wave of prosperity. He bought luxury watches, expensive clothing, and several cars, among them a $40,000 Corvette—paid for in cash. Winkler set up several businesses, including a limousine service, a jewelry distributorship, and facilities for a daycare center he planned to establish with his wife. He spent lots of money gambling, which he used as an explanation for his Rich and Famous mode of living. "I gamble a lot. I win a lot," he said. "The pit bosses in the Bahamas taught me how to play, so I win almost all the time—simple as that. Just lucky, I guess." Stine knew this was bunk. Nobody was that lucky, not over two years. Winkler's wave of wealth pushed the "Lifestyle Changes, You Lose" button in the game of fraud examination. "You see this in many of these employee defalcation, or employee fraud, cases," comments Stine. "Someone is making $50,000 a year, but they're buying a $500,000 home, driving a $75,000 car. And unless someone died and left them an inheritance, it doesn't add up."

In the civil trial for fraud and negligence, Winkler maintained his innocence—and his arrogance. Carriuolo and Stine presented evidence to show how the route deposits cash had been embezzled and covered for by the office deposits, explaining to the jury with charts and graphs and crash-course accounting presentations what crimes had occurred. The employee records, and the broad authority necessary to pull the scheme off, pointed the finger at Winkler. No one else, Carriuolo maintained, had the "unique access to, and knowledge of Mogel's Inc.'s computerized accounting systems" besides Winkler. Winkler's response? He dismissed (or lost) his attorney and declared he would represent himself. Little or no legal expertise was necessary for his defense: "It wasn't me, it must have been one of those other guys." When he cross-examined Don Stine, who has twelve years in litigation consulting, Winkler announced he had only one question: "Mr. Stine, do you know for certain who took the money?" Stine answered, "No," not with absolute, unconditional, ontological certainty. Happy to show there was no smoking gun, Winkler rested his case.

But the jury was unconvinced by Winkler's tactics. After a brief recess, they returned a guilty verdict for the $353,000 lost by Mogel's, plus treble damages, for a total judgment of over a million dollars. And it seems that Winkler remains unreconstructed, since he was recently named in a complaint filed by the company he worked for after Mogel's. His high life keeps seeking new lows.

Obviously, receivables skimming schemes are more difficult to conceal than sales skimming schemes. When fraudsters attempt to skim receivables, they generally use one of the following techniques to conceal the thefts:

- Lapping
- Force balancing
- Stolen statements
- Fraudulent write-offs or discounts
- Debiting the wrong account
- Document destruction

Lapping Lapping customer payments is one of the most common methods of concealing receivables skimming. Lapping is the crediting of one account through the abstraction of money from another account. It is the fraudster's version of "robbing Peter to pay Paul." Suppose a company has three customers: A, B, and C. When A's payment is received, the fraudster takes it for himself instead of posting it to A's account. Customer A expects that his account will be credited with the payment he has made, but this payment has actually been stolen. When A's next statement arrives, he will see that the check was not applied to his account and will complain. To avoid this, some action must be taken to make it appear that the payment was posted.

When B's check arrives, the fraudster takes this money and posts it to A's account. Payments now appear to be up-to-date on A's account, but B's account is short. When C's payment is received, the perpetrator applies it to B's account. This process continues indefinitely until one of three things happens: (1) someone discovers the scheme, (2) restitution is made to the accounts, or (3) some concealing entry is made to adjust the accounts receivable balances.

In the Mogel's case study, we saw that one of the ways Stefan Winkler concealed his thefts was to lap payments on customer accounts. Anecdotal evidence indicates that lapping is perhaps the most common concealment technique for skimming schemes. It should be noted that, though lapping is more commonly used to conceal skimmed receivables, it could also be used to disguise the skimming of sales. In Case 2128, for instance, a store manager stole daily receipts and replaced them with the following day's incoming cash. She progressively delayed making the company's bank deposits as more and more money was taken. Each time a day's receipts were stolen, it took an extra day of collections to cover the missing money. Eventually, the banking irregularities became so great that an investigation was ordered. It was discovered that the manager had stolen nearly $30,000, and had concealed the theft by lapping her store's sales.

Because lapping schemes can become very intricate, fraudsters sometimes keep a second set of books on hand detailing the true nature of the payments received. In many skimming cases, a search of the fraudster's work area will reveal a set of records tracking the actual payments made and how they have been misapplied to conceal the theft. It may seem odd that someone would keep records of his illegal activity on hand, but many lapping schemes become increasingly complicated as more and more payments are misapplied. The second set of records helps the perpetrator keep track of what funds he has stolen, and what accounts need to be credited to conceal the fraud. Uncovering these records, if they exist, will greatly aid the investigation of a lapping scheme.

Force Balancing Among the most dangerous receivables skimming schemes are those in which the perpetrator is in charge of collecting and posting payments. If a fraudster has a hand in both ends of the receipting process, he can falsify records to conceal the theft of receivables payments. For example, the fraudster might post an incoming payment to a customer's receivables account, even though the payment will never be deposited. This keeps the receivable from aging, but it creates an imbalance in the cash account. The perpetrator hides the imbalance by forcing the total on the cash account, overstating it to match the total postings to accounts receivable.

Stolen Statements Another method used by employees to conceal the misapplication of customer payments is the theft or alteration of account statements. If a customer's payments are stolen and not posted, his account will become delinquent. When this happens, he should receive late notices or statements that show that his account is past due. The purpose of altering a customer's statements is to keep him from complaining about the misapplication of his payments.

To keep a customer unaware about the true status of his account, some fraudsters will intercept his account statements or late notices; this might be accomplished, for example, by changing the customer's address in the billing system. The statements will be sent directly to the employee's home, or to an address where he can retrieve them. In other cases, the address is changed so that the statement is undeliverable, which causes the statements to be returned to the fraudster's desk. In either situation, once the employee has access to the statements, he can do one of two things.

The first option is to throw the statements away, but this will not be particularly effective if the customer ever requests information about his account after not having received a statement.

Therefore, the fraudster may instead choose to alter the statements, or to produce counterfeit statements to make it appear that the customer's payments have been properly posted. The fraudster then sends these fake statements to the customer. The false statements lead the customer to believe that his account is up to date, keeping him from complaining about stolen payments.

Fraudulent Write-Offs or Discounts Intercepting the customer's statements will keep him in the dark as to the status of his account, but the problem still remains: as long as the customer's payments are being skimmed, his account is slipping further and further past due. The fraudster must find some way to bring the account back up to date in order to conceal his crime. As we have discussed, lapping is one way to keep accounts current as the employee skims from them. Another way is to fraudulently write off the customer's account. In Case 2435, for example, an employee skimmed cash collections and wrote off the related receivables as "bad debts." Similarly, in Case 442, a billing manager was authorized to write off certain patient balances as hardship allowances. This employee accepted payments from patients, and then instructed billing personnel to write off the balance in question. The payments were never posted, because the billing manager intercepted them. She covered approximately $30,000 in stolen funds by using her authority to write off patients' account balances.

Instead of writing off accounts as bad debts, some employees cover their skimming by posting entries to contra revenue accounts such as "discounts and allowances." If, for instance, an employee intercepts a $1,000 payment, he would create a $1,000 "discount" on the account to compensate for the missing money.

Debiting the Wrong Account Fraudsters might also debit existing or fictitious accounts receivable in order to conceal skimmed cash. In Case 1996, for example, an office manager in a health care facility took payments from patients for herself. To conceal her activity, the office manager added the amounts taken to the accounts of other patients that she knew would soon be written off as uncollectable. The employees who use this method generally add the skimmed balances to accounts that either are very large or that are aging and about to be written off. Increases in the balances of these accounts are not as noticeable as in other accounts. In the case above, once the old accounts were written off, the stolen funds would be written off along with them.

Rather than existing accounts, some fraudsters set up completely fictitious accounts and debit them for the cost of skimmed receivables. The employees then simply wait for the fictitious receivables to age and be written off, knowing that they are uncollectable. In the meantime, they carry the cost of a skimming scheme where it will not be detected.

Destroying or Altering Records of the Transaction

Finally, when all else fails, a perpetrator may simply destroy an organization's accounting records in order to cover his tracks. For instance, we have already discussed the need for a salesperson to destroy the store's copy of a receipt in order for the sale to go undetected. Similarly, cash register tapes may be destroyed to hide an off-book sale. In Case 788, two management-level employees skimmed approximately $250,000 from their company over a four-year period. These employees tampered with cash register tapes that reflected transactions in which sales revenues had been skimmed. The perpetrators either destroyed entire register tapes or cut off large portions where the fraudulent transactions were recorded. In some circumstances, the employees then fabricated new tapes to match the cash on hand and make their registers appear to balance.

Discarding transaction records is often a last-ditch method for a fraudster to escape detection; the fact that records have been destroyed may itself signal that fraud has occurred. Nevertheless, without the records it can be very difficult to reconstruct the missing transactions and prove that someone actually skimmed money. Furthermore, it may be difficult to prove who was involved in the scheme.

Preventing and Detecting Receivables Skimming

Receivables skimming schemes typically succeed when there is a breakdown in an organization's controls, particularly when one individual has too much control over the process of receiving and recording customer payments, posting cash receipts, and issuing customer payments. If the accounting duties associated with accounts receivable are properly separated so that there are independent checks of all transactions, skimming of these payments is very difficult to commit, and very easy to detect. For example, when force balancing is used to conceal skimming of receivables, this causes a shortage in the organization's cash account, since incoming payments are received but never deposited. By simply reconciling its bank statement regularly and thoroughly, an organization ought to be able to catch this type of fraud. Similarly, when an individual skims receivables but continues to post the payments to customer accounts, postings to accounts receivable will exceed what is reflected in the daily deposit. If an organization assigns an employee to independently verify that deposits match accounts receivable postings, this type of scheme ought to be quickly detected—or, more likely, will not be attempted at all. It is also a good idea to have that employee spot check deposits to accounts receivable to ensure that payments are being applied to the proper accounts. If a check were received by Customer A but the payment posted to Customer B's account, this would indicate a lapping scheme.

As was discussed earlier, lapping schemes can become very complicated and may require the perpetrator to spend long hours at work trying to shift funds around in order to conceal the crime. Ironically, it is very common in these cases for the perpetrator to actually develop a reputation as a model employee because of all the overtime he puts in at the office. After the frauds come to light, the employers frequently express shock not only because they were defrauded, but also because they had considered the perpetrator to be one of their best employees. The point is that a lapping scheme can only succeed through the constant vigilance of the perpetrator. Because of this fact, many organizations mandate that their employees take a vacation every year, or regularly rotate job duties among employees. Both of these tactics can be successful in uncovering lapping schemes, because they effectively take control of the books out of the perpetrator's hands for a period of time; when this happens, the lapping scheme will quickly become apparent.

It is also important to mandate supervisory approval for write-offs or discounts to accounts receivable. As we have seen, fraudulent write-offs and discounts are a common means by which receivables skimming is concealed; they enable the fraudster to wipe the stolen funds off the books. However, if the person who receives and records customer payments has no authority to make these adjustments, then the perceived opportunity to commit the crime is severely diminished.

While strong internal controls are a valuable preventative tool, the fact remains that fraud can and will continue to occur, regardless of the existence of controls designed to prevent it. Organizations must also be able to detect fraud once it has occurred. Some detection methods are very simple. For example, fraudsters sometimes conceal the theft of receivables by making alterations or corrections to books and records. Physical alterations to financial records, such as erasures or cross-outs, are often a sign of fraud, as are irregular entries to miscellaneous accounts. Audit staff should be trained to investigate these red flags.

It is also important for organizations to proactively search out accounting clues that point to fraud. This can be tedious, time-consuming work, but computerized audit tools allow organizations to automate many of these tests and greatly aid in the process of searching out fraudulent conduct.

The key to successfully using automated tests is in designing them to highlight the red flags typically associated with a particular scheme. For example, we have seen that fraudsters often conceal the skimming of receivables by writing off the amount of funds they have stolen from the targeted account. To detect this kind of activity, organizations can run reports summarizing the number of discounts, adjustments, returns, write-offs, and so on generated by location, department, or employee. Unusually high levels may be associated with skimming schemes and could warrant further investigation. Because some fraudsters conceal their skimming by debiting accounts that are aging or that typically have very little activity, it may also be helpful to run reports looking for unusual activity in otherwise dormant accounts.

Trend analysis on aging of customer accounts can likewise be used to highlight a skimming scheme. A significant rise in the number or size of overdue accounts could be a result of an employee's having stolen customer payments without ever posting them, thereby causing the accounts to run past due. If skimming is suspected, an employee who is independent of the accounts receivable function should confirm overdue balances with customers.

There are several audit tests that can be used to help detect various forms of occupational fraud. In each chapter of this book where fraud schemes are examined, we will provide a set of proactive computer audit tests that are tailored to that particular category of fraud. These tests were developed and accumulated by Richard Lanza, working through the Institute of Internal Auditors Research Foundation.[2]

PROACTIVE COMPUTER AUDIT TESTS DETECTING SKIMMING[3]

Title	Category	Description	Data file(s)
Summarize net sales by employee, and extract top 10 employees with low sales.	All	Employees with lower sales may be suspect. This test may also prove more valuable when executed over a trend in time.	• Sale system register
Summarize by location discounts, returns, inventory adjustments, accounts receivable write-offs, and voids charged.	All	Locations with high adjustments may signal actions to hide skimming schemes.	• Sale system register • Invoice sales register • Inventory adjustments
Summarize by employee discounts, returns, inventory adjustments, accounts receivable write-offs, and voids charged.	All	Employees with high adjustments may signal actions to hide skimming schemes.	• Sale system register • Invoice sales register • Inventory adjustments
List top 100 employees by dollar size (one for discounts, one for refunds, one for inventory adjustments, one for accounts receivable write-offs, and one for sale voids).	All	Employees with high adjustments may signal actions to hide skimming schemes.	• Sale system register • Invoice sales register • Inventory adjustments
List top 100 employees who have been on the top 100 list for three months (one for discounts, one for refunds, one for inventory adjustments, one for accounts receivable write-offs, and one for sale voids).	All	Employees with high adjustments may signal actions to hide skimming schemes.	• Sale system register • Invoice sales register • Inventory adjustments
List top 10 locations that have been on the top 10 list for three months (one for discounts, one for refunds, one for inventory adjustments, one for accounts receivable write-offs, and one for sale voids).	All	Locations with high adjustments may signal actions to hide skimming schemes.	• Sale system register • Invoice sales register • Inventory adjustments
Compute standard deviation for each employee for the last three months and list those employees that provided three times the standard deviation in the current month (separately for discounts, for refunds, for inventory adjustments, for accounts receivable write-offs, and for sale voids).	All	Employees with high adjustments may signal actions to hide skimming schemes.	• Sale system register • Invoice sales register • Inventory adjustments

(Continued)

(*Continued*)

Title	Category	Description	Data file(s)
Compare adjustments to inventory to the void/refund transactions summarized by employee.	All	First, a summary of adjustments by inventory number (SKN number) and employee is completed, which is then compared to credit adjustments (to inappropriately decrease inventory that was supposedly returned) by inventory number.	• Sales system register • Inventory detail register
Summarize user access for the sales, accounts receivable, inventory, and general ledger systems for segregation of duties reviews.	All	User access to systems may identify segregation of duties issues. For example, if an employee can make changes to the accounts receivable system and then post other concealment entries in the general ledger, such nonsegregation of duties would allow an employee to hide his actions. User access should be reviewed from the perspective of adjustments within the application and adjustments to the data itself.	• System user access logs • System user access master file
Summarize user access for the sales, accounts receivable, inventory, and general ledger systems in nonbusiness hours.	All	Many times, concealment adjustments are made in nonbusiness hours. User access should be reviewed from the perspective of adjustments within the application and adjustments to the data itself.	• System user access logs
Compute the percentage of assigned to unassigned time for employees.	All	Service employees that have a high majority of unassigned time may be charging the customer and pocketing the proceeds.	• Employee timecard system
Review telephone logs for calls during nonbusiness hours.	All	Service employees that are completing transactions during nonbusiness hours will probably use company lines to effectuate their services.	• Detail telephone record
Extract sales with over x% discount and summarized by employee.	Understated Sales	Employees with high discount adjustments may signal actions to hide understated sales schemes.	• Sale system register

Extract invoices with partial payments.	Understated Sales, Refunds & Other	Employees who are using lapping to hide their skimming scheme may find it difficult to apply a payment from one customer to another customer's invoices in a fully reconciled fashion.	• Invoice sales register
Join the customer statement report file to accounts receivable and review for balance differences.	Understated Sales, Refunds & Other	Through the matching of the customer statement report file (the file that is used to print customer statements) and the open invoices to that customer, any improper changes to customer statements to mask skimming schemes will be detected.	• Customer statement report file • Invoice sales register
Extract customer open invoice balances that are in a credit position.	Understated Sales, Refunds & Other	Customers with a credit position account may be due to improper credit entries posted to the customer account to hide cash skimming.	• Invoice sales register
Extract customers with no telephone or tax ID number.	Understated Sales, Refunds & Other	Customers without this information may have been created for use in posting improper entries to hide a skimming scheme.	• Customer master file
Identify customers added during the period under review.	Understated Sales, Refunds & Other	The issuers of new customer additions should be reviewed using this report to determine whether an employee is using a phony customer account as part of a lapping scheme by crediting that account for cash misappropriation.	• Customer master file
Match the customer master file to the employee master file on various key fields.	Understated Sales, Refunds & Other	Compare telephone number, address, tax ID numbers, numbers in the address, PO box, and ZIP code in customer file to employee file, especially for those employees working in the accounts receivable department. Questionable customer accounts should be reviewed using this report to determine whether an employee is using a phony customer account as part of a lapping scheme by crediting that account for cash misappropriation.	• Customer master file • Employee master file

SUMMARY

Skimming is defined as the removal of cash from an organization prior to its entry into the books and records. Most skimming schemes follow the same basic pattern: an employee steals incoming funds before they are recorded by the victim organization. These schemes can be subdivided based on whether they involve the theft of sales or receivables. The character of the incoming funds affects how the frauds are concealed, which is the key to sustaining an occupational fraud scheme.

Because skimming schemes are off-book frauds, they leave no direct audit trail. This can make it difficult for victim organizations to detect that cash has been stolen, let alone detect who committed the crime.

The most basic skimming scheme involves the unrecorded sale of goods. There are a number of variations of sales

skimming. These include register manipulations, after-hours sales, skimming by off-site employees, understated sales, check-for-currency substitutions, and theft of incoming checks received through the mail.

Receivables skimming is more difficult than sales skimming, because the payments that are stolen are *expected* by the victim organization. In order to succeed at a receivables skimming scheme, the perpetrator must conceal the thefts from the victim organization and, in many cases, from the customer whose payment was stolen. Receivables skimming is generally concealed by one of the following methods: lapping, force balancing, stolen statements, fraudulent write-offs or discounts, debits to the wrong account, or document destruction.

ESSENTIAL TERMS

Skimming Theft of cash prior to its entry into the accounting system.

Sales skimming Skimming that involves the theft of sales receipts, as opposed to payments on accounts receivable. Sales skimming schemes leave the victim organization's books in balance, because neither the sales transaction nor the stolen funds are ever recorded.

Off-book fraud A fraud that occurs outside the financial system and that therefore has no direct audit trail. There are several kinds of off-book frauds that will be discussed in this book. Skimming is the most common off-book fraud.

Understated sales A variation of a sales skimming scheme in which only a portion of the cash received in a sales transaction is stolen. This type of fraud is not off-book, because the transaction is posted to the victim organization's books but for a lower amount than the perpetrator collected from the customer.

Check-for-currency substitution A skimming method whereby the fraudster steals an unrecorded check and substitutes it for recorded currency in the same amount.

Receivables skimming Skimming that involves the theft of incoming payments on accounts receivable. This form of skimming is more difficult to detect than sales skimming, because the receivables are already recorded on the victim organization's books. In other words, the incoming payments are expected by the victim organization. The key to a receivables skimming scheme is to conceal either that the payment was stolen, or that the payment was due.

Lapping A method of concealing the theft of cash designated for accounts receivable by crediting one account while abstracting money from a different account. This process must be continuously repeated to avoid detection.

Force balancing A method of concealing receivables skimming whereby the fraudster falsifies account totals to conceal the theft of funds. This is also sometimes known as "plugging." Typically, the fraudster will steal a customer's payment but nevertheless post it to the customer's account so that the account does not age past due. This causes an imbalance in the cash account.

REVIEW QUESTIONS

2-1 (Learning objective 2-1) How is "skimming" defined?

2-2 (Learning objective 2-2) What are the two principal categories of skimming?

2-3 (Learning objective 2-3) How do sales skimming schemes leave a victim organization's books in balance, despite the theft of funds?

2-4 (Learning objective 2-3) Under what circumstances are incoming checks that are received through the mail typically stolen?

2-5 (Learning objective 2-4) How do "understated sales" schemes differ from "unrecorded sales"?

2-6 (Learning objective 2-5) How is the cash register manipulated to conceal skimming?

2-7 (Learning objective 2-6) Give examples of skimming during nonbusiness hours and of skimming of off-site sales.

2-8 (Learning objective 2-8) What are the six principal methods used to conceal receivables skimming?

2-9 (Learning objective 2-9) What is "lapping," and how is it used to conceal receivables skimming?

2-10 (Learning objective 2-10) List four types of false entries a fraudster can make in the victim organization's books to conceal receivables skimming.

DISCUSSION ISSUES

2-1 (Learning objective 2-3) Sales skimming is called an "off-book" fraud. Why?

2-2 (Learning objective 2-3) In the case study of Brian Lee, the plastic surgeon, what kind of skimming scheme did he commit?

2-3 (Learning objectives 2-5 and 2-12) If you suspected skimming of sales at the cash register, what is one of the first things you would check?

2-4 (Learning objective 2-3) Assume that a client who owns a small apartment complex in a different city than where he lives has discovered that the apartment manager has been skimming rental receipts, which are usually paid by check. The manager endorsed the checks with the apartment rental stamp, then endorsed her own name and deposited the proceeds into her own checking account. Because of the size of the operation, hiring a separate employee to keep the books is not practical. How could a scheme like this be prevented in the future?

2-5 (Learning objectives 2-8 and 2-11) What is the most effective control to prevent receivables skimming?

2-6 (Learning objectives 2-3 and 2-7) In many cases involving skimming, employees steal checks from the incoming mail. What are some of the controls that can prevent such occurrences?

2-7 (Learning objectives 2-7 and 2-11) In the case study of Stefan Winkler, chief financial officer for a beverage company in Florida, how did he conceal his skimming scheme? How could the scheme have been prevented or discovered?

ENDNOTES

1. Throughout the text, numbered case examples are provided to illustrate the various occupational fraud schemes. These examples are derived from responses to ACFE Fraud Surveys.
2. Richard B. Lanza, CPA, PMP, Copyright 2003, *Proactively Detecting Occupational Fraud Using Computer Audit Reports*, by The Institute of Internal Auditors Research Foundation, 247 Maitland Avenue, Altamonte Springs, Florida 32701-4201 U.S.A. Reprinted with permission.
3. Lanza, pp. 41–44.

Cash Larceny Schemes

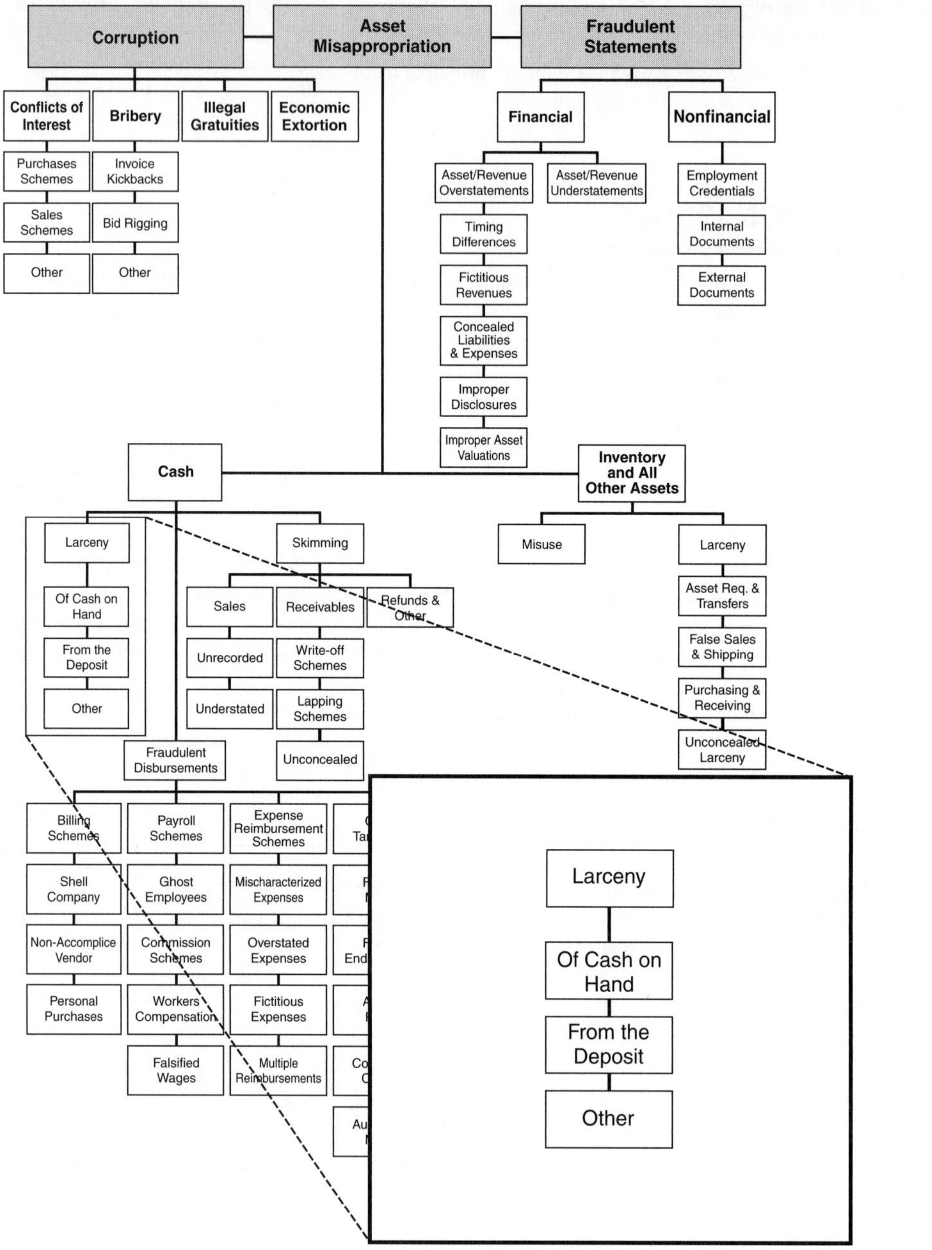

EXHIBIT 3-1

CHAPTER 3

CASH LARCENY

LEARNING OBJECTIVES

After studying this chapter, you should be able to:

3-1 Define cash larceny

3-2 Understand how cash receipts schemes differ from fraudulent disbursements

3-3 Recognize the difference between cash larceny and skimming

3-4 Understand the relative frequency and cost of cash larceny schemes as opposed to other forms of cash misappropriations

3-5 Identify weaknesses in internal controls as inducing factors to cash larceny schemes

3-6 Understand how cash larceny is committed at the point of sale

3-7 Discuss measures that can be used to prevent and detect cash larceny at the point of sale

3-8 Understand and identify various methods used by fraudsters to conceal cash larceny of receivables

3-9 Understand schemes involving cash larceny from deposits including lapping and deposits in transit

3-10 Understand controls and procedures that can be used to prevent and detect cash larceny from bank deposits

3-11 Be familiar with proactive audit tests that can be used to detect cash larceny schemes

CASE STUDY: BANK TELLER GETS NABBED FOR THEFT[1]

Laura Grove worked at Rocky Mountain Bank in Nashville, Tennessee, for five years. As a teller, she thought to herself, she wasn't getting any richer. She and her husband owed about $14,000 in credit card bills, which seemed to get higher and higher each month, especially after adopting a five-year-old girl the year before.

When she transferred to a branch bank in Cheetboro, Tennessee, the bank promoted her to head teller. In this new position, Laura had authority to open the night depository vault with another teller. For security reasons, the bank allowed each teller to possess only half the combination to the vault.

[1] Several names and details have been changed to preserve anonymity.

Every morning, Laura saw the bank night deposit vault door open and close after the removal of all customer night deposit bags. The bank placed only one camera on the night vault, which was turned on at 8:00 a.m. when the bank opened for business. Laura thought it would be easy to get into the night depository and take the bags. These thoughts were reinforced when a customer reported his bag missing and the bank quickly paid his money without a thorough investigation. So one Friday morning, Laura made up her mind that she could take about $15,000 with little risk of being identified. But before she actually took the money, she observed. When she opened the night vault with her co-worker Frank Geffen, she saw him dial the first half of the combination and was careful to memorize the numbers. After entering the second half of the combination, they opened it as usual, removed and listed each night deposit bag, and shut the vault behind them. This time, however, Laura did not lock the vault.

Here, Laura made her first mistake. She thought she could leave the vault door open and return Monday to take the money. But just before the bank closed and employees prepared to leave, teller Melissa Derkstein checked the vault one more time. Seeing that the vault was open, she spun the dial, shaking the handle to ensure the door was locked.

Laura and the other bank employees punched their security codes on the outside door and left for the day. During the weekend, Laura considered her plot. Should she enter the combination by herself this time and place the money into a personal tote bag? Should she stay at work all day with the goods underneath her feet?

Monday morning, she still was not sure how to pull it off but had resolved to go through with the plan anyway. Arriving at 7:15 a.m., Laura was the first person in the bank that morning. After punching in her security code, she placed her tote bag and personal belongings on her chair. Immediately, she went to the night vault and dialed the full combination. Nothing happened. Her mind raced. "Maybe this won't work; this is too risky." Her fingers tried the combination again, and once again, until she heard a click and the vault opened.

Inside, Laura removed the two customer deposit bags, ones that she knew contained large sums of cash. She placed both bags in her tote bag and walked back to her teller window. She stuffed her Weight Watchers book and purse inside the tote bag, on top of the deposit bags. She then hung her bag on the door of the storage room and returned to the teller window, straightening up her work area.

Fifteen minutes later, the branch manager, Harvey Lebrand, entered, looking surprised that Laura was already at her desk. He asked Laura why she had come into work so early this Monday.

"Oh, I just needed to get organized early, because I need to take my Bronco into the shop later today and knew I wouldn't have much time," Laura said.

"You need to get your truck repaired?" Mr. Lebrand asked. "Why don't you go now?"

"Okay, I can get my mother to give me a ride back," Laura said. "See you soon, Mr. Lebrand."

Laura rushed to the storage area, grabbed the tote bag and left the bank. She drove directly to her home and emptied the contents of the bag, watching the many bills and checks spill onto her bed. She lit up with uneasy excitement. Sorting the checks into a separate pile, she gathered the money into a large heap and did a quick count. She estimated she had taken about $15,000. Placing the bills into manila envelopes, she hid them in the headboard storage compartment of the bed. The checks were placed in a small plastic bag. She then phoned her mother and asked her to meet her at the Sears Auto Center.

Laura knew there was an apartment complex next to Sears that had a large blue dumpster. After the checks had been deposited in the dumpster, Laura drove to Sears. Her mother arrived a little later to take her back to work.

A day later, Rocky Mountain Bank Audit Investigator Stacy Boone received a call from Laura's manager, informing her that two customers had not gotten credit for the deposits they'd made the night before. Each deposit was for $8,000.

Boone's investigation quickly led her to suspect Grove. The first one in the bank that morning, Grove also came in before the surveillance cameras turned on. As head teller, she had one-half of the combination to the night depository. Other employees said they "didn't trust her." But when the investigators questioned her, Grove strongly denied any knowledge of the theft.

"During our interview with her, she broke out in a red rash" (which suggested stress). "I have seen innocent people break out into a red rash, but she was the only one we interviewed that day who did," Boone said.

Boone also suspected Grove because the branch bank from which she'd transferred "had a lot of unexplained shortages, and she was a suspect there, but we could never pin down that she took the money. She had bought a lot of new jewelry, wore a lot of expensive clothes, but had filed bankruptcy at one point that year."

The investigation came to a swift conclusion, however, when Boone received a call on her answering machine from Grove's husband, a former neighbor. "I was afraid he wanted to know why we were investigating his wife, and hesitated to call him right back," Boone said.

Boone decided she "might as well get this over with and tell him I could not talk about it [the investigation]. When I called him, he told me he found the bank's money in his attic and suspected his wife. His wife had told him of the bank's investigation, but had not admitted any theft.

"Their daughter had overheard a conversation they had the day of the theft" in which Laura had expressed anxiety to her husband about the bank's investigation, Boone said. "His daughter had told him that she saw [Laura] put something in the attic. So, when she wasn't there, the husband went up in the attic and looked, and found two bags of money."

Boone said the husband was also suspicious because his wife had lied to him before. "He told me that his mother-in-law, her mother, always won all these prizes. She had even won a car through a contest. One night, he came home and found a new big-screen LCD HDTV in the living room, and asked his wife where it came from. She said 'Oh, Mom won that.' At the time, he really didn't think anything about it. But a couple days later, Kirby's Electronics, where the TV came from, called in regard to her credit application. They told him that she charged that TV."

Faced with this evidence, Laura and her husband delivered the $16,000 in cash as restitution. The bank dismissed Grove and she was prosecuted for the crime but received probation in lieu of prison time.

A year later, Boone received a call from one of the bank's tellers who had seen Grove working at another bank in a small city outside of Nashville. Boone called one of the personnel employees there and talked with her.

"They were a bank that did not do fingerprint checks, so they had no knowledge that she had been convicted. She did get into another bank to work, but not for very long."

OVERVIEW

In the occupational fraud setting, a *cash larceny* may be defined as the intentional taking away of an employer's cash (the term *cash* includes both currency and checks) without the consent, and against the will, of the employer. In the case study above, Laura Grove's theft of approximately $16,000 from her employer is an example of a cash larceny.

How do cash larceny schemes differ from other cash frauds? In order to understand the distinction in our classifications, it is helpful first to break down the cash schemes into two broad groups, the first being the *fraudulent disbursement schemes* and the second being what we will loosely term the *cash receipts schemes*. Fraudulent disbursement schemes are those in which a distribution of funds is made from some company account in what appears to be a normal manner. The method for obtaining the funds may be the forging of a check, the submission of a false invoice, the doctoring of a timecard, and so forth. The key is that the money is removed from the company in what appears to be a legitimate disbursement of funds. Fraudulent disbursements will be discussed later in this book.

Cash receipts schemes, on the other hand, are what we typically think of as the outright stealing of cash. The perpetrator does not rely on the submission of phony documents or the forging of signatures; he simply grabs the cash and takes it. The cash receipts schemes fall into two categories: *skimming*, which we have already discussed, and *cash larcenies*. Remember that skimming was defined as the theft of off-book funds. Cash larceny schemes, on the other hand, involve the theft of money that has already appeared on a victim company's books.

Cash Larceny Data from the ACFE *2009 Global Fraud Survey*

In the ACFE study, cash larceny schemes were the least common form of cash misappropriations. Thirteen percent of all cash schemes in our survey involved cash larceny. The median loss for these cases was $100,000, which is more than the median loss for skimming schemes, but only two-thirds as much as the median loss for fraudulent disbursements (see Exhibits 3-2 and 3-3).

CASH LARCENY SCHEMES

A cash larceny scheme can take place in any circumstance in which an employee has access to cash. Every company must deal with the receipt, deposit, and distribution of cash (if not, it certainly won't be a very long-lived company!), so every company is potentially vulnerable to this form of fraud. Although the circumstances in which an

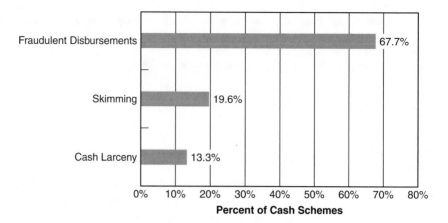

EXHIBIT 3-2 *2009 Global Fraud Survey*: Frequency of Cash Misappropriations[a]

[a]The sum of these percentages exceeds 100 percent because some cases involved multiple fraud schemes that fell into more than one category.

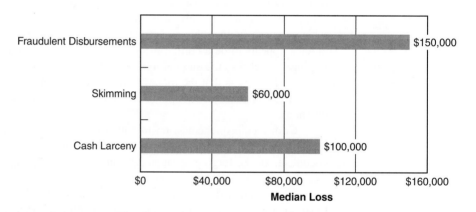

EXHIBIT 3-3 *2009 Global Fraud Survey*: Median Loss of Cash Misappropriations

employee might steal cash are nearly limitless, most larceny schemes involve the theft of cash:

- At the point of sale
- From incoming receivables
- From the victim organization's bank deposits

Larceny at the Point of Sale

A large percentage of the cash larceny schemes in our research occurred at the point of sale, and for good reason—that's where the money is. The cash register (or similar cash collection points like cash drawers or cash boxes) is usually the most common point of access to ready cash for employees, so it is understandable that larceny schemes would frequently occur there. Furthermore, there is often a great deal of activity at the point of sale—particularly in retail organizations—with multiple transactions requiring the handling of cash by employees. This activity can serve as a cover for the theft of cash. In a flurry of activity, with cash being passed back and forth between customer and

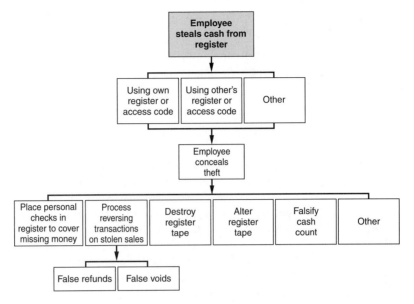

EXHIBIT 3-4   Cash Larceny from the Register

employee, a fraudster is more likely to be able to slip currency out of the cash drawer and into his pocket without getting caught.

This is the most straightforward scheme: Open up the register and remove currency (see Exhibit 3-4). It might be done as a sale is being conducted, to make the theft appear to be part of the transaction, or perhaps when no one is around to notice the perpetrator digging into the cash drawer. In Case 1252, for instance, a teller simply signed onto a cash register, rang a "no sale," and took currency from the drawer. Over a period of time, the teller took approximately $6,000 through this simple method.

Recall that the benefit of a skimming scheme is that the transaction is unrecorded and the stolen funds are never entered on company books. The employee who is skimming either underrings the register transaction so that a portion of the sale is unrecorded or completely omits the sale by failing to enter it at all on his register. This makes the skimming scheme difficult to detect, because the register tape does not reflect the presence of the funds that have been taken. In a larceny scheme, on the other hand, the funds that the perpetrator steals are already reflected on the register tape. As a result, an imbalance will result between the register tape and the cash drawer. This imbalance should be a signal that alerts a victim organization to the theft.

The actual method for taking money at the point of sale—opening a cash drawer and removing currency—rarely varies; it is the methods used by fraudsters to avoid getting caught that distinguish larceny schemes. Oddly, in many cases the perpetrator has no plan for avoiding detection. A large part of fraud is rationalizing; the fraudster convinces himself that he is somehow entitled to what he is taking, or that what he is doing is not actually a crime. Cash larceny schemes frequently begin when perpetrators convince themselves that they are only "borrowing" the funds to cover a temporary monetary need. These people might carry the missing cash in their registers for several days, deluding themselves that they will one day repay the funds, and hoping their employers will not perform a surprise cash count until the missing money is replaced.

The employee who does nothing to camouflage his crimes is easily caught; more dangerous is the person who takes active steps to hide his misdeeds. In the cash larceny schemes we reviewed, there were several methods used to conceal larceny that occurred at the point of sale:

- Thefts from other registers
- Death by a thousand cuts
- Reversing transactions
- Altering cash counts or register tapes
- Destroying register tapes

Thefts from Other Registers   One basic way for an employee to disguise the fact that he is stealing currency is to take money from someone else's cash register. In some retail organizations, employees are assigned to certain registers. Alternatively, one register is used and each employee has an access code. When cash is missing from a cashier's register, the most likely suspect for the theft is obviously that cashier. Therefore, by stealing from another employee's register, or by using someone else's access code, the fraudster makes sure that another employee will be the prime suspect in the theft. In Case 1252 discussed above, for example, the employee who stole money did so by waiting until another teller was on break, then logging onto that teller's register, ringing a "no sale," and taking the cash. The resulting cash shortage therefore appeared in the register of an honest employee, deflecting attention from the true thief. In another case the ACFE reviewed, Case 2127, a cash office manager stole over $8,000, in part by taking money from cash registers and making it appear that the cashiers were stealing.

Death by a Thousand Cuts   A very unsophisticated way to avoid detection is to steal currency in very small amounts over an extended period of time. This is the "death by a thousand cuts" larceny scheme: $15 dollars here, $20 there—and slowly, as in Case 709, the culprit bleeds his company. Because the missing amounts are small, the shortages may be credited to errors rather than theft. Typically, the employee becomes dependent on the extra money he is pilfering, and his thefts increase in scale or become more frequent, which causes the scheme to be uncovered. Most retail organizations track overages or shortages by employee, making this method largely ineffectual.

Reversing Transactions   Another way to conceal cash larceny is to use reversing transactions, such as false voids or refunds, which cause the register tape to reconcile to the amount of cash on hand after the theft. By processing fraudulent reversing transactions, an employee can reduce the amount of cash reflected on the register tape. For instance, in Case 2147, a cashier received payments from a customer and recorded the transactions on her system. She later stole those payments, and then destroyed the company's receipts that reflected the transactions. To complete the cover-up, the cashier went back and voided the transactions, which she had entered at the time the payments were received. The reversing entries brought the receipt totals into balance with the cash on hand. (These schemes will be discussed in more detail in Chapter 8.)

Altering Cash Counts or Cash Register Tapes   A cash register is balanced by comparing the transactions on the register tape to the amount of cash on hand. Starting at a known balance, sales, returns, and other register transactions are added to or subtracted from the balance to arrive at a total for the period in question. The actual cash is then counted and the two totals are compared. If the register tape shows that there should be more cash in the register than what is present, it may be because of larceny. To conceal cash larceny, some fraudsters alter the cash counts from their registers to match the total receipts reflected on their register tape. For example, if an employee processes $1,000 worth of transactions on a register, then steals $300, there will be only $700 left in the cash drawer. The employee will falsify the cash count by recording that $1,000 is on hand so that the cash count balances to the register tape. This type of scheme occurred in Case 1806, when a fraudster not only discarded register tapes to conceal her thefts, but also erased and rewrote cash counts for the registers from which she pilfered. The new totals on the cash count envelopes were overstated by the amount of money she had stolen, reflecting the actual receipts for the period and balancing with the cash register tapes. Under the victim company's controls, this employee was not supposed to have access to cash. Ironically, coworkers praised her dedication for helping them count cash when it was not one of her official duties.

Instead of altering cash counts, some employees will manually alter the register tape from their cash registers. Again, the purpose of this activity is to force a balance between the cash on hand and the record of cash received. In Case 788, for instance, a department manager altered and destroyed cash register tapes to help conceal a fraud scheme that went on for four years.

Destroying Register Tapes If the fraudster cannot make the cash and the tape balance, the next best thing is to prevent others from computing the totals and discovering the imbalance. Employees who are stealing at the point of sale sometimes destroy detail tapes, which would implicate them in a crime.

Preventing and Detecting Cash Larceny at the Point of Sale Most cash larceny schemes only succeed because of a lack of internal controls. In order to prevent this form of fraud, organizations should enforce separation of duties in the cash receipts process and make sure there are independent checks over the receipting and recording of incoming cash.

When cash is received over the counter, the employee conducting the transaction should record each transaction. The transaction is generally recorded on a cash register or on a prenumbered receipt form. At the end of the business day, each salesperson should count the cash in his cash drawer and record the amount on a memorandum form.

Another employee then removes the register tape or other records of the transactions. This employee also counts the cash to make sure the total agrees with the salesperson's count and with the register tape. By having an independent employee verify the cash count in each register or cash box at the end of each shift, an organization reduces the possibility of long-term losses due to cash theft. Cash larceny through the falsification of cash counts can be prevented by this control, and suspicions of fraud will be immediately raised if sales records have been purposely destroyed.

Once the second employee has determined that the totals for the register tape and cash on hand reconcile, the cash should be taken directly to the cashier's office. The register tape, memorandum form, and any other pertinent records of the day's transactions are sent to the accounting department, where the totals are entered in the cash receipts journal.

Obviously, to detect cash larceny at the point of sale, the first key is to look for discrepancies between sales records and cash on hand. Large differences will normally draw attention, but those who reconcile the two figures should also be alert to a high frequency of small-dollar occurrences. Fraudsters sometimes steal small amounts in the hopes that they will not be noticed, or that such shortfalls will be too small to review. A pattern of small shortages may indicate the presence of this type of scheme.

Organizations should also periodically run reports showing the number of discounts, returns, adjustments, write-offs, and other concealing transactions issued by employee, department, or location. These transactions may be used to conceal cash larceny. Similarly, all journal entries to cash accounts could be scrutinized, as these are often used to hide missing cash.

Larceny of Receivables

Not all cash larceny schemes occur at the point of sale. As was discussed in Chapter 2, employees will frequently steal incoming customer payments on accounts receivable. Generally, these schemes involve skimming—the perpetrator steals the payment but never records it. In some cases, however, the theft occurs after the payment has been recorded, which means that it is classified as cash larceny. In Case 2758, for example, an employee posted all records of customer payments to date, but stole the money received. In a four-month period, this employee took over $200,000 in incoming payments. Consequently, the cash account was significantly out of balance, which led to discovery of the fraud. This was one of the cases in the ACFE studies, incidentally, in which the employee justified the theft by saying she planned to pay the money back. This case illustrates the central weakness of cash larceny schemes—the resulting imbalances in company accounts. In order for an employee to succeed at a cash larceny scheme, he must be able to hide the imbalances caused by the fraud. Larceny of receivables is generally concealed through one of three methods:

- Force balancing
- Reversing entries
- Destruction of records

Force Balancing   Those fraudsters who have total control of a company's accounting system can overcome the problem of out-of-balance accounts. In Case 1663, an employee stole customer payments and posted them to the accounts receivable journal in the same manner as the fraudster discussed in Case 2758 above. As in the previous case, this employee's fraud resulted in an imbalance in the victim company's cash account. The difference between the two frauds is that the perpetrator of Case 1663 had control over the company's deposits and all its ledgers. She was therefore able to conceal her crime by *force balancing*: making unsupported entries in the company's books to produce a fictitious balance between receipts and ledgers. This case illustrates how poor separation of duties can allow the perpetuation of a fraud that ordinarily would be easy to detect.

Reversing Entries   In circumstances in which payments are stolen but nonetheless posted to the cash receipts journal, reversing entries can be used to balance the victim company's accounts. For instance, in Case 1886, an office manager stole approximately $75,000 in customer payments from her employer. Her method in a number of these cases was to post the payment to the customer's account, and then to later reverse the entry on the books with unauthorized adjustments such as "courtesy discounts."

Destruction of Records   A less elegant way to hide a crime is to simply destroy all records that might prove that the perpetrator has been stealing. Destroying records en masse does not prevent the victim company from realizing that it is being robbed, but it may help conceal the identity of the thief. A controller in Case 1550 used this "slash-and-burn" concealment strategy. The controller, who had complete control over the books of her employer, stole approximately $100,000. When it became evident that her superiors were suspicious of her activities, the perpetrator entered her office one night after work, stole all the cash on hand, destroyed all records (among them her personnel file), and left town.

Cash Larceny from the Deposit

At some point in most revenue-generating businesses, someone must physically take the company's currency and checks to the bank. This person or persons, literally left holding the bag, will have an opportunity to take a portion of the money prior to depositing it into the company's accounts.

Typically, when a company receives cash, someone is assigned to tabulate the receipts, list the form of payment (currency or check), and prepare a deposit slip for the bank. Then another employee, preferably one not involved in the preparing of the deposit slip, takes the cash and deposits it in the bank. The person who made out the deposit generally retains one copy of the slip. This copy is matched to a receipted copy of the slip stamped by the bank when the deposit is made.

This procedure is designed to prevent theft of funds from the deposit, but thefts still occur, often because the process is not adhered to (see Exhibit 3-5). In Case 1277, for example, an employee in a small company was responsible for preparing and making the deposits, recording the deposits in the company's books, and reconciling the bank statements. This employee took several thousand dollars from the company deposits and concealed it by making false entries in the books that corresponded to falsely prepared deposit slips. Similarly, in a retail store where cash registers were not used—in Case 2833—sales were recorded on prenumbered invoices. The controller of this organization was responsible for collecting cash receipts and making the bank deposits. This controller

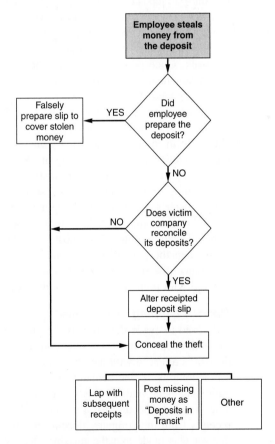

EXHIBIT 3-5 Cash Larceny from the Deposit

was also the only person who reconciled the totals on the prenumbered receipts to the bank deposit. Therefore, he was able to steal a portion of the deposit with the knowledge that the discrepancy between the deposit and the day's receipts would not be detected.

Another oversight in procedure is failure to reconcile the bank copy of the deposit slip with the office copy. When the person making the deposit knows that his company does not reconcile the two deposit slips, he can steal cash from the deposit on the way to the bank and alter the deposit slip so that it reflects a lesser amount. In some cases sales records will also be altered to match the diminished deposit.

When cash is stolen from the deposit, the receipted deposit slip will of course be out of balance with the company's copy of the deposit slip (unless the perpetrator also prepared the deposit). To correct this problem, some fraudsters alter the bank copy of the deposit slip after it has been validated. This brings the two copies back into balance. In Case 1446, for example, an employee altered twenty-four deposit slips and validated bank receipts in the course of a year to conceal the theft of over $15,000. These documents were altered with correction fluid or ballpoint pen to match the company's cash reports. Of course, cash having been stolen, the company's book balance will not match its actual bank balance. If another employee regularly balances the checking account, this type of theft should be easily detected.

Another mistake that can be made in the deposit function, and one that is a departure from common sense, is entrusting the deposit to the wrong person. For instance, in Case 693, a bookkeeper who had been employed for only one month was put in charge of making the deposit. She promptly diverted the funds to her own use. This is not to say that all new employees are untrustworthy—but it is advisable to have some sense of a person's character before handing that person a bag full of money.

Still another commonsense issue is the handling of the deposit on the way to the bank. Once prepared, the deposit should be immediately put in a safe place until it is taken to the bank. In a few of the cases we studied, the deposit was carelessly left unattended. In Case 2232, for example, a part-time employee learned that it was the bookkeeper's habit to leave the bank bag in her desk overnight before taking it to the bank the following morning. For approximately six months, this employee pilfered checks from the deposit and got away with it. He was able to endorse the checks at a local establishment, without using his own signature, in the name of the victim company. The owner of the check-cashing institution did not question the fact that this individual was cashing company checks because, as a pastor of a sizable church in the community, the fraudster's integrity was thought to be above reproach.

As with other cash larceny schemes, stealing from the company deposit can be rather difficult to conceal. In most cases these schemes are successful for a long duration only when the person who counts the cash also makes the deposit. In any other circumstance, the success of the scheme depends primarily on the inattentiveness of those charged with preparing and reconciling the deposit.

Deposit Lapping   One method ACFE studies have identified as having been successfully used to evade detection is the lapping method. Lapping occurs when an employee steals the deposit from day one, and then replaces it with day two's deposit. Day two's deposit is replaced with day three's, and so on. The perpetrator is always one day behind, but as long as no one demands an up-to-the minute reconciliation of the deposits to the bank statement, and if the size of the deposits does not drop precipitously, he may be able to avoid detection for a period of time. In Case 1993, a company officer stole cash receipts from the company deposit and withheld the deposit for a time. Eventually the deposit was made and the missing cash was replaced with a check received at a later date. Lapping is discussed in more detail in Chapter 2.

Deposits in Transit A final concealment strategy with stolen deposits is to carry the missing money as deposits in transit. In Case 1716, an employee was responsible for receiving collections, issuing receipts, posting transactions, reconciling accounts, and making deposits. Such a lack of separation of duties leaves a company extremely vulnerable to fraud. This employee took over $20,000 in collections from her employer over a five-month period. To hide her theft, the perpetrator carried the missing money as deposits in transit, meaning that the missing money would appear on the next month's bank statement. Of course, it never did. The balance was carried for several months as "d.i.t." until an auditor recognized the discrepancy and put a halt to the fraud.

Preventing and Detecting Cash Larceny from the Deposit The most important factor in preventing cash larceny from the deposit is separating duties. Calculating daily receipts, preparing the deposit, delivering the deposit to the bank, and verifying the receipted deposit slip are duties that should be performed independently of one another. So long as this separation is maintained, shortages in the deposit should be quickly detected.

All incoming revenues should be delivered to a centralized department where an itemized deposit slip is prepared, listing each individual check or money order along with currency receipts. Itemizing the deposit slip is a key antifraud control. It enables the organization to track specific payments to the deposit and may help detect larceny as well as lapping schemes and other forms of receivables skimming. It is very important that the person who prepares the deposit slip be separated from the duty of receiving and logging incoming payments so that he can act as an independent check on these functions. Before it is sent to the bank, the deposit slip should be matched to the remittance list to ensure that all payments are accounted for.

Typically, the cashier will deliver the deposit to the bank, while a cash-receipts clerk posts the total amount of receipts in the cash receipts journal. In some cases, the cashier does the posting, while a separate individual delivers the deposit. In either case, the duties of posting cash receipts and delivering the deposit should be separated. If a single person performs both functions, that individual can falsify the deposit slip or cash receipts postings to conceal larceny from the deposit.

Once the deposit has been totaled and matched to the remittance list, it should be secured and taken immediately to the bank, along with two copies of the deposit slip (one of which will be retained by the bank). A third copy of the deposit slip should be retained by the organization. When the deposit is made, one copy of the deposit slip is stamped (authenticated) by the bank as received. The bank then delivers this copy back to the depositing organization.

The authenticated deposit slip should be compared with the organization's copy of the deposit slip, the remittance list, and the general ledger posting of the day's receipts. If all four totals match, this verifies that the deposit was properly made. It is critical that someone other than the person who prepared the deposit reconcile the authenticated deposit slip. If the cashier, for example, is allowed to prepare and reconcile the deposit, the control function designed to prevent cash larceny at this stage is effectively destroyed. The cashier could falsify the deposit slip or force totals to conceal larceny. If fraud is suspected, verify each deposit prior to dispatch without the suspect's knowledge; then call the bank to verify that the entire deposit was made.

In order to further safeguard against larceny, two copies of the bank statement should be delivered to different persons in the organization. Each person should verify deposits on the bank statement to postings in the general ledger and to receipted deposit slips. If deposits in transit show up on a bank reconciliation, they should clear within two days of the date of reconciliation. Any instance in which a deposit in transit exceeds the two-day clear should be investigated.

To prevent deposit lapping, organizations can require that deposits be made in a night drop at the bank and verify each deposit at the beginning of the next day's business.

The following case study has been selected as an example of how an employee stole cash from his company's bank deposits. Bill Gurado, a branch manager for a consumer-loan finance company, took his branch's deposits to the bank himself, where he placed the money into his own account rather than his employer's. CFE Harry Smith audited Gurado's branch to determine the scope of his scheme. This case provides an excellent example of how an employee's perception of his company's controls can be valuable in preventing and detecting fraud.

CASE STUDY: THE OL' FAKE SURPRISE AUDIT GETS 'EM EVERY TIME[2]

Some people would say that auditors have no sense of humor—that they are a straight-laced, straight-faced bunch. Bill Gurado knows better.

Gurado worked as a branch manager for Newfund, a consumer-loan finance company in New Orleans. He was the highly respected leader of the company's oldest, largest, and most successful branch. With such a high profile, Gurado commanded a lot of respect. Other managers wanted to be like him. Employees respected him. Everyone in the company considered him a good guy.

For reasons not entirely clear, Gurado began stealing from the company. He did not take a lot of money. His scheme was less than brilliant. And because he did not appreciate an auditor's sense of humor, his fraud was brought to light just weeks after it began.

Newfund employed good controls, both from an accounting as well as a management standpoint. One control on which Barry Ecker, the company's internal auditor, relied was the surprise audit. He normally sprang surprise audits at least once, and sometimes twice, a year on each of Newfund's thirty branches. Due to the size of Gurado's branch, Ecker could not perform a surprise audit by himself. He would have to coordinate with the external audit staff. During these surprise audits, Ecker came in and took control from the start. He was extremely thorough. Harry J. Smith, one of the external auditors whose team would accompany him, describes Ecker as "your typical old-time sleuth-type auditor. A little bitty, short, pudgy guy who got a lot of psychic pleasure out of scaring the hell out of branch people. He'd come in and he'd be quiet and very secure about his papers and his area. He'd stare people down. He'd stare at ledger cards looking for irregularities. He'd just make people quake." Adds Smith, "He was really fun to watch. When he was in his character, he was one for the books." Having been through several surprise audits, Gurado knew the extent of Ecker's

investigating. He probably had that in the back of his mind when he ran into Ecker at a store by chance over the weekend.

They had a brief conversation, and as might be expected from someone like Ecker, who enjoyed putting a little fear into people, he mentioned he was about to launch a surprise audit at Gurado's branch. "Well, I'll see you Monday," he said without cracking a smile. "Harry and I are going to pull an audit on your branch on Monday morning." Of course, he had no plans to audit the branch any time in the near future. As they parted, Gurado said, "Great. See you then." But Gurado was not looking forward to seeing Ecker at all. He knew that Ecker, with all his searching and checking, would find some irregularities. He would piece together Gurado's fraud without much trouble at all. It would not take much effort to learn that Gurado had diverted company money into his own bank account.

Newfund's clientele was such that it received a lot of cash. For about a week Gurado took the daily deposits to the bank himself and deposited the money in his personal account. He made certain all the daily reports were sent to headquarters as usual—except, of course, the receipted bank deposit slips. It was only a few thousand dollars. But he had not yet had a chance to replace any of the money (if he had ever intended to), and he would not have time to cover his tracks before the "surprise" audit.

"He was absolutely convinced that had we audited his branch, we would find it," says Smith. "And we probably would have. Barry Ecker did an old-style audit where you go in and seal the file cabinets and take immediate control of the cash drawers and the ledger tubs. It's a complete instantaneous control and tie-out. I'm pretty sure we'd have found it. I know the branch manager was convinced his boat was sunk."

Gurado did some deep soul-searching that weekend. On Sunday night, he called on the president of the company, a man with a reputation of being a hard-driving, authoritarian individual. "I know it was a giant step for the branch

[2]Several names and details have been changed to preserve anonymity.

manager to call him up that night," Smith says. At the president's house that Sunday evening, Gurado came clean. "I know the auditors are coming tomorrow morning," he said. Then he confessed to taking money from the company. He was immediately fired.

On Monday morning, Ecker called Smith at the accounting firm. He told Smith what had transpired, and then said, "Look, we gotta go audit the branch." Smith and Ecker pulled out all the stops to get an audit team over to the branch to make sure there was nothing else going on.

They found exactly what Gurado had reported and nothing else. Looking back on this case, Smith feels certain the fraud would have been detected even without the misunderstood joke. Newfund practiced a control procedure that probably would have turned up the missing money within fifteen days. Because of that fact, he surmises that Gurado might have been covering some kind of short-term debt with the intent of repaying it.

Since Gurado returned the funds immediately and because he had confessed, the company did not pursue any criminal or civil action against him, feeling it a better course of action to keep the matter out of the public eye.

Word did travel quickly around the company, however—upper management made sure of that. The fact that this esteemed branch manager tripped himself up and immediately got caught went a long way toward reinforcing the importance of following proper procedures.

"People commonly measure auditing's benefit by the substance of its findings and recommendations," Smith says. "Auditing's role in preventing abuse is hard to observe and measure and is often unappreciated. But this case clearly shows that the specter of having an audit certainly affects peoples' behavior."

PROACTIVE COMPUTER AUDIT TESTS FOR DETECTING CASH LARCENY[1]

Title	Category	Description	Data file(s)
Summarize by employee the difference between the cash receipt report and the sales register system.	All	Focus should be given to employees with high-dollar differences, especially when manifested as high occurrence of small-dollar differences.	• Sales system register • Cash receipts register
Summarize by employee by day the difference between the cash receipt report and the sales register system.	All	Focus should be given to employees with high-dollar differences, especially high occurrences of small-dollar differences.	• Sales system register • Cash receipts register
Summarize by location discounts, returns, cash receipt adjustments, accounts receivable write-offs, and voids charged.	All	Locations with high adjustments may signal actions to hide cash larceny schemes.	• Sales system register • Invoice sales register • Cash receipts register
Summarize by employee discounts, returns, cash receipt adjustments, accounts receivable write-offs, and voids charged.	All	Employees with high adjustments may signal actions to hide cash larceny schemes.	• Sales system register • Invoice sales register • Cash receipts register
List top 100 employees by dollar size (one for discounts, one for refunds, one for cash receipt adjustments, one for accounts receivable write-offs, and one for sale voids).	All	Employees with high adjustments may signal actions to hide cash larceny schemes.	• Sales system register • Invoice sales register • Cash receipts register

(Continued)

(Continued)

Title	Category	Description	Data file(s)
List top 100 employees who have been on any top-100 list for three months (whether for discounts, for refunds, for cash receipt adjustments, for accounts receivable write-offs, or for sale voids).	All	Employees with high adjustments may signal actions to hide cash larceny schemes.	• Sales system register • Invoice sales register • Cash receipts register
List top 10 locations that have been on a top-10 list for three months (whether for discounts, for refunds, for cash receipt adjustments, for accounts receivable write-offs, or for sale voids).	All	Locations with high adjustments may signal actions to hide cash larceny schemes.	• Sales system register • Invoice sales register • Cash receipts register
Compute standard deviation for each employee for the last three months and list those employees that provided three times the standard deviation in the current month (separately for discounts, for refunds, for cash receipt adjustments, for accounts receivable write-offs, and for sale voids).	All	Employees with high adjustments may signal actions to hide cash larceny schemes.	• Sales system register • Invoice sales register • Cash receipts register
Compare adjustments to inventory to the void/refund transactions summarized by employee.	All	First, a summary of adjustments by inventory item number and employee is completed, which is then compared to credit adjustments (to inappropriately decrease inventory that was supposedly returned) by inventory number.	• Sales system register • Inventory detail register
Review unique journal entries in cash accounts.	All	All journal entries in cash accounts, especially those that appear to be unique adjustments, should be reviewed as concealment actions to a cash larceny scheme.	• General ledger detail
Summarize user access for the sales, accounts receivable, cash receipt, and general ledger systems for segregation of duties reviews.	All	User access to systems may identify segregation of duties issues. For example, if an employee can make changes to the accounts receivable system and then post other concealment entries in the general ledger, such nonsegregation of duties would allow an employee to hide his actions. User access should be reviewed from the perspective of adjustments within the application and adjustments to the data itself.	• System user access logs or System user access master file
Summarize user access for the sales, accounts receivable, cash receipt, and general ledger systems in nonbusiness hours.	All	Concealment adjustments often are made in nonbusiness hours. User access should be reviewed from the perspective of adjustments within the application and adjustments to the data itself.	• System user access logs

SUMMARY

Cash larceny is the intentional taking away of an employer's cash, currency, or checks, without the consent, and against the will, of the employer. Cash larceny schemes differ from skimming in that they are *on-book* frauds; they involve the theft of money that has been recorded in the employer's books, whereas skimming involves the theft of unrecorded cash. Because cash larceny schemes target recorded cash, these frauds leave a victim organization's books out of balance; cash on hand is reduced by the theft even as recorded cash remains constant. Cash larceny frauds are sometimes discovered as a result of this imbalance, but the perpetrator of a cash larceny scheme will often take steps to conceal the imbalance on the organization's books.

Most cash larceny schemes take place at the point of sale. Several methods can be used to conceal this type of fraud, most of them fairly uncomplicated. The perpetrator might steal from a cash register other than the one he is logged onto in order to keep from being a suspect. Another common scheme involves the repeated theft of very small amounts in hopes that the shortages will be disregarded by the organization. Reversing transactions such as fraudulent refunds can be processed to account for the missing funds. Cash counts or sales records may be altered to produce a false balance, or records may be destroyed altogether to prevent others from reconciling cash on hand to recorded sales. When employees steal receivables, as opposed to incoming sales, these thefts are typically concealed by force balancing, processing fraudulent discounts or other reversing entries, or destroying records of the transaction in question.

Cash larceny schemes also frequently target the victim organization's bank deposits. The perpetrator steals currency or checks after the deposit has been prepared but before it has been taken to the bank. These schemes frequently succeed when one person is in charge of calculating daily receipts, preparing the deposit, delivering the deposit to the bank, and verifying the receipted deposit slip. This breakdown in controls allows the perpetrator to steal cash without anyone detecting the resulting imbalances in the company's accounting records. In some cases, the perpetrator will lap daily receipts or list missing deposits as "deposits in transit" to further conceal the crime.

ESSENTIAL TERMS

Cash larceny The theft of an organization's cash after it has been recorded in the accounting system.

Cash receipts schemes Frauds that target incoming sales or receivables. Typically, the perpetrators in these schemes physically abscond with the victim organization's cash instead of relying on phony documents to justify the disbursement of the funds. Cash receipts frauds generally fall into two categories: skimming and cash larceny.

Deposit lapping A method of concealing deposit theft that occurs when an employee steals part or all of the deposit from one day and then replaces it with receipts from subsequent days.

Fraudulent disbursements Schemes in which an employee illegally or improperly causes the distribution of funds in a way that appears to be legitimate. Funds can be obtained by forging checks, submission of false invoices, or falsifying time records.

Reversing transactions A method used to conceal cash larceny. The perpetrator processes false transactions to void a sale or refund cash, which cause sales records to reconcile to the amount of cash on hand after the theft.

REVIEW QUESTIONS

3-1 (Learning objective 3-1) What is cash larceny?

3-2 (Learning objective 3-2) How do cash larceny schemes differ from fraudulent disbursements?

3-3 (Learning objective 3-3) What is the difference between cash larceny and skimming?

3-4 (Learning objective 3-4) Where do cash larceny schemes rank among cash misappropriations in terms of frequency? In terms of median loss?

3-5 (Learning objective 3-5) What are the main weaknesses in an internal control system that permit fraudsters the opportunity to commit cash larceny schemes?

3-6 (Learning objective 3-6) What are the five methods discussed in this chapter that are used to conceal cash larceny that occurs at the point of sale? Explain how each works.

3-7 (Learning objective 3-8) How do employees commit cash larceny of incoming receivables? How are the schemes concealed?

3-8 (Learning objective 3-8) What is force balancing, and how is it used to conceal cash larceny?

3-9 (Learning objective 3-9) How do fraudsters commit cash larceny from the bank deposit?

3-10 (Learning objectives 3-5, 3-7, and 3-10) What are some basic internal control procedures to deter and detect cash larceny schemes?

DISCUSSION ISSUES

3-1 (Learning objectives 3-1, 3-6, 3-8, and 3-9) Briefly describe some common types of cash larceny schemes.

3-2 (Learning objective 3-3) Why is it generally more difficult to detect skimming than cash larceny?

3-3 (Learning objectives 3-2 and 3-3) In the case study of bank teller Laura Grove, what type of fraud did she commit?

3-4 (Learning objective 3-5) What are the internal control weaknesses that failed to deter and detect the fraud in Laura Grove's case?

3-5 (Learning objectives 3-6 and 3-7) Other than falsifying a company's records of cash receipts, how might an employee conceal larceny from a cash register?

3-6 (Learning objectives 3-10 and 3-11) What steps might an organization take to protect outgoing bank deposits from cash larceny schemes?

3-7 (Learning objective 3-8) How is the larceny of receivables often detected?

3-8 (Learning objective 3-11) In the case study "The Ol' Fake Surprise Audit Gets 'Em Every Time," how did Newfund's accounting and management controls contribute to the detection of Gurado's fraud scheme? How did the resulting actions of management help to deter future frauds?

3-9 (Learning objective 3-11) Among the proactive audit techniques suggested in this chapter are (1) a summary, by employee, of the difference between cash receipt reports and the sales register system and (2) a summary, by employee, of discounts, returns, cash receipt adjustments, accounts receivable write-offs, and voids processed. Why would these two tests be effective in detecting cash larceny?

ENDNOTES

1. Lanza, pp. 38–40.

Billing Schemes

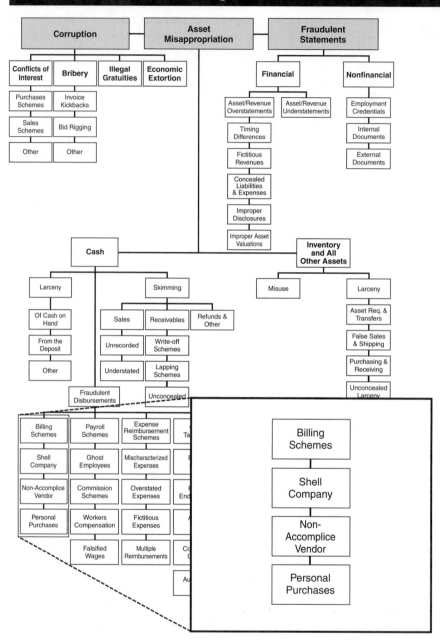

Corruption

Conflicts of Interest	Bribery	Illegal Gratuities	Economic Extortion
Purchases Schemes	Invoice Kickbacks		
Sales Schemes	Bid Rigging		
Other	Other		

Asset Misappropriation

Fraudulent Statements

Financial		Nonfinancial
Asset/Revenue Overstatements	Asset/Revenue Understatements	Employment Credentials
Timing Differences		Internal Documents
Fictitious Revenues		External Documents
Concealed Liabilities & Expenses		
Improper Disclosures		
Improper Asset Valuations		

Cash

Larceny	Skimming		
Of Cash on Hand	Sales	Receivables	Refunds & Other
From the Deposit	Unrecorded	Write-off Schemes	
Other	Understated	Lapping Schemes	

Fraudulent Disbursements — Unconcealed

Billing Schemes	Payroll Schemes	Expense Reimbursement Schemes	
Shell Company	Ghost Employees	Mischaracterized Expenses	
Non-Accomplice Vendor	Commission Schemes	Overstated Expenses	
Personal Purchases	Workers Compensation	Fictitious Expenses	
	Falsified Wages	Multiple Reimbursements	

Inventory and All Other Assets

Misuse	Larceny
	Asset Req. & Transfers
	False Sales & Shipping
	Purchasing & Receiving
	Unconcealed Larceny

Billing Schemes

- Billing Schemes
- Shell Company
- Non-Accomplice Vendor
- Personal Purchases

EXHIBIT 4-1

CHAPTER 4

BILLING SCHEMES

LEARNING OBJECTIVES

After studying this chapter, you should be able to:

4-1 List the five major categories of fraudulent disbursements

4-2 Define billing schemes

4-3 List the three categories of billing schemes

4-4 Understand what a shell company is, and how it is formed

4-5 List and understand the four ways false invoices are approved for payment

4-6 Understand why most shell company schemes involve the purchase of services rather than goods

4-7 Understand how a pass-through scheme differs from the usual shell company schemes

4-8 Be familiar with the methods identified in this chapter for preventing and detecting shell company schemes

4-9 Understand how pay-and-return schemes work

4-10 Understand how non-accomplice vendor schemes work

4-11 Be familiar with the methods identified in this chapter for preventing and detecting non-accomplice vendor schemes

4-12 Understand how personal purchases schemes work

4-13 Be familiar with the methods identified in this chapter for preventing and detecting personal purchases schemes

4-14 Be familiar with proactive audit tests that can be used to detect billing schemes

CASE STUDY: MEDICAL SCHOOL TREATS FRAUD AND ABUSE[1]

Fraud seemed to plague a certain Southeastern medical college, with one bad case erupting after another. One supervisor's minor transgression opened a Pandora's box of fraud perpetrated by his assistant. It all began when Bruce Livingstone, a married supervisor at the college's three-person business office, took his girlfriend on a business trip using school funds drawn from a suspense account (a temporary account in which entries of credits or charges are made until their proper disposition can be determined). Livingstone did not submit an expense report to offset the charges that

month, a violation of a policy governing the college's extensive travel budget.

Once officials realized that employees had grown lax about submitting timely expense reports, they attempted to reconcile the suspense account by requiring employees to settle their own accounts before receiving their paychecks. Not wanting his indiscretion revealed, Livingstone had to disguise the additional expense of taking his girlfriend on a business trip. He submitted a phony expense report in which he unwisely named a female senior auditor at the college as his traveling partner. He forged the auditor's signature on a letter that stated she had participated.

As luck would have it, the unsuspecting auditor herself reviewed the bogus report. She was quite surprised to

[1]Several names and details have been changed to preserve anonymity.

find she'd taken a trip with Livingstone. She immediately informed Harold Dore, the director of internal audit for the institution, of the forgery. Dore alerted others.

Following a short interview with college officials, Livingstone admitted his wrongdoing and was promptly terminated. The executive vice president authorized Dore to conduct a full fraud examination. As they were soon to find out, they had not seen the worst of it yet. Livingstone's amorous business trip was just the tip of the iceberg.

"Whenever there's fraud found here," said Dore, "I automatically conduct what I call a 'magnitude investigation.'" He has learned that perpetrators rarely limit themselves to the fraud initially uncovered: "Chances are, they did something else."

As part of the information-gathering portion of his investigation, Dore decided to interview Cheryl Brown, the 30-year-old administrative assistant who had worked under Livingstone for three years. The interview was to be conducted with the dean of the dental school president, so Dore headed across campus toward the business office.

But Brown left before Dore arrived. She told coworkers that her uncle had been shot and that she had to depart for California immediately. In her haste to get away, she even left her paycheck behind.

Taking that as a sign, Dore immediately sealed the empty office Brown and Livingstone shared and began searching its contents. The search uncovered bags of expensive dental tools and prostheses, which it turned out he had been illegally selling to dental students for years.

Knowing vendor kickbacks are common—and since one of the main functions of the business office was to process invoices submitted by vendors—Dore started by reviewing the master file. The list had never been purged and contained tens of thousands of names—all the vendors who had ever supplied goods and services as part of the college's annual budget of $55 million. He selected 50 vendors, deliberately choosing those without a phone number or street address.

Then Dore took his list to the next stop in the payment process, the accounts payable department. After methodically pulling all corresponding documentation, he quickly focused on one vendor: Armstrong Supply Company. It regularly billed two or three times a month for strange items named but unknown by Dore, and always for amounts under $4,500, thus eliminating the necessity of two authorized signatures. All of the request-for-funds forms attached to the invoices either bore the signature of Livingstone or the dean of the dental school. Furthermore, Dore could find no vendor application on file for Armstrong Supply. He also failed to find any competitive bidding process in place.

"Once I looked at the actual invoices, that really got me going," said the fraud examiner. Some carried invoice numbers; others did not, but they did carry a four-digit post office box number. (Subsequent research revealed that postal authorities had switched to five-digit and six-digit PO boxes years earlier.) Billed items included such things as "3 dozen TPM pins" (the identity of which baffled even the long-time stockroom manager).

"The invoices just smelled fake," said Dore, who packs more than 20 years of auditing experience. What's more, he later found blank invoices for Armstrong Supply in one of Brown's desk drawers. He even noticed one completed invoice that had been readied for submission. (Apparently, Brown left in too much of a hurry to dispose of the smoking gun.)

Based on those questionable invoices, the accounts payable department would issue a check for the stated amount. On the request-for-funds forms attached, Brown always indicated that she would personally present the check to Armstrong Supply. (Due to lax controls, vendors and employees were allowed to pick up checks.) Canceled checks revealed that a man named Claude Armstrong III cashed them at various check-cashing services, which sometimes called Cheryl Brown for additional verification, as noted on the backs of the checks.

Further research showed yet another scam, according to Dore. The office mail contained a department store gift card with a note from a vendor to Brown, thanking her for her recent business. The California vendor had billed the college for roughly $42,000 worth of copy machine cartridges—running $4,500 apiece—and Brown had processed the invoices. After a fruitless search for this valuable cache in the school's storerooms and copy centers, Dore called local dealers and discovered that their most expensive cartridge cost only $483. Under his direction, private investigators located the vendor's "corporate headquarters" in a rental unit at a retail postal center, but the college abandoned their long-distance pursuit of recovery when it proved too costly.

Although Dore tried to keep his three-month-long investigation quiet, the campus buzzed with news of his activities. Brown's many friends, including two in the accounts payable department, kept her abreast of his movements.

Next he pulled in Livingstone for a chat about the new evidence supporting vendor fraud and kickbacks, as well as his backroom sale of orthodontic supplies. According to Dore, it became apparent during the interview that the philanderer knew nothing about the vendor schemes. Brown had perpetrated the $63,000 vendor fraud without Livingstone's help. He seemed quite taken aback that it had occurred under his nose by someone he trusted so much. In some cases, Brown had forged the signatures of her supervisor and the dean of the dental school. In others, the unwitting bosses actually signed the bogus forms.

At the same time the Livingstone interview was being conducted, the school's general counsel received a call from Brown's lawyer. "He asked if we had ever given leniency to an errant employee in the past, if he were to admit to everything," said Dore. Once the general counsel deemed it a possibility, they scheduled a meeting for September. It was to be attended by both attorneys, Dore, the executive vice president of the college, and Brown, who had never returned to work since her hasty departure. Her lawyer also relayed her request to bring along a friend as a character witness, a nurse for whom she had once worked and who could attest to the good nature of this unmarried mother supporting three small children.

Brown was quiet and cooperative at the meeting. Dore took her through his voluminous file folder on Armstrong Supply, the sham company she had created. She willingly identified each and every document that detailed her duplicity, which had begun five months after her hire. Dire cash emergencies prompted the first few deceptions, she said. As Brown realized how easy it was in light of the weak controls, her confidence grew and she stepped up her thefts with no signs of stopping. "It became addictive, in her words," recalled Dore.

To illustrate her need, she explained that her husband had developed a drug and alcohol problem and that she had been dragged into drug abuse as well. She claimed that after she had become addicted, her husband abandoned her and the small children. She then broke down and cried, the first of many times during the interview. Brown went on to point out that she was seeing a doctor for her addictive behavior. When Dore asked how long she had been seeing her doctor, "She said her first visit was going to be next week." (Months later, a casual conversation between Dore and a coworker who had once dated Brown raised doubts about her excuses. "He swore she never touched drugs or alcohol," said Dore.)

She said her accomplice, Claude Armstrong III, was a friend with a history of drug abuse. (Background checks showed an arrest and conviction on drug charges for Armstrong; Brown had no prior arrests or convictions, and her references proved favorable.) She also admitted that her cover story about the uncle in California was fabricated.

After Brown expressed remorse over the fake invoices, Dore asked her about her relationship with the phony cartridge supply firm. She totally disavowed any knowledge of that scam. She insisted that the invoices were legitimate and the cartridges were stacked in a storeroom. (Note: No one has found the cartridges to date.)

Even without owning up to the recent $42,000 cartridge scam, Brown seemed surprised to learn that her Armstrong Supply fraud had netted $63,000 over two years.

Given the small percentage of the annual budget that was pilfered, college officials were not surprised that the fraud went undetected by the Big Four firm that served as their external auditor. Their contract stated that "audit tests are not all-inclusive and not designed to find fraud," a disclaimer that auditors rely on to absolve them from possible culpability. "If they were that detailed, nobody could afford an external audit," said Dore, also a certified internal auditor.

Looking back, he saw that some good stemmed from the frauds. Since then, the college has instituted much stronger controls and makes sure to enforce them. Dore said tales of his dogged investigation enhanced respect for the audit function, "[a]nd probably instilled a bit of fear among the 4,500 employees, because the college officials did pursue a criminal prosecution against Brown."

During the course of her trial, the district attorney informed Dore that his testimony was not needed, even though it would have shown hell-bent intent on the part of the defendant. With her lawyer acting on her behalf, Brown struck a deal with the prosecutor. She was placed on probation and ordered to pay partial restitution. (Brown was found three-fourths culpable and Armstrong one-fourth. Because half of the stolen funds came from federal grants, $30,000 was charged off to the federal granting authority.)

As part of the deal, Brown was also sentenced to six months' house arrest—with exceptions granted for her to attend work and church.

OVERVIEW

In Chapter 2, we saw that the vast majority of asset misappropriations target cash, as opposed to noncash assets. We also saw that cash misappropriations are subdivided into three categories in the fraud tree: *skimming, cash larceny*, and *fraudulent disbursements*. Skimming and cash larceny have already been covered, so we will now turn our attention in the next five chapters to fraudulent disbursement schemes. There are five major categories of fraudulent disbursement in the fraud tree:

- Billing schemes
- Check tampering
- Payroll schemes

- Expense reimbursement schemes
- Register disbursement schemes

The first category of fraudulent disbursements to be covered is *billing schemes*. These may be loosely defined as schemes in which a fraudster causes the victim organization to issue a fraudulent payment by submitting invoices for fictitious goods or services, inflated invoices, or invoices for personal purchases. As the data from ACFE research shows, billing schemes are among the most costly, and the most common, forms of occupational fraud.

Billing Scheme Data from the ACFE *2009 Global Fraud Survey*

Among the fraudulent disbursement categories, billing schemes were most commonly reported in the *2009 Global Fraud Survey* (see Exhibit 4-2). Of 921 reported fraudulent disbursement cases, 52 percent involved billing fraud. Billing schemes were also the second most costly form of fraudulent disbursement, with a reported median loss of $128,000 (see Exhibit 4-3).

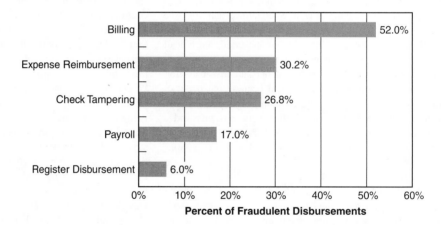

EXHIBIT 4-2 *2009 Global Fraud Survey*: Frequency of Fraudulent Disbursements[a]

[a]The sum of these percentages exceeds 100 percent because some cases involved multiple fraud schemes that fell into more than one category

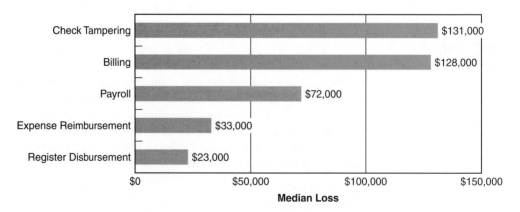

EXHIBIT 4-3 *2009 Global Fraud Survey*: Median Loss of Fraudulent Disbursements

BILLING SCHEMES

In a billing scheme, the perpetrator uses false documentation—such as an invoice, purchase order, credit card or purchasing card bill, and so on—to cause his employer to issue a payment for some fraudulent purpose. The actual disbursement of funds is performed by the organization in the same manner as would be a legitimate disbursement. The crux of the fraud is not that a bogus payment is issued; instead, the key to these schemes is that the fraudster is able to deceive his employer so that the organization willingly and unwittingly issues the bogus payment.

Billing schemes generally fall into one of three categories:

- Shell company schemes
- Non-accomplice vendor schemes
- Personal purchases schemes

Shell Company Schemes

Shell companies, for the purposes of our discussion, are fictitious entities created for the sole purpose of committing fraud. As we saw in the case study at the beginning of this chapter, they may be nothing more than a fabricated name and a post office box that an employee uses to collect disbursements from false billings. However, since the payments received will be payable to the shell company, the perpetrator will normally also set up a bank account in his new company's name, listing himself as an authorized signer on the account (see Exhibit 4-4).

Forming a Shell Company In order to open a bank account for a shell company, a fraudster will probably have to present the bank with a certificate of incorporation or an assumed-name certificate. These are documents that a company must obtain through a state or local government. These documents can be forged, but it is more likely that the perpetrator will simply file the requisite paperwork and obtain legitimate documents from his state or county. This can usually be accomplished for a small fee, the cost of which can be more than offset by a successful fraud scheme.

If it is discovered that a company is being falsely billed by a vendor, fraud examiners for the victim company may try to trace the ownership of the vendor. The documents used to start a bank account in a shell company's name can sometimes assist examiners in determining who is behind the fraudulent billings. If the corrupt employee formed his shell company under his own name, a search of public records at the local court house may reveal the person as the fraudster.

For this reason, the corrupt employee will sometimes form his shell company in the name of someone other than himself. For example, in Case 4737, an employee stole approximately $4 million from his company via false billings submitted from a shell company set up in his wife's name. Using a spouse's name adds a buffer of security to an employee's fraud scheme. When a male employee sets up a shell company, he sometimes does so in his wife's maiden name to further distance himself from the fictitious company.

A more effective way for a fraudster to hide his connection to a false company is to form the company under a fictitious name. In Case 4455 an employee used a coworker's identification to form a shell vendor. The fraudster then proceeded to bill his employer for approximately $20,000 in false services. The resulting checks were deposited in the

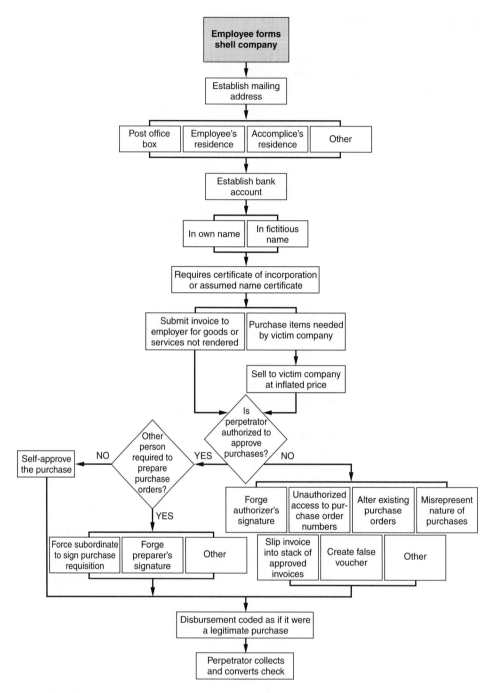

EXHIBIT 4-4   False Billings from Shell Companies

account of the shell company, and currency was withdrawn from the account through an ATM.

The other issue involved in forming a shell company is the entity's address—the place where fraudulent checks will be collected. Often, an employee rents a post office box and lists it as the mailing address of his shell company. Some employees list their home address instead. In Case 4434, a department head set up a dummy company using his residence as the mailing address. Over a two-year period, this man submitted over $250,000 worth of false invoices. Eventually, the scheme was detected by a newly hired clerk. The clerk was processing an invoice when she noticed that the address of the vendor was the same as her boss's address. (By a lucky coincidence, the clerk had typed a personal letter for her boss earlier that day and remembered his address.) Had the department head used a post office box instead of his home address on the invoices, his scheme might have continued indefinitely.

One reason employees might be hesitant to use post office boxes in shell company schemes is that some businesses are especially wary of sending checks to vendors that do not have street addresses. Such an address, as we have already discussed, can signal fraud. For this reason, fraudsters may use the address of a relative, friend, or accomplice as a collection point for fraudulent checks.

Submitting False Invoices Once a shell company is formed and a bank account has been opened, the corrupt employee is in a position to begin billing his employer. Invoices can be manufactured by various means such as a professional printer or a personal computer. As we saw in the case study at the beginning of this chapter, false invoices do not always have to be of professional quality to generate fraudulent disbursements. The phony invoices Cheryl Brown used to bill from Armstrong Supply Company "just smelled fake," according to Harold Dore, yet they were sufficient to generate checks.

Self-Approval of Fraudulent Invoices The difficulty in a shell-company scheme is not usually in producing the invoices, but in getting the victim company to pay them. Authorization for the fictitious purchase (and therefore payment of the bill) is the key. In a large percentage of the shell company cases in the ACFE studies, the fraudster was in a position to approve payment on the very invoices he was fraudulently submitting. In Case 446, for example, a manager authorized payment of $6 million worth of phony invoices from a dummy company he had formed. Similarly, an employee in Case 982 set up a bogus freight company and personally approved $50,000 worth of bogus invoices from it. It is only logical that those with authority to approve purchases would be among the most likely to engage in billing schemes, since they have fewer hurdles to overcome than other employees.

A slight twist to this method was used in Case 4542. The victim organization in this case properly required vouchers to be prepared and approved by different persons. The fraudster in this case had approval authority, but was not allowed to prepare the vouchers that he approved. Therefore, this person created false vouchers and forged a coworker's initials as the preparer. Then the perpetrator approved the voucher for payment under his own authority. It therefore appeared that two employees had signed off on the voucher, as mandated by the organization's controls.

Not all companies require the completion of payment vouchers before they will issue payments. In some enterprises, payments are issued based on less formal procedures. In Case 4436, for example, the CEO of a nonprofit company simply submitted "check requests" to the accounting department. As the CEO, his "requests" obviously carried great weight in the organization. The company issued checks to whatever company was listed on the request in whatever amount was specified. The CEO used these forms to obtain over $35,000 in payments for fictitious services rendered by a shell company he had formed. In this case, invoices were not even required to authorize the payments. The check request forms simply listed the payee, the amount, and a brief narrative regarding the reason for the check. This made it so easy for the CEO to generate fraudulent disbursements that he eventually had three separate companies billing the victim company at the same time. It is obvious that, as CEO, the fraudster in this case had a wide degree of latitude within the company and was unlikely to be obstructed by one of his subordinates. Nevertheless, this case should illustrate how the failure to require proper support for payments can lead to fraud.

"Rubber Stamp" Supervisors   If an employee cannot authorize payments himself, the next best thing is if the person who has that authority is inattentive or overly trusting. "Rubber stamp" supervisors like this are destined to be targeted by unethical employees. In Case 4759, for example, an employee set up a fake computer supply company with an accomplice and "sold" parts and services to his employer. The perpetrator's supervisor did not know much about computers and therefore could not accurately gauge whether the invoices from the dummy company were excessive—or even necessary. The supervisor was therefore forced to rely on the perpetrator of the scheme to verify the authenticity of the purchases. Consequently, the victim company suffered approximately $20,000 in losses.

Reliance on False Documents   When an employee does not have approval authority for purchases and does not have the benefit of a rubber stamp supervisor, he must run vouchers through the normal accounts payable process. The success of this kind of scheme will depend on the apparent authenticity of the false voucher he creates. If the fraudster can generate purchase orders and receiving reports that corroborate the information on the fraudulent invoice from his shell company, he can fool accounts payable into issuing a payment.

Collusion   Collusion among several employees is sometimes used to overcome well-designed internal controls of a victim company. For example, in a company with proper separation of duties, the functions of purchasing goods or services, authorizing the purchase, receiving the goods or services, and making the payment to the vendor should be separated. Obviously, if this process is strictly adhered to, it will be extremely difficult for any single employee to commit a false-billing scheme. As a result, the ACFE studies included several schemes in which employees conspired to defeat the fraud prevention measures of their employer. In Case 444, for example, a warehouse foreman and a parts-ordering clerk conspired to purchase approximately $300,000 of nonexistent supplies. The parts-ordering clerk initiated the false transactions by obtaining approval to place orders for parts he claimed were needed. The orders were then sent to a vendor who, acting in conjunction with the two employee fraudsters, prepared false invoices that were sent to the victim company. Meanwhile, the warehouse foreman verified receipt of the fictitious shipments of incoming supplies. The perpetrators were therefore able to compile complete vouchers for the fraudulent purchases without overstepping their normal duties. Similarly, in Case 4099, three employees set up a shell company to bill their employer for services and supplies. The first employee, a clerk, was in charge of ordering parts and services. The second employee, a purchasing agent, helped authorize these orders by falsifying purchasing reports regarding comparison pricing, and so on. The clerk was also responsible for receiving the parts and services; a third conspirator, a manager in the victim company's accounts payable department, ensured that payments were issued on the fraudulent invoices.

The cases above illustrate how collusion among several employees with separate duties in the purchasing process can be very difficult to detect. Even if all controls are followed, at some point a company must rely on its employees to be honest. One of the purposes of separating duties is to prevent any one person from having too much control over a particular business function; it provides a built-in monitoring mechanism whereby every person's actions are in some way verified by another person. But if everyone is corrupt, even proper controls can be overcome.

Purchases of Services Rather Than Goods   Most of the shell company schemes in our survey involved the purchase of services rather than goods. Why is this so? The primary reason is that services are not tangible. If an employee sets up a shell company to make fictitious sales of goods to his employer, these goods will obviously never arrive. By comparing its purchases to its inventory levels, the victim company might detect the fraud. It is much more difficult, however, for the victim company to verify that the services were never rendered. For this reason, many employees involved in shell company schemes bill their employers for things like "consulting services."

Pass-through Schemes   In the schemes discussed so far, the victim companies were billed for completely fictitious goods or services. This is the most common formula for a shell company fraud, but there is a subcategory of shell company schemes in which actual goods or services are sold to the victim company. These are known as pass-through schemes.

Pass-through schemes are usually undertaken by employees in charge of purchasing on behalf of the victim company. Instead of buying merchandise directly from a vendor, the employee sets up a shell company and purchases the merchandise through that fictitious entity. He then resells the merchandise to his employer from the shell company at an inflated price, thereby making an unauthorized profit on the transaction.

One of the best examples of a pass-through scheme in the ACFE studies came from Case 4763, in which a department director was in charge of purchasing computer equipment. Because of his expertise on the subject and his high standing within the company, he was unsupervised in this task. The director set up a shell company in another state and bought used computers through the shell company, then turned around and sold them to his employer at a greatly exaggerated price. The money from the victim company's first installment on the computers was used to pay the shell company's debts to the real vendors. Subsequent payments were profits for the bogus company. The scheme cost the victim company over $4 million.

Preventing and Detecting Shell Company Schemes   Because shell company schemes are among the most costly of all forms of occupational fraud, it is imperative that organizations have controls in place to prevent these frauds. As is the case with all forms of billing fraud, it is critical that duties in the purchasing process be separated. Most billing schemes succeed when an individual has control over one or more aspects of purchasing, authorizing purchases, receiving and storing goods, and issuing payments. If these duties are strictly segregated, it will be very difficult for an employee to commit most forms of billing fraud, including shell company schemes.

Because shell company schemes, by definition, involve invoicing from fictitious vendors, one of the best ways to counter this type of fraud is to maintain and regularly update an approved vendor list. The legitimacy of all vendors on the list should be verified by someone independent of the purchasing function, and whenever an invoice is received from a vendor not on the list, independent verification of that company should be required before the invoice is paid.

Identifying Shell Company Invoices   In addition to controls aimed at generally preventing billing fraud, auditors, accounting personnel, and other employees should be trained to identify fraudulent invoices. One common red flag is a lack of detail on the fraudulent invoice. For example, the invoice might lack a phone number, fax number, invoice number, or tax identification number, or other information that usually appears on legitimate invoices. Another common sign of fraud is an invoice that lacks detailed descriptions of the items for which the victim organization is being billed. Finally, the mailing address on an invoice can indicate that it is fraudulent. In most shell company schemes, the mailing address for payments is a mail drop or a residential address. Any invoice that calls for a payment to one of these locations should be scrutinized, and the existence of the vendor should be verified before a check is mailed.

In some cases, a fraudster will print or create several invoices and then submit them to his employer one at a time over an extended period so that the amount he is stealing will be spread out, making it less noticeable. These schemes can sometimes be detected because the invoices used by the perpetrator will be consecutively numbered. In other words, the invoice numbers might be 4002, 4003, 4004, and so forth. This is clearly a sign of a shell company, because it indicates that the vendor in question is only sending invoices to the victim. Suppose, for example, that an organization receives invoice #4002 from a vendor on September 1, and receives invoice #4003 on October 1. This would indicate that the vendor issued only a single invoice in September—the invoice received by the company in question. Obviously, a legitimate company could not operate this way and survive.

Organizations can detect this sort of anomaly by regularly reviewing the payables account and sorting payments by vendor and invoice number. Also, in many shell company schemes the perpetrator will repeatedly bill for identical or similar amounts. If the perpetrator has purchase authority, these amounts will tend to be just below the perpetrator's approval limit. So if Employee X is committing a shell company scheme and is authorized to approve purchases up to $10,000, his shell company invoices might tend to fall in the $9,000 to $9,999 range. This can be detected by sorting payments by vendor and amount.

Testing for Shell Company Schemes   As discussed above, sorting payments by vendor, amount, and invoice number is one way to search out red flags that might indicate a shell company scheme. There are a number of other trends and red flags that are frequently associated with these frauds, and organizations should regularly test for them as part of a proactive fraud detection program.

Billing schemes will typically cause an organization's expenses to exceed budget projections, so organizations should be alert to large budget overruns, and to departments that regularly exceed their budgets. Billing schemes will also tend to cause an increase in expenses from previous years. In a small company a billing scheme could significantly affect the financial statements and could be detected through horizontal analysis (comparison of financials on a year-to-year basis). In a very large company, a billing scheme might not have a significant impact on the overall financials, but it could still be detected by analyzing expense trends on a departmental or project basis. Obviously, by fraudulently increasing purchasing expenses, billing schemes will also tend to cause an increase in cost of goods sold relative to sales, and therefore will tend to negatively impact profits.

Because billing schemes generally involve the purchase of fictitious goods or services, a review of purchase levels can help detect this form of fraud. As we have stated, most shell company schemes involve purchases of fictitious services, since these "soft account" items cannot be traced to inventory, leaving no physical evidence that the transaction was fraudulent. However, these schemes will cause an increase in service-related expenses. So, for instance, a large, unexplained rise in consulting or training expenses could indicate a shell company scheme. When this red flag shows up, the underlying purchases should be reviewed, and both the performance of the service and the legitimacy of the provider should be confirmed. By tracking approval authority for all purchases, organizations can also run comparison reports looking for employees or managers who approve an unusually high level of services based on their job function.

In cases where a shell company bills for goods, these goods either will be nonexistent or will be overpriced as part of a pass-through scheme. In either case, this will cause expenses and cost of goods sold to rise, as discussed above. Furthermore, if an individual causes his organization to buy nonexistent goods, that means the quantity of items purchased will increase by the number of fictitious items bought from the shell company. Unexplained increases in the quantity of goods purchased should be investigated, particularly when the increase does not translate to increased sales. Purchases of nonexistent goods will also cause inventory shortages, because the purchased items will be added to the organization's perpetual inventory system but will never enter the physical inventory. Purchases that cannot be traced to inventory are a clear red flag of shell company schemes.

Alternatively, if the shell company sells existing goods as part of a pass-through scheme, then the price for these items will be substantially marked up. Organizations should monitor trends in average unit price of goods purchased. Significant increases could signal not only pass-through schemes, but also kickback schemes and other types of billing fraud. If prices on a particular transaction or set of transactions seem out of line, other vendors should be contacted to determine the industry norm. Assuming the pricing is way out of line, the organization should review the transaction to determine how the vendor was approved, and what employees were involved in the transaction. In addition, steps should be taken to confirm that the vendor is legitimate, as discussed below.

In addition to reviewing *quantities* purchased, organizations should also pay attention to *types* of goods and services that are purchased. In many shell company schemes and other forms of billing fraud, the nature of the purchases is patently unreasonable, but the invoices in question are nevertheless rubber-stamped. For instance, when a law firm buys a truckload of gravel, red flags should immediately go up. This kind of test is really an issue of common sense, and it requires that auditors, managers, and accounting personnel have a good understanding of how their organizations function.

Because employees sometimes run shell company schemes using their home address to collect payments, organizations should periodically run comparison reports for vendor addresses and employee addresses. If a match occurs, the employee in question is probably engaging in a shell company scheme.

Fraudulent vouchers are also generally run through the payables system more quickly than legitimate ones. The employees who commit these schemes try to get their bogus invoices paid as quickly as possible, both because they want their money immediately and because once the invoice gets paid the likelihood of the scheme being detected drops considerably. A report showing the average turnaround time on invoices sorted by vendor might show that a particular company tends to have its invoices paid much more quickly than other vendors. If so, steps should be taken to confirm that the company exists, and that the purchases were appropriate.

Verifying Whether a Shell Company Exists   It is usually fairly simple to determine whether a particular vendor is legitimate. A good first step is to simply look up the vendor in the phone book. The absence of a phone number for a vendor is generally an indication that the company is a shell. It is also a good idea to contact others in your industry to determine whether they are familiar with the vendor. If the vendor only appears to have billed your company, or if no one else in your community seems to have heard of it, the company may not actually exist. Finally, if questions persist about whether the vendor is a shell, someone from the victim organization should verify the vendor's address through a personal visit or using satellite imaging software.

Identifying the Employee behind a Shell Company Even when a company has been identified as a shell, there is still the matter of determining who is behind the scheme. In most cases, the perpetrator will have been involved in selecting the vendor or approving the purchase. However it may be necessary to gather independent verification to prove the identity of the fraudster. This can make it easier to obtain a confession during an investigative interview, and it will also serve as useful evidence if the matter eventually goes to trial—a possibility that exists in any fraud investigation. There are a number of ways to verify the identity of the person or persons operating a shell company.

In many cases the person who creates a shell company will register the company with the appropriate government authority, because such registration is necessary to open a bank account in the shell's name. These documents require the name, address, and signature of the person who is forming the company. Therefore, a search of the company's registration, which is a matter of public record, may indicate who committed the fraud. Articles of incorporation are maintained by the secretary of state (or the state corporation bureau or corporate registry office) in every state. DBA (Doing Business As) information can usually be obtained at the county level. These public records can be obtained without a subpoena.

When conducting a records search, it is important to remember that fraudsters might set up a company under a false name to avoid being identified with the shell. One common technique is to establish the shell in the name of a relative or accomplice who does not work for the victim organization. If the perpetrator is male and is married, he might also form the shell under his wife's maiden name. When checking public records, investigators should be alert for related names, as well as addresses, phone numbers, Social Security numbers, or other identifiers that may match an employee's personnel information.

Rather than conduct a records search, it may be possible to confirm the identity of the fraudster based on other factors. For instance, a company could compare checks that have been converted by the shell company with information from the suspect's payroll checks or direct deposits. Matching account numbers or signatures would indicate that the payments were deposited into the same bank account. Similarly, handwriting samples on business filings or communications from the suspected vendor can be matched against the handwriting of suspected employees.

Another way to identify the perpetrator behind a shell company scheme is to conduct surveillance of the mail drop to determine who collects checks on behalf of the shell company. Finally, if a suspect or suspects have been identified, a search of their office or workspace might also reveal trash. Many shell company schemes are detected when a vendor's invoices or letterhead are discovered in an employee's work area. However, any workplace search must be done carefully, ensuring that the employee's privacy rights are not violated. Workplace searches should be conducted only after consulting with an attorney.

BILLING SCHEMES INVOLVING NON-ACCOMPLICE VENDORS

Pay-and-Return Schemes

Rather than use shell companies as vessels for overbilling schemes, some employees generate fraudulent disbursements by using the invoices of non-accomplice vendors. In pay-and-return schemes, these employees do not prepare and submit the vendor's invoices; rather, they intentionally mishandle payments that are owed to the legitimate vendors (see Exhibit 4-5). One way to do this is to purposely double-pay an invoice. In Case 4020, for instance, a secretary was responsible for opening mail, processing claims, and authorizing payments. She intentionally paid some bills twice, then requested the recipients to return one of the checks. She would intercept these returned checks and deposit them into her own bank account.

Another way to accomplish a pay-and-return scheme is to intentionally pay the wrong vendor. In Case 756, an accounts payable clerk deliberately put vendor checks in the wrong envelopes. After they had been mailed, she called the vendors to explain the "mistake," and requested that they return the checks to her. She deposited these checks in her personal bank account and ran the vouchers through the accounts payable system a second time to pay the appropriate vendors.

Finally, an employee might pay the proper vendor, but intentionally overpay him. In Case 2649, an employee intentionally caused a check to be issued to a vendor for more than the invoice amount, then requested that the vendor return the excess. This money was

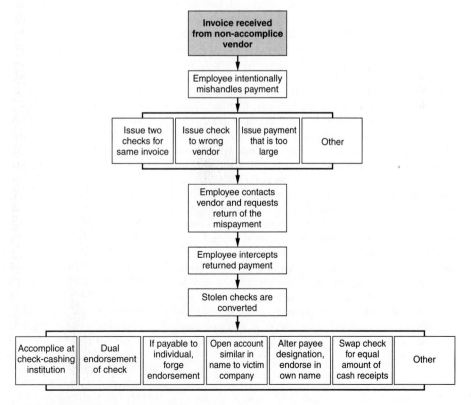

EXHIBIT 4-5 Pay-and-Return Schemes

taken by the fraudster and deposited into her own account. Similarly, an employee might intentionally purchase excess merchandise, return the excess, and pocket the refund.

Overbilling with a Non-Accomplice Vendor's Invoices

In some cases employees use invoices in the name of existing vendors to generate fraudulent payments. This occurs in kickback schemes when the vendor is an accomplice in the fraud, but it can also occur when the vendor is unaware of the crime. The perpetrator either manufactures a fake invoice for a vendor who regularly deals with the victim organization or reruns an invoice that has already been paid. The perpetrator submits the fraudulent invoice and intercepts the resulting payment. Since the bill is fictitious, the existing vendor is not out any money. The only victim is the employer's organization, which pays for goods or services that it does not receive. In the following case study, Albert Miano took a copy of a contractor's invoice, replicated it, and used the phony invoices to bill his employer for over a million dollars' worth of false work. CFE Terence McGrane put a stop to Miano's scheme.

CASE STUDY: COVER STORY: INTERNAL FRAUD[2]

Sometimes fraud is discovered by chance instead of deliberate effort. In the $4 million embezzlement fraud by an employee of a magazine publisher, more than one coincidence brought down the perpetrator.

A popular magazine and large direct-mail publishing house decided to outsource much of its direct-mail operations to specialized mail vendors. The company began converting its plant in Pleasantville, New York, from a direct-mail-order factory to an office complex. Part of the office complex construction involved building an auditorium that was to be identical to another auditorium in historic Williamsburg, Virginia. Terrence McGrane had just begun his third day on the job as chief internal auditor. In an effort to get to know his new company, he had scheduled a series of interviews with all the vice presidents. His first interview was with the vice president of administrative services, Harold J. Scott, who was in charge of many construction projects and maintenance services. Because of the massive renovation project, it was not unusual for hundreds of invoices to be forwarded to Scott.

Coincidence one: McGrane stopped by the accounts payable department and retrieved a series of recently submitted invoices for various trade expenses related to the auditorium construction project. "One of the things I wanted to accomplish was to understand how the accounting codes worked—what was capitalized; what was expensed; how it was recorded, etc." So he grabbed a stack of processed invoices with accounting codes and went up to the construction site to meet with the vice president for an hour-long interview.

[2]Several names and details have been changed to preserve anonymity.

As the two walked around the grounds, McGrane asked the vice president if he could explain the accounting codes to him: "He stared at the [top] invoice for approximately 30 seconds and said: 'That is not my signature on the invoice!'

As he looked through the stack, he found what appeared to be about three or four other forgeries. He was completely baffled."

The initial investigation revealed that all of the forgeries were in the painting division, budgeted at approximately $500,000 a year. The company employed only one person to oversee the painting operations in its facilities department: Albert Miano.

Miano, a 35-year-old from New Fairfield, Connecticut, earned about $30,000 a year. It was his job to coordinate time-and-materials contracts with the scores of painters, carpenters, electricians, and plumbers who toiled daily on the renovation, repair, and construction of the building complex. As facilities supervisor, Miano regularly forwarded invoices to the vice president of administration services for approval.

Miano launched his scheme by crafting false invoices for the jobs done by the painters. He took a copy of a trade invoice from an existing painting contractor and, using his home computer, created a replica into which he would record slightly different hours for the trade contractors' work.

McGrane related a probable scenario of how Miano executed his scheme. "Let's say he knew that during the month of February, as an example," McGrane said, "there were twenty-seven painters on the grounds during the course of one week." Miano also knew the total number of hours and the volume of materials used in that time. "He would create invoices that were similar in nature, but record only eleven painters on the grounds," McGrane said. Miano would not reinvoice exactly the same work done during a week, but he would make it look so similar that no one's suspicions were ever aroused. Effectively, there were no work orders on the "phantom work" he created on these invoices. Miano always listed fewer painters on the false invoice than the actual number who had worked that week, and he registered less time for their services than they had actually worked.

As part of his job, he regularly brought the trade invoices into the administrative VP's office for signature approval. After delivering a stack of these invoices, he would return to collect them within the next day or two and deliver the approved invoices to the accounts payable department. "It was this opportunity," McGrane said, "that this individual was allowed to go and collect the approved invoices and insert his own replicated fraudulent invoices as approved. This was the first piece of an 'electronic circuit' that allowed him to commit the fraud." The second piece of the circuit for the fraud to ignite, McGrane said, was allowing this same employee to transport the invoices to the accounts payable department, and ultimately to collect the check.

After seeing how easy it was to slip in his own false invoices in the stack of approved ones, Miano became bolder in his scheme. He began calling accounts payable, claiming that a carpenter or painter had arrived on the grounds and needed his check "immediately." To keep the project flowing, the employees in the accounts payable department accommodated him. Many employees knew and liked Miano, who had worked for the company for nearly 15 years.

Eventually, this routine became so familiar to employees in accounts payable that Miano did not even need to make up an excuse to pick up checks. Each time he would collect them, he stashed the check for the false invoice in his pocket. When he returned home to New Fairfield, Connecticut, he took the check to his bank, forged the contractor's name on the back, then endorsed it with his own name and deposited the check.

McGrane explains that Miano was able to pull off the scam due to failure of internal controls and employees not following standard accounting procedures. "For any business transaction, the invoices should be dispatched independently to the approving authority. Once signed, the approved invoices should be sent independently to accounts payable. When the check is prepared by accounts payable, they should mail it directly to the third party. Under a strong internal control system, the employees and/or contractors should not be allowed to come in and collect checks directly. Direct contacts with accounts payable personnel make it too tempting for someone to try to misappropriate funds."

Accounts payable also failed to combine the invoices into a single check—they wrote a check for each invoice. "Had they combined it," McGrane said, "his false invoice would have been added into the legitimate painter's monthly invoice summary, and the money would be mailed to the legitimate contractor," McGrane said. Accounts payable neglected to study the invoice signatures for forgeries, and the accounting department dropped the ball by not perusing processed

checks for dual endorsements, another red flag for potentially misappropriated funds.

Miano's first transaction totaled $1,200. His second transaction jumped to $6,000—his third, $12,000. His largest single transaction came to over $66,000. Miano refined his strategy by pacing, on a parallel basis, a certain amount below the total due the painter. "If the painter submitted an invoice for $20,000 a month," McGrane said, "Miano would submit an invoice for, say, $14,000. If the painter submitted a $6,000 invoice, he'd submit one for $3,000." The individual invoice amounts, because of the continuing construction, would not have alarmed even an auditor.

Miano's behavior at the office was the same as ever. He dressed the same way, drove the same car to work, and shared little of his private life with other workers. He had not taken a vacation in over four years, and his boss thought he should be promoted (a move Miano resisted, for reasons now obvious). After hours, however, Miano was a different person.

Coincidence two: McGrane's secretary was not only on Miano's bowling team, she was also his neighbor. They saw each other regularly at the local bowling alley. She took notice when Miano's behavior became somewhat extravagant. At first he took to buying the team drinks, a habit most appreciated by his teammates. However, the secretary began wondering where all the money was coming from when he showed up in his new Mercedes (one of five cars he bought) and talked about a new $18,000 boat. He also invested in real estate and purchased a second home costing $416,000.

McGrane's secretary approached Miano one night after he had spent some $800 on drinks for the team. "Did you win the lottery, or what?" she asked. He explained that his father-in-law had recently died and left a substantial inheritance to his wife and him. Miano's father-in-law was actually quite alive, but no one ever bothered to check out the claim. No one suspected Miano of doing anything sinister or criminal. All of his associates considered him "too dumb" to carry out such a scheme. One person described him as "dumb as a box of rocks."

Coincidence three: After four years without a vacation, Miano took what he considered a well-deserved trip to Atlantic City. But he wasn't there long before he was called back to Pleasantville. One can imagine his chagrin at having to leave the casinos and boardwalks and head back to the office. Little did he know that things were about to get a lot worse.

Upon his return, Miano found himself confronted by the auditor, the vice president, and two attorneys from the district attorney's office. He readily admitted guilt. "He said he had expected to get caught," McGrane said. "He did it strictly based on greed. Miano claimed there was no one else involved, and the sum total of his fraud was about $400,000." But the internal audit found that Miano had forged endorsements on more than fifty checks in those four years, totaling $1,057,000. Ironically, the auditors could only identify about $380,000 spent on tangible items (boats, cars, down payment on a home, etc.). The investigators could not account for the other $700,000, although they knew Miano had withdrawn at least that much from the bank.

Miano served only two years of an eight-year sentence in a state penitentiary. At the time of his indictment, his wife filed for divorce, claiming she knew nothing of her husband's crimes. Miano told a reporter in jail that the loss of his family and the public humiliation had taught him his lesson.

"For a nickel or for $5 million, it doesn't pay," Miano said. "You enjoy the money for a while, but you lose your pride and your self-respect. It ends up hurting your family, and no money can ever change that."

Preventing and Detecting Fraudulent Invoices from a Non-Accomplice Vendor

Prevention of non-accomplice vendor invoicing schemes is largely dependent on the purchasing function controls already discussed in this chapter. Efforts at detecting these schemes should focus on several red flags that are common to non-accomplice vendor invoicing. For example, if an employee produces invoices designed to mimic those of a known vendor, the mailing address or electronic payment information might differ from that of the real vendor. This variation is necessary so that the perpetrator can collect the payment. As discussed previously, organizations should maintain up-to-date approved vendor lists that include contact, mailing, and electronic payment information for approved vendors. Deviations from this information, such as a change in mailing address or electronic payment information, should be flagged, and the changes verified as legitimate before a disbursement is issued. In addition, a fraudulent invoice prepared by an employee to mimic that of a legitimate vendor might have an invoice number that is significantly out of sequence. A sort of disbursements by vendor, date, and invoice number could reveal this type of anomaly.

Instead of producing fraudulent vendor invoices, some employees simply rerun invoices from existing vendors and divert the payments that result from the second run. This type of fraud should be easily detectable if an organization has an effective duplicate checking system to ensure that the same invoice cannot be run through the payables system twice. In manual systems, every paid voucher should be clearly marked "paid" to prevent reprocessing. In an electronic system, duplicate invoice numbers should be automatically flagged. In order to dodge a duplicate checking system, some fraudsters will slightly alter the invoice number. For instance, invoice #44004 might be changed to #44004a, or a zero in the number might be changed to the letter *O* so that the number will look the same to the naked eye but will not show up as a duplicate in the accounting system. However, a sort of invoice numbers from a particular vendor in ascending or descending order will reveal these as out of sequence.

Pay-and-return schemes can be mostly prevented if the duties of purchasing, authorizing, and distributing payments are separated and if all invoices are matched to purchase orders before payments are issued. Incoming mail should also never be delivered directly to an employee. All incoming mail should be opened by mailroom personnel to ensure that every incoming check is recorded. In addition, each incoming check should be photocopied, with the copy attached to the remittance advice. This will help prevent a dishonest employee from being able to recover an amount that was intentionally double-paid.

When the targeted vendor in a pay-and-return scheme returns an overpayment to the fraudster, it is often as a check payable to the victim organization. To make it more difficult to convert such a check, organizations should instruct their banks not to cash checks payable to the organization.

Finally, if a pay-and-return scheme is suspected, organizations should spot-check past accounts payable files for overpayments. Identify all persons involved in processing any overpayment, and review their transactions for similar "mistakes."

PERSONAL PURCHASES WITH COMPANY FUNDS

Instead of undertaking billing schemes to generate cash, many fraudsters simply purchase personal items with their company's money. Company accounts are used to buy items for fraudsters, their businesses, their families, and so on. In Case 649, for instance, a supervisor started a company for his son and directed work to the son's company. In addition to this unethical behavior, the supervisor saw to it that his employer purchased all the materials and supplies necessary for the son's business. In addition, the supervisor purchased materials through his employer that were used to add a room to his own house. All in all, the perpetrator bought nearly $50,000 worth of supplies and materials for himself using company money.

Conceptually, one might wonder why a purchases fraud is not classified as a theft of inventory or other assets rather than a billing scheme. After all, in purchase schemes the fraudster buys something with company money, then takes the purchased item for himself. In Case 649 discussed in the preceding paragraph, for example, the supervisor took building materials and supplies. How does this differ from those frauds that will be discussed in Chapter 9, whereby employees steal inventory, supplies, and other materials? At first glance, the schemes appear very similar. In fact, the perpetrator of a purchases fraud is stealing inventory just as he would in any other inventory theft scheme. Nevertheless, the heart of the scheme is not the *taking* of the inventory but the *purchasing* of the inventory. In other words, when an employee steals merchandise from a warehouse, he is stealing an asset that the company needs, an asset that it has on hand for a particular reason. The harm to the victim company is not only the cost of the asset, but also the loss of the asset itself. In a purchasing scheme, on the other hand, the asset that is taken is superfluous. The perpetrator causes the victim company to order and pay for an asset that it does not really need, so the only damage to the victim company is the money lost in purchasing the particular item. This is why purchasing schemes are categorized as billing frauds.

Personal Purchases through False Invoicing

Most of the employees in our studies who undertook purchases schemes did so by running unsanctioned invoices through the accounts payable system. The fraudster in this type of fraud buys an item and submits the bill to his employer as if it represented a purchase on behalf of the company (see Exhibit 4-6). The goal is to have the company pay the invoice. Obviously, the invoice that the employee submits to his company is not legitimate. The main hurdle for a fraudster to overcome, therefore, is to avoid scrutiny of the invalid invoice and obtain authorization for the bill to be paid.

The Fraudster as Authorizer of Invoices As was the case in the shell company schemes we reviewed, the person who engages in a purchases scheme is often the very person in the company whose duties include *authorizing* purchases. Obviously, proper controls should preclude anyone from approving his own purchases. Such poorly separated functions leave little other than his conscience to dissuade an employee from fraud.

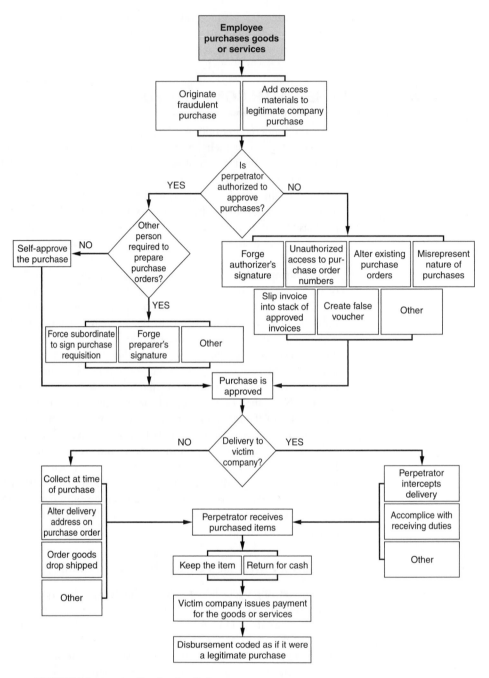

EXHIBIT 4-6 Invoice Purchasing Schemes

Nevertheless, we saw several examples of organizations in which this lapse in controls existed. As we continue to point out, fraud arises in part because of a perceived opportunity. An employee who sees that no one is reviewing his actions is more likely to turn to fraud than one who knows that his company diligently works to detect employee theft.

An example of how poor controls can lead to fraud was found in Case 888, where a manager of a remote location of a large, publicly traded company was authorized to both order supplies and approve vendor invoices for payment. For over a year, the manager routinely added personal items and supplies for his own business to orders made on behalf of his employer. The orders often included a strange mix of items; technical supplies and home furnishings might, for instance, be purchased in the same order. Because the manager was in a position to approve his own purchases, he could get away with such blatantly obvious frauds. In addition to ordering personal items, the perpetrator changed the delivery address for certain supplies so that they would be delivered directly to his home or side business. This scheme cost the victim company approximately $300,000 in unnecessary purchases. In a similar case, 770, an employee with complete control of purchasing and storing supplies for his department bought approximately $100,000 worth of unnecessary supplies using company funds. The employee authorized both the orders and the payments. The excess supplies were taken to the perpetrator's home, where he used them to manufacture a product for his own business. It should be obvious from the examples cited above that not only do poor controls pave the way for fraud, a lack of oversight regarding the purchasing function can allow an employee to take huge chunks out of his company's bottom line.

In some situations, the perpetrator is authorized to approve purchases, but controls prevent him from also initiating purchase requests. This procedure is meant to prevent the kinds of schemes discussed above. Unfortunately, those with authority to approve purchases are often high-level employees with a good deal of control over their subordinates. These persons can use their influence to force subordinates to assist in purchases scheme. In Case 95, for example, purchases under $1,000 at a certain utility company could be made with limited-value purchase orders (LPOs), which required two signatures—the originator of a purchase request and the approver of the request. An LPO attached to an invoice for less than $1,000 would be paid by the accounts payable department. In this case, a manager bought goods and services on company accounts, and prepared LPOs for the purchases. (In some cases, the LPO would falsely describe the item to conceal the nature of the purchase.) Once the LPO was prepared, the manager forced a clerk in his department to sign the document as the originator of the transaction. The clerk, intimidated by her boss, did not question the authenticity of the LPOs. With two signatures affixed, the LPO appeared to be legitimate and the bills were paid. The scheme cost the victim company at least $25,000.

Falsifying Documents to Obtain Authorization Not all fraudsters are free to approve their own purchases; those who cannot must rely on other methods to get their personal bills paid by the company. The chief control document in many vouchers is the purchase order. When an employee wants to buy goods or services, he submits a purchase requisition to a superior. If the purchase requisition is approved, a purchase order is sent to a vendor. A copy of this purchase order, retained in the voucher, tells accounts payable that the transaction has been approved. Later, when an invoice and receiving report corresponding to this purchase order are assembled, accounts payable will issue a check.

So in order to make their purchases appear authentic, some fraudsters generate false purchase orders. In Case 634, for example, an employee forged the signature of a division controller on purchase orders; thus, the purchase orders appeared to be authentic and the employee was able to buy approximately $3,000 worth of goods at his company's expense. In another instance, Case 434, a part-time employee at an educational institution obtained unused purchase order numbers and used them to order computer equipment under a fictitious name. The employee then intercepted the equipment as it arrived at the school and loaded the items into his car. Eventually, the employee began using fictitious purchase order numbers instead of real ones. The scheme came to light when the perpetrator inadvertently selected the name of a real vendor. After scrutinizing the documents, the school knew that it had been victimized. In the meantime, the employee had bought nearly $8,000 worth of unnecessary equipment.

Altering Existing Purchase Orders   Purchase orders can also be altered by employees who seek to obtain merchandise at their employer's expense. In Case 1334, for example, several individuals conspired to purchase over $2 million worth of materials for their personal use. The ringleader of the scheme was a low-level supervisor who had access to the computer system that controlled the requisition and receipt of materials. This supervisor entered the system and either initiated orders of materials that exceeded the needs of a particular project or altered existing orders to increase the amount of materials being requisitioned. Because the victim organization had poor controls, it did not compare completed work orders on projects to the amount of materials ordered for those projects. This allowed the inflated orders to go undetected. In addition, other employees involved in the scheme were in charge of receiving deliveries. These employees were able to divert the excess materials and falsify receiving reports to conceal the missing items. In addition, the victim institution did not enforce a central delivery point, meaning that employees were allowed to pick up materials from the vendors in their personal vehicles. This made it very easy to misappropriate the excess merchandise. The supervisor's ability to circumvent controls and initiate false orders or alter genuine ones, though, was the real key to the scheme.

False Purchase Requisitions   Another way for an employee to get a false purchase approved is to misrepresent the nature of the purchase. In many companies, those with the power to authorize purchases are not always attentive to their duties. If a trusted subordinate vouches for an acquisition, for instance, busy supervisors often give rubber stamp approval to purchase requisitions. Additionally, employees sometimes misrepresent the nature of the items they are purchasing in order to pass a cursory review by their superiors. For example, in Case 1015, an engineer bought over $30,000 worth of personal items. The engineer dealt directly with vendors and was also in charge of overseeing the receipt of the materials he purchased. He was therefore able to misrepresent the nature of the merchandise he bought, calling it "maintenance items." Vendor invoices were altered to agree to this description.

Of course, the problem with lying about what one is buying is that when delivery occurs, it is the perpetrator's personal items that arrive, not the business items listed on the purchase requisition. In the case discussed above, the problem of detection at this stage of the crime was avoided because the engineer who made the fraudulent purchases was also in charge of receiving the merchandise. He could therefore falsify receiving reports to perpetuate the fraud. We have also encountered cases in which fraudsters in the purchasing department enlisted the aid of employees in the receiving department to conceal their crimes.

Another way to avoid detection at the delivery stage is to change the delivery address for purchases. Instead of being shipped to the victim company, the items the employee buys are sent directly to his home or business. In a related scenario, an accounts payable supervisor in Case 592 purchased supplies for her own business by entering vouchers in the accounts payable system of her employer. Checks were cut for the expenses during normal daily check runs. To avoid problems with receiving the unauthorized goods, the perpetrator ordered the supplies from the vendor and had them shipped directly to a client of her side business.

Personal Purchases on Credit Cards or Other Company Accounts

Instead of running false invoices through accounts payable, some employees make personal purchases on company credit cards, purchasing cards, or running accounts with vendors. As with invoicing schemes, the key to getting away with a false credit card purchase is avoiding detection. Unlike invoicing schemes, however, prior approval for purchases is not required. An employee with a company credit card or purchasing card can buy an item merely by signing his name (or forging someone else's) at the time of purchase. Later review of the card statement, however, may detect the fraudulent purchase. In invoicing schemes we saw how those who committed the frauds were often in a position to approve their own purchases. The same is often true in credit card and purchasing card schemes. A manager in Case 446, for example, reviewed and approved his own credit card statements. This allowed him to make fraudulent purchases on the company card for approximately two years.

Of course, only certain employees are authorized to use company credit cards or issued purchase cards. The manager in Case 446 above, for instance, had his own company card. Employees without this privilege can make fraudulent purchases with a company card only if they first manage to get hold of one. To this end, company cards are sometimes stolen or "borrowed" from authorized users. A more novel approach was used by an accountant in Case 1481, who falsely added her name to a list of employees to whom cards were to be issued. She used her card to make fraudulent purchases, but forged the signatures of authorized cardholders to cover her tracks. Since no one knew she even had a company card, she would not be a prime suspect in the fraud even if someone questioned the purchases. For over five years this employee continued her scheme, racking up a six-figure bill on her employer's account. In addition, she had control of the credit card statement and was able to code her purchases to various expense accounts, thereby further delaying detection of her crime.

An executive secretary in Case 521 used her access to the statement for a different purpose. After making hundreds of thousands of dollars' worth of fraudulent purchases on corporate cards, this employee destroyed both the receipts from her purchases and the monthly credit card statements. Eventually, duplicate statements were requested from the credit card company, and the fraud was discovered. The fact that no statements were received by the company therefore led to detection of the scheme. Some fraudsters, having destroyed the real copies of credit card statements, produce counterfeit copies on which their fraudulent purchases are omitted. By taking this extra step, the fraudster is able to keep his employer in the dark about the true activity on the account.

Charge Accounts Some companies keep charge accounts with vendors with whom they do regular business. Office supply companies are a good example of this kind of vendor. Purchases on charge accounts may require a signature or other form of authorization from a designated company representative. Obviously, that representative is in a position to buy personal items on the company account. Other employees might do the same by forging the signature of an authorized person at the time of a fraudulent purchase. In some informal settings, purchases can be verified by as little as a phone call, making it very easy to make fraudulent purchases.

Returning Merchandise for Cash The cases we have discussed in the fraudulent purchases section to this point have all involved the false purchase of merchandise for the sake of obtaining the merchandise. In some cases, however, the fraudster buys items and then returns them for cash. The best example of this type of scheme in our survey was Case 1510, in which an employee made fraudulent gains from a business travel account. The employee began by purchasing tickets for herself and her family through her company's travel budget. Poor separation of duties allowed the fraudster to order the tickets, receive them, prepare claims for payments, and distribute checks. The only review of her activities was made by a busy and rather uninterested supervisor who approved the employee's claims without requiring supporting documentation. Eventually, the employee's scheme evolved. She began to purchase airline tickets and return them for their cash value. An employee of the travel agency assisted in the scheme by encoding the tickets as though the fraudster had paid for them herself. That caused the airlines to pay refunds directly to the fraudster rather than to her employer. In the course of two years, this employee embezzled over $100,000 through her purchases scheme.

Preventing and Detecting Personal Purchases on Company Credit Cards and Purchasing Cards

The most important step in preventing credit card and purchasing card fraud is conducting thorough reviews of each card statement. This duty should be performed by someone independent of those who have signature authority on the account. During review, a business purpose should be verified for each listing on the statement, and the person who incurred the expense should be required to provide original support for the expense.

To prevent falsifications of the statement, organizations should direct the card issuer to send two copies of the statement to two different individuals within the organization. Both individuals should reconcile the statements separately and then compare the results. In the case of credit cards, it is advisable to establish spending limits for credit card users in order to prevent large abuses.

Card statements should be compared with employee expense vouchers for duplications, and card expenses should be monitored for any unexplained increase in purchasing levels. Excess purchases can be traced to a particular cardholder, and that person can be interviewed to determine the reason for the increase.

PROACTIVE COMPUTER AUDIT TESTS FOR DETECTING BILLING SCHEMES[1]

Title	Category	Description	Data file(s)
Perform a trend analysis of vendor payments.	All	Special note should be given to vendors that have had minimal purchases in prior periods, yet have large payments in current periods.	• Invoice payment
Identify duplicate payments based on various means.	All	Duplicate payment tests can be enacted on the vendor, invoice number, and amount. More complicated tests can look for instances in which the same invoice and amount are paid, yet the payment is made to two different vendors. Another advanced test is to search for same vendor and invoice when a different amount is paid.	• Invoice payment

Summarize debit memos by vendor, issuer, and type.	All	Debit memo trends that appear unusual should be investigated as attempts to cover unauthorized payments.	• Invoice payment
Summarize accounts payable activity by general ledger account, sort from high to low, and review for reasonableness.	All	Expense account trends that appear unusual should be investigated as attempts to cover unauthorized payments.	• Invoice payment • General Ledger distribution
Extract manual checks and summarize by vendor and issuer.	All	Manual checks are more prone to abuse and therefore should be scrutinized, especially if a particular issuer is drafting the majority of manual checks.	• Check register
Extract all purchases having no purchase order and summarize by vendor and issuer.	All	Purchases having no purchase order are more prone to abuse and therefore should be scrutinized, especially if a particular issuer is drafting the majority of payments without purchase orders.	• Invoice payment
Extract all round-dollar payments.	All	Round-dollar payments have a higher likelihood of being fabricated and, therefore, fraudulent.	• Invoice payment
Calculate the ratio of the largest purchase to next-largest purchase by vendor.	All	By identifying the largest purchase to a vendor and the next-largest purchase, any large ratio difference may identify a fraudulently issued "largest" check.	• Invoice payment
Compare check register to invoice payment file to identify any checks with no related system invoices.	Shell Company	Check payments that do not appear on the invoice register may be an attempt to hide unauthorized payments.	• Invoice payment and check register
Match vendor master file to accounts payable invoice file.	Shell Company	Identify payments to a potentially unapproved vendor by joining the vendor to the invoice file on vendor number. The joining of these two files should be done in an "unmatched" format so that only those vendor numbers in the invoice file not appearing in the vendor file are shown.	• Vendor master • Invoice payment
Extract vendors having no telephone or tax ID number.	Shell Company	Vendors without this information are more prone to abuse and should be scrutinized.	• Vendor master
Identify vendors added during the period under review.	Shell Company	The issuers of new vendor additions should be reviewed using this report to determine whether a particular issuer is drafting the majority of vendor additions.	• Vendor master

(*Continued*)

(*Continued*)

Title	Category	Description	Data file(s)
List all vendors having an address that is not designated as a business address.	Shell Company	The identification of whether an address is legitimately a business address can be done using some software databases.	• Vendor master
List all vendors who had multiple invoices immediately below an approval limit (e.g., many $999 payments to a vendor when there is a $1,000 approval limit), highlighting a circumvention of the established control.	Shell Company	Invoices below an approval limit may be an attempt to circumvent a management review.	• Invoice payment
Match the vendor master file to the employee master file on various key fields.	Shell Company	Compare telephone number, address, tax ID numbers, numbers in the address, zip code, and post office box in the vendor file to those in the employee file, especially those of employees working in the accounts payable department.	• Vendor master • Employee master
Review payments having little or no sequence between invoice numbers.	Shell Company	Employees developing shell companies often invoice the company with no gaps in invoice sequence, highlighting that the victim company is the shell company's only customer.	• Invoice payment
List payments to any vendor that exceed the twelve-month average payments to that vendor by a specified percentage (e.g., 200%).	Shell Company and Non-Accomplice Vendor	Large payments are unusual and should be scrutinized as potentially fraudulent.	• Invoice payment
Extract vendor payments that are a specified percentage (e.g., 200%) greater than the last largest payment to that vendor.	Shell Company and Non-Accomplice Vendor	Large payments are unusual and should be scrutinized as potentially fraudulent.	• Invoice payment
Sample vendor open invoices for confirmation with vendor.	Non-Accomplice Vendor	Vendor invoices may remain open on the subledger when the vendor believes such invoices have been paid.	• Invoice payment
Extract SIC codes from card payments normally associated with personal purchases.	Personal Purchases	Personal purchases with company cards may be a sign of abuse.	• Procurement card
Extract multiple charges of the same product type (using SIC code) below a predefined card expense limit.	Personal Purchases	Charges below an approval limit may be an attempt to circumvent a management review.	• Procurement card
Summarize card use by employee and sort from high to low.	Personal Purchases	High usage of credit or purchasing cards by certain employees may be a sign of abuse.	• Procurement card

List all vendors with differing billing and delivery addresses.	Personal Purchases	Company purchases sent to a delivery address different from the billing address may signal personal purchases made on account of the company.	• Vendor master
Extract all delivery addresses that do not correspond to company locations.	Personal Purchases	Company purchases should normally be sent to known company locations. Shipments to other locations are a potential sign of fraud.	• Vendor master

SUMMARY

Billing schemes may be loosely defined as frauds in which an employee causes the victim organization to issue a fraudulent payment by submitting invoices for fictitious goods or services, inflated invoices, or invoices for personal purchases. Billing schemes are among the most costly, and the most common, forms of occupational fraud. These frauds generally fall into one of three categories: shell company schemes, non-accomplice vendor schemes, and personal purchases schemes.

A shell company is a fictitious entity set up for the sole purpose of committing fraud and may be nothing more than a fabricated name and an account number or a post office box that an employee uses to collect disbursements from false billings. Shell company schemes usually involve the purchase of fictitious goods or services, although in pass-through schemes a shell company might supply a real product or service by simply acting as the middleman between a real vendor and the victim organization, inflating the purchase price along the way.

In non-accomplice vendor schemes, a fraudster overbills his organization using the invoices of a legitimate vendor that is uninvolved in the fraud. This can be accomplished by producing counterfeit copies of a legitimate vendor's invoices, or by simply running an invoice through the payables system twice and keeping one of the resulting disbursements. A distinct subcategory is the pay-and-return scheme, in which a fraudster intentionally overpays an invoice and steals the excess payment when it is returned by the vendor.

An employee may make personal purchases with company money or using company credit cards or purchasing cards. In the first case, the employee purchases a personal item and runs the invoice through the accounts payable system; in the second, the employee makes personal purchases using company credit cards or running accounts with vendors.

ESSENTIAL TERMS

Billing scheme A scheme in which a fraudster causes the victim organization to issue a fraudulent payment by submitting invoices for fictitious goods or services, inflated invoices, or invoices for personal purchases.

Shell company A fictitious entity created for the sole purpose of committing fraud.

Collusion A situation in which two or more employees work together to commit fraud by overcoming a well-designed internal control system.

Pass-through scheme A subcategory of a shell company scheme in which actual goods or services are sold to the victim company, with the fraudster acting as a middleman and inflating the prices of the goods or services.

Pay-and-return scheme A fraud in which an employee intentionally mishandles payments that are owed to legitimate companies, then steals the excess payments when they are returned by the vendor.

Personal purchases scheme A category of billing scheme in which an employee simply buys personal items with his company's funds, credit card, or purchasing card.

REVIEW QUESTIONS

4-1 (Learning objective 4-1) What are the five categories of fraudulent disbursements, and where did billing schemes rank in terms of frequency and cost in the *2009 Global Fraud Survey*?

4-2 (Learning objectives 4-2 and 4-3) How is the term *billing schemes* defined, and what are the three categories of billing schemes covered in this chapter?

4-3 (Learning objective 4-4) What is the purpose of a shell company, and how is it normally formed?

4-4 (Learning objective 4-5) There are four ways that fraudulent invoices are approved for payment. What are they?

4-5 (Learning objective 4-5) Why does collusion among employees in the purchasing process make it very difficult to detect billing schemes?

4-6 (Learning objective 4-6) Why do most shell company schemes involve the purchase of services rather than goods?

4-7 (Learning objective 4-7) What is a pass-through scheme, and how does it differ from a typical shell company billing scheme?

4-8 (Learning objective 4-9) What is a pay-and-return scheme? List three examples of how this type of fraud can be committed.

4-9 (Learning objective 4-10) How does an employee use a non-accomplice vendor's invoice to generate a fraudulent payment?

4-10 (Learning objective 4-12) How does an employee make personal purchases on company credit cards, purchasing cards, or running charge accounts?

DISCUSSION ISSUES

4-1 (Learning objectives 4-3 and 4-4) In the case study of Cheryl Brown, the administrative assistant at a Southeastern medical school, what type of billing scheme did she commit?

4-2 (Learning objectives 4-8, 4-11, and 4-13) Explain how separation of duties contributes to the prevention and detection of billing schemes.

4-3 (Learning objectives 4-8 and 4-14) List and explain at least four proactive audit tests that could be performed to help detect a shell company scheme.

4-4 (Learning objectives 4-4, 4-5, and 4-8) What are some of the ways shell company invoices can be identified?

4-5 (Learning objectives 4-4 and 4-7) Sharon Forsyth worked in the purchasing department of a retail store. She was in charge of ordering merchandise inventory and various supplies for the organization. She purchased merchandise through a fictitious shell company and then resold it to her employer at an inflated price. What is the name for this type of fraud?

4-6 (Learning objective 4-9) Karen Martinis was responsible for opening mail, processing vendor claims, and authorizing payments. She was involved in a scheme in which she either double-paid vendor invoices, paid the wrong vendors, or overpaid the right vendors. What type of billing scheme is being described in this case?

4-7 (Learning objective 4-9) What type of internal controls can be utilized to help prevent pay-and-return billing schemes?

4-8 (Learning objective 4-12) In terms of classifying frauds under the fraud tree system, how does a scheme in which an employee fraudulently orders merchandise for his personal use differ from a scheme in which an employee steals merchandise from his company's warehouse?

ENDNOTES

1. Lanza, pp. 48–50.

Check Tampering Schemes

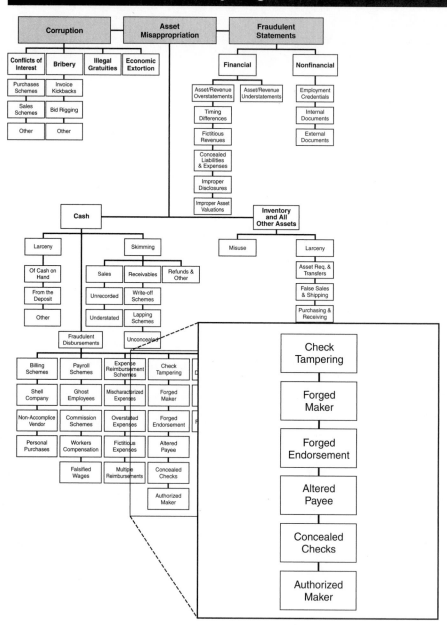

EXHIBIT 5-1

CHAPTER 5

CHECK TAMPERING

LEARNING OBJECTIVES

After studying this chapter, you should be able to:

5-1 Define check tampering

5-2 Understand the five principal categories of check tampering

5-3 Detail the means by which employees fraudulently obtain company checks

5-4 Understand how forged signatures are created on blank check stock

5-5 Be familiar with the methods identified in this chapter for preventing and detecting forged maker schemes

5-6 Differentiate between forged maker and forged endorsement schemes

5-7 Detail the methods employees use to intercept outgoing checks before they are delivered to the intended payee

5-8 Be able to discuss methods that can be used to prevent and detect the theft and alteration of outgoing company checks

5-9 Understand how authorized maker schemes work and why they are especially difficult to prevent

5-10 Explain how check tampering is hidden in a company's accounting records

5-11 Describe measures companies can take to prevent and detect fraudulent electronic payments

5-12 Be familiar with proactive audit tests that can be used to detect check tampering

CASE STUDY: A WOLF IN SHEEP'S CLOTHING[1]

Melissa Robinson was a devoted wife and the mother of two adorable children. She was very active at her children's school and was known as a charitable person, giving both her time and money to various organizations throughout the community.

She spent a good portion of her time working for a worldwide charitable organization chapter in Nashville as the executive secretary. In fact, her fellow employees and club members perceived Robinson's donation of time and hard work as nothing less than a godsend. "Even if somebody had told [the board of directors] that this lady was stealing," recalls certified fraud examiner and CPA David Mensel, also

a member of the organization, "they would have said, 'Impossible, she'd never do it.'"

However, all these accolades could not obscure one cold fact: Melissa Robinson was a thief. As executive secretary, she was one of two people in the organization allowed to sign checks on its bank accounts. As a result, the club was bilked out of more than $60,000 over five years, until club members put an end to Robinson's scam. The Nashville chapter of the organization was very much like other charitable entities—they engaged in fundraising activities, such as selling peanuts or candy bars on street corners around the holiday seasons. Although a percentage came in check form, most of the fundraising revenue was naturally cash.

"There was no oversight in those currency collections," says Mensel. "If I had gone out on a collecting route, I'd

[1] Several names and details have been changed to preserve anonymity.

come back with a bag of money and drop it on the secretary's desk and be gone."

Mensel suspects that Robinson stole far more than the $60,800 that the audit team ultimately established, because the amount of currency that flowed through her office was undocumented. "It is just a supposition, given her behavior with the checking accounts," Mensel explains. "As well, we saw a basic decline in collections from some activities that the organization had been involved in for many years."

Robinson's fraudulent activities were made possible by the relaxed operations of the Nashville chapter's board of directors. The organization's charter mandated that an independent audit be performed annually. However, during Robinson's tenure as executive secretary, not one yearly audit was completed. Mensel describes the board of directors during that tenure as "lackadaisical."

Robinson arrived at the executive secretary's desk through hard work; she was one of the most dedicated employees the company had, giving as much time as she could to help out. Once she earned the executive secretary position, Robinson apparently began pilfering from the organization's three bank accounts a little at a time. Although the accounts required two signatures per check, Robinson was able to write checks to herself and others by signing her own name and forging the second signature. Mensel says she would usually write a check to herself or to cash and record the transaction in the organization's books as a check to a legitimate source. If anyone glanced at the books, they would see plenty of hotels and office supply stores, names that were expected to show up in the ledger.

"The club meetings were regularly held in a hotel in town or at one of these executive meeting clubs," Mensel recalls, "and those bills would run from two to four thousand dollars a month. The executive secretary would... post in the checkbook that she had paid the hotel, but the actual check would be made out to someone else."

Mensel also remembers that Robinson repeatedly refused to convert her manual checking system into the computerized system the organization wanted her to use. "Now we know why," says Mensel.

Mensel and another associate were very involved in a fundraising operation when Robinson began her reign as executive secretary. Mensel observed that whenever he asked for any financial information from Robinson, she would stonewall him or make excuses. Mensel became suspicious and took the matter up with the board of directors. But when he told the board that he thought it was very peculiar that he couldn't get much financial data from Robinson, the board quite definitely sided with the executive secretary.

"The officers of the board essentially jumped down my throat, told me I was wrong and that I was being unreasonable," Mensel says. "And since I had no substantiation, just a bad feeling... I let it pass."

Mensel felt that the current treasurer was personally offended by his inquiry, as though he were suggesting that the treasurer was not doing his job properly. The treasurer acted defensively and did not check into Robinson's dealings.

As a result, the organization, which Mensel describes as previously "financially very sound," began to feel some financial strain. There simply wasn't as much money to run the organization as in the past, and it was at this point Robinson made what was perhaps her most ingenious maneuver. She convinced the board of directors that because the organization was experiencing some economic troubles, they ought to close the office space rented out for the executive secretary. This office was considered the financial center of the organization. Supposedly out of the goodness of her heart, Robinson told the board members that she would be happy to relinquish her precious space and run the financial matters of the club from her home. The board members agreed.

This allowed Robinson to carry out her embezzlement in small doses—Mensel recalls that Robinson wrote several checks for only $200 to $300. All this time, the board did nothing to impede Robinson's progress, even when she would not divulge financial information on request. When she came to club meetings, board members would sometimes ask her for information about the finances or ask to look at her books. Robinson would apologize and explain that she had forgotten them.

However, during the last year of the embezzlement, a new group of officers was elected, including a new treasurer. The first thing the treasurer did was ask Robinson for the books. Robinson repeatedly denied his requests, until the new chapter president went to Robinson's house and demanded them. "[The president] stood on her doorstep until she gave the books to him. He said he wouldn't leave until she gave them to him," Mensel recalls. "Once [the board] got their hands on the books ... they could see that something was definitely very wrong."

In comparing the books with many of the returned checks, the organization could immediately see that not only had some checks been altered or forged, but also many of the checks were simply missing. At that point, the board of directors assigned Mensel and two other club members, one a CPA, to investigate Robinson's alleged wrongdoings. As Mensel and the other audit committee members looked at the checks, they realized that Robinson hardly attempted to cover up her scams at all.

"She did physically erase some checks and sometimes even used correction fluid to rewrite the name of the payee that was in the checkbook after the check had cleared," Mensel laughs. "But of course, on the back of the check was her name, as the depositor of the check."

The peculiar thing, in Mensel's mind, was the varying nature of Robinson's check writing. Although Mensel says several of the checks were written to casinos such as the Trump Taj Mahal and weekend getaway spots like the Mountain View Chalet, many more of the checks were written to other charities, and to the school Robinson's children attended. She apparently didn't use the embezzled money to substantially improve her lifestyle, which Mensel describes as "a very standard middle-class life here in Nashville. She and her husband were not wealthy people by any means."

Robinson was immediately excused from her executive secretary position. She was indicted by a grand jury, and was tried and found guilty. In addition, she was ordered to pay restitution to the club and its insurance company.

Robinson appeared to be one of the most dedicated volunteers in a charitable organization, giving of her time and efforts. The workers around her praised her generosity and work ethic, yet all the while she was stealing from them. If there is a lesson to be learned here, it is that audit functions are in place for a reason, and should never be overlooked. Unfortunately, this charitable organization was reminded of this lesson the hard way.

OVERVIEW

The story of Melissa Robinson is an example of one of the most common forms of fraudulent disbursement, the *check tampering* scheme. Check tampering occurs when an employee converts an organization's funds by either (1) fraudulently preparing a check drawn on the organization's account for his own benefit or (2) intercepting a check drawn on the organization's account that is intended for a third party, and converting that check to his own benefit. Remember: check tampering is a form of fraudulent *disbursement*, and applies only to payments drawn on the victim organization's bank accounts. If the perpetrator steals an incoming check from a customer that is payable to the victim organization, such a theft is classified as either *skimming* or *cash larceny*, depending on whether the check was recorded before it was stolen.

Because the vast majority of business payments are currently still made by check, the bulk of this chapter will focus on how traditional check-based payments can be manipulated by dishonest employees. However, businesses are increasingly using electronic forms of payment—such as wire transfers, ACH debits, and online bill-pay services—to pay vendors and other third parties. Consequently, the specific implications and considerations of these types of payments will be discussed in a separate section at the end of this chapter.

Check Tampering Data from the ACFE 2009 Global Fraud Survey

Check tampering, as we have stated, is a form of fraudulent disbursement in which the perpetrator converts an organization's funds by forging or altering a check drawn on one of the organization's bank accounts, or steals a check the organization has legitimately issued to another payee. Among fraudulent disbursement cases in the 2009 study, 27 percent involved check tampering (see Exhibit 5-2). This ranked check tampering as the third most common form of fraudulent disbursement in both studies, behind billing and expense reimbursement schemes.

As shown in Exhibit 5-3, the median loss due to check tampering schemes in the 2009 survey was $131,000, making it the most expensive of the fraudulent disbursement schemes.

CHECK TAMPERING SCHEMES

Check tampering is unique among fraudulent disbursements because it is the one group of schemes in which the perpetrator physically prepares the fraudulent check. In most fraudulent disbursement schemes, the culprit generates a payment to himself by submitting

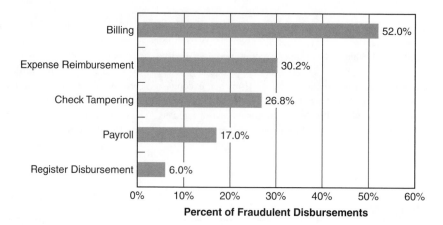

EXHIBIT 5-2 *2009 Global Fraud Survey:* Frequency of Fraudulent Disbursements[a]

[a]The sum of these percentages exceeds 100 percent because some cases involved multiple fraud schemes that fell into more than one category.

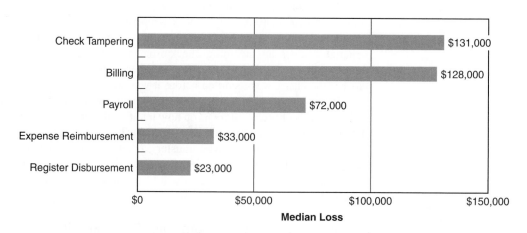

EXHIBIT 5-3 *2009 Global Fraud Survey:* Median Loss of Fraudulent Disbursements

some false document to the victim company such as an invoice or a timecard. The false document represents a claim for payment and causes the victim company to issue a check that the perpetrator then converts. These frauds essentially amount to trickery; the perpetrator fools the company into handing over its money.

But check tampering schemes are fundamentally different. In these frauds, the perpetrator takes physical control of a check and makes it payable to himself through one of several methods. Check tampering schemes depend on factors such as access to the company check stock, bank statements, and cash disbursements journal, as well as the ability to forge signatures or alter other information on the face of the check. Five principal methods are used to commit check tampering:

- Forged maker schemes
- Forged endorsement schemes
- Altered payee schemes

- Concealed check schemes
- Authorized maker schemes

Forged Maker Schemes

The legal definition of forgery includes not only the signing of another person's name to a document (such as a check) with a fraudulent intent, but also the fraudulent alteration of a genuine instrument.[1] This definition is so broad that it would encompass all check tampering schemes, so we have narrowed the term to fit our needs. Because we are interested in distinguishing the various methods used by individuals to tamper with checks, we will constrain the concept of "forgeries" to those cases in which an individual signs another person's name on a check.

The person who signs a check is known as the "maker" of the check. A forged maker scheme, then, may be defined as a check tampering scheme in which an employee misappropriates a check and fraudulently affixes the signature of an authorized maker thereon (see Exhibit 5-4). Frauds that involve other types of check tampering, such as the alteration of the payee or the changing of the dollar amount, are classified separately.

As one might expect, forged check schemes are usually committed by employees who lack signatory authority on company accounts. Melissa Robinson's case is something of an exception because, although she did have signatory authority, her organization's checks required two signatures. Robinson therefore had to forge another person's signature.

In order to forge a check, an employee must have access to a blank check, must be able to produce a convincing forgery of an authorized signature, and must be able to conceal his crime. If the fraudster cannot hide the crime from his employer, the scheme is sure to be short-lived. Concealment is a universal problem in check tampering schemes; the methods used are basically the same for all categories of check tampering. Therefore, concealment issues will be discussed as a group at the end of the chapter.

Obtaining the Check

Employees with Access to Company Checks   One cannot forge a company check unless one first possesses a company check. The first hurdle that a fraudster must overcome in committing a forgery scheme is to figure out how to get his hands on a blank check. Most forgery schemes are committed by accounts payable clerks, office managers, bookkeepers, or other employees whose duties typically include the preparation of company checks. Like Melissa Robinson, these are people who have access to a company's check stock on a regular basis and are therefore in the best position to steal blank checks. If an employee spends his workday preparing checks on behalf of his company, and if that employee has some personal financial difficulty, it takes only a small leap in logic (and a big leap in ethics) to see that his financial troubles can be solved by writing fraudulent checks for his own benefit. Time and again we see that employees tailor their fraud to the circumstances of their jobs. It stands to reason that those with access to the company's checks would be prone to committing forgery schemes.

Employees Lacking Access to Company Checks   If the perpetrator does not have access to the check stock through her work duties, she will have to find other means of misappropriating a check. The method by which a person steals a check depends largely on how blank checks are handled within a particular company. In some circumstances checks are poorly guarded, left in unattended areas where anyone can get to them. In

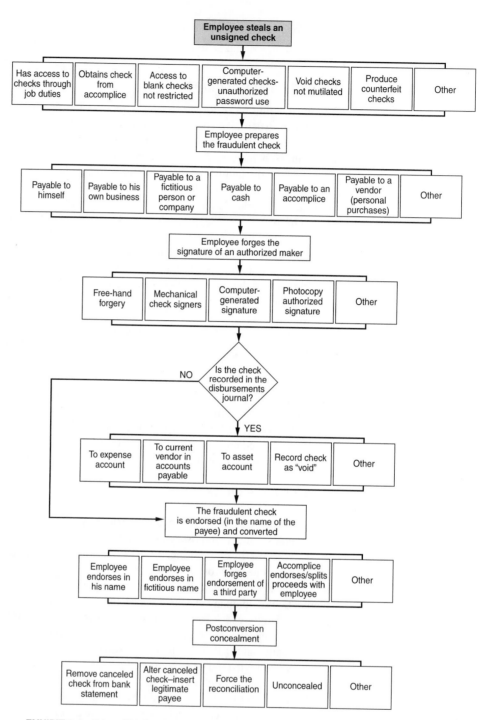

EXHIBIT 5-4 Forged Maker Schemes

other companies, the check stock may be kept in a restricted area, but the perpetrator may have obtained a key or combination to this area, or may know where an employee with access to the checks keeps his copy of the key or combination. An accomplice may provide blank checks for the fraudster in return for a portion of the stolen funds. Perhaps a secretary sees a blank check left on a manager's desk, or a custodian comes across the check stock in an unlocked desk drawer.

In some companies, checks are computer-generated. When this is the case, an employee who knows the password that allows checks to be prepared and issued may be able to obtain as many unsigned checks as he desires. There are an unlimited number of ways to steal a check, each dependent on the way in which a particular company guards its blank checks.

A fraudster may also be able to obtain a blank check when the company fails to properly dispose of unused checks. In Case 669, for example, a company used voided checks to line up the printer that ran payroll checks. These voided checks were not mutilated. A payroll clerk collected the voided checks after the printer was aligned and used them to issue herself extra disbursements through the payroll account.

Producing Counterfeit Checks   In more sophisticated forgery schemes, the perpetrator may produce counterfeit check stock with the organization's bank account number on the counterfeit checks. These counterfeit checks can be practically indistinguishable from the company's legitimate stock. In Case 1460, for example, the perpetrator had an accomplice who worked for a professional check-printing company and who printed blank checks for the bank account of the perpetrator's employer. The perpetrator then wrote over $100,000 worth of forgeries on these counterfeit checks.

Safeguarding the Organization's Check Stock   Organizations should take steps to safeguard their check stock and proactively seek out stolen and forged checks. These goals can be achieved through a number of relatively simple prevention and detection techniques that may avert a very large fraud scheme.

Clearly, blank checks should be maintained under lock and key and access should be severely limited to those whose duties include check preparation. (If checks are computer-generated, access to the code or password that allows issuance of checks should likewise be restricted.) Boxes of blank checks should be sealed with security tape to make it obvious when a new box has been opened, and on a periodic basis, someone independent of the check preparation function should verify the security of unused checks. Organizations should also promptly destroy any voided checks. These checks, if carelessly discarded, may be stolen and forged by employees.

The type of paper a check is printed on can sometimes help distinguish a legitimate check from a counterfeit. Organizations should print their checks on watermark paper supplied by a company independent of its check printer. (This will prevent a dishonest employee of the printer from using the company's watermarked paper.) Security threads or other markers can also be incorporated to help verify that company checks are legitimate. If an organization uses high-quality, distinctly marked paper for its checks, counterfeits will be easier to detect. In addition, it is a good idea to periodically rotate check printers and check stock to help make counterfeits stand out.

There are certain indicators that organizations can look for to help spot stolen or forged checks. Obviously, as stated above, if checks are noticed missing, or if there are signs of tampering with unused check stock, this is a clear indicator of theft. In addition, out-of-sequence checks or duplicate check numbers that show up on an organization's bank statement may signal theft. When employees steal blank checks, they will often take them from the bottom of the box with the hope that the missing check will not be noticed for some time. When these checks are converted, they should be noted as out-of-sequence on the bank statement. Employees who reconcile the statement should be trained to look for this red flag. Similarly, counterfeit checks often have numbers either that are completely out of sequence or that duplicate numbers of checks that have already been issued.

Employees who steal blank checks often do so after hours, when there are fewer people around to witness the theft. As a matter of practice, at the start of each business day, organizations should reconcile the first check in the check stock to the last check written on the previous day. If there is a gap, it should be promptly investigated.

To Whom Is the Check Made Payable?

Payable to the Perpetrator   Once a blank check has been obtained, the fraudster must decide to whom it should be made payable. He can write the check to anyone, though in most instances forged checks are payable to the perpetrator himself so that they are easier to convert. A check made payable to a third person, or to a fictitious person or business, may be difficult to convert without false identification. The tendency to make forged checks payable to oneself seems to be a result of fraudsters' laziness rather than a decision integral to the successful operation of their schemes; checks payable to an employee are clearly more likely to be recognized as fraudulent than checks made out to other persons or entities.

If the fraudster owns his own business or has established a shell company, he will usually write fraudulent checks to these entities rather than to himself. When the payee on a forged check is a vendor rather than an employee of the victim company, the checks are not as obviously fraudulent on their faces. At the same time, these checks are easy to convert, because the fraudster owns the entity to which the checks are payable.

Payable to an Accomplice   If a fraudster is working with an accomplice, she can make the forged check payable to that person; the accomplice then cashes the check and splits the money with the employee-fraudster. Because the check is payable to the accomplice in her true identity, it is easily converted. An additional benefit to using an accomplice is that a canceled check payable to a third-party accomplice is not as likely to raise suspicion as a canceled check to an employee. The obvious drawback to using an accomplice in a scheme is that the employee-fraudster usually has to share the proceeds of the scheme.

In some circumstances, however, the accomplice may be unaware that she is involved in a fraud. An example of how this can occur was found in Case 729, in which a bookkeeper wrote several fraudulent checks on company accounts, then convinced a friend to allow her to deposit the checks in the friend's account. The fraudster claimed the money was revenue from a side business she owned and the subterfuge was necessary to prevent creditors from seizing the funds. After the checks were deposited, the friend withdrew the money and gave it to the fraudster.

Payable to "Cash"   The fraudster may also write checks payable to "cash" in order to avoid listing himself as the payee. Checks made payable to cash, however, must still be endorsed. The fraudster will have to sign his own name, or forge the name of another, in order to convert the check. In addition, checks payable to "cash" are usually viewed more skeptically than checks payable to persons or businesses.

Payable to a Vendor   The employee who forges company checks may do so not to obtain currency, but to purchase goods or services for his own benefit. When this is the case, forged checks are made payable to third-party vendors who are uninvolved in the fraud. For instance, we saw in the case study at the beginning of this chapter how several of Melissa Robinson's checks were written to casinos and hotels, apparently for personal vacations.

Forging the Signature   After the employee has obtained and prepared a blank check, he must forge an authorized signature in order to convert the check. The most obvious method, and the one that comes to mind when we think of the word *forgery*, is to simply take pen in hand and sign the name of an authorized maker.

Free-Hand Forgery   The difficulty a fraudster encounters when physically signing the authorized maker's name is in creating a reasonable approximation of the true signature. If the forgery appears authentic, the perpetrator will probably have no problem cashing the check. In truth, the forged signature may not have to be particularly accurate. Many organizations do not verify the signatures on cancelled checks when they reconcile their bank statements, so even a poorly forged signature may go unnoticed.

Photocopied Forgeries   To guarantee an accurate forgery, some employees make photocopies of legitimate signatures and affix them to company checks. The fraudster is thus assured that the signature appears authentic. This method was used by a bookkeeper in Case 2514 to steal over $100,000 from her employer. Using her boss's business correspondence and the company Xerox machine, she made transparencies of his signature. These transparencies were then placed in the copy machine so that when she ran checks through the machine the boss's signature was copied onto the maker line of the check. The bookkeeper now had a signed check in hand. She made the fraudulent checks payable to herself, but falsified the check register so that the checks appeared to have been written to legitimate payees.

Automatic Check-Signing Mechanisms   Companies that issue a large number of checks sometimes utilize automatic check-signing mechanisms in lieu of signing each check by hand. Automated signatures are either produced with manual instruments like signature stamps or are printed by computer. Obviously, a fraudster who gains access to an automatic check-signing mechanism will have no trouble forging the signatures of authorized makers. Even the most rudimentary control procedures should severely limit access to these mechanisms. Nevertheless, several of the forged maker schemes the ACFE reviewed were accomplished through use of a signature stamp. In Case 838, for instance, a fiscal officer maintained a set of manual checks that were unknown to other persons in the company. The company used an automated check signer, and the custodian of the signer let the officer have uncontrolled access to it. Using the manual checks and the company's check signer, the fiscal officer was able to write over $90,000 worth of fraudulent checks to himself over a period of approximately four years.

The same principle applies to computerized signatures. Access to the password or program that prints signed checks should be restricted, specifically excluding those who prepare checks and those who reconcile the bank statement. The fraudster in Case 2342, for example, was in charge of preparing checks. The fraudster managed to obtain the issuance password from her boss, then used this password to issue checks to a company she owned on the side. She was able to bilk her employer out of approximately $100,000 using this method.

The beauty of automated check signers, from the fraudster's perspective, is that they produce perfect forgeries. Nothing about the physical appearance of the check will indicate that it is fraudulent. Of course, forged checks are written for illegitimate purposes, so they may be detectable when the bank statement is reconciled, or when accounts are reviewed. The ways in which fraudsters avoid detection through these measures will be discussed later in this chapter.

Preventing and Detecting Forged Maker Schemes   Obviously, a key to preventing forgeries is to maintain a strict set of procedures for the handling of outgoing checks, which includes safeguarding blank check stock, establishing rules for custody of checks that have been prepared but not signed, and separating the duties of check preparation and check signing. Organizations should establish a restrictive list of authorized check signers, and should see to it that checks that have been prepared are safeguarded until they are presented to these signatories.

To the extent possible, organizations should rotate authorized check signers and keep track of who is approved to sign checks during a given period. Rotating this duty can help prevent abuse by an authorized signatory, but also, if a canceled check shows a signature from the wrong signer for the date of the disbursement, this could indicate fraud. Also, on a periodic basis an organization should have authorized check signers verify their signatures on returned checks, or another employee should be required to spot-check signatures against an established signature file.

In organizations that use a signature stamp, access to the stamp should be strictly limited, and a custodian should maintain a log of who uses the signature stamp and at what time. If it is suspected that someone is misusing the signature stamp, temporarily suspend use of the stamp and instruct the bank to honor only checks bearing original signatures.

Miscoding Fraudulent Checks   Miscoding a check is actually a form of concealment, a means of hiding the fraudulent nature of the check. We will discuss the ways fraudsters code their forged checks in the concealment section at the end of this chapter. It should be noted here, however, that miscoding is typically used as a concealment method only by those employees who have access to the cash disbursements journal. If a forged maker scheme is undertaken by an employee without access to the cash disbursements journal, she usually makes no entry whatsoever to conceal her scheme.

Converting the Check   In order to convert the forged check, the perpetrator must endorse it. The endorsement is typically made in the name of the payee on the check. Since identification is generally required when one seeks to convert a check, the fraudster usually needs fake identification if he forges checks to real or fictitious third persons. As discussed earlier, checks payable to "cash" require the endorsement of the person converting them. Without fake ID, the fraudster will likely have to endorse these checks in his own name. Obviously, an employee's endorsement on a canceled check is a red flag.

Forged Endorsement Schemes

Forged endorsement frauds are those check tampering schemes in which an employee intercepts a company check intended for a third party and converts the check by signing the third party's name on the endorsement line of the check (see Exhibit 5-5). In some instances the fraudster also signs his own name as a second endorser. The term *forged endorsement schemes* would seem to imply that these frauds should be categorized along with the forged maker schemes discussed in the previous section. It is true that both kinds of fraud involve the false signing of another person's name on a check, but there

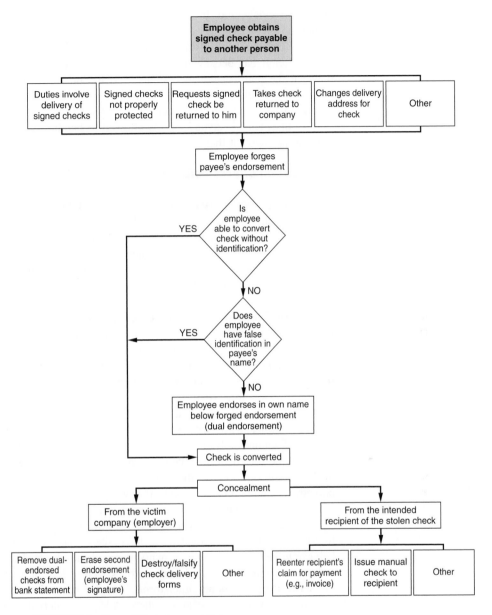

EXHIBIT 5-5 Forged Endorsement Schemes

are certain distinctions that cause forged endorsement schemes to be categorized here rather than with the other forgeries.

In classifying fraud types, we look to the heart of the scheme. What is the crucial point in the commission of the crime? In a forged maker scheme, the perpetrator is normally working with a blank check. The trick to this kind of scheme is in gaining access to blank checks and producing a signature that appears authentic.

In a forged endorsement scheme, on the other hand, the perpetrator is tampering with a check that has already been written, so the issues involved in the fraud are different. The key to these schemes is obtaining the checks after they are signed but before they are properly delivered. If this is accomplished, the actual forging of the endorsement is somewhat secondary.

A fraudster's main dilemma in a forged endorsement case is gaining access to a check after it has been written and signed. The fraudster must either steal the check between the point where it is signed and the point where it is delivered, or he must reroute the check, causing it to be mailed to a location where he can retrieve it. The manner used to steal a check depends largely on the way the company handles outgoing disbursements—anyone who is allowed to handle signed checks may be in a good position to intercept them.

Intercepting Checks before Delivery

Employees Involved in Delivery of Checks Obviously, the employees in the best position to intercept signed checks are those whose duties include the handling and delivery of signed checks. The most obvious example is a mailroom employee who opens outgoing mail containing signed checks and steals the checks. Other personnel who have access to outgoing checks might include accounts payable employees, payroll clerks, secretaries, and so forth.

Poor Control of Signed Checks Unfortunately, fraudsters are often able to intercept signed checks because of poor internal controls. For instance, in Case 1000, signed checks were left overnight on the desks of some employees because processing on the checks was not complete. One of the janitors on the overnight cleaning crew found these checks and took them, forged the endorsements of the payees, and cashed them at a liquor store. Another example of poor observance of internal controls appeared in Case 933. In this scheme a high-level manager with authority to disburse employee benefits instructed accounts payable personnel to return signed benefits checks to him instead of immediately delivering them to their intended recipients. These instructions were not questioned, despite the fact that they presented a clear violation of the separation-of-duties concept, due to the manager's level of authority within the company. The perpetrator simply took the checks that were returned to him and deposited them into his personal bank account, forging the endorsements of the intended payees.

Case 933 represents what seems to be the most common breakdown of controls in forged endorsement frauds. We have seen repeated occurrences of signed checks being returned to the employee who prepared the check. This typically occurs when a supervisor signs a check and hands it back to the clerk or secretary who presented it to the supervisor; it is done either through negligence or because the employee is highly trusted and thought to be above theft. Adequate internal controls should prevent the person who prepares company disbursements from having access to signed checks. This separation of duties is elemental; its purpose is to break the disbursement chain so that no one person controls the entire payment process.

Theft of Returned Checks Another way to obtain signed checks is to steal checks that have been mailed, but have been returned to the victim company for some reason such as an incorrect address. Employees with access to incoming mail may be able to intercept these returned checks from the mail and convert them by forging the endorsement of the intended payee. In Case 2288, for example, a manager took and converted approximately $130,000 worth of checks that were returned due to noncurrent addresses. (He also stole outgoing checks, cashed them, and then declared them lost.) The fraudster was well known at his bank and was able to convert the checks by claiming that he was doing it as a favor to the real payees, who were "too busy to come to the bank." The fraudster was able to continue with his scheme because the nature of his company's business was such that the recipients of the misdelivered checks were often not aware that the victim company owed them money. Therefore, they did not complain when their checks failed to arrive. In addition, the perpetrator had complete control over the bank reconciliation, so he could issue new checks to those payees who did complain and then "force" the reconciliation, making it appear that the bank balance and book balance matched when in fact they did not. Stealing returned checks is obviously not as common as other methods for intercepting checks, and it is more difficult for a fraudster to plan and carry out on a long-term basis. But it is also very difficult to detect, and can lead to large-scale fraud, as the previous case illustrates.

Rerouting the Delivery of Checks   The other way an employee can go about misappropriating a signed check is to alter the address to which the check is to be mailed. The check either is delivered to a place where the fraudster can retrieve it, or is purposely misaddressed so that he can steal it when it is returned as discussed above. As we have said before, proper separation of duties should preclude anyone who prepares disbursements from being involved in their delivery. Nevertheless, this control is often overlooked, allowing the person who prepares a check to address it and mail it as well.

In some instances in which proper controls are in place, fraudsters are still able to cause the misdelivery of checks. In Case 1470, for instance, the fraudster was a clerk in the customer service department of a mortgage company where her duties included changing the mailing addresses of property owners. She was assigned a password that gave her access to make address changes. The clerk was transferred to a new department where one of her duties was the issuance of checks to property owners. Unfortunately, her supervisor forgot to cancel her old password. When the clerk realized this oversight, she requested checks for certain property owners, then signed onto the system with her old password and changed the addresses of the property owners. The checks were then sent to her. The next day, the employee used her old password to reenter the system and replace the proper address so that there would be no record of where the check had been sent. This fraudster's scheme resulted in a loss of over $250,000 to the victim company.

Converting the Stolen Check   Once the check has been intercepted, the perpetrator can cash it by forging the payee's signature, hence the term *forged endorsement scheme*. Depending on where he tries to cash the check, the perpetrator may or may not need fake identification at this stage. As we alluded to earlier, many fraudsters cash their stolen checks at places where they are not required to show an ID.

If a fraudster is required to show identification in order to cash his stolen check, and if he does not have a fake ID in the payee's name, he may use a dual endorsement to cash or deposit the check. In other words, the fraudster forges the payee's signature as though the payee had transferred the check to him then the fraudster endorses the check in his own name and converts it. When the bank statement is reconciled, double endorsements on checks should always raise suspicions, particularly when the second signer is an employee of the company.

Preventing and Detecting the Theft of Outgoing Company Checks   It is very important that the functions of cutting checks, signing checks, and delivering checks be separated. If a check preparer is also allowed to have custody of signed checks, it is easy to commit check tampering. The individual can draft a check for a fraudulent purpose, wait for it to be signed, and simply pocket it. However, if the individual knows he will not see the check again after it has been signed, that person is less likely to attempt this kind of scheme because of the diminished perceived opportunity for success.

In addition to establishing controls designed to prevent the theft of outgoing checks, organizations should train their employees to look for this kind of scheme, and should establish routine procedures designed to help detect it if and when it does occur. These proactive detection techniques are generally not very complicated and do not require sophisticated procedures or investigative methods; all that is required is that an organization devote a minimal amount of time to routinely checking for thefts.

If an employee steals a check payable to a vendor and does not issue a replacement, the vendor will almost certainly complain about the nonpayment. This is the point at which most forged endorsement schemes should be detected. Therefore, every organization should have a structure in place to handle both vendor and customer complaints. All complaints should be investigated by someone independent of the payables function so that the fraudster will not be able to cover her tracks. When a complaint regarding nonpayment is received, it should be a relatively simple matter to track the missing check and identify when it was converted, and by whom. As a proactive measure, it may be advisable—particularly in organizations in which check theft has been a problem—to have independent personnel randomly contact vendors to confirm receipt of payments.

As was previously discussed, some employees who steal outgoing checks will cause a replacement check to be issued so that the vendor will not complain. In order to detect these schemes, an organization's accounting system should be set up to detect duplicate payments. Paid vouchers should immediately be stamped "paid," and computerized systems should automatically flag duplicate invoice numbers. In addition, payables reports sorted by payee and amount should be periodically generated in order to detect duplicates when invoice numbers have been altered for the second check.

Instead of stealing checks on the company premises, some employees will cause them to be misdelivered by changing the mailing address of the intended recipient in the organization's payables system. For this reason, authority to make changes to vendor records should be restricted, and the organization's accounting system should automatically track who makes changes to vendor records. This will make it easier to identify the perpetrator if an outgoing check is stolen. Periodically, a report listing all changes to vendor addresses, payment amounts, payees, and so on can be generated to determine if there have been an inordinate amount of changes, especially when a vendor's address is temporarily changed before a check is issued, then restored after the check has been mailed.

To convert an intercepted check, the perpetrator may have to use a dual endorsement. Any canceled checks with more than one endorsement should be investigated, as should any nonpayroll check that an employee has endorsed. The employee or employees who reconcile the bank statement should be required to review the backs of canceled checks for suspicious endorsements as a matter of course.

Another procedure that all organizations should have in place is to chart the date of mailing for every outgoing check. In the event that a signed check is stolen, the date of mailing can be compared to work records of mailroom personnel and other employees who have contact with outgoing checks to determine a list of possible suspects.

Finally, organizations should consider installing surveillance cameras in their mailrooms. Mailroom personnel are in a good position to steal outgoing checks, and also to skim incoming revenues or merchandise shipments. If a theft is discovered, security camera tapes may help identify the wrongdoer. More important, the presence of surveillance cameras can help deter employees from stealing.

Altered Payee Schemes

The second type of intercepted check scheme is the altered payee scheme. This is a type of check tampering fraud in which an employee intercepts a company check intended for a third party and alters the payee designation so that the check can be converted by the employee or an accomplice (see Exhibit 5-6). The fraudster inserts his own name, the name of a fictitious entity, or some other name on the payee line of the check. Altering the payee designation eliminates many of the problems associated with converting the check that would be encountered in a forged endorsement fraud. Because the alteration essentially makes the check payable to the fraudster (or an accomplice), there is no need to forge an endorsement, and no need to obtain false identification. The fraudster or his accomplice can endorse the check in his own name and convert it.

Of course, if canceled checks are reviewed during reconciliation of the bank statement, a check made payable to an employee is likely to cause suspicion, especially if the alteration to the payee designation is obvious. This is the main obstacle that must be overcome by fraudsters in altered payee schemes.

Altering Checks Prepared by Others: Inserting a New Payee

The method used to alter the payee designation on a check depends largely on how that check is prepared and intercepted. (Incidentally, the amount of the check may also be altered at the same time and by the same method as the payee designation.) Checks prepared by others can be intercepted by any of the methods discussed in the forged endorsements section above. When the fraudster intercepts a check that has been prepared by someone else, there are essentially two methods that may be employed. The first is to insert the false payee's name in place of the true payee's. This is usually done by rather unsophisticated means: The true name might be scratched out with a pen or covered up with correction fluid, and another name entered on the payee designation. These kinds of alterations are usually simple to detect.

A more intricate method occurs when the perpetrator of the fraud enters the accounts payable system and changes the names of payees, as occurred in Case 1112: An accounts payable employee in this case was so trusted that her manager allowed her to use his computer password in his absence. The password permitted access to the accounts payable address file. This employee waited until the manager was absent, then selected a legitimate vendor with whom her company did a great deal of business. She held up the vendor's invoices for the day, then after work used the manager's logon to change the vendor name and address to that of a fictitious company. The new name and address were run through the accounts payable cycle with an old invoice number, causing a fraudulent check to be issued. The victim company had an automated duplicate invoice test, but the fraudster circumvented it by substituting "1" for I and "0" (zero) for capital O. The next day, the employee replaced the true vendor's name and address, and mutilated the check register so that the check payable to the fictitious vendor was concealed. Approximately $300,000 in false checks were issued using this method.

Altering Checks Prepared by Others: "Tacking On"

The other method that can be used by fraudsters to alter checks prepared by others is "tacking on" additional letters or words to the end of the real payee designation. This rather unusual approach to check tampering occurred in Case 153, in which an employee took checks payable to "ABC" company and altered them to read "A.B. Collins." She then deposited these checks in an account that had been established in the name of A.B. Collins. The simple inclusion of a filler line after the payee designation would have prevented the loss of over $60,000

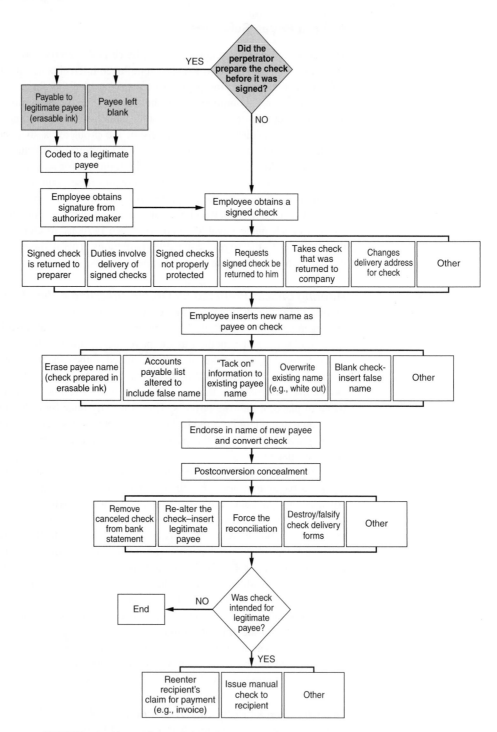

EXHIBIT 5-6 Altered Payee Schemes

in this case. In addition to altering the payee designation, the amount of the check can be altered by tacking on extra numbers if the person preparing the check is careless and leaves space for extra numbers in the "amount" portion of the check.

Altering Checks Prepared by the Fraudster: Erasable Ink When the fraudster prepares the check that is to be altered, the schemes tend to be a bit more sophisticated. The reason for this is obvious: when the perpetrator is able to prepare the check himself, he can prepare it with the thought of how the payee designation will be altered. But if the perpetrator is preparing the check, why not make the check payable to himself or an accomplice to begin with? In order to get an authorized maker to sign the check, the fraudster must make it appear that the check is made out to a legitimate payee. Only after a legitimate signature is obtained does the fraudster in an altered payee scheme set about tampering with the check.

One of the most common ways to prepare a check for alteration is to write or type the payee's name (and possibly the amount) in erasable ink. After the check is signed by an authorized maker, the perpetrator retrieves the check, erases the payee's name, and inserts his own. One example of this type of fraud was found in Case 2212, in which a bookkeeper typed out small checks to a local supplier and had the owner of the company sign them. The bookkeeper then used her erasing typewriter to lift the payee designation and amount from the check. She entered her own name as the payee and raised the amount precipitously. For instance, the owner might sign a $10 check that later became a $10,000 check. These checks were entered in the disbursements journal as payments for aggregate inventory to the company's largest supplier, who received several large checks each month. The bookkeeper stole over $300,000 from her employer in this scheme. The same type of fraud can be undertaken using an erasable pen. In some cases, fraudsters have even obtained signatures on checks written in pencil.

We have already discussed how, with a proper separation of duties, a person who prepares a check should not be permitted to handle the check after it has been signed. Nevertheless, this is exactly what happens in most altered payee schemes. When fraudsters prepare checks with the intent of altering them later, those fraudsters obviously have a plan for reobtaining the checks once they have been signed. Usually, the fraudster knows that there is no effective separation of controls in place, and knows that the maker of the check will return it to him.

Altering Checks Prepared by the Fraudster: Blank Checks The most egregious example of poor controls in the handling of signed checks is one in which the perpetrator prepares a check, leaves the payee designation blank, and submits it to an authorized maker who signs the check and returns it to the employee. Obviously, it is quite easy for the fraudster to designate himself or an accomplice, as the payee when this line has been left blank. Common sense tells us that one should not give a signed, blank check to another person. Nevertheless, this happened in several cases in our studies, usually when the fraudster was a longtime, trusted employee. In Case 1616, for example, an employee gained the confidence of the owner of his company, whom he convinced to sign blank checks for office use while the owner was out of town. The employee then filled in his own name as the payee on one of the checks, cashed it, and altered the check when it was returned along with the bank statement. The owner's blind trust in his employee cost him nearly $200,000.

Converting Altered Checks As with all other types of fraudulent checks, conversion is accomplished by endorsing the checks in the name of the payee. Conversion of fraudulent checks has already been discussed in previous sections and will not be reexamined here.

Preventing and Detecting the Alteration of Company Checks Most successful altered payee schemes occur when the person who prepares checks also has access to those checks after they have been signed. As with all forms of check tampering, altered payee schemes can usually be prevented by separating the duties of check preparation, signing, and delivery. It is also critical that the duty of reconciling the bank statement be separated from other check-preparation functions. Altered payee schemes should be very simple to detect during reconciliation, simply because the name or amount on the fraudulent check will not match the entry in the books or the support for the check. In almost all successful altered payee schemes, the perpetrator was able to prepare checks and reconcile the bank statement.

In addition to diligently matching all bank statement items to canceled checks, organizations might consider the use of carbon copy checks. Even if these instruments are altered after they have been cut, the copy will still reflect the intended payee and amount. Another simple method is to require that all checks be drafted in permanent ink to prevent schemes in which the payee and amount are erased and rewritten after a check is signed.

Concealed Check Schemes

Another scheme that requires a significant breakdown in controls and common sense is the concealed check scheme. These are check tampering frauds in which an employee prepares a fraudulent check and submits it along with legitimate checks to an authorized maker who signs it without a proper review (see Exhibit 5-7). Although not nearly as common as the other check tampering methods, it is worth mentioning for its simplicity, its uniqueness, and the ease with which it could be prevented.

The perpetrator of a concealed check scheme is almost always a person responsible for preparing checks. The steps involved in a concealed check scheme are similar to those in a forged maker scheme, except for the way in which the employee gets the fraudulent check signed. These schemes work as follows: The perpetrator prepares a check made out to himself, an accomplice, a fictitious person, and so on. Instead of forging the signature of an authorized maker, the employee takes the check to the authorized maker, usually concealed in a stack of legitimate checks awaiting signatures. The checks are typically delivered to the signer during a busy time of day when he is rushed and will be less likely to pay close attention to them. Generally, the checks are fanned out on the signer's desk so that the signature lines are exposed but the names of the payees are concealed. If a particular authorized maker is known to be inattentive, the checks are given to him.

The maker signs the checks quickly, and without adequate review. Because he is busy or generally inattentive, or both, he simply does not look at what he is signing. He does not demand to see supporting documentation for the checks, and does nothing to verify their legitimacy. Once the checks have been signed they are returned to the employee, who removes his check and converts it. This appears to be one of the methods used by Ernie Philips in the case study at the end of this chapter. Philips slipped several checks payable to himself into a stack of company checks, then took them to the operations manager, who was designated to sign checks when the business's owner was out of town. The operations manager apparently did not check the names of the payees and unknowingly signed several company checks to Philips.

A similar example of the concealed check method took place in Case 2474, where a bookkeeper took advantage of the owner of her company by inserting checks payable

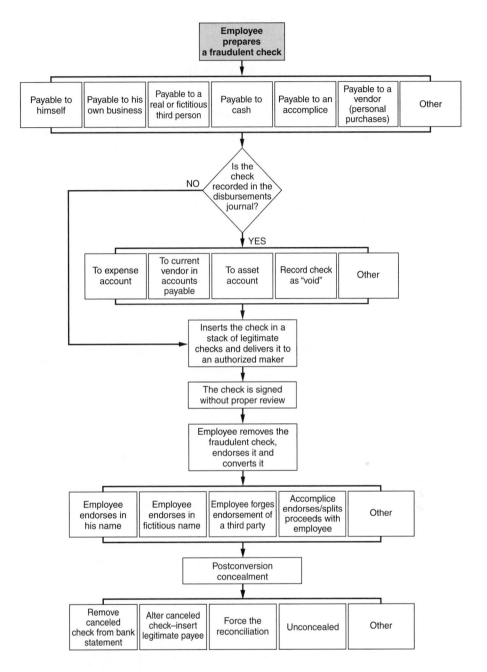

EXHIBIT 5-7   Concealed Check Schemes

to herself into batches of checks given to the owner for signature. The owner simply never looked at whom he was paying when he signed the checks.

The perpetrator of a concealed check scheme banks on the inattentiveness of the check signer. If the signer were to review the checks he was signing, he would certainly discover the fraud. It should be noted that the fraudster in these cases could make the fraudulent check payable to an accomplice, a fictitious person, or a fictitious business instead of payable to himself. This is more common and certainly a lot less dangerous for the employee (but not nearly as exciting).

Authorized Maker Schemes

The final check tampering scheme, the authorized maker scheme, may be the most difficult to defend against. An authorized maker scheme is a type of check tampering fraud in which an employee with signatory authority on a company account writes fraudulent checks for his own benefit and signs his own name as the maker (see Exhibit 5-8). The perpetrator in these schemes can write and sign fraudulent checks without assistance; he does not have to alter a preprepared instrument or forge the maker's signature.

Overriding Controls through Intimidation   When a person is authorized to sign company checks, preparing the checks is easy. The employee simply writes and signs the

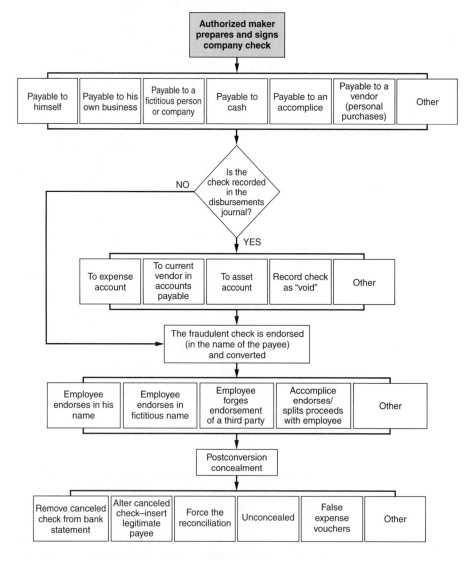

EXHIBIT 5-8   Authorized Maker Schemes

instruments the same way he would with any legitimate check. In most situations, check signers are owners, officers, or otherwise high-ranking employees, and thus have or can obtain access to all the blank checks they need. Even if company policy prohibits check signers from handling blank checks, the perpetrator's influence normally can be used to overcome this impediment. What employee is going to tell the CEO that he can't have a blank check?

The most basic way an employee accomplishes an authorized maker scheme is to override controls designed to prevent fraud. We have already stated that most authorized signatories have high levels of influence within their companies. This influence may be used by the perpetrator to deflect questions about fraudulent transactions. The most common example is one in which a majority owner or sole shareholder uses his company as a sort of alter ego, paying personal expenses directly out of company accounts. If this arrangement is disclosed and agreed to by other owners, there may be nothing illegal about it—after all, one cannot steal from oneself. On the other hand, in the absence of an agreement between all owners, these disbursements amount to embezzlement. Instead of paying personal expenses, the fraudster might cut checks directly to himself, his friends or family. Using fear for job security as a weapon, the owner can maintain a work environment in which employees are afraid to question these transactions.

High-level managers or officers may also use their authority to override controls in those companies whose ownership is either absent or inattentive. Intimidation can play a large part in the commission and concealment of any type of occupational fraud where powerful individuals are involved. In Case 878, for example, the manager of a sales office stole approximately $150,000 from his employers over a two-year period. This manager had primary check-signing authority and abused this power by writing company checks to pay his personal expenses. The manager's fraudulent activities were well known by certain members of his staff, but these employees' careers were controlled by the perpetrator. Fear of losing their jobs combined with lack of a proper whistleblowing structure prevented the manager's employees from reporting his fraud.

Poor Controls   Although overriding controls is the most blatant way to execute an authorized maker scheme, it is not the most common. Far more of these schemes occur because no one is paying attention to the accounts and few controls are present to prevent fraud. In Case 740, for example, a manager of a small business wrote company checks to purchase assets for his own business. He took approximately $800,000 from his employer, hiding the missing money in accounts receivable because he knew that those accounts were reviewed only once a year. Before audits, the manager would borrow money from the bank to replace the missing funds, then begin the whole process again when the books were closed. This unfortunate scheme ended in tragedy as the manager and his wife committed suicide when the fraud came to light. Setting aside the personal catastrophe that occurred in this case, it is obvious that if the books had been more closely monitored, or if there had been a threat of surprise audits in addition to the regularly scheduled reviews, this fraud might not have gotten so far out of hand.

The failure to closely monitor accounts is supplemented by lack of internal controls, specifically the absence of separation of duties in the cash disbursements process. In Case 2802, for instance, the perpetrator was in charge of signing all company checks, as well as reconciling the bank accounts for a small business. This put the fraudster in perfect position to write fraudulent checks to herself and her husband. Similarly, in Case 196, the bookkeeper of a medium-sized company was charged with paying all bills and preparing the company payroll. She had access to an automatic check signer and total control over company bank accounts. The bookkeeper wrote extra checks to herself, coded the expenditures to payroll, and destroyed the canceled checks when they were returned with the bank statement. Had the duties of preparing checks and reconciling accounts been separated, as they should be, the fraudster would not have been able to complete her scheme.

Preventing and Detecting Check Tampering by Authorized Makers   Check tampering committed by authorized signers can be among the most difficult forms of occupational fraud to prevent, simply because the check signer is relied on by an organization to serve as a control against fraud by reviewing prepared checks and affixing her signature only to legitimate disbursements. When the check signer is herself a part of the fraud, this control evaporates.

As with all forms of check tampering, the most important preventative measure is to establish a firm separation of duties in the check-writing function—specifically, to separate the duties of preparing and signing checks, and to ensure that check signers do not have access to blank checks. If an authorized maker has access only to checks that have already been prepared by someone else, then she cannot create a fraudulent check on her own.

Another control that can help limit losses caused by authorized maker schemes is to require dual signatures for disbursements over a threshold amount. This will not prevent fraudulent checks below the threshold, but it will limit the damage a single fraudster can do by abusing his check-signing authority.

Organizations should also maintain up-to-date vendor lists and confirm all disbursements to the list, giving scrutiny to checks written to unknown vendors. Payments to known vendors in unusual amounts or at unusual times should also be investigated. In addition, canceled checks should be spot-checked for proper support and to verify the business purpose of the disbursements. Obviously, all of these tests should be performed by persons who are independent of the disbursements function.

CONCEALING CHECK TAMPERING

Because most check tampering schemes do not consist of a single occurrence but instead continue over a period of time, concealing the fraud is arguably the most important aspect of the scheme. If a fraudster intended to steal a large sum of money and skip to South America, hiding the fraud might not be so important. But the vast majority of occupational fraudsters remain employees of their companies as they continue to steal from them. Therefore, hiding the fraud is extremely important. Concealment of the fraud means not only hiding the identity of the criminal, but, in most cases, hiding the fact of the fraud. The most successful frauds are those in which the victim company is unaware that it is being robbed. Obviously, once a business learns that it is being victimized it will take steps to stanch its bleeding and the end of the fraudster's scheme will be at hand.

Check tampering schemes can present especially tricky concealment problems for fraudsters. In other types of fraudulent disbursements such as invoice or payroll schemes, the fraudulent payment is entered in the books as a legitimate transaction by someone other than the fraudster. Remember that the payments in those schemes are generated by the production of false documents that cause accounts payable personnel to think that money is owed to a particular person or vendor. When accounts payable issues a disbursement for a bogus invoice, it does so because it believes the invoice to be genuine. The payment is then entered in the books as a legitimate payment. In other words, the perpetrator generally does not have to worry about concealing the payment in the books, because someone else unwittingly does it for him.

Check tampering schemes do not always afford this luxury to the fraudster. In forgery and authorized maker schemes the perpetrator is the one writing the check, and he is also usually the one coding the check in the disbursements journal. He must "explain" the check on the books. Forged endorsement schemes and altered payee schemes are different because they involve the alteration of checks that were already prepared and coded by someone else. Nevertheless, they create a problem for the fraudster, because the intercepted check was intended for a legitimate recipient. In short, someone is out there waiting for the check that the fraudster has taken. The culprit in these schemes must worry not only about hiding the fraud from his employer, but also about appeasing the intended payee. If the intended recipient of the check does not receive his payment, the person will complain to the fraudster's employer about the nonpayment. This could trigger an investigation into the whereabouts of the missing check, something the fraudster definitely wants to avoid.

The Fraudster Reconciling the Bank Statement

Many of those who perpetrate check tampering frauds are involved in reconciling the company's bank statement. The bank statement that a company receives normally includes the canceled checks that have been cashed in the preceding period. A person who reconciles the accounts is therefore in a position to hide the existence of any fraudulent checks that he has written to himself. He can remove the fraudulent checks or doctor the bank statement, or both.

We said earlier that in forged maker and authorized maker schemes, the perpetrator usually has to code the check in the disbursements journal. The most fundamental way to hide the check is to code it as "void," or to include no listing at all in the journal. Then, when the bank statement arrives, the perpetrator removes the fraudulent check from the returned checks and destroys it or alters the bank statement. Now there is no record of the payment in the journal, and no physical evidence of the check on hand. Of course, the bank will have a copy of the check, but unless someone questions the missing check there will be little chance that the company will routinely discover the problem. And since the perpetrator is the one who reconciles the account, it is unlikely that anyone will even notice that the check is missing.

The problem with simply omitting the fraudulent check from the disbursements journal is that the bank balance will not reconcile to the book balance. For instance, if the fraudster wrote a $25,000 check to himself and did not record it, then the book balance will be $25,000 higher than the bank balance ($25,000 was taken out of the bank account by the fraudster, but was not credited out of the company's cash account). Fraudsters usually omit their illicit checks from the disbursements journal only in situations in which they personally reconcile the bank statement and no one reviews their work, thus allowing the fraudster to force the reconciliation. In other words, the fraudster reports that the bank balance and book balance match when in fact they do not. These are circumstances in which the employer basically takes the perpetrator's word that the book balance and bank balance reconcile.

Some of the victim companies in our studies simply did not reconcile their accounts regularly. Because no one was reconciling the book balance and the bank balance, the fraudster was able to write checks without recording them. In a system in which controls are so lax, almost any concealment method will be effective to disguise fraud. In fact, no effort to conceal the crime may even be necessary in such circumstances.

Fraudsters might physically alter the bank statement to cause it to match the company's book balance. For instance, a person engaging in a forged maker scheme may decide to steal blank checks from the bottom of the check stock. These checks are out of sequence and therefore will be listed last on the bank statement. The employee then deletes this clump of checks and alters the final total to match the victim company's books. We will see this method of concealment used in the following case study.

In some cases, although employee's duties do not include reconciling the bank accounts, he is nevertheless able to intercept bank statements and alter them to hide his crimes. In the following case study, Ernie Philips was able to persuade his company's bank to send the bank statements directly to him instead of to his boss. Philips then altered the bank statements to conceal his fraudulent activities. This case describes how CFE James Sell put an end to Philips's scheme.

CASE STUDY: WHAT ARE FRIENDS FOR?[2]

Ernie Philips had fallen on hard times. Several back operations left him barely able to move around. He became addicted to the pills that made the pain bearable. His CPA practice was going under. He and his wife had six adopted children to support. Not surprisingly, he suffered from depression and chronic anxiety. But Ernie's luck changed when he ran into his old friend, James Sell. The two men had worked together at a federal agency and known each other more than 20 years. Ernie talked about the trouble he was having, and James said he could help. At the time, Ernie was in a rehabilitation program for his substance abuse, so James told him, "Let me know when you're finished with that, and I'll have some work for you."

James rented Ernie an office and started sending a few small projects his way. "I wanted to try him out, see how he would do," Sell remarks. "He seemed like he was trying to get himself together." Ernie completed the work on time, and performed well, so when James got a big account with the Arizona and Nevada governments, he brought his friend into the main office. They agreed on a salary just over $68,000 a year, which James upped to $74,000 after six months.

Sell was appointed receiver for CSC Financial Services in Arizona and Nevada. CSC owners had been caught diverting $5.5 million of customer escrow funds from its operations in Arizona and Nevada. The computer equipment used in the operation dated from the 1960s, and a lack of supervision and proper controls had obviously allowed the embezzlement to take place. The company didn't use a double-entry system, so management could alter ending totals with wide latitude. Even after a regulatory audit discovered that things were in disarray at CSC, the Arizona administrators had allowed the offending owners to continue operating for a year and a half. So when Sell finally took over, he found a rather large mess. That's part of the game, he says: "When you get a company as receiver, you try to survive with what you inherit." The receivership involved more than 15,000 active accounts,

with about $285 million in in-house payments each year, and more than 30,000 transactions a month. Sorting out the trouble wouldn't be easy. Sell knew Ernie had experience, so he tapped him for the job. "One of the reasons I brought him in," Sell says, "was to establish controls where there were none before."

But Ernie had little respect for controls. When James asked the mailroom clerk about the bank statements for a particular month, he told him that Ernie had them. "Why is that?" James asked. "He knows those are supposed to come to me unopened. He shouldn't have them." The clerk said Ernie needed the statements for a reconciliation. James didn't want to overreact, but he was nervous. "There's limited control over any position and even less over a key financial position," he says, "and any time you lose a control point, you're in jeopardy. So you have to take a strong position in order to restore the process." He discussed the matter with Ernie and thought they had an understanding.

Ernie was having problems with other people in the company too. He and the operations manager had a heated exchange when the manager retrieved some account papers from Ernie's desk. Ernie had been out and the papers were needed right away. When Ernie aired his grievance, James sided with the operations manager. There shouldn't be any problem, James said. It wasn't like anyone was rifling Ernie's desk. Besides, Sell traveled frequently, and spent a lot of time in the Nevada office, so having open access in the Arizona office allowed for informal oversight. Sell muses, "One of the best controls in the world is to create an atmosphere of uncertainty. Usually embezzlement doesn't occur unless the person thinks he can hide what he's doing. So I figured this would be a way to keep things on the up and up."

The uncertainty didn't prevent the fraud, but it did help detect what was going on. The operations manager discovered Ernie's scheme during a search for accounting records. He brought Sell a company check from Ernie's desk, made out in the name of Ernie Philips for $2,315. It wasn't Ernie's payroll check, so what was it? The check hadn't been cashed, but Sell's signature had been forged. Not sure yet about the

[2]Several names and details have been changed to preserve anonymity.

situation, Sell arranged to meet Ernie away from the main office.

Sell had been out of town and needed some updates on the escrow operations, so he dropped by Ernie's private office one afternoon. After they finished their discussion, James said, "There's one more thing I wanted to ask you about." He pulled a copy of the check from his briefcase and told Ernie, "I was hoping you could explain this."

There was a long silence. Ernie stared at the check, pursing his lips and scratching his hands across the desktop. The pause stretched into what seemed like minutes. Finally he confessed, "I've been taking money."

"I could tell from the look on his face this was trouble," Sell reports. The worst was confirmed. He had been hoping there was an explanation, an innocuous one, despite all the signs. Still, he had come prepared. "I wanted to confront him away from the main office so if there was anything he could get to and destroy, I'd be protected." James had also brought a copy of the check so it wouldn't be apparent when he showed the check to Ernie that it wasn't cashed. "I wanted to make him believe I knew more than I did. Nailing down this operation would have meant reviewing pages and pages of bank statements, verifying checks and payments. Before I went to that trouble, I wanted to know there was a reason to look."

Sell barred Ernie from both his offices, and began tracing his friend's activities over the past seven months. In some cases, Sell's name was forged onto the checks in handwriting that wasn't his and which bore a resemblance to Ernie's. Others were marked with the signature stamp that was supposed to remain locked in a clerk's office except when she was using it for a very limited set of transactions. Somehow, Ernie had been able to slip the stamp away and mark his checks.

He covered his tracks by taking checks out of sequence so they would show up at the end of the bank statement. Then he'd intercept the statement, and alter the report at the end, returning a copy of the statement to the clerk for filing. After the clerk told Sell about Ernie having the statement, Ernie arranged with the bank for the statements to come addressed to his attention. Without getting authorization, the bank agreed; Ernie could then doctor the statement, copy it, and send it down the line. If someone did ask about an unidentified disbursement, Ernie told them the money went to a supply vendor, and since he was the controller, he was taken at his word. He even managed on a couple of occasions to slip checks made out to himself into a regular batch, which the operations manager—who was authorized to sign checks in Sell's absence—signed.

Sell was, to put it mildly, chagrined. He had believed that his office was set up to avoid the kind of flagrant defalcation he was facing now. But, he admits, "No matter how good a system you design, one knowledgeable person can circumvent it... The trick is to make sure the procedures you set up are followed. I don't know if there's a system in the world that's immune. The key is to limit and control the extent of any one person's action, so you can at least detect when things go awry."

Sell figured his losses at about $109,000. He got a complete run of the bank statements from Ernie's tenure, identified checks out of sequence, or gaps in issued checks, and then verified to whom they were payable and the stated purpose. The scheme had required some footwork, but wasn't terribly sophisticated. The checks were written in odd-number amounts—$4,994.16, for example—but Ernie had made the payments in his own name. He had left behind some of his personal bank statements, which showed deposits correlated with the money he'd taken from Sell. (The amounts didn't always match, because Ernie would take cash back from the deposit, but they were close enough to link the transactions.)

Ernie's brief era of good feelings had ended. He had used the proceeds from his finagling for a lavish family vacation, a new car, a new computer, and improvements on the house where he lived with his wife and their adopted family, but in the fallout of his dismissal Ernie's house went into foreclosure. He was charged around the same time with driving under the influence. The CPA board revoked his license and fined him for ethics violations. He made no defense at his civil trial, where a judgment was rendered against him for the $109,000 he took, plus treble damages. While he was out on bail for the criminal charges against him, Ernie took his family and fled; Sell was able to locate him through an Internet search service. But Ernie died shortly thereafter. "He threw everything away," Sell laments. "For $109,000 he fouled up his life, and his family."

Sell takes the matter philosophically. There are plenty of cases that echo Ernie's. For example, Sell just investigated a paralegal who not only wrote company checks to herself, but also sent one to the County Attorney's office—to pay the fine she owed for writing bad checks. "Typically, these people don't take the time to set up a new identity or a dummy company," James says. "They just want the money fast and grab it the easiest way they can."

"And often enough," he adds, "they want to get caught... Ernie knew he was out of control; we had been friends for so long. He knew he was doing more than just breaking the law. During one of our conversations after this he told me, 'You know, the first check was real hard to write. But I had clients I had borrowed from, I owed money all over the place, I had a family. As it went on, writing the checks just got easier.'"

Re-Altering Checks

In altered payee schemes, remember that it is common for the perpetrator to take a check intended for a legitimate recipient, then doctor the instrument so that he is designated as the payee. A company check payable to an employee will obviously raise suspicions of fraud when the canceled check is reconciled with the bank statement. To prevent this, some employees re-alter their fraudulent checks when the bank statement arrives. We have already discussed how some fraudsters alter checks by writing the payee's name in erasable ink or type when the check is prepared. These employees obtain a signature for the check, then erase the true payee's name and insert their own. When these checks return with the statement, the employee erases his own name and reenters the name of the proper payee; thus, there will be no appearance of mischief. The fraudster in Case 1616 used the re-alteration method to hide over $185,000 in fraudulent checks.

The re-alteration method is not limited to altered payee schemes; the concealment will be equally effective in forged maker schemes, authorized maker schemes, and concealed check schemes. Re-altered checks will match the names of legitimate payees listed in the disbursements journal.

Falsifying the Disbursements Journal

Rather than omit a fraudulent check from the disbursements journal or list it as void, the perpetrator might write a check payable to himself but list a different person as the payee on the books. Usually, the fake payee is a regular vendor—a person or business that receives numerous checks from the victim company. Employees tend to pick known vendors for these schemes, because one extra disbursement to a regular payee is less likely to stand out.

The false entry is usually made at the time the fraudulent check is written, but in some cases the fraudster makes alterations to existing information on the book. In the opening case study in this chapter, for instance, Melissa Robinson used correction fluid and an eraser to change the payee names in her company's checkbook. Obviously, alterations found in a company's books should be carefully scrutinized to make sure they are legitimate.

The fraudster can also conceal a fraudulent check by falsely entering the amounts of legitimate checks in the disbursements journal. He overstates the amounts of legitimate disbursements in order to absorb the cost of a fraudulent check. For instance, assume that a company owes $10,000 to a particular vendor. The fraudster would write a check to the vendor for $10,000, but enter the check in the disbursements journal as a $15,000 payment. The company's disbursements are now overstated by $5,000. The fraudster can write a $5,000 check to himself and list that check as void in the disbursements journal. The bank balance and the book balance will still match, because the cost of the fraudulent check was absorbed by overstating the amount of the legitimate check. Of course, the fact that the canceled checks do not match the entries in the journal should indicate potential fraud. This type of concealment is really effective only when the bank accounts are not closely monitored or when the employee is also in charge of reconciling the accounts.

If possible, fraudsters will try to code their fraudulent checks to existing accounts that are rarely reviewed or to accounts that are very active. In Case 804, for instance, the perpetrator charged his checks to an intercompany payables account because it was reviewed only at the end of the year, and not in great detail. The perpetrator in this case might also have coded his checks to an account with extensive activity in the hopes that his fraudulent check would be lost in the crowd of transactions on the account. In the cases the ACFE researchers reviewed, most checks were coded to expense accounts or liability accounts.

This particular method can be very effective in concealing fraudulent checks, particularly when the victim company is not diligent in reconciling its bank accounts. For instance, in Case 1761, the victim company reconciled its accounts by verifying the amount of the checks with the check numbers, but did not verify that the payee on the actual check matched the payee listed in the disbursements journal. As a result, the company was unable to detect that the checks had been miscoded in the disbursements journal. As we discussed in the previous section, the fraudster might also intercept the bank statement before it is reconciled and alter the payee name on the fraudulent check to match the entry he made in the disbursements journal.

Reissuing Intercepted Checks

We mentioned before that in intercepted check schemes, the employee faces detection not only through his employer's normal control procedures, but also by the intended recipients of the checks he steals. After all, when these people do not receive their payments from the victim company, they are likely to complain; these complaints, in turn, could trigger a fraud investigation.

Some employees head this problem off by issuing new checks to the people whose initial checks they stole. In Case 579, for instance, an employee stole checks intended for vendors and deposited them into her own checking account. She then took the invoices from these vendors and reentered them in the company's accounts payable system, adding a number or letter to avoid the computerized system's duplicate check controls. This assured that the vendors received their due payment and therefore would not blow the whistle on her scheme, which netted approximately $200,000.

Another example of reissuance was provided by an accounts payable troubleshooter in Case 1328. The employee in this case was in charge of auditing payments to all suppliers, reviewing supporting documents, and mailing checks. Every once in a while, she purposely failed to mail a check to a vendor. The vendor, of course, called accounts payable about the late payment and was told that his invoice had been paid on a certain date. Since accounts payable did not have a copy of the canceled check (because the fraudster was still holding it), they would call the troubleshooter to research the problem. Unfortunately for the company, the troubleshooter was the one who had stolen the check; she told accounts payable to issue another check to the vendor while she stopped payment on the first. Thus the vendor received his payment, and instead of stopping payment on the first check, the troubleshooter deposited it into her own account.

The difference between these two schemes is that in the latter, two checks were issued for a single invoice. The troubleshooter in Case 1328 did not have to worry about this problem because she performed the bank reconciliations for her company and was able to force the totals. Once again, we see that access to the bank statement is a key to concealing a check tampering scheme.

Bogus Supporting Documents

Whereas some fraudsters attempt to wipe out all traces of their fraudulent disbursements by destroying the checks, forcing the bank reconciliation, and so on, others opt to justify their checks by manufacturing fake support for them. These fraudsters prepare false payment vouchers, including false invoices, purchase orders, or receiving reports, to create an appearance of authenticity. This concealment strategy is practical only when the employee writes checks payable to someone other than himself (e.g., an accomplice or a shell company). A check made payable to an employee may raise suspicions regardless of any supporting documents he manufactures.

Conceptually, the idea of producing false payment vouchers may seem confusing in a chapter on check tampering. If the fraudster is using fake vouchers, shouldn't the crime be classified as a billing scheme? Not necessarily. In a check tampering scheme, the fraudster generates the disbursement by writing the check himself. He may create fake support to justify the check, but the support—the voucher—had nothing to do with the disbursement being made. Had the fraudster not created a fake invoice, he would still have had a fraudulent check.

In a billing scheme, on the other hand, the fraudster uses the false voucher to *cause a payment to be generated*. Without a fake voucher in these schemes, there would be no fraudulent disbursement at all, because the employee depends on someone else to actually cut the check. In other words, the false voucher is a means of creating the unwarranted payment in these schemes, rather than an attempt to hide it.

ELECTRONIC PAYMENT TAMPERING

As businesses move to using electronic payments—such as automated clearing house (ACH) payments, online bill payments, and wire transfers—in addition to or instead of traditional checks, fraudsters are adapting their methods to manipulate these payments as well. Some of these fraudsters abuse their legitimate access to their employer's electronic payment system; these schemes are similar to traditional check tampering frauds carried out by authorized makers. Others gain access through social engineering or password theft, or by exploiting weaknesses in their employer's internal control or electronic payment system. Regardless of the means by which they log in to the system, the dishonest employees use this access to fraudulently initiate or divert electronic payments to themselves or their accomplices.

As with other schemes, once the fraudulent payment has been made, the employee must cover his tracks. However, the lack of physical evidence and forged signatures can make concealment of fraudulent electronic payments less challenging than other check tampering schemes. Some fraudsters attempt to conceal their schemes by altering the bank statement, miscoding transactions in the accounting records, or sending fraudulent payments to a shell company with a name similar to that of an existing vendor. Others merely rely on the company's failure to monitor or reconcile its accounts.

Prevention and Detection

Internal Controls One of the most important internal controls for preventing and detecting electronic payment fraud is separation of duties. For example, in the case of online bill payments, such as those made through a bank's website or a third-party business-to-business payment service, separate individuals should be responsible for maintaining payments templates, entering payments, and approving payments. For wire transfers, duties for creating, approving, and releasing wires should be segregated. And to prevent attempts to conceal fraudulent electronic payment activity, no individual involved in the payment process should reconcile the bank statement, or even have access to it. In addition to separating duties, companies should consider segregating their bank accounts in order to maintain better control over them—for example, separate accounts can be used for paper and electronic transactions.

Account monitoring and reconciliation should be performed daily so as to quickly spot and notify the bank of any unusual transactions. Depending on the accounting software in use at the company and the account reconciliation offerings of its bank, much of the reconciliation process can be automated. Additionally, many banks are able to provide daily itemized reports of outstanding payments in addition to a list of those payments that have already cleared.

In guarding against improper access to electronic payment systems, proper management and protection of user access and account information are essential. All log-in information, such as usernames and passwords, should be heavily guarded, with passwords changed frequently and user access immediately deactivated for any user who no longer has a need for it (e.g., a terminated employee or an employee who has changed roles). Although most electronic payment systems will eventually time out, users should log off immediately when they are finished using the system or if they need to leave their computer unattended, even if only for a short time. Unattended computers that are logged on to a payment system provide fraudsters with a free pass to the company's bank account. For example, in Case 5777, an employee who was working in the company's electronic payment system left his computer unattended for less than ten minutes so that he could grab a cup of coffee. During that time, another employee who shared an office with him was able to wire $3,273 to an existing vendor with whom he was in collusion. Because the victim company performed daily account reconciliations, the fraud was caught the next day. The fraudster was fired immediately, and the individual who left his computer unattended while logged into the system was reprimanded.

Bank Security Services   Most large banks offer a number of security services that can help business account holders mitigate fraud through early detection and prevention of fraudulent electronic payments. For example, ACH blocks allow account holders to notify their banks that ACH debits—whether authorized or not—should not be allowed on specific accounts. ACH filters enable account holders to provide their banks with a list of defined criteria (such as the sending company ID, account number, and transaction code) against which banks can filter ACH debits and reject any unauthorized transactions. Positive pay for ACH is another security feature offered by banks to their account holders, in which banks match the details of ACH payments with those on a list of legitimate and expected payments provided by the account holder. Only authorized electronic transactions are allowed to be withdrawn from the account; exceptions are reported to the customer for review.

Organizations can also set up their commercial banking software to restrict access to specific banking activities—such as viewing transactions, viewing bank statements, initiating electronic payments, or setting up ACH blocks or filters—to designated individuals. Companies should incorporate this feature into their internal control system to enhance separation of duties. For example, any individual authorized to make payments should not be permitted to set up ACH blocks or filters, or to submit positive pay information. In addition, businesses can customize their banking software to incorporate features such as dual authorization for certain transactions and daily or individual transaction limits.

Companies can further enhance their protection against unauthorized access to an electronic payment system through the use of their banks' multifactor authentication tools, mechanisms that combine two or more methods to validate the identity of the person attempting to access the system. These tools—such as tokens (physical devices that authorized users provide in addition to their passwords to prove their identities electronically), digital certificates, smart cards, and voiceprint recognition software—can help businesses overcome the problem of compromised credentials, such as usernames and passwords.

PROACTIVE COMPUTER AUDIT TESTS FOR DETECTING CHECK TAMPERING SCHEMES[2]

Title	Category	Description	Data file(s)
Extract all voided checks and summarize by issuer for reasonableness.	All	Checks may be voided in the system and then cashed (which requires another entry in the bank reconciliation to conceal the fraud).	• Check register
Extract all reconciling items per the bank reconciliation and summarize for reasonableness.	All	Because most of the concealment of check tampering is done between the bank balance and the general ledger, these adjusting entries should be closely scrutinized.	• General ledger detail
Summarize debit memos by vendor, issuer, and type.	All	Debit memo trends that appear unusual should be investigated as attempts to cover unauthorized payments.	• Invoice payment
Identify duplicate payments based on various means.	All	Duplicate payments are made to properly pay down open vendor balances when another payment, intended for the vendor, is diverted. Duplicate payment tests can be enacted on the vendor, invoice number, and amount. More complicated tests can look for instances in which the same invoice and amount are paid, yet the payment is made to two different vendors. Another advanced test is to search for identical vendor and invoice but different amounts.	• Invoice payment
Summarize accounts payable activity by general ledger account, sort from high to low, and review for reasonableness.	All	Expense account trends that appear unusual should be investigated as attempts to cover unauthorized payments.	• Invoice payment general ledger distribution
Compare balance per accounts payable subledger to vendor account balances per their accounts receivable system.	All	Vendors that are not paid will show their customer account from the defrauded company as an old receivable. In order to obtain an electronic file of all customer account statements, it may be necessary to request statements and enter them into a spreadsheet. Please note that even vendors having no balance should be requested to provide customer statements.	• Accounts payable subledger • Customer account statements (from all vendors)

Extract users who can write checks or initiate electronic payments and also post entries to the general ledger.	All	Users who can make payments and also subsequently conceal the misappropriation through adjustments to the general ledger cash accounts can take advantage of nonsegregation of duties to conceal their fraud. User access should be reviewed from the perspective of adjustments within the application and adjustments to the data itself.	• Check register user access master file • General ledger user access master file • Check register user access log file • General ledger user access log file
Extract all employee payments equal to zero in any given pay period.	All	Reports unusual check amounts to employees for review. Check amounts may be written in after printing.	• Check register
Extract all checks payable to "cash" and summarize by issuer for reasonableness.	Forged maker	Checks issued to "cash" have a higher incidence of fraud.	• Check register
Extract manual checks and summarize by vendor and issuer	Forged maker	Manual checks are more prone to abuse and therefore should be scrutinized, especially if a particular issuer is drafting the majority of manual checks.	• Check register
Extract all purchases with no purchase orders and summarize by vendor and issuer.	Forged maker	Purchases with no purchase orders are more prone to abuse and therefore should be scrutinized, especially if a particular issuer is drafting the majority of payments without purchase orders.	• Invoice payment
Sequence gaps in checks.	Forged maker	Checks that are stolen will normally not appear in the check register and therefore will be seen as a gap in the check sequence.	• Check register
Extract checks that are out of the normal sequence.	Forged maker, concealed check, and authorized maker	Checks that are fabricated or stolen will oftentimes not be in the same general sequence as the company's normal check sequence.	• Check register
Sample vendor open invoices for confirmation with vendor.	Forged maker, concealed check, and authorized maker	Much as with the above comparison test, vendor invoices may appear paid on the subledger when the vendor believes such invoices have not been paid.	• Invoice payment

*Please note that "check register" may designate the vendor check register but may also refer to the payroll check register.

SUMMARY

Check tampering is a form of occupational fraud in which an employee converts an organization's funds by fraudulently preparing a company check for his own purposes, or by intercepting and converting an organization's check that is intended for a third party. Most check tampering frauds fall into one of five categories: (1) forged maker schemes, (2) forged endorsement schemes, (3) altered payee schemes, (4) concealed check schemes, and (5) authorized maker schemes.

In a forged maker scheme, the perpetrator obtains or counterfeits an organization's blank check and makes it payable to himself, to an accomplice, or to a third party. The perpetrator forges the signature of an authorized check signer (or "maker") to convert the fraudulent instrument.

A forged endorsement scheme occurs when an employee intercepts an outgoing check intended for a third party and converts the check by forging the intended payee's name on the endorsement line of the check. A third form of check tampering—the altered payee scheme—also involves the theft of outgoing checks. In this type of fraud, the perpetrator alters the name of the payee on the stolen check so that he will be able to convert it. It should be remembered that these schemes are classified as check tampering only if they involve the theft of outgoing checks drawn on the organization's bank accounts. This is because check tampering is a form of fraudulent disbursement; thus there must be a disbursement of the organization's funds. If an employee intercepts an incoming check that is payable to the organization, that scheme will be classified as either skimming or cash larceny (see Chapters 2 and 3).

A fourth category of check tampering is the authorized maker scheme, in which an employee who has check-signing authority abuses the trust of his employer by writing fraudulent checks on organization accounts. Finally, an employee lacking signatory authority can obtain signatures on fraudulent checks by concealing them within a large group of legitimate checks awaiting signature, where they are likely to avoid scrutiny.

Check tampering frauds occur primarily because of the lack of adequate internal controls. The most effective control is to segregate duties among those employees who have access to the organization's checks, including the preparation, posting, signing, delivery, and reconciliation functions. Additional controls include a routine review of supporting documentation, canceled checks, out-of-sequence check numbers, and changes to vendor addresses. Also, check stock should be adequately safeguarded to preclude theft.

Electronic payments, such as ACH payments, online bill payments, and wire transfers, can also be manipulated by dishonest employees. Employers can best defend against fraudulent electronic payments through a combination of solid internal controls and bank security services.

ESSENTIAL TERMS

Check tampering A type of fraudulent disbursement that occurs when an employee converts an organization's funds by either (1) fraudulently preparing a check drawn on the organization's account for his own benefit or (2) intercepting a check drawn on the organization's account that is intended for a third party, and converting that check to his own benefit.

Forgery The signing of another person's name to a document (such as a check) with fraudulent intent, or the fraudulent alteration of a genuine instrument.

Maker The person who signs a check.

Forged maker scheme A check tampering scheme in which an employee misappropriates a check and fraudulently affixes the signature of an authorized maker thereon.

Forged endorsement scheme A check tampering scheme in which an employee intercepts a company check intended for a third party and converts the check by signing the third party's name on the endorsement line of the check.

Forced reconciliation A method of concealing a check tampering scheme by manipulating the bank reconciliation so that the bank balance and the book balance match.

Altered payee scheme A check tampering scheme in which an employee intercepts a company check intended for a third party and alters the payee designation so that the check can be converted by the employee or an accomplice.

Concealed check scheme A check tampering scheme whereby an employee prepares a fraudulent check and submits it, usually along with legitimate checks, to an authorized maker who signs it without a proper review.

Authorized maker scheme A check tampering scheme in which an employee with signatory authority on a company account writes fraudulent checks for his own benefit and signs his own name as the maker.

Electronic payment A payment alternative to traditional paper checks that enables payers to transmit funds electronically over the Internet or other medium; examples include ACH payments, online bill payments, and wire transfers.

REVIEW QUESTIONS

5-1 (Learning objective 5-1) Assume that there are two thefts of checks at ABC Company. In the first case, an employee steals an outgoing check that is drawn on ABC's account and that is payable to "D. Jones." The perpetrator forges the endorsement of "D. Jones" and cashes the check. In the second case, an employee steals an incoming check from "D. Jones" that is payable to ABC Company. The employee fraudulently endorses the check and cashes it. Which of these schemes would be classified as check tampering? Why?

5-2 (Learning objective 5-2) There are five principal categories of check tampering frauds. What are they?

5-3 (Learning objective 5-3) What are the methods discussed in this chapter by which fraudsters gain access to blank company checks as part of a forged maker scheme?

5-4 (Learning objective 5-4) Perpetrators of check tampering schemes must obtain a signature on the check. What are methods used to affix a signature to the check?

5-5 (Learning objective 5-5) How can the type of paper on which an organization's checks are printed be a factor in preventing and detecting forged maker schemes?

5-6 (Learning objective 5-6) What are the differences between a forged maker scheme and a forged endorsement scheme?

5-7 (Learning objective 5-7) What are some methods of intercepting a check intended for a third party?

5-8 (Learning objective 5-9) What is an authorized maker scheme, and why are these frauds especially difficult to prevent using normal internal controls?

5-9 (Learning objective 5-7) How can a perpetrator conceal check tampering activity from others in the organization?

5-10 (Learning objectives 5-5, 5-8, and 5-10) There are several duties that should be segregated among employees to minimize the opportunity for check tampering. List these duties.

5-11 (Learning objective 5-11) What measures can companies can take to prevent and detect fraudulent electronic payments?

DISCUSSION ISSUES

5-1 (Learning objectives 5-5 and 5-10) In the case study of Melissa Robinson, Melissa was able to steal over $60,000 from her employer. Why was she able to commit her fraud without detection?

5-2 (Learning objectives 5-5, 5-8, and 5-10) Assume you are a new hire in the accounting department of an organization. One of your responsibilities is the reconciliation of the operating account. After the end of the month you are given a copy of the bank statement and the canceled checks, and are instructed to perform your reconciliation. You notice that there are some faint markings on a portion of the bank statement that could be alterations. What steps would you take in performing the reconciliation?

5-3 (Learning objective 5-3) If a fraudster does not have legitimate access to check stock, he must obtain access to the check stock in order to commit a forged maker scheme. What are some ways blank checks can be fraudulently obtained, and what measures could an organization take to prevent this from occurring?

5-4 (Learning objectives 5-3 and 5-5) Access to an organization's funds can be gained through counterfeiting the organization's check stock. What types of controls would help detect a counterfeit check?

5-5 (Learning objectives 5-4 and 5-5) Checks can be forged by several methods: free-hand forgeries, photocopies of legitimate signatures, and obtaining access to an automatic check-signing mechanism. What are some controls an organization could institute to minimize the chance that a forgery will occur?

5-6 (Learning objectives 5-6, 5-7, and 5-8) Forged endorsement schemes and altered payee schemes both involve the theft of outgoing checks that are intended for third parties for some legitimate purpose (e.g., a check payable to a vendor for services rendered). In this respect, these schemes differ from other forms of check tampering, in which the check is usually drafted by the perpetrator for a fraudulent purpose. Discuss how this distinction affects the way in which forged endorsement and altered payee schemes must be concealed.

5-7 (Learning objective 5-8) In altered payee schemes, the perpetrator changes the name of the intended third party and negotiates the check himself. This can be done by adding a second payee or by changing the original payee's name. What is the best method for detecting this type of fraud?

5-8 (Learning objectives 5-5 and 5-10) In the Ernie Philips case, $109,000 was stolen through check tampering. How was this scheme accomplished, and what could management have done differently to prevent the scheme from occurring?

ENDNOTES

1. Henry Campbell Black, Black's Law Dictionary, 5th ed. (St. Paul: West Publishing, 1979), p. 585.

2. Lanza, pp. 58–60.

Payroll Schemes

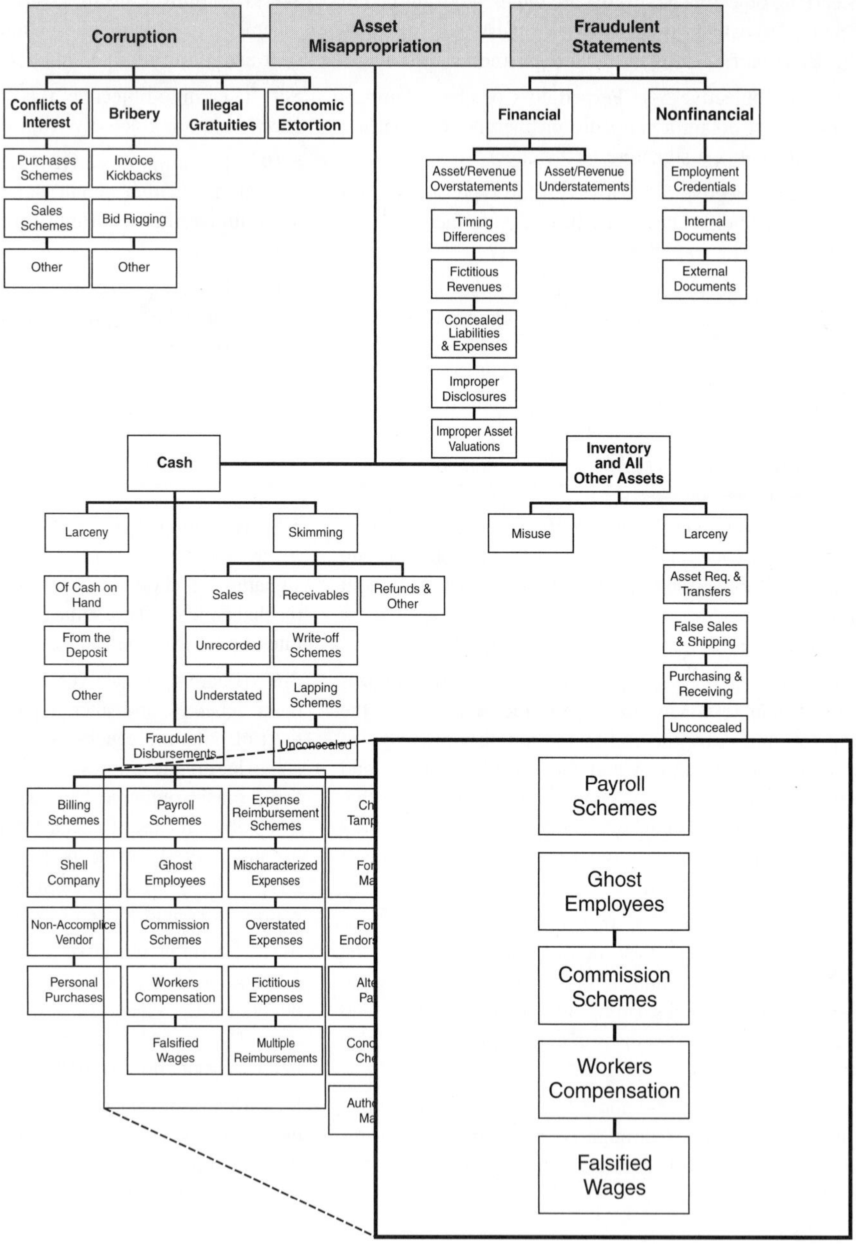

Corruption | **Asset Misappropriation** | **Fraudulent Statements**

Corruption
- **Conflicts of Interest**
  - Purchases Schemes
  - Sales Schemes
  - Other
- **Bribery**
  - Invoice Kickbacks
  - Bid Rigging
  - Other
- **Illegal Gratuities**
- **Economic Extortion**

Fraudulent Statements
- **Financial**
  - Asset/Revenue Overstatements
    - Timing Differences
    - Fictitious Revenues
    - Concealed Liabilities & Expenses
    - Improper Disclosures
    - Improper Asset Valuations
  - Asset/Revenue Understatements
- **Nonfinancial**
  - Employment Credentials
  - Internal Documents
  - External Documents

Asset Misappropriation

Cash
- **Larceny**
  - Of Cash on Hand
  - From the Deposit
  - Other
- **Skimming**
  - Sales
    - Unrecorded
    - Understated
  - Receivables
    - Write-off Schemes
    - Lapping Schemes
    - Unconcealed
  - Refunds & Other
- **Fraudulent Disbursements**
  - Billing Schemes
    - Shell Company
    - Non-Accomplice Vendor
    - Personal Purchases
  - Payroll Schemes
    - Ghost Employees
    - Commission Schemes
    - Workers Compensation
    - Falsified Wages
  - Expense Reimbursement Schemes
    - Mischaracterized Expenses
    - Overstated Expenses
    - Fictitious Expenses
    - Multiple Reimbursements
  - Check Tampering
    - Forged Maker
    - Forged Endorsement
    - Altered Payee
    - Concealed Checks
    - Authorized Maker

Inventory and All Other Assets
- **Misuse**
- **Larceny**
  - Asset Req. & Transfers
  - False Sales & Shipping
  - Purchasing & Receiving
  - Unconcealed

Payroll Schemes (detail)
- Payroll Schemes
- Ghost Employees
- Commission Schemes
- Workers Compensation
- Falsified Wages

EXHIBIT 6-1

CHAPTER **6**

PAYROLL SCHEMES

LEARNING OBJECTIVES

After studying this chapter, you should be able to:

6-1 List and understand the three main categories of payroll fraud

6-2 Understand the relative cost and frequency of payroll frauds

6-3 Define a ghost employee

6-4 List and understand the four steps of making a ghost employee scheme work

6-5 Understand how separation of duties in payroll and human resources functions can reduce the threat of payroll fraud

6-6 Be familiar with methods identified in this chapter for preventing and detecting ghost employee schemes

6-7 List and understand the four ways that employees can obtain authorization for a falsified timecard in a manual system

6-8 Understand the role that payroll controls play in preventing falsified hours and salary schemes

6-9 Discuss the methods identified in this chapter for preventing and detecting falsified hours and salary schemes

6-10 Understand how employees commit commission schemes

6-11 Identify red flags that are typically associated with commission schemes

6-12 Be familiar with proactive audit tests that can be used to detect various forms of payroll fraud

CASE STUDY: SAY CHEESE![1]

Every once in a while, a person devises a fraud scheme so complex that it is virtually undetectable. Intricate planning allows the person to cheat a company out of millions of dollars with little chance of getting caught.

Jerry Harkanell is no such person.

Harkanell's payroll scheme put only about $1,500 in his pocket before a supervisor detected his fraud, less than half a year after it began.

Harkanell worked as an administrative assistant for a unit of a large San Antonio hospital. His duties consisted mostly of clerical tasks, including the submission of payroll information for the unit.

An exception report for the month of March listed some unusual activity on Harkanell's timesheet. He had posted

[1]Several names and details have been changed to preserve anonymity.

eight hours that resulted in overtime wages for a particular pay period. The pay period coincided with a time of low occupancy in Harkanell's unit. During times of low occupancy, there is no need for anyone—especially an administrative assistant—to work overtime.

When his supervisor confronted Harkanell about the eight hours, he confessed. He said he posted the time because of financial problems and threats from his wife to leave him. He immediately submitted his resignation, a hospital administrator accepted it, and Jerry Harkanell became a former hospital employee.

The hospital administrator shared the specifics of this incident with Oscar Straine, director of internal auditing for the hospital and a certified fraud examiner.

"Nobody leaves for just eight hours," Straine said. "There must be a lot more there."

153

When Straine delved into the records, he found exactly what he had suspected. Since October of the previous year, Harkanell had been overstating his hours. He had recorded hours that he had not actually worked; he had posted his hours to shifts for which pay was higher; he had reported vacation time as time worked, drawing not only additional pay but extra vacation time, too.

Unfortunately for Harkanell, his method of cheating his employer left a well-marked paper trail. In his administrative role, he collected and submitted the unit's manually prepared timesheets to his supervisor. She signed the timesheets, made copies to retain for her records, and returned them to Harkanell for delivery to the payroll department. Harkanell then altered his original timesheet before he delivered the approved documents to the payroll department. Amazingly, he completed his timesheets in pencil, allowing him simply to erase the old numbers and make changes.

The audit staff compared the supervisor's copies of timesheets with the timesheets on file in the payroll department. Discrepancies between the two stood out. The investigation lasted less than a month. The results revealed that during a twenty-six-week period, Jerry Harkanell defrauded the hospital of $1,570.

Interviews conducted with coworkers and supervisors revealed one detail that might have tipped Harkanell's hand even earlier, had anyone recognized a suspicious act for what it was.

One Friday before payday when Harkanell had the day off, he showed up at the hospital anyway. This was more than a minor inconvenience since he didn't own a car. But Harkanell took the bus to work just so he could personally get the unit's timesheets approved and turned in to payroll. At the time, no one questioned why he didn't simply ask someone to cover for him.

At the completion of the investigation, the hospital filed a claim with the district attorney's office. Evidence consisted of copies of the approved timesheets, copies of the altered timesheets, and affidavits from Harkanell's supervisors.

An assistant district attorney in charge of the case called the hospital shortly after receiving the case. She had uncovered some interesting details about Harkanell's past during a routine background check. A computer search revealed that he had a criminal history, and that he was currently on parole. In fact, the assistant district attorney reported, Harkanell had previously been sentenced to life in prison for armed robbery.

The news that the hospital had unknowingly hired a convicted felon distressed Oscar Straine. He discovered that the hospital's ability to conduct thorough background checks on prospective employees was restricted by money and access to records. The hospital routinely checked criminal records in Bexar County (where the hospital is located) and any counties where an applicant reported having a history. But cost and time prohibited the hospital from checking records in all 254 Texas counties, especially when hiring a low-salaried employee like Harkanell.

The complaint against Harkanell went to the grand jury quickly. Straine testified, the grand jury issued an indictment, and a warrant was issued for Harkanell's arrest.

The sheriff's department attempted to locate Harkanell several times, but with no success. He had moved and, not surprisingly, left no forwarding address. The DA's office notified the hospital that Harkanell had disappeared, and that it had no immediate plans to continue the search.

Harkanell remained at large for several months, but luck was on the hospital's side—or, perhaps more accurately, stupidity was on Harkanell's. Just as he had done with his timesheet fraud, he left a clue behind, this time concerning his whereabouts. This was no subtle hint, either. He might as well have mailed the hospital an invitation with a map.

The following January, Straine was talking to a woman in the human resources department who had worked on Jerry Harkanell's original case. Straine called this woman to talk about his continuing concerns over the hospital's inability to do a more thorough background check on prospective hires. During the conversation, the woman asked, "By the way, did you happen to see the paper a few weeks ago?"

"I don't know what you're talking about," he replied.

"Oh—well, Jerry Harkanell's picture was on the front page of the business section of the *Express*."

"You have to be kidding." But she wasn't.

Straine immediately searched online for a copy of the article. Within minutes, he'd found a story about a nonprofit organization that helps low-income families buy houses with low-interest loans and no down payment.

Right in the middle of the article was a picture, and right in the middle of that picture was Jerry Harkanell. He and his family were sitting on the front porch of the new home the nonprofit group had helped him purchase. The article detailed Harkanell's story, commenting on how hard he had worked to get his house. And though it never mentioned the address, the article contained enough information to pinpoint the location. The Harkanells lived near a new shopping center, and across the street from a park. Theirs was the only new house on the block.

It took Straine ten minutes to find the house from his office. He knew the location of the shopping center, and he drove there, then located the park.

Straine said, "It was weird driving up the street with the photograph, and there's his house. We could even identify the design on the front door and match it with the photograph in the newspaper as we drove up the street."

As soon as he returned to his office, Straine called the assistant district attorney. Harkanell was arrested the next day.

Harkanell appealed for assistance from the nonprofit organization that had helped him buy his house. They agreed to help him—on the condition that he promise to come clean. The organization contacted the hospital's community outreach program to request that the charge be dropped, or at least decreased from a felony to a misdemeanor.

The hospital declined to drop the charge. The nonprofit group pleaded Harkanell's case, pointing out that he had a wife and a sick child who would have to go on welfare if he were convicted of a felony.

Straine made it clear that the hospital would pursue a conviction, whether a felony or a misdemeanor. The hospital's position was that Harkanell should at least have to face a judge. (Later, the assistant district attorney revealed that had Harkanell pleaded guilty to the felony charge, the judge would have sentenced him to twenty-five years.)

While Harkanell continued to try to get the charges dropped, another piece of his past caught up with him. A separate party filed a forgery claim with the district attorney's office. As soon as the nonprofit organization got word of this development, it refused to provide any additional assistance to Harkanell.

A judge sentenced Jerry Harkanell to thirty-five years in prison. Law enforcement officials escorted him from the courtroom directly to a jail cell.

OVERVIEW

Payroll schemes are similar to billing schemes in that they are based on a fraudulent claim for payment that causes the victim company to unknowingly make a fraudulent disbursement. In billing schemes, the false claim is usually based on an invoice (coupled, perhaps, with false receiving reports, purchase orders, and purchase authorizations) that shows that the victim organization owes money to a vendor. Payroll schemes are typically based on fraudulent timecards or payroll registers, and they show that the victim organization owes money to one of its employees. In the preceding case study, for example, Jerry Harkanell turned in false timesheets, which caused his employer to overpay his wages.

Payroll Scheme Data from the ACFE *2009 Global Fraud Survey*

In the ACFE's 2009 survey, payroll schemes ranked fourth among fraudulent disbursements in terms of frequency; 17 percent of the fraudulent disbursement cases reviewed contained some form of payroll fraud (see Exhibit 6-2).

As illustrated in Exhibit 6-3, the median loss among payroll frauds in the 2009 survey was $72,000. Payroll frauds ranked third among fraudulent disbursements in terms of median loss.

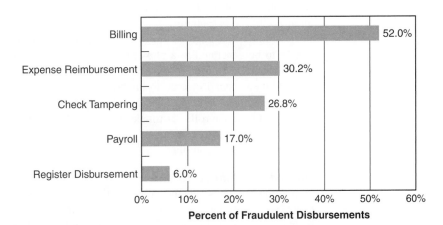

EXHIBIT 6-2 *2009 Global Fraud Survey*: Frequency of Fraudulent Disbursements[a]

[a]The sum of these percentages exceeds 100 percent because some cases involved multiple fraud schemes that fell into more than one category.

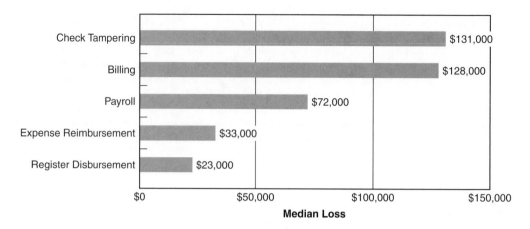

EXHIBIT 6-3 *2009 Global Fraud Survey:* Median Loss of Fraudulent Disbursements

PAYROLL SCHEMES

Payroll schemes may be defined as occupational frauds in which a person who works for an organization causes that organization to issue a payment by making false claims for compensation. There are three main categories of payroll fraud:

- Ghost employee schemes
- Falsified hours and salary schemes
- Commission schemes

Ghost Employees

The term *ghost employee* refers to someone on the payroll who does not actually work for the victim company. The ghost employee may be a fictitious person, or a real individual who simply does not work for the victim employer. When the ghost is a real person, it is often a friend or relative of the perpetrator. In some cases, the ghost employee is an accomplice of the fraudster who cashes the fraudulent paychecks and then splits the money with the perpetrator.

Through the falsification of personnel or payroll records, a fraudster causes paychecks to be generated to a ghost; then the paychecks are converted by the fraudster or an accomplice (see Exhibit 6-4). Use of a ghost employee scheme by a fraudster can be like adding a second income to his household.

For a ghost employee scheme to work, four things must happen: (1) the ghost must be added to the payroll, (2) timekeeping and wage rate information must be collected, (3) a paycheck must be issued to the ghost, and (4) the check must be delivered to the perpetrator or an accomplice.

Adding the Ghost to the Payroll The first step in a ghost employee scheme is entering the ghost on the payroll. In some businesses, all hiring is done through a centralized personnel department; in others, the personnel function is spread over the managerial responsibilities of various departments. Regardless of how hiring of new employees is handled within a business, the person or persons who have authority to add new employees are in the best position to put ghosts on the payroll. In Case 2432, for example, a manager who was responsible for hiring and scheduling janitorial work added over eighty ghost employees to his payroll. The ghosts in this case were actual people who worked at other jobs for different companies. The manager filled out timesheets for the fictitious employees and authorized them, then took the resulting paychecks to

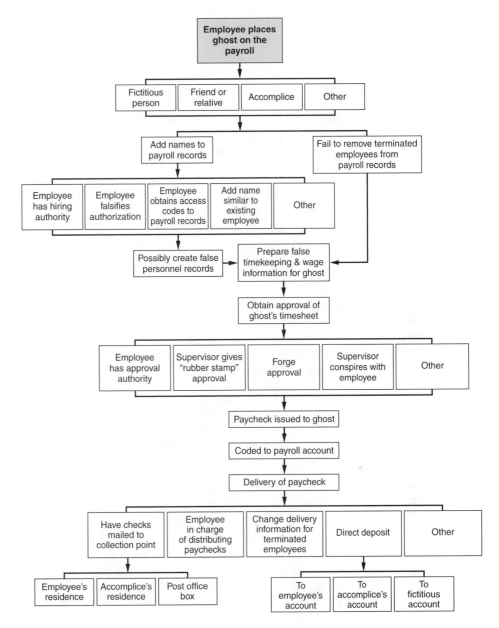

EXHIBIT 6-4 Ghost Employees

the ghost employees, who cashed them and split the proceeds with the manager. It was this manager's authority in the hiring and supervision of employees that enabled him to perpetrate this fraud.

Another area where the opportunity exists to add ghosts is payroll accounting. In a perfect world, every name listed on an organization's payroll would be verified against personnel records to make sure that those persons receiving paychecks actually work for the company, but in practice this does not always happen. Thus, persons in payroll accounting may be able to generate fraudulent paychecks by adding fictitious employees to the roll. Access to payroll records is usually restricted, so it may be that only managers have access to make changes to payroll accounting records—making these managers the most likely suspects in a ghost employee scheme. On the other hand, lower-level employees often gain access to payroll records, either through poor observance of controls or by surreptitious means. In Case 1042, for instance, an employee in the payroll department was given the authority to enter new employees into the payroll system, make corrections to payroll information, and distribute paychecks. This employee's manager gave rubber-stamp approval to the employee's actions because of a trusting relationship between the two. The lack of separation of duties and the absence of review made it simple for the culprit to add a fictitious employee into the payroll system.

One way to help conceal the presence of a ghost on the payroll is to create a fictitious employee with a name very similar to that of a real employee. The name on the fraudulent paycheck, then, will appear to be legitimate to anyone who glances at it. The perpetrator of Case 970, a bookkeeper who made off with $35,000 in fraudulent wages, used this method.

Instead of adding new names to the payroll, some employees undertake ghost employee schemes by failing to remove the names of terminated employees. Paychecks to the terminated employee continue to be generated even though he no longer works for the victim company. The perpetrator intercepts these fraudulent paychecks and converts them to his own use. For instance, in Case 1738, an accountant delayed the submission of resignation notices of certain employees, and then she falsified timesheets for these employees to make it appear that they still worked for the victim company. This accountant was also in charge of distributing paychecks to all employees of the company, so when the fraudulent checks were generated she simply took them out of the stack of legitimate checks and kept them for herself.

Collecting Timekeeping Information   The second thing that must occur in order for a paycheck to be issued to a ghost employee, at least in the case of hourly employees, is the collection and computation of timekeeping information. The perpetrator must provide payroll accounting with a timecard or other instrument showing how many hours the fictitious employee worked over the most recent pay period. This information, along with the wage rate information contained in personnel or payroll files, will be used to compute the amount of the fraudulent paycheck.

Timekeeping records can be maintained in a variety of ways. In many organizations, computer systems are used to track employees' hours. Alternatively, employees might manually record their hours on timecards or might punch time clocks that record the time at which a person starts and finishes his work.

When a ghost employee scheme is in place, someone must create documentation for the ghost's hours. This essentially amounts to preparing a fake timecard showing when the ghost was allegedly present at work. Depending on the normal procedure for recording hours, a fraudster might log into the computerized system and record the ghost employee's hours, create a timecard and sign it in the ghost's name, punch the time clock for the ghost, or so on. The preparing of the timecard is not a great obstacle to the perpetrator. The real key to the timekeeping document is obtaining approval of the timecard.

A supervisor should approve timecards of hourly employees. This verifies to the payroll department that the employee actually worked the hours that are claimed on the card. A ghost employee, by definition, does not work for the victim company, so approval will have to be fraudulently obtained. Often, the supervisor himself is the one who creates the ghost. When this is the case, the supervisor fills out a timecard in the name of the ghost, and then affixes his approval. The timecard is thereby authenticated, and a paycheck will be issued. When a nonsupervisor is committing a ghost employee scheme, he will typically forge the necessary approval and then forward the bogus timecard directly to payroll accounting, bypassing his supervisor.

In computerized systems, a supervisor's signature might not be required. In lieu of the signature, the supervisor inputs data into the payroll system, and the use of his password serves to authorize the entry. If an employee has access to the supervisor's password, he can input any data he wants, and it arrives in the payroll system with a seal of approval.

If the fraudster creates ghost employees who are salaried rather than hourly employees, it is not necessary to collect timekeeping information; salaried employees are paid a certain amount each pay period, regardless of how many hours they work. Because the timekeeping function can be avoided, it may be easier easy for a fraudster to create a ghost employee who works on salary. However, salaried employees typically are fewer, and are more likely to be members of management; the salaried ghost may therefore be more difficult to conceal.

Issuing the Ghost's Paycheck Once a ghost is entered on the payroll and his timecard has been approved, the third step in the scheme is the actual issuance of the paycheck. The heart of a ghost employee scheme is in the falsification of payroll records and timekeeping information. Once this falsification has occurred, the perpetrator does not generally take an active role in the issuance of the check. The payroll department issues the payment—based on the bogus information provided by the fraudster—as it would any other paycheck.

Delivery of the Paycheck The final step in a ghost employee scheme is the distribution of the checks to the perpetrator. Paychecks might be hand delivered to employees while at work, mailed to employees at their home addresses, or direct-deposited into the employees' bank accounts. If employees are paid in currency rather than by check, the distribution is almost always conducted in person and on site.

Ideally, those in charge of payroll distribution should not have a hand in any of the other functions of the payroll cycle. For instance, the person who enters new employees in the payroll system should not be allowed to distribute paychecks because, as in Case 1738, this person can include a ghost on the payroll, then simply remove the fraudulent check from the stack of legitimate paychecks she handles as she disburses pay. Obviously, when the perpetrator of a ghost employee scheme is allowed to mail checks to employees or pass them out at work, he is in the best position to ensure that the ghost's check is delivered to himself.

In most instances, the perpetrator does not have the authority to distribute paychecks, and so must make sure that the victim employer sends the checks to a place from which he can recover them. When checks are not distributed in the workplace, they are either mailed to employees or deposited directly into those employees' accounts.

If the fictitious employee was added into the payroll or personnel records by the fraudster, the problem of distribution is usually minor. When the ghost's employment information is input, the perpetrator simply lists an address or bank account to which the payments can be sent. In the case of purely fictitious ghost employees, the address is often the perpetrator's own (the same goes for bank accounts). The fact that two employees (the perpetrator and the ghost) are receiving payments at the same destination may indicate that fraud is afoot. Some fraudsters avoid this problem by having payments sent to a post office box or to a separate bank account. In Case 1042, for example, the perpetrator set up a fake bank account in the name of a fictitious employee and arranged for paychecks to be deposited directly into this account.

As we have said, the ghost is not always a fictitious person; it may instead be a real person who is conspiring with the perpetrator to defraud the company. In Case 687, for instance, an employee listed both his wife and his girlfriend on the company payroll. When real persons conspiring with the fraudster are falsely included on the payroll, the perpetrator typically sees to it that checks are sent to the homes or bank accounts of these persons, in this way avoiding the problem of duplicating addresses on the payroll.

Distribution is a more difficult problem when the ghost is a former employee who was simply not removed from the payroll. In Case 146, for instance, a supervisor continued to submit timecards for employees who had been terminated. Payroll records will obviously reflect the bank account number or address of the terminated employee in this situation. The perpetrator, then, has two courses of action. In companies where paychecks are distributed by hand or are left at a central spot for employees to collect, the perpetrator can ignore the payroll records and simply pick up the fraudulent paychecks. If the paychecks are to be distributed through the mail or by direct deposit, the perpetrator will have to enter the terminated employee's records and change his delivery information.

Preventing and Detecting Ghost Employee Schemes

Preventing and Detecting Ghost Employee Schemes It is very important to separate the hiring function from other duties associated with payroll. Most ghost employee schemes succeed when the perpetrator has the authority to add employees to the payroll and approve the timecards of those employees; it therefore follows that if all hiring is done through a centralized human resources department, an organization can substantially limit its exposure to ghost employee schemes.

Personnel records should be maintained independently of payroll and timekeeping functions, and the personnel department should verify any changes to payroll. The personnel department should also conduct background checks and reference checks on all prospective employees in advance of hire. These simple verification procedures should eliminate most ghost employee schemes by making it impossible for a single individual to add a ghost to an organization's payroll. If employees know that payroll changes are verified against personnel records, this will deter most ghost employee schemes. Furthermore, if personnel and payroll records are maintained separately, a simple comparison report should identify persons on the payroll who have no personnel file. Organizations should also periodically check the payroll against personnel records for terminated employees, and unauthorized wage or deduction adjustments.

Another way to proactively test for ghost employees is to have someone in the organization who is independent of the payroll function periodically run a report looking for employees who lack Social Security numbers, who have no deductions on their paychecks for withholding taxes or insurance, or who show no physical address or phone number. Fraudsters who create ghost employees often fail to attend to these details, the omission of which is a clear red flag. Similarly, reports should be run periodically looking for multiple employees who share a Social Security number, bank account number, or physical address. All these conditions tend to indicate the presence of a ghost on the payroll.

A comparison of payroll expenses to production schedules might also uncover a ghost employee scheme. The distribution of hours to activity or departments should be reviewed by supervisors in those departments, and payroll expenses should be compared to budgeted amounts. Significant budget overruns could signal payroll fraud.

Finally, by simply keeping signed paychecks in a secure location, and by verifying that they are properly distributed, an organization can thwart most ghost employee schemes. The employee or manager who adds a ghost to the payroll must be able to collect the ghost's check. In most cases, he is able to do that because he has access to payroll checks prior to distribution, or because he is in charge of distributing paychecks himself. If an organization assigns the task of distributing paychecks to a person who is independent of the payroll functions and who has no authority to add personnel, this can make it difficult for the perpetrator to obtain the ghost's paycheck. The duty of distributing paychecks should be rotated among several employees to further guard against fraud. Employees should be required to provide identification to receive their paychecks to ensure that every employee receives only his own check, and if pay is deposited directly into bank accounts, a report should be run every pay period searching for multiple employees who share an account number.

Falsified Hours and Salary

The most common method of misappropriating funds from the payroll is through the overpayment of wages. For hourly employees, the size of a paycheck is based on two essential factors: the number of hours worked, and the rate of pay. It is therefore obvious that for an hourly employee to fraudulently increase the size of his paycheck, he must either falsify the number of hours he has worked or change his wage rate (see Exhibit 6-5). Because salaried employees do not receive compensation based on their

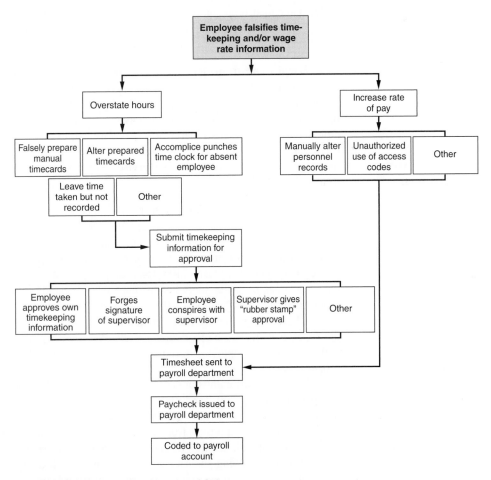

EXHIBIT 6-5 Falsified Hours and Salary

time at work, in most cases these employees generate fraudulent wages by increasing their rates of pay.

When we discuss payroll frauds that involve overstated hours, we must first understand how an employee's time at work is recorded. As we have already discussed, time is generally kept by one of three methods. Time clocks may be used to mark the time when an employee begins and finishes work. The employee inserts a card into the clock at the beginning and end of work, and the clock imprints the current time on the card. In more sophisticated systems, computers may automatically track the time employees spend on the job based on login codes or some other similar tracking mechanism. Finally, paper or computerized timecards showing the number of hours an employee worked on a particular day are often prepared manually by the employee and approved by his manager.

Manually Prepared Timecards

When hours are recorded manually, an employee typically fills out his timecard to reflect the number of hours he has worked and then presents it to his supervisor for approval. The supervisor verifies the accuracy of the timecard, signs or otherwise approves the card to indicate his authorization, and then forwards it to the payroll department so that a paycheck can be issued. Most of the payroll frauds we encountered in our studies stemmed from abuses of this process.

Obviously, if an employee fills out his own timecard, it may be easy to falsify his hours worked. He simply records the wrong time, showing that he arrived at work earlier or left later than he actually did. The difficulty is not in falsifying the timecard, but in getting the fraudulent card approved by the employee's supervisor. There are basically four ways for the employee to obtain the authorization he needs.

Forging a Supervisor's Signature

When using this method, an employee typically withholds his paper timecard from those being sent to the supervisor for approval, forges the supervisor's signature or initials, and then adds the timecard to the stack of authorized cards that are sent to payroll. In an electronic payroll environment, an employee who learns his supervisor's password can log into the system and authorize his own timecard surreptitiously. The fraudulent timecard then arrives at the payroll department with what appears to be a supervisor's approval, and a paycheck is subsequently issued.

Collusion with a Supervisor

The second way to obtain approval of a fraudulent timecard is to collude with a supervisor who authorizes timekeeping information. In these schemes, the supervisor knowingly approves false timecards and usually takes a portion of the fraudulent wages. In some cases, the supervisor may take the entire amount of the overpayment. In Case 2406, for example, a supervisor assigned employees to better work areas or better jobs, but in return she demanded payment. The payment was arranged by the falsification of the employees' timecards, which the supervisor authorized. The employees were paid for fictitious overtime, which was then kicked back to the supervisor. It may be particularly difficult to detect payroll fraud when a supervisor colludes with an employee, because managers are often relied on as a control to assure proper timekeeping.

But in payroll collusion schemes, the supervisor does not always take a cut of the overpayment. Case 749, for instance, involved a temporary employee who added fictitious hours to her timesheet. Rather than get the approval of her direct supervisor, the employee obtained approval from an administrator at another site. The employee was a relative of this administrator, who authorized her overpayment without receiving any compensation for doing so. And in another case, 2314, a supervisor needed to enhance the salary of an employee in order to keep him from leaving for another job. The supervisor authorized the payment of $10,000 in fictitious overtime to the employee. But two part-time employees who did not even bother to show up for work committed perhaps the most unique case in the ACFE studies. One of the fraudsters did not perform any verifiable work for nine months; the other was apparently absent for *two years!* The timecards for these employees were completed by a timekeeper based on their work schedules, and a supervisor approved the timecards. This supervisor was also a part-time employee who held another job, in which he was supervised by one of the fraudsters. Thus, the supervisor was under pressure to authorize the fraudulent timecards in order to keep his second job.

Rubber Stamp Supervisors   The third way to obtain approval of fraudulent timecards is to rely on a supervisor to approve them without reviewing their accuracy. The "lazy manager" method seems risky—so much so that one would think that it would be uncommon—but it actually occurs quite frequently. A recurring theme in ACFE studies is the reliance of fraudsters on the inattentiveness of others. When an employee sees an opportunity to make a little extra money without getting caught, that employee is more likely to be emboldened to attempt a fraud scheme. The fact that a supervisor is known to rubber-stamp timecards, or even ignore them, can be a factor in an employee's decision to begin stealing from his company.

For instance, in Case 1615 a temporary employee noticed that his manager did not reconcile the expense journal on a monthly basis. Thus, the manager did not know how much was being paid to the temporary agency. The fraudster completed fictitious time reports that were sent to the temporary agency and that caused the victim company to pay over $30,000 in fraudulent wages. Because the fraudster controlled the mail and the manager did not review the expense journal, this extremely simple scheme went undetected for some time. In another example of poor supervision, Case 503, a bookkeeper whose duties included the preparation of payroll checks, inflated her checks by adding fictitious overtime. This person added over $90,000 of unauthorized pay to her wages over a four-year period before an accountant noticed the overpayments.

Poor Custody Procedures   One form of control breakdown that occurred in several cases in our studies was the failure to maintain proper control over authorized timecards. In a properly run system, once management authorizes timecards, they should be sent directly to payroll. Those who prepare the timecards should not have access to them after they have been approved. Similarly, computerized timesheets should be blocked from modification by the employee once supervisor authorization has been given. When these procedures are not observed, the person who prepared a timecard can alter it after his supervisor has approved it but before it is delivered to payroll. This is precisely what happened in several cases in our studies. In the case study at the beginning of this chapter, for instance, Jerry Harkanell was in charge of compiling weekly timesheets (including his own), obtaining his supervisor's approval on the sheets, and delivering the approved sheets to payroll. As we saw, Harkanell waited until his supervisor signed the unit's timesheets, then overstated his hours or posted hours he had worked to higher-paid shifts. Since the supervisor had authorized the timesheet, payroll assumed that the hours were legitimate.

Another way hours are falsified is in the misreporting of leave time. This is not as common as timecard falsification, but nevertheless can be problematic. Incidentally, it is the one instance in which salaried employees commit payroll fraud by falsifying their hours.

The way a leave scheme works is very simple. An employee takes a certain amount of time off of work as paid leave or vacation, but does not report the absence. Employees typically receive a certain amount of paid leave per year. If a person takes a leave of absence but does not report it, those days are not deducted from his allotted days off. In other words, he gets more leave time than he is entitled to. The result is that the employee shows up for work less, yet still receives the same pay. This was another method used by Jerry Harkanell to increase his pay. Another example of this type of scheme was found in Case 1315, where a senior manager allowed certain persons to be absent from work without submitting leave forms to the personnel department. Consequently, these employees were able to take excess leave amounting to approximately $25,000 worth of unearned wages.

Time Clocks and Other Automated Timekeeping Systems   In companies that use time clocks to collect timekeeping information, payroll fraud is usually uncomplicated. In the typical scenario, the time clock is located in an unrestricted area, and a timecard for each employee is kept nearby. The employees insert their timecards into the time clock at the beginning and end of their shifts and the clock imprints the time. The length of time an employee spends at work is thus recorded. Supervisors should be present at the beginning and end of shifts to assure that employees do not punch the timecards of absent coworkers, yet this simple control is often overlooked.

AFCE researchers encountered very few time clock fraud schemes, and those they did come across followed a single, uncomplicated pattern. When one employee is absent, a friend of that person punches his timecard so that it appears as if the absent employee was at work that day. The absent employee is therefore overcompensated on his next paycheck. This method was used in Cases 478 and 2673.

Rates of Pay   While the preceding discussion focused on how employees overstate the number of hours they have worked, it should be remembered that an employee could also generate a larger paycheck by changing his pay rate. An employee's personnel or payroll records reflect his rate of pay. If an employee can gain access to these records, or has an accomplice with access to them, he can adjust the pay rate to increase his compensation.

Preventing and Detecting Falsified Hours and Salary Schemes   As with most other forms of occupational fraud, falsified hours and salaries schemes generally succeed because an organization fails to enforce proper controls. As a rule, payroll preparation, authorization, distribution, and reconciliation should be strictly segregated. In addition, the transfer of funds from general accounts to payroll accounts should be handled independently of the other functions. This will prevent most instances of falsified hours and salary schemes.

The role of the manager in verifying hours worked and authorizing timecards is critical to preventing and detecting this form of payroll fraud. Organizations should have a rule stating that no overtime will be paid unless a supervisor authorizes it in advance. This control is not only a good antifraud mechanism, it is also key to maintaining control over payroll costs. Sick leave and vacation time should also not be granted without a supervisor's review. Leave and vacation time should be monitored for excesses by an independent human resources department.

A designated official should verify all wage rate changes. These changes should be administered through a centralized human resources department. Any wage rate change not properly authorized by a supervisor and recorded by human resources should be denied.

After a supervisor has approved timecards for her employees, those timecards should be sent directly to the payroll department, and employees should not have access to their timecards after they have been approved. One of the most common falsified hours and salary schemes is to simply alter a timecard after it has been approved. Maintaining proper custody of approved timecards will go a long way toward eliminating this type of fraud.

If a time clock is used, timecards should be secured and a supervisor should be present whenever timecards are punched. This supervisor should work independently of hiring and other payroll functions. A different supervisor should approve timecards.

In addition to controls aimed at preventing payroll fraud, organizations should run tests that actively seek out fraudulent payroll activity. For example, in a document-based system, supervisors should maintain copies of their employees' timecards. These copies can be spot-checked against a payroll distribution list or against timecards on file in the payroll department. Any discrepancies likely indicate fraud. In an electronic environment, tests should be run to determine whether any timecards were accessed or altered after the supervisor's approval; exceptions should be confirmed with the approving supervisor for legitimacy.

Because many falsified hours and salary schemes involve fraudulent claims for overtime pay, organizations should actively test for overtime abuses. Comparison reports can illustrate instances in which a particular individual has been paid significantly more overtime than other employees who have similar job duties, or in which a particular department tends to generate more overtime expenses than are warranted. Other tests that can highlight falsified hours and salary schemes include the following:

- Perform a trend analysis comparing payroll expenses to budget projections or prior years' totals. This analysis can be done by company or by department.
- Generate exception reports testing for any employee whose compensation has increased from the prior year by a disproportionately large percentage. For example, if an organization generally awards raises of no more than 3 percent, then it would be advisable to double-check the records of any employee whose wages have increased by more than 3 percent.
- Verify that payroll taxes for the year equal federal tax forms.
- Compare net payroll to payroll checks issued.

Commission Schemes

Commission is a form of compensation calculated as a percentage of the amount of sales a salesperson or other employee generates. It is a unique form of compensation that is not based on hours worked or a set yearly salary, but rather on an employee's revenue output. A commissioned employee's wages are based on two factors: the amount of sales he generates and the percentage of those sales he is paid. In other words, there are two ways an employee on commission can fraudulently increase his pay: (1) falsify the amount of sales made or (2) increase his rate of commission (see Exhibit 6-6).

Fictitious Sales An employee can falsify the amount of sales he has made in two ways, the first being the creation of fictitious sales. In Case 531, for example, an unscrupulous insurance agent took advantage of his company's incentive commissions, which paid $1.25 for every $1.00 of premiums generated in the first year of a policy. The agent wrote policies to fictitious customers, paid the premiums, and received his commissions, which created an illicit profit on the transaction. For instance, if the fraudster paid $100,000 in premiums, he received $125,000 in commissions, a $25,000 profit. No payments were made on the fraudulent policies after the first year.

The way in which fictitious sales are created depends on the organization for which the fraudster works. A fictitious sale might be constructed by the creation of fraudulent sales orders, purchase orders, credit authorizations, packing slips, invoices, and so on. On the other hand, a fraudster might simply ring up a false sale on a cash register. The

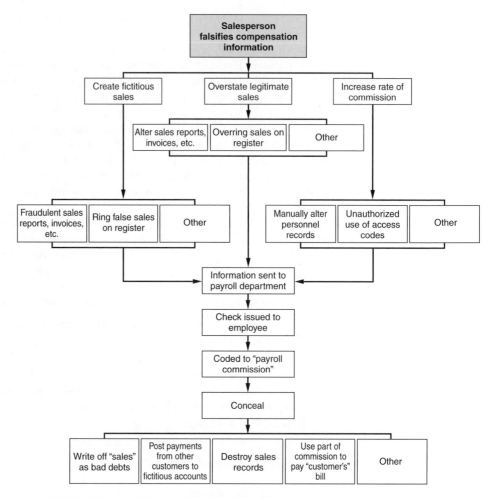

EXHIBIT 6-6 Commission Schemes

key is that a fictitious sale is created, that it appears to be legitimate, and that the victim company reacts by issuing a commission check to the fraudster.

Altered Sales The second way for a fraudster to falsify the value of sales he has made is to alter the prices listed on sales documents; in other words, the fraudster charges one price to a customer, but records a higher price in the company books. This results in the payment of a commission that is larger than the fraudster deserves. Case 1681 provides an example of this type of scheme. In this situation a salesman quoted a certain rate to his customers, and billed them at this rate and collected their payments—but overstated his sales reports. The fraudster intercepted and altered the outgoing invoices from these transactions so that his customers would not detect the fraud. He also overstated the revenues received from his customers. Since the fraudster's commissions were based on the amount of revenues he billed out, he was overcompensated.

As mentioned above, the other way to manipulate the commission process is to change the employee's rate of commission, This would likely necessitate the alteration of payroll or personnel records, which should be off-limits to the sales staff.

Detecting Commission Schemes Generally, there should be a linear correlation between sales figures and commission expenses. Periodic reports should be run to confirm this relationship. If commission expenses increase as a percentage of total sales, this might indicate fraud. An employee who is independent of the sales department should investigate the reason for the increase.

If a salesperson is engaged in a commission scheme, his commissions earned will tend to rise compared to other members of the sales department. Organizations should routinely test for this type of fraud by running a comparative analysis of commission earned by each salesperson, verifying rates and calculation accuracy.

In addition, organizations should track uncollected sales generated by each member of their sales department. One of the most common commission schemes involves the creation of fictitious sales to bolster commission earnings. Obviously, these fictitious sales will most likely go uncollected. Therefore, if an employee tends to generate a much higher percentage of uncollected sales than his coworkers, this could indicate fraud. A review of the support for the uncollected sales should be conducted to verify that they were legitimate transactions.

Overstated sales or fictitious sales can also be detected by conducting a random sample of customers. Verify that the customer exists, that the sale is legitimate, and that the amount of the sale corresponds to the customer's records. Someone independent of the sales force must perform this confirmation.

CASE STUDY: THE ALL-AMERICAN GIRL[2]

If you put 100 people in a room and asked them to pick out the criminal, chances are about 99 other people would get selected before anybody would think to point a finger at Katie Jordan. At about five feet, three inches, with short blonde hair and a bubbly personality, looking barely old enough to be out of high school—much less college—Katie seemed to personify the image of the all-American Girl Next Door. But somewhere along the way, Katie made a bad choice, and that led to another bad choice—and on and on until things had spiraled out of control. Before anybody knew what had happened, Katie Jordan had taken over $65,000 from her employer.

Susan Evers, the CFE who investigated Katie Jordan's case, says the incident was typical of many occupational frauds she encounters, in which "a person starts stealing because they're in a bad spot financially, and they think it's just temporary." But of course, it rarely is. "They may think they'll pay back the money, but they never do. Usually, before they know it they've taken so much there's no way they could ever pay it all back."

When Katie Jordan began working for Aramis Properties, she had no intention of defrauding the company. It was her first job out of college, and she was excited about the opportunity, eager to do a good job and move up. And that's what she did. Aramis owned several apartment complexes in the Dallas–Fort Worth area, and Katie was hired as an on-site

manager at one of those locations. She showed apartments to prospective tenants, collected rents, oversaw a maintenance crew, and generally ran the day-to-day operations of the complex. She reported to Gil Fleming, who worked in the company's corporate offices and who oversaw several properties, including the one Katie managed. Fleming took a liking to Katie because of her enthusiasm and because she did a good job. "She was very excited about work," he says. "I never had a single complaint about her performance in any way."

Katie did such a good job, in fact, that two years later, when the company acquired a large apartment complex in the Houston area, its first property in that market, Gil asked Katie to move to Houston to run it. "Of all the people that worked for me, she was the one I trusted most to do a good job, which is why we sent her," says Fleming. The new job would leave Katie with very little supervision, since the company's offices were in Dallas and Fleming had little time to travel to Houston to personally oversee her work.

Katie settled into her new job in Houston, and her life pretty much went on as it had before. Things changed, however, when her fiancé suffered an accident. His name was David Green, and in his spare time he was a semiprofessional motocross racer. There wasn't much money in it, and not a lot of security either, but he loved the speed and excitement of the sport. Unfortunately, when he flipped his bike and shattered his leg during a race, he was left hobbled—with no insurance and no income. Money became very tight for David and Katie, who were living together at the time.

Around that same time, one of the employees on the complex maintenance crew, a man named Manuel, quit his job.

[2]Several names and details have been changed to preserve anonymity.

Under normal circumstances, Katie would have filled out paperwork showing that this employee had left the company and sent it into headquarters, and then she would have begun looking for a replacement. But these were not normal circumstances, and it occurred to Katie that if she did not tell anybody at headquarters that Manuel had quit, then there would be no reason for them to stop issuing his paychecks. So when the next pay period rolled around, Katie collected timesheets for the four employees who worked under her and sent them off to the payroll department in Dallas, just as she always had. But she also filled out a timesheet for Manuel, and included it with the others. Under the company's system, paychecks were mailed back to Katie, who distributed them to the employees. When the paychecks arrived, she took the check made out to Manuel and cashed it at a liquor store.

Suddenly there was some money to help Katie and David get by, and nobody said a word. Every two weeks, she sent in another timesheet for Manuel and received another check. There was no way for anyone who worked at the complex to know what she was doing, because they never saw the books. Nobody at corporate headquarters had any idea, because from their end no changes had been made to the payroll. Gil Fleming visited the site a couple of times, but he never checked to make sure Manuel was still on staff. Why would he? "There was nothing unusual at all," says Fleming. "Nothing that made us suspect any kind of fraud."

Eventually Katie had to hire another maintenance man to take up the slack for Manuel's absence. "Her plan had been to float on Manuel's checks for a few weeks to get by," says Susan Evers, "then she would hire a new maintenance guy and stop taking the checks, and everything would go back to normal." But when it came time to bring in a new employee, Katie did not want to give up her new source of income. So instead of dropping Manuel off the books, she hired a new employee and kept right on paying Manuel. She even called Fleming at headquarters to let him know she was hiring extra maintenance staff. "She told him there were some problems with the structure, they were getting a lot of repair requests and she needed the extra help," says Evers. "He's not there. He trusts her. There wasn't any reason why he wouldn't okay it."

When Katie saw how easy it was to add an employee, that's when her scheme escalated. "I think that's when she first really figured out how much autonomy she had," says Evers. "About a month later, she hired an 'assistant' to help her at the office. The only problem was, the 'assistant' didn't exist." Katie now had two ghosts on the payroll, Manuel and her new assistant 'Wendy.' Between them, they made more than Katie. With very little effort, she'd more than doubled her income.

"The money had originally been for her fiancée, but it got way past that," says Evers. "Even after she'd taken enough to pay his medical bills, she kept on stealing. She got hooked on the easy money." It didn't take long before the scheme came unraveled. Katie may have been good at managing apartments, but she was lousy at committing fraud. "She hadn't really thought it through," says Evers. "The second ghost was supposed to be her assistant, but there wasn't even a desk for her in the office." Shortly after Wendy went on the books, Fleming made a routine visit to the property. He was standing in the office speaking to Katie and another employee when he casually asked about the new assistant. He immediately knew something was wrong. "The other girl looked confused, and Katie got very flustered," says Fleming. "Then I started looking around and noticed there was no sign of anybody else working there at all. Then I thought 'uh oh.'" Katie asked him to come into her office, and she confessed right there. "The whole thing, from the moment I brought it up, took about five minutes," says Flemming. "She spilled everything and started crying. She told me how sorry she was. Honestly, I think she was relieved to tell me."

What she didn't tell him was how much she'd stolen. Katie confessed to adding 'Wendy' to the payroll, but she said nothing about Manuel. "I don't know why," says Fleming, "She had to know we'd go back over the books."

Evers has a theory: "People have a hard time admitting to what they've done. Even when they get caught, they can't admit it was as bad as it really was. They try to downplay it."

Evers was brought in by the company to go over the books and determine how much Katie had stolen. After reviewing the records and talking to a couple of employees, it didn't take long to figure out that Manuel hadn't worked there in over six months. She also found out that Katie had been skimming rents by taking cash from certain tenants and listing their units as vacant. When she finally interviewed Katie, Evers found out that after the medical bills had been paid off, she had been using the company's funds to pay for her upcoming wedding. She'd bought a dress and put a down payment on a reception hall. She'd also bought a new car.

Katie offered to make good on what she had stolen, but she was only able to pay back about $12,000, less than a fifth of her take. "She was shocked when I told her how much she'd stolen," says Evers. "She didn't have any idea it was that much, mostly because she didn't want to know. After all, she was the one who was cashing all the checks."

After Evers filed her report, the company dismissed Katie and pressed charges against her. She was convicted, but served no jail time. Evers also helped the company set up internal controls to provide better checks and balances on the company's accounting and personnel policies. But according to Evers, having strong internal controls is not enough: "Companies have to realize that any employee, under the right circumstances, can commit fraud." Even an all-American girl.

PROACTIVE COMPUTER AUDIT TESTS FOR DETECTING PAYROLL FRAUD[1]

Title	Category	Description	Data file(s)
Age employee payments by check date.	All	Focuses audit efforts on periods of increased activity.	• Payroll register
Stratify on hourly rates, hours worked, net pay amount, commission amount, and overtime hours.	All	Focuses audit efforts on high rates.	• Payroll register
Compare salaried employee gross pay from one pay period to the next.	All	Review changes in salaried payroll for areas of potential fraud.	• Payroll register
Age customer open invoices by salesperson.	Commission	Identifies salespeople that have unusually old receivable balances, which may be phony invoices used to bolster commission payments.	• Sales register (open invoices designated)
Extract all round-dollar payments.	All	Round-dollar payments have a higher likelihood of being fraudulent.	• Invoice payment
Compare current year to prior year payroll file to detect additional/terminated employees.	Ghost employees	Highlights new and terminated employees for agreement to authorization records. New employees should be reviewed closely to determine whether ghost employees accepting fraudulent payments exist.	• Payroll register • Employee master file
Compare employees reported per timecard system to payroll system.	Ghost employees	Isolates differences between the employee register in the timecard system and the payroll register. Focus should be on employees in the payroll register who do not appear in the timecard system and thus may have been fraudulently added.	• Payroll register • Timecard system
Compare payroll data files to human resource data files to test for differences between the files.	Ghost employees	Ensures agreement between human resource and payroll records. Isolate potential unauthorized payroll payments. Detect new or terminated employees for agreement to authorized forms.	• Payroll register • Employee master file
Extract all employee payments with no deductions/taxes withheld.	Ghost employees	Highlights payments without taxes/deductions, which are, by their nature, more prone to fraud.	• Payroll register

(Continued)

(*Continued*)

Title	Category	Description	Data file(s)
Extract all employees without an employee number or Social Security number.	Ghost employees	Reports potential ghost employees who may have unauthorized payments. Please note that this field may be blank or filled with the series 999999999.	• Payroll register • Employee master file
Extract employee payments having payment dates after employee termination dates.	Ghost employees	Reports potentially unauthorized payments to terminated employees that may be made and intercepted by an employee.	• Payroll register • Employee master file
Extract employees without names.	Ghost employees	Reports potential ghost employees who may have unauthorized payments or payments made with payees being written in after check printing.	• Payroll register • Employee master file
Sequence duplicate Social Security numbers paid in the same pay period.	Ghost employees	Lists possible duplicate payments to employees, which are highly prone to fraud.	• Payroll register • Employee master file
Sequence duplicate direct deposit numbers paid in the same pay period.	Ghost employees	Lists possible duplicate payments to employees, which are highly prone to fraud.	• Payroll register • Employee master file
Sequence possible duplicate payments based on the absolute value of the net pay and the check date.	Ghost employees	Lists possible duplicate payments to employees, which are highly prone to fraud.	• Payroll register
Sequence duplicate mailing address numbers paid in the same pay period.	Ghost employees	Lists possible duplicate payments to employees, which are highly prone to fraud.	• Payroll register • Employee master file
Extract users who can issue paychecks and also add new employees in the payroll and timecard system.	Ghost employees, Falsified hours, Falsified salary	Users who can enter new employees, enter time, and issue a fraudulent paycheck can take advantage of nonsegregation of duties to commit their fraud. User access should be reviewed from the perspective of adjustments within the application and adjustments to the data itself.	• Payroll register user access master file • Timecard user access master file • Payroll register user access log file • Timecard user access log file
Calculate the percentage of bonus to gross pay (on a person-by-person basis) and sort from high to low.	Falsified hours, Falsified salary	Reports high and potentially unauthorized bonus payments.	• Payroll register

Calculate the percentage of fringe expense to the gross pay (on a person-by-person basis) and sort from high to low.	Falsified hours, Falsified salary	Reports unusually high fringe payments. Also, payments with fringe payments equal to zero are, by their nature, more prone to fraud.	• Payroll register
Calculate the percentage of overtime to gross pay (on a person-by-person basis) and sort from low to high.	Falsified hours, Falsified salary	Reports high and potentially unauthorized overtime expenses.	• Payroll register
Calculate the average payroll per employee and sort from high to low.	Falsified hours, Falsified salary, Commission schemes	Reports high and potentially unauthorized employee payments.	• Payroll register
Compare bonus payments to budget or prior year on an employee-by-employee basis.	Falsified hours, Falsified salary	Reports large changes and potentially unauthorized bonus payments.	• Payroll register
Compare current year to prior year payroll file to detect changes in pay rates.	Falsified hours, Falsified salary	Highlights changes in rates that can be reviewed for unusual trends, exceptions, and unauthorized changes.	• Payroll register • Employee master file
Compare hours reported per timecard system to payroll system.	Falsified hours, Falsified salary	Isolates differences between the hours worked and the hours paid to employees. Overpayments may be detected if more hours are paid for than worked or unauthorized deductions of hours may be occurring.	• Payroll register • Timecard system
Compare overtime hours to budget or prior year by department.	Falsified hours, Falsified salary	Reports large changes and potentially unauthorized overtime payments.	• Payroll register
Compare payroll data files to human resource data files to test for differing salary rates.	Falsified hours, Falsified salary	Ensures agreement between human resource and payroll records. Isolates potential unauthorized payroll payments. Detects new or terminated employees for agreement to authorized forms.	• Payroll register • Employee master file
Extract all employees paid more than 25 percent of their gross pay in overtime.	Falsified hours, Falsified salary	Reports large and potentially unauthorized overtime payments.	• Payroll register
Extract all employees with over x hours per pay period.	Falsified hours, Falsified salary	Reports large and potentially unauthorized hours charged by employees. One basic test is to review any employees with over 168 hours (more than the weekly limit).	• Payroll register

(*Continued*)

(*Continued*)

Title	Category	Description	Data file(s)
Recalculate gross pay.	Falsified hours, Falsified salary	Recalculate gross pay for agreement to company records. Any differences may signal a control weakness in the computer system or a fraudulently adjusted payment.	• Payroll register
Recalculate net pay.	Falsified hours, Falsified salary	Recalculate net pay for agreement to company records. Any differences may signal a control weakness in the computer system or a fraudulently adjusted payment.	• Payroll register
Recalculate the hours reported per the timecard system by employee.	Falsified hours, Falsified salary	Recalculate hours per timecard system for agreement to payroll check-writing system. Any differences may signal a control weakness in the computer system or fraudulently adjusted payment.	• Timecard system
Summarize commissions paid by product line, region, and salesperson.	Commission schemes	Focus should be on areas of high ratios for potential fraudulently inflated sales/commissions.	• Payroll register
Complete a trend analysis of commission to sale ratios by salesperson.	Commission schemes	Sales and commission ratios should work in a linear fashion over time and should not appear overstated in relation to the sales.	• Payroll register • Sales register
Recalculate commissions based on current year sales and other required performance measures.	Commission schemes	Recalculate commissions for agreement to company records. Any differences may signal a control weakness in the computer system or a fraudulently adjusted payment.	• Payroll register • Sales register
Classify sales prices by salesperson and calculate an average price per salesperson.	Commission schemes	Focus should be on areas of high sales prices for potential fraudulently inflated sales/commissions.	• Sales register
Sequence possible duplicate sales invoices based on the absolute value of the invoice and customer.	Commission schemes	Lists possible duplicate invoices that may be used to inflate sales and associated commissions.	• Sales register
Dormant customer accounts for the past six months that post a sale in the last two months of the year.	Commission schemes	Customers that have been dormant may be used as accounts to post fraudulent activity, increasing any associated commissions.	• Sales register
Calculate the ratio of the largest sale to next largest sale by customer.	Commission schemes	By identifying the largest sale to a customer and the next largest sale, any large ratio difference may identify a fraudulently recorded "largest" sale made to increase any associated commissions.	• Sales register

Extract customer sales that exceed the twelve-month average sales from that customer by a specified percentage (i.e., 200%).	Commission schemes	This test may identify a large fraudulently recorded sale, made to increase any associated commissions.	• Sales register
Extract customer sale balances that exceed the customer credit limit.	Commission schemes	This test may identify a large fraudulently recorded sale, made to increase any associated commissions.	• Sales register • Customer master file
Compare the customer master file to the sales register to check for phony customers.	Commission schemes	Phony customers added could be used to post fraudulent invoices that could be used to inflate commissions.	• Sales register • Customer master file
Extract customers who have no telephone number or tax ID.	Commission schemes	Customers without this information are more prone to abuse and should be scrutinized as possible phantom customers.	• Customer master file
Identify customers added during the period under review.	Commission schemes	New customer additions should be reviewed using this report to determine whether any phantom customers are being created.	• Customer master file
Extract any salesperson users who can enter sales orders/adjustments and also can create customer accounts.	Commission schemes	Users who can create new customers and then post orders/adjustments to those customers can take advantage of nonsegregation of duties to commit their fraud. User access should be reviewed from the perspective of adjustments within the application and adjustments to the data itself.	• Sales register user access master file • Customer master user access master file • Sales register user access log file • Customer master access log file

SUMMARY

Payroll schemes are a form of fraudulent disbursement in which an organization makes a payment to an individual who either works for the organization or claims to work for the organization. Payroll schemes fall into three categories: (1) ghost employees, (2) falsified hours and salary, and (3) commission schemes.

Ghost employees can be either fictitious persons or real persons who do not work for the organization. When the ghost is a real person, it is often a friend or relative of the perpetrator who cashes the fraudulent paychecks and splits the money with the perpetrator.

The most common method of misappropriating funds from the payroll occurs when employees falsify the number of hours they have worked. These schemes usually succeed when organizations fail to segregate the duties of payroll preparation, authorization, distribution, and reconciliation. Corrupt employees can also make unauthorized adjustments to their wage rates to increase the size of their paychecks, though this is not as common as falsifying hours.

Employees who work on commission can defraud a company by falsifying the amount of sales they have made or by falsifying the prices of items they have sold. Salespersons might also change the rate of their commissions to increase their pay.

ESSENTIAL TERMS

Ghost employee An individual on the payroll of a company who does not actually work for the company. This individual can be real or fictitious.

Salaried employees Employees who are paid a set amount of money per period (weekly, biweekly, monthly, etc.). Unlike hourly employees, salaried employees are paid a set amount regardless of the actual number of hours they work.

Rubber stamp supervisor A supervisor who neglects to review documents, such as timecards, before signing or approving them for payment.

Commission A form of compensation calculated as a percentage of the amount of sales an employee generates. A commissioned employee's wages are based on two factors: the amount of sales generated, and the percentage of those sales he is paid.

REVIEW QUESTIONS

6-1 (Learning objective 6-1) According to this chapter, what are the three main categories of payroll fraud?

6-2 (Learning objective 6-2) In terms of median losses, which causes larger ones: billing schemes, or payroll schemes? Can you offer a possible explanation for why this is so?

6-3 (Learning objective 6-3) What is a "ghost employee"?

6-4 (Learning objective 6-3) Four steps must be completed in order for a ghost employee scheme to be successful. What are they?

6-5 (Learning objective 6-3) Within a given organization, who is the individual most likely to add ghost employees to the payroll system?

6-6 (Learning objective 6-6) The key to a falsified hours scheme in a manual system is for the perpetrator to obtain authorization for the falsified timecard. There were four methods identified in this chapter by which employees achieved this. What were they?

6-7 (Learning objectives 6-7 and 6-8) What is meant by the term *rubber stamp supervisor*, and how are these individuals utilized in a payroll fraud scheme?

6-8 (Learning objective 6-8) List at least three tests that could be performed to detect falsified hours and salary schemes.

6-9 (Learning objective 6-9) There are two ways that an employee working on commission can fraudulently increase his pay. What are they?

DISCUSSION ISSUES

6-1 (Learning objective 6-1) List and explain at least three computer-aided audit tests that can be used to detect a ghost employee scheme.

6-2 (Learning objectives 6-4 and 6-5) The ability to add ghost employees to a company's payroll system is often the result of a breakdown in internal controls. What internal controls prevent an individual from adding fictitious employees to payroll records?

6-3 (Learning objective 6-7) In the case study of Jerry Harkanell, what internal controls could have prevented the falsification of his timesheet?

6-4 (Learning objective 6-7) In terms of preventing payroll fraud, why is it important for hiring and wage rate changes to be administered through a centralized and independent human resources department?

6-5 (Learning objective 6-10) If you suspect that a salesperson is inflating his commissions, what would you do to determine whether this were occurring?

6-6 (Learning objective 6-10) Beta is one of ten salespeople working for ABC Company. Over a given period, 15 percent of Beta's sales are uncollectable, as opposed to an average of 3 percent for the rest of the department. Explain how this fact could be related to a commission scheme by Beta.

ENDNOTES

1. Lanza, pp. 51–55.

Expense Reimbursement Schemes

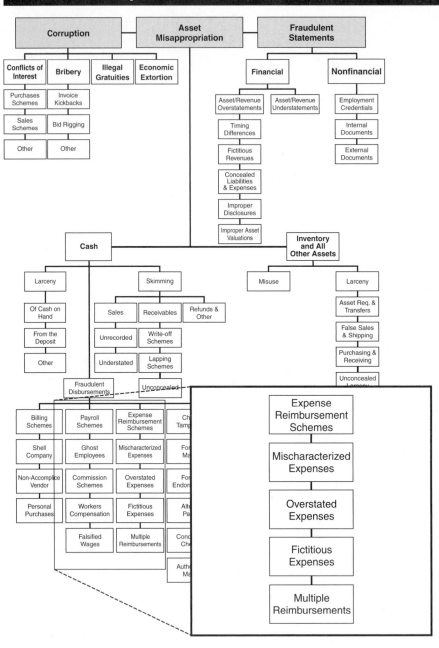

Corruption
- **Conflicts of Interest**
  - Purchases Schemes
  - Sales Schemes
  - Other
- **Bribery**
  - Invoice Kickbacks
  - Bid Rigging
  - Other
- **Illegal Gratuities**
- **Economic Extortion**

Asset Misappropriation

Fraudulent Statements
- **Financial**
  - Asset/Revenue Overstatements
    - Timing Differences
    - Fictitious Revenues
    - Concealed Liabilities & Expenses
    - Improper Disclosures
    - Improper Asset Valuations
  - Asset/Revenue Understatements
- **Nonfinancial**
  - Employment Credentials
  - Internal Documents
  - External Documents

Cash
- **Larceny**
  - Of Cash on Hand
  - From the Deposit
  - Other
- **Skimming**
  - Sales
    - Unrecorded
    - Understated
  - Receivables
    - Write-off Schemes
    - Lapping Schemes
  - Refunds & Other
- **Fraudulent Disbursements**
  - Billing Schemes
    - Shell Company
    - Non-Accomplice Vendor
    - Personal Purchases
  - Payroll Schemes
    - Ghost Employees
    - Commission Schemes
    - Workers Compensation
    - Falsified Wages
  - Expense Reimbursement Schemes
    - Mischaracterized Expenses
    - Overstated Expenses
    - Fictitious Expenses
    - Multiple Reimbursements
  - Check Tampering
    - Forged Maker
    - Forged Endorsement
    - Altered Payee
    - Concealed Checks
    - Authorized Maker
- **Unconcealed**

Inventory and All Other Assets
- **Misuse**
- **Larceny**
  - Asset Req. & Transfers
  - False Sales & Shipping
  - Purchasing & Receiving
  - Unconcealed Larceny

Expense Reimbursement Schemes
- Mischaracterized Expenses
- Overstated Expenses
- Fictitious Expenses
- Multiple Reimbursements

EXHIBIT 7-1

CHAPTER 7

EXPENSE REIMBURSEMENT SCHEMES

LEARNING OBJECTIVES

After studying this chapter, you should be able to:

7-1 Explain what constitutes expense reimbursement fraud

7-2 Discuss the data on expense reimbursement fraud from the *2009 Global Fraud Survey*

7-3 Understand how mischaracterized expense reimbursement schemes are committed

7-4 Be familiar with the controls identified in this chapter for preventing and detecting mischaracterized expense schemes

7-5 Identify the methods employees use to overstate otherwise legitimate expenses on their expense reports

7-6 Understand controls that can be used to prevent and detect overstated expense schemes

7-7 Explain what a fictitious expense reimbursement scheme is and differentiate it from other forms of expense reimbursement fraud

7-8 Identify red flags that are commonly associated with fictitious expense schemes

7-9 Discuss what a multiple reimbursement scheme is and how this kind of fraud is committed

7-10 Discuss the controls identified in this chapter for preventing and detecting multiple reimbursement schemes

7-11 Be familiar with proactive audit tests that can be used to detect various forms of expense reimbursement fraud

CASE STUDY: FREQUENT FLIER'S FRAUD CRASHES[1]

In his ten years at a regional office of Tyler & Hartford, Marcus Lane had spent more time on the road than at home—which means he often whispered a long-distance goodnight to his kids over his cell phone. The 35-year-old Ph.D. traveled all over North and South America for his job as a geologist for the privately held firm specializing in environmental management and engineering services. Its extensive client list represented all types of industries and included municipalities, construction firms, petroleum companies, and manufacturers with multimillion-dollar projects. As part of a team assembled by a project manager from Tyler & Hartford, Lane was regularly called on to oversee drilling operations, conduct sampling tests, or assist with a formal site analysis.

Going from site to site, the road warrior adhered to the basic rules of business travel: Try to get a room on the top floor, away from the elevators and the ice machine. Request a seat in an emergency exit row on the airplane, where there is more leg room. Always get documentation for any travel

[1]Several names and details have been changed to preserve anonymity.

expense—and so on. But Lane broke a basic rule of ethics: never cheat on your expense report.

His transgression was discovered by Heidi McCullough, an accountant who worked out of Tyler & Hartford's East Coast headquarters. As she was processing Lane's most recent expense report, she noticed a discrepancy between the departure times listed on the flight receipt and boarding pass for Flight 4578 from Minneapolis to San Antonio. Whereas the receipt indicated that the flight had been scheduled to depart at 6:15 p.m., the boarding pass indicated a departure time of 6:15 a.m. McCullough figured that the discrepancy was most likely due to an error on the part of the airline. After all, Lane was a highly trusted and well respected employee who traveled regularly on company business. But, being the prudent employee she was, she decided she'd better bring the discrepancy to the attention of Tina Marie Williams, manager of the internal audit department.

"I was immediately suspicious," recalled Williams, who was newly accredited as a CFE at the time. "Although it was possible that the airline had made an error, it seemed much more likely that either the flight receipt, the boarding pass, or both had been doctored. This was a situation that needed to be looked into." The first thing Williams did was contact the airline to verify whether the flight number in question was even a legitimate flight, and, if so, what the correct scheduled departure time was. She learned that flight 4578 was, in fact, an actual flight and that it had been scheduled to depart—and did depart—at 6:15 p.m. But because Lane had booked the flight using his own credit card, she was unable to confirm with the airline whether he actually took the flight.

Next Williams proceeded to carefully review the rest of the Lane's travel receipts for his trip to San Antonio. Two of the receipts stood out. One was for a car rental, which indicated that the car was picked up by Lane at noon on the day of his flight to San Antonio. The second was a receipt for lunch at a restaurant located near the San Antonio International Airport, also on the day of the flight.

Williams suspected that Lane had not actually boarded flight 4578, but had created a phony boarding pass to make it appear as though he had. As an experienced auditor, Williams was familiar with a common expense reimbursement scheme in which an employee books two separate flights to the same location, but with a huge cost difference; he uses the cheaper ticket for the actual flight and returns the more expensive ticket for credit. And, of course, he submits the more expensive ticket for reimbursement.

"Company policy is that employees must book all travel through the company travel agent. But Lane has been booking his own travel since long before I started working here. When I mentioned my concerns over this to senior management I was told to let it be—that Lane was a loyal and trustworthy employee, and that I had nothing to worry about."

Playing by the book, Williams called the legal department at Tyler & Hartford to apprise it of the situation and ask for any advice on procedure. Williams said that the legal department put the case under protective privilege.

She then overnighted her collection of evidence along with her detailed analysis of the airfare scheme to Lane's immediate supervisor at the regional office, who in turn showed it to his boss at his earliest availability. Right on time, the two managers scheduled a private meeting with Lane, bright and early on the following Monday morning.

Without mincing words, one of the managers asked Lane, "How is it that you were able to pick up a rental car at noon and have lunch in San Antonio when your flight from Minneapolis didn't depart until 6 p.m.?" Lane, knowing that he had been caught, immediately confessed to double-booking flights and creating fictitious boarding passes using his home computer, in order to make it appear as though he took a more expensive flight than he had actually taken. He explained that he was experiencing temporary financial problems as the result of his recent divorce, that he just needed some money to tide him over. He said that he intended to pay the money back as soon as possible. According to Williams, who heard the account second-hand, Lane vowed, "I only did it for four months." He swore that he padded his expense account for just a brief period; he urged the managers to check out all the other expense reports he had submitted in his ten years at Tyler & Hartford and voluntarily agreed to surrender his personal credit card and bank records. He also agreed to provide his own accounting of the crime.

All in all, Lane had swindled the company out of $4,100. He agreed to pay back the stolen money. "He paid us $2,000 in one lump sum initially, then $150 every two months after that," Williams recalled.

Lane was promptly terminated, but Tyler & Hartford decided not to prosecute the geologist. They kept their month-long investigation quiet as well. "No one found out about it except through the grapevine." Even then, others only knew that somebody got in trouble for fudging an expense report, said Williams.

True to the company's culture of taking decisive action, Williams and her team resolved this case in just under one month from the time of its detection. "This is the smoothest case we've ever had," she admitted.

"We discovered that it was a very easy fraud to perpetrate, especially since it is so simple to create phony airline tickets and boarding passes. On behalf of Tyler & Hartford, Williams later launched a target audit to uncover other travel scams, and found some. Lane's scam, unfortunately, was not an isolated incident.

After Lane's fraud was exposed, Williams received full support from senior management for clarification and better enforcement of the policy that all travel for the entire company, including all fifty regional offices, must be booked through the company travel agent using a designated company credit card. "That makes our auditing lives so much easier. It gives us better control, as well as better cost data," said Williams.

Williams also recommended that employees only use a company credit card to charge all other business expenditures. Top management accepted the recommendation and issued a mandate. Williams was pleased, as the billing statement for a company credit card provides a strong audit tool and an easy-access audit trail.

OVERVIEW

Expense reimbursement schemes, as the name implies, occur when employees make false claims for reimbursement of fictitious or inflated business expenses. This is a very common form of occupational fraud and one that, by its nature, can be extremely difficult to detect. Employees who engage in this type of fraud generally seek to have the company pay for their personal expenses, or they pad the amount of business expenses they have incurred in order to generate excess reimbursements. In most cases, the travel and entertainment expenses at issue were incurred away from the office where there was no direct supervision and no company representative (other than the fraudster) present to verify that the expenses were, indeed, incurred. Thus, these frauds generally are detected through indirect means—trend analysis, comparisons of expenses to work schedules, and so forth. If a fraudster is smart and does not get too greedy, it can be virtually impossible to catch an expense reimbursement scheme. But then, most fraudsters eventually get greedy.

Expense Reimbursement Data from the ACFE
2009 Global Fraud Survey

In the ACFE's study, expense reimbursement fraud was cited in 30 percent of fraudulent disbursement cases, ranking second in terms of frequency (see Exhibit 7-2). In contrast,

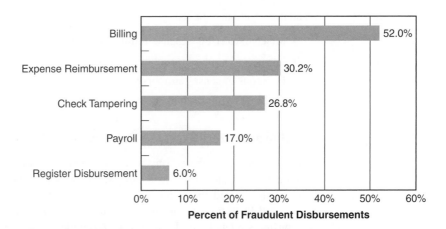

EXHIBIT 7-2 *2009 Global Fraud Survey*: Frequency of Fraudulent Disbursements[a]

[a]The sum of these percentages exceeds 100 percent because some cases involved multiple fraud schemes that fell into more than one category

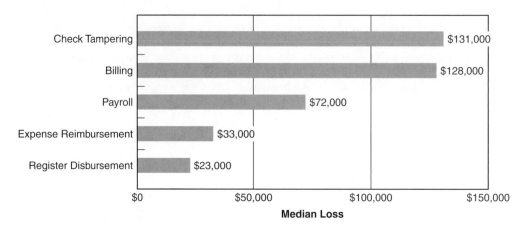

EXHIBIT 7-3 *2009 Global Fraud Survey*: Median Loss of Fraudulent Disbursements

expense reimbursement fraud schemes were the second least costly form of fraudulent disbursement in the study, resulting in a median loss of $33,000 (see Exhibit 7-3).

EXPENSE REIMBURSEMENT SCHEMES

Expense reimbursements are usually paid by organizations in the following manner. An employee submits a report detailing an expense incurred for a business purpose, such as a business lunch with a client, airfare, hotel bills associated with business travel, and so on. In preparing an expense report, an employee usually must explain the business purpose for the expense, as well as the time, date, and location in which it was incurred. Attached to the report should be support documentation for the expense—typically, a receipt. In some cases, canceled checks written by the employee, or copies of a personal credit card statement showing the expense, are allowed. The report usually must be authorized by a supervisor in order for the expense to be reimbursed.

There are four methods by which employees typically abuse this process to generate fraudulent reimbursements:

- Mischaracterized expense reimbursements
- Overstated expense reimbursements
- Fictitious expense reimbursements
- Multiple reimbursements

Mischaracterized Expense Reimbursements

Most companies reimburse only certain expenses of their employees. Which expenses a company will pay depends to an extent on policy, but in general, business-related travel, lodging, and meals are reimbursed. One of the most basic expense schemes is perpetrated by simply requesting reimbursement for a personal expense, claiming that it is business-related (see Exhibit 7-4). Examples of mischaracterized expenses include claiming personal travel as a business trip, listing dinner with a friend as "business development," and so on. Fraudsters may submit the receipts from their personal expenses along with their reports and provide business reasons for the incurred costs.

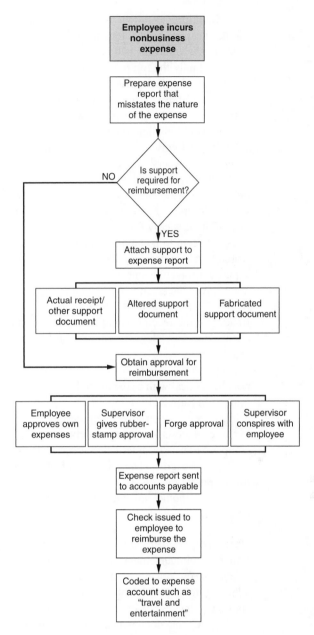

EXHIBIT 7-4 Mischaracterized Expenses

The false expense report induces the victim company to issue a check, reimbursing the perpetrator for his personal expenses. A mischaracterization is a simple scheme. In cases involving airfare and overnight travel, a mischaracterization can sometimes be detected by simply comparing the employee's expense reports to his work schedule. Often, the dates of the so-called "business trip" coincide with a vacation or day off. Detailed expense reports allow a company to make this kind of comparison and are therefore very helpful in preventing expenses schemes.

Requiring detailed information means more than just supporting documents; it should mean precise statements of what was purchased, as well as when and where. In Case 479, a fraudster submitted credit card statements as support for expenses, but he submitted only the top portion of the statements, not the portion that describes what was purchased. Over 95 percent of his expenses that were reimbursed were of a personal rather than a business nature. Of course, in this particular example the scheme was made easier because the perpetrator was the CEO of the company, making it unlikely that anyone would challenge the validity of his expense reports.

Interestingly, many mischaracterized expense schemes are undertaken by high-level employees, owners, or officers. Many times, such a perpetrator actually has authority over the account from which expenses were reimbursed. In other cases, the perpetrators simply fail to submit detailed expense reports, or even any expense reports at all. Obviously, when a company is willing to reimburse employee expenses without any verifying documentation, it is easy for an employee to take advantage of the system. Nevertheless, there does not seem to be anything inherent in the nature of a mischaracterization scheme that would preclude its use in a system in which detailed reports are required. As an example, suppose a traveling salesman goes on a trip and runs up a large bar bill one night in his hotel, saves his receipt, and lists this expense as "business entertainment" on an expense report. Nothing about the time, date, or nature of the expense would readily point to fraud, and the receipt would appear to substantiate the expense. Short of contacting the client who was allegedly entertained, there is little hope of identifying the expense as fraudulent.

One final note is that mischaracterization schemes can be extremely costly. They do not always deal with a free lunch here or there, but instead may involve very large sums of money. In Case 2249, for example, two mid-level managers ran up $1 million in inappropriate expenses over a two-year period. Their travel was not properly overseen, and their expense requests were not closely reviewed, allowing them to spend large amounts of company money on international travel, lavish entertainment of friends, and the purchase of expensive gifts. They simply claimed that they incurred these expenses entertaining corporate clients. Though this was more costly than the average mischaracterization scheme, it should underscore the potential harm that can occur if the reimbursement process is not carefully attended to.

Preventing and Detecting Mischaracterized Expense Reimbursements

Expense reimbursement fraud is very common and can be difficult to detect. It is important for organizations to focus on preventing these crimes by establishing and adhering to a system of controls that makes fraud more difficult to commit. As a starting point, every organization should require detailed expense reports that include original support documents, dates and times of business expenses, method of payment, and descriptions of the purpose for the expenses. All travel and entertainment expenses should be reviewed by a direct supervisor of the requestor. In no circumstance should expenses be reimbursed without an independent review.

Organizations should establish a policy that clearly states what types of expenses will and will not be reimbursed, that explains what are considered invalid reasons for incurring business expenses, and that sets reasonable limits for expense reimbursements. This policy must be publicized to all employees, particularly those who are likely to incur travel and entertainment expenses, and employees should sign a statement acknowledging that they understand the policy and will abide by it. This serves two purposes: first, it educates employees about what are considered acceptable reimbursable expenses; second, in the event that an employee tries to claim reimbursement for personal or nonreimbursable expenses, the signed statement will provide evidence that the employee knew the company's rules, which will help establish that the expense report in question was intentionally fraudulent, not the result of an honest mistake.

In some cases, fraud perpetrators try to get personal expenses approved by having their expense reports reviewed by a supervisor outside their department. The idea is that these supervisors will not be as familiar with the employee's work schedule, duties, and so on, so, for instance, if the perpetrator is claiming expenses for dates when she was on vacation, a direct supervisor might spot this anomaly, but a supervisor from another department might not. Therefore, organizations should scrutinize any expense report that was approved by a supervisor outside the requestor's department.

Because so many mischaracterized expense schemes involve personal expenses incurred during nonwork hours, one way to catch these crimes is to compare dates of claimed expenses to work schedules. For example, an organization could set up its accounting system so that any payment coded as an expense reimbursement is automatically compared to vacation or leave time requested by the employee in question. Expenses incurred on weekends or at unusual times could also be flagged for follow-up.

Organizations can also use trend analysis to detect these frauds. Current expense reimbursement levels should be compared to prior years and to budgeted amounts. If travel and entertainment expenses seem to be excessive, attempt to identify any legitimate business reasons for the increase. Also compare expense reimbursements per employee looking for a particular individual whose expense reimbursements seem excessive.

Overstated Expense Reimbursements

Instead of seeking reimbursement for personal expenses, some employees overstate the cost of actual business expenses (see Exhibit 7-5). This can be accomplished in a number of ways.

Altered Receipts   The most fundamental example of overstated expense schemes occurs when an employee doctors a receipt or other supporting documentation to reflect a higher cost than what he actually paid. The employee may use correction fluid, a ball-point pen, or some other method to change the price reflected on the receipt before submitting his expense report. If the company does not require original documents as support, the perpetrator generally attaches a copy of the receipt to his expense report. (Alterations are usually less noticeable on a photocopy than on an original document.) For precisely this reason, many businesses require original receipts and ink signatures on expense reports.

As with other expense frauds, overstated expense schemes often succeed because of poor controls. In companies in which supporting documents are not required, for example, fraudsters simply lie about how much they paid for a business expense. With no support available, it may be very difficult to disprove an employee's false expense claims.

Overpurchasing   The case of Marcus Lane at the beginning of this chapter illustrated another way to overstate a reimbursement form: the "overpurchasing" of business expenses. As we saw, Lane purchased two tickets for his business travel, one expensive and one cheap. He returned the expensive ticket, but used the receipt for it, along with a phony boarding pass, to overstate his expense report. Meanwhile, he used the cheaper

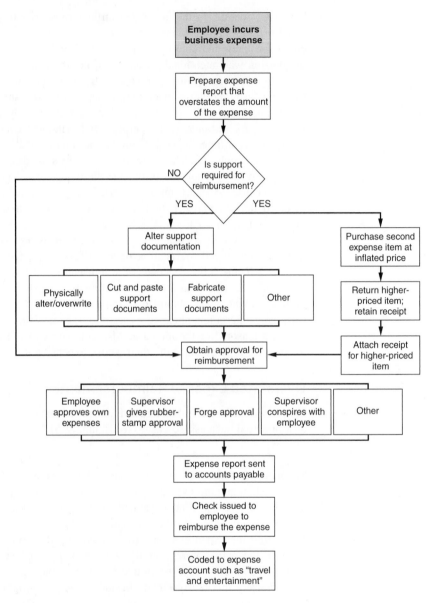

EXHIBIT 7-5 Overstated Expenses

ticket for his trip. In this manner, he was able to be reimbursed for an expense that was larger than what he had actually paid.

Overstating Another Employee's Expenses Overstated expense schemes are not only committed by the person who incurs the expense. In addition, they may be committed by someone else who handles or processes expense reports. Such an example occurred in Case 2389, where a petty cashier whited-out other employees' requests for travel advances and inserted larger amounts. The cashier then passed on the legitimate travel advances and pocketed the excess.

This kind of scheme is most likely to occur in a system in which expenses are reimbursed in currency rather than by a check, since the perpetrator would be unable to extract her "cut" from a single check made out to another employee.

Orders to Overstate Expenses   Finally, AFCE researchers have seen a few cases in which employees knowingly falsified their own reports, but did so at the direction of their supervisors. In Case 1971, for instance, a department head forced his subordinates to inflate their expenses and return the proceeds to him. The employees went along with this scheme, presumably for fear of losing their jobs. The fraud lasted for 10 years and cost the victim company approximately $6 million. Similarly, in Case 1974, a sales executive instructed his salesmen to inflate their expenses in order to generate cash for a slush fund that was then used to pay bribes and to provide improper forms of entertainment for clients and customers.

Preventing and Detecting Overstated Expense Reimbursement Schemes   In addition to the prevention and detection methods that have already been discussed, it is particularly important, for dealing with overstated expense reimbursement schemes, that an organization require *original* receipts for all expense reimbursements. Alterations to original receipts should be very obvious, whereas it can be difficult to detect alterations to photocopies. Any policy addressing expense reimbursements should clearly state that expenses will be reimbursed only when supported by original receipts.

Comparison reports that show reimbursed expenses can be useful in detecting overstated expense reimbursement schemes. If one employee's travel and entertainment expenses are consistently higher than those of coworkers who have similar travel schedules, this is a red flag. Also, a comparison of similar expenses incurred by different individuals may highlight fraud. For example, if two salespeople regularly fly to the same city, does one tend to seek higher levels of reimbursement?

If an organization has had problems with expense reimbursement fraud, it may be helpful to spot-check expense reports with customers, confirming business dinners, meetings, and so forth.

Fictitious Expense Reimbursement Schemes

Expense reimbursements are sometimes sought by employees for wholly fictitious items. Instead of overstating a real business expense or seeking reimbursement for a personal expense, an employee simply invents a purchase to be reimbursed (see Exhibit 7-6).

Producing Fictitious Receipts   One way to generate a reimbursement for a fictitious expense is to create bogus support documents, such as false receipts. Personal computers enable employees to create realistic-looking counterfeit receipts at home. Such was the scheme in Case 1275, in which an employee manufactured fake receipts using his computer and laser printer. The counterfeits were very sophisticated, even including the logos of the stores where he had allegedly made business-related purchases.

Computers are not the only means for creating support for a fictitious expense. The fraudster in Case 1275 used several methods for justifying fictitious expenses as his scheme progressed. He began by using calculator printouts to simulate receipts, then advanced to cutting and pasting receipts from suppliers before finally progressing to using computer software to generate fictitious receipts.

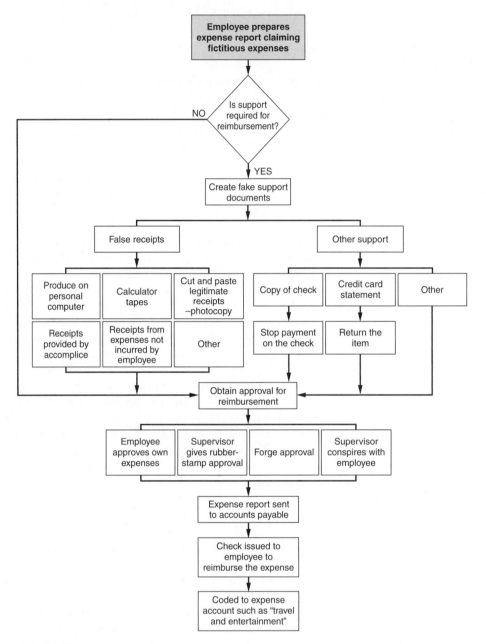

EXHIBIT 7-6 Fictitious Expenses

Obtaining Blank Receipts from Vendors If receipts are not created by the fraud-ster, they can be obtained from legitimate suppliers in a number of ways. A manager in Case 2830 simply requested blank receipts from waiters, bartenders, and so on. He then filled in these receipts to "create" business expenses, including the names of clients whom he allegedly entertained. The fraudster usually paid all his expenses in cash to prevent an audit trail. One thing that undid this culprit was the fact that the last digit on most of the prices on his receipt was usually a zero or a five. This fact, noted by an astute employee, raised questions about the validity of his expenses.

A similar scheme was found in Case 1980, in which an employee's girlfriend worked at a restaurant near the victim company. This girlfriend validated credit card receipts and gave them to the fraudster so that he could submit them with his expense reports.

Instead of asking for blank receipts, some employees simply steal them. In some cases a fraudster will steal an entire stack of blank receipts and submit them over time to verify fictitious business expenses. This type of fraud should be identifiable by the fact that the perpetrator is submitting consecutively numbered receipts from the same establishment even though his expense reports are spread out over time.

Claiming the Expenses of Others Another way that fraudsters use actual receipts to generate unwarranted reimbursements is by submitting expense reports for expenses that were paid by others. For instance, in Case 2619 an employee claimed hotel expenses that had actually been paid by his client. Photocopies of legitimate hotel bills were attached to the expense report as though the employee had paid for his own room.

As we have stated, not all companies require receipts to be attached to expense reports. Checks written by the employee or copies of his personal credit card bill might be allowed as support in lieu of a receipt. In Case 2075 a person wrote personal checks that appeared to be for business expenses, then photocopied these checks and attached them to reimbursement requests. In actuality, nothing was purchased with the checks; they were destroyed after the copies were made. This enabled the fraudster to receive a reimbursement from his employer without ever actually incurring a business expense. The same method can be used with credit cards, when a copy of a statement is used to support a purchase. Once the expense report is filed, the fraudster returns the item and receives a credit to his account.

In many expense reimbursement schemes the perpetrator is not required to submit any support at all. This makes it much easier to create the appearance of an expense that does not actually exist.

Preventing and Detecting Fictitious Expense Reimbursement Schemes A number of red flags may indicate an employee is seeking reimbursement for fictitious travel and entertainment expenses. One of the most common is the employee who claims items—particularly high-dollar items—were paid for in cash. This enables him to explain why there is no audit trail for the expense (i.e., why the item did not show up on his company credit card statement). Organizations should be alert for patterns in which an employee uses credit cards for low-dollar expenses but pays cash for high-dollar expenses. Other common red flags include the following:

- Expenses that are consistently rounded off, ending with a "0" or a "5," which tends to indicate that the employee is fabricating the numbers
- Patterns in which expenses are consistently for the same amount (e.g., a salesperson's business dinners always cost $120)

- Reimbursement requests from an employee that consistently fall at or just below the organization's reimbursement limit
- Receipts from a restaurant that are submitted over an extended period of time, yet are consecutively numbered; this tends to indicate that the employee has obtained a stack of blank receipts and is using them to support fictitious expenses
- Receipts or other support that do not look professional or lack information about the vendor such as phone numbers, physical addresses, or logos

Multiple Reimbursement Schemes

The least common of the expense reimbursement schemes as revealed in the ACFE's research is the multiple reimbursement. This type of fraud involves the submission of a single expense several times to receive multiple reimbursements. The most frequent example of a duplicate reimbursement scheme is the submission of several types of support for the same expense. An example arose in Case 89, in which an employee used, for example, an airline ticket receipt and a travel agency invoice on separate expense reports so that he could be reimbursed twice for the cost of a single flight. The fraudster had his division president authorize one report and the vice president authorize the other so that neither saw both reports. In addition, the perpetrator allowed a time lag of about a month between the filing of the two reports, so that the duplication would be less noticeable.

In cases in which a company does not require original documents as support, some employees even use several copies of the same support document to generate multiple reimbursements.

Rather than file two expense reports, employees may charge an item to the company credit card, save the receipt, and attach it to an expense report as if they paid for the item themselves. The victim company therefore ends up paying twice for the same expense.

Perhaps the most interesting case of duplicated expenses in our studies involved a government official who had responsibilities over two distinct budgets. The perpetrator of Case 83 took business trips and made expense claims to the travel funds of each of his budgets, thereby receiving a double reimbursement. In some cases the culprit charged the expenses to another budget category and still submitted reports through both budgets, generating a triple reimbursement. Eventually this person began to fabricate trips when he was not even leaving town, which led to the detection of his scheme.

Preventing and Detecting Multiple Reimbursement Schemes Organizations should enforce a policy against accepting photocopies as support for business expenses. This practice will help prevent schemes whereby copies of the same receipt are submitted several times. If photocopies are submitted, verify the expense and check it against previous requests before issuing a reimbursement. An organization's accounting system should be set up to flag duplicate payment amounts that are coded as travel and entertainment expense.

It is also important to clearly establish what types of support will be accepted with an expense report. For instance, some fraudsters use a restaurant receipt to claim reimbursement for a business dinner, then use their credit card statement to claim reimbursement for the meal a second time. If the organization accepts only original receipts, this scheme will not succeed.

Expense reports that are approved by supervisors outside the requestor's department should be carefully scrutinized, and in general organizations should require that expense reports be reviewed and approved by a direct supervisor. Employees may take an expense report to a manager from another department because they know that manager will not be familiar enough with their work schedule to spot an inconsistency on the report, or they may try to have two managers approve the same report as part of a multiple reimbursement scheme.

Some employees obtain reimbursement for a business expense, maintain a copy of the receipt, and resubmit the expense after a few weeks. Organizations should establish a policy whereby expenses must be submitted within a certain time frame. Any expenses more than 60 days old, for example, would be denied.

CASE STUDY: THE EXTRAVAGANT SALESMAN[2]

Dan Greenfield is a CFE who has been investigating fraud for over 15 years, and in that time he's developed a feel for when somebody is being dishonest with him. It's not always the same thing: some people are too defensive, some too nervous, some too angry. And then there are people like Cy Chesterly, who are just too helpful. The first time Dan Greenfield met Cy Chesterly, he quickly got the feeling that Chesterly was trying to put something over on him: "He was just way too friendly, shaking hands, slapping my back. His whole approach was very slick. I definitely got the feeling he was trying to 'sell' me."

And selling is what Cy Chesterly did best. Chesterly was the vice president in charge of sales for Stemson, Inc., one of the largest machine parts manufacturers in the upper Midwest. Greenfield, who specializes in internal investigations, had been called in by the company's new president to look into some disturbing numbers in the company's travel and entertainment expenses. The initial clues pointed to Chesterly as the most likely perpetrator. "You never go into a case trying to pin a fraud on somebody, but you usually start out with a theory of the most reasonable explanation for the losses," says Greenfield. And in this case, the evidence Greenfield had already pointed to Chesterly. "Then when you meet the guy and he's way too eager, much more than a normal person would be, that is a clue that you're on the right track."

Chesterly had been with Stemson, Inc., for over ten years, and in that time he'd helped build it into one of the most successful companies in its sector. Chesterly had the gift of the salesman; he could glad-hand and schmooze with the best of them. He had a familiar good ol' boy charm (he was originally from Texas) that drew people in. He knew every customer by name, and he knew their family members' names, too. Everyone he did business with was "Hoss"

or "Buddy," or "Sweetie" if she was a woman. It may not have been politically correct, but it won him customers, and it built Stemson, Inc.'s business. The company's founder, Charlie Stemson, considered Chesterly his top employee; he even promoted him from sales manager to vice president. Chesterly was the face of the company to all its biggest clients. He was a star.

The biggest weapon in Chesterly's sales arsenal was the company expense account. He wined and dined customers and prospects: steak dinners, golf outings, bars, strip clubs, fishing trips, expensive birthday presents, gifts for their kids, anything it took to ingratiate himself. "He built relationships with his customers, which is what a good salesman does," says Greenfield. "And he was a heck of a salesman. These people loved him. We interviewed a few customers in the course of the investigation, and they all said what a great guy he was. You send somebody's kid a birthday present, they're going to respond to that. It was a great touch."

Charlie Stemson, the company owner, knew that Chesterly was running up big expenses with his customers, and he encouraged it. The returns more than justified the investment. Chesterly kept bringing in more and more business, and over time everybody just kind of stopped paying attention to his expense account. "There were no controls on his expenses whatsoever, as far as we could tell," says Greenfield.

All of that might have gone on indefinitely, if not for a bad turn of luck: Charlie Stemson had a heart attack. He survived, but after that Stemson began looking to retire and bring someone else in to run the business. When Stemson finally found a replacement, his choice was a little shocking. Into this informally run machine parts manufacturing company stepped the new president, Stuart Rusk.

Rusk was a CPA and an MBA, a man who had worked for years in upper management for a major Midwestern wholesaler. He was straight business school, button-down shirt,

[2]Several names and details have been changed to preserve anonymity.

blue blazer, the works. He was the last person on earth who would seem to fit in at Stemson, Inc., where men like Cy Chesterly and Charlie Stemson wore jeans to work and didn't even have college degrees.

"What happened is, the company had outgrown itself," says Greenfield. "They started as a sort of mom and pop operation; they didn't have any formal business plan or structure, no controls, nothing like that. When they got big, that system didn't work for the business anymore." Stemson may have been retiring, but he wanted to make sure his company continued to grow. "He decided that they were going to have to start acting like a big-time business if they wanted to keep growing," Greenfield says. "That's why he brought in Rusk." As Charlie Stemson said, they already knew the manufacturing end of the business. They needed somebody who knew the business end of the business.

Rusk did not personally know Stemson, but he knew a friend of Stemson's, and that friend provided the connection. They met for an interview at which Rusk gave Stemson a detailed plan for the company's future; how to maximize profits, reach new markets, cut costs, the works. Stemson was sold. Within a few weeks Rusk took over Stemson, Inc.

"One of the first things he did was look at the books," says Greenfield, "and when he did, the travel and entertainment expense just jumped off the page at him. It was ridiculous." Chesterly had apparently started using his expense account for more than just entertaining customers. Entertainment expenses had been rising much faster than sales, and they were way higher than anyone could think was reasonable. Just looking at a few of the most recent company credit card statements, Rusk immediately knew he had a problem. "There was lawn furniture on one statement. Another one had a Ping Pong table," says Greenfield. "He didn't even try to hide it. He just charged the stuff to the company credit card. Nobody ever looked at it. They just sent in the check."

Rusk immediately decided to call in a fraud expert to sort everything out. That's where Greenfield entered the picture. His firm was brought in to determine how big a problem there was, and who was behind it. "Of course, everything immediately pointed to Chesterly," says Greenfield. "He was the guy making most of the sales trips, dealing with most of the customers. Plus you had the charges they'd already found on the credit card."

But proving what was going on turned out to be somewhat difficult. "There was no support of any kind on any of Chesterly's expense reports," says Greenfield. "We went back four or five years and probably didn't find ten receipts. The items on the credit cards you could track down, but he had trips, meals, car rentals, you name it, that he'd supposedly paid for in cash or charged to his own credit card. He got reimbursed for all of it." Some of the items on Chesterly's expense reports weren't even what he said they were. For

instance, on one report he claimed $600 for an airline ticket, paid for by check; it turned out to be a motorcycle he'd bought for his son.

Gradually, Greenfield and his associates began to sort through all the financial mess. When they did, the information was shocking. "He'd been abusing the system at just an amazing rate," says Greenfield. "Over the preceding four years, we found about $50,000 in expenses that were definitely fraudulent, and probably twice that much in stuff we suspected but couldn't prove." Chesterly was using the company's money to bolster his lifestyle. "Vacations, restaurants, furniture, jewelry for his wife, you name it," says Greenfield. They even found that he had charged professional escort services to the company credit card. "We don't know if that was for him or for his customers. We don't really want to know. It's fraud either way."

The investigation of Chesterly's expense account abuse eventually turned up other frauds as well. He was cutting special deals to his customers and getting kickbacks in return. "He had an enormous amount of latitude to negotiate prices, expend funds, whatever," says Greenfield. "There was very little oversight. He took advantage of it."

Eventually, Greenfield and an associate interviewed Chesterly about the fraud. By that time, they had enough documentation to prove he'd done it. But he never confessed. "He came into the room, told us what a good job we were doing, called me 'Hoss,' the whole bit," says Greenfield. "He kept going on about how much he wanted to help us. But he never said a thing. We caught him lying, we caught him contradicting himself, we showed him proof on some of the frauds. Most people, if you do that they'll confess because they know they're caught." But not Chesterly. "It didn't even faze him. He was probably the slipperiest guy I've ever interviewed. He'd just keep lying, even when it didn't make sense." Of course, the fact that Chesterly never confessed didn't mean that the interview was wasted. "When you get somebody who absolutely won't confess, you can at least still document that they're being contradictory," says Greenfield. "You document the lies and then later you use that in your case."

In the end, Greenfield documented over $200,000 in losses caused by Chesterly, "and that was just when we stopped counting. I'm sure there was more. But at that point we had enough to go to management." Chesterly was fired but the company never prosecuted. Greenfield thinks the reason is because of the change in management and the fact that some of the company's customers might have been involved in Chesterly's schemes. "They had an unstable situation at the time and I think they just didn't want to rock the boat any further. Obviously, I don't think it was the right decision. But those things are the client's call; all we can do is give them the information."

PROACTIVE COMPUTER AUDIT TESTS FOR DETECTING EXPENSE REIMBURSEMENT SCHEMES[1]

Title	Category	Description	Data file(s)
Age employee payments by check date.	All	Focuses audit efforts on periods of increased activity.	• Invoice payment
Stratify by expense payment amount.	All	Focuses audit efforts on high invoice payments.	• Invoice payment
Extract multiple charges of the same product type (using SIC code) below a predefined credit card expense limit.	All	Charges below an approval limit may be an attempt to circumvent a management review.	• Procurement card
Summarize credit card use by employee and sort from high to low.	All	High usage of credit cards by certain employees may be a sign of abuse.	• Procurement card
Extract all round-dollar payments.	All	Round-dollar payments have a higher likelihood of being fraudulent.	• Invoice payment
Extract payments to employees for expenses that were incurred during periods when the employee was on vacation.	Mischaracterized expenses	Expenses for business are rarely charged when the employee is also on vacation.	• Invoice payment • Procurement card
Extract SIC codes from credit card payments normally associated with personal purchases.	Mischaracterized expenses	Personal purchases with company cards may be a sign of abuse.	• Procurement card
Sequence possible duplicate expenses based on the absolute value of the amount and receipt date.	Multiple reimbursements	Lists possible duplicate invoices that may be used to inflate sales and associated commissions.	• Invoice payment

SUMMARY

Expense reimbursement schemes occur when employees make false claims for reimbursement of fictitious or inflated business expenses. There are four principal methods by which fraudsters attempt to generate fraudulent reimbursements from their employers. The first is to mischaracterize personal expenses—such as airfare or hotel costs—as business-related expenses. The second method is to overstate the cost of actual business expenses by altering receipts or by purchasing more than is necessary for business purposes. Employees can also seek reimbursement for fictitious expenses that were never incurred. Finally, employees may attempt to obtain multiple reimbursements for the same expense.

ESSENTIAL TERMS

Mischaracterized expense scheme An attempt to obtain reimbursement for personal expenses by claiming that they are business-related expenses.

Overstated expense reimbursements Schemes in which business-related expenses are inflated on an expense report so that the perpetrator is reimbursed for an amount greater than the actual expense.

Overpurchasing A method of overstating business expenses whereby a fraudster buys two or more business expense items (such as airline tickets) at different prices. The perpetrator returns the more expensive item for a refund, but claims reimbursement for this item. As a result, he is reimbursed for more than his actual expenses.

Fictitious expense reimbursement schemes A scheme in which an employee seeks reimbursement for wholly nonexistent items or expenses.

Multiple reimbursement schemes A scheme in which an employee seeks to obtain reimbursement more than once for a single business-related expense.

REVIEW QUESTIONS

7-1 (Learning objective 7-1) Explain what constitutes expense reimbursement fraud, and list the four categories of expense reimbursement schemes.

7-2 (Learning objective 7-3) Alpha is a salesperson for ABC Company. In July, Alpha flies to Miami for two weeks of vacation. Instead of buying a coach class ticket, he flies business class, which is more expensive. A few weeks later, Alpha prepares an expense report and includes the Miami flight on it. He lists the reason for the flight as "customer development." What category of expense reimbursement fraud has Alpha committed?

7-3 (Learning objective 7-5) Why is it important to require original receipts as support for expenses listed on a travel and entertainment expense report?

7-4 (Learning objective 7-5) What is meant by the term *overpurchasing*?

7-5 (Learning objective 7-7) Provide two examples of how an employee can commit a fictitious expense reimbursement scheme.

7-6 (Learning objective 7-9) How is a multiple reimbursement scheme committed?

7-7 (Learning objective 7-5) Beta is an auditor for ABC Company. He runs a report that extracts payments to employees for business expenses incurred on dates that do not coincide with scheduled business trips or that were incurred while the employee was on leave time. What category or categories of expense reimbursement scheme would this report most likely identify?

DISCUSSION ISSUES

7-1 (Learning objective 7-4) What internal controls can be put into place to prevent an employee from committing a mischaracterized expense scheme?

7-2 (Learning objectives 7-4, 7-6, and 7-8) In the case study "Frequent Flier's Fraud Crashes," what internal controls could have detected the fraud earlier?

7-3 (Learning objectives 7-4, 7-6, 7-8, and 7-10) Discuss how establishing travel and entertainment budgets can help an organization detect expense reimbursement fraud.

7-4 (Learning objectives 7-5 and 7-6) ABC Company has three in-house salespeople (Red, White, and Blue) who all make frequent trips to Santa Fe, New Mexico, where one of the company's largest customers is based. A manager at ABC has noticed that the average airfare expense claimed by Red for these trips is $755 round trip. The average airfare expense claimed by White is $778. The average airfare expense claimed by Blue is $1,159. What type of expense reimbursement fraud might this indicate, and what controls

would you recommend to the company to prevent this kind of scheme?

7-5 (Learning objectives 7-7 and 7-8) Baker is an auditor for ABC Company. He is reviewing the expense reports that Green, a salesperson, has submitted over the last 12 months. Baker notices that Green's expenses for "customer development dinners" consistently range between $160 and $170, and the amounts are almost always a round number. ABC Company has a policy that limits reimbursement for business dinners to $175 unless otherwise authorized. In addition, most of the expense reports show that Green paid for the meals in cash, even though he has been issued a company credit card that he usually uses for other travel and entertainment expenses. What kind of expense reimbursement scheme is Green most likely perpetrating, based on these circumstances?

7-6 (Learning objective 7-10) What internal controls would help prevent an employee from claiming an expense more than once?

ENDNOTES

1. Lanza, pp. 56–57.

Register Disbursement Schemes

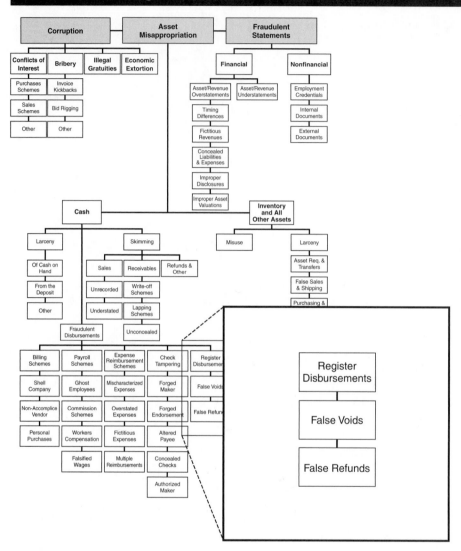

Corruption
- **Conflicts of Interest**
  - Purchases Schemes
  - Sales Schemes
  - Other
- **Bribery**
  - Invoice Kickbacks
  - Bid Rigging
  - Other
- **Illegal Gratuities**
- **Economic Extortion**

Asset Misappropriation

Fraudulent Statements
- **Financial**
  - Asset/Revenue Overstatements
    - Timing Differences
    - Fictitious Revenues
    - Concealed Liabilities & Expenses
    - Improper Disclosures
    - Improper Asset Valuations
  - Asset/Revenue Understatements
- **Nonfinancial**
  - Employment Credentials
  - Internal Documents
  - External Documents

Cash
- **Larceny**
  - Of Cash on Hand
  - From the Deposit
  - Other
- **Skimming**
  - Sales
    - Unrecorded
    - Understated
  - Receivables
    - Write-off Schemes
    - Lapping Schemes
    - Unconcealed
  - Refunds & Other
- **Fraudulent Disbursements**
  - Billing Schemes
    - Shell Company
    - Non-Accomplice Vendor
    - Personal Purchases
  - Payroll Schemes
    - Ghost Employees
    - Commission Schemes
    - Workers Compensation
    - Falsified Wages
  - Expense Reimbursement Schemes
    - Mischaracterized Expenses
    - Overstated Expenses
    - Fictitious Expenses
    - Multiple Reimbursements
  - Check Tampering
    - Forged Maker
    - Forged Endorsement
    - Altered Payee
    - Concealed Checks
    - Authorized Maker
  - Register Disbursements
    - False Voids
    - False Refunds

Inventory and All Other Assets
- **Misuse**
- **Larceny**
  - Asset Req. & Transfers
  - False Sales & Shipping
  - Purchasing &

Register Disbursements
- False Voids
- False Refunds

EXHIBIT 8-1

CHAPTER 8

REGISTER DISBURSEMENT SCHEMES

LEARNING OBJECTIVES

After studying this chapter, you should be able to:

8-1   Explain what constitutes a register disbursement scheme

8-2   Differentiate register disbursements from skimming and cash larceny schemes

8-3   List the two basic categories of register disbursements

8-4   Explain how false refund schemes are committed

8-5   Explain how false void schemes are committed

8-6   Understand how register disbursement schemes cause shrinkage

8-7   Discuss the methods by which fraudulent register disbursements are concealed

8-8   Understand the methods identified in this chapter for preventing and detecting register disbursement schemes

8-9   Be familiar with proactive audit tests that can be used to detect register disbursement schemes

CASE STUDY: DEMOTION SETS FRAUD IN MOTION[1]

Following a demotion and consequent pay cut, Bob Walker silently vowed to even the score with his employer. In six months Walker racked up $10,000 in ill-gotten cash from his employer, who was caught completely off-guard, before someone blew the whistle.

The whistleblower was Emily Schlitz, who worked weekends as a backup bookkeeper at a unit of Thrifty PayLess, a chain of 1,000 discount drugstores crossing ten Western states.

One October, while reviewing her store's refund log, Schlitz noticed an unusually large number of protocol breaches by the head cashier—one Bob Walker—who naturally handled most refunds. In issuing cash refunds for big-ticket items, for instance, Walker frequently failed to record the customer's phone number. Often, he neglected to attach sales receipts to the refund log, noting that the customers wanted to keep their receipts. Schlitz questioned the high proportion of these irregularities and notified the store manager, who in turn called the asset protection (security)

[1] Several names and details have been changed to preserve anonymity.

department at headquarters to investigate what he termed "strange entries."

Thrifty PayLess pays serious attention to such phone calls, according to its director of asset protection, James Hansen, who celebrated his thirteenth anniversary with the retailer that year. In 57 percent of the fraud cases for that year, Hansen reported, investigators received their first alert directly from store managers, as in this case.

The strange entries that Schlitz found called for immediate action. Hansen dispatched a field investigator, Raymond Willis, to review the findings and conduct a brief background check of Walker—a thirty-two-year-old single male who had been employed by Thrifty PayLess for five years.

Willis soon learned that six months earlier the store manager, citing poor performance, had demoted Walker from a management position to head cashier, which also brought a $300 a month pay cut for Walker. To Willis, that information alone raised some red flags that signal potential fraud by employees: personal or financial problems, lifestyle changes or pressures, and low morale or feelings of resentment.

Further inquiry revealed Walker blamed management for the demotion.

But those red flags paled next to the wealth of evidence Willis uncovered during his investigation. He began by calling customers listed in the refund log to politely inquire about the service they received at the drugstore, discreetly looking for verification or vilification. Next, he compared the number of refunds for food processors—by far the most popular merchandise item Walker accepted for return—to the number originally received in shipment minus those sold. These numbers were in turn compared to the food processors actually in stock. The investigator discovered major discrepancies.

Willis brought the case to a conclusion in just three days. "He stayed awake nights working on this one because he quickly saw the enormity of the take," recalled boss Hansen. "It just fueled his fire."

"The perpetrator had really gotten carried away with his activity. As will often happen, over time he got greedy. And once Walker got greedy, he got careless and sloppy," said Hansen.

Although aggressive in his investigation, Willis kept it quiet. He limited his interviews to just two or three of Walker's fellow employees. "Several coworkers had previously told managers that Walker seemed disgruntled and somewhat upset. But outwardly, his frustration never peaked enough to warrant the need for management to keep an eye on this guy," explained Hansen.

At the end of Willis's third day in the field, it was time to interview Walker. Initially, Willis asked general questions about store policies and procedures. He went on to focus more on cashiering methods. Walker seemed at ease in the beginning, helpful and responsive. At one point, Walker even offered the suggestion that "more controls should be placed on refunds."

As the interview progressed, however, Walker got more and more nervous. The smooth talker began to stutter and stammer. Willis asked Walker if he knew the definition of shrinkage. He haltingly replied, "for one, loss of cash or inventory due to customer or employee theft."

Willis then asked, "What have you personally done to cause shrinkage?" Walker became very quiet. After a long pause, he asked in a hushed tone, "Well, what if I did do it?" Willis laid out the consequences and continued to query the formerly trusted employee.

Walker vented his anger toward the managers who had "unjustly" demoted him. He confessed to writing fake cash refunds in retaliation. While the fraud began in May as an occasional act, it soon increased in frequency and flagrancy. At first, to fulfill the blanks on the customer information part of the refund log, he pulled names at random from the phone book. Later he simply made up names and phone numbers, he said. As his greed escalated, he altered legitimate refunds that he had issued earlier in the day, adding merchandise to inflate their monetary value and pocketing the difference.

Although store policy dictated that management approval was required for refunds totaling more than $25 or in the absence of a sales receipt, Walker deliberately thumbed his nose at those rules and others. No one ever questioned the signature authority of this recently defrocked member of the management team.

To further justify his actions, Walker detailed his previous financial problems, which he said were exacerbated by the $300 monthly pay cut.

Proceeds from the fraud initially went toward his two mortgage payments, which equaled $800 a month. His ongoing booty subsequently financed his insurance premiums and living expenses, which were now mounting. He easily paid off his credit cards. The single man also used the cash for fancy dinners out on the town.

During the two-hour-long confrontation, Walker claimed ignorance about the exact amount he'd filched, saying he had never tallied the score. He did admit, however, that he played this lucrative game with a growing ardor and intensity.

As it turned out, all three refunds Walker had issued the day of the interview proved fraudulent. Yet he still seemed shocked that his fraud totaled upwards of $10,000—more than five-and-a-half times the total pay cut he had endured over the past six months.

In a store that generates $4 million in annual sales, $10,000 over six months represents a small percentage of loss. In the retailing industry, such shrinkage may be explained away by shoplifting, bad checks, accounting or paperwork errors, breakage or spoilage, shipping shortages, or numerous other reasons. Employee theft, of course, is also a significant factor in shrinkage, said Hansen, who began his career as a store detective.

"In my mind, a comprehensive loss prevention program is well balanced between preventive and investigative efforts." He said Thrifty PayLess maintains an outstanding educational program for all employees. They attend mandated training classes in both the prevention and detection of fraud. Crucial to the success of the antifraud program, employees are always made to feel like an integral part of Thrifty PayLess's whole loss prevention effort. Hansen and his asset protection staff regularly visit the stores to introduce themselves, become familiar to employees, form and maintain rapport, and build a level of trust in confidentiality. To further encourage communication, the retailer established a hotline that employees can call with anonymous tips about suspected fraud or abuse.

As evidenced by the part-time bookkeeper's suspicions and subsequent actions in this case, Thrifty PayLess's efforts obviously work, said the head of security. "It's not that our controls were in any way inadequate; it's that a local manager was not properly enforcing those controls. Generally, he got lax with a 'trusted' employee." (Needless to say, the store manager suffered some repercussions as a result of this case.)

As a result of the Walker experience, manager approval is now required for all refunds over $5. A sales receipt must also accompany all refunds, said Hansen. Thrifty PayLess's internal audit and asset protection departments perform audits regularly, checking for compliance.

"Proper implementation is the key." Hansen continued, "You cannot prevent fraud 100 percent. The best you can do is to limit it through your proactive educational, awareness, and audit programs. Of course, aggressively investigating all red flags or tips as well." Hansen's asset protection department concludes over 1,400 employee theft and fraud cases and 30,000 customer shoplifting cases annually.

Owing to the grand scale of theft in this case, Walker was arrested immediately after his interview, booked on felony charges of embezzlement, and held pending bail. He faced criminal and civil prosecution. Walker made bail within hours, then disappeared without a trace. All investigative efforts to locate him thus far have failed.

To this day Bob Walker remains a fugitive of justice.

OVERVIEW

We have so far discussed two ways in which fraud is committed at the cash register—skimming and cash larceny. These schemes are what we commonly think of as outright theft. They involve the surreptitious removal of money from a cash register. When money is taken from a register in a skimming or larceny scheme, there is no record of the transaction—the money is simply missing.

In this chapter we will discuss fraudulent disbursements at the cash register. These schemes differ from the other register frauds in that when money is taken from the cash register, the removal of money is recorded on the register tape. A false transaction is recorded as though it were a legitimate disbursement to justify the removal of money. Bob Walker's fraudulent refunds were an example of such a false transaction.

Register Disbursement Data from the ACFE
2009 Global Fraud Survey

Register disbursements were reported less frequently than any other fraudulent disbursement scheme in the 2009 survey; they accounted for 6 percent of the reported fraudulent disbursements. It should be remembered, however, that the survey only asked respondents to report one case they had investigated; it was not designed to measure the overall frequency of various types of schemes within a particular organization. Thus, the low response rate for register disbursements does not necessarily reflect how often these schemes occur. Furthermore, the type of fraud that occurs within an organization is, to some extent, determined by the nature of business the organization conducts. For example, register disbursement schemes would tend to be much more common in a large retail store that employs several cash register clerks than in a law firm, where a cash register would not even be present. Readers should keep in mind that the frequency statistics presented in this book only represent the frequency of cases that were reported by the survey respondents (see Exhibit 8-2).

In addition to being the least frequently reported type of fraudulent disbursement, register disbursements were the least costly, with a median loss of $23,000. The typical register disbursement scheme in the survey caused about one-sixth the losses of the typical check tampering scheme (see Exhibit 8-3).

REGISTER DISBURSEMENT SCHEMES

Two basic fraudulent disbursement schemes take place at the cash register: *false refunds* and *false voids*. Although these schemes are largely similar, a few differences between the two merit discussing them separately.

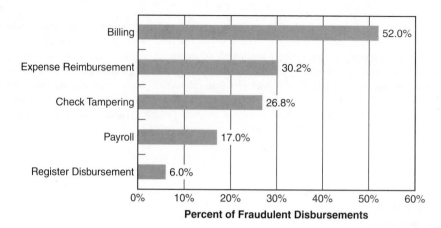

EXHIBIT 8-2 *2009 Global Fraud Survey:* Frequency of Fraudulent Disbursements[a]

[a]The sum of these percentages exceeds 100 percent because some cases involved multiple fraud schemes that fell into more than one category

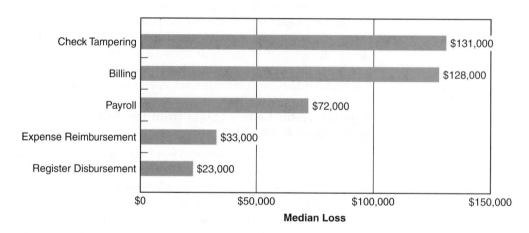

EXHIBIT 8-3 *2009 Global Fraud Survey:* Median Loss of Fraudulent Disbursements

False Refunds

A refund is processed at the register when a customer returns an item of merchandise purchased from that store. The transaction that is entered on the register indicates that the merchandise is being replaced in the store's inventory, and that the purchase price is being returned to the customer. In other words, a refund shows a disbursement of money from the register as the customer gets his money back (see Exhibit 8-4).

Fictitious Refunds In a fictitious refund scheme, a fraudster processes a transaction as if a customer were returning merchandise, even though no actual return takes place. Two things result from this fraudulent transaction, First, the fraudster takes cash from the register in the amount of the false return. Since the register tape shows that a merchandise return has been made, the disbursement appears legitimate. The register tape balances with the amount of money in the register, because the money that was taken by the fraudster is supposed to have been removed, given to a customer as a refund. These kinds of

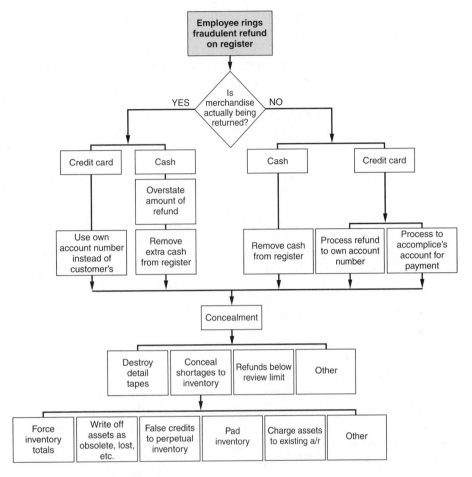

EXHIBIT 8-4   False Refunds

fraudulent transactions were used by Bob Walker in the case study at the beginning of this chapter.

As we also saw in that case study, the second thing that happens in a fictitious refund scheme is that a debit is made to the inventory system showing that the merchandise has been returned to the inventory. Because the transaction is fictitious, no merchandise is actually returned. As a result, the company's inventory is overstated. For instance, in Case 1583, a manager created $5,500 worth of false returns, resulting in a large shortage in the company's inventory. He was able to carry on his scheme for several months, however, because (1) inventory was not counted regularly, and (2) the perpetrator, a manager, was one of the people who performed inventory counts.

Overstated Refunds   Rather than create an entirely fictitious refund, some fraudsters merely overstate the amount of a legitimate refund and steal the excess money. This occurred in Case 1875, in which an employee sought to supplement his income by processing fraudulent refunds. In some cases he rang up completely fictitious refunds, making up names and phone numbers for his customers. In other instances he added to the value of legitimate refunds, overstating the value of a real customer's refund, paying the customer the actual amount owed for the returned merchandise, and keeping the excess portion of the return for himself.

Credit Card Refunds When purchases are made with a credit card rather than cash, refunds appear as credits to the customer's credit card rather than as cash disbursements. Some fraudsters process false refunds on credit card sales in lieu of processing a normal cash transaction. One benefit of the credit card method is that the perpetrator does not have to physically take cash from the register and carry it out of the store, the most dangerous part of a typical register scheme (since managers, coworkers, or security cameras may detect the culprit in the process of removing the cash). By processing the refunds to a credit card account, a fraudster reaps an unwarranted financial gain and avoids the potential embarrassment of being caught red-handed taking cash.

In a typical credit card refund scheme, the fraudster rings up a refund on a credit card sale, though the merchandise is not actually being returned. Rather than use the customer's credit card number on the refund, the employee inserts his own. As a result, the cost of the item is credited to the perpetrator's credit card account.

A more creative and wide-ranging application of the credit card refund scheme was used by Joe Anderson in the following case study. Anderson processed merchandise refunds to the accounts of other people, and in return received a portion of the refund as a kickback. CFE Russ Rooker discovered Anderson's scheme, which cost Greene's department store at least $150,000. This case is also a bribery scheme, because Anderson took illicit payments in exchange for creating fraudulent transactions. It serves as an excellent example of how the cash register can be used as a tool for theft.

CASE STUDY: A SILENT CRIME[2]

"A silent crime"—that's the way Russ Rooker refers to the theft he uncovered at a Detroit-area Greene's department store. "It takes only about 30 seconds, and you can have a thousand bucks," explains the regional investigation specialist.

Joe Anderson, a 15-hour-a-week employee in that store's shoe department, was an expert at that silent crime—ringing up fictitious returns and crediting credit cards for the cash.

During his five-year tenure with the store, Anderson did this time and time again. Rooker documented at least $150,000 in losses, but believes it was closer to $500,000, and wouldn't be surprised if the fraud exceeded $1 million. "We're scared to even know," he says.

This was a scam that was right up Rooker's analytical alley. At the time of the investigation, he had worked in retail security for about a decade—first as a credit fraud investigator checking the external, or customer, side of credit card fraud. Then he went into internal investigation, searching out employee theft and fraud.

At Greene's store, records showed that the store's shoe department was losing money because it had an exceedingly high rate of returns on its shoes. Rooker decided to investigate by using his "FTM" formula—Follow the Money.

He ordered up five months of sales data for the department from ten sales terminals. Rooker had returns divided into categories of cash, proprietary credit cards (i.e., Greene's cards), and third-party credit cards such as Visa and MasterCard.

And he saw a trend. Around the twenty-eighth of each month, certain credit card numbers would be credited for a return of approximately $300. "Two hundred ninety-seven dollars and sixty cents to be exact," says Rooker. There was never a corresponding sale recorded for the returns. And each month, each credit card number was credited only once—thus, if Rooker had chosen to study only one month's data, the crime would not have been discovered.

He eventually found that one part-time employee, Joe Anderson, was crediting more than 200 credit cards belonging to 110 persons. Each week, Anderson credited $2,000 to $3,000 in returns to his friends', neighbors', and relatives' accounts. In return, Anderson was paid up to 50 percent of the credit. For instance, if a friend was running $300 short at the end of the month and still needed to make his house payment, he'd phone Anderson. According to Rooker, the word around Detroit was if you needed money, "Call Joe. Give him $150 and he'll double your money."

The friend might contact Anderson at the home he shared with his girlfriend, or he might meet Anderson at the local bar or in the back of his souped-up van. Or he might simply text him a credit card number.

[2]Several names and details have been changed to preserve anonymity.

Either way, the friend gave Anderson his credit card number and promised to pay him $150 for the money. Then, Anderson, in thirty-second increments at the cash register, punched in the credit. Next, just as rapidly, he'd phone the friend and tell him the deal was done. Finally, the friend would go to the nearest ATM, swipe through his credit card, and—knowing that he had a $300 credit to his account—get $300 in cash.

"So it was basically turning the money right into cash," says Rooker. "You can see the drug connection here." Yet a drug connection was never actually proven. What was proven, to quote Rooker, was that a man who "worked fifteen hours a week at Greene's was living the high life. He dressed like a million bucks. He ate at fancy restaurants." And he wore lots of gold jewelry—and drove a "fully decked out" conversion van.

The majority of his "customers" looked as though they lived an upper-middle-class life, too, but appearances can be deceiving. Most of them were in the lower-income bracket—Anderson had helped them move up. Sometimes he gave them a $300 pair of shoes to go along with their $300 credit; that way, they could go to another Greene's location, return the shoes, and get an additional $300. One customer was credited $30,000 in one year, says Rooker.

One regular customer was Anderson's girlfriend, who owned the house in which the two lived. And, although she worked as a branch manager for a major bank in Detroit, she was not prosecuted; the Secret Service and the U.S. Attorney, whom Rooker called into the investigation upon his discovery of the perpetrator, decided who was prosecuted.

Anderson was well known by many; he had friends and acquaintances just about everywhere. The fifteen-hour-a-week employee with the big, illegal income was a mover and shaker of sorts. Rooker thinks that was part of Anderson's motive—Anderson hung out with the upper-middle class and was well accepted in their stratum. He wanted to stay in that social group, but the only way he could find to do that was to commit fraud.

Rooker also believes that Anderson simply got "caught up in it" because people came to expect the fraud of him. In fact, they came directly into the store and asked for Anderson: only he could wait on them. Those people were often the ones to whom he gave a pair of shoes as well.

The Secret Service told Rooker that if he would document a minimum of $10,000 in returns via video surveillance, they would go from there. So Rooker had video surveillance equipment installed throughout the shoe department, and at the point-of-sale registers. The first day the equipment was up and running, Anderson was up and running as well; he credited $5,000 that day.

According to Rooker, Anderson simply reached into the inside pocket of his expensive suit jacket, pulled out a list, and started ringing up credits. One day, he gave a single customer a $300 cash refund, a $300 credit refund, and a $300 pair of shoes.

This wreaked havoc on Greene's inventory. Let's say the store's inventory reports showed that there were ten pairs of style 8730 in stock. But then along came Anderson, ringing up a return for style 8730. Suddenly the inventory reports showed eleven pairs of style 8730 in stock, even though there were still only the original ten pairs.

Five thousand dollars of returns in one day caused inventory to be overstated by approximately seventeen pairs of shoes. Seventeen pairs of shoes, five workdays a week, 4.3 weeks per month—and Greene's had a lot of invisible shoes in stock.

Six weeks after the start of in-store surveillance, $30,000 in losses was recorded on videotape—put another way, that's 100 pairs of non-existent shoes that were falsely reported as in-stock.

Most of those losses were documented at the end of each month, because by then, Anderson's customers were in a typical end-of-the-month money crunch. "They came to really depend on this money," explains Rooker.

The certified fraud examiner next started matching customers to credit card numbers. That was easy to do with the Greene's cards, but it was a slightly harder task for the third-party cards, which were responsible for the majority of the returns.

By working his professional connections, Rooker was able to contact fraud investigators at various banks to find out informally "what was going on" from the banks' perspectives. That's how he learned that some of Anderson's customers were Anderson's friends and relatives.

Ironically, the part-time employee never carried a credit card. He was a cash customer only. His only known asset was his conversion van. The house he shared with his girlfriend was held in her name.

The Secret Service put Anderson under surveillance. Over two weeks, they discovered how he was making his contacts. All day long, friends, relatives, and neighbors streamed in and out of the home he shared with his banker girlfriend. In essence, his fifteen-hour-a-week job demanded more than fifteen hours a week. And often the same people who were observed going into his home received credits that same day.

Anderson had apparently started his "side" job as a bit of a lark and charged only 10 percent of the fictitious refund as his fee. As the scam and his renown grew, he upped his percentage to 25, then 50 percent. Everyone in town, everyone in his shoe department knew he was doing something fishy, reports Rooker, but they were scared to report him. Anderson allegedly carried a gun. And though many liked Anderson, many also feared him.

But that did not deter Rooker and the Secret Service. "The Secret Service was very aggressive," says Rooker.

They promised to pursue any co-conspirator who had earned at least $5,000 in returns over two years. That led them to Ohio, where they interviewed a middle-aged couple.

(Most of Anderson's customers were between the ages of 30 and 50.)

This couple had once lived in the Detroit area. After getting the couple to turn state's evidence (as the Secret Service did with numerous co-conspirators during this investigation), the law enforcement officers learned Anderson's entire scam.

Soon thereafter, four armed U.S. Secret Service agents entered the store, grabbed Anderson, pulled him through the stock room, and arrested him. When confronted with the crime, Anderson told the agents and Rooker, "Pound sand." He had $5,000 in cash stuffed into his socks. In his coat pocket, he had a list of fifteen third-party credit card numbers with dollar amounts to credit.

Having those fifteen numbers on his person, says Rooker, was enough to charge the perpetrator. Eventually, though, Rooker learned that $60,000 in refunds had been credited to those fifteen numbers over the previous two years.

Anderson was led through the mall, in handcuffs, by the Secret Service. As he exited, mall store manager after store manager stood at their doors and yelled, "Hey, Joe, what's going on?"

They were worried. They were losing one of their best cash customers.

Local and federal charges for embezzlement and financial transaction card fraud against Anderson and twenty-seven conspirators are pending.

Not pending are new internal controls at Greene's. Rooker implemented them immediately. Over time, another fifty to sixty employees were determined to be pulling off the same scam, at losses of $10,000 to $30,000 to Greene's. The only difference was that these employees were crediting their own charge cards; Anderson only credited other people's charge cards, silently, in thirty-second increments.

False Voids

False voids are similar to refund schemes in that they generate a disbursement from the register. When a sale is voided on a register, a copy of the customer's receipt is usually attached to a void slip, along with the signature or initials of a manager that indicate that the transaction has been approved (see Exhibit 8-5). In order to process a false void, then, the first thing the fraudster needs is the customer's copy of the sales receipt. Typically, when an employee sets about processing a fictitious void, or she simply withholds the customer's receipt at the time of the sale. If the customer requests the receipt, the clerk can produce it, but in many cases customers simply do not notice that they didn't receive a receipt.

With the customer copy of the receipt in hand, the culprit rings a voided sale. Whatever money the customer paid for the item is removed from the register as though it were being returned to a customer. The copy of the customer's receipt is attached to the void slip to verify the authenticity of the transaction.

Before the voided sale will be perceived as valid, a manager generally must approve it. In many of the cases in the ACFE studies, the manager in question simply neglected to verify the authenticity of the voided sale. Such managers signed essentially anything presented to them, thus leaving themselves vulnerable to a voided sales scheme. An example of this kind of managerial nonchalance occurred in Case 1753. In this case a retail clerk kept customer receipts and "voided" their sales after the customers left the store; the store manager signed the void slips on these transactions without taking any action to verify their authenticity. A similar breakdown in review was detected in Case 1787, where an employee processed fraudulent voids, kept customer receipts, and presented them to her supervisors for review at the end of her shift, long after the alleged transactions had taken place. Her supervisors approved the voided sales, and the accounts receivable department failed to notice the excessive number of voided sales processed by this employee.

It was not a coincidence that the perpetrators of these crimes presented their void slips to a manager who happened to be lackadaisical about authorizing them. Generally, such managers are essential to the employee's schemes.

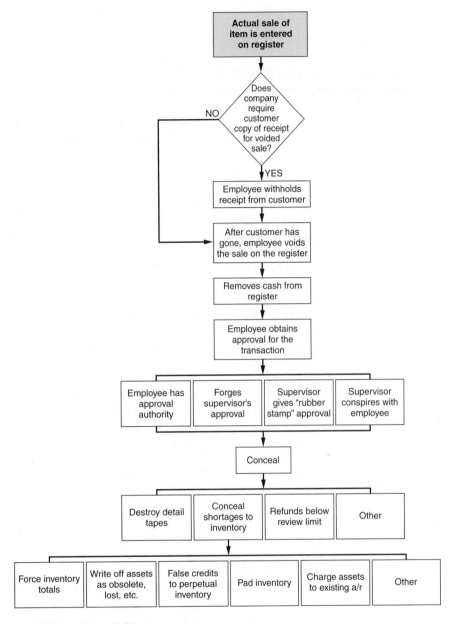

EXHIBIT 8-5 False Voids

Because not all managers are willing to provide rubber-stamp approval of voided sales, some employees take affirmative steps to get their voided sales "approved." This usually amounts to forgery, as in Case 1753 (previously noted), whereby the fraudster eventually began forging his supervisor's signature as the employee's false voids became more and more frequent.

Finally, it is possible that a manager will conspire with a register employee and approve false voids in return for a share of the proceeds. Although ACFE researchers did not encounter any cases like this in their studies, they did come across several examples of managers helping employees to falsify timecards or expense reimbursement requests. There is no reason why the same kind of scheme would not also work with false voids.

CONCEALING REGISTER DISBURSEMENTS

As we discussed above, when a false refund or void is entered into the register, two things happen. First, the employee who is committing the fraud removes cash from the register; second, the item allegedly being returned is debited back into inventory. This leads to shrinkage: a situation in which there is less inventory actually on hand than the inventory records reflect. A certain amount of shrinkage is expected in any retail industry, but too much of it raises concerns of fraud.

Remember: inventory is accounted for by a two-step process. The first part of the process is the perpetual inventory, which is essentially a running tabulation of how much inventory *should be on hand*. When a sale of merchandise is made, the perpetual inventory is credited to remove this merchandise from the records; the amount of merchandise that should be on hand is reduced. Periodically, someone from the company takes a physical count of the inventory, going through the stockroom or warehouse and counting the amount of inventory that *is actually on hand*. The two figures are then compared to see if there is a discrepancy between the perpetual inventory (what should be on hand) and the physical inventory (what is on hand). When a fraudulent refund or void has been recorded, the amount of inventory that is actually on hand will be less than the amount that should be on hand.

Typically, fraudsters do not make any effort to conceal the shrinkage that results from their schemes. In many register disbursement cases, the amount of shrinkage is not large enough to raise a red flag, but in large-scale cases the amount of shrinkage caused by a fraudster can be quite significant. For example, in the previous case study, Joe Anderson, a part-time employee, rang up $150,000 in documented fictitious returns in a scheme that had a significant effect on the victim company's inventory. An excessive number of reversing transactions, combined with increased levels of shrinkage, would generally be considered a strong indicator of register disbursement fraud. For a discussion of how fraudsters attempt to conceal shrinkage, please see Chapter 9.

Aside from shrinkage, a register disbursement scheme leaves the victim organization's books in balance. The whole purpose of recording a fraudulent refund or void, after all, is to account for the stolen funds, and to justify their removal from the cash drawer. Therefore, fraudsters often take no further steps to conceal a register disbursement scheme. However, a register disbursement scheme can still be detected if someone notices abnormal levels of refunds or voids. There are two methods that fraudsters often use to avoid this form of detection.

Small Disbursements

One common concealment technique is to keep the sizes of the disbursements low. Many companies set limits below which management review of a refund is not required. When this is the case, fraudsters simply process copious numbers of refunds that are small enough that they need not be reviewed. In Case 791, for example, an employee created over 1,000 false refunds, all under the review limit of $15. He was eventually caught because he began processing refunds before store hours; another employee noticed that refunds were appearing on the system before the store opened. Nevertheless, before his scheme was detected, the employee made off with over $11,000 of his employer's money.

Destroying Records

One final means of concealing a register scheme, as with many kinds of fraud, is to destroy all records of the transaction. Most concealment methods are concerned with keeping management from realizing that fraud has occurred. When an employee resorts to destroying records, however, he typically has conceded that management will discover his theft. The purpose of destroying records is usually to prevent management from determining who the thief is. In Case 2728, for example, a woman was creating false inventory vouchers that were reflected on the register tape. She then discarded all refund vouchers, both legitimate and fraudulent. Because documentation was missing on all transactions, it was extremely difficult to distinguish the good from the bad. Thus, it was hard to determine who was stealing.

PREVENTING AND DETECTING REGISTER DISBURSEMENT SCHEMES

The best way for organizations to prevent fraudulent register disbursements is to always maintain appropriate separation of duties. Management approval should be required for all refunds and voided sales in order to prevent a rogue employee from generating fraudulent disbursements at his cash register. Access to the control key or management code that authorizes reversing transactions should be closely guarded, and cashiers should not be allowed to reverse their own sales.

In addition to management review, voided transactions should be properly documented. Require a copy of the customer's receipt from the initial purchase, which should be attached to a copy of a void slip or other documentation of the transaction. This documentation should be retained on file.

Every cashier or sales clerk should be required to maintain a distinct login code for work at the register, allowing voids and refunds to be traced back to the employee who processed them. Periodically, organizations should generate reports of all reversing transactions at the register, looking for employees who tend to process an inordinate number of these transactions. Recurring transaction amounts, particularly in round numbers such as $50, $100, and so on, are also common indicators of register disbursement fraud.

If the organization requires management approval only for voids and refunds above a certain amount, look for large numbers of transactions just below this amount. For instance, if the minimum review amount is $20, fraudsters may process multiple refunds for $19 in order to avoid review.

One way to help deter register disbursements is to place signs or institute store policies encouraging customers to ask for and examine their receipts. For example, offer a discount to any customer who does not receive a receipt. This will prevent employees from retaining customer receipts to use as support for false voids or refunds.

Random customer service calls can also be made to customers who have returned merchandise or voided sales as a way of verifying that these transactions actually took place. This type of verification is effective only if the persons who make the customer service calls are independent of the cash receipts function.

PROACTIVE COMPUTER AUDIT TESTS FOR DETECTING REGISTER DISBURSEMENT SCHEMES[1]

Title	Category	Description	Data file(s)
Summarize by location refunds and voids charged.	All	Locations with high adjustments may signal actions to hide register disbursement schemes.	• Sales system register
Summarize by employee refunds and voids charged.	All	Employees with high adjustments may signal actions to hide register disbursement schemes.	• Sales system register
List top 100 employees by dollar size (once for refunds and once for sale voids).	All	Employees with high adjustments may signal actions to hide register disbursement schemes.	• Sales system register
List top 100 employees who have been on the top 100 list for three months (once for refunds and once for sale voids).	All	Employees with high adjustments may signal actions to hide register disbursement schemes.	• Sales system register
List top 10 locations that have been on the top 10 list for three months (once for discounts and once for sale voids).	All	Locations with high adjustments may signal actions to hide register disbursement schemes.	• Sales system register
Compute standard deviation for each employee for the last three months and list those employees that provided three times the standard deviation in the current month (once for discounts and once for sale voids).	All	Employees with high adjustments may signal actions to hide cash larceny schemes.	• Sales system register
Compare adjustments to inventory to the void/refund transactions summarized by employee.	All	First, a summary of adjustments by inventory number (SKN number) and employee is completed, which is then compared to credit adjustments (to inappropriately decrease inventory that was supposedly returned) by inventory number.	• Sales system register • Inventory detail register
Extract users who can enter and approve void and refund transactions.	All	Users who can enter the void/refund and subsequently approve it have a nonsegregation of duties that gives an opportunity for fraud.	• Sales system user access master file • Sales system user access log file
Extract users who can post refunds and voids as well as inventory adjustments.	All	Users who can enter the void/refund and subsequently conceal the misappropriation through adjustments to the inventory system have a nonsegregation of duties that gives an opportunity for fraud. User access should be reviewed from the perspective of adjustments within the application and adjustments to the data itself.	• Sales system user access master file • Inventory system user access master file • Sales system user access log file • Inventory system user access log file

Compare customer sales and refunds within the same day.	All	Although possible, it is improbable that a customer would return a product in the same day. Such refund transactions may be fraudulently invoked.	• Sales system register
Compare customer sales posted to one card but with refunds posted to another card.	Credit card refunds	A common fraud is to have a customer make a purchase of a product and then fraudulently charge the refund to a fraud perpetrator or accomplice's credit card.	• Sales system register

SUMMARY

Two basic types of fraudulent disbursement schemes take place at the cash register: *false refunds* and *false voids*. In a false refund scheme, an employee fraudulently records a return of merchandise and a corresponding disbursement of cash from his register. The false transaction accounts for the theft of cash and keeps the register in balance, because the amount of money stolen is equal to the amount of the fraudulent disbursement. Typically, false refund schemes involve wholly fictitious transactions, though in some cases an actual refund will be overstated and the perpetrator will steal the excess amount. Although most false refund schemes involve the fraudulent disbursement of cash from the register, in some cases perpetrators run a bogus refund to a credit card account, whether their own or an accomplice's.

False voids are similar to false refunds. They occur when a perpetrator uses a confiscated customer sales slip to void a sale. The scheme is consummated when the employee takes cash from the register in an amount equaling the amount on the sales slip.

In many cases, there is no effort made to conceal register disbursements, because the fraudulent transaction is designed to account for the stolen funds and the cash register remains in balance after the theft. But it may still be necessary to conceal the fact that an inordinate number of reversing transactions have been processed. To accomplish this, fraudsters typically either process fraudulent voids or refunds in small amounts that fall below review limits, or destroy records of the fraudulent transactions.

ESSENTIAL TERMS

False refund scheme One of two main categories of register disbursements, in which a fraudulent refund is processed at the cash register to account for stolen cash.

Fictitious refund scheme A false refund scheme in which an employee processes a fake refund transaction as if a customer were actually returning merchandise and pockets the cash instead.

Overstated refund scheme A false refund scheme in which an employee overstates the amount of a legitimate customer refund, then gives the customer the actual amount of the refund and steals the excess.

False void scheme One of two main categories of register disbursements. A scheme in which an employee accounts for stolen cash by voiding a previously recorded sale.

REVIEW QUESTIONS

8-1 (Learning objective 8-1) What is a register disbursement scheme?

8-2 (Learning objective 8-2) How do register disbursement schemes differ from skimming and cash larceny, both of which frequently involve thefts of cash from cash registers?

8-3 (Learning objective 8-3) What are the two main categories of register disbursement schemes?

8-4 (Learning objective 8-4) What is the difference between a fictitious refund scheme and an overstated refund scheme?

8-5 (Learning objective 8-5) How are fraudulent void schemes used to generate a disbursement from a cash register?

8-6 (Learning objective 8-6) How do register disbursement schemes cause shrinkage?

8-7 (Learning objective 8-7) How can the processing of low-dollar refunds help a fraudster conceal a register disbursement scheme?

8-8 (Learning objective 8-8) Why is it important for all cashiers to maintain distinct login codes for work at the cash register?

DISCUSSION ISSUES

8-1 (Learning objective 8-4) In the case study involving Bob Walker at the beginning of this chapter, what type of register disbursement schemes did he commit? Discuss the role his recent demotion played in the scheme.

8-2 (Learning objective 8-2) In the *2009 Global Fraud Survey*, register disbursements were reported far less frequently than any other fraudulent disbursement scheme. Discuss some reasons why this result might not reflect the true frequency of register disbursements.

8-3 (Learning objectives 8-8 and 8-9) What are some tests that can help detect fictitious refund schemes that involve the overstatement of inventories?

8-4 (Learning objective 8-4) In the "silent crime" case study mentioned in the chapter, how did Joe Anderson involve other individuals in his credit card refund scheme?

8-5 (Learning objectives 8-8 and 8-9) Explain how each of the following three conditions could be a red flag for a register disbursement scheme.

1. Able, a cash register teller, is authorized to approve sales refunds; he is also authorized to make inventory adjustments.

2. Baker, a cashier, processed fifteen refunds in the last week. No other cashier processed more than five during that same period. Each of the transactions was for between $13.50 and $14.99.

3. Over 70 percent of the refunds processed by Chase, a cash register clerk, were run on the same date as the original sale.

ENDNOTES

1. Lanza, pp. 61–62.

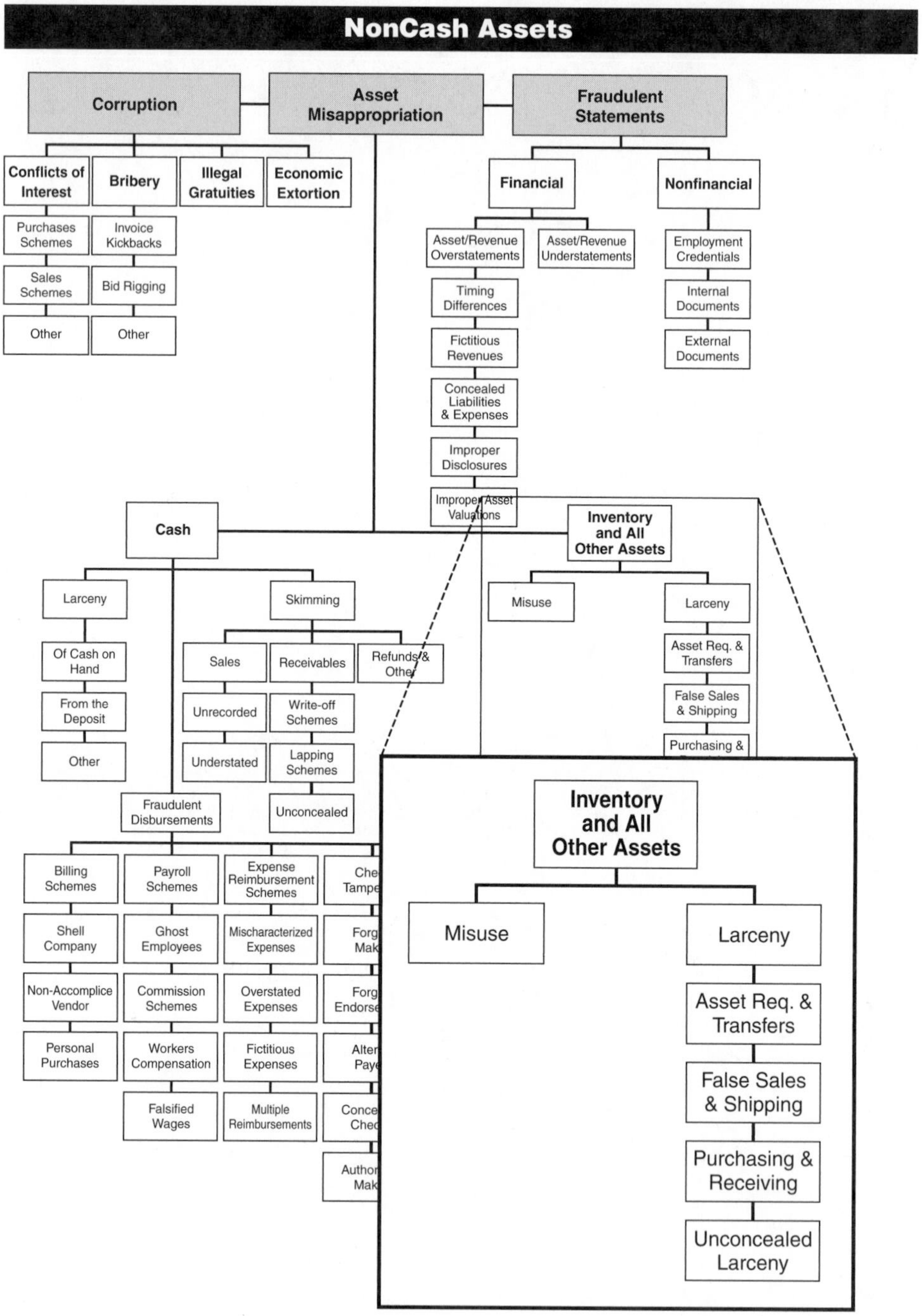

NonCash Assets

Corruption

- **Conflicts of Interest**
  - Purchases Schemes
  - Sales Schemes
  - Other
- **Bribery**
  - Invoice Kickbacks
  - Bid Rigging
  - Other
- **Illegal Gratuities**
- **Economic Extortion**

Asset Misappropriation

Cash

- **Larceny**
  - Of Cash on Hand
  - From the Deposit
  - Other
- **Skimming**
  - Sales
    - Unrecorded
    - Understated
  - Receivables
    - Write-off Schemes
    - Lapping Schemes
    - Unconcealed
  - Refunds & Other
- **Fraudulent Disbursements**
  - Billing Schemes
    - Shell Company
    - Non-Accomplice Vendor
    - Personal Purchases
  - Payroll Schemes
    - Ghost Employees
    - Commission Schemes
    - Workers Compensation
    - Falsified Wages
  - Expense Reimbursement Schemes
    - Mischaracterized Expenses
    - Overstated Expenses
    - Fictitious Expenses
    - Multiple Reimbursements
  - Check Tampering
    - Forged Maker
    - Forged Endorsement
    - Altered Payee
    - Concealed Check
    - Authorized Maker

Inventory and All Other Assets

- **Misuse**
- **Larceny**
  - Asset Req. & Transfers
  - False Sales & Shipping
  - Purchasing & Receiving

Fraudulent Statements

- **Financial**
  - Asset/Revenue Overstatements
    - Timing Differences
    - Fictitious Revenues
    - Concealed Liabilities & Expenses
    - Improper Disclosures
    - Improper Asset Valuations
  - Asset/Revenue Understatements
- **Nonfinancial**
  - Employment Credentials
  - Internal Documents
  - External Documents

Inventory and All Other Assets

- **Misuse**
- **Larceny**
  - Asset Req. & Transfers
  - False Sales & Shipping
  - Purchasing & Receiving
  - Unconcealed Larceny

EXHIBIT 9-1

NONCASH ASSETS

LEARNING OBJECTIVES

After studying this chapter, you should be able to

9-1 List the five categories of tangible noncash misappropriations discussed in this chapter

9-2 Discuss the data on noncash misappropriations from the *2009 Global Fraud Survey*

9-3 Explain how misuse of noncash assets can negatively affect organizations

9-4 Understand how and why unconcealed larceny of noncash assets occurs

9-5 Be familiar with internal controls and tests that can be used to prevent and detect noncash larceny

9-6 Understand how weaknesses in internal asset requisition and transfer procedures can lead to the misappropriation of noncash assets

9-7 Explain how purchasing and receiving schemes are used to misappropriate noncash assets

9-8 Understand how the theft of noncash assets through the use of fraudulent shipments is accomplished

9-9 Define shrinkage

9-10 Describe how fraudsters conceal the theft of noncash assets on the victim organization's books

9-11 Understand how employees can misappropriate intangible assets, as well as how companies can protect themselves from such schemes

9-12 Be familiar with proactive audit tests that can be used to detect misappropriations of noncash assets

CASE STUDY: CHIPPING AWAY AT HIGH-TECH THEFT[1]

Nineteen-year-old Larry Gunter didn't know much about computers, but he worked as a shipping clerk in a computer manufacturer's warehouse. Like many other companies in Silicon Valley, this company produced thousands of miniature electronic circuits—microprocessor chips—the building block of personal computers.

Gunter didn't work in the plant's "clean room" building, where the chips were manufactured. The company moved the

[1]Several names and details have been changed to preserve anonymity.

chips, along with other computer components, next door to the warehouse for processing and inventory.

On the open market, one of these computer chips, which is comprised of hundreds of millions of transistors packed into a space no bigger than a fingernail, is worth about $40. Over 1,000 chips were packaged in plastic storage tubes inside a company-marked cardboard box.

Gunter knew they were worth something, but he didn't know how much. One day, he took a chip from a barrel in the warehouse and gave it to his girlfriend's father, Grant Thurman, whom he knew operated some type of computer salvage business. He told Thurman that the company had discarded the chip as "scrap."

"I asked him if he knew anyone who would buy scrap chips," Gunter said, and Thurman said he did. "So after about another week or two I stole three boxes of computer chips and brought them to Grant to sell them to his computer guy. Around a week later I got paid by Grant Thurman in the amount of $5,000 in a personal check."

Gunter knew the chips were not scrap, since the boxes, each about the size of a shoebox, bore the marking "SIMMS," signifying that the chips were sound. In fact, the manufacturer maintained a standard procedure for scrap chips, taking them to another warehouse on the company's grounds and sealing the components for shipment to another plant for destruction.

Gunter concealed the boxes from the security guards by placing them on the bottom of his work cart, with empty boxes on top. He pushed the cart out of the warehouse as if he were just taking empty boxes to the trash. Once in the parking lot, where there were no security guards, he loaded the three boxes of chips into his truck.

Shortly after the theft, an inventory manager filling an order noticed that many company chips were missing and immediately went to his supervisor, the warehouse manager. The manager verified that they were missing about ten cartons of chips, worth over $30,000. They contacted the company's director of operations, who accelerated the product inventory process at the plant. Instead of taking product inventory once a month, he began taking it once a week.

Gunter still found it easy to steal, he said, because the security guards didn't pay much attention and because it was easy to evade the stationary surveillance cameras in the warehouse. About two weeks after his first theft, he stole four boxes of new chips, for which Thurman paid him $10,000. Excited about his new conquest, Gunter told his young friend and coworker, Larry Spelber, about the easy profit to be made. The two could split $50,000 from a theft of six boxes of chips, he told Spelber—enough to quit work and finance their schooling.

By this time, however, the company had detected the second loss and contacted private investigator and fraud examiner Lee Roberts. Roberts, head of Roberts Protection & Investigations, had worked with the company's attorney before.

"They knew exactly how much of their product they were missing," Roberts said, "because no product was supposed to leave the building unless they had the paper for loading it on the truck to fill a specific order. However, there was a flaw in the system. The company's operation was separated in two buildings, about 300 feet apart... They would receive an extremely valuable product, and it would go from one building to the other simply by being pushed by employees with carts through this 300-foot parking lot. Consequently, they would end up with an overstock of product that needed to leave the warehouse and be returned to

Building One. Of course, that generated no internal paperwork; someone would simply say 'I'm taking this product to Building Two' or vice versa, and that was such a common occurrence that the security guards started to think nothing about it."

"My immediate concern was," Roberts said, "if we've got something leaving the building in the ordered process, then we must have supervisors involved, drivers involved, and the like. It would be a fairly massive operation, and maybe that was their concern."

Roberts suspected the thefts occurred between these interbuilding transfers. Since the employees who did these transfers were the thirty or so warehouse floor workers, he had many potential suspects.

To catch the thieves, however, a new video surveillance system would need to be set up at the warehouse. "We looked at their video surveillance system and found their cameras were improperly positioned, and they were not saving their tapes in the library long enough to go back and look at them." Roberts's firm, which partly specializes in alarms and security protection, set up an additional sixteen hidden video cameras inside the warehouse, as well as additional cameras in the parking lots.

"We agreed to pretend that nothing had happened," Roberts said of the thefts, "which would give the suspects a false sense of security, and the company agreed to restock the computer chips."

The warehouse manager and his assistant began to surreptitiously track interbuilding transfers on a daily basis. With access to the paperwork and new video, "we were able to freeze-frame images" in order to look at all sides of an employee's cart. This time, the warehouse manager knew exactly how many boxes an employee was supposed to be taking to the other building.

Unbeknownst to Gunter and Spelber, the video cameras recorded them talking in the aisleways and other areas of the warehouse. Coupled with the daily inventory check, the record showed that the two employees frequently had more than the number of boxes they were supposed to be moving.

About 3:30 one afternoon, Gunter and Spelber removed six boxes from the shelves, placed them on a cart with empty boxes on top, and moved the cart outside. In the parking lot, Spelber loaded the boxes into his truck and returned to work. After work, they drove their own vehicles down the street and transferred the boxes to Gunter's car.

At home, Gunter removed the company labels from the chips and drove to Thurman's house. Thurman promised to pay him $50,000 for this stock.

Gunter and Spelber never saw that money. The next day, company security confronted them with the evidence. They quickly admitted their guilt and identified Thurman as the receiver of the stolen equipment. When police interviewed Thurman at his home, he denied knowing that the computer chips were stolen, but he admitted to reselling the chips to an acquaintance named Marty for $180,000, paid for with cashier's checks.

Interviews with Marty, along with check receipts, revealed that the amount was actually much greater—Marty had paid approximately $697,000 to Thurman for the chips (a profit of about 50 cents on the dollar, as compared to the 10 cents on the dollar Gunter received). Although investigators could not uncover any stolen equipment, they believed that Marty had sold the goods to the aerospace industry, and possibly to federal agencies.

The next day, police arrested Thurman after he attempted to make a large withdrawal from his credit union. Thurman and Gunter both served over a year in the state pen for grand theft and embezzlement; Spelber got nine months in a work furlough program. The police were never able to tag anything on Marty, who made the most money in the open market for the chips. Since none of the product could be found in his store, and since investigators could not prove he knew the property was stolen, they could not criminally prosecute him.

Roberts said the case was unique in that, at the time, it represented the largest internal theft in the history of this California county. The company, though unable to recover most of the stolen property, learned a valuable lesson from the fraud. Afterward, managers conducted tighter controls on transfers of property between buildings, produced more frequent inventory audits, and established enhanced physical security, which included a new chain-link fence between the two buildings.

"I think this fraud was difficult to detect because the audit controls that they set up, and the manner in which they had set them up, were improper," Roberts said. "That's a common thing that we see as fraud examiners or investigators. Often people spend a great deal of money to set up audit controls—they set up physical security; they install alarms—and we often say to them: Simply buying that piece of equipment or putting those procedures into place is not enough. You need a trained, experienced professional to tell you how to do it and how to use them. If you don't do it the right way, it's worthless."

OVERVIEW

Up to this point in the book, our discussion of asset misappropriations has focused on cash schemes. While the vast majority of asset misappropriation schemes involve cash, it should be remembered that other assets can be stolen as well. Although schemes involving the misappropriation of noncash assets are not as common as cash schemes, they are nevertheless potentially disastrous. As Larry Gunter's scheme illustrates, thefts of inventory can run into the millions of dollars. In this chapter we will discuss the ways in which employees misappropriate noncash assets, such as inventory, supplies, equipment, and information.

Noncash Misappropriation Data from the ACFE *2009 Global Fraud Survey*

Frequency and Cost Noncash schemes were not nearly as common as cash schemes in the ACFE survey, accounting for only 20 percent of asset misappropriations (see Exhibit 9-2). Additionally, as indicated in Exhibit 9-3, noncash schemes had a lower median cost than frauds that targeted cash.

Types of Noncash Assets Stolen By far, physical assets, including inventory and equipment, were the most commonly misappropriated noncash asset in the ACFE study. Fraudsters embezzled physical assets in 75 percent of the cases involving noncash misappropriations (see Exhibit 9-4).

Although *securities* were the least likely asset to be misappropriated (15 cases), the median loss in cases involving securities theft was significantly higher than in any other category, at $10,000,000 (see Exhibit 9-5).

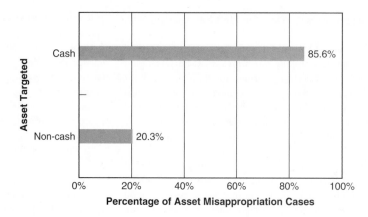

EXHIBIT 9-2 *2009 Global Fraud Survey:* Comparison of Frequency of Asset Misappropriations[a]

[a]The sum of these percentages exceeds 100 percent because some cases involved multiple fraud schemes that fell into more than one category. Similarly, other charts in this chapter may also reflect percentages totaling in excess of 100 percent.

EXHIBIT 9-3 *2009 Global Fraud Survey:* Comparison of Median Loss of Asset Misappropriations

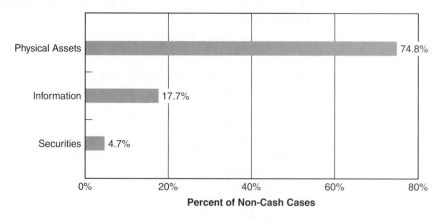

EXHIBIT 9-4 *2009 Global Fraud Survey*: Noncash Cases by Type of Asset Misappropriated

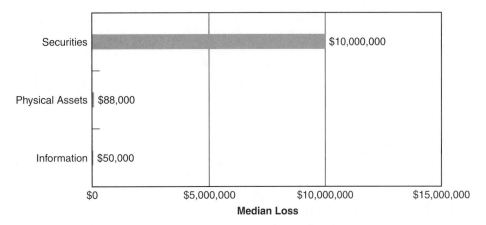

EXHIBIT 9-5 *2009 Global Fraud Survey:* Median Loss in Noncash Cases by Type of Asset Misappropriated

NONCASH MISAPPROPRIATION SCHEMES

Noncash tangible assets, such as inventory and equipment, are misappropriated by employees in a number of ways. These schemes can range from taking a box of pens home from work to the theft of millions of dollars' worth of company property. In general, misappropriations of noncash tangible assets fall into one of the following categories:

- Misuse
- Unconcealed larceny
- Asset requisitions and transfers
- Purchasing and receiving schemes
- Fraudulent shipments

Misuse of Noncash Assets

There are basically two ways a person can misappropriate a company asset. The asset can be misused (or "borrowed"), or it can be stolen. Simple misuse is obviously the less egregious of the two. Assets that are misused, but not stolen, typically include company vehicles, company supplies, computers, and other office equipment. In Case 1421, for example, an employee made personal use of a company vehicle while on an out-of-town assignment. The employee provided false information, both written and verbal, regarding the nature of his use of the vehicle. The vehicle was returned unharmed and the cost to the perpetrator's company was only a few hundred dollars, but such unauthorized use of a company asset does amount to fraud when a false statement accompanies the use.

Computers, supplies, and other office equipment are also used by some employees to do personal work on company time. For instance, an employee might use his computer at work to write letters, print invoices, or do other work connected with a business that he runs on the side. In many instances, these side businesses are of the same nature as the employer's business, so the employee is essentially using his employer's equipment to compete with the employer. An example of how employees misuse company assets to compete with their employers was provided by Case 1406, in which a group of employees not only stole company supplies, but also used the stolen supplies, in conjunction with their employer's equipment, to manufacture their own product. The fraudsters then removed the completed product from their work location and sold it in competition with their employer. In a similar scheme, the perpetrator of Case 2579 used his employer's machinery to run his own snow removal and excavation business for approximately nine months. He generally did his own work on weekends and after hours, falsifying the logs that recorded mileage and usage on the equipment. The employee had formerly owned all the equipment himself, but had sold it in order to avoid bankruptcy. As a term of the sale, he had agreed to go to work for the new owner operating the equipment, but in truth, he never stopped running his old business.

The preceding cases offer a good illustration of how a single scheme can encompass more than one type of fraud. Though the perpetrators in these schemes were misusing company materials and equipment—a case of asset misappropriation—they were also competing with their employers for business—a conflict of interest. The categories ACFE researchers have developed for classifying fraud are helpful in that they allow examiners to track certain types of schemes, noting common elements, victims, methods, and so on; but those involved in fraud prevention should remember that every crime will not fall neatly into one category. Frauds often expand as opportunity and need allow; a scheme that begins small may grow into a massive crime that can cripple a business.

The Costs of Inventory Misuse   The costs of noncash asset misuse are difficult to quantify. To many individuals this type of fraud is viewed not as a crime, but rather as "borrowing." In truth, the cost to a company from this kind of scheme may often be immaterial. When a perpetrator borrows a stapler for the night or takes home some tools to perform a household repair, the cost to his company is negligible, as long as the assets are returned unharmed.

But misuse schemes can also be very costly. Take, for example, situations such as those discussed above in which an employee uses company equipment to operate a side business during work hours. Since the employee is not performing his work-related duties, the employer suffers a loss in productivity. If the low productivity continues, the employer might have to hire additional employees to compensate, diverting more capital to wages. If the employee's business is similar to the employer's, lost business could be an additional cost; had the employee not contracted work for his own company, the business would presumably have gone to his employer. Unauthorized use of equipment can also mean additional wear and tear, causing the equipment to break down sooner than it would have under normal business conditions. Additionally, when an employee "borrows" company property, there is no guarantee that he will bring it back. This is precisely how some theft schemes begin. Despite some opinions to the contrary, asset misuse is not always a harmless crime.

Unconcealed Larceny Schemes

Though the misuse of company property might be a problem, the *theft* of company property is obviously of greater concern. As we have seen, losses resulting from larceny of company assets can run into the millions of dollars. The means employed to steal noncash assets range from simple larceny—just walking off with company property—to more complicated schemes involving the falsification of company documents and ledgers.

The textbook definition of larceny is too broad for our purposes, as it would encompass every kind of theft. In order to gain a more specific understanding of the methods used to steal noncash assets, we have narrowed the definition of larceny. For our purposes, larceny is the most basic type of theft, exhibited in schemes in which an employee simply takes property from the company premises without attempting to conceal it in the

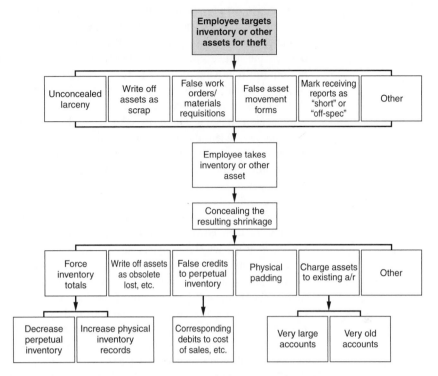

EXHIBIT 9-6 Noncash Larceny

books and records (see Exhibit 9-6). In other fraud schemes, employees may create false documentation to justify the shipment of merchandise or tamper with inventory records to conceal missing assets, but larceny is more blunt. The culprit in these crimes simply takes company assets, without trying to account for their absence. In the case study at the beginning of this chapter, for instance, Larry Gunter simply walked out of his warehouse with several hundred thousand dollars' worth of computer chips.

Most noncash larceny schemes are not very complicated. They are typically committed by employees (such as warehouse personnel, inventory clerks, and shipping clerks) who have access to inventory and other assets. A typical example of this type of scheme was committed by the perpetrator of Case 968, a warehouse clerk who simply removed inventory from outgoing shipments and left it in plain sight on the warehouse floor as he went about his duties. If someone noticed that a shipment was short, the fact that the merchandise was sitting out in the open made it appear that the omission had been an oversight rather than an intentional removal. In most cases, however, no one noticed that shipments were short, leaving the excess inventory available for the perpetrator to take. If customers complained about receiving short shipments, the company sent the missing items without performing any follow-up to see where the missing inventory had gone. The culprit was eventually caught when someone noticed that he was involved in the preparation of an inordinate number of short shipments.

When we speak of inventory theft, we tend to conjure up images of late-night rendezvous at the warehouse or merchandise stuffed hastily under clothing as a nervous employee beats a path to his car. Although sometimes this is how employees go about stealing inventory and other assets, in many instances fraudsters do not have to go to these extremes. In several of the cases in our studies, employees took items openly during business hours, in plain view of their coworkers. How does this happen? The truth is that people tend to assume that their friends and acquaintances are acting honestly. When they see a trusted coworker taking something out of the office, people are likely to assume that the culprit has a legitimate reason for removing the asset. In most cases, people just don't assume that fraud is going on around them. Such was the situation in Case 728, in which a university faculty member was leaving his offices to take a position at a new school. This person was permitted to take a small number of items to his new job, but certainly exceeded the intentions of the school when he loaded two trucks full of university lab equipment and computers worth several hundred thousand dollars. The perpetrator simply packed up these stolen assets along with his personal items and drove away.

Though it is true that employees sometimes misappropriate assets in front of coworkers who do not suspect fraud, it is also true that employees may be fully aware that one of their coworkers is stealing, yet refrain from reporting the crime. There are several reasons why employees might ignore illegal conduct, among them a sense of duty to friends, a "management versus labor" mentality, intimidation by the thief, or poor channels of communication—or the coworkers may be assisting in the theft. When high-ranking personnel are stealing from their companies, employees often overlook the crime for fear that they will lose their jobs if they report it. For example, a school superintendent in Case 2462 was not only pilfering school accounts, but also stealing school assets. A search of his residence revealed a cellar filled with school property. A number of school employees knew or suspected the superintendent was involved in illegal dealings, but he was very powerful, and people were afraid to report him for fear of retaliation. As a result, he was able to steal from the school for several years. Similarly, in Case 144, a city manager ordered subordinates to install air conditioners—known to be city property—in his home and in the homes of several influential citizens. Although there was no question that this violated the city's code of ethics, no one reported the manager because of a lack of a proper whistleblowing procedure in the department.

Ironically, employees who steal company property are often highly trusted within their organizations. This trust can provide employees with access to restricted areas, safes, supply rooms, or even keys to the business. Such access, in turn, makes it easy for employees to misappropriate company assets. Case 716 provides an example of how an employee abused his position of trust to misappropriate noncash assets. In this case, a long-term employee of a contractor was given keys to the company parts room. It was his job to deliver parts to job sites. This individual used his access to steal high-value items that he then sold to another contractor. The scheme itself was uncomplicated, but because the employee had a long history of service to the company, and because he was highly trusted, inventory counts were allowed to lapse and his performance went largely unsupervised. As a result, the scheme continued for over two years and cost the company over $200,000.

Employees who have keys to company buildings are able to misappropriate assets during nonbusiness hours, when they can avoid the prying eyes of their fellow employees as well as management and security personnel. The ACFE studies revealed several schemes in which employees entered their places of business to steal assets during weekends, as well as before or after normal working hours. Case 1766 provided an example of this after-hours activity. In this scheme two employees in management positions at a manufacturing plant would set finished items aside at the end of the day, then return the next day an hour before the morning shift and remove the merchandise before other employees arrived. These perpetrators had keys to the plant's security gate, which allowed them to enter the plant before normal hours. Over the course of several years, these two fraudsters removed and sold approximately $300,000 worth of inventory from their company.

It can be unwise for a fraudster to physically carry inventory and other assets off the premises of his company. This practice carries with it the inherent risk and potential embarrassment of being caught red-handed with stolen goods on his person. Some fraudsters avoid this problem by mailing company assets to a location where they can pick them up without having to worry about security, management, or other potential observers. In Case 1465, for instance, a spare-parts custodian took several thousand dollars' worth of computer chips and mailed them to a company that had no business dealings with the custodian's employer. He then reclaimed the merchandise as his own. By taking the step of mailing the stolen inventory, the fraudster allowed the postal service to unwittingly do his dirty work for him.

The Fake Sale   Asset misappropriations are not always undertaken solely by employees of the victim organization. In many cases, corrupt employees use outside accomplices to help steal an organization's property. The fake sale is one method that depends on an accomplice for its success. Like most larceny schemes, the fake sale is not complicated. As reflected in Case 1963, a fake sale occurs when the accomplice of the employee-fraudster "buys" merchandise but the employee does not ring up the sale; the accomplice takes the merchandise without making any payment. To a casual observer, it will appear that the transaction is a normal sale. The employee bags the merchandise, and may act as though a transaction is being entered on the register, but in fact, the "sale" is not recorded. The accomplice may even pass a nominal amount of money to the employee to complete the illusion. In Case 1963 the perpetrator went along with these fake sales in exchange for gifts from her accomplice, though in other cases the two might split the stolen merchandise.

Accomplices are also sometimes used to return the inventory that an employee has stolen. This is an easy way for the employee to convert the inventory into cash when he has no need for the merchandise itself and has no means of reselling it on his own.

Preventing and Detecting Larceny of Noncash Assets   In order to prevent larceny of noncash assets, the duties of requisitioning, purchasing, and receiving these assets should be segregated. To provide additional checks and balances, the payables function should be segregated from all purchasing and receiving duties. In addition, physical controls are a key to preventing theft of noncash assets. All merchandise should be physically guarded and locked, with access restricted to authorized personnel only. Access logs can be used to track those who enter restricted areas, or each authorized individual could be given a personalized entry code. In either case, a log will be created that shows who had access to restricted assets, and at what times. Not only will this help identify the perpetrator in the event that a theft occurs, but—more important—it will help deter employees from attempting to steal company merchandise.

Another potentially effective deterrence method is the installation of security cameras in warehouses or on sales floors. If security cameras are to be used, their presence should be made known to employees to deter misconduct. Security guards can also be used for the same purpose.

In order to help detect inventory thefts in a timely manner, organizations should conduct physical inventory counts on a periodic basis, and someone independent of the purchasing and warehousing functions should conduct these counts. Physical counts should be comprehensive. Also, boxes should be inspected to make sure they actually contain inventory. Physical inventory counts should be subject to recounts or spot checks by independent personnel. Also, shipping and receiving activities should be suspended during physical counts to ensure a proper cutoff. Significant discrepancies between physical counts and perpetual inventory (shrinkage) should be investigated before adjustments are made to inventory records.

One common way to commit inventory theft is to remove items from outgoing shipments of merchandise. It is therefore important for organizations to have in place a mechanism for receiving customer complaints regarding, among other things, "short" shipments. An employee who is independent of the purchasing and warehousing functions should be assigned to follow up on complaints. If a large number of complaints are received, the dates of shipment can be compared to employee work schedules to help identify suspects.

Asset Requisitions and Transfers

Asset requisitions or other documentation that enable noncash assets to be moved from one location in a company to another can be used to facilitate the misappropriation of those assets. Fraudsters use these internal documents to gain access to merchandise that they otherwise might not be able to handle without raising suspicion. Transfer documents do not account for missing merchandise the way false sales do, but they allow a fraudster to move assets from one location to another. In the process of this movement, the fraudster takes the merchandise for himself (see Exhibit 9-6).

The most basic scheme occurs when an employee requisitions materials to complete a work-related project, then steals the materials instead. In some cases the fraudster simply overstates the amount of supplies or equipment it will take to complete his work, and pilfers the excess. In more extreme cases, the fraudster might completely fabricate a project that necessitates the use of certain assets he intends to steal. In Case 2744, for instance, an employee of a telecommunications company used false project documents to request approximately $100,000 worth of computer chips, allegedly to upgrade company computers. Knowing that this type of requisition required verbal authorization from another source, the employee set up an elaborate phone scheme to get the "project" approved. The fraudster used his knowledge of the company's phone system to forward calls from four different lines to his own desk. When the confirmation call was made, it was the perpetrator who answered the phone and authorized the project.

Dishonest employees sometimes falsify property transfer forms so that they can remove inventory or other assets from a warehouse or stockroom. Once the merchandise is in their possession, the fraudsters simply take it home with them. In Case 653, for example, a manager requested that merchandise from the company warehouse be displayed on a showroom floor. But the pieces he requested never made it to the showroom, because he loaded them into a pickup truck and took them home. In some instances he actually took the items in broad daylight and with the help of another employee. The obvious problem with this type of scheme is that the person who orders the merchandise will usually be the primary suspect when it turns up missing. In many cases the fraudster simply relies on poor communication between different departments in his company and hopes no one will piece the crime together. The individual in this case, however, thought he was immune to detection, because the merchandise was requested via computer, using a management-level security code. Because the code was not specific to any one manager, he thought there would be no way of knowing which manager had ordered the merchandise. Unfortunately for the thief, the company was able to record the computer terminal from which the request originated. The manager had used his own computer to make the request, which led to his undoing.

When inventory is stored in multiple locations, the transfer of assets from one building to another can create opportunities for employees to pilfer. Larry Gunter, in the case study at the beginning of this chapter, stole over $1 million worth of computer chips by adding extra merchandise to his cart as he transferred materials between two company buildings or as he took out the trash. He simply took a detour and loaded the stolen chips in his truck before continuing on his route. As is the case in many businesses, Larry Gunter's company required no internal paperwork when product was moved between its two buildings, so it was very difficult to track the movement of assets. Consequently, it was easy for Gunter to steal from the company.

Purchasing and Receiving Schemes

The purchasing and receiving functions of a company can also be manipulated by dishonest employees to facilitate the theft of noncash assets (see Exhibit 9-6). It might at first seem that any purchasing scheme should fall under the heading of false billings, but there is a distinction between purchasing schemes that are classified as false billings and those that are classified as noncash misappropriations. If an employee causes his company to purchase merchandise that the company does not need, this is a false billing scheme: the harm to the company comes in paying for assets for which it has no use. For instance, in Case 1693 a carpenter was allowed control over the ordering of materials for a small construction project. No one bothered to measure the amount of materials ordered against the size of the carpenter's project, so the carpenter was able to order excess, unneeded lumber, which was then delivered to his home, to build a fence for himself. The essence of the fraud in this case was the *purchase* of unneeded materials.

On the other hand, if the assets were intentionally purchased by the company but simply misappropriated by the fraudster, this is classified as a noncash scheme. In the preceding example, assume that the victim company wanted to keep a certain amount of lumber on hand for odd jobs. If the carpenter took this lumber home, the crime is a theft of lumber. The difference is that, in the second example, the company is deprived not only of the cash it paid for the lumber, but also of the lumber itself. It will now have to purchase more lumber to replace what it is missing. In the first example, the company's only loss was the cash it paid in the fraudulent purchase of the materials it did not need.

Falsifying Incoming Shipments One of the most common ways for employees to abuse the purchasing and receiving functions is for a person charged with receiving goods on behalf of the victim company—such as a warehouse supervisor or receiving clerk—to falsify the records of incoming shipments. In Case 684, for instance, two employees conspired to misappropriate incoming merchandise by marking shipments as short. If 1,000 units of a particular item were received, for example, the fraudsters would indicate that only 900 were received. They were then able to steal the 100 units that were unaccounted for.

The obvious problem with this kind of scheme is that if the receiving report does not match the vendor's invoice, there will be a problem with payment. In the above example, if the vendor bills for 1,000 units but the accounts payable voucher shows receipt of only 900 units of merchandise, then someone will have to explain where the extra 100 units went. Obviously, the vendor will indicate that a full shipment was made, so the victim company's attention will likely turn to whoever signed the receiving reports.

In this case, the fraudsters attempted to avoid this problem by altering only one copy of the receiving report. The copy that was sent to accounts payable indicated receipt of a full shipment, so that the vendor would be paid without any questions. The copy used for inventory records indicated a short shipment so that the assets on hand would equal the assets in the perpetual inventory.

Instead of marking shipments short, the fraudster might reject portions of a shipment as not being up to quality specifications. The perpetrator then keeps the "substandard" merchandise rather than sending it back to the supplier. The result is the same as if the shipment had been marked short.

False Shipments of Inventory and Other Assets

To conceal thefts of inventory, fraudsters sometimes create false shipping documents and false sales documents to make it appear that missing inventory was not actually stolen but was instead sold (see Exhibit 9-7). The document that tells the shipping department to release inventory for delivery is usually the packing slip. By creating a false packing slip, a corrupt employee can cause inventory to be fraudulently delivered to himself or to an

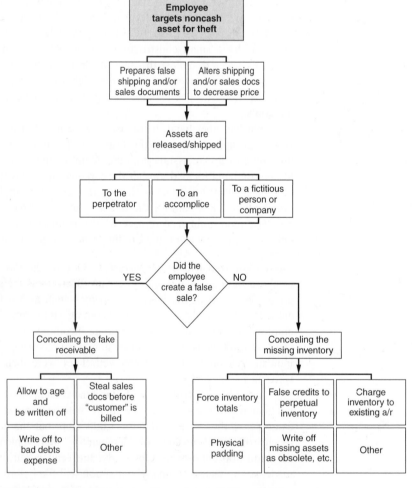

EXHIBIT 9-7 False Shipments of Inventory and Other Assets

accomplice. The "sales" reflected in the packing slips are typically made to a fictitious person, a fictitious company, or an accomplice of the perpetrator. In Case 1598, for instance, an inventory control employee used his position to create fraudulent paperwork that authorized the shipment of over $30,000 worth of inventory to his accomplices. The fraudsters were then able to sell the inventory for their own profit.

One benefit to using false shipping documents to misappropriate inventory or other assets is that someone other than the fraudster can remove the product from the warehouse or storeroom. The perpetrator of the scheme does not have to risk being caught stealing company inventory. Instead, the victim company unknowingly delivers the targeted assets to him.

Packing slips allow inventory to be shipped from the victim company to the perpetrator, but they alone do not conceal the fact that inventory has been misappropriated. In order to hide the theft, fraudsters may also create a false sale so that it appears that the missing inventory was shipped to a customer. In this way, the inventory is accounted for. Depending on how the victim organization operates, the fraudster may have to create a false purchase order from the "buyer," a false sales order, and a false invoice along with the packing slip to create the illusion of a sale.

The result is that a fake receivable account goes into the books for the price of the misappropriated inventory. Obviously, the "buyer" of the merchandise will never pay for it. How do fraudsters deal with these fake receivables? In some cases, the fraudster simply lets the receivable age on his company's books until it is eventually written off as uncollectable. In other instances the employee may take steps to remove the sale—and the delinquent receivable that results—from the books. For instance, in Case 1683, the perpetrator generated false invoices and delivered them to the company warehouse for shipping. The invoices were then marked "delivered" and sent to the sales office. The perpetrator removed all copies of the invoices from the files before they were billed to the fictitious customer. In other scenarios, the perpetrator might write the receivables off himself, as did a corrupt manager in Case 651; in a five-year scheme, the perpetrator took company assets and covered up the loss by setting up a fake sale. A few weeks after the fake sale went into the books, the perpetrator wrote off the receivable to an account for "lost and stolen assets." More commonly, however, the fake sale will be written off to discounts and allowances or a bad debt expense account.

Instead of completely fabricated sales, some employees understate legitimate sales so that an accomplice is billed for less than is delivered. The result is that a portion of the merchandise is sold at no cost. For instance, in Case 998 a salesman filled out shipping tickets, which he forwarded to the warehouse. After the merchandise was delivered, he instructed the warehouse employees to return the shipping tickets to him for "extra work" before they went to the invoicing department. But the extra work the salesman did was simply to alter the shipping tickets, reducing the quantity of merchandise on the ticket so that the buyer (an accomplice of the salesman) was billed for less than he received.

The following case study was selected as an example of a false shipping scheme. In this case, a marketing manager, with the help of a shipping clerk, delivered several computer hard drives to a computer company in return for a substantial cash payment. The victim company in this case had poor controls that allowed merchandise to be shipped without receipts, leaving the company extremely vulnerable to such a scheme. Harry D'Arcy, CFE, investigated this crime and eventually helped bring the culprits to justice.

CASE STUDY: HARD DRIVES AND BAD LUCK[2]

Someone had stolen 1,400 hard drives from a computer warehouse in Toronto. That much was certain. But the question remained: who took them? The answer was more than academic; it could mean the difference between the distributor's continuing operation and a total crash. Swainler's Technology averaged $8–$9 million a year in sales, but with an 8 percent profit margin, the company didn't have much financial room to maneuver. The company was a joint venture, overseen by a group of investors who were, to put it mildly, nervous. They had theft insurance, but with a particularly sticky clause that said that the policy wouldn't cover theft committed by a Swainler's employee. In order to collect on the $600,000 worth of disk drives missing from the warehouse, the investors had to show that the theft was an outside job.

Their report showed just that. Employees and management agreed that the skids bearing the equipment had been safe and sound until the week that a competitor of Swainler's, Hargrove Incorporated, had sent delivery drivers over for an exchange. Evidently, some of Hargrove's people had swiped the equipment during the several days they were working in the Swainler's warehouse. Hargrove and Swainler's worked together when they had to, but they were in hot competition, and at different times each company had lost business—and employees—to the other. Since all Swainler's employees checked out, management concluded that the theft must have been committed by someone from Hargrove.

Doug Andrews was an independent adjuster hired by Swainler's Technology's insurance company. Besides conducting routine loss estimates, he's also a certified fraud examiner who is willing, as he puts it, "to see things other people either don't see or choose to ignore." Although the Swainler's board assured Andrews this was a simple case, he wasn't convinced: "I wasn't sure it wasn't an inside job. Too many questions were left hanging. How did the Hargrove people get the stuff out without being seen? The date management was setting for the loss seemed awfully convenient. It seemed like at the least someone at Swainler's had to be involved," Andrews remembers. He needed some help chasing down these hunches, so Andrews hired Harry D'Arcy to assist. D'Arcy worked for the Canadian Insurance Crime Prevention Bureau as a CFE and investigator. He and Andrews interviewed everyone at the warehouse and on the investors' board, returning two or three times if necessary to get their questions answered. They traced serial numbers and possible distribution routes to turn up some sign of the hard drives. D'Arcy says, "We met at least twice a week to come up with a way to solve this. It was like a think tank, bouncing ideas

and options off each other: 'What tack should we take now? Should we call out to California? Do we need to go to that shop in Ottawa?' We knew we were being stymied. We just had to find a way around the blocks they put in front of us."

The main thing bothering Harry D'Arcy was that the board was presenting them with what appeared to be an open and shut case. Everyone's stories matched like precision parts. "It was too good to be true, too neat," D'Arcy says. The board members had seen the material on the Friday before Hargrove came; they noticed it was gone afterward; they had reason to suspect their competitor was behind it. Yes, they knew their insurance policy wouldn't pay if an employee did the hit, but that was beside the point. The board trusted its employees. Many of the people at Swainler's, from clerks to warehouse personnel, were either related to, or friends of, the management. D'Arcy and Andrews were encountering what Andrews later described as "an active campaign of misinformation."

Once he got a sense of the system of operation at Swainler's, D'Arcy had some material for a new round of questioning. He noticed that as skids of equipment were prepared for shipping, the entire apparatus was wrapped in a thick plastic sealant and moved from the warehouse floor into the shipping dock. "Now," he asked one of the investors, "if those disk drives were ready for shipping on the Friday you say, then they would have already been wrapped, right?"

"Sure."

"Then, how did you know what you were seeing if the wrapping was already on? You can't see through the wrapping."

"I knew that batch was supposed to go out for the next week," the man replied.

"Then the skids should have been moved to the loading dock," D'Arcy interjected.

"I don't see your point."

"You said you saw them in the warehouse," D'Arcy reminded the man. "You couldn't have seen them in the warehouse if they had been moved to the dock for shipping."

The witness, feeling stymied himself, shifted and said, "Well, maybe they hadn't been taken over yet."

D'Arcy had a full house of questions for the initially talkative managers. Why would they notice a particular skid of drives on a particular day? Why were their memories so specific on this one shipment? How often did management tour the warehouse for an informal inventory? D'Arcy reports, "Once I had them shaken up, I would ask them point blank, 'Are you parroting something you heard somebody else say?'" The men would declare that, no, they'd seen the material themselves.

"Did you discuss this with other board members?" D'Arcy asked.

[2]Several names and details have been changed to preserve anonymity.

"We talked about it in board meetings, sure," came the answer.

"And did you all agree on what you would say when you gave a statement?"

"No."

"But your statements all match."

"We agreed that we remembered the drives being there on the same day."

Doug Andrews was feeling fed up: "We were getting this string of non-answers. I felt like we were coming up dry."

Swainler's had hired a private investigator of its own to work the case. Harry D'Arcy talked with the man, who was convinced he had the material to show an outside job. The PI had been to Hargrove and spoken with employees there, including a man who had once worked for Swainler's. "I don't know if somebody here took the stuff or not," the man said. "But those guys at Swainler's deserve everything they get." He claimed Swainler's required its employees to work long hours with little pay or benefits, that workers were little more than switches on a processing board. To Swainler's investigator, then, this was a classic case of employee resentment, a common excuse for fraud.

D'Arcy said he disagreed, but the investigator persisted. Swainler's Technology was now claiming its expenses for the investigation, finally totaling $125,000. During one week alone, the PI billed $45,000 when he conducted a stakeout in another city. An anonymous tip to the executive vice president at Swainler's placed the stolen disks at a storage facility in London, Ontario. The investigator took a team of people and equipment, and after a weekend surveillance, it observed a man opening the unit. When the team approached, it found nothing inside but the man's personal belongings.

Meanwhile, D'Arcy and Andrews pursued their own strategy. They notified the manufacturer's representatives throughout Canada and the United States to be on the lookout for a set of serial numbers. Sure enough, a call came in from a dealer in California; one of the disk drives had shown up for repair. Invoices showed the drive had been shipped from upstate New York and was purchased in Ottawa, Canada. The Ottawa shop had received the drive from a distributor in Montreal. Doug Andrews went to the Montreal warehouse but found it empty. Canvassing the neighborhood, he was told the people renting the warehouse had moved to another area in northern Montreal.

When Andrews got to the new address, he questioned four or five of the workers there about his case. They had never heard of Swainler's and knew nothing about the stolen drives. But when Andrews pressured them to look through their records with him, he found documents matching his serial numbers. Then, one of the missing drives turned up inside the warehouse.

Andrews wasn't ready to celebrate, though. "I was feeling beat. We'd been spending all this time, running back and forth, interviewing and reinterviewing. I said, 'I don't know, we may not get this one.'" The invoices he'd looked at were dated five weeks earlier than the time Swainler's had listed the theft. The discrepancy might help disprove the company's outside perpetrator theory, but could also be used to throw Andrews's largely circumstantial case into further confusion. As he was driving back to Toronto, Andrews got a call from Harry D'Arcy. "I've been doing some work based on what you found there," D'Arcy told him excitedly. "When you get back they'll be in chains."

Since D'Arcy now knew that at least some of the merchandise had gone through the warehouse in Montreal, he had looked for phone calls from that city in the phone logs at Swainler's. The marketing manager, Frederic Boucher, had not only received a large number of calls from Montreal, the calls were coming from the warehouse Andrews had just visited, the one claiming it had never heard of Swainler's. D'Arcy spoke again with people in the warehouse, one of whom admitted that the skids had disappeared much earlier than first reported. He guessed the actual date was about a month earlier than the one management had given. This, of course, coincided with the invoices Andrews had found in Montreal. At a special meeting, the board of directors reviewed D'Arcy's findings and confronted Frederic Boucher with the evidence pointing toward him. Boucher denied any involvement, and the board supported his story.

The next morning, Boucher told a different story. He had talked with his wife and a lawyer and was ready to come clean. He said he'd met the people from the Montreal warehouse at a conference. Together they worked out a deal in which Boucher would provide them with a supply of hard drives at a sweet price. With the help of a Swainler's shipping clerk, Boucher sent sixty low-end drives to Kingston, halfway between Montreal and Toronto, for $20,000 paid in cash. The atmosphere at Swainler's was ripe for this sort of offense. Harry D'Arcy recalls, "The bookkeeping system wasn't controlled. It was nothing to find things going out with no receipts. The operation was mainly run on trust. The men who headed up the company were all old friends, and they hired people they knew or to whom they were connected in one way or another. It ran on blind trust and nepotism." Encouraged by their first success, Boucher and his accomplices then arranged to make the big sale: 1,400 top-quality hard drives for a $600,000 take. They didn't have to worry about covering their tracks, because management was eager to point the finger outside the company and collect on their insurance.

With Boucher's confession, Doug Andrews could make a happy report to his client that they weren't liable for the claim. Boucher was sentenced to make restitution for the theft, and to two years' imprisonment, while the shipping clerk and the Montreal distributor were given one year each. All the sentences were suspended and the defendants placed on probation. The executives at Swainler's were, according to Harry D'Arcy, "cautioned regarding their complicity in the matter." Swainler's survived the loss but was later purchased by a prominent Canadian investment group and now operates under that umbrella.

Doug Andrews, who lectures and writes articles on insurance fraud in addition to conducting investigations, finds that people resist seeing cases like Swainler's as a real crime.

"There's a belief that perpetrating fraud against an insurer is a victimless crime." Reports from the KPMG accounting firm and the Canadian Coalition Against Insurance Fraud place the insurance losses in Canada between $1 billion and $2.6 billion a year. But Andrews believes that "[you can] take the middle figure of $2 billion and double it." Though a significant portion of those losses is related to occupational crimes,

an accurate account is not yet available. That's because some of the major acts that occur in business felonies—like supplier and kickback fraud—aren't included in the insurance industry figures. Nevertheless, these crimes are serious and proliferating. "They are frequent," Andrews says, "and often systematic and well organized. Especially since insurance companies don't advertise as aggressively in Canada as they do in the United States, people see insurance as a kind of faceless bureaucracy." With the tremendous amounts of money changing hands in this industry every day, "there's a mindset that labels these companies fair game... But people see the difference in the end, when they pay their premiums."

Other Schemes

Because employees tailor their thefts to the security systems, record-keeping systems, building layout, and other day-to-day operations of their companies, the methods used to steal inventory and other assets vary. The preceding categories comprised the majority of schemes in our studies, but there were a couple of other schemes that did not fit any established category, yet that merit discussion.

Write-offs are often used to conceal the theft of assets after they have been stolen. In some cases, however, assets are written off in order to make them available for theft. In Case 894 a warehouse foreman abused his authority to declare inventory obsolete. He wrote off perfectly good inventory, then "gave" it to a dummy corporation that he secretly owned. This fraudster took over $200,000 worth of merchandise from his employer. Once assets are designated as "scrap," it may be easier to conceal their misappropriation. Fraudsters may be allowed to take the "useless" assets for themselves, buy them or sell them to an accomplice at a greatly reduced price, or simply give the assets away.

One final unique example was presented in Case 2188. In this scheme a low-level manager convinced his supervisor to approve the purchase of new office equipment to replace existing equipment, which was to be retired. When the new equipment was purchased, the perpetrator took it home and left the existing equipment in place. His boss assumed that the equipment in the office was new, even though it was actually the same equipment that had always been there. If nothing else, this case illustrates that sometimes a little bit of attentiveness by management is all it takes to halt fraud.

CONCEALING INVENTORY SHRINKAGE

When inventory is stolen, the key concealment issue for the fraudster is shrinkage. Inventory shrinkage is the unaccounted-for reduction in the company's inventory that results from theft. For instance, assume that a computer retailer has 1,000 computers in stock. After work one day, an employee loads ten computers into a truck and takes them home. Now the company only has 990 computers, but since there is no record that the employee took ten computers, the inventory records still show 1,000 units on hand. The company has experienced inventory shrinkage in the amount of ten computers.

Shrinkage is one of the red flags that signal fraud. When merchandise is missing and unaccounted for, the obvious question is, "Where did it go?" The search for an answer to this question can uncover fraud. The goal of the fraudster is to proceed with his scheme undetected, so it is in his best interest to prevent anyone from looking for missing assets. This means concealing the shrinkage that occurs from theft.

Inventory is typically tracked through a two-step process. The first step, the perpetual inventory, is a running count that records how much should be on hand. When new shipments of supplies are received, for instance, these supplies are entered into the perpetual inventory. Similarly, when goods are sold, they are removed from the perpetual inventory records. In this way, a company tracks its inventory on a day-to-day basis.

Periodically, companies should make a physical count of assets on hand. In this process, someone actually goes through the storeroom or warehouse and counts everything that the company has in stock. This total is then matched to the amount of assets reflected in the perpetual inventory. A variation between the physical inventory and the perpetual inventory totals is shrinkage. While a certain amount of shrinkage may be expected in any business, large shrinkage totals may indicate fraud.

Altered Inventory Records

One of the simplest methods for concealing shrinkage is to change the perpetual inventory record so that it will match the physical inventory count. This is also known as a *forced reconciliation* of the account. Basically, the perpetrator just changes the numbers in the perpetual inventory to make them match the amount of inventory on hand. In Case 1465, a supervisor involved in the theft of inventory credited the perpetual inventory and debited the cost of sales account to bring the perpetual inventory numbers into line with the actual inventory count. Once these adjusting entries were made, a review of inventory would not reveal any shrinkage. Rather than use correcting entries to adjust perpetual inventory, some employees simply alter the numbers by deleting or covering up the correct totals and entering new numbers.

There are two sides to the inventory equation, the perpetual inventory and the physical inventory. Instead of altering the perpetual inventory, a fraudster who has access to the records from a physical inventory count can change those records to match the total of the perpetual inventory. Going back to the computer store example, assume that the company counts its inventory every month and matches it to the perpetual inventory. The physical count should come to 990 computers, since that is what is actually on hand. If the perpetrator is someone charged with counting inventory, he can simply write down that there are 1,000 units on hand.

Fictitious Sales and Accounts Receivable

We have already discussed how fraudsters create fake sales to mask the theft of assets. When the perpetrator made an adjusting entry to the perpetual inventory and cost of sales accounts in Case 1465, above, the problem was that there was no sales transaction on the books that corresponded to these entries. Had the perpetrator wished to fix this problem, he would have entered a debit to accounts receivable and a corresponding credit to the sales account to make it appear that the missing goods had been sold.

Of course, the problem of payment then arises, because no one is going to pay for the goods that were "sold" in this transaction. There are two routes that a fraudster might take in this circumstance. The first is to charge the sale to an existing account. In some cases, fraudsters charge fake sales to existing receivables accounts that are so large that the addition of the assets that the fraudster has stolen will not be noticed. Other corrupt employees charge the "sales" to accounts that are already aging and will soon be written off. When these accounts are removed from the books, the fraudster's stolen inventory effectively disappears.

The other adjustment that is typically made is a write-off to discounts and allowances or bad debt expense. In Case 2790, an employee with blanket authority to write off up to $5,000 in uncollectable sales per occurrence used this authority to conceal false sales of inventory to nonexistent companies. The fraudster bilked his company out of nearly $180,000 using this method.

Write Off Inventory and Other Assets

We have already discussed Case 894, in which a corrupt employee wrote off inventory as obsolete, then "gave" the inventory to a shell company that he controlled. Writing off inventory and other assets is a relatively common way for fraudsters to remove assets from the books before or after they are stolen. Again, this is beneficial to the fraudster because it eliminates the problem of shrinkage that inherently exists in every case of noncash asset misappropriation. Examples of this method include Case 705, in which a manager wrote supplies off as lost or destroyed, then sold the supplies through his own company; and Case 720, in which a director of maintenance disposed of fixed assets by reporting them as broken, then took the assets for himself.

Physical Padding

Most methods of concealment deal with altering inventory records, either by changing the perpetual inventory or by miscounting during the physical inventory. As an alternative, some fraudsters try to make it appear that there are more assets present in the warehouse or stockroom than there actually are. Empty boxes, for example, may be stacked on shelves to create the illusion of extra inventory. In Case 5, for example, employees stole liquor from their stockroom and restacked the containers for the missing merchandise. This made it appear that the missing inventory was present when in fact there were really empty boxes on the stockroom shelves. In a period of approximately eighteen months, this concealment method allowed employees to steal over $200,000 of liquor.

The most egregious case of inventory padding in our studies occurred in Case 1666, in which the fraudsters constructed a facade of finished product in a remote location of a warehouse and cordoned off the area to restrict access. Though there should have been a million dollars' worth of product on hand, there was actually nothing behind the wall of finished product, which was constructed solely to create the appearance of additional inventory.

PREVENTING AND DETECTING THEFTS OF NONCASH TANGIBLE ASSETS THAT ARE CONCEALED BY FRAUDULENT SUPPORT

In the purchasing function, it is important to separate the duties of ordering goods, receiving goods, maintaining perpetual inventory records, and issuing payments. Invoices should always be matched to receiving reports before payments are issued in order to help prevent schemes where inventory is stolen from incoming shipments.

To prevent fraudulent shipments of merchandise, organizations should make sure that every packing slip (sales order) is matched to an approved purchase order and that every outgoing shipment is matched to the sales order before the merchandise goes out. Shipments of inventory should be periodically matched to sales records to detect signs of fraud. Whenever a shipment shows up that cannot be traced to a sale, this should be investigated. Another red flag that may indicate a fraudulent shipping scheme is an increase in bad debt expense. As was discussed earlier, some employees will create a fraudulent sale to justify a shipment of merchandise, then will either cancel the sale or write it off as a bad debt after the goods have left the victim organization. Customer shipping addresses can also be matched against employee addresses to find schemes in which an employee has inventory or equipment delivered to his home address.

Carefully review any unexplained entries in perpetual inventory records. Make sure all reductions to the perpetual inventory records are supported by proper source documents. Look for obvious signs of alterations. Make sure that the beginning balance for each month's inventory ties to the ending balance from the previous month. Also determine that the dollar value of ending inventory is reasonably close to previous comparable amounts. Reconcile the inventory balance on the inventory report to the inventory balance in the general ledger. Investigate any discrepancies.

Another fairly common scheme involves employees who overstate the amount of materials needed for a project and steal the excess materials. To prevent this kind of fraud, organizations should reconcile materials ordered for projects to the actual work done. Make sure all materials requisitions are approved by appropriate personnel and require both the requestor and the approver to sign materials requisitions so that if fraud occurs, the culprit can be identified.

In some circumstances employees will write off stolen inventory or equipment as "scrap" either to make it easier to steal (because the organization has fewer safeguards over its scrap items) or to account for the missing assets on the organization's books. In either case, organizations should periodically perform trend analysis on the amount of inventory that is being designated as scrap. Significant increase in scrap levels could indicate an inventory theft scheme. Similarly, look for unusually high levels of reorders for particular items, which could indicate that a particular item of inventory is being stolen.

Assets should be removed from operations only with the proper authority. For example, if a journal entry is used to record abandonment of a fixed asset, the journal entry should be supported by the responsible person's approval. Control should be maintained over assets during disposal. If the organization sells assets that have been designated as scrap, they should be turned over to the selling agent on approval of the disposal. The asset custodian should maintain contact with the selling agent to report on the disposition of the asset in question. Proceeds from the sale of scrap items should follow normal cash receipt operations. The person responsible for asset disposition should not be responsible for receipt of the proceeds.

MISAPPROPRIATION OF INTANGIBLE ASSETS

Misappropriation of Information

In addition to misappropriation of tangible noncash assets, organizations are vulnerable to theft of proprietary information, which can undermine their value, reputation, and competitive advantages, and result in legal liabilities. According to the *ACFE 2009 Global*

Fraud Survey, fraudsters misappropriated information in 18 percent of the cases involving noncash misappropriations.

Companies frequently make sizeable technological investments in protecting their information from external information thieves, but often the biggest threats are internal. Employees are the most likely to be in a position to exploit their employers' information security. After all, who has more insider information and access to proprietary records and data than an employee or former employee?

Information misappropriation schemes commonly include theft by employees of competitively sensitive information, such as customer lists, marketing strategies, trade secrets, new products, or details on development sites. For example, in Case 5565, an employee who felt a sense of entitlement for having contributed to a new product design stole the design in attempt to get ahead in a new job with a competitor. And in Case 5582, a disgruntled former employee sold a company trade secret to a competitor in order to retaliate for what he felt was unfair treatment.

It is critical that companies identify their most valuable information and take steps to protect it. This process must be a cross-departmental endeavor, involving specialists from corporate security/risk management, information technology, human resources, marketing, research and development, and so on. If in-house capabilities do not exist, companies can bring in information security experts to assist them in designing an effective information security system, including awareness training for employees. An information security system may include measures such as limiting access to networks, systems, or data to those who have a legitimate need for access, protecting company data through the use of firewalls and virus scanning software, implementing and enforcing confidentiality agreements and restrictive covenants where appropriate, performing adequate background checks on employees, establishing and enforcing a security policy, and much more.

Misappropriation of Securities

According to the *ACFE 2009 Global Fraud Survey*, although securities were the least likely asset to be misappropriated (5 percent of cases), the median loss in cases involving securities theft was significantly higher than in any other category, at $10,000,000 (see Exhibits 9-4 and 9-5). In order to avoid falling victim to a misappropriation of securities scheme, companies must maintain proper internal controls over their investment portfolio, including proper separation of duties, restricted access to investment accounts, and periodic account reconciliations.

In Case 5234, the director of accounting and finance, who was responsible for making trades, left his computer unattended for a short time while signed into to one of the company's investment accounts. Another employee, a senior accountant, took the opportunity to access the director's computer to sell $15,000 worth of investments and have the proceeds mailed to the company. Due to lax internal controls, she was able to intercept the check and deposit it into her own bank account. Because this employee was in charge of reconciling the investment accounts and had the access needed to enter and post journal entries to the general ledger, she was able to easily hide her scheme by writing off a "loss" on investments to an expense account. It wasn't until almost a year later, when auditors were reviewing the company's books, that the scheme was uncovered. By that time, the thief was nowhere to be found.

PROACTIVE COMPUTER AUDIT TESTS FOR DETECTING NONCASH MISAPPROPRIATIONS[1]

Title	Category	Description	Data file(s)
Identify delivery of inventory to employee addresses by joining employee address file to shipment address file.	All	Inventory may be shipped directly to an employee address.	• Shipment register • Employee address list
Identify delivery of inventory to addresses not designated as business addresses.	All	Inventory may be shipped to an employee address that is entered into the system to appear as a regular business address. The identification of whether an address is legitimately a business one can be done using software databases such as Select Phone Pro.	• Shipment register
Inventory actual to standard price.	All except larceny	Inventory prices may be adjusted in an attempt to conceal inventory larceny schemes.	• On-hand inventory
List top 100 employees by dollar size (once for inventory adjustments, once for asset transfers, and once for accounts receivable write-offs).	All except larceny	Employees with high adjustments may signal actions to hide inventory larceny schemes.	• Invoice sales register • inventory adjustments • Shipment register
List top 100 employees who have been on the top 100 list for three months (once for inventory adjustments, once for asset transfers, and once for accounts receivable write-offs).	All except larceny	Employees with high adjustments may signal actions to hide inventory larceny schemes.	• Invoice sales register • Inventory adjustments • Shipment register
List top 10 locations that have been on the top 10 list for three months (once for inventory adjustments, once for asset transfers, and once for accounts receivable write-offs).	All except larceny	Locations with high adjustments may signal actions to hide inventory larceny schemes.	• Invoice sales register • inventory adjustments • Shipment register
Compute standard deviation for each employee for the last three months and list those employees that provided three times the standard deviation in the current month (once for inventory adjustments, once for asset transfers, and once for accounts receivable writeoffs).	All except larceny	Employees with high adjustments may signal actions to hide inventory larceny schemes.	• Invoice sales register • Inventory adjustments • Shipment register

(Continued)

(*Continued*)

Title	Category	Description	Data file(s)
Summarize user access for the receiving, inventory adjustments, shipping, and customer account systems for segregation of duties reviews.	All except larceny	User access to systems may identify segregation-of-duties issues. For example, if an employee posts a fraudulent shipment to his home address and then writes off the receivable, this nonsegregation would facilitate the fraud. User access should be reviewed from the perspective of adjustments within the application and adjustments to the data itself.	• System user access logs • System user access master file
Duplicate inventory listing by amount and description, as well as quantity and amount.	All except larceny	Inventory may be fraudulently listed in duplicate in the on-hand register to appear to be on hand, concealing the inventory larceny.	• On-hand inventory
Inventory price greater than retail price.	All except larceny	Inventory prices may be adjusted in an attempt to conceal inventory larceny schemes.	• On-hand inventory
Extract all inventory coded as obsolete that possess reorder points within the inventory system.	Purchasing and receiving schemes	Inventory that has been written off as obsolete while also having reorder points may be a sign that the items were written off fraudulently to conceal an inventory larceny.	• Inventory master file • Inventory adjustments
Receipts per receiving report in the receiving system that do not agree to the receipts per the accounts payable invoice.	Purchasing and receiving schemes	Receipts per the receiving log may be fraudulently lowered to conceal an inventory larceny and then increased when passed to accounts payable to effectuate the payment to the vendor.	• Receiving log • Invoice payment
Inventory receipts per inventory item that exceed the economic order quantity or maximum for that item.	Purchasing and receiving schemes	Overordering of product so that it may be taken fraudulently may be detected through this analysis.	• Receiving log • Inventory master file
Inventory with a negative quantity balance.	False shipments	Employees posting fraudulent shipments may erroneously enter more shipments than there is inventory for a stated inventory item.	• On-hand inventory
Dormant customer accounts for the past six months that post a sale in the last two months of the year.	False shipments	Customers that have been dormant may be used as accounts to post fraudulent sales, concealing an inventory larceny.	• Sales register
Calculate the ratio of the largest sale to next-largest sale by customer.	False shipments	By identifying the largest sale to a customer and the next-largest sale, any large ratio difference may identify a fraudulently recorded "largest" sale. This would essentially be made to conceal an inventory larceny.	• Sales register
Shipping documents with no associated sales order.	False shipments	A false shipment concealing an inventory larceny may be posted to the sales journal with no corresponding shipment entry, thereby avoiding detection of the entry.	• Sales register • Shipment register

SUMMARY

Asset misappropriation schemes are subdivided based on whether the perpetrator steals cash or noncash assets such as inventory, supplies, equipment, information, and securities. As the data from the *2009 Global Fraud Survey* show, noncash schemes are less common than cash schemes, and the median loss in noncash schemes is slightly lower.

In this chapter, we discussed five types of schemes used to misappropriate noncash tangible assets: *misuse, unconcealed larceny, asset requisitions and transfers, purchasing and receiving schemes*, and *fraudulent shipments*. Misuse schemes occur when an employee makes an unauthorized use of his organization's property without actually stealing the property. Unconcealed larceny, as its name implies, involves the theft of noncash assets without the use of fraudulent bookkeeping entries to conceal the theft.

Fraudulent asset requisitions and transfers schemes involve the use of internal documents to cause inventory, supplies, or equipment to be moved from one location to another or allocated to a particular project. These documents do not necessarily account for missing property, but they enable the perpetrator to gain access to and transport the property and thus provide an opportunity to steal it.

In purchasing and receiving schemes, an employee steals incoming merchandise by fraudulently marking incoming shipments as "short" to conceal the theft. Fraudulent shipments are a category of noncash theft in which a fraudster causes his organization to ship out merchandise as though it had been sold. The shipments are typically sent to the perpetrator or an accomplice.

The key concealment issue for a fraudster in a noncash theft case is shrinkage, which may be defined as the unaccounted-for reduction in an organization's inventory that results from theft. Inventory shrinkage is generally concealed on the victim organization's books through the alteration of inventory records (either manually or by false entry), the creation of fictitious sales and receivables, the fraudulent writing off of noncash assets as "scrap," or physical padding (in which empty boxes or containers are used to create the appearance of extra inventory on hand).

We also addressed misappropriation of intangible asset schemes, specifically the misappropriation of information and securities. Because theft of company information—including customer information, trade secrets, new product designs, and marketing plans—can undermine a company's value, reputation, and competitive advantages, the information must be protected through an effective information security system. In addition, companies must maintain proper internal controls to protect their securities and other noncash investments from misappropriation.

ESSENTIAL TERMS

Unconcealed larceny Schemes in which an employee steals an asset without attempting to conceal the theft in the organization's books and records.

Fraudulent write-offs A method used to conceal the theft of noncash assets by justifying their absence on the books. Stolen items are removed from the accounting system by being classified as scrap, lost or destroyed, damaged, bad debt, scrap shrinkage, discounts and allowances, returns, and so forth.

Shrinkage The unaccounted-for reduction in an organization's inventory that results from theft. Shrinkage is a common red flag of fraud.

Perpetual inventory A method of accounting for inventory in the records by continually updating the amount of inventory on hand as purchases and sales occur.

Physical inventory A detailed count and listing of assets on hand.

Forced reconciliation A method of concealing fraud by manually altering entries in an organization's books and records or by intentionally miscomputing totals. In the case of noncash misappropriations, inventory records are typically altered to create a false balance between physical and perpetual inventory.

Physical padding A fraud concealment scheme in which the fraudsters try to create the appearance that there are more assets on hand in a warehouse or stockroom than there actually are (e.g., by stacking empty boxes to create illusion of extra inventory).

REVIEW QUESTIONS

9-1 (Learning objective 9-1) What are the five categories of schemes used to misappropriate noncash tangible assets identified in this chapter?

9-2 (Learning objective 9-2) According to the *2009 Global Fraud Survey*, how do noncash misappropriations compare with cash misappropriations in terms of frequency and cost?

What two types of noncash assets were most commonly misappropriated?

9-3 (Learning objective 9-3) What are some examples of asset misuse? Give at least three.

9-4 (Learning objective 9-4) What is an "unconcealed larceny" scheme?

9-5 (Learning objective 9-6) Able is a job-site supervisor for ABC Construction. Able is responsible for overseeing the construction of a number of residential homes, and for making sure each of his crews has sufficient materials to complete its work. All of ABC's lumber and other building materials are stored in a central warehouse and are released upon signed authorization from job-site supervisors as needed. Able requests twice the amount of lumber that is actually needed for a particular job. He uses the excess materials to build a new deck on his home. How would Able's scheme be categorized?

9-6 (Learning objective 9-9) What is "shrinkage"?

9-7 (Learning objectives 9-8 and 9-10) Baker works in the sales department of ABC Company, which manufactures computer chips. Baker creates false documentation indicating that XYZ, Inc. (a nonexistent company) has agreed to purchase a large quantity of computer chips. The computer chips are shipped to XYZ, Inc. "headquarters," which is really Baker's house. How would Baker's scheme be categorized, and what are some red flags that might occur as a result of the scheme?

9-8 (Learning objective 9-7) How do employees use falsified receiving reports as part of schemes to steal inventory?

9-9 (Learning objective 9-10) What is meant by the term *physical padding*?

9-10 (Learning objective 9-10) What are the four methods identified in this chapter by which employees conceal inventory shrinkage?

9-11 (Learning objective 9-11) Provide an example of a misappropriation of intangibles scheme.

DISCUSSION ISSUES

9-1 (Learning objective 9-3) Jones is the manager of ABC Auto Repair. Unknown to his employer, Jones also does freelance auto repair work to earn extra cash. He sometimes uses ABC's facilities and tools for these jobs. Discuss the costs and potential costs that ABC might suffer as a result of Jones's actions.

9-2 (Learning objectives 9-4 and 9-5) Discuss how establishing a strong system of communication between employees and management can help deter and detect inventory larceny.

9-3 (Learning objectives 9-5 and 9-6) In the case study "Chipping Away at High-Tech Theft," do you believe the procedures and controls maintained by the manufacturer contributed to the theft? Why, or why not?

9-4 (Learning objective 9-5) Discuss the controls that an organization should have in place to effectively prevent and detect larceny of inventory.

9-5 (Learning objective 9-7) Baker was in charge of computer systems for ABC Company. As part of a general upgrade, the company authorized the purchase of twenty new computers for the employees in its marketing department. Baker secretly changed the order so that twenty-one computers were purchased. When they were delivered, he stole the extra computer. Later, ten more new computers were purchased for the ten employees in the company's research and development department. Baker also stole one of these computers. How should these two schemes be classified under the fraud tree?

9-6 (Learning objectives 9-8 and 9-12) Baker is an auditor for ABC Company. As part of a proactive fraud audit, Baker runs the following tests: (1) a review of the sales register for dormant customer accounts that posted a sale within the last two months; and (2) a comparison of the sales register and the shipment register for shipping documents that have no associated sales order. Taken together, what type of noncash scheme is Baker most likely to find with these tests? Explain how each one might identify fraud.

9-7 (Learning objective 9-8) Explain why the following circumstances might indicate that one or more employees are stealing merchandise: (1) an increase in uncollectable sales from previous periods and (2) an increase in damaged or obsolete inventory from previous periods.

ENDNOTES

1. Lanza, pp. 41–44.

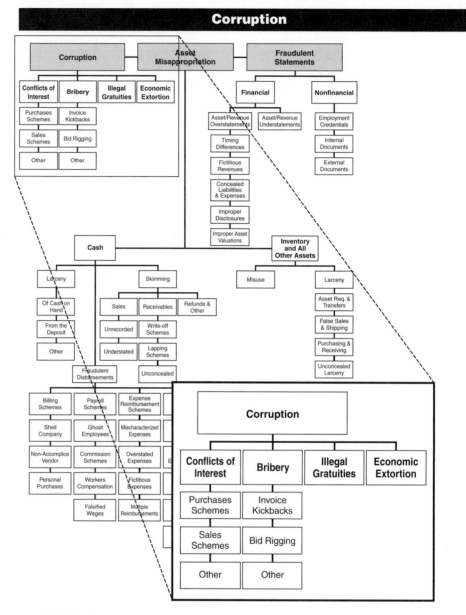

EXHIBIT 10-1

CHAPTER 10

CORRUPTION

LEARNING OBJECTIVES

After studying this chapter, you should be able to

10-1 Define corruption

10-2 Identify the four categories of corruption

10-3 Define bribery

10-4 Compare and contrast bribery, extortion, and illegal gratuities

10-5 Identify the two categories of bribery schemes

10-6 Understand kickback schemes and how they are committed

10-7 Understand bid-rigging schemes and explain how they are categorized

10-8 Describe the types of abuses that are committed at each stage of the competitive bidding process

10-9 Be familiar with the controls and techniques that can be used to prevent and detect bribery

10-10 Define conflicts of interest

10-11 Differentiate conflicts of interest from bribery schemes and billing schemes

10-12 List and understand the two major categories of conflicts of interest

10-13 Be familiar with proactive audit tests that can be used to detect corruption schemes

---

CASE STUDY: WHY IS THIS FURNITURE FALLING APART?[1]

A number of years ago, the *Washington Post* ran a series of articles detailing charges of waste, fraud, and abuse in the General Services Administration (GSA), the federal government's housekeeping agency. In particular, for more than a decade a furniture manufacturer in New Jersey had churned out $200 million worth of defective and useless furniture that GSA purchased.

Despite years of complaints from GSA's customers about the shoddiness of the furniture and equipment, the GSA had done little to investigate the contractor, Art Metal U.S.A. Government agencies that had been issued the furniture, like the Internal Revenue Service, the Central Intelligence Agency, and the State Department,

told horror stories about furniture that fell apart, desks that collapsed, and chairs with one leg shorter than the others.

When federal employees complained to the GSA, they were ignored or rebuffed. "You didn't fill out the right form," GSA would say, or "You have to pay to ship it back to the contractor and wait two years and you might get a replacement." After several years, this behavior naturally gave rise to the speculation that bribery and corruption were the cause of the problem.

A series of articles in the *Washington Post* led to a congressional investigation. Peter Roman, then chief investigator for a subcommittee of the U.S. Senate Committee on Government Affairs, recalled when Senator Lawton Chiles of Florida, chairman of the subcommittee, called him to his office. "He wanted a full investigation into all the practices

[1]Several names and details have been changed to preserve anonymity.

of GSA," Roman said. Unlike a private audit, a congressional investigation involves a thorough review of financial and operational records, interviews, and sworn testimony, when necessary. If there is enough evidence to show a crime has been committed, then the U.S. Justice Department prosecutes. Roman said this was "one of the few white-collar fraud investigations the Senate had done in years, with the exception of the Investigation Subcommittee's organized crime inquiries."

The first step in such an analysis involved general oversight hearings for the Subcommittee on Federal Spending Practices and Open Government. At one of the first hearings, Mr. Phillip J. Kurans, president of the Art Metal furniture company, appeared, uninvited, and demanded an opportunity to testify. He told Senator Chiles that his company produced good-quality furniture at bargain prices and challenged the subcommittee to prove otherwise. He invited the senator to the plant in Newark, New Jersey, to inspect their records.

"Chiles had me in his office the next morning," Roman recalls. "He said, 'Tell them we accept their offer. Get up to New Jersey and find out what happened.'"

Roman assembled an investigation team borrowed from other federal agencies. The principals were Dick Polhemus, CFE, from the Treasury Department; Marvin Doyal, CFE, CPA; and Paul Granetto from the U.S. General Accounting Office. "We agreed that the logical approach was to do a cash flow analysis," Roman recalls. "If the furniture was defective, then someone had to generate cash to bribe somebody else to accept it. All of us had experience in following the money, so we went off to Newark to look for it."

Together, they paid a visit to Art Metal U.S.A. on behalf of the senator. Kurans grudgingly sent them into a large room filled with thirty years of financial records. In the past, the sheer volume of paper had caused two GSA investigations to end without incident and the company's own auditors to find nothing untoward. Half the team began controlling the checks, separating them out into operations and payroll, while the others reviewed the canceled checks to do a pattern analysis.

"Marvin Doyal and I still argue over which one of us first found the checks to a subcontractor that had been cashed rather than deposited," Roman says. "As we began to review the operational checks," he remembers, "one of the items that stood out were checks made out to one company, but under three different names: I. Spiegel, Spiegel Trucking Company, and Spiegel Trucking, Inc." Were the bookkeepers careless in writing the wrong name? The investigators discovered that the checks made out to I. Spiegel (which were folded into threes, like one would fold a personal check to be placed in a wallet) were cashed by one Isador Spiegel. These checks were not run through any Spiegel Trucking Co. business account and had been used solely for cash. The checks to Spiegel Trucking Co., on the other hand, "looked like they

had been used for actual delivery of furniture to various GSA depots or customers," Roman said.

The other item that caught the investigators' eyes involved checks made out simply to "Auction Expenses" for even sums of money. Kurans told them that the company bought used machinery for cash at auctions throughout the East Coast. That was the reason, he said, that the company spent large amounts of cash.

Yet when the team called operators of furniture auctions they found that auctions required the buyer to show up with a certified check for 10 percent of the amount bought. The rest was also to be paid with certified checks. Over four years, Art Metal generated $482,000 in cash through so-called "auction expenses." More than $800,000 flowing to Spiegel was converted into cash. This was enough evidence to garner Kurens a subpoena to appear before the subcommittee. The subpoena enabled investigators to obtain "literally a truckfull of documents" from Art Metal, Roman said, "which filled a whole room in the basement of the Russell Senate Office Building."

With over $1 million in cash discovered, the next step for the investigating team was to look for evidence of bribery. They painstakingly interviewed every furniture inspector in GSA's Region Two, eventually focusing on a former regional inspector of the GSA. Over the past four years, this man had bought eleven racehorses at an average price of $13,000 each—much more money than a GSA furniture inspector could afford. At this point, Senator Chiles authorized bringing in a special counsel. This was Charles Intriago, Esq., a former Miami Strike Force prosecutor. When confronted, the inspector availed himself of his Fifth Amendment rights, and the search for another witness continued. They found one: Louis Arnold, a retired bookkeeper at Art Metal. Arnold would testify that Art Metal management was paying off GSA inspectors. Arnold revealed a third source of cash, a petty cash fund totaling about $100,000 that was used to pay for the inspectors' lunches and hotel expenses.

Based on Arnold's testimony, investigators subpoenaed three banks that had photographed all of their cash transactions: "We found pictures of the treasurer, the plant manager, and occasionally one of the partners cashing these 'auction expense' checks and taking the money in twenties."

During the Senate hearings, several senior agency officials testified to the shoddiness of the furniture. Roman, who spent some time on the floor of the plant, saw many examples of shabby workmanship. For example, although plant managers claimed they had bought a quality paint machine to paint filing cabinets, Roman said all he ever saw was a man wearing a gas mask, with a hand-held paint sprayer, wildly spraying at cabinets that darted past him on a conveyor belt. "It was like seeing a little kid playing laser tag, and the target appears for half a second, and he takes a wild shot at it and hopes he hits the target," he said.

Marvin Doyal testified to the generation of $1.3 million in cash, a company official testified that the money had been used to bribe (unnamed) GSA inspectors, and company officials and GSA inspectors availed themselves of their Fifth Amendment rights. Interagency problems between the subcommittee and the Justice Department played a major role in a failed plea bargain with a former GSA official. At this point, Senator Chiles and the staff decided that the subcommittee had gone as far as it could go.

Why did Art Metal not make an attempt to hide their fraud? "In the first place," Roman said, "they thought nobody would ever come. Secondly, they had been the subject of two GSA-appointed investigations" that uncovered nothing.

The result of the investigations proved disappointing to Senator Chiles and the subcommittee staff. "In the end,"

however, Senator Chiles later said, "we achieved our legislative mission. We were disappointed that the plea bargain and other subcommittee efforts didn't pay off as fully as they might have, but we sure got GSA's attention."

Embarrassed by the subcommittee disclosures, GSA stopped awarding government furniture contracts to Art Metal U.S.A. Having lost what amounted to its sole customer, Art Metal soon went bankrupt. Its plant manager and general counsel were convicted of related offenses within two years. The investigations into the GSA prompted a housecleaning of that agency. At the time of the hearings, GSA had 27,000 employees; today, it employs about 13,000. GSA's role as the federal government's chief purchasing agent has been greatly diminished. The Art Metal case showed that centralized purchasing is not always a good idea.

OVERVIEW

In Chapter 1, we learned that occupational frauds fall into three major categories: *asset misappropriations, corruption*, and *fraudulent statements*. We have already covered the various forms of asset misappropriations in Chapters 2 through 9. Now, we turn our attention to corruption.

Black's Law Dictionary defines *corrupt* as "spoiled; tainted; vitiated; depraved; debased; morally degenerate. As used as a verb, to change one's morals and principles from good to bad." It further defines *corruption* as "an act done with an intent to give some advantage inconsistent with official duty and the rights of others. The act of an official or fiduciary person who unlawfully and wrongfully uses his station or character to procure some benefit for himself or for another person, contrary to duty and the rights of others." This strikes at the heart of what corruption is: an act in which a person uses his position to gain some personal advantage at the expense of the organization he represents.

Corruption Data from the ACFE *2009 Global Fraud Survey*

Frequency and Cost   Of 1,843 cases in the ACFE's 2009 survey, 33 percent involved a corruption scheme. Although corruption schemes were far less common than asset misappropriations, which have already been discussed, they were more costly. The median loss of corruption cases in the survey ($250,000) was nearly twice as large as the median loss of asset misappropriation schemes ($135,000) (see Exhibit 10-2 and 10-3).

Types of Corruption Schemes   In the fraud tree, corruption schemes can be broken down into four distinct categories: bribery, conflicts of interest, economic extortion, and illegal gratuities. As Exhibit 10-4 shows, approximately 56 percent of the corruption cases the ACFE researchers reviewed involved bribery, while 53 percent involved conflicts of interest.

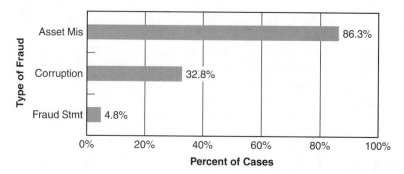

EXHIBIT 10-2 *2009 Global Fraud Survey*: Frequency of Three Major Fraud Categories[a]

[a]The sum of these percentages exceeds 100 percent because some cases involved multiple fraud schemes that fell into more than one category. Other charts in this chapter may reflect percentages that total in excess of 100 percent for similar reasons

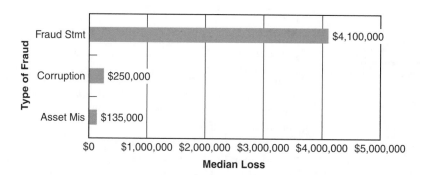

EXHIBIT 10-3 *2009 Global Fraud Survey*: Median Loss of Three Major Fraud Categories

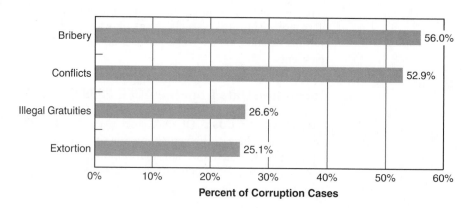

EXHIBIT 10-4 *2009 Global Fraud Survey*: Frequency of Corruption Schemes by Type

CORRUPTION SCHEMES

As previously mentioned, corruption schemes in the ACFE studies are broken down into four classifications:

- Bribery
- Illegal gratuities
- Economic extortion
- Conflicts of interest

Before discussing how corruption schemes work, we must understand the similarities and differences that exist among bribery, illegal gratuities, and extortion cases. *Bribery* may be defined as the offering, giving, receiving, or soliciting any thing of value to influence an official act. The term *official act* means that traditional bribery statutes proscribe only payments made to influence the decisions of government agents or employees. In the case of Art Metal U.S.A., this is exactly what happened. The furniture supplier paid off government inspectors to accept substandard merchandise.

Many occupational fraud schemes, however, involve *commercial bribery*, which is similar to the traditional definition of bribery except that something of value is offered to influence a business decision rather than an official act of government. Of course, payments are made every day to influence business decisions, and these payments are perfectly legal. When two parties sign a contract agreeing that one will deliver merchandise in return for a certain sum of money, this is a business decision that has been influenced by the offer of something of value. Obviously, this transaction is not illegal. In a commercial bribery scheme, however, the payment is received by an employee without his employer's consent. In other words, commercial bribery cases deal with the acceptance of under-the-table payments in return for the exercise of influence over a business transaction. Notice also that *offering* a payment can constitute a bribe, even if the illicit payment is never actually made.

Illegal gratuities are similar to bribery schemes, except that something of value is given to an employee to *reward* a decision rather than influence it. In an illegal gratuities scheme, a decision is made that happens to benefit a certain person or company. This decision is not influenced by any sort of payment. The party who benefited from the decision then rewards the person who made the decision. For example, in Case 1739 an employee of a utility company awarded a multimillion-dollar construction contract to a certain vendor and later received an automobile from that vendor as a reward.

At first glance, it may seem that illegal gratuities schemes are harmless if the business decisions in question are not influenced by the promise of payment. But most company ethics policies forbid employees from accepting unreported gifts from vendors. One reason is that illegal gratuities schemes can (and do) evolve into bribery schemes. Once an employee has been rewarded for an act such as directing business to a particular supplier, an understanding might be reached that future decisions beneficial to the supplier will also be rewarded. Additionally, even though an outright promise of payment has not been made, employees may direct business to certain companies in the hope that they will be rewarded with money or gifts.

Economic extortion cases are the "pay up or else" corruption schemes. Whereas bribery schemes involve an offer of payment intended to influence a business decision, economic extortion schemes are committed when one person demands payment from another. Refusal to pay the extorter results in some harm such as a loss of business. For instance, in Case 2234, an employee demanded payment from suppliers and in return awarded those suppliers subcontracts on various projects. If the suppliers refused to pay the employee, the subcontracts were awarded to rival suppliers, or were held back until the fraudster got his money.

Bribery, illegal gratuities, and economic extortion cases all bear a great deal of similarity in that they all involve an illicit payment from one party to another, either to influence a decision or as a reward for a decision already made. But conflicts of interest are different in nature. A conflict of interest occurs when an employee, manager, or executive has an undisclosed economic or personal interest in a transaction that adversely affects the organization. As with other corruption cases, conflict schemes involve the exertion of an employee's influence to the detriment of his employer. But whereas in bribery schemes a fraudster is paid to exercise his influence on behalf of a third party, in a conflict of interest scheme the perpetrator engages in *self*-dealing. The distinction between conflicts of interest and other forms of corruption will be discussed in greater detail later in this chapter.

BRIBERY

At its heart, a bribe is a business transaction, albeit an illegal or unethical one. As in the GSA case discussed above, a person "buys" something with the bribes he pays. What he buys is the influence of the recipient. Bribery schemes generally fall into two broad categories: *kickbacks* and *bid-rigging schemes*.

Kickbacks are undisclosed payments made by vendors to employees of purchasing companies. The purpose of a kickback is usually to enlist the corrupt employee in an overbilling scheme. Sometimes vendors pay kickbacks simply to get extra business from the purchasing company. Bid-rigging schemes occur when an employee fraudulently assists a vendor in winning a contract through the competitive bidding process.

Kickback Schemes

Kickback schemes are usually very similar to the billing schemes described in Chapter 4. They involve the submission of invoices for goods and services that are either overpriced or completely fictitious (see Exhibit 10-5).

Kickbacks are classified as corruption schemes rather than asset misappropriations because they involve collusion between employees and vendors. In a common type of kickback scheme, a vendor submits a fraudulent or inflated invoice to the victim company, and an employee of that company helps make sure that a payment is made on the false invoice. For his assistance, the employee-fraudster receives some form of payment from the vendor. This payment is the kickback.

Kickback schemes almost always attack the purchasing function of the victim company, so it stands to reason that these frauds are often undertaken by employees who have purchasing responsibilities. Purchasing employees often have direct contact with vendors and therefore have an opportunity to establish a collusive relationship. In Case 119, for instance, a purchasing agent redirected orders to a company owned by a supplier with whom he was conspiring. In return for the additional business, the supplier paid the purchasing agent over half the profits from the additional orders.

Diverting Business to Vendors   In some instances, an employee-fraudster receives a kickback simply for directing excess business to a vendor. There might be no overbilling involved in these cases; the vendor simply pays the kickbacks to ensure a steady stream

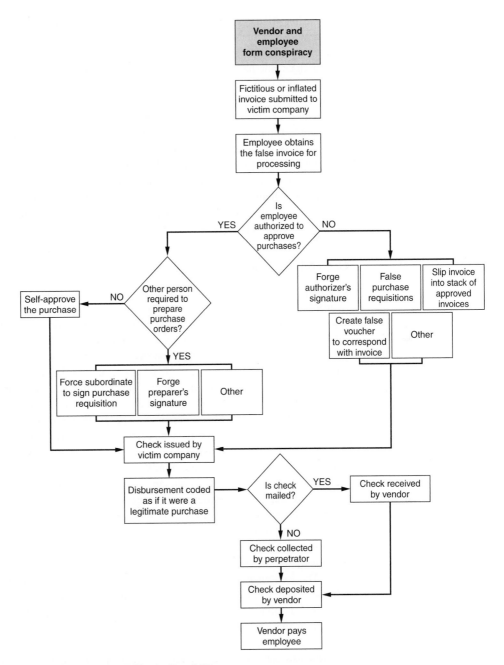

EXHIBIT 10-5 Kickbacks/Overbilling

of business from the purchasing company. In Case 1987, for instance, the president of a software supplier offered a percentage of ownership in his company to an employee of a purchaser in exchange for a major contract. Similarly, a travel agency in Case 1211 provided free travel and entertainment to the purchasing agent of a retail company. In return, the purchasing agent agreed to book all corporate trips through the travel agent.

If no overbilling is involved in a kickback scheme, one might wonder where the harm lies. Assuming the vendor simply wants to get the buyer's business and does not increase his prices or bill for undelivered goods and services, how is the buyer harmed? The problem is that, having bought off an employee of the purchasing company, a vendor is no longer subject to the normal economic pressures of the marketplace. This vendor does not have to compete with other suppliers for the purchasing company's business, and so has no incentive to provide a low price or quality merchandise. In these circumstances the purchasing company almost always ends up overpaying for goods or services, or getting less than it paid for. In Case 1211, described above, the victim company estimated that it paid $10,000 more for airfare over a two-year period by booking through the corrupt travel agency than if it had used a different company.

Once a vendor knows that he has an exclusive purchasing arrangement, his incentive is to raise prices to cover the cost of the kickback. Most bribery schemes end up as overbilling schemes even if they do not start that way. This is one reason why most business codes of ethics prohibit employees from accepting undisclosed gifts from vendors. In the long run, the employee's company is sure to pay for his unethical conduct.

Overbilling Schemes

Employees with Approval Authority   In most instances, kickback schemes begin as overbilling schemes in which a vendor submits inflated invoices to the victim company. The false invoices either overstate the cost of actual goods and services or reflect fictitious sales. In Case 520, an employee with complete authority to approve vouchers from a certain vendor authorized payment on over 100 fraudulent invoices in which the vendor's rates were overstated. Because no one was reviewing her decisions, the employee could approve payments on invoices at above-normal rates without fear of detection.

The ability to authorize purchases (and thus to authorize fraudulent purchases) is usually a key to kickback schemes. The fraudster in Case 520, for example, was a nonmanagement employee who had approval authority for purchases made from the vendor with whom she colluded. She authorized approximately $300,000 worth of inflated billings in less than two years. Similarly, in Case 127, a manager was authorized to purchase fixed assets for his company as part of a leasehold improvement. The assets he ordered were of a cheaper quality and lower price than what was specified, but the contract he negotiated did not reflect this. Therefore, the victim company paid for high-quality materials but received low-quality materials. The difference in price between what the company paid and what the materials actually cost was diverted back to the manager as a kickback.

The existence of purchasing authority can be critical to the success of kickback schemes. The ability of a fraudster to authorize payments himself means that he does not have to submit purchase requisitions to an honest superior who might question the validity of the transaction.

Fraudsters Lacking Approval Authority   Though the majority of the kickback schemes the ACFE researchers reviewed involved people with authority to approve purchases, this authority is not an absolute necessity. When an employee cannot approve fraudulent purchases himself, he can still orchestrate a kickback scheme if he can circumvent purchasing controls. In some cases, all that is required is the filing of a false purchase requisition. If a trusted employee tells his superior that the company needs certain materials or services, this is sometimes sufficient to get a false invoice approved for payment. Such schemes are generally successful when the person with approval authority is inattentive, or when she is forced to rely on her subordinates' guidance in purchasing matters.

Corrupt employees might also prepare false vouchers to make it appear that fraudulent invoices are legitimate. When proper controls are in place, a completed voucher is required before accounts payable will pay an invoice. One key is for the fraudster to create a purchase order that corresponds to the vendor's fraudulent invoice. The fraudster might forge the signature of an authorized party on the purchase order to show that the acquisition has been approved. If the payables system is computerized, an employee who has access to a restricted password can enter the system and authorize payments on fraudulent invoices.

In less sophisticated schemes, a corrupt employee might simply take a fraudulent invoice from a vendor and slip it into a stack of prepared invoices before they are input into the accounts payable system. (A more detailed description of how false invoices are processed is found in Chapter 4.)

Kickback schemes can be very difficult to detect. In a sense, the victim company is being attacked from two directions. Externally, a corrupt vendor submits false invoices that induce the victim company to unknowingly pay for goods or services that it does not receive. Internally, one or more of the victim company's employees waits to corroborate the false information provided by the vendor.

Other Kickback Schemes   Bribes are not always paid to employees to process phony invoices. In some circumstances outsiders seek other fraudulent assistance from employees of the victim company. In the case study at the beginning of this chapter, for instance, Art Metal U.S.A. paid huge sums to quality insurance inspectors so that the General Services Administration would accept Art Metal's substandard equipment. In this case the vendor was not overbilling the agency; he was instead trying to dump substandard products in lieu of providing equipment that met government specifications.

In other cases, bribes come not from vendors who are trying to sell something to the victim company, but rather from potential purchasers who seek a lower price from the victim company. In Case 1866, for instance, an advertising salesman not only sold ads, but was also authorized to bill for and collect on advertising accounts. He was also authorized to issue discounts to clients. In return for benefits such as free travel, lodging, and various gifts, this individual either sold ads at greatly reduced rates or gave free ads to those who bought him off. His complete control over advertising and a lack of oversight allowed this employee to "trade away" over $20,000 in advertising revenues. Similarly, in Case 986 the manager of a convention center accepted various gifts from show promoters. In return, he allowed these promoters to rent the convention center at prices below the rates approved by the city that owned the center.

Slush Funds   Every bribe is a two-sided transaction. In every case in which a vendor bribes a purchaser, there is someone on the vendor's side of the transaction who is making an illicit payment. It is therefore equally likely that employees are paying bribes as accepting them.

In order to obtain the funds to make these payments, employees usually divert company money into a slush fund, a noncompany account from which bribes can be made. Assuming that the briber's company does not authorize bribes, he must find a way to generate the funds necessary to illegally influence someone in another organization. Therefore, the key to the crime from the briber's perspective is the diversion of money into the slush fund. This fraudulent disbursement of company funds is usually accomplished by writing company checks to a fictitious entity or submitting false invoices in the name of the false entity. In Case 1605, for example, an officer in a very large health care organization created a fund to pay public officials and influence pending legislation.

This officer used check requests for several different expense codes to generate payments that went to one of the company's lobbyists, who placed the money in an account from which bribe money could be withdrawn. Most of the checks in this case were coded as "fees" for consulting or other services.

It is common to charge fraudulent disbursements to nebulous accounts like "consulting fees." The purchase of goods can be verified by a check of inventory, but there is no inventory for these kinds of services. It is therefore more difficult to prove that the payments are fraudulent. The discussion of exactly how fraudulent disbursements are made is found in Chapters 4 and 5.

Preventing and Detecting Kickback Schemes Kickback schemes are in most respects very similar to billing schemes, which were discussed in Chapter 4, with the added component that they include the active participation of a vendor in the fraud. Because of their similarity to billing schemes, the controls discussed earlier relating to billing fraud—separation of purchasing, authorization, receiving and storing goods, and cash disbursements; maintenance of an updated vendor list; and proper review and matching of all support in disbursement vouchers—may be effective in detecting or deterring some kickback schemes.

These controls, however, do not fully address the threat of kickback fraud, because they are principally designed to ensure the proper accounting of purchases and to spot abnormalities in the purchasing function. For example, separation of duties will help prevent a billing scheme in which an employee sets up a shell company and bills for nonexistent goods, because independent checks in authorization, receiving, and disbursements should identify circumstances in which a vendor does not exist or goods or services were never received. But this is not an issue in most kickback schemes, because the vendors in these frauds do exist, and in most cases these vendors provide real goods or services, albeit at an inflated price. Similarly, because the vendor is conspiring with a purchasing agent or another of the victim's employees, the fraudulent price will usually be agreed to by both parties at the outset, so that the terms on the vendor's invoices will match the terms on purchase orders, receiving reports, and so forth. On the face of the documents in the disbursements voucher, there will be no inconsistency or abnormality.

Many kickback schemes begin as legitimate, nonfraudulent transactions between the victim organization and an outside vendor. It is only after a relationship has been established between the vendor and an employee of the victim organization (e.g., a purchasing agent) that the conspiracy to overbill the victim organization begins. Since the vendors in these schemes were selected for legitimate reasons, controls such as independent verification of new vendors or independent approval of purchases will also not help detect or deter many kickback schemes.

In working to prevent and detect kickbacks, organizations must tailor their efforts to the specific red flags and characteristics of kickback schemes. For example, the key component to most kickback schemes is price inflation: the vendor fraudulently increases the price of goods or services to cover the cost of the kickback. Organizations should routinely monitor the prices paid for goods and services, comparing them to market rates. If more than one supplier is used for a certain type of good or service, prices should be compared among these suppliers as well. If a certain vendor is regularly charging above market rates, this could indicate a kickback scheme.

Organizations should also monitor trends in the cost of goods and services that are purchased. If a supplier raises its prices to cover the cost of kickbacks, this increase may be noticeable. Furthermore, kickbacks, like most other fraud schemes, often start small and increase over time as the fraudsters become emboldened by their success. Kickback schemes often start with relatively small 5 percent or 10 percent overcharges, but as these frauds progress, the supplier and corrupt employee may begin to bill for several times the legitimate purchase price.

In order to help detect overcharges, price thresholds should be established for materials purchases. Deviations from these thresholds should be noted and the reasons for the deviations verified in advance of payment. In addition, organizations should maintain an up-to-date vendor list, and purchases should be made only from suppliers who have been approved. As part of the approval process, organizations should take into account the honesty, integrity, and business reputation of prospective vendors.

Kickback schemes not only frequently result in overcharges, but they may also result in the purchase of excessive quantities of goods or services from a corrupt supplier. Organizations should track purchase levels by vendor and routinely monitor these trends for excessive purchases from a certain supplier or deviations from a standard vendor rotation, if one exists. Unusually high-volume purchases from a vendor that do not appear to be justified by business need are frequently a sign of fraud.

It is important to monitor not only the number of transactions per vendor, but also the amount of materials being ordered in any given transaction. Purchases should be routinely reviewed to make sure materials are being ordered at the optimal reorder point. If inventory is overstocked with materials provided by a particular vendor, this may indicate a kickback scheme.

On the other hand, some kickback schemes progress to the point at which a corrupt employee will pay invoices without any goods or services actually being delivered by the vendor. In these cases, inventory shortages—purchases that cannot be traced to inventory—can also signal fraud.

Another potential sign of fraud is the purchase of inferior-quality inventory or merchandise. This may result from kickback schemes in which a corrupt employee initiates a purchase of premium-quality merchandise from a vendor but the vendor delivers lower-quality (less expensive) merchandise. The difference in price between the materials that were contracted for and those that were actually delivered is kicked back to the corrupt purchasing agent or split between the purchasing agent and the vendor.

As with any form of billing fraud, kickback schemes have the potential to create budget overruns, either because of overcharges or excessive quantities purchased, or both. Actual expenditures should be compared to budgeted amounts and to prior years, with follow-up for significant deviations.

As a preventative measure, organizations should assign an employee who is independent of the purchasing function to routinely review the organization's buying patterns for signs of fraud such as those discussed above. In order to provide an appropriate audit trail for this type of review, organizations should require that all purchase decisions be adequately documented, showing who initiated the purchase, who approved it, who received the materials, and so on.

Because any investigation of a kickback scheme will likely necessitate a review of the corrupt vendor's books, all contracts with suppliers should contain a "right-to-audit" clause, a standard provision in many purchasing contracts that requires the supplier to retain and make available to the purchaser support for all invoices issued under the contract. In short, a right-to-audit clause gives an organization the right to review the supplier's internal records to determine whether fraud occurred.

Finally, organizations should establish written policies prohibiting employees from soliciting or accepting any gift or favor from a customer or supplier. These policies should also expressly forbid employees from engaging in any transaction on behalf of the organization when they have an undisclosed personal interest in the transaction. This should be a standard part of any organizational ethics policy, and it serves two purposes: (1) it clearly explains to employees what types of conduct are considered to be improper, and (2) it provides grounds for termination if an employee accepts a bribe or kickback while preventing the employee from claiming that she did not know that such conduct was prohibited.

Bid-Rigging Schemes

As we have said, when one person pays a bribe to another, he does so to gain the benefit of the recipient's influence. The competitive bidding process, in which several suppliers or contractors are vying for contracts in what can be a very cutthroat environment, can be tailor-made for bribery. Any advantage one vendor can gain over his competitors in this arena is extremely valuable. The benefit of "inside influence" can ensure that a vendor will win a sought-after contract. Many vendors are willing to pay for this influence.

In the competitive bidding process, all bidders are legally supposed to be placed on the same plane of equality, bidding on the same terms and conditions. Each bidder competes for a contract based on the specifications set forth by the purchasing company. Vendors submit confidential bids stating the price at which they will complete a project in accordance with the purchaser's specifications.

The way competitive bidding is rigged depends largely on the level of influence of the corrupt employee. The more power a person has over the bidding process, the more likely the person is to be able to influence the selection of a supplier. Therefore, employees involved in bid-rigging schemes, like those in kickback schemes, tend to have a good measure of influence or access to the competitive bidding process. Potential targets for accepting bribes include buyers, contracting officials, engineers and technical representatives, quality or product assurance representatives, subcontractor liaison employees, and anyone else with authority over the awarding of contracts.

Bid-rigging schemes can be categorized based on the stage of bidding at which the fraudster exerts his influence. Bid-rigging schemes usually occur in the presolicitation phase, the solicitation phase, or the submission phase of the bidding process (see Exhibit 10-6).

The Presolicitation Phase

In the presolicitation phase of the competitive bidding process—before bids are officially sought for a project—bribery schemes can be broken down into two distinct types. The first is the need recognition scheme, whereby an employee of a purchasing company is paid to convince his company that a particular project is necessary. The second reason to bribe someone in the presolicitation phase is to have the specifications of the contract tailored to the strengths of a particular supplier.

Need Recognition Schemes

The typical fraud in the need recognition phase of the contract negotiation is a conspiracy between the buyer and contractor whereby an employee of the buyer receives something of value and in return recognizes a "need" for a particular product or service. The result of such a scheme is that the victim company purchases unnecessary goods or services from a supplier at the direction of the corrupt employee.

There are several trends that may indicate a need recognition fraud. Unusually high requirements for stock and inventory levels may reveal a situation in which a corrupt employee is seeking to justify unnecessary purchase activity from a certain supplier. An employee might also justify unnecessary purchases of inventory by writing off large numbers of surplus items to scrap. As these items leave the inventory, they open up

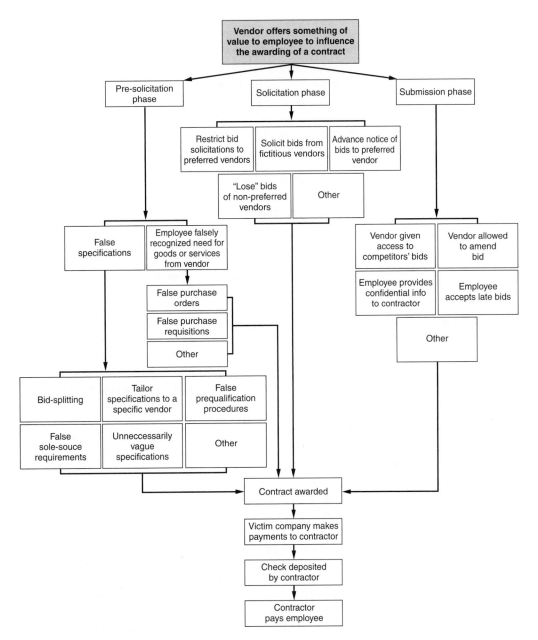

EXHIBIT 10-6 Bid-Rigging (Bribery)

spaces to justify additional purchases. Another indicator of a need recognition scheme is the defining of a "need" that can be met only by a certain supplier or contractor. In addition, the failure to develop a satisfactory list of backup suppliers may reveal an unusually strong attachment to a primary supplier—an attachment that is explainable by the acceptance of bribes from that supplier.

Specifications Schemes The other type of presolicitation fraud is a specifications scheme. The specifications of a contract are a list of the elements, materials, dimensions, and other relevant requirements for completion of the project. Specifications are prepared to assist vendors in the bidding process, telling them what they are required to do and providing a firm basis for making and accepting bids.

One corruption scheme that occurs in this process is the fraudulent tailoring of specifications to a particular vendor. In these cases, the vendor pays off an employee of the buyer who is involved in the preparation of specifications for the contract. In return, the employee sets the specifications of the contract to accommodate that vendor's capabilities. In Case 1063, for instance, a supplier paid an employee of a public utility to write contract specifications that were so proprietary that they effectively eliminated all competition for the project. For four years this supplier won the contract, which was the largest awarded by the utility company. The fraud cost the utility company in excess of $2 million.

The methods used to restrict competition in the bidding process may include the use of "prequalification" procedures that are known to eliminate certain competitors. For instance, the bid may require potential contractors to have a certain percentage of female or minority ownership. There is nothing illegal with such a requirement, but if it is placed in the specifications as a result of a bribe rather than as the result of other factors, then the employee has sold his influence to benefit a dishonest vendor—a clear case of corruption.

Sole-source or noncompetitive procurement justifications may also be used to eliminate competition and steer contracts to a particular vendor. In Case 2015, a requisitioner distorted the requirements of a contract up for bid, claiming the specifications called for a sole-source provider. Based on the requisitioner's information, competitive bidding was disregarded and the contract was awarded to a particular supplier. A review of other bids received at a later date showed that certain materials were available for up to $70,000 less than what the company paid in the sole-source arrangement. The employee had helped divert the job to the contractor in return for a promise of future employment. Competitive bidding was also disregarded in Case 1075, wherein management staff of a state entity took bribes from vendors to authorize purchases of approximately $200,000 in fixed assets.

Another type of specifications scheme is the deliberate writing of vague specifications. In this type of scheme, a supplier pays an employee of the purchasing company to write specifications that will require amendments at a later date. This will allow the supplier to raise the price of the contract when the amendments are made. As the buyer's needs become more specific or more detailed, the vendor can claim that, had he known what the buyer actually wanted, his bid on the project would have been higher. In order to complete the project as defined by the amended specifications, the supplier will have to charge a higher price.

Another form of specifications fraud is bid-splitting. In Case 1797, a manager of a federal employer split a large repair job into several component contracts in order to divert the jobs to his brother-in-law. Federal law required competitive bidding on projects over a certain dollar value. The manager broke the project up so that each smaller project was below the mandatory bidding level. Once the contract was split, the manager hired his brother-in-law to handle each of the component projects. Thus, the brother-in-law got the entire contract while avoiding competitive bidding.

A less egregious, but still unfair, form of bid-rigging occurs when a vendor pays an employee of the buyer for the right to see the specifications earlier than her competitors are able to. The employee does not alter the specifications to suit the vendor, but rather simply gives her a head start on planning her bid and preparing for the job. The extra planning time gives the vendor an advantage over her competitors in preparing a bid for the job.

The Solicitation Phase In the solicitation phase of the competitive bidding process, fraudsters attempt to influence the selection of a contractor by restricting the pool of competitors from whom bids are sought. In other words, a corrupt vendor pays an employee of the purchasing company to assure that one or more of the vendor's competitors do not get to bid on the contract. In this manner, the corrupt vendor is able to improve his chances of winning the job.

One type of scheme involves the sales representative who deals on behalf of a number of potential bidders. The sales representative bribes a contracting official to rig the solicitation, ensuring that only those companies represented by him get to submit bids. It is not uncommon in some sectors for buyers to "require" bidders to be represented by certain sales or manufacturing representatives. These representatives pay a kickback to the buyer to protect their clients' interests. The result of this transaction is that the purchasing company is deprived of the ability to get the best price on its contract. Typically, the group of "protected" vendors will not actually compete against each other for the purchaser's contracts, but instead engage in "bid-pooling."

Bid-Pooling Bid-pooling is a process by which several bidders conspire to split up contracts and ensure that each gets a certain amount of work. Instead of submitting confidential bids, the vendors decide in advance what their bids will be so that they can guarantee that each vendor will win a share of the purchasing company's business. For example, if vendors A, B, and C are up for three separate jobs, they may agree that A's bid will be the lowest on the first contract, that B's bid will be the lowest on the second contract, and that C's bid will be the lowest on the third contract. None of the vendors gets all three jobs, but each is at least guaranteed to get one. Furthermore, since they plan their bids ahead of time, the vendors can conspire to raise their prices; the purchasing company suffers as a result of the scheme.

Fictitious Suppliers Another way to eliminate competition in the solicitation phase of the selection process is to solicit bids from fictitious suppliers. In Case 1797 discussed above (the bid-splitting case), the brother-in-law submitted quotes in the names of several different companies and performed work under these various names. Although confidential bidding was avoided in this case, the perpetrator used quotes from several of the brother-in-law's fictitious companies to demonstrate price reasonableness on the final contracts. In other words, the brother-in-law's fictitious price quotes were used to validate his actual prices.

Other Methods In some cases, competition for a contract can be limited by severely restricting the time for submitting bids. Certain suppliers are given advance notice of contracts before bids are solicited. These suppliers are therefore able to begin preparing their bids ahead of time. With the short time frame for developing bid proposals, the supplier with advance knowledge of the contract will have a decided advantage over his competition.

Bribed purchasing officials can also restrict competition for their co-conspirators by soliciting bids in obscure publications where they are unlikely to be seen by other vendors. Again, this is done to eliminate potential rivals and create an advantage for the corrupt suppliers. Some schemes have also involved the publication of bid solicitations during holiday periods when those suppliers not "in the know" are unlikely to be looking for potential contracts. In more blatant cases, the bids of outsiders are accepted but are "lost" or improperly disqualified by the corrupt employee of the purchaser.

Typically, when a vendor bribes an employee of the purchasing company to assist him in any kind of solicitation scheme, the cost of the bribe is included in the corrupt vendor's bid. Therefore, the purchasing company ends up bearing the cost of the illicit payment, in the form of a higher contract price.

The Submission Phase In the actual submission phase of the process, wherein bids are proffered to the buyer, several schemes may be used to win a contract for a particular supplier. The principal offense tends to be abuse of the sealed-bid process. Competitive bids are confidential; they are, of course, supposed to remain sealed until a specified date when all bids are opened and reviewed by the purchasing company. The person or persons who have access to sealed bids are often the targets of unethical vendors who are seeking an advantage in the process. In Case 1170, for example, gifts and cash payments were given to a majority owner of a company in exchange for preferential treatment during the bidding process. The supplier who paid the bribes was allowed to submit his bids last, knowing what prices his competitors had quoted, or, alternatively, was allowed to actually see his competitors' bids, and adjust his own accordingly.

Vendors also bribe employees of the purchaser for information on how to prepare their bid. In Case 613, the general manager for a purchasing company provided confidential pricing information to a supplier that enabled the supplier to outbid his competitors and win a long-term contract. In return, both the general manager and his daughter received payments from the supplier. Other reasons to bribe employees of the purchaser include to ensure receipt of a late bid or to falsify the bid log, to extend the bid opening date, and to control bid openings.

Preventing and Detecting Bid-Rigging Schemes Bid-rigging is a form of bribery similar to kickback schemes, which were already discussed, and in many instances this type of fraud involves the payment of kickbacks to corrupt employees of the purchasing organization. Therefore, many of the antifraud measures discussed earlier under the heading "Preventing and Detecting Kickback Schemes" will also be effective in dealing with bid-rigging frauds. In addition, a number of prevention and detection methods are specifically applicable to the competitive bidding process.

Bid-rigging schemes are often uncovered because of unusual bidding patterns that emerge during the process. Perhaps the most common indicator of collusive bidding practices is an unusually high contract price. For example, if two or more contractors conspire with an employee in the bidding process, or if an employee incorporates bids from fictitious vendors to artificially inflate the contract price, the winning bid (or in some cases all bids submitted) will be excessively high compared to expected prices, previous contracts, budgeted amounts, and so forth. Organizations should monitor price trends for such instances.

Another red flag sometimes arises in bid-rigging cases when low-bid awards are frequently followed by change orders or amendments that significantly increase payments to the contractor. This may indicate that the contractor has conspired with somebody in the purchasing organization who has the authority to amend the contract. The contractor submits a very low bid to ensure that its bid will win the contract, knowing that the final price will be inflated after the award.

Very large, unexplained price differences among bidders can also indicate fraud. As noted in the preceding paragraph, this condition may arise when one supplier submits a very low bid with the understanding that the final contract price will later be inflated. Significant cost differences among bidders can also occur when an honest bidder submits a proposal in a competitive bidding process that was previously dominated by a group of suppliers who were conspiring, by means of a bid-pooling scheme, to keep prices artificially high.

Red flags might also appear from certain patterns within the bidding process. For example, if the last contractor to submit a bid repeatedly wins the contract, this would tend to indicate that an employee of the purchasing organization is allowing vendors to see their competitors' bids. The corrupt supplier would wait until all other bids have been submitted, then would use its inside knowledge to narrowly undercut the competition with a last-minute proposal. This narrow margin of victory can itself be a sign of fraud. If the winning bidder repeatedly wins contracts by a very slim margin, this could also indicate that the bidder has an accomplice working within the purchasing organization.

In bid-pooling schemes, as discussed above, several vendors conspire to fix their bids so that each one wins a certain number of contracts, thereby removing the competitive element of the bidding prices and enabling the corrupt suppliers to collectively inflate their prices. These schemes may result in a predictable rotation of bid winners, something that would not be expected in a truly competitive bidding process. Any sort of predictable pattern of contract award that is based on a factor other than price or quality should be investigated.

Another red flag consistent with collusive bidding occurs when losing bidders frequently appear as subcontractors on the project. This tends to indicate that the suppliers conspired to divide the proceeds of the contract, agreeing that one would win the award while others would receive a certain portion of the project through subcontracting arrangements. In some cases, the low bidder will withdraw and subsequently become a subcontractor after the job has been awarded to another supplier.

A corrupt employee or vendor will sometimes submit bids from fictitious suppliers to create the illusion of competition where none really exists. In some cases, these frauds have been detected because the same calculations or errors occurred on two or more bids, or because two or more vendors had the same address, phone number, officer, and so forth.

Fraud may be indicated by a situation in which qualified bidders fail to submit contract proposals, or in which significantly fewer bidders than expected respond to a request for proposals. This type of red flag is consistent with schemes in which a corrupt employee purposely fails to advertise the contract up for bid. This eliminates competition and helps ensure that a certain supplier will be awarded the contract. Similarly, the number of bids might be reduced because a corrupt employee has destroyed or fraudulently disqualified the bids of contractors who submitted more favorable proposals than the employee's co-conspirator.

Finally, bid-rigging may be indicated by the avoidance of competitive bidding altogether, such as occurs when an employee splits a large project into several smaller jobs that fall beneath a bidding threshold, then makes sole-source awards to favored suppliers.

Something of Value

Bribery was defined at the beginning of this chapter as "offering, giving, receiving, or soliciting any thing of value to influence an official act." A corrupt employee helps the briber obtain something of value, and in return the employee gives something of value. There are several ways for a vendor to "pay" an employee to surreptitiously aid the vendor's cause. The most common, of course, is money. In the most basic bribery scheme, the vendor simply gives the employee currency. This is what we think of in the classic bribery scenario—an envelope stuffed with currency being slipped under a table, a roll of bills hastily stuffed into a pocket. These payments are preferably made with currency rather than checks, because the payment is harder to trace. But currency may not be practical when large sums are involved. When this is the case, slush funds are usually set up to finance the illegal payments. In other cases, checks may be drawn directly from company accounts. These disbursements are usually coded as "consulting fees," "referral commissions," or the like.

Instead of cash payments, some employees accept promises of future employment as bribes. In Case 1590, for instance, a government employee gave a contractor inside information in order to win a bid on a multimillion-dollar contract in return for the promise of a high-paying job. As with money, the promise of employment might be intended to benefit a third party rather than the corrupt employee. In Case 1584, a consultant who worked for a particular university hired the daughter of one of the university's employees.

In Case 1987, we also discussed how a corrupt individual diverted a major purchase commitment to a supplier in return for a percent of ownership in the supplier's business. This is similar to a bribe effected by the promise of employment, but also contains elements of a conflict of interest scheme. The promise of part ownership in the supplier amounts to an undisclosed financial interest in the transaction for the corrupt employee.

Gifts of all kinds may also be used to corrupt an employee. The types of gifts used to sway an employee's influence can include free liquor and meals, free travel and accommodations, cars, other merchandise, and even sexual favors.

Other inducements include the paying off of a corrupt employee's loans or credit card bills, the offering of loans on very favorable terms, and transfers of property at substantially below market value. The list of things that can be given to an employee in return for the exercise of his influence is almost endless. Anything that the employee values is fair game, and may be used to sway his loyalty.

ILLEGAL GRATUITIES

As stated, illegal gratuities are similar to bribery schemes, except there is not necessarily intent to influence a particular business decision. An example of an illegal gratuity was found in Case 2294, in which a city commissioner negotiated a land development deal with a group of private investors. After the deal was approved, the commissioner and his wife were rewarded with a free international vacation, all expenses paid. While the promise of this trip may have influenced the commissioner's negotiations, this would be difficult to prove. However, merely accepting such a gift amounts to an illegal gratuity, an act that is prohibited by most government and private company codes of ethics.

ECONOMIC EXTORTION

As stated earlier, economic extortion is basically the flip side of a bribery scheme. Instead of a vendor offering a payment to an employee to influence a decision, the employee demands a payment from a vendor in order to make a decision in that vendor's favor. In any situation in which an employee might accept bribes to favor a particular company or person, the situation could be reversed so that the employee extorts money from a potential purchaser or supplier. In Case 802, for example, a plant manager for a utility company started his own business on the side. Vendors who wanted to do work for the utility company were forced by the manager to divert some of their business to his own company. Those who did not "play ball" lost their business with the utility.

CONFLICTS OF INTEREST

As we stated earlier in this chapter, a conflict of interest occurs when an employee, manager, or executive has an undisclosed economic or personal interest in a transaction that adversely affects the company. The key word in this definition is *undisclosed*. The crux of a conflict case is that the fraudster takes advantage of his employer; the victim organization is unaware that its employee has divided loyalties. If an employer knows of the employee's interest in a business deal or negotiation, there can be no conflict of interest, no matter how favorable the arrangement is for the employee.

Most conflict cases occur because the fraudster has an undisclosed *economic* interest in a transaction. But the fraudster's hidden interest is not necessarily economic. In some scenarios an employee acts in a manner detrimental to his employer in order to provide a benefit to a friend or relative, even though the fraudster receives no financial benefit from the transaction himself. In Case 1797, for instance, a manager split a large repair project into several smaller projects to avoid bidding requirements. This allowed the manager to award the contracts to his brother-in-law. Though there was no indication that the manager received any financial gain from this scheme, his actions nevertheless amounted to a conflict of interest.

Any bribery scheme could potentially be considered a conflict of interest—after all, an employee who accepts a bribe clearly has an undisclosed economic interest in the transaction (in the form of the bribe that he is paid), and he is clearly not working with his employer's best interests at heart. The reason that some schemes are classified as briberies but others are classified as conflicts of interest is a question of motive.

If an employee approves payment on a fraudulent invoice submitted by a vendor in return for a kickback, this is bribery. But if an employee approves payment on invoices submitted by her own company (and if the ownership is undisclosed), this is a conflict of interest. This was the situation in Case 1132, in which an office service employee recommended his own company to do repairs and maintenance on office equipment for his employer. The fraudster approved invoices for approximately $30,000 in excessive charges.

The distinction between the two schemes is obvious. In the bribery case, the fraudster approves the invoice in return for a kickback, whereas in a conflict of interest case he approves the invoice because of his own hidden interest in the vendor. Aside from the employee's motive for committing the crime, the mechanics of the two transactions are practically identical. The same duality can be found in bid-rigging cases, wherein an employee influences the selection of a company in which he has a hidden interest, rather than influencing the selection of a vendor who has bribed him.

However, conflict schemes do not always simply mirror bribery schemes. There are vast numbers of ways in which an employee can use his influence to benefit a company in which he has a hidden interest. The majority of conflict schemes fit into one of two categories:

- Purchasing schemes
- Sales schemes

In other words, most conflicts of interest arise when a victim company unwittingly *buys* something at a high price from a company in which one of its employees has a hidden interest, or unwittingly *sells* something at a low price to a company in which one of its employees has a hidden interest. Most of the other conflict cases the ACFE researchers reviewed involved employees who stole clients or diverted funds from their employer.

CASE STUDY: WORKING DOUBLE DUTY[2]

After grabbing a quick bite to eat at the mall, Troy Biederman spent the rest of his lunch hour shopping for clothes. He liked to present a professional appearance as a sales manager at ElectroCity, an electronics and appliance chain. While waiting on a charge approval at a small menswear store, Biederman spotted its promotion for a free La-Z-Boy and tossed his business card into the drawing fishbowl on the counter. Suddenly his eye caught a familiar name on top of the pile—Rita Mae King, the full-time purchasing agent at ElectroCity. The card, however, read: Rita Mae King, account executive at Spicewood Travel.

"He put two and two together and it smelled fishy," explained Bill Reed, the vice president of loss prevention at ElectroCity. Biederman knew Spicewood Travel was the agency his company used to book incentive trips for its sales force, of which he was a member. He also knew King enjoyed close ties with Spicewood—now he wondered how close. Biederman snatched King's card from the pile and discreetly turned it in to his boss that afternoon.

Within two weeks the business card had made its way up to the executive vice president of ElectroCity, a company that rings up annual sales of $450 million. Not wanting to jump to any conclusions, yet also suspecting that his purchasing agent might be in cahoots with a travel vendor, the EVP handed the card over to Bill Reed "to investigate the extent of the relationship."

Reed immediately requisitioned the accounts payable department for all corporate travel billings for the past three years. Early entries showed that the company had been using Executive Travel for most of its travel needs. In her first year as purchasing agent, however, King had introduced Spicewood and had placed it at the top of the travel vendor list. Reed said that although ElectroCity had never designated any one agency as its sole vendor, under the direction of the corporation's purchaser, Spicewood had squeezed out Executive Travel for the store's business—which now exceeded $200,000.

Corporate fraud examiners then phoned numerous other travel agencies, asking for quotes on similar services for the same period in an effort to compare prices. They found that many of the bills were inflated between 10 and 30 percent over the other agencies' package trips to destinations such as Trump Castle in Atlantic City and Bally's in Las Vegas. Calls to other branches of Spicewood Travel further confirmed significant overcharging by the local office, which King used exclusively.

Six days into his investigation, Reed took a statement from the corporate merchandising buyer at ElectroCity, who had experienced difficulties with King on several occasions

about competitively priced trips. He said King was insistent on using Spicewood. In his written account of a recent episode, the merchandising buyer told of personally shopping for a better price on an incentive vacation to the Cayman Islands. "With this trip, I went to an outside agent first and then gave Rita Mae the information to price this trip.

Spicewood came in almost $100 higher per person. Rita Mae did not book the trip through the lower-priced agent, but went back and had Spicewood requote for what was supposed to be the same trip. When I asked to have Spicewood's now lower requote spelled out exactly, I found that the airfare included an additional stopover, which lowered the airfare."

In order to establish King's relationship with the travel agency, Reed had one of his investigators call its local office and ask to speak with account executive Rita Mae King. Without missing a beat, the receptionist transferred him to Janet Levy, manager of corporate services. The investigator identified himself as an interested traveler who had King's business card and wanted her to book a good deal to the Bahamas. Levy assured him it would not be a problem since she worked closely with King. Levy then asked him to call King at another phone number. It turned out to be her number at ElectroCity.

"She was essentially running her own travel shop out of her office here," said Reed. Although she had no access to an online computer, she jerry-rigged a system for her travel customers. "Apparently, if King fed business to Spicewood, they would add that to her credit arrangement."

King operated out of a beehive of activity littered with paperwork, said Reed. The fifty-one-year-old married woman often kept two or three conversations going in her workplace at the same time. "She was a very take-charge, bossy kind of person—very outgoing, but also caustic in a lot of her interactions with other employees. Also quick to denigrate and complain." On the flip side, "She can be very ingratiating and very nice when she wants." Through her work, King became well networked in the travel industry, with many friends and lots of contacts.

After having established an outside business link between King and Spicewood, Reed then reviewed personnel records for her travel activity. Working on a hunch, he honed in on a vacation King took the previous December when she and a companion flew to the Caribbean island of Antigua via American Airlines.

Reed, a former police officer, scrutinized King's personal credit card statements from that time. An examination of the statements revealed a MasterCard charge from the Royal Antiguan Hotel. Again, Reed had one of his investigators place a call. Posing as "Mr. Lowell King," the investigator phoned the hotel claiming to need help with his travel

[2]Several names and details have been changed to preserve anonymity.

records in preparation for an IRS audit. The hotel book-keeper graciously faxed the "guest" a copy of the King hotel bill.

On the bill, King had listed her occupation as a travel agent, giving her business address as the local office of Spice-wood Travel. To receive a 50 percent discount on her room rate—a savings worth $412—she furnished the manager with her business card and an Airline Reporting Corporation number, a code issued by an international clearinghouse to identify every travel-booking agency. Though Reed suspected King might have gone on other company-subsidized trips, "Antigua was the only one we flushed out. We only needed one."

Further analysis of King's credit statements showed that she charged three other airline tickets over a seven-month period and received three corresponding credits that canceled out the price of the trips, saving her $834.

The fraud examiners clearly proved that King had breached her duty to act in the company's best interests in connection with her role as the company's purchasing agent. And she had also derived some benefit from a vendor—another violation of corporate policy. ElectroCity's personnel handbook addresses both issues: "Employees must disclose any outside financial interest that might influence their corporate decisions or actions. If the company believes that such activities are in conflict with the company's welfare, the employee will be expected to terminate such interests. Such interests include but are not limited to personal or family ownership or interest in a business deemed a customer, supplier, or competitor."

King broke other rules listed in the personnel handbook as well: "Employees may not use corporate assets for their personal use or gain. Employees and their families must never accept any form of under-the-table payments, kickbacks, or rebates, whether in cash or goods, from suppliers." Contrary to company policy, King had set up an off-site mini-agency using the company's phone, accepted travel discounts from a vendor for continued and increased business, and received an estimated 10 percent of the agency's billings in kickbacks.

Based on their findings, the examiners also determined that King violated the state's commercial bribery statute and could be liable for civil damages if the company decided to press charges. While Reed said that her transgressions warranted immediate termination, the ex-cop recommended against pursuing criminal action, given King's age and the ill health of her unemployed husband. "When you take someone to court, the only options you have are fines or prison."

He takes full responsibility for the decision not to prosecute King. Like police officers, security professionals must make appropriate assessments based on the circumstances,

Reed said. "The bad ones always follow the book, regardless of what's best for the community."

"We made the case, corrected the system within the company, and damaged her professionally," Reed said. Electro-City now requires all vendors to sign agreements acknowledging prohibitive behavior and gifts to all its employees, who now number 3,200. The errant employee was not required to make restitution.

Reed next brought the results of their fraud examination to the president of Spicewood Travel, who reacted with total silence and stunned disbelief. "The documentation was there. They knew they were going to lose business." The company also made verbal legal threats against the agency in the beginning. They held prolonged negotiations to recover $20,000, an estimate of two years of overcharges, "but another VP dropped that ball," said Reed.

The corporation's director of investigations conducted a corporate interview with King to make a final determination of the nature and extent of her relationship with Spicewood and to elicit evidence of any other kickback arrangements that might have adversely affected the company. Reed suggested that King be asked to furnish investigators with a full written disclosure of her interests and activities in connection with Spicewood and any other suppliers.

During the interview, King composed her thoughts in a handwritten letter to the president of ElectroCity:

> Dear Mr. Smith:
>
> I must say that I am sorry. It never dawned on me that what I did was in conflict of my trusted position here at ElectroCity. I truly screwed up; there is no explanation other than that. There was no consideration on my part that a reduced price was anything other than that. I never even thought about it. I am truly sorry, especially because I feel I have broken a trust that we have built over the years. Please understand that I meant nothing against ElectroCity or anyone. Additionally, I didn't even see that special rate as a benefit from a supplier, only as a manner by which I could save some dollars personally.
>
> Respectfully,
> Rita Mae King

King had misused her authority as a purchasing agent and had violated her duty to ElectroCity. "She was remorseful in the sense that she was now going to have to bite the bullet," said Reed. "I think she probably kicked herself because she didn't get more out of the scam. She felt that she was a woman who worked very hard at a very difficult job, was unappreciated, and was not compensated properly by a male-dominated class system in corporate America."

Purchasing Schemes

The majority of conflict schemes in our studies were purchasing schemes, and the most common of these was the overbilling scheme, the kind of fraud Rita Mae King committed in the preceding case study. We have already briefly discussed conflict schemes that involved false billings (see Case 1132, above). Because these frauds are very similar to the billing schemes discussed in Chapter 4 of this book, it will be helpful to discuss the distinction we have drawn between traditional billing schemes and purchasing schemes that are classified as conflicts of interest.

Though it is true that any time an employee assists in the overbilling of her company there is probably some conflict of interest (the employee causes harm to her employer because of a hidden financial interest in the transaction), this does not necessarily mean that every instance of false billing will be categorized as a conflict scheme. In order for the scheme to be classified as a conflict of interest, the employee (or a friend or relative of the employee) must have some kind of ownership or employment interest in the vendor that submits the invoice. This distinction is easy to understand if we look at the nature of the fraud. Why does the fraudster overbill her employer? If she engages in the scheme only for the cash, the scheme is a fraudulent disbursement billing scheme. If, on the other hand, she seeks to better the financial condition of her business at the expense of her employer, this is a conflict of interest. In other words, the fraudster's *interests* lie with a company other than her employer. When an employee falsifies the invoices of a third-party vendor to whom she has no relation, this is not a conflict of interest scheme, because the employee has no interest in that vendor. The sole purpose of the scheme is to generate a fraudulent disbursement.

One might wonder, then, why shell company schemes are classified as fraudulent disbursements rather than conflicts of interest. After all, the fraudster in a shell company scheme owns the fictitious company and therefore must have an interest in it. Remember, though, that shell companies are created for the sole purpose of defrauding the employer. The company is not so much an entity in the mind of the fraudster as it is a tool. In fact, a shell company is usually little more than a post office box and a bank account. The fraudster has no interest in the shell company that causes a division of loyalty; he simply uses the shell company to bilk his employer. Shell company schemes are therefore classified as false billing schemes.

A short rule of thumb can be used to distinguish between overbilling schemes that are classified as asset misappropriations and those that are conflicts of interest: If the bill originates from a *real company* in which the fraudster has an economic or personal interest, and if the fraudster's interest in the company is undisclosed to the victim company, then the scheme is a conflict of interest.

Now that we know what kinds of purchasing schemes are classified as conflicts of interest, the question is: How do these schemes work? After our lengthy discussion about distinguishing between conflicts and fraudulent disbursements, the answer is somewhat anticlimactic. The schemes work the same either way. The distinction between the two kinds of fraud is useful only to distinguish the status and purpose of the fraudster. The mechanics of the billing scheme, whether conflict or fraudulent disbursement, do not change (see Exhibit 10-7). In Case 464, for instance, a purchasing superintendent defrauded his employer by purchasing items on behalf of his employer at inflated prices from a certain vendor. The vendor in this case was owned by the purchasing superintendent but established in his wife's name and run by his brother. The perpetrator's interest in the company was undisclosed. The vendor would buy items on the open market, then inflate the prices and resell the items to the victim company. The purchasing

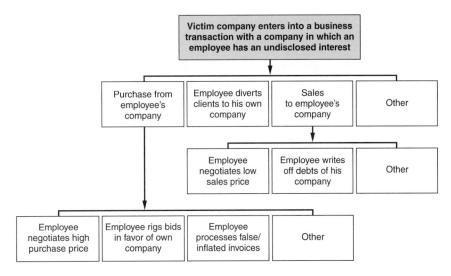

EXHIBIT 10-7 Conflicts of Interest

superintendent used his influence to ensure that his employer continued doing business with the vendor and paying the exorbitant prices. (A more detailed analysis of overbilling frauds is found in Chapter 4.)

Fraudsters also engage in bid-rigging on behalf of their own companies. The methods used to rig bids were discussed in detail earlier in this chapter. Briefly stated, an employee of the purchasing company is in a perfect position to rig bids, because he has access to the bids of his competitors. Since the fraudster can find out the amounts of the bids of other vendors, he can easily tailor his own company's bid to win the contract. Bid waivers are also sometimes used by fraudsters to avoid competitive bidding outright. In Case 1473, for instance, a manager processed several unsubstantiated bid waivers in order to direct purchases to a vendor in which one of his employees had an interest. The conflict was undisclosed, and the scheme cost the victim company over $150,000.

In other cases a fraudster might ignore his employer's purchasing rotation and direct an inordinate number of purchases or contracts to his own company. Any way by which a fraudster exerts his influence to divert business to a company in which he has a hidden interest is a conflict of interest.

But not all conflict schemes occur in the traditional vendor–buyer relationship. Several of the cases in our survey involved employees' negotiating for the purchase of some unique, typically large asset such as land or a building in which the employee had an undisclosed interest. It is in the process of these negotiations that the fraudster violates his duty of loyalty to his employer. Because he stands to profit from the sale of the asset, the employee does not negotiate in good faith on behalf of his employer; he does not attempt to get the best price possible. After all, the fraudster will reap a greater financial benefit if the purchase price is high.

An example of this type of scheme was found in Case 2421, in which a senior vice president of a utility company was in charge of negotiating and approving mineral leases on behalf of his company. Unknown to his employer, the vice president also owned the property on which the leases were made. The potential harm in this type of relationship is obvious—there was no financial motive for the vice president to negotiate a favorable lease for his employer.

Turnaround Sales   A special kind of purchasing scheme that we have encountered in the ACFE studies is called the turnaround sale, or flip. In this type of scheme an employee knows his employer is seeking to purchase a certain asset, and takes advantage of the situation by purchasing the asset himself (usually in the name of an accomplice or shell company). The fraudster then turns around and resells the item to his employer at an inflated price. We have already seen one example of this kind of scheme in Case 464 discussed above, in which a purchasing supervisor set up a company in his wife's name to resell merchandise to his employer. Another interesting example of the turnaround method occurred in Case 1379, in which the CEO of a company, conspiring with a former employee, sold an office building to the CEO's company. What made the transaction suspicious was that the former employee had purchased the building on the same day that it was resold to the victim company, and for $1.2 million less than the price charged to the CEO's company.

Sales Schemes

The ACFE studies identified two principal types of conflict schemes associated with the victim company's sales. The first and most harmful is the underselling of goods or services. Just as a corrupt employee can cause his employer to overpay for goods or services sold by a company in which he has a hidden interest, so, too, can he cause the employer to undersell to a company in which he maintains a hidden interest (see Exhibit 10-7).

Underbillings   In an underbilling scheme, the perpetrator sells goods or services below fair market value to a vendor in which he has a hidden interest. This results in a diminished profit margin, or even a loss on the sale, depending on the size of the discount. Two employees who sold their employer's inventory to their own company at off-spec prices, causing a loss of approximately $100,000, used this method in Case 2427. Another example was found in Case 2684, when an employee disposed of his employer's real estate by selling it below fair market value to a company in which he had a hidden interest, causing a loss of approximately $500,000.

Writing Off Sales   The other type of sales scheme involves tampering with the books of the victim company to decrease or write off the amount owed by an employee's business. For instance, after an employee's company purchases goods or services from the victim company, credit memos may be issued against the sale, causing it to be written off to contra accounts such as Discounts and Allowances. A plant manager in Case 2197 used this method; this fraudster assisted favored clients by delaying billing on their purchases for up to sixty days. When the receivable on these clients' accounts became delinquent, the perpetrator issued credit memos against the sales to delete them.

A large number of reversing entries to sales may be a sign that fraud is occurring in an organization. The fraudster in Case 2197 avoided the problem of too many write-offs by issuing new invoices on the sales after the "old" receivables were taken off the books. In this way, the receivables could be carried indefinitely on the books without ever becoming past due.

In other cases, the perpetrator might not write off the scheme, but simply delay billing. This is sometimes done as a favor to a friendly client, not as outright avoidance of the bill but rather as a dilatory tactic. The victim company eventually gets paid, but loses time value on the payment that arrives later than it should.

Other Conflict of Interest Schemes

Business Diversions In Case 1258, an employee started his own business to compete directly with his employer. While still employed by the victim company, this employee began siphoning off clients for his own business. This activity clearly violated the employee's duty of loyalty to his employer. There is nothing unscrupulous about free competition, but when a person acts as a representative of his employer it is certainly improper to try to undercut the employer and take clients. Similarly, the fraudster in Case 2161 steered potential clients away from his employer and toward his own business. There is nothing unethical about pursuing an independent venture (in the absence of restrictive employment covenants such as noncompete agreements), but if the employee fails to act in the best interests of his employer while carrying out his duties, then this employee is violating the standards of business ethics.

Resource Diversions Finally, some employees divert the funds and other resources of their employers to the development of their own business. In Case 209, for example, a vice president of a company authorized large expenditures to develop a unique type of new equipment used by a certain contractor. Another firm subsequently took over the contractor, as well as the new equipment. Shortly after that, the vice president retired and went to work for the firm that had bought out the contractor. The fraudster had managed to use his employer's money to fund a company in which he eventually developed an interest. This scheme involves elements of bribery, conflicts of interest, and fraudulent disbursements. In this particular case, if the vice president had financed the equipment in return for the promise of a job, his actions might have been properly classified as a bribery scheme. Case 209 nevertheless illustrates a potential conflict problem. The fraudster could just as easily have authorized the fraudulent expenditures for a company in which he secretly held an ownership interest.

 While these schemes are clearly corruption schemes, the funds are diverted through the use of a fraudulent disbursement. The money could be drained from the victim company through a check tampering scheme, a billing scheme, a payroll scheme, or an expense reimbursement scheme. (For a discussion of the methods used to generate fraudulent disbursements, please refer to Chapters 4–8.)

Financial Disclosures Management has an obligation to disclose to the shareholders significant fraud committed by officers, executives, and others in positions of trust. Management does not have the responsibility of disclosing uncharged criminal conduct of its officers and executives. However, if and when officers, executives, or other persons in trusted positions become subjects of a criminal indictment, disclosure is required.

 The inadequate disclosure of conflicts of interest is among the most serious of frauds. Inadequate disclosure of related-party transactions is not limited to any specific industry; it transcends all business types and relationships.

Preventing and Detecting Conflicts of Interest

Conflict of interest schemes are violations of the rule that a fiduciary, agent, or employee must act in good faith, with full disclosure, in the best interest of the principal or employer. Most schemes are a violation of the maxim that a person "cannot serve two masters." Some of the more common schemes involve an employee's, manager's, or executive's interest in a customer or supplier and receipt of gifts. Often, the employee, manager, or executive is compensated for her interest in the form of "consulting fees."

The prevention of conflicts of interest can be difficult. The primary resource for heading off this complex act is a company ethics policy that specifically addresses the problems and illegalities associated with conflicts of interest and related offenses. The purpose of the policy is to make the position of the company absolutely clear, to define what constitutes a conflict or an improper relationship, and to express in no uncertain terms that conflicts are not appropriate and will not be tolerated. The absence of a clear policy leaves an opportunity for a perpetrator to rationalize his behavior or to claim ignorance of any wrongdoing.

A policy requiring employees to complete an annual disclosure statement is also an excellent proactive approach to preventing conflicts of interest. Comparing the disclosed names and addresses with the vendor list may reveal real conflicts of interest and the appearance of such. Communication with employees regarding their other business interests is also advisable.

In order to detect conflicts of interest, organizations should concentrate on establishing an anonymous reporting mechanism to receive tips and complaints; this is how most conflict of interest cases are detected. Complaints typically come from employees who are aware of a coworker's self-dealing, or from vendors who have knowledge that a competing vendor who has ties to an employee of the organization is being favored.

Another detection method that can be helpful is to periodically run comparisons between vendor and employee addresses and phone numbers. Obviously, if a vendor is owned or run by an employee of the organization without that fact having been disclosed, this would constitute a conflict of interest.

PROACTIVE COMPUTER AUDIT TESTS FOR DETECTING CORRUPTION[1]

Title	Category	Description	Data file(s)
Stratify vendor payments by approval limits, especially directly under (e.g., 5%) the approval limit.	All	A high incidence of invoice payments directly below an approval limit may be an attempt to circumvent a management review.	• Paid invoice
Stratify inventory actual to standard price.	All	Inventory prices may be agreed to that are higher than normal as part of the fraud schemes. This stratification will direct audit efforts on those parts exceeding the standard price.	• On-hand inventory
Identify trends in obsolete inventory over two or more periods.	All	Inventory that has been overpurchased will generally result in obsolescence, which should be identified through trend analysis.	• On-hand inventory
Age inventory by the date of last part issuance.	All	Inventory that has been overpurchased will generally result in obsolescence, which should be identified through trend analysis.	• On-hand inventory
Calculate number of months of inventory that is on hand (on a part-by-part basis) and extract those with a high number of months.	All	Inventory that has been overpurchased will generally result in obsolescence, which should be identified through trend analysis.	• On-hand inventory • Shipment log

Extract all parts greater than zero in cost that have had no usage in the current year.	All	Inventory that has been overpurchased will generally result in obsolescence, which should be identified through trend analysis.	• On-hand inventory • Shipment log
Identify inventory price greater than retail price (if inventory is for sale).	All	Inventory prices may be agreed to that are higher than normal as part of the fraud schemes.	• On-hand inventory
Identify inventory receipts per inventory item that exceed the economic order quantity or maximum for that item.	All	Inventory quantities may be agreed to that are higher than normal as part of the fraud schemes.	• Receiving log • Inventory master file
Identify duplicate payments based on various means that would be made with intent by the employee and accepted with intent by the vendor.	All	Duplicate payment tests can be enacted on the vendor, invoice number, amount. More complicated tests can look where the same invoice and amount are paid yet the payment is made to two different vendors. Another advanced test would be to search for same vendor and invoice when a different amount is paid.	• Paid invoice
Calculate the ratio of the largest purchase to next-largest purchase by vendor.	All	By identifying the largest purchase to a vendor and the next-largest purchase, any large ratio difference may identify a fraudulently issued "largest" purchase.	• Paid invoice
Calculate the annualized unit price changes in purchase orders for the same product in the same year.	All	Assesses price changes in purchases for potential fraudulent company purchases and employee payments.	• Purchase order
List all vendors who had multiple invoices immediately below an approval limit (e.g., many $999 payments to a vendor when there is a $1,000 approval limit), highlighting a circumvention of the established control.	All	Multiple invoices below an approval limit may be an attempt to circumvent a management review.	• Paid invoice
Extract round-dollar payments and summarize by vendor.	All	Payments made in round dollars have a higher incidence of being fraudulent and should be scrutinized closely.	• Paid invoice
Review payments with little or no sequence between invoice numbers.	All	Vendors issuing phony invoices many times will invoice the company with no gaps in invoice sequence.	• Paid invoice
List payments to any vendor that exceed the twelve-month average payments to that vendor by a specified percentage (e.g., 200%).	All	Large payments are unusual and should be scrutinized as potentially being fraudulent.	• Paid invoice

(*Continued*)

(*Continued*)

Title	Category	Description	Data file(s)
List payments to any vendor that exceed the twelve-month average payments to any vendor within the purchase category (e.g., supplies, fixtures) by a specified percentage (e.g., 200%).	All	Large payments are unusual and should be scrutinized as potentially being fraudulent, especially when analyzed in relation to other vendors of similar products.	• Paid invoice
Summarize invoice payment general ledger activity by type of purchase, and identify areas with less than three vendors.	All	By summarizing general ledger activity, the vendors by type of purchase (e.g., fixtures, transportation) can be identified. Types with less than three vendors could identify an area where few vendors are being used, reducing competitive influence, and providing the opportunity for fraudulent activity.	• Paid invoice • General ledger distribution
Calculate the average payment by general ledger activity type and review for payments made that exceed that average by a large percentage (e.g., 100%).	All	By summarizing general ledger activity by type of purchase (e.g., fixtures, transportation) high value payments may be identified to fraudulent vendors.	• Paid invoice • General ledger distribution
Summarize by vendor the number of inferior goods based on number of returns.	All	Inferior quality may be reduced to companies with employees receiving fraudulent payments.	• Receiving log
Identify delivery of inventory to employee address by joining employee address to shipment address file.	All	Inventory may be shipped directly to an employee address to act as consideration to the employee for fraudulent activity.	• Shipment register • Employee address
Identify delivery of inventory to addresses not designated as business addresses.	All	Inventory may be shipped to an employee address that is entered into the system to appear as a regular business address. Such a shipment would act as consideration to the employee for fraudulent activity. The identification of whether an address is legitimately a business one can be done via software databases such as Select Phone Pro.	• Shipment register
Match the vendor master file to the employee master file on various key fields.	All	Compare telephone number, address, tax ID numbers, numbers in the address, PO Boxes, and ZIP code in vendor file to information in employee files, especially for employees working in the accounts payable department.	• Vendor master file • Employee master file
Identify vendor addresses not designated as business addresses.	All	The identification of whether an address is legitimately a business one can be done using software databases such as Select Phone Pro.	• Vendor master file
Review Internet resources, online newspaper archives, background check, and commercial credit databases for related parties of employees.	All	Review of Internet resources such as AuditNet.org, online newspapers such as newyorktimes.com and wsj.com, and other online background databases may identify employee related parties.	• N/A

SUMMARY

As we learned in Chapter 1, occupational fraud can be divided into three major categories: asset misappropriations, corruption, and fraudulent statements. Corruption occurs when an employee of an organization wrongfully uses his influence in a transaction to procure some benefit for himself or another person, contrary to the employee's duty to the organization for which he works. Corruption schemes are broken down into four categories: *bribery, illegal gratuities, economic extortion*, and *conflicts of interest*.

Bribery is the offering, giving, receiving, or soliciting any thing of value to influence an official act or business decision. Bribery schemes generally fall into two categories: kickbacks and bid-rigging schemes. Kickbacks involve collusion between employees and vendors and almost always strike the purchasing function of the target company. Kickbacks typically involve the overbilling of the victim organization, though in some schemes the goal is only to divert extra business to a particular vendor. Bid-rigging schemes can be categorized based on the stage of bidding at which the perpetrator exerts his influence. This type of scheme may take place in the presolicitation phase, the solicitation phase, or the submission phase of the bidding process.

Although illegal gratuities are similar to bribery schemes, they differ in that an illegal gratuity is paid as a *reward* for a decision that has already been made, rather than in an attempt to influence an impending decision. Illegal gratuity schemes can, and do, develop into bribery schemes when an understanding results that future business decisions benefiting the person or company that gave the illegal gratuity will be rewarded.

The third category of corruption is economic extortion, which occurs when one person demands a payment from another in order to make a decision that will either benefit the payer or prevent the occurrence of economic harm, such as loss of business.

Conflicts of interest are the fourth category of corruption. They occur when an employee, manager, or executive has an undisclosed economic or personal interest in a transaction that adversely affects the perpetrator's employer. Most conflict of interest schemes fit into one of two main categories: purchasing schemes and sales schemes. Purchasing schemes generally involve a perpetrator who has a hidden interest in a vendor and who helps that vendor overbill his employer. Turnaround sales are another type of purchasing scheme that takes place when an employee knows his company is about to purchase an asset (such as land), acquires it, and then sells it to the company at an inflated price.

In sales schemes, the perpetrator typically causes her employer to sell goods or services at below fair market value to a vendor in which she has a hidden interest. Another form of sales scheme occurs when an employee writes off sales to a vendor in which she has a secret interest, or generates fraudulent discounts on behalf of that vendor.

Other conflict of interest schemes include business diversions, in which the perpetrator steals customers from his employer, and resource diversions, in which the perpetrator uses his employer's cash or property for the benefit of a company he secretly owns.

ESSENTIAL TERMS

Bid-pooling A process by which several bidders conspire to split contracts, thereby ensuring that each gets a certain amount of work.

Bid-rigging A process by which an employee assists a vendor to fraudulently win a contract through the competitive bidding process.

Bid-splitting A fraudulent scheme in which a large project is split into several component projects so that each sectional contract falls below the mandatory bidding level, thereby avoiding the competitive bidding process.

Bribery The offering, giving, receiving, or soliciting of something of value for the purpose of influencing an official act.

Business diversions A scheme that typically involves a favor done for a friendly client. Business diversions can include situations in which an employee starts his own company and, while still employed by the victim, steers existing or potential clients away from the victim and toward his own new company.

Collusion A secret agreement between two or more people for a fraudulent, illegal, or deceitful purpose, such as overcoming the internal controls of their employer.

Commercial bribery The offering, giving, receiving, or soliciting of something of value for the purpose of influencing a business decision without the knowledge or consent of the principal.

Conflict of interest A situation in which an employee, manager, or executive has an undisclosed economic or personal interest in a transaction that adversely affects the company as a result.

Economic extortion The obtaining of property from another when the other party's "consent" has been induced by wrongful use of actual or threatened force or fear.

Illegal gratuities The offering, giving, receiving, or soliciting of something of value for, or because of, an official act.

Kickbacks Schemes in which a vendor pays back a portion of the purchase price to an employee of the buyer in order to influence the buyer's decision.

Need recognition scheme A presolicitation-phase bid-rigging conspiracy between the buyer and contractor whereby an employee of the buyer receives something of value to convince his company that it has a "need" for a particular product or service.

Official act The decisions or actions of government agents or employees. Traditionally, bribery statutes proscribed only payments made to influence public officials.

Purchasing scheme A conflict of interest scheme in which a victim company unwittingly buys something at a high price from a company in which one of its employees has a hidden interest.

Resource diversions The diversion of assets from the victim company.

Sales scheme A conflict of interest scheme in which a victim company unwittingly sells something at a low price to a company in which one of its employees has a hidden interest.

Slush fund A noncompany account into which company money has been fraudulently diverted and from which bribes can be paid.

Specifications scheme A presolicitation bid-rigging conspiracy between the buyer and vendor wherein an employee of the buyer receives something of value to set the specifications of the contract to accommodate that vendor's capabilities.

Turnaround sales A purchasing scheme wherein an employee knows that his company plans to purchase a certain asset, takes advantage of the situation by purchasing the asset himself, and then sells the asset to his employer at an inflated price.

Underbilling A sales scheme that occurs when an employee underbills a vendor in which she has a hidden interest. As a result, the company ends up selling its goods or services at less than fair market value, which creates a diminished profit margin or loss on the sale.

REVIEW QUESTIONS

10-1 (Learning objective 10-2) What are the four categories of corruption?

10-2 (Learning objective 10-4) How are bribery, extortion, and illegal gratuities different?

10-3 (Learning objective 10-5) What are the two classifications of bribery schemes?

10-4 (Learning objective 10-6) What are some of the different types of kickback schemes?

10-5 (Learning objective 10-7) What is a bid-rigging scheme?

10-6 (Learning objective 10-7) How are bid-rigging schemes categorized?

10-7 (Learning objective 10-8) How might competition be eliminated in the solicitation phase of a bid-rigging scheme?

10-8 (Learning objective 10-8) What types of abuses may be found in the submission phase of a bid-rigging scheme?

10-9 (Learning objective 10-11) What is a conflict of interest?

10-10 (Learning objective 10-12) What is meant by the term *turnaround sale*?

10-11 (Learning objective 10-12) How are underbillings usually accomplished?

10-12 (Learning objective 10-12) What is the difference between business diversions and resource diversions?

DISCUSSION ISSUES

10-1 (Learning objective 10-3) Offering a payment can constitute a bribe, even if the illegal payment is never actually made. Why?

10-2 (Learning objective 10-1) What is the common ingredient shared by the four classifications of corruption?

10-3 (Learning objective 10-3) What is the difference between official bribery and commercial bribery?

10-4 (Learning objectives 10-6 and 10-9) If you suspected someone of being involved in a kickback scheme, what would you look for?

10-5 (Learning objective 10-6) An employee can implement a kickback scheme regardless of whether she has approval authority over the purchasing function. How might this be accomplished?

10-6 (Learning objectives 10-7, 10-8, and 10-9) What are some clues that might alert you to possible fraudulent activity at the different stages of a bid-rigging scheme?

10-7 (Learning objective 10-11) How do conflicts of interest differ from bribery?

10-8 (Learning objective 10-12) Compare the characteristics of purchasing schemes to sales schemes.

10-9 (Learning objectives 10-10 and 10-12) Assume that an employee is responsible for purchasing an apartment complex on behalf of his company. The employee owns stock in the management company that operates the apartment complex.

The employee, who does not let his company know about his stock ownership, makes the purchase. Why does this example represent a conflict of interest?

10-10 (Learning objectives 10-9 and 10-13) What are some of the ways organizations can determine whether a particular vendor is being favored?

ENDNOTES

1. Lanza, pp. 22–24.

CHAPTER 11

ACCOUNTING PRINCIPLES AND FRAUD

LEARNING OBJECTIVES

After studying this chapter, you should be able to:

11-1 Define fraud as it relates to financial statements

11-2 Identify the three main groups of people who commit financial statement fraud

11-3 List the three primary reasons people commit financial statement fraud

11-4 Describe the three general methods used to commit financial statement fraud

11-5 Define overstatements

11-6 Define understatements

11-7 Describe the conceptual framework for financial reporting

11-8 List examples of various types of financial statements

FRAUD IN FINANCIAL STATEMENTS

In this chapter, we will examine some underlying principles that permit financial statement frauds to occur. Additionally, we will summarize the key provisions of the 2002 Sarbanes–Oxley Act, designed to deter these offenses. Financial statement frauds are caused by a number of factors occurring at the same time, the most significant of which is the pressure on upper management to show earnings. Preparing false financial statements is made easier by the subjective nature of the way books and records are kept. The accounting profession has long recognized that, to a large extent, accounting is a somewhat arbitrary process, subject to judgment. The profession also indirectly recognizes that numbers are subject to manipulation. After all, a debit on a company's books can be recorded as either an expense or an asset. A credit can be a liability or equity. Therefore, there can be tremendous temptation—when a strong earnings showing is needed—to classify expenses as assets, and liabilities as equity.

In the next chapter we will explore the five major methods by which financial statement fraud is committed, but before we delve into the mechanics of these schemes it is important to first consider three general questions that go to the heart of these crimes:

- Who commits financial statement fraud?
- Why do people commit financial statement fraud?
- How do people commit financial statement fraud?

Who Commits Financial Statement Fraud?

There are three main groups of people who commit financial statement fraud. In descending order of likelihood of involvement, they are as follows:

- *Senior management.* In 2010, the Committee of Sponsoring Organizations of the Treadway Commission (COSO) released *Fraudulent Financial Reporting: 1998–2007*, a study of 347 alleged financial statement frauds from 1998 to 2007. The SEC named the CEO and/or CFO for involvement in 89 percent these fraud cases. And within two years of the completion of the SEC investigation, about 20 percent of the CEOs/CFOs had been indicted. Over 60 percent of those indicted were convicted. Motives for senior managers to commit financial statement fraud are varied and are described below.

- *Mid- and lower-level employees.* This category of employees may falsify financial statements for their area of responsibility (subsidiary, division, or other unit) to conceal their poor performance or to earn bonuses based on the higher performance.

- *Organized criminals.* This group may use this type of scheme to obtain fraudulent loans from a financial institution, or to hype a stock they are selling as part of a "pump-and-dump" scheme.

Why Do People Commit Financial Statement Fraud?

Senior managers (CEO, CFO, etc.) and business owners may "cook the books" for several key reasons:

- *To conceal true business performance.* This may be to overstate or understate results.

- *To preserve personal status/control.* Senior managers with strong egos may be unwilling to admit that their strategy has failed and that business performance is bad, since doing so may lead to their termination.

- *To maintain personal income/wealth* from salary, bonus, stock, and stock options.

We can better deter and detect fraud if we first understand the different pressures that senior managers and business owners can face that might drive them to commit fraud. If we understand the motivating factors behind these crimes, it stands to reason that we will be in a better position to recognize circumstances that might motivate or pressure people into committing financial statement fraud. We will also increase our likelihood of detecting these crimes by knowing the most likely places to look for fraud on an organization's financials.

As with other forms of occupational fraud, financial statement schemes are generally tailored to the circumstances that exist in the organization. In other words, the evaluation criteria used by those with power over management will tend to drive management behavior in fraud cases. For example, tight loan covenants might drive managers to misclassify certain liabilities as long-term rather than current in order to improve the entity's current ratio (current assets to current liabilities) without affecting reported earnings.

The following are some of the more common reasons why senior management will *overstate* business performance to meet certain objectives:

- To meet or exceed the earnings or revenue growth expectations of stock market analysts

- To comply with loan covenants
- To increase the amount of financing available from asset-based loans
- To meet a lender's criteria for granting/extending loan facilities
- To meet corporate performance criteria set by the parent company
- To meet personal performance criteria
- To trigger performance-related compensation or earn-out payments
- To support the stock price in anticipation of a merger, acquisition, or sale of personal stockholding
- To show a pattern of growth to support a planned securities offering or sale of the business

Alternatively, senior management may *understate* business performance to meet certain objectives:

- To defer "surplus" earnings to the next accounting period. If current period budgets have been met and there is no reward for additional performance, corporate managers may prefer to direct additional earnings into the next period to help meet their new targets.
- To take all possible write-offs in one "big bath" now so future earnings will be consistently higher.
- To reduce expectations now so future growth will be better perceived and rewarded.
- To preserve a trend of consistent growth, avoiding volatile results.
- To reduce the value of an owner-managed business for purposes of a divorce settlement.
- To reduce the value of a corporate unit whose management is planning a buyout.

How Do People Commit Financial Statement Fraud?

The mechanics of the major types of financial statement fraud will be discussed in the next chapter. As you review that material, keep in mind that, regardless of method, there are three general ways in which fraudulent financial statements can be produced. By being aware of these three approaches, those who investigate financial statement fraud can be alert for evidence of attempts to manipulate the accounting and financial reporting process, or to go outside it. Financial statement frauds may involve more than one of these three methods, though they will commonly start with the first method and progressively add the other two methods as the fraud grows. The three general methods are as follows:

- *Playing the accounting system.* In this approach, the fraudster uses the accounting system as a tool to generate the results he wants. For example, in order to increase or decrease earnings to a desired figure, a fraudster might manipulate the assumptions used to calculate depreciation charges, allowances for bad debts, or allowances for excess and obsolete inventory. To avoid recognizing expenses and liabilities, vendor invoices might not be recorded on a timely basis. Genuine sales might be recorded prematurely. Transactions recorded in the accounting system have a basis in fact, even if they are improperly recorded. There is a documentary trail to support the results reported in the financial statements, though the assumptions shown in some of those documents may be questionable.
- *Beating the accounting system.* In this approach, the fraudster feeds false and fictitious information into the accounting system to manipulate reported results

by an amount greater than can be achieved by simply "playing the accounting system." Fictitious sales may be recorded to legitimate or phony customers. Inventory and receivables figures may be invented, with documents later being forged to support the claimed numbers. Senior financial management might determine allowances for bad debts and for excess and obsolete inventory without regard to the formulae or methods historically used in the entity to determine these amounts. Journal entries might be disguised in an attempt to conceal their fraudulent intent (e.g., splitting big round-sum adjustments into many smaller entries of odd amounts), or transactions may be hidden through use of intercompany accounts to conceal the other side of a transaction. Some transactions recorded in the accounting system may have no basis in fact, and some that do may be improperly recorded. There will be no documentary trail to support certain transactions or balances unless the fraudster prepares forged or altered documents to help support this fraud.

- *Going outside the accounting system.* In this approach, the fraudster produces whatever financial statements he wishes. These financial statements could be based on the results of an accounting and financial reporting process for an operating entity, with additional manual adjustments to achieve the results desired by the fraudster. Alternatively, they could just be printed up using phony numbers supplied by the fraudster. In some cases, the fraudster may go back and enter false data in the accounting system to support the phony financial statements. In other cases, he may not bother, or there might be no accounting system. So not all transactions may be recorded in an accounting system, and some or all transactions may have no basis in fact. To catch this type of fraud, it is usually necessary to start by tracing the published financial statements back to the output of the accounting system. As in the previous situation, there will be no documentary trail to support certain transactions or balances reported in the financial statements unless the fraudsters prepare forged or altered documents to help support this fraud.

CONCEPTUAL FRAMEWORK FOR FINANCIAL REPORTING

Over the years, businesses have found numerous ingenious ways to overstate their true earnings and assets. As a result, a number of accounting guidelines, or what are termed generally accepted accounting principles (GAAP), have developed. The Financial Accounting Standards Board (FASB), an independent public watchdog organization responsible for standard setting, has codified most historic accounting principles. Statement on Auditing Standards (SAS) No. 69 (AU 411), "The Meaning of Present Fairly in Conformity With Generally Accepted Accounting Principles," indicates the primary sources of generally accepted accounting principles as FASB Standards and Interpretations, APB Opinions, and AICPA Accounting Research Bulletins. Although accounting students should already be familiar with these concepts, we will review them again here with the emphasis on fraud. The following is a conceptual framework for financial reporting:

I. Recognition and measurement concepts

    A. Assumptions
      i. Economic entity
     ii. Going concern
    iii. Monetary unit
    iv. Periodicity

    B. Principles
        i. Historical cost
        ii. Revenue recognition
        iii. Matching
        iv. Full disclosure

    C. Constraints
        i. Cost-benefit
        ii. Materiality
        iii. Industry practice
        iv. Conservatism

II. Qualitative characteristics

    A. Relevance and reliability

    B. Comparability and consistency

Economic Entity

The premise of the economic entity assumption is that the activity of a business enterprise should be kept separate and distinct from its owners and other business entities. The entity concept does not rely on a legal basis, but rather on substance. The concept of the entity is becoming ever more difficult to define. Companies with subsidiaries, joint ventures, or special-purpose entities (SPEs), like those established by Enron, have raised further questions about how to account for the entity in order to prevent fraudulent manipulation of the financial statements.

Going Concern

In valuing a firm's assets for financial statement purposes, it is assumed that the business is one that will continue into the future. That is because the worth of the business, if it is any good, will always be higher than the value of its hard assets. For example, if you wanted to buy a business that paid you a 10 percent return, then you would pay up to a million dollars for an investment that earned $100,000 a year. The value of the actual assets underlying the business, if they were sold at auction, would typically not bring nearly a million dollars. The going concern concept assumes that the business will go on indefinitely in the future. If there is serious doubt about whether a business can continue, this must be disclosed as a footnote in the financial statements.

    Fraud in the going concern concept will usually result from attempts by an entity to conceal its terminal business condition. For example, assume a company is in the computer parts manufacturing business. Last year, the company earned $100,000 after taxes. This year, management is aware that new technology will make its business totally obsolete, and by next year, the business will likely close. The company's auditors might not know this fact. And when they prepare the financial statements for their company, management has the duty to inform the accountants of the business's future ability to earn money. The auditors, in turn, will insist that the financial statements for the current period reflect this future event.

Monetary Unit

In order to measure and analyze financial transactions, a common standard is necessary. In our society, that common denominator is money. The U.S. dollar has remained reasonably stable, but some countries, as a result of persistent economic volatility, use "inflation accounting" to adjust for price-level changes in their currency. International companies that deal with foreign currency transactions may be subject to fraudulent abuse of monetary exchange rates.

Periodicity

This "time period" assumption advises that economic activity be divided into specific time intervals, such as monthly, quarterly, and annually. With shorter reporting periods, however, the data tends to be subject to greater human error and manipulation and, therefore, is less reliable.

Historical Cost

Generally accepted accounting principles (GAAP) require that assets be carried on the financial statements at the price established by the exchange transaction. This figure is referred to as historical or acquisition cost, and is generally the most conservative and reliable method. However, there are some exceptions to the historical cost principle. For example, if inventory is worth less than its cost, this lower value is to be reported on the financials. This approach is referred to as the lower of cost or market. Furthermore, many investments are reported at fair value. But there are other methods of valuation, too. The net realizable value of an asset is the amount of money that would be realized upon the sale of the asset, less the costs to sell it. The problem arises when attempting to establish a sales value, without selling it. If companies were required to place a sales value on every asset in order to determine net income, the resulting figure would be materially affected by opinion. The potential for fraud, in this case, is evident. Similar arguments have been made against using replacement value.

Revenue Recognition

According to generally accepted accounting principles, the accrual basis of accounting should be used for financial reporting. As such, revenues are recognized and reported in the period in which they are earned. Intentional manipulation of the timing for revenues earned could be a potential area for fraudulent abuse.

Matching

The matching concept requires that the books and records and the resultant financial statements match revenue and expense in the proper accounting period. Fraud can occur when purposeful attempts are made to manipulate the matching concept. For example, through controlling the year-end cut-off in financial figures, many companies boost their current net income by counting revenue from the following year early and by delaying the posting of this year's expenses until the following year.

Full Disclosure

The principle behind full disclosure, as in the previous example, is that any material deviation from generally accepted accounting principles must be explained to the reader of the financial information. In addition, any known event that could have a material impact on future earnings must be explained or disclosed. For example, as we discussed earlier, suppose a company is aware that competitors are making its principal manufacturing method for computer parts obsolete. Such an event must be disclosed. If the company is being sued and is in danger of a material monetary judgment, that must be disclosed, too. In actuality, any potential adverse event of a material nature must be disclosed in the financials. Many major financial frauds have been caused by the purposeful omission of footnote disclosures to the statements.

Cost-Benefit

In formulating standards for financial reporting, the FASB considers the tradeoff between the cost of providing certain information and the related benefit to be derived by the users of the information. The specific costs and benefits, however, are not always readily apparent. Some costs, such as the cost to collect, distribute, and audit data, are more easily measured than, for example, the cost of disclosure to competitors. This constraint should not be construed as an excuse to purposely and fraudulently omit material information from the financial statements.

Materiality

Financial statements are not meant to be perfect, only reasonable and fair. There are doubtless many small errors in the books of corporations of all sizes, but what does it really mean when considering the big picture? The answer is that it depends on who is looking at the financial statements and making decisions based on them. If a company's estimated earnings are $1 million a year on its financial statements, and it turns out that figure is actually $990,000 (or $1,010,000), who cares? Probably not many people. But suppose that $1 million in earnings on the financial statements is actually $500,000—half what the company showed. Then many people—investors and lenders, primarily—would care a great deal.

Materiality, then, according to GAAP, is a user-oriented concept. If a misstatement is so significant that reasonable, prudent users of the financial statements would make a different decision than they would if they had been given correct information, then the misstatement is material and requires correction.

A typical issue involving materiality and fraud would be asset misappropriations. Many of them, taken separately, are quite small and not material to the financial statements as a whole. But what of the aggregate? If many steal small amounts, the result could indeed be material.

Industry Practice

Reporting practices may exist within certain industries that deviate from generally accepted accounting principles. For example, due to the utility industry's highly capital-intensive nature, noncurrent assets are listed first on the balance sheet, rather than listing the assets in order of liquidity. In the event of deviations from GAAP, a determination should be made regarding whether there is justification for the departure.

Conservatism

The conservatism constraint requires that when there is any doubt, we should avoid overstating assets and income. The intention of this principle is to provide a reasonable guideline in a questionable situation. If there is no doubt concerning an accurate valuation, this constraint need not be applied. An example of conservatism in accounting is the use of the "lower of cost or market" rule as it relates to inventory valuation. If a company's financial statements intentionally violate the conservatism constraint, they could be fraudulent.

Relevance and Reliability

"Qualitative Characteristics of Accounting Information" as outlined in Statement of Financial Accounting Concepts No. 2 identifies relevance and reliability as two primary qualities of usefulness for decision making. Relevance implies that certain information will make a difference in arriving at a decision. Reliability, on the other hand, means that the user can depend on the factual accuracy of the information. It is precisely when the factual accuracy of information is intentionally distorted, in order to influence a decision by the user of the financial statements, that fraud occurs.

Comparability and Consistency

In order for financial information to be useful for analytical purposes, it must possess the secondary qualitative characteristics of comparability and consistency. For example, one easy way for the value of assets and income to be inflated is through the depreciation methods companies use on their books. Assume a valuable piece of equipment was purchased by a company for $99,000 and was expected to last three years with no salvage value at the end of its useful life. That means under *straight-line* depreciation, the write-off in the first year would be $33,000. Using the *double declining balance* method of depreciation, the write-off would be $66,000 the first year. By switching depreciation methods from one year to the next, the company could influence its net income by as much as $33,000. By manipulating income in this manner, the user is comparing apples and oranges. So if a company changes the way it keeps its books from one year to the next, and if these changes have a material impact on the financial statements, they must be disclosed in a footnote to the financials. Fraud occurs when consistency is intentionally avoided to show false profits.

RESPONSIBILITY FOR FINANCIAL STATEMENTS

Financial statements are the responsibility of company management. Therefore, it is hard to imagine that financial statement fraud can be committed without some knowledge or consent of management, although financial statement fraud can be perpetrated by anyone who has the opportunity and the motive to omit or misstate the data presented in furtherance of his purpose.

Recall that financial statement fraud is generally instigated by members of management, or, at the least, by persons under the direction and control of management. In the instances where management does not investigate suspected frauds, how can management assure itself that fraud will be deterred and, if fraud does occur, that it will be detected?

A company's board of directors and senior management generally set the code of conduct for the company. This code of conduct is often referred to as the company's "ethic." The ethic is the standard by which all other employees will tend to conduct themselves. It stands to reason, therefore, that if the company's ethic is one of high integrity, the company's employees will tend to operate in a more honest manner. If, on the other hand, the ethic is corrupt, employees will view that as a license to also be corrupt. However, an unimpeachable company ethic does not, in and of itself, ensure that financial statement fraud will not occur; additional measures are required in order for management to discharge its responsibilities with respect to deterrence and detection of fraudulent financial reporting.

USERS OF FINANCIAL STATEMENTS

Financial statement fraud schemes are most often perpetrated against potential users of financial statements by management. These users of financial statements include company ownership and management, lending organizations, and investors. Fraudulent statements are used for a number of reasons. The most common is to increase the apparent prosperity of the organization in the eyes of potential and current investors. This not only may induce new investment, but it can help keep current investors satisfied. Fraudulent financial statements can be used to dispel negative perceptions of an organization in the open market. Company management often uses financial statements to judge employee or management performance. Employees are tempted to manipulate statements to ensure continued employment and additional compensation that is potentially tied to performance. Certain internal goals, such as satisfying budgets, contribute added pressure to the manager responsible. The following diagram displays the role of financial information and statements in the decision-making process of the users.

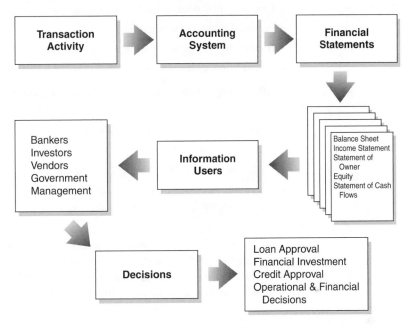

TYPES OF FINANCIAL STATEMENTS

According to the Statement on Auditing Standards (SAS) No. 62 (AU 623), "Special Reports," published by the AICPA Auditing Standards Board, financial statements include presentations of financial data and accompanying notes prepared in conformity with either generally accepted accounting principles or some other comprehensive basis of accounting. The following is a list of such financial statements:

- Balance sheet
- Statement of income or statement of operations
- Statement of retained earnings
- Statement of cash flows
- Statement of changes in owners' equity
- Statement of assets and liabilities that does not include owners' equity accounts
- Statement of revenue and expenses
- Summary of operations

- Statement of operations by product lines
- Statement of cash receipts and disbursements

Although not specifically noted in SAS No. 62 (AU 623), financial statements also typically include other financial data presentations, such as:

- Prospective financial information
- Pro forma financial statements
- Proxy statements
- Interim financial information
- Current value financial representations
- Personal financial statements
- Bankruptcy financial statements
- Registration statement disclosures

Other comprehensive bases of accounting, according to SAS No. 62 (AU 623), include:

- Government or regulatory agency accounting
- Tax basis accounting
- Cash receipts and disbursements, or modified cash receipts and disbursements
- Any other basis with a definite set of criteria applied to all material items, such as the price-level basis of accounting

As we see from the preceding lists, the term *financial statement* includes almost any financial data presentation prepared according to generally accepted accounting principles or in accord with another comprehensive basis of accounting. Throughout this chapter and the next, the term *financial statements* will include the above forms of reporting financial data, including the accompanying footnotes and management's discussion.

THE SARBANES–OXLEY ACT OF 2002

The Sarbanes–Oxley Act of 2002 was signed into law on July 30, 2002, to address corporate governance and accountability as well as public accounting responsibilities in improving the quality, reliability, integrity, and transparency of financial reports. The Act provides sweeping measures aimed at:

- Establishing higher standards for corporate governance and accountability
- Creating an independent regulatory framework for the accounting profession
- Enhancing the quality and transparency of financial reports
- Developing severe civil and criminal penalties for corporate wrongdoers
- Establishing new protections for corporate whistleblowers

The Act authorized the Securities and Exchange Commission (SEC) to issue implementation rules on many of its provisions intended to improve corporate governance, financial reporting, and audit functions. As part of these directives, the SEC has implemented rules pertaining to the following:

- Management's report on internal control over financial reporting and certification of disclosure in periodic reports

- Improper influence on conduct of audits
- New standards of professional conduct for attorneys
- Standards and procedures related to listed company audit committees
- Strengthening the commission's requirements regarding auditor independence
- Disclosure in management's discussion and analysis about off–balance sheet arrangements and aggregate contractual obligations
- Disclosures regarding a code of ethics for senior financial officers and audit committee financial expert
- Retention of records relevant to audits and reviews
- Insider trades during pension fund blackout periods
- Conditions for use of non-GAAP financial measures
- Certification of disclosure in companies' quarterly and annual reports

These implementation rules are expected to create an environment that promotes strong marketplace integrity, improves the probability of detection and deterrence of corporate misstatements, and restores public trust in the quality and transparency of financial information. Exhibit 11-1 summarizes important provisions of the Act aimed at improving corporate governance, financial reports, and audit functions to restore investor confidence and public trust in financial information.

CORPORATE GOVERNANCE AND ACCOUNTING PROVISIONS OF THE SARBANES–OXLEY ACT OF 2002

Section	Provisions
101	**Establishment of Public Company Accounting Oversight Board (PCAOB):** 1. The PCAOB will have five financially literate members. 2. Members are appointed by the SEC for five-year terms, will serve on a full-time basis, and may be removed by the SEC "for good cause." 3. Two of the members must be or must have been CPAs, and the remaining three must not be and cannot have been CPAs. 4. The chair may be held by one of the CPA members, who must not have been engaged as a practicing CPA for five years.
103	**The PCAOB Shall:** 1. Register public accounting firms (foreign and domestic) that prepare audit reports for issuers. 2. Establish, or adopt, by rule, auditing, quality control, ethics, independence, and other standards relating to the preparation of audit reports for issuers. 3. Conduct inspections of registered public accounting firms. 4. Conduct investigations and disciplinary proceedings and impose appropriate sections. 5. Enforce compliance with the Act, the rules of the Board, and other applicable rules and regulations. 6. Establish budget and manage the operations of the Board and its staff.
107	**Commission Oversight of the Board:** 1. The SEC shall have oversight and enforcement authority over the PCAOB. 2. The SEC can, by rule or order, give the PCAOB additional responsibilities. 3. The PCAOB is required to file proposed rules and proposed rule changes with the SEC. 4. The SEC may approve, reject, or amend such rules. 5. The PCAOB must notify the SEC of pending investigations and coordinate its investigation with the SEC Division of Enforcement.

EXHIBIT 11-1

Section	Provisions
	6. The PCAOB must notify the SEC when it imposes any final sanction on any accounting firm or associated person. 7. The PCAOB findings and sanctions are subject to review by the SEC, which may enhance, modify, cancel, reduce, or require remission of such sanction.
108	**Accounting Standards:** 1. The SEC may recognize as "generally accepted" any accounting principles that are established by a standard-setting body that meets the Act's criteria. 2. The SEC shall conduct a study on the adoption of a principles-based accounting system.
201	**Auditor Independence: Services Outside the Scope of Practice of Auditors:** 1. Registered public accounting firms are prohibited from providing any nonaudit services to an issuer contemporaneously with the audit including but not limited to (a) bookkeeping or other services related to the accounting record or financial statement of the audit client; (b) financial information systems design and implementation; (c) appraisal or valuation services; (d) actuarial services; (e) internal audit outsourcing services; (f) management functions or human resources; (g) broker or dealer, investment advisor, or investment banking; (h) legal services and expert services unrelated to the audit; and (i) any other services that the PCAOB determines, by regulation, is impermissible. 2. The PCAOB may, on a case-by-case basis, exempt from these prohibitions any person, issuer, public accounting firm, or transaction, subject to review by the SEC. 3. Nonaudit services not explicitly prohibited by the Act, such as tax services, can be performed upon preapproval by the audit committee and full disclosure to investors.
203	**Audit Partner Rotation:** 1. The lead audit or coordinating partner and reviewing partner of the registered accounting firm must rotate off of the audit every five years.
204	**Auditor Reports to Audit Committees:** The registered accounting firm must report to the Audit Committee 1. All critical accounting policies and practices to be used 2. All alternative treatments of financial information within generally accepted accounting principles, ramifications of the use of such alternative disclosures and treatments, and the preferred treatment 3. Other material written communication between the auditor and management
206	**Conflicts of Interest:** Registered accounting firms are prohibited from performing audits for any issuer whose CEO, CFO, controller, chief accounting officer, or other person in an equivalent position was employed by the accounting firm during the one-year period preceding the audit.
207	**Study of Mandatory Rotation of Registered Public Accounting Firms:** The Comptroller General of the United States will conduct a study on the potential effects of requiring the mandatory rotation of public accounting firms.
301	**Public Company Audit Committees:** 1. Each member of the audit committee shall be an independent member of the board of directors. 2. To be considered independent, the member of the audit committee should not receive any compensations other than for service on the board, nor accept any consulting, advisory, or other compensatory fee from the company, and not be an affiliated person of the issuer, or any subsidiary thereof. 3. The SEC may make exemptions for certain individuals on a case-by-case basis. 4. The audit committee shall be directly responsible for the appointment, compensation, and oversight of the work of any registered public accounting firm associated by the issuer. 5. The audit committee shall establish procedures for the receipt, retention, and treatment of complaints received by the issuer regarding accounting, internal accounting controls, or auditing matters and the confidential, anonymous submission by employees of the issuer of concerns regarding questionable accounting or auditing matters. 6. The audit committee shall have the authority to engage independent counsel and other advisors necessary to carry out its duties. 7. The audit committee shall be properly funded.

EXHIBIT 11-1 *(Continued)*

Section	Provisions
302	**Corporate Responsibility for Financial Reports:** 1. The signing officers (e.g., CEO, CFO) shall certify in each annual or quarterly report filed with the SEC that (a) the report does not contain any untrue statement of a material fact or omitted material facts that cause the report to be misleading; and (b) financial statements and disclosures fairly present, in all material respects, the financial condition and results of operations of the issuer. 2. The signing officers are responsible for establishing and maintaining adequate and effective controls to ensure reliability of financial statements and disclosures. 3. The signing officers are responsible for proper design of, periodic assessment of the effectiveness of, and disclosure of material deficiencies in internal controls to external auditors and the audit committee.
303	**Improper Influence on Conduct of Audits:** It shall be unlawful for any officer or director of an issuer to take any action to fraudulently influence, coerce, manipulate, or mislead auditors in the performance of financial audit of the financial statements.
304	**Forfeiture of Certain Bonuses and Profits:** 1. CEOs and CFOs who revise company's financial statements for the material noncompliance with any financial reporting requirements must pay back any bonuses or stock options awarded because of the misstatements. 2. CEOs and CFOs shall reimburse the issuer for any bonus or other incentive-based or equity-based compensation received or any profits realized from the sale of securities during that period for financial restatements due to material noncompliance with financial reporting and disclosure requirements.
306	**Insider Trades during Pension Fund Blackout Periods:** 1. It shall be unlawful for any directors or executive officers directly or indirectly to purchase, sell, or otherwise acquire or transfer any equity security of the issuer during any blackout periods. 2. Any profits resulting from sales in violation of this section shall inure to and be recoverable by the issuer.
401	**Disclosures in Periodic Reports:** 1. Each financial report that is required to be prepared in accordance with GAAP shall reflect all material correcting adjustments that have been identified by the auditors. 2. Each financial report (annual and quarterly) shall disclose all material off–balance sheet transactions and other relationships with unconsolidated entities that may have a material current or future effect on the financial conditions of the issuer. 3. The SEC shall issue final rules providing that pro forma financial information filed with the Commission (a) does not contain an untrue statement of a material fact or omitted material information and (b) reconciles with the financial condition and results of operations. 4. The SEC shall study the extent of off–balance sheet transactions including assets, liabilities, leases, losses, and the use of special-purpose entities and whether the use of GAAP reflects the economics of such off–balance sheet transactions.
402	**Extended Conflict of Interest Provisions:** It is unlawful for the issuer to extend credit to any directors or executive officers.
404	**Management Assessments of Internal Controls:** 1. Each annual report filed with the SEC shall contain an internal control report which shall (a) state the responsibility of management for establishing and maintaining an adequate internal control structure and procedures for financial reporting and (b) contain an assessment of the effectiveness of the internal control structure and procedures as of the end of the issuer's fiscal year. 2. Auditors shall attest to, and report on, the assessment of the adequacy and effectiveness of the issuer internal control structure and procedures as part of audit of financial reports in accordance with standards for attestation engagements.
406	**Code of Ethics for Senior Financial Officers:** The SEC shall issue rules to require each issuer to disclose whether it has adopted a code of ethics for its senior financial officers and the nature and content of such code.
407	**Disclosure of Audit Committee Financial Expert:** The SEC shall issue rules to require each issuer to disclose whether at least one member of its audit committee is a "financial" expert as defined by the Commission.

EXHIBIT 11-1 *(Continued)*

Section	Provisions
409	**Real-Time Issuer Disclosures:** Each issuer shall disclose information on material changes in the financial condition or operations of the issuer on a rapid and current basis.
501	**Treatment of Securities Analysts:** Registered securities associations and national securities exchanges shall adopt rules designed to address conflicts of interest for research analysts who recommend equities in research reports.
602	**Practice before the Commission:** 1. The SEC may censure any person or temporarily bar or deny any person the right to appear or practice before the SEC if the person does not possess the requisite qualifications to represent others, has willfully violated federal securities laws, or lacks character or integrity. 2. The SEC shall conduct a study of "securities professionals" (e.g., accountants, investment bankers, brokers, dealers, attorneys, and investment advisors) who have been found to have aided and abetted a violation of federal securities laws. 3. The SEC shall establish rules setting minimum standards for professional conduct for attorneys practicing before the commission.
701	**GAO Study and Report Regarding Consolidation of Public Accounting Firms:** The GAO shall conduct a study regarding consolidation of public accounting firms since 1989 and determine the consequences of the consolidation, including the present and future impact and solutions to any problems that may result from the consolidation.
802	**Criminal Penalties for Altering Documents:** 1. It is a felony to knowingly alter, destroy, falsify, cover up, conceal, or create documents to impede, obstruct, or influence any existing or contemplated federal investigation. 2. Registered public accounting firms are required to maintain all audit or review workpapers for five years.
903 904 906	**White-Collar Crime Penalty Enhancements:** 1. The maximum penalty for mail and wire fraud is ten years. 2. The SEC may prohibit anyone convicted of securities fraud from being a director or officer of any public company. 3. Financial reports filed with the SEC (annual, quarterly) must be certified by the CEO and CFO of the issuer. The certification must state that the financial statements and disclosures fully comply with provisions of Securities Acts and that they fairly present, in all material respects, financial results and conditions of the issuer. Maximum penalties for willful and knowing violations of these provisions of the Act are a fine of not more than $500,000 and/or imprisonment of up to five years.
1001	**Corporate Tax Returns:** The federal income tax return of public corporations should be signed by the CEO of the issuer.
1105	**Authority of the SEC:** The Commission may prohibit a person from serving as a director or officer of a publicly traded company if the person has committed securities fraud.

Public Company Accounting Oversight Board

Title I of Sarbanes–Oxley establishes the Public Company Accounting Oversight Board, whose purpose is

> to oversee the audit of public companies that are subject to the securities laws, and related matters, in order to protect the interests of investors and further the public interest in the preparation of informative, accurate, and independent audit reports for companies the securities of which are sold to, and held by and for, public investors.
>
> [Section 101]

In short, the Board is charged with overseeing public company audits, setting audit standards, and investigating acts of noncompliance by auditors or audit firms. The Board is appointed and overseen by the Securities and Exchange Commission. It is made up of five persons, two who are or have been CPAs and three who have never been CPAs. The Act lists the Board's duties, which include:

- Registering public accounting firms that audit publicly traded companies
- Establishing or adopting auditing, quality control, ethics, independence, and other standards relating to audits of publicly traded companies
- Inspecting registered public accounting firms
- Investigating registered public accounting firms and their employees, conducting disciplinary hearings, and imposing sanctions where justified
- Performing such other duties as are necessary to promote high professional standards among registered accounting firms, to improve the quality of audit services offered by those firms, and to protect investors
- Enforcing compliance with the Sarbanes–Oxley Act, the rules of the Board, professional standards, and securities laws relating to public company audits

Registration with the Board   Public accounting firms must be registered with the Public Company Accounting Oversight Board in order to legally prepare or issue an audit report on a publicly traded company. In order to become registered, accounting firms must disclose, among other things, the names of all public companies they audited in the preceding year, the names of all public companies they expect to audit in the current year, and the annual fees they received from each of their public audit clients for audit, accounting, and nonaudit services.

Auditing, Quality Control, and Independence Standards and Rules   Section 103 of the Act requires the Board to establish standards for auditing, quality control, ethics, independence, and other issues relating to audits of publicly traded companies. Adopted rules do not take effect until the SEC approves them, as detailed in Section 107 of the Act. Although the Act places the responsibility on the Board to establish audit standards, it also sets forth certain rules that the Board is required to include in those auditing standards. These rules include the following:

- Audit workpapers must be maintained for at least seven years.
- Auditing firms must include a concurring or second-partner review and approval of audit reports, and concurring approval in the issuance of the audit report by a qualified person other than the person in charge of the audit.
- All audit reports must describe the scope of testing of the company's internal control structure and must present the auditor's findings from the testing, including an evaluation of whether the internal control structure is acceptable and a description of material weaknesses in internal controls and any material noncompliance with controls.

Inspections of Registered Public Accounting Firms   The Act also authorizes the Board to conduct regular inspections of public accounting firms to assess their degree of compliance with laws, rules, and professional standards regarding audits. Inspections are to be conducted once a year for firms that regularly audit more than 100 public companies, and at least once every three years for firms that regularly audit 100 or fewer public companies.

Investigations and Disciplinary Proceedings   The Board has the authority to investigate registered public accounting firms (or their employees) for potential violations of the Sarbanes–Oxley Act, professional standards, any rules established by the Board, or any securities laws relating to the preparation and issuance of audit reports. During an investigation, the Board has the power to compel testimony and document production.

The Board has the power to issue sanctions for violations or for noncooperation with an investigation. Sanctions can include temporary or permanent suspension of a firm's registration with the Board (which would mean that firm could no longer legally audit publicly traded companies), temporary or permanent suspension of a person's right to be associated with a registered public accounting firm, prohibition from auditing public companies, and civil monetary penalties of up to $750,000 for an individual and up to $15,000,000 for a firm.

Certification Obligations for CEOs and CFOs

One of the most significant changes effected by the Sarbanes–Oxley Act is the requirement that the chief executive officer and the chief financial officer of public companies personally certify annual and quarterly SEC filings. These certifications essentially require CEOs and CFOs to take responsibility for their companies' financial statements and prevent them from delegating this responsibility to their subordinates and then claiming ignorance when fraud is uncovered in the financial statements.

There are two types of officer certifications mandated by Sarbanes–Oxley: criminal certifications, which are set forth in Section 906 of the Act and codified at 18 USC § 1350, and civil certifications, which are set forth in Section 302.

Criminal Certifications (Section 906) Periodic filings with the SEC must be accompanied by a statement, signed by the CEO and CFO, which certifies that the report fully complies with the SEC's periodic reporting requirements and that the information in the report fairly presents, in all material respects, the financial condition and results of operation of the company.

These certifications are known as "criminal certifications" because the act imposes criminal penalties on officers who violate the certification requirements.

- Corporate officers who *knowingly* violate the certification requirements are subject to fines of up to $1,000,000 and up to ten years' imprisonment, or both.

- Corporate officers who *willfully* violate the certification requirements are subject to fines of up to $5,000,000 and up to twenty years' imprisonment, or both.

Civil Certifications (Section 302) Section 302 of the Act requires the CEO and CFO to personally certify the following in their reports:

1. They have personally reviewed the report.

2. Based on their knowledge, the report does not contain any material misstatement that would render the financials misleading.

3. Based on their knowledge, the financial information in the report fairly presents in all material respects the financial condition, results of operations, and cash flow of the company.

4. They are responsible for designing, maintaining, and evaluating the company's internal controls, they have evaluated the controls within ninety days prior to the report, and they have presented their conclusions about the effectiveness of those controls in the report.

5. They have disclosed to the auditors and the audit committee any material weaknesses in the controls and any fraud, whether material or not, that involves management or other employees who have a significant role in the company's internal controls.

6. They have indicated in their report whether there have been significant changes in the company's internal controls since the filing of the last report.

Note that in items 2 and 3 the CEO and CFO are not required to certify that the financials are accurate or that there is no misstatement. They are simply required to certify that *to their knowledge* the financials are accurate and not misleading. However, this does not mean that senior financial officers can simply plead ignorance about their companies' SEC filings in order to avoid liability. The term *fairly presents* in item 3 is a broader standard than that required by GAAP. In certifying that their SEC filings meet this standard, the CEO and CFO essentially must certify that the company (1) has selected appropriate accounting policies to ensure the material accuracy of the reports, (2) has properly applied those accounting standards; and (3) has disclosed financial information that reflects the underlying transactions and events of the company. Furthermore, the other new certification rules (see 1 and 4–6 above) mandate that CEOs and CFOs take an active role in their companies' public reporting, and in the design and maintenance of internal controls.

It is significant that in item 4, the CEO and CFO not only have to certify that they are responsible for their companies' internal controls, but also that they have evaluated the controls *within ninety days prior to their quarterly or annual report*. Essentially, this certification requirement mandates that companies actively and continually reevaluate their control structures to prevent fraud.

Item 5 requires the CEO and CFO to certify that they have disclosed to their auditors and their audit committee any material weaknesses in the company's internal controls, and also any fraud, *whether material or not*, that involves management or other key employees. Obviously, this is a very broad reporting standard that goes beyond the "material" standard. The CEO and CFO now must report to their auditors and audit committee *any fraud* committed by management. This places a greater burden on the CEO and CFO to take part in antifraud efforts and to be aware of fraudulent activity within their companies in order to meet this certification requirement.

Item 6 is significant because periodic SEC filings must include statements detailing significant changes to the internal controls of publicly traded companies.

Management Assessment of Internal Controls In conjunction with the Section 302 certification requirements on the responsibility of the CEO and CFO for internal controls, Section 404 of Sarbanes–Oxley requires all annual reports to contain an internal control report that (1) states management's responsibility for establishing and maintaining an adequate internal control structure and procedures for financial reporting; and (2) contains an assessment of the effectiveness of the internal control structure and procedures of the company for financial reporting. The filing company's independent auditor will also be required to issue an attestation report on management's assessment of the company's internal control over financial reporting. This attestation report must be filed with the SEC as part of the company's annual report.

New Standards for Audit Committee Independence

Audit Committee Responsibilities Section 301 of the Act requires that the audit committee for each publicly traded company shall be directly responsible for appointing, compensating, and overseeing the work of the company's outside auditors. The Act also mandates that the auditors must report directly to the audit committee—not to management—and makes it the responsibility of the audit committee to resolve disputes between management and the auditors. Section 301 also requires that the audit committee must have the authority and funding to hire independent counsel and any other advisors it deems necessary to carry out its duties.

Composition of the Audit Committee   The Sarbanes–Oxley Act mandates that each member of a company's audit committee must be a member of its board of directors and must otherwise be "independent." The term *independent* means that the audit committee member can receive compensation from the company only for his service on the board of directors, the audit committee, or another committee of the board of directors. The company may not pay them for any other consulting or advisory work.

Financial Expert   Section 407 of the Act requires every public company to disclose in its periodic reports to the SEC whether the audit committee has at least one member who is a "financial expert," and, if the committee does not, to explain the reasons why. The Act defines a "financial expert" as a person who, through education and experience as a public accountant or auditor, or a CFO, comptroller, or a similar position (1) has an understanding of generally accepted accounting principles and financial statements; (2) has experience in preparing or auditing financial statements of comparable companies and in the application of such principles in accounting for estimates, accruals, and reserves; (3) has experience with internal controls; and (4) has an understanding of audit committee functions.

Establishing a Whistleblowing Structure   The Act makes it the responsibility of the audit committee to establish procedures (e.g., a hotline) for receiving and dealing with complaints and anonymous employee tips regarding irregularities in the company's accounting methods, internal controls, or auditing matters.

New Standards for Auditor Independence

Restrictions on Nonaudit Activity   Perhaps the greatest concern arising out of the public accounting scandals of 2001 and 2002 was the fear that public accounting firms that received multimillion-dollar consulting fees from their public company clients could not maintain an appropriate level of objectivity and professional skepticism in conducting audits for those clients. In order to address this concern, Congress, in Section 201 of the Sarbanes–Oxley Act, established a list of activities that public accounting firms are now prohibited from performing on behalf of their audit clients. The prohibited services are as follows:

- Bookkeeping services
- Financial information systems design and implementation
- Appraisal or valuation services, fairness opinions, or contribution-in-kind reports
- Actuarial services
- Internal audit outsource services
- Management functions or human resources
- Broker or dealer, investment advisor, or investment banking services
- Legal services and expert services unrelated to the audit
- Any other service that the Public Company Accounting Oversight Board proscribes

There are certain other nonaudit services—most notably, tax services—that are not expressly prohibited by Sarbanes–Oxley. However, in order for a public accounting firm to perform these services on behalf of an audit client, that service must be approved in advance by the client's audit committee. Approval of the nonaudit services must be disclosed in the client's periodic SEC reports.

Mandatory Audit Partner Rotation   Section 203 of the Act requires public accounting firms to rotate the lead audit partner or the partner responsible for reviewing the audit every five years.

Conflict of Interest Provisions   Another provision of Sarbanes–Oxley aimed at improving auditor independence is Section 206, which seeks to limit conflicts or potential conflicts that arise when auditors cross over to work for their former clients. The Act makes it unlawful for a public accounting firm to audit a company if, within the prior year, the client's CEO, CFO, controller, or chief accounting officer worked for the accounting firm and participated in the company's audit.

Auditor Reports to Audit Committees   Section 301 requires that auditors report directly to the audit committee, and Section 204 makes certain requirements as to the contents of those reports. In order to help ensure that the audit committee is aware of questionable accounting policies or treatments that were used in the preparation of the company's financial statements, Section 204 states that auditors must make a timely report of the following to the audit committee:

- All critical accounting policies and practices used
- Alternative GAAP methods that were discussed with management, the ramifications of the use of those alternative treatments, and the treatment preferred by the auditors
- Any other material written communications between the auditors and management

Auditors' Attestation to Internal Controls   As was stated previously, Section 404 of the Act requires every annual report to contain an internal control report that states that the company's management is responsible for internal controls and that it also assesses the effectiveness of the internal control structures. Section 404 requires the company's external auditors to attest to and issue a report on management's assessment of internal controls.

Improper Influence on Audits   The Act also makes it unlawful for any officer or director of a public company to take any action to fraudulently influence, coerce, manipulate, or mislead an auditor in the performance of an audit of the company's financial statements. This is yet another attempt by Congress to ensure the independence and objectivity of audits in order to prevent accounting fraud and strengthen investor confidence in the reliability of public company financial statements.

Enhanced Financial Disclosure Requirements

Off–Balance Sheet Transactions   The Sarbanes–Oxley Act directs the SEC to issue rules that require the disclosure of all material off–balance sheet transactions by publicly traded companies. As directed by Section 401 of the Act, the rules require disclosure of "all material off–balance sheet transactions, arrangements, obligations (including contingent obligations), and other relationships the company may have with unconsolidated entities or persons that may have a material current or future effect on the company's financial condition, changes in financial condition, liquidity, capital expenditures, capital resources, or significant components of revenues or expenses." These disclosures are required in all annual and quarterly SEC reports.

Pro Forma Financial Information   Section 401 also directs the SEC to issue rules on pro forma financial statements. These rules require that pro forma financials must not contain any untrue statements or omissions that would make them misleading, and they require that the pro forma financials be reconciled to GAAP. These rules apply to all pro forma financial statements that are filed with the SEC or that are included in any public disclosure or press release.

Prohibitions on Personal Loans to Executives Section 402 makes it illegal for public companies to make personal loans or otherwise extend credit, either directly or indirectly, to or for any director or executive officer. There is an exception that applies to consumer lenders if the loans are consumer loans of the type the company normally makes to the public, and on the same terms.

Restrictions on Insider Trading Section 403 establishes disclosure requirements for stock transactions by directors and officers of public companies, or by persons who own more than 10 percent of a publicly traded company's stock. Reports of changes in beneficial ownership by these persons must be filed with the SEC by the end of the second business day following the transaction.

Under Section 306, directors and officers are also prohibited from trading in the company's securities during any pension fund blackout periods. This restriction applies only to securities that were acquired as a result of their employment or service to the company. A blackout period is defined as any period of more than three consecutive business days in which at least 50 percent of the participants in the company's retirement plan are restricted from trading in the company's securities. If a director or officer violates this provision, he can be forced to disgorge to the company all profits received from the sale of securities during the blackout period.

Codes of Ethics for Senior Financial Officers Pursuant to Section 406 of the Act, the SEC established rules that require public companies to disclose whether they have adopted a code of ethics for their senior financial officers, and if not, to explain the reasons why. The new rules also require immediate public disclosure any time there is a change in the code of ethics or a waiver of the code of ethics for a senior financial officer.

Enhanced Review of Periodic Filings Section 408 of the Act requires the SEC to make regular and systematic reviews of disclosures made by public companies in their periodic reports to the SEC. Reviews of a company's disclosures, including its financial statements, must be made at least once every three years. Prior to this enactment, reviews were typically minimal and tended to coincide with registered offerings.

Real-Time Disclosures Under Section 409, registered companies must publicly disclose information concerning material changes in their financial condition or operations. These disclosures must be "in plain English" and must be made "on a rapid and current basis."

Protections for Corporate Whistleblowers under Sarbanes–Oxley

The Sarbanes–Oxley Act establishes broad new protections for corporate whistleblowers. There are two sections of the Act that address whistleblower protections: Section 806 deals with civil protections and Section 1107 establishes criminal liability for those who retaliate against whistleblowers.

Civil Liability Whistleblower Protection Section 806 of the Act, which is codified at 18 USC §1514A, creates civil liability for companies that retaliate against whistleblowers. It should be noted that this provision does not provide universal whistleblower protection; it protects only employees of publicly traded companies. Section 806 makes it unlawful to fire, demote, suspend, threaten, harass, or in any other manner discriminate against an employee for providing information or aiding in an investigation of securities fraud. In order to trigger Section 806 protections, the employee must report the suspected misconduct to a federal regulatory or law enforcement agency, a member of Congress or a committee of Congress, or a supervisor. Employees are also protected against retaliation for filing, testifying in, participating in, or otherwise assisting in a proceeding filed or about to be filed relating to an alleged violation of securities laws or SEC rules.

The whistleblower protections apply even if the company is ultimately found not to have committed securities fraud. As long as the employee reasonably believes she is reporting conduct that constitutes a violation of various federal securities laws, then she is protected. The protections cover retaliatory acts not only of the company, but also of any officer, employee, contractor, subcontractor, or agent of the company.

If a public company is found to have violated Section 806, the Act provides for an award of compensatory damages sufficient to "make the employee whole." Penalties include reinstatement; back pay with interest; and compensation for special damages including litigation costs, expert witness fees, and attorneys' fees.

Criminal Sanction Whistleblower Protection Section 1107 of Sarbanes–Oxley—codified at 18 USC §1513—makes it a crime to knowingly, with the intent to retaliate, take any harmful action against a person for providing truthful information relating to the commission or possible commission of any federal offense. This protection is triggered only when information is provided to a law enforcement officer; it does not apply to reports made to supervisors or to members of Congress, as is the case under Section 806.

In general, the coverage of Section 1107 is much broader than the civil liability whistleblower protections of Section 806. While the Section 806 protections apply only to employees of publicly traded companies, Section 1107's criminal whistleblower protections cover all individuals (and organizations) regardless of where they work. Also, Section 806 applies only to violations of securities laws or SEC rules and regulations, whereas Section 1107 protects individuals who provide truthful information about the commission or possible commission of *any federal offense*.

Violations of Section 1107 can be punished by fines of up to $250,000 and up to ten years in prison for individuals. Corporations that violate the act can be fined up to $500,000.

Enhanced Penalties for White-Collar Crime

As part of Congress's general effort to deter corporate accounting fraud and other forms of white-collar crime, the Sarbanes–Oxley Act also enhances the criminal penalties for a number of white-collar offenses.

Attempt and Conspiracy The Act amends the mail fraud provisions of the United States Code (Chapter 63) to make "attempt" and "conspiracy to commit" offenses subject to the same penalties as the offense itself. This applies to mail fraud, wire fraud, securities fraud, bank fraud, and health care fraud.

Mail Fraud and Wire Fraud Sarbanes–Oxley amends the mail fraud and wire fraud statutes (18 USC §§1341, 1343), increasing the maximum jail term from five to twenty years.

Securities Fraud Section 807 of the Act makes securities fraud a crime under 18 USC §1348, providing for fines up to $250,000 and up to twenty-five years in prison.

Document Destruction Section 802 of the Act makes destroying evidence to obstruct an investigation or any other matter within the jurisdiction of any U.S. department illegal and punishable by a fine of up to $250,000 and up to twenty years in prison.

The final rules adopted by the SEC under Section 802 specifically require that accountants who perform audits on publicly traded companies must maintain all audit or review workpapers for a period of seven years. Although the original provisions of Section 802 only required a retention period of five years, the SEC extended the requirement to be consistent with the seven-year retention period required under the Auditing Standards promulgated by the Public Company Accounting Oversight Board (PCAOB) per Section 103 of the Act. Violations of the final SEC rules may be punished by fines up to $250,000 and up to ten years in jail for individuals, or fines up to $500,000 for corporations.

Section 1102 of the Act amends Section 1512 of the U.S. Code to make it a criminal offense to corruptly alter, destroy, mutilate, or conceal a record or document with the intent to impair its integrity or use in an official proceeding, or to otherwise obstruct, influence, or impede any official proceeding or attempt to do so. Violations of this section are punishable by fines up to $250,000 and imprisonment for up to twenty years.

Freezing of Assets During an investigation of possible securities violations by a publicly traded company or any of its officers, directors, partners, agents, controlling persons, or employees, the SEC can petition a federal court to issue a forty-five-day freeze on "extraordinary payments" to any of the foregoing persons. If granted, the payments will be placed in an interest-bearing escrow account while the investigation commences. This provision was enacted to prevent corporate assets from being improperly distributed while an investigation is underway.

Bankruptcy Loopholes Section 803 amends the bankruptcy code so that judgments, settlements, damages, fines, penalties, restitution, and disgorgement payments resulting from violations of federal securities laws are nondischargeable. This is intended to prevent corporate wrongdoers from sheltering their assets under bankruptcy protection.

Disgorgement of Bonuses One of the most noteworthy aspects of the Sarbanes–Oxley Act is Section 304, which states that if a publicly traded company is required to prepare an accounting restatement due to the company's material noncompliance, as a result of "misconduct," with any financial reporting requirement under securities laws, then the CEO and CFO must reimburse the company for:

- Any bonus or other incentive-based or equity-based compensation received during the twelve months after the initial filing of the report that requires restating
- Any profits realized from the sale of the company's securities during the same twelve-month period

While the Act requires the CEO and CFO to disgorge their bonuses if the company's financial statements have to be restated because of "misconduct," it makes no mention of whose misconduct triggers this provision. There is nothing in the text of Section 304 that limits the disgorgement provision to instances of misconduct by the CEO and CFO. Presumably, then, the CEO and CFO could be required to disgorge their bonuses and profits from the sale of company stock even if they had no knowledge of and took no part in the misconduct that made the restatement necessary.

Now that we understand the underlying accounting principles that allow financial statement frauds to occur, and the impact of the Sarbanes–Oxley Act to discourage these acts, we will turn, in the next chapter, to the mechanics of how such frauds are committed.

FINANCIAL STATEMENT FRAUD DATA FROM THE ACFE
2009 GLOBAL FRAUD SURVEY

Frequency and Cost

Financial statement frauds were by far the least common method of occupational fraud in our study. Of 1,843 cases in the 2009 survey, only 5 percent involved financial statement fraud (see Exhibit 11-2).

Although they were the least frequently reported category of occupational fraud, financial statement schemes were the most costly by far. The median loss associated with fraudulent financial statement schemes in our survey was $4.1 million, sixteen times the median loss caused by corruption schemes and more than thirty times the median loss for asset misappropriations (see Exhibit 11-3).

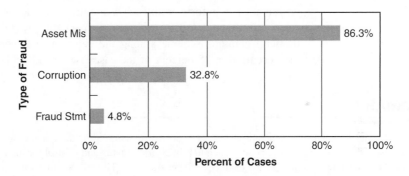

EXHIBIT 11-2   *2009 Global Fraud Survey*: Frequency of Three Major Categories[a]

[a]The sum of these percentages exceeds 100 percent because some cases involved multiple fraud schemes that fell into more than one category. Various charts in this chapter may reflect percentages that total in excess of 100 percent for similar reasons

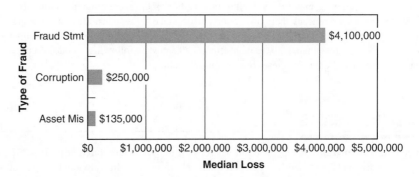

EXHIBIT 11-3   *2009 Global Fraud Survey:* Median Loss of Three Major Categories

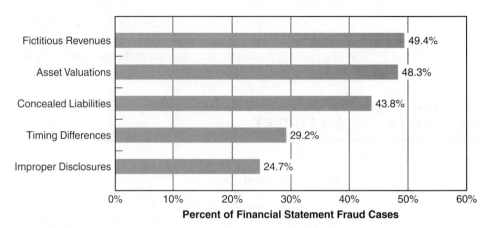

EXHIBIT 11-4   *2009 Global Fraud Survey:* Fraudulent Financial Statement Schemes by Category

Types of Fraudulent Financial Statement Schemes

Financial statement frauds can be broken down into five distinct categories: *fictitious revenues, improper asset valuations, concealed liabilities and expenses, timing differences*, and *improper disclosures*. As Exhibit 11-4 shows, the distribution of these scheme types was somewhat uniform, with each of the first three categories occurring in at least 40 percent of the fraudulent financial statement schemes reviewed. Improper disclosures were the least common scheme among the eighty-nine financial statement frauds reviewed; they occurred in 25 percent of the cases (see Exhibit 11-4).

SUMMARY

Fraud in financial statements generally takes one of two forms: overstated assets or revenue, or understated liabilities or expenses. Although they are conceptually distinct, both general forms result in increased equity and net worth for a company, all as a result of fraud.

There are three main groups of people who commit financial statement fraud. Sometimes it is committed by organized criminals, who may engage in this type of fraud as part of a scheme to obtain fraudulent loans or to promote a stock. Mid- and lower-level employees may be involved in falsification of financial statements to conceal their own poor performance or for other related reasons. Most commonly, senior-level management perpetrates financial statement fraud schemes for various reasons. Some of these reasons may include concealing their actual business performance, preserving their status and control, or maintaining their personal wealth.

The three primary methods of committing financial statement fraud include *playing the accounting system, beating the accounting system*, and using methods *outside of the accounting system*. In order to attempt to prevent the overstatement of assets or revenues, guidelines have developed over the years, and have been codified by the Financial Accounting Standards Board into what has become known as generally accepted accounting principles (GAAP). Financial statements are the responsibility of a company's management, and management can attempt to deter financial statement fraud by setting and following a code of conduct.

ESSENTIAL TERMS

Financial statement fraud A type of fraud whereby an individual or individuals purposefully misreport financial information about an organization in order to mislead those who read it.

Overstatements Type of financial statement fraud in which an individual exaggerates a company's assets or revenues to meet certain objectives.

Understatements Type of financial statement fraud in which an individual minimizes a company's liabilities or expenses to meet certain objectives.

Generally accepted accounting principles Recognition and measurement concepts that have evolved over time and have been codified by the Financial Accounting Standards Board and its predecessor organizations. The standards serve to guide regular business practices and deter financial statement fraud.

Comparability and consistency Secondary qualitative characteristics that state that a company's information must be presented with the same consistent method from year to year, in order for it to be useful for analytical purposes in decision making.

Relevance and reliability Primary qualitative characteristics of financial reports as they relate to usefulness for decision making. Relevance implies that certain information will make a difference in arriving at a decision. Reliability means that the user can depend on the factual accuracy of the information.

Periodicity A "time period" assumption, which deems that economic activity be divided into specific time intervals, such as monthly, quarterly, and annually.

Full disclosure A standard for financial reporting that states that any material deviation from generally accepted accounting principles must be explained to the reader of the financial information. Any potential adverse event must be disclosed in the financial statements.

REVIEW QUESTIONS

11-1 (Learning objective 11-1) Why are the fraudulent statement methods under discussion referred to as "financial statement fraud"?

11-2 (Learning objective 11-2) There are three main groups of people who commit financial statement fraud. Who are they?

11-3 (Learning objective 11-3) What are the three primary reasons people commit financial statement fraud?

11-4 (Learning objective 11-4) What are the three general methods commonly used to commit financial statement fraud?

11-5 (Learning objective 11-5) What is meant by the term *overstatement*?

11-6 (Learning objective 11-6) What is meant by the term *understatement*?

11-7 (Learning objective 11-7) What are the components of the conceptual framework for financial reporting?

11-8 (Learning objective 11-8) Define the term *financial statement* and provide examples of types of financial statements used in companies.

DISCUSSION ISSUES

11-1 (Learning objective 11-1) Why is financial statement fraud commonly referred to as "cooking the books"?

11-2 (Learning objectives 11-2 and 11-3) Compare the three main groups of people who may commit financial statement fraud, and describe their potential reasons for the fraud.

11-3 (Learning objective 11-4) Although three general methods of producing fraudulent statements have been identified, one of these methods is typically used first. Which method is this, and why is it more likely to be selected first as opposed to the other two?

11-4 (Learning objective 11-7) What is the generally accepted accounting principle known as matching? Describe how a company may be involved in fraud that violates this principle.

11-5 (Learning objective 11-7) Management of a cellular phone company learns that a new technological advance will occur within the next year that will make the company's current phones and related products obsolete. As a result, there is a strong chance that the company will close. When financial statements appear for auditors, management does not reveal its knowledge of the new technology. In this case, what accounting concepts are involved?

11-6 (Learning objective 11-8) In an organization, who is generally responsible for the financial statements, and how can those responsible help to deter financial statement fraud?

Fraudulent Financial Statement Schemes

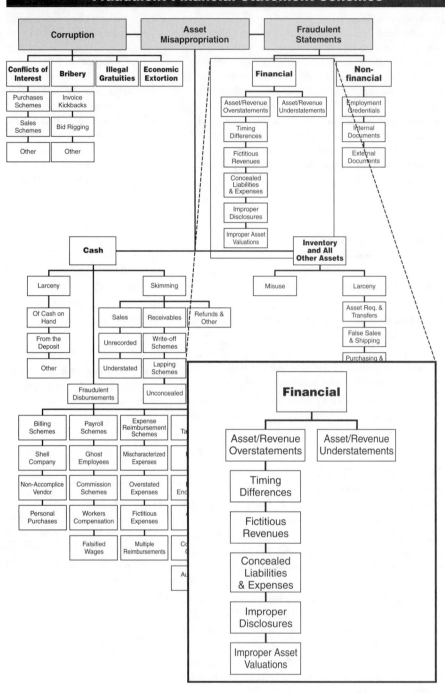

Corruption

- **Conflicts of Interest**
  - Purchases Schemes
  - Sales Schemes
  - Other
- **Bribery**
  - Invoice Kickbacks
  - Bid Rigging
  - Other
- **Illegal Gratuities**
- **Economic Extortion**

Asset Misappropriation

Fraudulent Statements

- **Financial**
  - Asset/Revenue Overstatements
  - Asset/Revenue Understatements
  - Timing Differences
  - Fictitious Revenues
  - Concealed Liabilities & Expenses
  - Improper Disclosures
  - Improper Asset Valuations
- **Non-financial**
  - Employment Credentials
  - Internal Documents
  - External Documents

Cash

- **Larceny**
  - Of Cash on Hand
  - From the Deposit
  - Other
- **Skimming**
  - Sales
    - Unrecorded
    - Understated
  - Receivables
    - Write-off Schemes
    - Lapping Schemes
    - Unconcealed
  - Refunds & Other

Fraudulent Disbursements

- **Billing Schemes**
  - Shell Company
  - Non-Accomplice Vendor
  - Personal Purchases
- **Payroll Schemes**
  - Ghost Employees
  - Commission Schemes
  - Workers Compensation
  - Falsified Wages
- **Expense Reimbursement Schemes**
  - Mischaracterized Expenses
  - Overstated Expenses
  - Fictitious Expenses
  - Multiple Reimbursements

Inventory and All Other Assets

- **Misuse**
- **Larceny**
  - Asset Req. & Transfers
  - False Sales & Shipping
  - Purchasing &

Financial

- Asset/Revenue Overstatements
- Asset/Revenue Understatements
- Timing Differences
- Fictitious Revenues
- Concealed Liabilities & Expenses
- Improper Disclosures
- Improper Asset Valuations

EXHIBIT 12-1

CHAPTER 12

FRAUDULENT FINANCIAL STATEMENT SCHEMES

LEARNING OBJECTIVES

After studying this chapter, you should be able to:

12-1 Define financial statement fraud and related schemes

12-2 Understand and identify the five classifications of financial statement fraud

12-3 Explain how fictitious revenues schemes are committed, as well as the motivation for, and result of, committing such fraud

12-4 Explain how timing difference schemes are committed, as well as the motivation for, and result of, committing such fraud

12-5 Describe the methods by which concealed liabilities and expenses are used to fraudulently improve a company's balance sheet

12-6 Understand how improper disclosures may be used to mislead potential investors, creditors, or other users of the financial statements

12-7 Recognize how improper asset valuation may inflate the current ratio

12-8 Identify detection and deterrence procedures that may be instrumental in dealing with fraudulent financial statement schemes

12-9 Understand financial statement analysis for detecting fraud

12-10 Identify and characterize current professional and legislative actions that have sought to improve corporate governance, enhance the reliability and quality of financial reports, and foster credibility and effectiveness of audit functions

CASE STUDY: THAT WAY LIES MADNESS[1]

"I'm Crazy Eddie!" a goggle-eyed man screams from the television set, pulling at his face with his hands. "My prices are *in-sane!*" Eddie Antar got into the electronics business in 1969, with a modest store called Sight and Sound. Less than twenty years later, he had become Crazy Eddie, a millionaire many times over and an international fugitive from justice. He was shrewd, daring, and self-serving; he was obsessive and greedy. But he was hardly *insane*. A U.S. Attorney said, "He was not Crazy Eddie. He was Crooked Eddie."

The man on the screen wasn't Eddie at all. The face so dutifully watched throughout New Jersey, New York, and Connecticut—that was an actor, hired to do a humiliating but effective characterization. The real Eddie Antar was not the kind of man to yell and rend his clothes. He was busy making money, and he was making a lot of it illegally. By the time his electronics empire folded, Antar and members of his family had distinguished themselves with a fraud of massive proportions, reaping more than $120 million. A senior official at the Securities and Exchange Commission (SEC) quipped, "This may not be the biggest stock fraud of all time, but for outrageousness it is going to be very hard to beat." The SEC was joined by the FBI, the Postal Inspection Service, and the

[1] Several names and details have been changed to preserve anonymity.

U.S. Attorney in tracking Eddie down. They were able to show a multipronged fraud in which Antar:

- Listed smuggled money from foreign banks as sales
- Made false entries to accounts payable
- Overstated Crazy Eddie, Inc.'s inventory by breaking into and altering audit records
- Took credit for merchandise as "returned" while also counting it as inventory
- "Shared" inventory from one store to boost other stores' audit counts
- Arranged for vendors to ship merchandise and defer the billing, besides claiming discounts and advertising credits
- Sold large lots of merchandise to wholesalers, then spread the money to individual stores as retail receipts

It was a long list, and a profitable one for Eddie Antar and the inner circle of his family. The seven action items were designed to make Crazy Eddie's look like it was booming. In fact, it was. It was the single biggest retailer of stereos and televisions in the New York metropolitan area, with a dominant and seemingly impregnable share of the market. But that wasn't enough for Eddie. He took the chain public, and then made some real money. Shares that initially sold at $8 each later peaked at $80, thanks to the Antar team's masterful tweaking of company accounts.

Inflating Crazy Eddie's stock price wasn't the first scam Antar had pulled. In the early days, as Sight and Sound grew into Crazy Eddie's and spawned multiple stores, Eddie was actually underreporting his earnings. Eddie's cousin, Sam Antar, remembered learning how the company did business by watching his father during the early days. "The store managers would drop off cash to the house after they closed at ten o'clock, and my father would make one bundle for deposit into the company account, and several bundles for others in the family," Sam Antar said. "Then he would drive over to their houses and drop off their bundles at two in the morning." For every few dollars to the company, the Antars took a dollar for themselves. The cash was secreted away into bank accounts at Bank Leumi of Israel. Eddie smuggled some of the money out of the country himself, by strapping stacks of large bills across his body. The Antars sneaked away with at least $7 million over several years. Skimming the cash meant tax-free profits, and one gargantuan nest egg waiting across the sea.

But entering the stock market was another story. Eddie anticipated the initial public offering (IPO) of shares by quietly easing money from Bank Leumi back into the operation. The company really was growing, but injecting the pilfered funds as sales receipts made the growth look even more impressive: Skim the money and beat the tax man, then draw out funds as you need them to boost sales figures. Keeps the ship running smooth and sunny.

But Paul Hayes, a special agent who worked the case with the FBI, pointed out Crazy Eddie's problem. "After building up the books, they set a pattern of double-digit growth, which they had to sustain. When they couldn't sustain it, they started looking for new ways to fake it," Hayes said.

Eddie, his brothers, his cousins, and several family loyalists all owned large chunks of company stock. No matter what actually happened at the stores, they wanted that stock to rise. So the seven-point plan was born. There was the skimmed money waiting overseas, being brought back and disguised as sales. But there were limits to how much cash the family had available and could get back into the country, so they turned to other methods of inflating the company's financials. In the most daring part of the expanded scam, Antar's people broke into auditors' records and boosted the inventory numbers. With the stroke of a pen, 13 microcassette players became 1,327.

Better than that, the Antars figured out how to make their inventory do double work. Debit memos were drawn up showing substantial lots of stereos or VCRs as "returned to manufacturer." Crazy Eddie's was given a credit for the wholesale cost due back from the manufacturer. But the machines were kept at the warehouse to be counted as inventory. In a variation of the inventory scam, at least one wholesaler agreed to ship Crazy Eddie truckloads of merchandise, deferring the billing to a later date. That way Crazy Eddie's had plenty of inventory volume, plus the return credits listed on the account book. And what if auditors got too close and began asking questions? Executives would throw the records away. A "lost" report was a safe report.

Eddie Antar didn't stop at simple bookkeeping and warehouse games; he "shared inventory" among his nearly forty stores. After auditors had finished counting a warehouse's holdings and had gone for the day, workers tossed the merchandise into trucks. The inventory was hauled overnight to an early morning load-in at another store. When the auditors arrived at that store, they found a full stockroom waiting to be counted. Again, this ruse carried a double payoff. The audit looked strong because of the inventory items counted multiple times, and the bookkeeping looked good because only one set of invoices was entered as payable to Eddie's creditors. Also, the game could be repeated for as long as the audit route demanded.

Eddie's trump card was the supplier network. He had considerable leverage with area wholesalers, because Crazy Eddie's was the biggest and baddest retail outlet in the region. Agent Paul Hayes remembers Eddie as "an aggressive businessman: He'd put the squeeze on a manufacturer and tell them he wasn't going to carry their product. Now, he was king of what is possibly the biggest consolidated retail market in the nation. Japanese manufacturers were fighting each other to get into this market... So when Eddie made a threat, that was a threat with serious potential impact."

Suppliers gave Crazy Eddie's buyers extraordinary discounts and advertising rebates. If they didn't, the Antars had another method: They made up the discount. For example, Crazy Eddie's might owe George-Electronics $1 million; by claiming $500,000 in discounts or ad credits, the bill was cut in half. Sometimes there was a real discount, sometimes there wasn't. (It wasn't easy, after Eddie's fall, to tell what was a shrewd business deal and what was fraud. "They had legitimate discounts in there," says Hayes, "along with the criminal acts. That's why it was tough to know what was smoke and what was fire.")

Eddie had yet another arrangement with manufacturers. For certain high-demand items—high-end stereo systems, for example—a producing company would agree to sell only to Crazy Eddie. Eddie placed an order big enough for what he needed, and then added a little more. The excess he sold to a distributor who had already agreed to send the merchandise outside Crazy Eddie's tristate area. And then the really good part: By arrangement, the distributor paid for the merchandise in a series of small checks—$100,000 worth of portable stereos would be paid off with 10 checks of $10,000 each. Eddie sprinkled this money into his stores as register sales. He knew that *Wall Street analysts use comparable store sales as a bedrock indicator*. New stores are compared with old stores, and any store open more than a year is compared with its performance during the previous term. The goal is to outperform the previous year. So the $10,000 injections made Eddie's "comps" look fantastic.

As the doctored numbers circulated in enthusiastic financial circles, CRZY stock doubled its earnings per share during its first year on the stock exchange. The stock split two-for-one in both of its first two fiscal terms as a publicly traded company. As chairman and chief executive, Eddie Antar used his newsletter to trumpet soaring profits, declining overhead costs, and a new 210,000-square-foot corporate headquarters. Plans were underway for a home-shopping arm of the business. Besides the electronics stores, there was now a subsidiary, Crazy Eddie Record and Tape Asylums, in the Antar fold. At its peak, the operation included forty-three stores and reported sales of $350 million a year. This was a long way from the Sight and Sound storefront operation where it all began.

It was almost eerie how deliberately the Antar conspirators manipulated investors, and how directly their crimes affected brokers' assessments. At the end of Crazy Eddie's second public year, a major brokerage firm issued a gushing recommendation to "buy." The recommendation was explicitly "based on 35 percent EPS [earnings per share] growth" and "comparable store sales growth in the low double-digit range." These double-digit expansions were from the "comps" that Eddie and his gang had cooked up with wholesalers' money and by juggling inventories. CRZY stock, the report predicted, would double and then some during the next year. As if following an Antar script, the brokers declared, "Crazy Eddie is the only retailer in our universe that has not reported a disappointing quarter in the last two years. We do not believe that is an accident... We believe Crazy Eddie is

becoming the kind of company that can continually produce above-average comparable store sales growth." The brokers could not have known what Herculean efforts were needed to yield just that impression. The report praised Eddie's management skills. "Mr. Antar has created a strong organization beneath him that is close-knit and directed... Despite the boisterous (less charitable commentators would say obnoxious) quality of the commercials, Crazy Eddie management is quite conservative."

Well, yes, in a manner of speaking. They were certainly holding tightly to the money as it flowed through the market. According to federal indictments, the conspiracy inflated the company's value during the first year by about $2 million. By selling off shares of the overvalued stock, the partners pocketed over $28.2 million. The next year they illegally boosted income by $5.5 million and retail sales by $2.2 million. This time the group cashed in their stock for a cool $42.2 million windfall. In the last year before the boom went bust, Eddie and his partners inflated income by $37.5 million and retail by $18 million. They didn't have that much stock left, though, so despite the big blowup they only cashed in for about $8.3 million.

Maybe he knew the end was at hand, but with takeovers looming, Eddie kept fighting. He had started his business with one store in Brooklyn almost twenty years before, near the neighborhood where he grew up, populated mainly by Jewish immigrants from Syria. Despite these humble beginnings he would one day be called "the Darth Vader of capitalism" by a prosecuting attorney, referring not just to his professional inveigling but to his personal life as well. Eddie's affair with another woman broke up his marriage and precipitated a lifelong break with his father. Eventually he divorced his wife and married his lover. Rumors hinted that Eddie had been unhappy because he had five daughters and no sons from his first marriage. Neighbors said the rest of the family sided with the ex-wife. Eddie and his brothers continued in business together, but they had no contact outside the company. Allen Antar, a few years younger, should have been able to sympathize—he had also been estranged from the family when he filed for a divorce and married a woman who wasn't Jewish. (Allen eventually divorced that woman and remarried his first wife.) Later at trial, the brothers Antar were notably cold to one another. Even Eddie's own lawyer called him a "huckster."

But this Darth Vader had a compassionate side. Eddie was known as a quiet man, and modest. He was seldom photographed and almost never granted interviews. He was said to have waited hours at the bedside of a dying cousin, Mort Gindi, whose brother, also named Eddie, was named as a defendant in the Antars' federal trial. His cousin Sam remembers him as "a leader, someone I looked up to since I was a kid. Eddie was strong, he worked out with weights; when the Italian kids wanted to come into our neighborhood and beat up on the Jewish kids, Eddie would stop them. That was when we were kids. Later, it turned out different."

Eddie had come a long way. He had realized millions of dollars by selling off company stock at inflated prices. This money was stashed in secret accounts around the world, held under various assumed identities. In fact, Eddie had done so well that he was left vulnerable as leader of the retail empire. When Elias Zinn, a Houston businessman, joined with the Oppenheimer-Palmieri Fund and waged a proxy battle for Crazy Eddie's, the Antars had too little shareholders' power to stave off the bid. They lost. For the first time, Crazy Eddie's was out of Eddie's hands.

The new owners didn't have long to celebrate. They discovered that their ship was sinking fast. Stores were alarmingly understocked, shareholders were suing, and suppliers were shutting down credit lines because they were being paid either late or not at all. An initial review showed the company's inventory had been overstated by $65 million—a number later raised to over $80 million. In a desperate maneuver, the new management set up a computerized inventory system and established lines of credit. They made peace with the vendors and cut 150 jobs to reduce overhead. But it was too late. Less than a year after the takeover, Crazy Eddie's was dead.

Eddie Antar, on the other hand, was very much alive. But nobody knew where. He had disappeared when it became apparent that the takeover was forcing him out. He had set up dummy companies in Liberia, Gibraltar, and Panama, along with well-supplied bank accounts in Israel and Switzerland. Sensing that his days as Crazy Eddie were numbered, he fled the United States, traveling the world with faked passports, calling himself, at different times, Harry Page Shalom and David Cohen. Shalom was a real person, a longtime friend of Eddie's, another in a string of chagrined and erstwhile companions.

It was as David Cohen that Eddie ended his flight from justice and reality. After twenty-eight months on the run, he stalked into a police station in Bern, Switzerland—but not to turn himself in. "David Cohen" was demanding help from the police. He was mad because bank officials refused to let him at the $32 million he had on account there. The bank wouldn't tell Cohen anything—just that he couldn't access those funds. But officials discreetly informed police that the money had been frozen by the U.S. Department of Justice. Affidavits in the investigation had targeted the account as an Antar line. It didn't take long to realize that David Cohen, the irate millionaire in the Bern police station, was Eddie Antar. It was the last public part Crazy Eddie would play for a while. He eventually pled guilty to racketeering and conspiracy charges and was sentenced to eight-two months in prison with credit for time served. This left him with about three and a half years of jail time. He was also ordered to repay $121 million to bilked investors. Almost $72 million was recovered from Eddie's personal accounts. "I don't ask for mercy," Eddie told the judge at his trial. "I ask for balance."

Eddie's brother, Mitchell, was first convicted and given four-and-a-half years, with $3 million in restitution burdens, but his conviction was overturned because of a prejudicial remark by the judge in the first trial. Mitchell later pled guilty to two counts of securities fraud, and the rest of the charges were dropped. Allen Antar was acquitted at the first trial, but he and his father, Sam, were both later found guilty of insider trading and ordered to pay $11.9 million and $57.5 million, respectively, in disgorgement and interest.

What happened to the Crazy Eddie stores? In 1998, Eddie's nephews attempted to revive the legacy and held a grand opening for a new electronics store in New Jersey. At the beginning of the new millennium, the store's doors closed and Crazy Eddie shifted focus to become a dotcom retailer. But by 2004, the company had once again faltered and closed, this time amid allegations that it had resold unauthorized products online.

OVERVIEW

Financial statement fraud continues to be a hot subject in the press, as scandals challenge the corporate responsibility and integrity of major companies such as American International Group (AIG) and General Electric (GE), each of whom recently has been alleged by the SEC to have committed financial statement fraud. Internationally, India's main criminal investigation agency, the Central Bureau of Investigation, recently filed new charges against Satyam Computer Services, alleging accounting fraud in the amount of $2.6 billion. And it wasn't too long ago that companies, including Lucent, Xerox, Rite Aid, U.S. Foodservice, Waste Management, MicroStrategy, Raytheon, Sunbeam, Enron, WorldCom, Global Crossing, Adelphia, Qwest, and Tyco, graced the headlines for the same transgression. Top management teams, including chief executive officers (CEOs) and chief financial officers (CFOs), of these companies, and of many more, have been accused of cooking the books. Ongoing occurrences of financial statement fraud by high-profile companies, coupled with the demise of accounting firm Arthur Andersen in 2002, have raised concerns about the integrity, transparency, and reliability of the financial reporting process and have challenged the role of corporate governance and audit functions in deterring and detecting financial statement fraud.

DEFINING FINANCIAL STATEMENT FRAUD

The definition of financial statement fraud can be found in a number of authoritative reports (e.g., The Treadway Commission's *Report of the National Commission on Fraudulent Financial Reporting* (1987) and the AICPA's Statement on Auditing Standards No. 99 (AU 316), "Consideration of Fraud in a Financial Statement Audit"). *Financial statement fraud* is defined as deliberate misstatements or omissions of amounts or disclosures of financial statements to deceive financial statement users, particularly investors and creditors. Financial statement fraud may involve the following schemes:

- Falsification, alteration, or manipulation of material financial records, supporting documents, or business transactions
- Material intentional omissions or misrepresentations of events, transactions, accounts, or other significant information from which financial statements are prepared
- Deliberate misapplication of accounting principles, policies, and procedures used to measure, recognize, report, and disclose economic events and business transactions
- Intentional omissions of disclosures or presentation of inadequate disclosures regarding accounting principles and policies and related financial amounts (Rezaee 2002)

Statement on Auditing Standards (SAS) No. 99 (AU 316), entitled "Consideration of Fraud in a Financial Statement Audit," issued by the Auditing Standards Board (ASB) of the American Institute of Certified Public Accountants (AICPA) in November 2002, defines two types of misstatements relevant to an audit of financial statements and auditors' consideration of fraud (AICPA 2002). The first type is misstatements arising from fraudulent financial reporting, which are defined as "intentional misstatements or omissions of amounts or disclosures in financial statements designed to deceive financial statement users" (AICPA 2002: 7). The second type is misstatements arising from misappropriation of assets, which are commonly referred to as theft or defalcation. The primary focus of this chapter is on misstatements arising from fraudulent reporting that directly causes financial reports to be misleading and deceptive to investors and creditors. Fraudulent financial statements can be used to unjustifiably sell stock, obtain loans or trade credit, and/or improve managerial compensation and bonuses. The important issues addressed in this chapter are how to effectively and efficiently deter, detect, and correct financial statement fraud.

COSTS OF FINANCIAL STATEMENT FRAUD

Published statistics on the possible costs of financial statement fraud—including those from the *2009 Global Fraud Survey* that were included in the previous chapter—are estimates, at best. It is impossible to determine the actual total costs because not all fraud is detected, not all detected fraud is reported, and not all reported fraud is legally pursued.

Nonetheless, it is safe to say that the full impact of financial statement fraud is astonishing. In addition to the direct economic losses resulting from such manipulations are legal costs; increased insurance costs; loss of productivity; adverse impacts on employees' morale, customers' goodwill, and suppliers' trust; and negative stock market reactions. Another important indirect cost of financial statement fraud is the loss of productivity due to dismissal of the fraudsters and their replacements. While these indirect costs cannot possibly be estimated, they should be taken into consideration when assessing the consequences of financial statement fraud. Loss of public confidence in quality and reliability of financial statements caused by the alleged fraudulent activities is the most damaging and costly effect of fraud.

Financial statement fraud is harmful in many ways. It:

- *Undermines the reliability, quality, transparency, and integrity of the financial reporting process*. In 2009, General Electric (GE) agreed to pay a $50 million fine to the SEC to settle charges that it misled investors through fraudulent accounting practices in 2002 and 2003. Prior to the 2009 settlement, GE had already restated some of its financial statements for the years 2001 through 2008. In the wake of scandals such as those involving Enron, WorldCom, Adelphia, and Tyco, these types of high-profile financial restatements and enforcement actions by the SEC against big corporations for alleged financial statement fraud severely undermine public confidence in the veracity of financial reports.

- *Jeopardizes the integrity and objectivity of the auditing profession, especially of auditors and auditing firms*. Arthur Andersen, one of the Big Five CPA firms, dismantled its international network and allowed officers to join rival firms after it became embroiled in a scandal involving its shredding of documents related to its audit work for Enron. Although the Supreme Court ultimately overturned Andersen's conviction for obstruction of justice, the accounting firm had already irreparably crumbled in the wake of the document destruction debacle.

- *Diminishes the confidence of the capital markets, as well as market participants, in the reliability of financial information*. The capital market and market participants, including investors, creditors, employees, and pensioners, are affected by the quality and transparency of financial information they use in making investment decisions.

- *Makes the capital markets less efficient*. Auditors reduce the information risk that may be associated with the published financial statements and thus make them more transparent. The information risk is the likelihood that financial statements are inaccurate, false, misleading, biased, and deceptive. By applying the same financial standards to diverse businesses and by reducing the information risk, accountants contribute to the efficiency of our capital markets.

- *Adversely affects the nation's economic growth and prosperity*. Accountants are expected to make financial statements among corporations more comparable by applying the same set of accounting standards to diverse businesses. This enhanced comparability makes business more transparent, the capital markets more efficient, the free enterprise system possible, and the economy more vibrant and prosperous. The efficiency of our capital markets depends on receiving objective, reliable, and transparent financial information. Thus, the accounting profession, especially practicing auditors, plays an important role in our free enterprise system and capital markets. However, the Enron, WorldCom, and Global Crossing debacles provide evidence that the role of accountants can be compromised.

- *Results in huge litigation costs.* Corporations and their auditors are being sued for alleged financial statement fraud and related audit failures by a diverse group of litigants including small investors in class action suits and the U.S. Justice Department. Investors are also given the right to sue and recover damages from those who aided and abetted securities fraud.

- *Destroys careers of individuals involved in financial statement fraud.* For example, top executives are being barred from serving on the boards of directors of any public companies, and auditors are being barred from the practice of public accounting.

- *Causes bankruptcy or substantial economic losses by the company engaged in financial statement fraud.* WorldCom and Enron make up two of the ten largest bankruptcies in U.S. history. Total assets at the time of filing were $104 billion for WorldCom and $66 billion for Enron.

- *Encourages regulatory intervention.* Regulatory agencies (e.g., the SEC) considerably influence the financial reporting process and related audit functions. The recent perceived crisis in the financial reporting process and audit functions ultimately encouraged lawmakers to establish accounting reform legislation (Sarbanes–Oxley Act of 2002). This Act is intended to drastically change the self-regulating environment of the accounting profession to a regulatory framework under the SEC oversight function.

- *Causes devastation in the normal operations and performance of alleged companies.* Even if a company manages to escape bankruptcy as a result of financial statement fraud, it won't likely do so without experiencing immense financial and reputational damage. Normal operations and performance are bound to suffer as the company faces stock price volatility, difficulties in raising capital, layoffs, fines, legal fees, diminished sales, and other negative consequences.

- *Raises serious doubt about the efficacy of financial statement audits.* The financial community is demanding high-quality audits, and auditors need to effectively address this issue to produce the desired assurance.

- *Erodes public confidence and trust in the accounting and auditing profession.* One message that comes through loud and clear these days in response to the increasing number of financial restatements and alleged financial statement fraud is that the public confidence in the financial reporting process and related audit functions is substantially eroded.

FICTITIOUS REVENUES

Fictitious or fabricated revenue schemes involve the recording of sales of goods or services that did not occur. Fictitious sales most often involve fake or phantom customers, but can also involve legitimate customers. For example, a fictitious invoice can be prepared (but not mailed) for a legitimate customer although the goods are not delivered or the services are not rendered. At the beginning of the next accounting period, the sale might be reversed to help conceal the fraud, but this may lead to a revenue shortfall in the new period, creating the need for more fictitious sales. Another method is to use legitimate customers and artificially inflate or alter invoices reflecting higher amounts or quantities than actually sold.

Generally speaking, revenue is recognized when it is (1) realized or realizable and (2) earned. The Securities and Exchange Commission (SEC) issued Staff Accounting Bulletin (SAB) Topic 13, "Revenue Recognition" (codified in FASB ASC 605, "Revenue Recognition"), to provide additional guidance on revenue recognition criteria and to rein in some of the inappropriate practices that had been observed. FASB ASC 605 states that revenue is typically considered realized or realizable, and earned, when all of the following criteria are met:

- Persuasive evidence of an arrangement exists
- Delivery has occurred or services have been rendered
- The seller's price to the buyer is fixed or determinable
- Collectibility is reasonably assured

FASB ASC 605 concedes that revenue may be recognized in some circumstances where delivery has not occurred, but sets out strict criteria that limit the ability to record such transactions as revenue.

At present, there are approximately 200 sources of standards and guidance on revenue recognition in U.S. GAAP, not all of which are based on consistent concepts. The current conceptual guidelines for revenue recognition are found in FASB Concepts Statement No. 5, "Recognition and Measurement in Financial Statements of Business Enterprises" and FASB Concepts Statement No. 6, "Elements of Financial Statements." Concepts Statement No. 6 defines revenue as "inflows or other enhancements of assets of an entity or settlements of its liabilities (or a combination of both) from delivering or producing goods, rendering services, or other activities that constitute the entity's ongoing major or central operations." However, because conflicts can arise between the guidance contained in the two applicable Concepts Statements, the FASB is currently working to develop coherent conceptual guidance on revenue recognition to eliminate existing inconsistencies and to provide a basis for a comprehensive accounting standard on revenue recognition.

As part of this initiative, the FASB and the International Accounting Standards Board (IASB) have partnered on a project to tackle the issue of revenue recognition with the goal of promoting convergence of international accounting standards. The Boards' current perspective on this subject concentrates on "changes in assets and liabilities." The concept of realization or completion of the earnings processes is not an integral part of their focus in this regard. This is consistent with FASB Concepts Statement No. 6. Although the Boards have arrived at several tentative decisions as part of the project, these decisions do not change current accounting policy until they have gone through extensive due process and deliberations.

Case 1760 details a typical example of fictitious revenue. Interested in inflating their financial standing, a publicly traded company engineered sham transactions for more than seven years. The company's management utilized several shell companies, supposedly making a number of favorable sales. The sales transactions were fictitious, as were the supposed customers. As the amounts of the sales grew, so did the suspicions of internal auditors. The sham transactions included the payment of funds for assets while the same funds were returned to the parent company as receipts on sales. The management scheme went undetected for so long that the company's books were eventually inflated by more than $80 million. The perpetrators were finally discovered and prosecuted in both civil and criminal courts.

An example of a sample entry from this type of case is detailed below. To record a purported purchase of fixed assets, a fictional entry is made by debiting fixed assets and crediting cash for the amount of the alleged purchase:

Date	Description	Ref.	Debit	Credit
12/01/Y1	Fixed Assets	104	350,000	
	Cash	101		350,000

A fictitious sales entry is then made for the same amount as the false purchase, debiting accounts receivable and crediting the sales account. The cash outflow that supposedly paid for the fixed assets is "returned" as payment on the receivable account, though in practice the cash might never have moved if the fraudsters hadn't bothered to falsify that extra documentary support.

Date	Description	Ref.	Debit	Credit
12/01/Y1	Accounts Receivable	120	350,000	
	Sales	400		350,000
12/15/Y1	Cash	101	350,000	
	Accounts Receivable	120		350,000

The result of the completely fabricated sequence of events is an increase in both company assets and yearly revenue. The debit could alternatively be directed to other accounts, such as inventory or accounts payable, or it could simply be left in accounts receivable if the fraud were committed close to year-end and the receivable could be left outstanding without attracting undue attention.

Sales with Conditions

Sales with conditions are a form of fictitious revenue scheme in which a sale is booked even though some terms have not been completed and the rights and risks of ownership have not passed to the purchaser. These transactions do not qualify for recording as revenue, but they may nevertheless be recorded in an effort to fraudulently boost a company's revenue. These types of sales are similar to schemes involving the recognition of revenue in improper periods since the conditions for sale may become satisfied in the future, at which point revenue recognition would become appropriate. Premature recognition schemes will be discussed later in this chapter in the section on timing differences.

Pressures to Boost Revenues

External pressures to succeed that are placed on business owners and managers by analysts, bankers, stockholders, families, and even communities often provide the motivation to commit fraud. For example, in addition to other charges, GE was alleged by the SEC to have manipulated earnings for two years in a row (2002 and 2003) in order to meet performance targets by recording $381 million in "sales" of locomotives to financial partners. Since GE hadn't ceded ownership of the assets and had agreed to maintain and secure them on its property, the transactions were, in reality, more like loans than sales. GE settled the SEC's charges in 2009 for $50 million, neither admitting nor denying guilt.

In a different case, the former Chairman of Satyam Computer Services, B. Ramalinga Raju, confessed to his board in January of 2009 that he had been falsifying revenue and profits for approximately six years to create a fictitious cash balance of $1 billion and hide poor performance. India's Central Bureau of Investigation, which is investigating the case, estimates the fraud to be significantly higher—at $2.6 billion.

In another example, in Case 2303, a real estate investment company arranged for the sale of shares that it held in a nonrelated company. The sale occurred on the last day of the year and accounted for 45 percent of the company's income for that year.

A 30 percent down payment was recorded as received, with a corresponding receivable recorded for the balance. With the intent to show a financially healthier company, the details of the sale were made public in an announcement to the press, but the sale of the stock was completely fabricated. To cover the fraud, off-book loans were made in the amount of the down payment. Other supporting documents were also falsified. The $40 million misstatement was ultimately uncovered, and the real estate company owner faced criminal prosecution.

In a similar instance, Case 710, a publicly traded textile company engaged in a series of false transactions designed to improve its financial image. Receipts from the sale of stock were returned to the company in the form of revenues. The fraudulent management team even went so far as to record a bank loan on the company books as revenue. At the time that the scheme was uncovered, the company books were overstated by some $50,000, a material amount to this particular company.

The pressures to commit financial statement fraud may also come from within a company. Departmental budget requirements including income and profit goals can create situations in which financial statement fraud is committed. In Case 1664, the accounting manager of a small company misstated financial records to cover its financial shortcomings. The financial statements included a series of entries made by the accounting manager designed to meet budget projections and to cover up losses in the company's pension fund. Influenced by dismal financial performance in recent months, the accountant also consistently overstated period revenues. To cover his scheme, he debited liability accounts and credited the equity account. The perpetrator finally resigned, leaving a letter of confession. He was later prosecuted in criminal court.

Red Flags Associated with Fictitious Revenues

- Rapid growth or unusual profitability, especially compared to that of other companies in the same industry
- Recurring negative cash flows from operations or an inability to generate cash flows from operations while reporting earnings and earnings growth
- Significant transactions with related parties or special-purpose entities not in the ordinary course of business or where those entities are not audited or are audited by another firm
- Significant, unusual, or highly complex transactions, especially those close to period end that pose difficult "substance over form" questions
- Unusual growth in the number of days' sales in receivables
- A significant volume of sales to entities whose substance and ownership is not known
- An unusual surge in sales by a minority of units within a company, or of sales recorded by corporate headquarters

TIMING DIFFERENCES

As we mentioned earlier, financial statement fraud may also involve timing differences—that is, the recording of revenue or expenses in improper periods. This can be done to shift revenues or expenses between one period and the next, increasing or decreasing earnings as desired.

Matching Revenues with Expenses

Remember, according to generally accepted accounting principles, revenue and corresponding expenses should be recorded or matched in the same accounting period; failing to do so violates GAAP's matching principle. For example, suppose a company accurately records sales that occurred in the month of December but fails to fully record expenses incurred as costs associated with those sales until January—in the next accounting period. The effect of this error would be to overstate the net income of the company in the period in which the sales were recorded, and also to understate net income in the subsequent period when the expenses are reported.

The following example depicts a sales transaction in which the cost of sales associated with the revenue is not recorded in the same period. A journal entry is made to record the billing of a project, which is not complete. Although a contract has been signed for this project, goods and services for this project have not been delivered, and the project is not even scheduled to start until January. In order to boost revenues for the current year, the following sales transaction is recorded fraudulently before year-end:

Date	Description	Ref.	Debit	Credit
12/31/Y1	Accounts Receivable	120	17,000	
	Sales—Project C	401		17,000
	To record sale of product and services for Project C			
	Fiscal Year-End—20Y1			

In January, the project is started and completed. The entries below show accurate recording of the $15,500 of costs associated with the sale:

Date	Description	Ref.	Debit	Credit
01/31/Y2	Cost of Sales—Project C	702	13,500	
	Inventory	140		13,500
	To record relief of inventory for Project C			
01/31/Y2	Labor Costs—Project C	550	2,000	
	Cash	101		2,000
	To record payroll expense for Project C			

If recorded correctly, the entries for the recognition of revenue and the costs associated with the sales would be recorded in the accounting period in which they actually occurred: January. The effect on the income statement for the company is shown on the next page.

This example depicts exactly how nonadherence to GAAP's matching principle can cause material misstatement in yearly income statements. When the income and expenses were stated in error, year 1 yielded a net income of $17,000 while year 2 produced a loss ($13,400). Correctly stated, revenues and expenses are matched and recorded together within the same accounting period showing a net income of $0 for year 1 and $3,600 for year 2.

Income Statements	Incorrectly Stated		Correctly Stated	
	Year 1	Year 2	Year 1	Year 2
Sales Revenue				
Project B	25,000		25,000	
Project C	17,000			17,000
Project D		26,500		26,500
Total Sales	42,000	26,500	25,000	43,500
Cost of Sales				
Project B	22,500		22,500	
Project C		15,500		15,500
Project D		21,400		21,400
Total Cost of Sales	22,500	36,900	22,500	36,900
Gross Margin	19,500	(10,400)	2,500	6,600
G & A Expenses	2,500	3,000	2,500	3,000
Net Income	17,000	(13,400)	0	3,600

Premature Revenue Recognition

Generally, revenue should be recognized in the accounting records when a sale is complete—that is, when title is passed from the seller to the buyer. This transfer of ownership completes the sale and is usually not final until all obligations surrounding the sale are complete and the four criteria set out in FASB ASC 605 have been satisfied. As mentioned previously, those four criteria are:

- Persuasive evidence of an arrangement exists
- Delivery has occurred or services have been rendered
- The seller's price to the buyer is fixed or determinable
- Collectibility is reasonably assured

Case 861 details how early recognition of revenue not only leads to financial statement misrepresentation but also can serve as a catalyst to further fraud. A retail drugstore chain's management got ahead of itself in recording income. In a scheme that was used repeatedly, management enhanced its earnings by recording unearned revenue prematurely, resulting in the impression that the drugstores were much more profitable than they actually were. When the situation came to light and was investigated, several embezzlement schemes, false expense report schemes, and instances of credit card fraud were also uncovered.

In Case 2639, the president of a not-for-profit organization was able to illicitly squeeze the maximum amount of private donations by cooking the company books. To enable the organization to receive additional funding, which was dependent on the amounts of already-received contributions, the organization's president recorded promised donations before they were actually received. By the time the organization's internal auditor discovered the scheme, the fraud had been perpetrated for more than four years.

When managers recognize revenues prematurely, one or more of the criteria set forth in FASB ASC 605 is typically not met. Examples of common problems with premature revenue recognition are set out below.

Persuasive Evidence of an Arrangement Does Not Exist

- No written or verbal agreement exists
- A verbal agreement exists, but a written agreement is customary
- A written order exists, but is conditional upon sale to end users (such as a consignment sale)
- A written order exists, but contains a right of return
- A written order exists, but a side letter alters the terms in ways that eliminate the required elements for an agreement
- The transaction is with a related party, but this fact has not been disclosed

Delivery Has Not Occurred or Services Have Not Been Rendered

- Shipment has not been made and the criteria for recognizing revenue on "bill-and-hold" transactions set out in FASB ASC 605 have not been met
- Shipment has been made not to the customer but to the seller's agent, to an installer, or to a public warehouse
- Some but not all of the components required for operation were shipped
- Items of the wrong specification were shipped
- Delivery is not complete until installation and customer testing and acceptance has occurred
- Services have not been provided at all
- Services are being performed over an extended period, and only a portion of the service revenues should have been recognized in the current period
- The mix of goods and services in a contract has been misstated in order to improperly accelerate revenue recognition

The Seller's Price to the Buyer Is Not Fixed or Determinable

- The price is contingent on some future events
- A service or membership fee is subject to unpredictable cancellation during the contract period
- The transaction includes an option to exchange the product for others
- Payment terms are extended for a substantial period and additional discounts or upgrades may be required to induce continued use and payment instead of switching to alternative products

Collectibility Is Not Reasonably Assured

- Collection is contingent on some future events (e.g., resale of the product, receipt of additional funding, or litigation)
- The customer does not have the ability to pay (e.g., it is financially troubled, it has purchased far more than it can afford, or it is a shell company with minimal assets)

Long-Term Contracts

Long-term contracts pose special problems for revenue recognition. Long-term construction contracts, for example, use either the completed contract method or the percentage of completion method, depending partly on the circumstances. The completed contract method does not record revenue until the project is 100 percent complete. Construction costs are held in an inventory account until completion of the project. The percentage of completion method recognizes revenues and expenses as measurable progress on a project is made, but this method is particularly vulnerable to manipulation. Managers can often easily manipulate the percentage of completion and the estimated costs to complete a construction project in order to recognize revenues prematurely and conceal contract overruns.

Channel Stuffing

Another difficult area of revenue recognition is "channel stuffing," which is also known as "trade loading." This refers to the sale of an unusually large quantity of a product to distributors, who are encouraged to overbuy through the use of deep discounts and/or extended payment terms. This practice is especially attractive in industries with high gross margins (cigarettes, pharmaceuticals, perfume, soda concentrate, and branded consumer goods) because it can increase short-term earnings. The downside is that stealing from the next period's sales makes it harder to achieve sales goals in the next period, sometimes leading to increasingly disruptive levels of channel stuffing and ultimately a restatement.

Although orders are received in a channel-stuffing scheme, the terms of the order might raise some question about the collectibility of accounts receivable, and there may be side agreements that grant a right of return, effectively making the sales consignment sales. There may be a greater risk of returns for certain products if they cannot be sold before their shelf life expires. This is particularly a problem for pharmaceuticals, because retailers will not accept drugs that have a short shelf life remaining. As a result, channel stuffing should be viewed skeptically as in certain circumstances it may constitute fraud.

Recording Expenses in the Wrong Period

The timely recording of expenses is often compromised due to pressures to meet budget projections and goals, or due to lack of proper accounting controls. As the expensing of certain costs is pushed into periods other than the ones in which they actually occur, they are not properly matched against the income that they help produce. Consider Case 1370, in which supplies were purchased and applied to the current-year budget but were actually used in the following accounting period. A manager at a publicly traded company completed eleven months of operations remarkably under budget when compared to total-year estimates. He therefore decided to get a head start on the next year's expenditures. In order to spend all current-year budgeted funds allocated to his department, the manager bought $50,000 in unneeded supplies. The supplies expense transactions were recorded against the current year's budget. Staff auditors noticed the huge leap in expenditures, however, and inquired about the situation. The manager came clean, explaining that he was under pressure to meet budget goals for the following year. Because the manager was not attempting to keep the funds for himself, no legal action was taken.

The correct recording of the above transactions would be to debit supplies inventory for the original purchase and subsequently expense the items out of the account as they are used. The example journal entries below detail the correct method of expensing the supplies over time.

Date	Description	Ref.	Debit	Credit
01/31/Y1	Supplies Inventory	109	50,000	
	Accounts Payable	201		50,000
	To record the purchase of supplies			
Record in	Supplies Expense	851	2,000	
Period Used	Supplies Inventory	109		2,000
	To record supplies consumed in current period			

Similar entries should be made monthly, as the supplies are used, until they are consumed and $50,000 in supplies expense is recorded.

Red Flags Associated with Timing Differences

- Rapid growth or unusual profitability, especially compared to that of other companies in the same industry
- Recurring negative cash flows from operations or an inability to generate cash flows from operations while reporting earnings and earnings growth
- Significant, unusual, or highly complex transactions, especially those close to period-end that pose difficult "substance over form" questions
- Unusual increase in gross margin or margin in excess of industry peers
- Unusual growth in the number of days' sales in receivables
- Unusual decline in the number of days' purchases in accounts payable

---

CASE STUDY: THE IMPORTANCE OF TIMING[2]

What about a scheme in which nobody gets any money? One that was never intended to enrich its players or to defraud the company they worked for? It happened in Huntsville, Alabama, on-site at a major aluminum products plant with over $300 million in yearly sales. A few shrewd men cooked the company's books without taking a single dime for themselves.

Terry Isbell was an internal auditor making a routine review of accounts payable. He was running a computer search to look at any transactions over $50,000 and found among the hits a bill for replacing two furnace liners. The payments went out toward the last of the year, to an approved vendor, with the proper signatures from Steven Leonyrd, a maintenance engineer, and Doggett Stine, the sector's purchasing manager. However, there was nothing else in the file. Maintenance and repair jobs of this sort were supposed to be done on a time-and-material basis. So there should have been work reports, vouchers, and inspection sheets in the file along with the paid invoices. But there was nothing.

[2]Several names and details have been changed to preserve anonymity.

Isbell talked with Steven Leonyrd, who showed him the furnaces, recently lined and working to perfection. So where was the paperwork? "It'll be in the regular work file for the first quarter," Leonyrd replied.

"The bill was for last year, November and December," Isbell pointed out. That was because the work was paid for in "advance payments," according to Leonyrd. There wasn't room in the work schedule to have the machines serviced in November, so the work was billed to that year's nonrecurring maintenance budget. Later, sometime after the first of the year, the work was actually done.

Division management okayed Isbell to make an examination. He found $150,000 in repair invoices without proper documentation. The records for materials and supplies, which were paid for in one year and received in the next, totaled $250,000. A check of later records and an inspection showed that everything paid for had in fact been received—just later than promised.

So it was back to visit Leonyrd, who said the whole thing was simple. "We had this money in the budget for maintenance and repair, supplies outside the usual scope of things. It was getting late in the year, looked like we were just going to lose those dollars, you know, they'd just revert back to the general fund. So we set up the work orders and made them on last year's budget. Then we got the actual stuff later." Who told Leonyrd to set it up that way? "Nobody. Just made sense, that's all."

Nobody, Isbell suspected, was the purchasing manager who handled Leonyrd's group, Doggett Stine. Stine was known as "a domineering-type guy" among the people who worked for him, a kind of storeroom bully. Isbell asked him about the arrangement with Leonyrd. "That's no big deal," Stine insisted. "Just spent the money while it was there. That's what it was put there for, to keep up the plant. That's what we did." It wasn't his idea, said Stine, but it wasn't really Leonyrd's either, just a discussion and an informal decision. The storeroom receiving supervisor agreed it was a grand idea, and made out the documents as he was told. Accounting personnel processed the invoices as they were told. A part-time bookkeeper said to Isbell she remembered some discussion about arranging to spend the money, but she didn't ask any questions.

Isbell was in a funny position, a little bit like Shakespeare's Malvolio, who spends his time in the play *Twelfth Night* scolding the other characters for having such a good time. Leonyrd hadn't pocketed anything, and neither had Stine; being a bully was hardly a fraudulent offense. There was about $6,000 in interest lost, supposing the money had stayed in company bank accounts, but that wasn't exactly the point. More seriously, this effortless cash-flow diversion represented a kink in the handling and dispersal of funds. Isbell wasn't thinking rules for their own sake or standing on ceremony—money this easy to come by just meant the company had gotten a break. The next guys might not be so civic-minded and selfless; they might start juggling zeros and signatures instead of dates.

Under Isbell's recommendation, the receiving department started reporting directly to the plant's general accounting division, and its supervisor was assigned elsewhere. Doggett Stine had subsequently retired. Steven Leonyrd was demoted and transferred to another sector; he was fired a year later for an unrelated scheme. He had approached a contractor to replace the roof on his house, with the bill to be charged against "nonrecurring maintenance" at the plant. But the contractor alerted plant officials to their conniving employee, who was also known to be picking up extra money for "consulting work" with plant-related businesses. *Rats*, Leonyrd must have thought, *foiled again*.

CONCEALED LIABILITIES AND EXPENSES

As previously discussed, understating liabilities and expenses is one of the ways that financial statements can be manipulated to make a company appear more profitable. Because pretax income will increase by the full amount of the expense or liability not recorded, this financial statement fraud method can have a significant impact on reported earnings with relatively little effort by the fraudster. This method is much easier to commit than falsifying many sales transactions. Missing transactions are generally harder for auditors to detect than improperly recorded ones, because there is no audit trail.

There are three common methods for concealing liabilities and expenses:

- Liability/expense omissions
- Capitalized expenses
- Failure to disclose warranty costs and liabilities

Liability/Expense Omissions

The preferred and easiest method of concealing liabilities/expenses is to simply fail to record them. Multimillion-dollar judgments against the company from a recent court decision might be conveniently ignored. Vendor invoices might be thrown away (they'll send another later) or stuffed into drawers rather than being posted into the accounts payable system, thereby increasing reported earnings by the full amount of the invoices. In a retail environment, debit memos might be created for chargebacks to vendors, supposedly to claim permitted rebates or allowances but sometimes just to create additional income. These items may or may not be properly recorded in a subsequent accounting period, but that does not change the fraudulent nature of the current financial statements.

One of the highest-profile liability omission cases of recent vintage involved Adelphia Communications. John Rigas, Adelphia's founder, purchased a small cable company in Coudersport, Pennsylvania for the sum of $300 in 1952. By 2002, it had grown to the nation's sixth-largest cable television company, with more than five million subscribers and $10 billion in assets.

Rigas, of Greek heritage, named his company Adelphia Communications Corporation, after the Greek word for "brothers." He and his brother Gus ran the company as their own—a style that came back to haunt him after the company went public. Later, his three sons Tim, Michael, and James—along with son-in-law Peter Venetis—became active in Adelphia's management. The family controlled the majority of the company's voting stock and constituted the majority on the board of directors. Accordingly, the family used Adelphia's money as their own. They also used company assets as their own. Three corporate jets took family members on exotic vacations, including African safaris. John Rigas was particularly egregious in his spending. At one time, he racked up personal debt of $66 million, forcing his son, Timothy, to put his father on a "budget" of $1 million a month in personal draws.

Adelphia CFO Timothy Rigas engineered the financial manipulations. He was in charge of manipulating the books to inflate the stock price in order to meet analysts' expectations. Investigators later discovered that the family members had looted the company to the tune of some $3 billion. The money transfers were made by journal entries that gave Adelphia debt that hadn't been disclosed. Among other things, the Rigas family used the funds to:

- Acquire other cable companies not owned by Adelphia
- Pay debt service on investments
- Purchase a controlling interest in the Buffalo Sabres Hockey Team
- Pay $700,000 in country club memberships
- Buy luxury vacation homes in Cancun, Beaver Creek (Colorado), and Hilton Head Island, as well as two apartments in Manhattan
- Purchase a $13 million golf course

The Rigas family's problems started with overexpansion in the late 1990s when they purchased Century Communications for the sum of $5.2 billion. By 2002, Adelphia's stock had fallen to historic lows and the company was unable to make payments on the debt it incurred to make acquisitions.

In July 2002, the SEC charged Adelphia with, among other things, fraudulently excluding over $2.3 billion in bank debt from its consolidated financial statements. According to the complaint filed by the SEC, Adelphia's founder and his three sons fraudulently excluded the liabilities from the company's annual and quarterly consolidated financial statements by deliberately shifting those liabilities onto the books of Adelphia's off–balance sheet unconsolidated affiliates. Failure to record this debt violated GAAP requirements and precipitated a series of misrepresentations about those liabilities by Adelphia and the defendants. This included the creation of (1) sham transactions backed by fictitious documents to give the false appearance that Adelphia had actually repaid debts when, in truth, it had simply shifted them to unconsolidated entities controlled by the founder and (2) misleading financial statements that, in their footnotes, gave the false impression that liabilities listed in the company's financials included all outstanding bank debt. This led to a freefall of Adelphia's stock; less than three months later, the company filed for bankruptcy.

Often, perpetrators of liability and expense omissions believe they can conceal their fraud in future periods. They often plan to compensate for their omitted liabilities with visions of other income sources such as profits from future price increases.

Just as they are easy to conceal, omitted liabilities are probably one of the most difficult financial statement schemes to uncover. A thorough review of all post-financial statement-date transactions, such as accounts payable increases and decreases, can aid in the discovery of omitted liabilities in financial statements, as can a computerized analysis of expense records. Additionally, if the auditor requested and was granted unrestricted access to the client's files, a physical search could turn up concealed invoices and unposted liabilities. Probing interviews of accounts payable and other personnel can reveal unrecorded or delayed items, too.

Capitalized Expenses

Capital expenditures are costs that provide a benefit to a company over more than one accounting period. Manufacturing equipment is an example of this type of expenditure. Revenue expenditures or *expenses*, on the other hand, directly correspond to the generation of current revenue and provide benefits for only the current accounting period. An example of expenses is labor costs for one week of service. These costs correspond directly with revenues billed in the current accounting period.

Capitalizing revenue-based expenses is another way to increase income and assets, since they are amortized over a period of years rather than expensed immediately. If expenditures are capitalized as assets and not expensed during the current period, income will be overstated. As the assets are depreciated, income in subsequent periods will be understated.

The improper capitalization of expenses was one of the key methods of financial statement fraud that was allegedly used by WorldCom, Inc., in its high-profile fraud, which came to light in early 2002. The saga of WorldCom, at one time the second-largest long-distance carrier in America (behind AT&T), began in 1983, when Bernie Ebbers drew a business plan on the back of a napkin at a coffee shop in Hattiesburg, Mississippi. Ebbers and his partners, attempting to benefit from the breakup of AT&T, decided to purchase long-distance time and sell it to local companies on a smaller scale. They named the fledgling business Long Distance Discount Service (LDDS).

Up until that time, Ebbers didn't know much about the telecommunications industry. He graduated from a small Mississippi college with a degree in physical education. He'd previously owned a small garment factory and several motels.

But LDDS turned out to be a success. The company was buying and selling a commodity—long-distance service—but it didn't have to invest in the costs of buying and installing expensive telephone lines. Along the way, LDDS acquired a half-dozen other communications companies.

In 1995, the business was renamed WorldCom, and the new company went on an acquisition rampage, purchasing over sixty companies. WorldCom's crown jewel was a $37 billion merger in 1997 with MCI, a much larger company. The following year, it bought Brooks Fiber Properties and CompuServe. In 1999, it attempted to acquire rival Sprint in a $115 billion merger, but the Federal Communications Commission blocked the deal to prevent breach of antitrust laws.

Because of increasing competition in the telecommunications industry, WorldCom's spectacular growth started slowing dramatically in 1998 and came to a halt in 1999, resulting in a precipitous drop in its stock price. To reverse declining margins, the company started reducing the reserves it had established to cover the undisclosed liabilities of companies it had acquired. Between 1998 and 2000, this amounted to $2.8 billion.

However, in the opinion of management, the reduction in reserves was insufficient. Scott Sullivan, the CFO, directed certain WorldCom staffers to reclassify as assets $3.35 billion in fees paid to lease phone networks from other companies and $500 million in computer expenses, both operating costs. Rather than suffering a $2.5 billion loss in 2001, the company reported a $1.4 billion profit. Andersen LLP, WorldCom's external auditors, uncovered none of these machinations.

In 2002, Sullivan directed a WorldCom employee to classify another $400 million in expenses as assets. The employee complained to Cynthia Cooper, CFE, WorldCom's internal auditor, who directed her staff to conduct an investigation. Cooper's team first discovered that the $500 million in computer expenses reclassified as assets had no documentation to support the expenditures. Then they uncovered another $2 billion in questionable entries.

Internal auditors met with the audit committee in June 2002 to explain their findings. On June 25, WorldCom made a public announcement that it had inflated revenues by $3.8 billion over the previous five quarters. Within three weeks, the company had filed for bankruptcy. Subsequent investigations would show that WorldCom had overstated its profits and income by about $11 billion.

These improper accounting practices were designed to, and did, inflate income to correspond with estimates by Wall Street analysts and to support the price of WorldCom's stock. As a result, several former WorldCom Executives, including former CEO Bernie Ebbers, former CFO Scott Sullivan, former Controller David F. Meyers, and former Director of General Accounting Buford "Buddy" Yates, Jr., were charged with multiple criminal offenses and received prison sentences ranging from one to twenty-five years for their participation in the scheme.

Expensing Capital Expenditures

Just as capitalizing expenses is improper, so is expensing costs that should be capitalized. An organization may want to minimize its net income due to tax considerations, or to increase earnings in future periods. Expensing an item that should be depreciated over a period of time helps accomplish just that—net income is lower, and so are taxes.

Returns and Allowances and Warranties

Improper recording of sales returns and allowances occurs when a company fails to properly record or present the expense associated with sales returns and customer allowances stemming from customer dissatisfaction. It is inevitable that a certain percentage of products sold will, for one reason or another, be returned. When this happens, management must record the related expense in a contra-sales account, which reduces the amount of net sales presented on the company's income statement.

Likewise, when a company offers a warranty on product sales, it must estimate the amount of warranty expense it reasonably expects to incur over the warranty period and accrue a liability for that amount. In warranty liability fraud, the warranty liability is usually either omitted or substantially understated. Another similar area is the liability resulting from defective products (product liability).

Red Flags Associated with Concealed Liabilities and Expenses

- Recurring negative cash flows from operations or an inability to generate cash flows from operations while reporting earnings and earnings growth
- Assets, liabilities, revenues, or expenses based on significant estimates that involve subjective judgments or uncertainties that are difficult to corroborate

- Nonfinancial management's excessive participation in or preoccupation with the selection of accounting principles or the determination of significant estimates
- Unusual increase in gross margin or margin in excess of industry peers
- Allowances for sales returns, warranty claims, and so on that are shrinking in percentage terms or are otherwise out of line with industry peers
- Unusual reduction in the number of days' purchases in accounts payable
- Reducing accounts payable while competitors are stretching out payments to vendors

IMPROPER DISCLOSURES

As we discussed earlier, accounting principles require that financial statements and notes include all the information necessary to prevent a reasonably discerning user of the financial statements from being misled. The notes should include narrative disclosures, supporting schedules, and any other information required to avoid misleading potential investors, creditors, or any other users of the financial statements.

Management has an obligation to disclose all significant information appropriately in the financial statements and in management's discussion and analysis. In addition, the disclosed information must not be misleading. Improper disclosures relating to financial statement fraud usually involve the following:

- Liability omissions
- Subsequent events
- Management fraud
- Related-party transactions
- Accounting changes

Liability Omissions

Typical omissions include the failure to disclose loan covenants or contingent liabilities. Loan covenants are agreements, in addition to or part of a financing arrangement, which a borrower has promised to keep as long as the financing is in place. The agreements can contain various types of covenants, including certain financial ratio limits and restrictions on other major financing arrangements. Contingent liabilities are potential obligations that will materialize only if certain events occur in the future. A corporate guarantee of personal loans taken out by an officer or a private company controlled by an officer is an example of a contingent liability. The company's potential liability, if material, must be disclosed.

Subsequent Events

Events occurring or becoming known after the close of the period may have a significant effect on the financial statements and should be disclosed. Fraudsters often avoid disclosing court judgments and regulatory decisions that undermine the reported values of assets, that indicate unrecorded liabilities, or that adversely reflect on management integrity. Public record searches can reveal this information.

Management Fraud

Management has an obligation to disclose to the shareholders significant fraud committed by officers, executives, and others in positions of trust. Withholding such information from auditors would likely also involve lying to auditors, an illegal act in itself.

Related-Party Transactions

Related-party transactions occur when a company does business with another entity whose management or operating policies can be controlled or significantly influenced by the company or by some other party in common. There is nothing inherently wrong with related-party transactions, as long as they are fully disclosed. If the transactions are not conducted on an arm's-length basis, the company may suffer economic harm, injuring stockholders.

The financial interest that a company official might have may not be readily apparent. For example, common directors of two companies that do business with each other, any corporate general partner and the partnerships with which it does business, and any controlling shareholder of the corporation with which he/she/it does business may be related parties. Family relationships can also be considered related parties. These relationships include all lineal descendants and ancestors, without regard to financial interests. Related-party transactions are sometimes referred to as "self-dealing." While these transactions are sometimes conducted at arm's length, they often are not.

In the highly publicized Tyco fraud case, which broke in 2002, the SEC charged former top executives of the company, including its former CEO, L. Dennis Kozlowski, with failing to disclose to shareholders hundreds of millions of dollars of low-interest and interest-free loans they took from the company. Moreover, Kozlowski forgave $50 million in loans to himself and another $56 million for fifty-one favored Tyco employees. Tyco's board approved none of the charges.

Kozlowski also engaged in undisclosed non-arm's-length real estate transactions with Tyco or its subsidiaries and received undisclosed compensation and perks, including rent-free use of large New York City apartments and personal use of corporate aircraft at little or no cost. The SEC complaint alleged that three former executives, including Kozlowski, also sold restricted shares of Tyco stock valued at $430 million dollars while their self-dealing remained undisclosed.

In addition, Kozlowski participated in numerous improper transactions to fund an extravagant lifestyle. In January 2002, several empty boxes arrived at Tyco's headquarters in Exeter, New Hampshire. They were supposed to contain art worth at least $13 million to decorate the modest, two-story facility. In fact, the art—consisting of original works by Renoir and Monet—was actually hanging on the walls in Kozlowski's lavish Fifth Avenue corporate apartment; the empty-box ruse had been staged in an effort to avoid New York State sales tax of 8.25 percent.

Less than six months later, Kozlowski resigned just before he was accused of evading payment of taxes on the art. But the art, paid for by Tyco, was just the tip of the iceberg. A subsequent investigation would accuse Kozlowski and CFO Mark Schwartz of systematically looting their employer for more than $170 million. Both men were later found guilty of twenty-two charges and sentenced to up to twenty-five years in prison.

Most of the stolen money was simply charged to Tyco even though it personally benefited Kozlowski. For example, his compensation was reported at $400 million, but, in addition, Tyco paid for such outrageous charges as:

- A $16.8 million apartment in New York City for Kozlowski
- $13 million in original art
- A $7 million apartment for Kozlowski's ex-wife
- An umbrella stand that cost $15,000
- A $17,000 traveling toilette box
- $5,960 for two sets of sheets
- A $6,300 sewing basket
- A $6,000 shower curtain
- Half of a $2.1 million birthday party for his wife
- Up to $80,000 a month in personal credit card charges

Although Kozlowski's embezzlements were not material to the financial statements as a whole, they were nonetheless substantial and vividly portray the ultimate in corporate greed.

Accounting Changes

FASB ASC 250, "Accounting Changes and Error Corrections," describes three types of accounting changes that must be disclosed to avoid misleading the user of financial statements: accounting principles, estimates, and reporting entities. Although the required treatment for each type of change is different, they are all susceptible to manipulation by determined fraudster. For example, fraudsters may fail to properly retroactively restate the financial statements for a change in accounting principle if the change causes the company's financial statements to appear weaker. Likewise, they may fail to disclose significant changes in estimates such as the useful lives and estimated salvage values of depreciable assets or the estimates underlying the determination of warranty or other liabilities. They may even secretly change the reporting entity, by adding entities owned privately by management or excluding certain company-owned units, in order to improve reported results.

Red Flags Associated with Improper Disclosures

- Domination of management by a single person or small group (in a non-owner-managed business) without compensating controls
- Ineffective board of directors or audit committee oversight over the financial reporting process and internal control
- Ineffective communication, implementation, support, or enforcement of the entity's values or ethical standards by management or the communication of inappropriate values or ethical standards
- Rapid growth or unusual profitability, especially compared to that of other companies in the same industry
- Significant, unusual, or highly complex transactions, especially those close to period end that pose difficult "substance over form" questions
- Significant related-party transactions not in the ordinary course of business or with related entities not audited or audited by another firm
- Significant bank accounts or subsidiary or branch operations in tax-haven jurisdictions for which there appears to be no clear business justification

- Overly complex organizational structure involving unusual legal entities or managerial lines of authority

- Known history of violations of securities laws or other laws and regulations, or claims against the entity, its senior management, or board members alleging fraud or violations of laws and regulations

- Recurring attempts by management to justify marginal or inappropriate accounting on the basis of materiality

- Formal or informal restrictions on the auditor that inappropriately limit access to people or information or the ability to communicate effectively with the board of directors or audit committee

IMPROPER ASSET VALUATION

Generally accepted accounting principles require that most assets be recorded at their historical (acquisition) cost. Under the "lower of cost or market value" rule, where an asset's cost exceeds its current market value (as happens often with obsolete technology), it must be written down to market value. With the exception of certain securities, asset values are not increased to reflect current market value. It is often necessary to use estimates in accounting. For example, estimates are used in determining the residual value and the useful life of a depreciable asset, the uncollectable portion of accounts receivable, or the excess or obsolete portion of inventory. Whenever estimates are used, there is an additional opportunity for fraud by manipulating those estimates.

Many schemes are used to inflate current assets at the expense of long-term assets. The net effect is seen in the current ratio. The misclassification of long-term assets as current assets can be of critical concern to lending institutions that often require the maintenance of certain financial ratios. This is of particular consequence when the loan covenants are on unsecured or undersecured lines of credit and other short-term borrowings. Sometimes these misclassifications are referred to as "window dressing."

Most improper asset valuations involve the fraudulent overstatement of inventory or receivables. Other improper asset valuations include manipulation of the allocation of the purchase price of an acquired business in order to inflate future earnings, misclassification of fixed and other assets, or improper capitalization of inventory or startup costs. Improper asset valuations usually fall into one of the following categories:

- Inventory valuation
- Accounts receivable
- Business combinations
- Fixed assets

Inventory Valuation

Since inventory must be valued at the acquisition cost except when the cost is determined to be higher than the current market value, inventory should be written down to its current value, or written off altogether if it has no value. Failing to write down inventory results in overstated assets and the mismatching of cost of goods sold with revenues. Inventory can also be improperly stated through the manipulation of the physical inventory count, by inflating the unit costs used to price out inventory, by failing to relieve inventory for costs of goods sold, or by other methods. Fictitious inventory schemes usually involve the creation of fake documents such as inventory count sheets, receiving reports, and similar items. Companies have even programmed special computer reports of inventory for auditors that incorrectly added up the line item values so as to inflate the overall inventory balance. Computer-assisted audit techniques can significantly help auditors to detect many of these inventory fraud techniques. Case 2481 involved an inventory valuation scheme in which the fraud was committed through tampering with the inventory count. During a routine audit of a publicly traded medical supply company, the audit team found a misstatement of the inventory value that could hardly be classified as routine. The client's inventory was measured in metric volumes, and apparently as the count was taken, an employee arbitrarily moved the decimal unit. This resulted in the inventory being grossly overstated. The discovery forced the company to restate its financial statements, resulting in a write-down of the inventory amount by more than $1.5 million.

One of the most popular methods of overstating inventory is through fictitious (phantom) inventory. For example, in Case 1666 a CFE conducting a systems control review at a large cannery and product wholesaler in the Southwest observed a forklift driver constructing a large façade of finished product in a remote location of the warehouse. The inventory was cordoned off and a sign indicated that it was earmarked for a national food processor. The cannery was supposedly warehousing the inventory until requested by the customer. When the CFE investigated, he discovered that the inventory held for the food processor was later resold to a national fast-food supplier.

A review of the accounts receivable aging report indicated sales of approximately $1.2 million to this particular customer in prior months, and the aging also showed that cash receipts had been applied against those receivables. An analysis of ending inventory failed to reveal any improprieties because the relief of inventory had been properly recorded with cost of sales. Copies of all sales documents to this particular customer were then requested. The product was repeatedly sold free on board (FOB) shipping point and title had passed. But bills of lading indicated that only $200,000 of inventory had been shipped to the original purchaser. There should have been a million dollars of finished product on hand for the food processor. However, there was nothing behind the façade of finished products. An additional comparison of bin numbers on the bill of lading with the sales documents revealed that the same product had been sold twice.

The corporate controller was notified and the plant manager questioned. He explained that "he was doing as he was told." The vice president of marketing and the vice president of operations both knew of the situation but felt there was "no impropriety." The CFO and president of the company felt differently, and fired the vice presidents. The company eventually was forced into bankruptcy.

Accounts Receivable

Accounts receivable are subject to manipulation in the same manner as sales and inventory, and in many cases, the schemes are conducted together. The two most common schemes involving accounts receivable are fictitious receivables and failure to write off accounts receivable as bad debts (or failure to establish an adequate allowance for bad debts). Fictitious receivables commonly arise from fictitious revenues, discussed earlier. Accounts receivable should be reported at net realizable value—that is, the amount of the receivable less amounts expected not to be collected.

Fictitious Accounts Receivable Fictitious accounts receivable are common among companies with financial problems, as well as with managers who receive a commission based on sales. The typical entry under fictitious accounts receivable is to debit (increase) accounts receivable and credit (increase) sales. Of course, these schemes are more common around the end of the accounting period, since accounts receivable should be paid in cash within a reasonable time. Fraudsters commonly attempt to conceal fictitious accounts receivable by providing false confirmations of balances to auditors. They get the audit confirmations because the mailing address they provide for the phony customers is typically either a mailbox under their control, a home address, or the business address of a co-conspirator. Such schemes can be detected by using satellite imaging software, business credit reports, public records, or even the telephone book to identify significant customers who have no physical existence or no apparent business need for the product sold to them.

Failure to Write Down Companies are required to accrue losses on uncollectible receivables when the criteria in FASB ASC 450, "Contingencies," are met, and to record impairment of long-lived assets and goodwill under FASB ASC 350, "Intangibles–Goodwill and Other." Companies struggling for profits and income may be tempted to omit the recognition of such losses because of the negative impact on income.

Business Combinations

Companies are required to allocate the purchase price they have paid to acquire another business to the tangible and intangible assets of that business. Any excess of the purchase price over the value of the acquired assets is treated as goodwill. Changes in goodwill accounting have decreased the incentive for companies to allocate an excessive amount to purchased assets, to minimize the amount allocated to goodwill that previously should have been amortized and which reduced future earnings. However, companies may still be tempted to overallocate the purchase price to in-process research and development assets, in order to then write them off immediately. Or they may establish excessive reserves for various expenses at the time of acquisition, intending to quietly release those excess reserves into earnings at a future date.

Fixed Assets

Fixed assets are subject to manipulation through several different schemes. Some of the more common schemes are:

- Booking fictitious assets
- Misrepresenting asset valuation
- Improperly capitalizing inventory and startup costs

Booking Fictitious Assets   One of the easiest methods of asset misrepresentation is in the recording of fictitious assets. This false creation of assets affects account totals on a company's balance sheet. The corresponding account commonly used is the owners' equity account. Because company assets are often physically found in many different locations, this fraud can sometimes be easily overlooked. One of the most common fictitious asset schemes is to simply create fictitious documents. For example, in Case 376 a real estate development and mortgage financing company produced fraudulent statements that included fictitious and inflated asset amounts and illegitimate receivables. The company also recorded expenses that actually were for personal, instead of business, use. To cover the fraud, the company raised cash through various illegal securities offerings, guaranteeing over $110 million with real estate projects. It subsequently defaulted. The company declared bankruptcy shortly before the owner passed away.

In other instances, equipment is leased, not owned, yet that fact is not disclosed during the audit of fixed assets. Bogus fixed assets can sometimes be detected because the fixed asset addition makes no business sense.

Misrepresenting Asset Value Fixed assets should be recorded at cost. Although assets may appreciate in value, this increase in value generally should not be recognized on company financial statements. Many financial statement frauds have involved the reporting of fixed assets at market values instead of the lower acquisition costs, or at even higher inflated values with phony valuations to support them. Further, companies may falsely inflate the value of fixed assets by failing to record impairments of long-lived assets and of goodwill as required by FASB ASC 350, "Intangibles—Goodwill and Other." Misrepresentation of asset values frequently goes hand in hand with other schemes.

One of the most high-profile asset-valuation fraud cases of recent years involved the collapse of Enron, the energy-trading company. Enron was created in 1985 as a merger between Houston Natural Gas and InterNorth, a Nebraska pipeline company. Although Enron began as a traditional natural gas supplier, under the lead of employee Jeffrey Skilling it quickly developed a new and innovative strategy to make money: the creation of a "gas bank," whereby the company would buy gas from a network of suppliers and sell to a network of consumers. Its profits would be derived from contractually guaranteeing both the supply and the selling price, charging a fee for its services.

This new business segment required Enron to borrow enormous amounts of money, but by 1990, the company was the market leader. Kenneth Lay, Enron's CEO, created Enron Finance Corp. (EFC) to handle the new business and picked Skilling to run it. Based on the initial success of EFC, and assisted by Skilling's new protégé, Andrew Fastow, the company's "gas bank" concept was expanded to include trading in a wide variety of areas: electricity, and futures contracts in coal, paper, water, steel, and other commodities.

Since Enron was either a buyer or a seller in every transaction, the company's credit was crucial. Eventually, in 2000, Enron expanded into the telecommunications business by announcing that it planned to build a high-speed broadband network, and to trade network capacity (bandwidth) in the same way it traded other commodities. Enron sunk hundreds of millions of dollars in borrowed money for this new venture, which quickly failed to produce the intended profits.

The money that Enron borrowed to finance its various ventures was kept off of its balance sheet by Fastow, using an accounting treatment called special-purpose entities (SPEs). Under accounting rules in place at the time, Enron could contribute up to 97 percent of an SPE's assets or equity. Then the SPE could borrow its own money, which would not show up on Enron's financial statements. But Enron could claim its profits (or losses).

In most of the SPEs established by Enron, the asset contributed was company stock. But since the stock contributed would have diluted earnings per share, Enron used another treatment, "mark-to-market accounting," to boost profits. Mark-to-market accounting required a company to book both realized and unrealized gains and losses on energy-related or other "derivative" contracts at the end of each quarter. Because there were no hard-and-fast rules on how to value such contracts, Enron consistently valued them to show gains, which would offset the effect of issuing more stock to fund the SPEs. Moreover, the accounting treatment that allowed Enron to keep the debt off of its balance sheet also allowed the company to claim the income from unrealized holding gains, which increased the return on assets. By 1999, Enron derived more than half of its $1.4 billion pretax net income from unrealized holding gains.

Fastow became the master of the SPE, eventually creating thousands of them for various purposes. However, when the economic boom of the 1990s started to wane, Enron's unrealized holding gains on its "derivative" contracts started turning into losses. To keep these losses from showing up on Enron's income statement, Fastow created SPEs to hide them. And in the process of creating SPEs, Fastow paid himself over $30 million in management fees; his wife was paid another $17 million.

One of the six transactions in the SEC's complaint against Fastow involved a special-purpose entity named Raptor I and a public company called Avici Systems, Inc. According to the complaint, Enron and the Fastow-controlled partnership, LJM2, engaged in complex transactions with Raptor I to manipulate Enron's balance sheet and income statement, as well as to generate profits for LJM2 and Fastow, at Enron's expense. In September 2000, Fastow and others used Raptor I to effectuate a fraudulent hedging transaction and thus avoid a decrease in the value of Enron's investment in the stock of Avici Systems, Inc. Specifically, Fastow and others back-dated documents to make it appear that Enron locked in the value of its investment in Avici in August 2000, when Avici's stock was trading at its all-time-high price.

The various deals that Enron cooked up should have been properly disclosed in footnotes to its financial statements. But a number of analysts questioned the transparency of those disclosures. One said, "The notes just don't make any sense, and we read notes for a living."

As in other cases involving profits built on paper and risky deals, Enron was unable to continue without massive infusions of cash. When that didn't materialize, Enron, in October 2001, was forced to disclose it was taking a $1 billion charge to earnings to account for poorly performing business segments. It also had to reverse $1.2 billion in assets and equities booked as a result of the failed SPEs. Later that month, it announced restatements that added $591 million in losses and $628 million in liabilities for the year ended in 2000.

The bubble had burst: On December 2, 2001, Enron filed for bankruptcy. Enron's auditor, Andersen & Co., closed its doors on August 30, 2002, for failing to discover the fraud. In the end, sixteen people pled guilty to crimes related to the scandal; five more were convicted at trial. Many of the company's top executives were sentenced to jail time for their part in the fraud, including Fastow, Skilling, and former treasurer Ben Glisan, Jr. Ken Lay was also found guilty of six counts of fraud, but died of a heart attack before sentencing.

Understating Assets In some cases, as with some government-related or government-regulated companies in which additional funding is often based on asset amounts, it may be advantageous to understate assets. This understatement can be done directly or through improper depreciation. In Case 507, for example, the management of the company falsified its financial statements by manipulating the depreciation of the fixed assets. The depreciation reserve was accelerated by the amount of $2.9 million over a six-month period. The purpose of the scheme was to avoid cash contributions to a central government capital asset acquisition account.

Capitalizing Non-Asset Cost   Excluded from the cost of a purchased asset are interest and finance charges incurred in the purchase. For example, as a company finances a capital equipment purchase, monthly payments include both principal liability reduction and interest payments. On initial purchase, only the original cost of the asset should be capitalized. The subsequent interest payments should be charged to interest expense and not to the asset. Without reason for intensive review, fraud of this type can go unchecked. In Case 921, a new investor in a closely held corporation sued for rescission of purchase of stock, alleging that the company compiled financial information that misrepresented the financial history of the business. A fraud examination uncovered assets that were overvalued due to capitalization of interest expenses and other finance charges. Also discovered was the fact that one of the owners was understating revenue by $150,000 and embezzling the funds. The parties subsequently settled out of court.

Misclassifying Assets   In order to meet budget requirements, and for various other reasons, assets are sometimes misclassified into general ledger accounts in which they don't belong. The manipulation can skew financial ratios and help comply with loan covenants or other borrowing requirements. In Case 2106, a purchasing employee at a retail jewelry firm feared being called to the carpet on some bad jewelry purchases. Instead of taking the blame for bad margins on many items, the employee arbitrarily redistributed costs of shipments to individual inventory accounts. The coverup did not take; the company's CFO detected the fraud after he initiated changes to control procedures. When the CFO created a separation of duties between the buying function and the costing activities, the dishonest employee was discovered and terminated.

Red Flags Associated with Improper Asset Valuation

- Recurring negative cash flows from operations or an inability to generate cash flows from operations while reporting earnings and earnings growth
- Significant declines in customer demand and increasing business failures in either the industry or overall economy
- Assets, liabilities, revenues, or expenses based on significant estimates that involve subjective judgments or uncertainties that are difficult to corroborate
- Nonfinancial management's excessive participation in or preoccupation with the selection of accounting principles or the determination of significant estimates
- Unusual increase in gross margin or margin in excess of industry peers
- Unusual growth in the number of days' sales in receivables
- Unusual growth in the number of days' purchases in inventory
- Allowances for bad debts, excess and obsolete inventory, and so on that are shrinking in percentage terms or that are otherwise out of line with those of industry peers
- Unusual change in the relationship between fixed assets and depreciation
- Adding to assets while competitors are reducing capital tied up in assets

DETECTION OF FRAUDULENT FINANCIAL STATEMENT SCHEMES

SAS No. 99 (AU 316)—Consideration of Fraud in a Financial Statement Audit

In response to the high-profile financial frauds that occurred in 2001 and 2002, the Auditing Standards Board of the AICPA replaced the preexisting fraud audit standard—SAS No. 82—with SAS No. 99 (AU 316) to give expanded guidance to auditors for detecting material fraud. The standard was issued as part of an effort to "restore investor confidence in U.S. capital markets and re-establish audited financial statements as a clear picture window into Corporate America."

Statement on Auditing Standards (SAS) No. 1 (AU 110), "Responsibilities and Functions of the Independent Auditor," states, "The auditor has a responsibility to plan and perform the audit to obtain reasonable assurance about whether the financial statements are free of material misstatement, whether caused by error or fraud." The purpose of SAS No. 99 (AU 316) is to "establish standards and provide guidance to auditors in fulfilling that responsibility." It is divided into ten main sections:

- Description and characteristics of fraud
- Importance of exercising professional skepticism
- Discussion among engagement personnel regarding risk of material misstatement due to fraud
- Obtaining information needed to identify risks of material misstatement due to fraud
- Identifying risks that may result in material misstatement due to fraud
- Assessing the identified risks after taking into account an evaluation of the entity's programs and controls
- Responding to the results of the assessment
- Evaluating audit evidence
- Communicating about fraud to management, the audit committee, and others
- Documenting the auditor's consideration of fraud

Following is a brief description of each of these sections.

Description and Characteristics of Fraud   This section emphasizes that the auditor should be interested in acts that result in a material misstatement of the financial statements. Misstatements can be the result of fraud or error depending on whether the misstatement was intentional or unintentional.

Two types of misstatements are considered relevant for audit purposes:

- Misstatements arising from fraudulent financial reporting
- Misstatements arising from misappropriation of assets

Misstatements Arising from Fraudulent Financial Reporting   This category is defined as intentional misstatements or omissions of amounts or disclosures in financial statements that are "designed to deceive financial statement users." Fraudulent financial reporting may be accomplished by the following:

- Manipulation, falsification, or alteration of accounting records or supporting documents
- Misrepresentation or intentional omission of events, transactions, or other significant information
- Intentional misapplication of accounting principles relating to amounts, classification, manner of presentation, or disclosure

Misstatements Arising from Misappropriation of Assets   Also referred to as theft or defalcation, this category includes the theft of an entity's assets such that the effect of the theft causes the financial statements, in all material respects, not to be in conformity with GAAP.

This section cautions the auditor that, by definition, fraud often is concealed, and management is in a position to perpetrate fraud more easily, because managers are in the position of being able to directly or indirectly manipulate accounting records. Auditors cannot obtain absolute assurance that material misstatements are not present, but auditors should be aware of the possibility that fraud may be concealed, and that employees may be in collusion with each other or with outside vendors. If the auditor notices records or activity that seem unusual, the auditor should at least consider the possibility that fraud may have occurred.

Importance of Exercising Professional Skepticism   SAS No. 1 (AU 110) states that due professional care requires the auditor to exercise professional skepticism. Because of the characteristics of fraud, the auditor should conduct the engagement "with a mindset that recognizes the possibility that a material misstatement due to fraud could be present." It also requires an "ongoing questioning" of whether information the auditor obtains could suggest a material misstatement due to fraud.

Discussion among Engagement Personnel Regarding Risk of Material Misstatement due to Fraud   Prior to or in conjunction with the information-gathering procedures discussed below, the members of the audit team should discuss the potential for material misstatements due to fraud. The discussion should include brainstorming among the audit team members about the following:

- How and where they believe the entity's financial statement might be susceptible to fraud
- How management could perpetrate or conceal fraud
- How assets of the entity could be misappropriated

This discussion should also include a consideration of known external and internal factors affecting the entity that might:

- Create incentives/pressures for management and others to commit fraud
- Provide the opportunity for fraud to be perpetrated
- Indicate a culture or environment that enables management and others to rationalize committing fraud

The discussion should also emphasize the need to maintain "a questioning mind" in gathering and evaluating evidence throughout the audit and to obtain additional information if necessary.

Obtaining Information Needed to Identify Risks of Material Misstatement due to Fraud   SAS No. 108 (AU 311), "Communications Between Predecessor and Successor Auditors," provides guidance on how the auditor obtains knowledge about the entity's business and industry. As part of that process, the auditor should perform the following procedures to obtain information to use in identifying the risks of material misstatement due to fraud:

- Make inquiries of management and others within the entity to obtain their views about the risks of fraud and how they are addressed
- Consider any unusual or unexpected relationships that have been identified in performing analytical procedures in planning the audit
- Consider whether one or more fraud risk factors exist
- Consider other information that may be helpful in the identification of risks of material misstatement due to fraud

Making Inquiries of Management about the Risks of Fraud and How They Are Addressed   This step involves asking management about a number of issues, including:

- Whether management has knowledge of fraud or suspected fraud
- Management's understanding of the risk of fraud
- Programs and controls the entity has established to help prevent, deter, or detect fraud
- Whether and how management communicates to employees its views on business practices and ethical behavior

The auditor should also question the audit committee directly about its views concerning the risk of fraud and whether the committee has knowledge of fraud or suspected fraud. The same should be done with the company's internal audit department.

Additionally, the auditor may need to conduct similar inquiries of the entity's other personnel if the auditor believes they may have additional information about the risks of fraud.

Considering the Results of Analytical Procedures Performed in Planning the Audit   SAS No. 99 (AU 316) requires that analytical procedures be performed in planning the audit with an objective of identifying the existence of unusual transactions or events, and amounts, ratios, and trends that might indicate matters "that have financial statement and audit planning implications." If the results of these procedures yield unusual or unexpected relationships, the auditor should consider the results in identifying the risks of material misstatement due to fraud.

Considering Fraud Risk Factors   As discussed above, even though fraud is concealed, the auditor may identify events or conditions that indicate incentives or pressures to commit fraud, opportunities to carry out fraud, or attitudes and rationalizations

to justify fraudulent conduct. These events and conditions are referred to as "fraud risk factors." The auditor should consider whether one or more of the fraud risk factors are present and should be considered in identifying and assessing the risks of material misstatement due to fraud. The appendix to SAS No. 99 (AU 316) contains a list of examples of fraud risk factors.

Considering Other Information in Identifying Risks of Material Misstatement due to Fraud   Finally, the auditor should also consider any other information that he may feel would be helpful in identifying the risks of material misstatement.

Identifying Risks That May Result in Material Misstatement due to Fraud

After gathering the information as discussed previously, the auditor should consider the information in the context of the three conditions present when fraud occurs—incentives/pressures, opportunities, and attitudes/rationalizations. Auditors should consider:

- The *type* of risk that may exist (i.e., whether it involves fraudulent financial reporting or misappropriation of assets)
- The *significance* of the risk (i.e., whether it is of a magnitude that could result in a possible material misstatement)
- The *likelihood* of the risk (i.e., the likelihood that it will result in a material misstatement)
- The *pervasiveness* of the risk (i.e., whether the potential risk is pervasive to the financial statement as a whole or is specifically related to a particular assertion, account, or class of transactions)

Assessing the Identified Risks after Taking into Account an Evaluation of the Entity's Programs and Controls

Auditors must obtain an understanding of each of the five components of internal controls sufficient to plan the audit. As part of this step, the auditor should evaluate whether the entity's programs and controls that address identified risks of fraud have been suitably designed and placed in operation. These programs and controls may involve:

- Specific controls designed to mitigate specific risks of fraud (e.g., controls to prevent misappropriation of particular, susceptible assets)
- Broader programs designed to deter and detect fraud (e.g., ethics policies)

Responding to the Results of the Assessment

Once the auditor has gathered the information and assessed the risk of fraud, he must determine what impact the assessment will have on how the audit is conducted. For example, the auditor may need to design additional or different auditing procedures to obtain more reliable evidence in support of account balances, transactions, and so forth, or obtain additional corroboration of management's explanations and representations concerning material matters (such as third-party confirmation, documentation from independent sources, use of a specialist, analytical procedures, etc.).

Overall Responses to the Risk of Material Misstatement Judgments about the risk of material misstatement due to fraud have an overall effect on how the audit is conducted in several ways:

- *Assignment of personnel and supervision.* The auditor may need to consult with specialists in a particular field.
- *Accounting principles.* The auditor should consider management's selection and application of significant accounting principles, particularly those related to subjective measurements and complex transactions.
- *Predictability of auditing procedures.* The auditor should incorporate an "element of unpredictability" in the selection of auditing procedures to be performed, such as using differing sampling methods at different locations or auditing on an unannounced basis.

Responses Involving the Nature, Timing, and Extent of Procedures to Be Performed to Address the Identified Risks This section notes that the auditing procedures performed in response to identified risks will vary depending on the type of risks identified. Such procedures may involve both substantive tests and tests of the operating effectiveness of the entity's programs and controls. However, because management may have the ability to override controls that may otherwise appear to be operating effectively, it is unlikely that the audit risk can be reduced appropriately by performing only tests of controls.

Therefore, the auditor's response to specifically identified risks of fraud should include the following:

- Changing the *nature* of the auditing procedures to obtain more reliable or additional corroborative information (such as through independent sources or physical inspection).
- Changing the *timing* of substantive tests. For example, the auditor may conduct substantive tests at or near the end of the reporting period.
- The *extent* of the procedures should also reflect the assessment of the risk of fraud, such as increasing the sample sizes or performing analytical procedures at a more detailed level.

EXAMPLES OF RESPONSES TO IDENTIFIED RISKS OF MISSTATEMENT ARISING FROM FRAUDULENT FINANCIAL REPORTING SAS No. 99 (AU 316) provides a number of examples of responses the auditor may take in regard to risks of misstatement arising from both fraudulent financial reporting and asset misappropriation.

Some examples concerning fraudulent financial reporting include:

- *Revenue recognition*—performing substantive analytical procedures relating to revenue using disaggregated data (for example, comparing revenue reported by month and by product line during the current reporting period with comparable prior periods), confirming with customers relevant contract terms, or questioning staff about shipments near the end of a period
- *Inventory quantities*—examining inventory records to identify locations or items that require specific attention during or after the physical inventory count, more rigorous examination of the count such as by examining contents of boxed items, or additional testing of count sheets, tags, or other records

- *Management estimates*—depending on the situation, engaging a specialist or developing an independent estimate for comparison to management's estimate; gathering further information may help the auditor evaluate the reasonableness of management's estimates and underlying assumptions

EXAMPLES OF RESPONSES TO IDENTIFIED RISKS OF MISSTATEMENT ARISING FROM MISAPPROPRIATION OF ASSETS   If the auditor identifies a risk of material misstatement due to fraud relating to misappropriation of assets, the auditor may wish to include additional procedures. For example, if a particular asset is highly susceptible to misappropriation, the auditor may wish to conduct further testing of the controls to detect and deter such misappropriation.

Responses to Further Address Risk of Management Override of Controls

Because management is in a unique position to override existing controls, if such a risk is identified, the auditor may need to perform further procedures to further address the risk of management override of controls.

Examining Journal Entries and Other Adjustments for Evidence of Possible Material Misstatement due to Fraud

Material misstatements of financial statements often involve recording inappropriate or unauthorized journal entries or making adjustments to amounts reported in the financial statements that are not reflected in journal entries (such as consolidating adjustments or reclassifications). Therefore, the auditor should design procedures to test the appropriateness of journal entries recorded in the general ledger and other adjustments (such as entries posted directly to financial statement drafts).

Reviewing Accounting Estimates for Biases That Could Result in Material Misstatement Due to Fraud

In preparing financial statements, management is responsible for making a number of judgments or assumptions that affect significant accounting estimates. Fraudulent financial reporting is often accomplished through intentional misstatement of these estimates. In performing the audit, the auditor should consider whether the differences between estimates supported by the audit evidence and the estimates included in the financial statements indicate a possible bias on the part of management. If so, the auditor should perform a retrospective review of significant accounting estimates of the prior year. This should provide the auditor with additional information about whether management may have a bias in presenting the current-year estimates.

Evaluating the Business Rationale for Significant Unusual Transactions

During the course of the audit, the auditor may become aware of significant transactions that are outside the normal course of the entity's business or appear unusual given the auditor's understanding of the entity's operations. The auditor should gain an understanding of the business rationale for these transactions and whether the rationale (or lack thereof) suggests that the transactions may have been entered into to engage in fraudulent financial reporting or to conceal misappropriation of assets. Some factors the auditor should consider include:

- Are the transactions overly complex?
- Has management discussed the transactions with the board of directors and audit committee?

- Has management placed more emphasis on the need for a particular accounting treatment than on the underlying economics of the particular transaction?
- Do the transactions involve unconsolidated, unrelated parties (including special-purpose entities), or parties that do not have the substance or financial strength to support the transaction?

Evaluating Audit Evidence

Assessing Risks of Material Misstatement due to Fraud throughout the Audit   During the performance of the audit, the auditor may identify conditions that either change or support a judgment regarding the assessment of risks. Examples include:

- Discrepancies in the accounting records (such as transactions that are not recorded, unsupported or unauthorized balances or transactions, or last-minute adjustments)
- Conflicting or missing evidential matter (such as missing or altered documents/records, unexplained items or reconciliations, or missing inventory)
- Problematic or unusual relationships between the auditor and management (such as denial of access to records, facilities, employees, or customers; complaints by management about the conduct of the audit team; unusual delays in providing information; or unwillingness to add or revise disclosures)

Evaluating Whether Analytical Procedures Indicate a Previously Unrecognized Risk of Fraud   Analytical procedures performed during the audit may result in identifying unusual or unexpected relationships that should be considered in assessing the risk of material misstatement due to fraud. Determining whether a particular trend or relationship is a risk of fraud requires professional judgment. Unusual relationships involving year-end revenue and income often are particularly relevant and might include (1) uncharacteristically large amounts of income reported in the last week or two of the reporting period from unusual transactions and (2) income that is inconsistent with trends in cash flow from operations.

Analytical procedures are useful because management or employees generally are unable to manipulate all the information necessary to produce normal or expected relationships. SAS No. 99 (AU 316) provides several examples, including:

- The relationship of net income to cash flows from operations may appear unusual because management recorded fictitious revenues and receivables but was unable to manipulate cash
- Changes in inventory, accounts payable, sales, or costs of sales from the prior period to the current period may be inconsistent, indicating a possible theft of inventory because the employee was unable to manipulate all of the related accounts
- An unexpected or unexplained relationship between sales volume as determined from the accounting records and production statistics maintained by operations personnel (which is more difficult for management to manipulate) may indicate a possible misstatement of sales

Evaluating Risks of Material Misstatement At or Near the Completion of Fieldwork   At or near the completion of fieldwork, the auditor should evaluate whether the accumulated results of auditing procedures and other observations affect the assessment of risk of material misstatements due to fraud made earlier. Such an evaluation may identify whether there is a need to perform further audit procedures.

Responding to Misstatements That May Be the Result of Fraud If the auditor believes that misstatements are or may be the result of fraud but the effect of the misstatements is not material to the financial statements, the auditor nevertheless should evaluate the implications, especially those dealing with the "organizational position" of the person involved, which may require a reevaluation of the assessment of the risk of material misstatement. An example is theft of cash from a small petty cash fund. The amount of the theft generally would not be of significance to the auditor, but if higher-level management perpetrated the theft, it may be indicative of a more pervasive problem, such as management integrity.

If the auditor believes that a misstatement is or may be the result of fraud, and either has determined that the effect of the misstatement is material to the financial statements, or has been unable to evaluate whether the effect is material, the auditor should:

- Attempt to obtain additional evidence to determine whether material fraud occurred and its effect on the financial statements
- Consider the implications for other aspects of the audit
- Discuss the matter and the approach for further investigation with an appropriate level of management that is at least one level above those involved, and with senior management and the audit committee
- If appropriate, suggest the client consult with legal counsel

Communicating about Possible Fraud to Management, the Audit Committee, and Others SAS No. 99 (AU 316) states, "Whenever an auditor has determined that there is evidence that fraud may exist, the matter should be brought to the attention of an appropriate level of management." It is considered appropriate to do so even if the matter might be considered inconsequential. Fraud involving senior management and fraud (by anyone) that causes a material misstatement should be reported directly to the audit committee.

If the auditor has identified risks of material misstatement due to fraud that have continuing control implications, the auditor should also consider whether these risks should be communicated to senior management and the audit committee. Conversely, the auditor should also consider whether the absence of controls to detect or deter fraud should also be reported.

The disclosure of possible fraud to parties other than the client's senior management and its audit committee is ordinarily not part of the auditor's responsibility and may be precluded by the auditor's legal or ethical obligations of confidentiality unless the matter is reflected in the auditor's report.

However, SAS No. 99 (AU 316) points out that there may be a duty to disclose the information to outside parties in the following circumstances:

- To comply with certain legal and regulatory requirements (such as SEC rules)
- To a successor auditor pursuant to SAS No. 84 (AU 315)
- In response to a subpoena
- To a funding agency or other specified agency in accordance with the requirements for audits of entities that receive governmental financial assistance

Documenting the Auditor's Consideration of Fraud SAS No. 99 (AU 316) concludes by requiring that auditors document the following:

- Discussion among engagement personnel regarding the susceptibility of the entity's financial statements to material misstatement due to fraud (including how and when the discussion occurred, the team members who participated, and the subject matter discussed)
- Procedures performed to obtain information necessary to identify and assess the risks of material misstatement due to fraud
- Specific risks of material misstatement due to fraud that were identified
- If the auditor has not identified improper revenue recognition as a risk, the reasons supporting the auditor's conclusion
- The results of the procedures performed to further address the risk of management override of controls
- Other conditions and analytical relationships that caused the auditor to believe that additional auditing procedures or other responses were required to address such risks
- The nature of the communication about fraud made to management, the audit committee, or others

Financial Statement Analysis

Comparative financial statements provide information for current and past accounting periods. Accounts expressed in whole-dollar amounts yield a limited amount of information. The conversion of these numbers into ratios or percentages allows the reader of the statements to analyze them based on their relationship to each other, as well as to major changes in historical totals. In fraud detection and investigation, the determination of the reasons for relationships and changes in amounts can be important. These determinations are the red flags that point an examiner in the direction of possible fraud. If large enough, a fraudulent misstatement will affect the financial statements in such a way that relationships between the numbers become questionable. Many schemes are detected because the financial statements, when analyzed closely, do not make sense. Financial statement analysis includes the following:

- Vertical analysis
- Horizontal analysis
- Ratio analysis

Percentage Analysis—Vertical and Horizontal Traditionally, there are two methods of percentage analysis of financial statements. *Vertical analysis* is a technique for analyzing the relationships between the items on an income statement, balance sheet, or statement of cash flows by expressing components as percentages. This method is often referred to as "common sizing" financial statements. In the vertical analysis of an income statement, net sales is assigned 100 percent; for a balance sheet, total assets is assigned 100 percent on the asset side, and total liabilities and equity is expressed as 100 percent. All other items in each of the sections are expressed as a percentage of these numbers.

Horizontal analysis is a technique for analyzing the percentage change in individual financial statement items from one year to the next. The first period in the analysis is considered the base, and the changes to subsequent periods are computed as a percentage of the base period. If more than two periods are presented, each period's changes are computed as a percentage of the preceding period. Like vertical analysis, this technique will not work for small, immaterial frauds.

The following is an example of financial statements that are analyzed by both vertical and horizontal analysis:

BALANCE SHEET	Vertical Analysis				Horizontal Analysis	
	Year 1		Year 2		Change	%Change
Assets						
Current Assets						
Cash	45,000	14%	15,000	4%	(30,000)	−67%
Acc'ts Receivable	150,000	45%	200,000	47%	50,000	33%
Inventory	75,000	23%	150,000	35%	75,000	100%
Fixed Assets (net)	60,000	18%	60,000	14%	−	0%
Total	330,000	100%	425,000	100%	95,000	29%
Accts Payable	95,000	29%	215,000	51%	120,000	126%
Long-term Debt	60,000	18%	60,000	14%	−	0%
Stockholder's Equity					−	
Common Stock	25,000	8%	25,000	6%	−	0%
Paid-in Capital	75,000	23%	75,000	18%	−	0%
Retained Earnings	75,000	23%	50,000	12%	(25,000)	−33%
Total	330,000	100%	425,000	100%	95,000	29%

INCOME STATEMENT	Vertical Analysis				Horizontal Analysis	
	Year 1		Year 2		Change	%Change
Net Sales	250,000	100%	450,000	100%	200,000	80%
Cost of Goods Sold	125,000	50%	300,000	67%	175,000	140%
Gross Margin	125,000	50%	150,000	33%	25,000	20%
Operating Expenses						
Selling Expenses	50,000	20%	75,000	17%	25,000	50%
Administrative	60,000	24%	100,000	22%	40,000	67%
Expenses						
Net Income	15,000	6%	(25,000)	−6%	(40,000)	−267%

Additional Information		
Average Net Receivables	155,000	210,000
Average Inventory	65,000	130,000
Average Assets	330,000	425,000

Vertical Analysis Discussion   Vertical analysis is the expression of the relationship or percentage of an item on a financial statement to a specific base item. In the above example, vertical analysis of the income statement includes net sales as the base amount, and all other items are then analyzed as a percentage of that total. Vertical analysis emphasizes the relationship of statement items within each accounting period. These relationships can be used with historical averages to determine statement anomalies.

In the above example, we can observe that accounts payable is 29 percent of total liabilities. Historically we may find that this account averages slightly over 25 percent.

In year 2, accounts payable increased to 51 percent. Although the change in the account total may be explainable through a correlation with a rise in sales, this significant rise might be a starting point in a fraud examination. Source documents should be examined to determine the cause of this percentage increase. With this type of examination, fraudulent activity may be detected. The same type of change can be seen as selling expenses decline as a part of sales in year 2 from 20 to 17 percent. Again, this change may be due to higher-volume sales or another bona fide situation. But close examination may possibly point a fraud examiner to uncover fictitious sales, since accounts payable rose significantly without a corresponding increase in selling expenses.

Horizontal Analysis Discussion   Horizontal statement analysis uses percentage comparison from one accounting period to the next. The percentage change is calculated by dividing the amount of increase or decrease for each item by the base period amount. It is important to consider the amount of change as well as the percentage in horizontal comparisons. A 5 percent change in an account with a very large dollar amount may actually be much more of a change than a 50 percent change in an account with much less activity.

In the above example, it is very obvious that the 80 percent increase in sales has a much greater corresponding increase in cost of goods sold, which rose 140 percent. These accounts are often used to hide fraudulent expenses, withdrawals, or other illegal transactions.

Ratio Analysis   *Ratio analysis* is a means of measuring the relationship between two different financial statement amounts. The relationship and comparison are the keys to the analysis, which allows for internal evaluations using financial statement data. Traditionally, financial statement ratios are used in comparisons to an entity's industry average. They can be very useful in detecting red flags for a fraud examination. As the financial ratios highlight a significant change in key areas of an organization from one year to the next, or over a period of years, it becomes obvious that there may a problem. As in all other analyses, specific changes can often be explained by changes in the business operations. Changes in key ratios are not, in and of themselves, proof of any wrongdoing. Whenever a change in specific ratios is detected, the appropriate source accounts should be researched and examined in detail to determine whether fraud has occurred. For instance, a significant decrease in a company's *current ratio* may have resulted from an increase in current liabilities or a reduction in assets, both of which could be used to conceal fraud. Like the statement analysis discussed previously, the analysis of ratios is limited by its inability to detect fraud on a smaller, immaterial scale. Some of key financial ratios include:

- Current ratio
- Quick ratio
- Receivable turnover
- Collection ratio
- Inventory turnover
- Average number of days inventory is in stock
- Debt-to-equity ratio
- Profit margin
- Asset turnover

There are many other kinds of financial ratios that are analyzed in industry-specific situations, but the nine listed previously are ratios that may lead to discovery of fraud. The following calculations are based on the sample financial statements presented earlier:

RATIO ANALYSIS

Ratio	Calculation	Year 1			Year 2		
Current Ratio	$\dfrac{\text{Current Assets}}{\text{Current Liabilities}}$	$\dfrac{270{,}000}{95{,}000}$	=	2.84	$\dfrac{365{,}000}{215{,}000}$	=	1.70
Quick Ratio	$\dfrac{\text{Cash} + \text{Securities} + \text{Receivables}}{\text{Current Liabilities}}$	$\dfrac{195{,}000}{95{,}000}$	=	2.05	$\dfrac{215{,}000}{215{,}000}$	=	1.00
Receivable Turnover	$\dfrac{\text{Net Sales on Account}}{\text{Average Net Receivables}}$	$\dfrac{250{,}000}{155{,}000}$	=	1.61	$\dfrac{450{,}000}{210{,}000}$	=	2.14
Collection Ratio	$\dfrac{365}{\text{Receivable Turnover}}$	$\dfrac{365}{1.61}$	=	226.30	$\dfrac{365}{2.14}$	=	170.33
Inventory Turnover	$\dfrac{\text{Cost of Goods Sold}}{\text{Average Inventory}}$	$\dfrac{125{,}000}{65{,}000}$	=	1.92	$\dfrac{300{,}000}{130{,}000}$	=	2.31
Average Number of Days Inventory Is in Stock	$\dfrac{365}{\text{Inventory Turnover}}$	$\dfrac{365}{1.92}$	=	189.80	$\dfrac{365}{2.31}$	=	158.17
Debt to Equity	$\dfrac{\text{Total Liabilities}}{\text{Total Equity}}$	$\dfrac{155{,}000}{175{,}000}$	=	0.89	$\dfrac{275{,}000}{150{,}000}$	=	1.83
Profit Margin	$\dfrac{\text{Net Income}}{\text{Net Sales}}$	$\dfrac{15{,}000}{250{,}000}$	=	0.06	$\dfrac{(25{,}000)}{450{,}000}$	=	(0.06)
Asset Turnover	$\dfrac{\text{Net Sales}}{\text{Average Assets}}$	$\dfrac{250{,}000}{330{,}000}$	=	0.76	$\dfrac{450{,}000}{425{,}000}$	=	1.06

Interpretation of Financial Ratios

CURRENT RATIO

$$\dfrac{\text{Current Assets}}{\text{Current Liabilities}}$$

The current ratio—current assets divided by current liabilities—is probably the most-used ratio in financial statement analysis. This comparison measures a company's ability to meet present obligations from its liquid assets. The number of times that current assets exceed current liabilities has long been a quick measure of financial strength.

In detecting fraud, this ratio can be a prime indicator of manipulation of accounts. Embezzlement will cause the ratio to decrease. Liability concealment will cause a more favorable ratio.

In the case example, the drastic change in the current ratio from year 1 (2.84) to year 2 (1.70) should cause an examiner to look at these accounts in more detail. For instance, a billing scheme will usually result in a decrease in current assets—cash—that will in turn decrease the ratio.

QUICK RATIO

$$\frac{\text{Cash + Securities + Receivables}}{\text{Current Liabilities}}$$

The quick ratio, often referred to as the acid-test ratio, compares assets that can be immediately liquidated. In this calculation the total of cash, securities, and receivables is divided by current liabilities. This ratio is a measure of a company's ability to meet sudden cash requirements. In turbulent economic times, it is used more prevalently, giving the analyst a worst-case look at the company's working capital situation.

An examiner will analyze this ratio for fraud indicators. In year 1 of the example, the company balance sheet reflects a quick ratio of 2.05. This ratio drops in year 2 to 1.00. In this situation, a fraud affecting the quick ratio might be fictitious accounts receivable that have been added to inflate sales in one year. The ratio calculation will be abnormally high and there will not be an offsetting current liability.

RECEIVABLE TURNOVER

$$\frac{\text{Net Sales on Account}}{\text{Average Net Receivables}}$$

Receivable turnover is defined as net sales divided by average net receivables. It measures the number of times accounts receivable is turned over during the accounting period. In other words, it measures the time between on-account sales and collection of funds. This ratio is one that uses both income statement and balance sheet accounts in its analysis. If the fraud involves fictitious sales, this bogus income will never be collected. As a result, the turnover of receivables will decrease.

COLLECTION RATIO

$$\frac{365}{\text{Receivable Turnover}}$$

Accounts receivable aging is measured by the collection ratio. This ratio divides 365 days by the receivable turnover ratio to arrive at the average number of days to collect receivables. In general, the lower the collection ratio, the faster receivables are collected. A fraud examiner may use this ratio as a first step in detecting fictitious receivables or larceny and skimming schemes. Normally, this ratio will stay fairly consistent from year to year, but changes in billing policies or collection efforts may cause a fluctuation. The example shows a favorable reduction in the collection ratio from 226.3 in year 1 to 170.33 in year 2. This means that the company is collecting its receivables more quickly in year 2 than in year 1.

INVENTORY TURNOVER

$$\frac{\text{Cost of Goods Sold}}{\text{Average Inventory}}$$

The relationship between a company's cost of goods sold and average inventory is shown through the inventory turnover ratio. This ratio measures the number of times inventory is sold during the period, and is a good determinant of purchasing, production, and sales efficiency. In general, a higher inventory turnover ratio is considered more favorable. For example, if cost of goods sold has increased due to theft of inventory (ending inventory has declined, but not through sales), then this ratio will be abnormally high. In the case example, inventory turnover increases in year 2, signaling the possibility that an embezzlement is buried in the inventory account. An examiner should look at the changes in the components of the ratio to determine a direction in which to discover possible fraud.

AVERAGE NUMBER OF DAYS INVENTORY IS IN STOCK

$$\frac{365}{\text{Inventory Turnover}}$$

The ratio of the average number of days inventory is in stock is a restatement of the inventory turnover ratio, expressed in days. This rate is important for several reasons. An increase in the number of days inventory stays in stock causes additional expenses, including storage costs, risk of inventory obsolescence, and market price reductions, as well as interest and other expenses incurred due to tying up funds in inventory stock. Inconsistency or significant variance in this ratio is a red flag for fraud investigators. Examiners may use this ratio to examine inventory accounts for possible larceny schemes. Purchasing and receiving inventory schemes can also affect the ratio, and false debits to cost of goods sold will result in an increase in the ratio. Significant changes in the inventory turnover ratio are good indicators of possible fraudulent inventory activity.

DEBT-TO-EQUITY RATIO

$$\frac{\text{Total Liabilities}}{\text{Total Equity}}$$

The debt-to-equity ratio is computed by dividing total liabilities by total equity. This ratio is one that is heavily considered by lending institutions. It provides a clear picture of the comparison between the long-term and short-term debt of the company, and the owner's financial injection plus earnings-to-date. This balance of resources provided by creditors and what the owners provide is crucial when analyzing the financial status of a company. Debt-to-equity requirements are often included as borrowing covenants in corporate lending agreements. The example displays a year 1 ratio of 0.89 and a year 2 ratio of 1.83. The increase in the ratio corresponds with the rise in accounts payable. Sudden changes in this ratio may signal an examiner to look for fraud.

PROFIT MARGIN

$$\frac{\text{Net Income}}{\text{Net Sales}}$$

Profit margin ratio is defined as net income divided by net sales. This ratio is often referred to as the efficiency ratio because it reveals profits earned per dollar of sales. The ratio of net income to sales relates not only to the effects of gross margin changes, but also charges to sales and administrative expenses. As fraud is committed, artificially inflated sales will not have a corresponding increase to cost of goods sold, net income will be overstated, and the profit margin ratio will be abnormally high. False expenses and fraudulent disbursements will cause an increase in expenses and a decrease in the profit margin ratio. Over time, this ratio should be fairly consistent.

ASSET TURNOVER

$$\frac{\text{Net Sales}}{\text{Average Assets}}$$

Net sales divided by average operating assets is the calculation used to determine the asset turnover ratio. This ratio is used to determine the efficiency with which asset resources are utilized. The case example reflects a greater use of assets in year 2 than in year 1.

DETERRENCE OF FINANCIAL STATEMENT FRAUD

Deterring financial statement fraud is more complex than deterring asset misappropriation and other frauds. Adding traditional internal controls is unlikely to be effective. As we saw earlier, the COSO study indicated that either the CEO or the CFO was involved in 89 percent of the financial statement frauds studied. People at this high level can use their authority to override most internal controls, so those controls will often be of limited value in preventing financial statement fraud. A different approach is needed.

Following the principles of the *fraud triangle*, introduced in Chapter 1, a general approach to reducing financial statement fraud is to:

- Reduce pressures to commit financial statement fraud
- Reduce the opportunity to commit financial statement fraud
- Reduce rationalization of financial statement fraud

Reduce Pressures to Commit Financial Statement Fraud

- Establish effective board oversight of the "tone at the top" created by management
- Avoid setting unachievable financial goals
- Avoid applying excessive pressure on employees to achieve goals
- Change goals if changed market conditions require it
- Ensure that compensation systems are fair and do not create too much incentive to commit fraud
- Discourage excessive external expectations of future corporate performance
- Remove operational obstacles blocking effective performance

Reduce the Opportunity to Commit Financial Statement Fraud

- Maintain accurate and complete internal accounting records
- Carefully monitor the business transactions and interpersonal relationships of suppliers, buyers, purchasing agents, sales representatives, and others who interface in the transactions between financial units
- Establish a physical security system to secure company assets, including finished goods, cash, capital equipment, tools, and other valuable items
- Divide important functions among employees, separating total control of one area

- Maintain accurate personnel records including background checks on new employees
- Encourage strong supervisory and leadership relationships within groups to ensure enforcement of accounting procedures
- Establish clear and uniform accounting procedures with no exception clauses

Reduce Rationalization of Financial Statement Fraud

- Promote strong values, based on integrity, throughout the organization.
- Have policies that clearly define prohibited behavior with respect to accounting and financial statement fraud.
- Provide regular training to all employees communicating prohibited behavior.
- Have confidential advice and reporting mechanisms to communicate inappropriate behavior.
- Have senior executives communicate to employees that integrity takes priority and that goals must never be achieved through fraud.
- Ensure management practices what it preaches and sets an example by promoting honesty in the accounting area. Dishonest acts by management, even if they are directed at someone outside the organization, create a dishonest environment that can spread to other business activities and other employees, internal and external.
- The consequences of violating the rules, and the punishment of violators, should be clearly communicated.

CASE STUDY: ALL ON THE SURFACE[3]

Michael Weinstein chuckled a lot. He smoked big cigars and laughed at the people who used to think he was just a chubby schmoe. *Forbes* and *Business Week* stoked the fire with adoring articles. *Business Week* called Weinstein's Coated Sales, Inc., "the fourth fastest growing company in the country" and predicted greater returns to come. Of Coated Sales' twenty competitors, eleven were either defunct or absorbed. "The survivors," observed a writer in *Forbes*, "are more likely to cower than laugh when they see Weinstein." In a few years' time, revenues at Coated had jumped from $10 to $90 million per annum. The stock was peaking at eight times its opening price. "One of my goals," Weinstein stated dramatically, "is to see us be almost alone."

Which didn't take long. Weinstein's auditors walked out on him. The Big-Six firm resigned and announced publicly they had no trust in the management of Coated Sales. Senior management scrambled en masse to get out of the way. Weinstein was suspended. New people started looking at the books. In two months, Coated Sales was filing for bankruptcy. The last laugh fell hollow down the empty hallways.

[3] Several names and details have been changed to preserve anonymity.

Michael Weinstein was once the All-American Businessman. At nineteen he borrowed $1,000 from his father and bought into a drugstore. At thirty-one he had a chain of stores, which he sold, and reaped several million dollars in take-home pay. Weinstein remembered thinking, "I have a problem." Just when all his contemporaries were reaching their thirty-something years, starting careers, raising their families, he was retiring. What to do with all that time?

His buddy Dick Bober talked him into the coated fabrics business. Weinstein didn't know anything about coated fabrics. But he wasn't a pharmacist either, and that venture had proved fortunate. Coating fabrics, he learned, was a crucial step in making lots of products, from conveyer belts to bulletproof vests. Things like parachutes, helmet liners, and camouflage suits all use coated fabrics. So there were some bulky government contracts waiting to be served. Uniforms and equipment have to be stainproofed, fungusproofed, waterproofed, and dyed. According to one estimate, coating adds from 10 to 50 percent to the base value of raw material, lending the luster of money to an otherwise workaday industry.

Weinstein threw himself into the business and eventually into the manufacturing process. As a pilot, he hated the life vests stowed on commercial airliners. "They had always bugged me," he said. "They [are] heavy and expensive to make," he told Coated researchers. They designed a prototype using coated nylon, which was 60 percent lighter than the standard, and 70 percent cheaper to make. Before his company's untimely demise, Weinstein could boast that every Western airline carried life vests manufactured with materials made by Coated Sales.

The Coated Sales laboratory helped develop a superproofed denim to protect oil rig workers, firemen, and people handling hazardous materials. Coated Sales employees worked on aircraft emergency slides, radiator hoses, telephone earpieces, a sewage filtration fabric, marine dive suits, backpacks, and, just for the flair of it, made some of the sailcloth for *Stars & Stripes*, the schooner piloted by Dennis Conner to win the America's Cup. Just two years before the crash, Weinstein became the first coated fabrics operator to own a large-scale finishing plant, a $27 million facility without rival in the industry.

At the same time, Weinstein's darling was digging its own grave. Expanding into new markets, developing cutting-edge product lines, herding new companies into the fold—all this takes money. Especially when the CEO and senior management like to live large and let people know about it. There's a constant cash crunch. Larger scale means larger crunch. Inside the workings of Coated Sales, shipments of fabric and equipment were being bought and sold quickly, often at a loss, just to get to the short-term money.

For years, Coated had used Main Hurdman for auditing, with no sign of trouble. But when Main Hurdman was acquired by Peat-Marwick, the new auditors saw a very different picture. One associate called a luggage manufacturer to ask about 750,000 pieces of merchandise purchased from Coated. The luggage company said they never placed an order like that. No idea. When audit team members spoke about their concerns, Coated sent in their legal counsel to talk with the auditors. Philip Kagan tried to get them to make a deal, to go ahead and let the financial statement slide; there were some problems, he admitted, but nothing beyond repair. The matter was being taken care of. No way, said the auditors, and walked out.

In two months' time, the company that flew higher than the rest had fallen into bankruptcy. Early estimates put shareholder losses at more than $160 million. Coated's top twenty creditors claimed they were out at least $17 million. The bankruptcy court appointed Coopers & Lybrand's insolvency and litigation practice to work with the debtor in possession. Besides the usual assessments, the group was to determine what went wrong, and just how wrong—in dollar amounts—it had gone. CFE Harvey Creem says, "We knew there was something of concern with a loan and how the money was used. Once we started poking around, the iceberg got larger." Creem worked with the debtor's lawyers, who determined that the proceeds of a bank loan had been

transferred to a brokerage account, one no longer carried in the ledgers. It was a supposedly dormant account from the company's first public offering, used for temporary investments until it was zeroed out. During the most recent fiscal year, there had been some activity on the account. Proceeds from a loan had been deposited into the brokerage account, transferred out to a cash account, and listed as if they were payments from customers against their accounts receivable. Coated Sales was due a lot of money, their receivables growing by $20 million a year. But a lot of the payments on those receivables were being made with Coated's own money, part of which originated from bank loans. The broad outline of the fraud was clear. "When you find a single check for, say $2 million, used to pay off several different accounts, you know something's up... Usually each customer sends their own check to pay off their own debt. In this case, a check listed under one name was used to pay off debts for several different people. Now, a company that not only pays its own debts, but the debts of other companies, too—that's not impossible, but it's not likely. The basics of the operation took two or three hours to break," says Creem. "Then it was tracking the scope of what happened."

Creem describes how he and his colleagues started at the bankruptcy filing date and "went in and analyzed the receivables in-depth... Large chunks of them were totally fallacious; they had nothing supporting them." The tracking effort was helped along by a number of lower-level employees: "Some of them didn't really know what was happening and they were willing to help. Some may have known, but they were repentant, so they were willing to talk." In about three years of scamming, Weinstein and his management had inflated their sales and profits, resulting in overstated equity by $55 million. They used these phony numbers to get loans from several banks, including a $52 million line of credit from BancBoston and a $15 million line from First Fidelity in Newark, New Jersey.

The rigged loans solved the cash-flow problem, and brought very pleasant side effects. Stock in Coated Sales—traded under the ticker symbol RAGS—had been headed through the roof. Huge leaps in revenue and a monstrous control of the market had propelled the stock to $12 a share, eight times more than what it opened for. The company's upper echelon, including President Ernest Glantz and Weinstein's longtime partner Vice President Dick Bober, was cashing in in a big way. By himself, Weinstein made more than $10 million in a short-term selling spree. Additionally, one of the myriad lawsuits against him accused Weinstein of departing with $968,000 in company cash.

Creem followed the trail of rigged profits into several intriguing corners. "To float this past the auditors for as long as they did, they found several ways to create the fiction that customers were actually paying the fake receivables. They would create a fake receivable, say $10,000 due from a company. They'd hold it as long as they could, sometimes doctoring the dates on the aging, so it looked more recent than it was." Creem says the next step was "rigging a way to pay the account off: They'd transmit their own cash to a vendor. The vendor presumably was in on the scheme, too, since they had submitted a fake invoice for the $10,000. This vendor keeps one to two percent for their trouble, and sends the rest back to Coated. That money would be reflected as a payment against the phony receivable."

Guys like Bernard Korostoff made the vendor trick work. Korostoff used his Kaye Mills International Corporation to create false invoices for several big Coated orders. Weinstein's team, having used their phony financials to get loans, sent out the money to Korostoff as if they were paying off a debt. Korostoff kept 1.5 percent for making the transaction possible, turning the rest back to Coated to pay off the falsified receivables. "I never really understood that," says Creem. "These guys are doing this for a measly little percentage. Why would they bother for no more than that? Maybe it was connected in other ways to the business."

The business, as it was being run, was a labyrinth of finagle and deception. Weinstein was faking how much he owed people in order to pay off receivables, which were also being faked. He was using receivables to get million-dollar loans and plowing chunks of the proceeds back into the system to keep suspicious eyes unaware. The false sales not only brought in loan dollars, they created portfolio dollars by driving RAGS stock higher and higher. To support the scam, Weinstein had three ways to keep his circle of money in motion: (1) he could move loan money from the hidden brokerage account to wherever it was needed, (2) he could use fake vendor invoices to launder funds back into the company, or (3) he and his associates could sell off their own stock in the company and apply some of the proceeds to the delinquent receivables.

Four years of this action and Weinstein had demolished Coated Sales. The company exaggerated its accounts receivable by millions, fictionalizing half or more of sales at any given point. At the time, it was the largest stock fraud ever in the state of New Jersey. Weinstein and nine other senior managers were charged with planning, executing, and profiting from the scheme. Weinstein—called "a tall, plump man with a domineering personality" by *Forbes*—owned more than ten airplanes and several helicopters. He had two Rolls-Royces, one at each of his two residences, besides five other luxury automobiles scattered about. He and the other conspirators had used some of the proceeds to buy themselves smaller companies. For flamboyance, he had no better, and for gall he was unrivaled. After Coated went belly up and federal

charges joined the pile of lawsuits against him, Weinstein bought a 13,000-square-foot house in Boca Raton, Florida, valued at $2 million, sitting on a $1 million property. Three different yachts were docked along the Florida coast in case Weinstein needed to get away from all the hassle.

But Weinstein wouldn't slip past this one. He and his inner circle were presented with a forty-six-page indictment. Bruce Bloom, Coated's chief financial officer, pled guilty and pointed at his cohorts. Coated's lead counsel, Philip Kagan, first declared himself "totally innocent of any wrongdoing," but later decided to plead guilty to the racketeering and conspiracy charges against him. Kagan confessed to helping dupe company auditors, and described trying to entice them into ignoring the facts of their ledgers. He also admitted that he had once accepted $115,000 in legal fees from Coated Sales without reporting the money to the SEC as required. Kagan was sentenced to eighteen months in prison. Jail terms for other low-level players ranged from one year to twenty-four months.

Coated President Ernest Glanz was given a year's sentence—part of a deal he made to cooperate with the government. Richard Bober, Weinstein's longtime friend, drew twenty months in prison and a $3 million fine, besides the $55.9 million civil judgment he shared with Weinstein. Creem remembers that when Bober testified in bankruptcy court, "The judge appeared shocked. He started asking Bober questions himself. I don't believe he had ever heard anything quite like this in his courtroom before."

Michael Weinstein struck a plea bargain, which nevertheless carried a pretty stout penalty. He forfeited virtually all of the properties, cars, and boats he had amassed, along with several businesses and numerous bank accounts worth several hundred thousand dollars each. He was given fifty-seven months in federal prison and charged to make restitution for any outstanding stockholder losses.

U.S. Attorney Michael Chertoff saw this as a decisive case, part of what he called "a new genre of corporate boardroom prosecutions." Fed up with the megascams of the megalomaniac executive, legal agencies began using the tough Securities Law Enforcement Remedies Act to go after the big players. "Major financial fraud," Chertoff told a press conference after Weinstein's guilty plea, "not only harms banking institutions but also infects the securities market, victimizing the thousands of persons who invest in stock. When dishonesty roams the boardroom, it is the creditors and investors who suffer."

SUMMARY

Financial statement fraud has become daily press, challenging the corporate governance and accountability of public companies as well as the professional responsibility and integrity of these companies' boards of directors, senior executives, and auditors. Financial statement fraud is defined as the deliberate misstatement or omission of amounts or disclosures to deceive financial statement users, particularly investors and creditors.

There are a variety of financial statement fraud schemes. The first is *fictitious revenues*, which includes using fictitious sales involving fake, phantom, and legitimate customers, and inflating or altering invoices for legitimate customers to increase assets and annual revenue. The motivation to commit this fraud comes from pressures that are placed on owners by bankers, stockholders, their families, and communities for the companies to succeed. Pressure also comes from departmental budget requirements, especially income and profit goals.

The second category is *timing differences*. These methods include not matching revenues with expenses, early revenue recognition, and recording expenses in the wrong period.

The third category is *concealed liabilities and expenses*. The three common methods for concealing liabilities and expenses are (1) liability/expense omissions, (2) capitalizing expenses, and (3) failure to disclose warranty costs and liabilities. Since

pretax income will increase by the full amount of the expense or liability not recorded, this fraud method can have a significant impact on reported earnings.

The fourth category is *improper disclosures*. This includes liability omission, significant events, management fraud, related-party transactions, and accounting changes.

The fifth category is improper asset valuation. The company's fraudulent overstatement of inventory or accounts receivable, booking fictitious assets, misrepresenting asset value, or misclassifying assets may cause inflation of the current ratio at the expense of long-term assets.

This chapter examines the incentives and opportunities to commit financial statement fraud and the rationalization and consequences of engaging in this type of fraud. It also presents financial statement fraud detection and deterrence recommendations, including the responsibilities of management, internal auditors, and external auditors as specified in SAS No. 99 (AU 316). Detection and deterrence of financial statement fraud is the responsibility of all corporate governance participants as well as those involved with the financial statements' supply chain, including the board of directors, the audit committee, management, internal auditors, and external auditors.

ESSENTIAL TERMS

Financial statement fraud Intentional misstatements or omissions of amounts or disclosures of financial statements to deceive investors, creditors, and other users of financial statements.

Fictitious revenue The recording of sales of goods or services that never occurred.

Liability/expense omissions Deliberate attempts to conceal liabilities and expenses already incurred.

Capitalized expenses When expenditures are capitalized as assets and not expensed off during the current period, income will be overstated. As the assets are depreciated, income in subsequent periods will be understated.

Related-party transactions Transactions that occur when a company does business with another entity whose management or operating policies can be controlled or significantly

influenced by the company or by some other party in common. There is nothing inherently wrong with related-party transactions, so long as they are fully disclosed.

Improper asset valuation Generally accepted accounting principles require that most assets be recorded at their historical (acquisition) cost with some exceptions. This type of fraud usually involves the fraudulent overstatement of inventory or receivables or the misclassification of fixed assets.

Horizontal analysis A technique for analyzing the percentage change in individual financial statement items from one year to the next.

Vertical analysis The expression of the relationship or percentage of component part items to a specific base item.

Ratio analysis A means of measuring the relationship between two different financial statement amounts.

REVIEW QUESTIONS

12-1 (Learning objective 12-1) What is financial statement fraud?

12-2 (Learning objective 12-2) List five different ways in which financial statement fraud can be committed.

12-3 (Learning objective 12-3) What are the two methods of engaging in fictitious revenues?

12-4 (Learning objective 12-3) What are the two most common pressures and motivations for committing financial statement fraud?

12-5 (Learning objective 12-4) List three methods of engaging in timing differences.

12-6 (Learning objective 12-4) What is the motivation for violating the generally accepted accounting principle of matching revenues with expenses? What is the result of committing this fraud?

12-7 (Learning objective 12-4) What is the motivation for early revenue recognition? What is the result of engaging in this type of fraud?

12-8 (Learning objective 12-5) List the three common methods for concealing liabilities and expenses.

12-9 (Learning objective 12-5) What is the motivation for concealing liabilities and expenses?

12-10 (Learning objective 12-6) List five common categories of improper disclosures.

12-11 (Learning objective 12-7) What are the four common forms of improper asset valuation?

12-12 (Learning objective 12-7) What is the likely result of committing an improper asset valuation?

12-13 (Learning objective 12-8) What is the difference between fraudulent financial reporting and misappropriation of assets?

12-14 (Learning objective 12-9) Describe three analytical techniques for financial statement analysis.

DISCUSSION ISSUES

12-1 (Learning objective 12-3) What is the most effective way to prevent fictitious revenue from being fraudulently reported in the financial statements?

12-2 (Learning objective 12-3) How can fictitious revenue be created through the use of false sales to shell companies? Discuss the method and result of committing this fraud.

12-3 (Learning objective 12-4) How might a company use timing differences to boost revenues for the current year? Discuss and analyze the method and result of committing the fraud.

12-4 (Learning objective 12-4) In the case study, "The Importance of Timing," what kind of fraud did the accountant commit? How could this fraud have been discovered?

12-5 (Learning objective 12-5) Liability/expense omission is the preferred and easiest method of concealing liabilities/expenses. Why? Discuss how to detect this type of fraud.

12-6 (Learning objective 12-7) What internal control activities and related test procedures can detect or deter overstated inventory?

12-7 (Learning objective 12-9) What financial reporting analysis techniques can help to detect fraudulent financial statement schemes?

12-8 (Learning objectives 12-3, 12-5, and 12-7) In the case study "That Way Lies Madness," what kind of fraud did Eddie Antar commit? How was the fraud committed? How could such fraud be discovered?

12-9 (Learning objective 12-10) During the audit of financial statements, an auditor discovers that financial statements might be materially misstated due to the existence of fraud. Describe (1) the auditor's responsibility according to SAS No. 99 (AU 316) for discovering financial statement fraud, (2) what the auditor should do if he is precluded from applying necessary audit procedures to discover the suspected fraud, and (3) what the auditor should do if he finds that the fraud materially affects the integrity of the financial statements.

CHAPTER 13

FRAUD RISK ASSESSMENT

LEARNING OBJECTIVES

After studying this chapter, you should be able to:

13-1 Describe the factors that influence an organization's vulnerability to fraud

13-2 Explain the difference between preventive and detective controls

13-3 Define and explain the objective of a fraud risk assessment

13-4 Discuss why organizations should conduct fraud risk assessments

13-5 Understand the characteristics of a good fraud risk assessment

13-6 Describe considerations for developing an effective fraud risk assessment

13-7 List actions that should be taken to prepare a company for a fraud risk assessment

13-8 Understand the steps involved in conducting a fraud risk assessment and how to apply a framework to them

13-9 Describe approaches to responding to an organization's residual fraud risks

13-10 Name important considerations when reporting the results of a fraud risk assessment

13-11 List actions management should take using the results of a fraud risk assessment

13-12 Explain how a fraud risk assessment can inform and influence the audit process

OVERVIEW

There are many measures organizations can and should take to minimize the risk that fraud might occur and go undetected. A fraud risk assessment can be a powerful proactive tool in the fight against fraud for any business. Regulators, professional standard-setters, and law enforcement authorities continue to emphasize the crucial role that fraud risk assessment plays in developing and maintaining effective fraud risk management programs and controls.

What Is Fraud Risk?

As discussed in Chapter 1, the fraud triangle, developed by Donald R. Cressey, tells us that there are three interrelated elements that enable someone to commit fraud: the *nonshareable financial need* that drives a person to want to commit the fraud, the *opportunity* that enables him to commit the fraud, and the *ability to rationalize* the fraudulent behavior. The vulnerability that an organization has to those capable of overcoming these three elements is *fraud risk*. Fraud risk can come from sources both internal and external to the organization.

Why Should an Organization Be Concerned about Fraud Risk?

Every organization is vulnerable to fraud—no organization has immunity to that risk. The key to reducing this vulnerability is to be consciously aware and realistic about the organization's weaknesses. Only then can management establish mechanisms that effectively prevent or detect fraudulent activities.

Organizational stakeholders expect their stewards to be thoughtful and prudent about protecting the business. Yet, even while tales of fraudsters receive much public attention, many organizations still have difficulty facing the reality of their susceptibility to fraud.

Factors That Influence Fraud Risk

The Nature of the Business   The types of risks an organization faces are directly connected to the nature of the business in which it is engaged. For example, the inherent fraud risks faced by hospitals and medical practices are vastly different from those faced by banks and financial institutions.

The Operating Environment   The environment in which the organization operates has a direct impact on its vulnerability to fraud. Brick-and-mortar businesses have a very different risk profile from that of Internet businesses. Likewise, local businesses have different risk profiles than those that operate in the international arena.

The Effectiveness of Its Internal Controls   A good system of internal controls, with the right balance of preventive and detective controls, can greatly reduce an organization's vulnerability to fraud. *Preventive controls* are those manual or automated processes designed to stop an undesirable event from occurring. *Detective controls* can also be manual or automated, but are designed to identify an undesirable event that has already occurred. No system of internal controls can fully eliminate the risk of fraud, but well-designed and effective internal controls can deter the average fraudster by reducing the opportunity to commit fraud.

The Ethics and Values of the Company and the People Within It   It is extremely difficult, if not impossible, to have a company made up of individuals whose ethics and values are fully aligned with those of the organization. Any gap in alignment can significantly increase an organization's fraud risk.

While many organizations have codes of conduct, those codes are not always clear in drawing the definitive line between acceptable and unacceptable behavior. That lack of clarity leaves room for fraudsters to rationalize their actions. For example, in most organizations, it is generally understood that manipulating financial records is unacceptable behavior that will result in termination; however, it is not always apparent whether taking home a pen or pencil that belongs to the company is unacceptable behavior or what the consequence, if any, would be.

An organization that is clear and consistent about its ethics, values, and expectations will reduce the potential fraudster's ability to rationalize his actions. Likewise, an organization that demonstrates consistency and predictability in how it handles and holds accountable employees who engage in unacceptable behaviors can significantly reduce its risk of fraud.

WHAT IS A FRAUD RISK ASSESSMENT?

Fraud risk assessment is a process aimed at proactively identifying and addressing an organization's vulnerabilities to internal and external fraud. As every organization is different, the fraud risk assessment process is often more of an art than a science. What gets evaluated and how it gets assessed should be tailored to the organization—there is no one-size-fits-all approach. Additionally, organizational fraud risks continually change. It is therefore important to think about a fraud risk assessment as an ongoing, continuous process rather than just an activity.

A fraud risk assessment starts with an identification and prioritization of fraud risks that exist in the business. The process evolves as the results of that identification and prioritization begin to drive education, communication, organizational alignment, and action around effectively managing fraud risk and identifying new fraud risks as they emerge.

What Is the Objective of a Fraud Risk Assessment?

In the simplest terms, the objective of a fraud risk assessment is to help an organization recognize what makes it most vulnerable to fraud. Through a fraud risk assessment, the organization is able to identify where fraud is most likely to occur, enabling proactive measures to be considered and implemented to reduce the chance that it could happen.

WHY SHOULD ORGANIZATIONS CONDUCT FRAUD RISK ASSESSMENTS?

Every organization should conduct a fraud risk assessment and build procedures to keep the assessment process current and relevant. Not only is this practice good corporate governance, it makes good business sense.

Improve Communication and Awareness about Fraud

A fraud risk assessment can be a great vehicle for an organization to open up communication and raise awareness about fraud. When employees are engaged in an open discussion about fraud, the conversations themselves can play a role in reducing fraud vulnerability. Employees are reminded that the organization does care about preventing fraud and are empowered to come forward if they suspect fraud is occurring in the organization. Open communication and awareness about fraud can also deter a potential fraudster by reducing his ability to rationalize bad behavior and increasing his perception that someone might catch on to his actions and report him.

Identify What Activities Are the Most Vulnerable to Fraud

Management must know where the company is most vulnerable to fraud in order to prevent it. For most companies, the normal course of business generally involves many different activities; however, not all the activities in which the company engages are equal in terms of increasing the business's exposure to fraud. The fraud risk assessment helps guide the organization to focus on the activities that put the company at the greatest risk.

Know Who Puts the Organization at the Greatest Risk

The actions of certain individuals can significantly increase the company's vulnerability to fraud. The risk can be driven by the way in which someone makes decisions, behaves, or treats others within and outside the organization. The fraud risk assessment can help hone in on those people and their activities that might increase the company's overall fraud risk.

Develop Plans to Mitigate Fraud Risk

If management knows where the greatest fraud risks are, it can put plans in place to reduce or mitigate those risks. The results of the fraud risk assessment can be used to gain alignment among various stakeholders and to drive preventive action.

Develop Techniques to Determine Whether Fraud Has Occurred in High-Risk Areas

Assessing an area as having a high fraud risk does not conclusively mean that fraud is actually occurring there. Nevertheless, the fraud risk assessment is useful in identifying areas that should be proactively investigated for evidence of fraud. In addition, putting high-risk areas under increased scrutiny can deter potential fraudsters by increasing their perception of detection.

Assess Internal Controls

Many organizations rely heavily on their internal control system to prevent and detect fraud. Although internal control plays a critical role in fraud prevention and detection, it is a dynamic system that requires constant reevaluation of its weaknesses. Performing a fraud risk assessment provides management with the opportunity to review the company's internal control system for effectiveness, taking into account the following considerations:

- Controls that may have been eliminated due to restructuring efforts (e.g., elimination of separation of duties due to downsizing)
- Controls that may have been eroded over time due to reengineering of business processes
- New opportunities for collusion
- Lack of internal controls in a vulnerable area
- Nonperformance of control procedures (e.g., control procedures compromised for the sake of expediency)
- Inherent limitations of internal controls, including opportunities for those responsible for a control to commit and conceal fraud (e.g., through management and system overrides)

Comply with Regulations and Professional Standards

Fraud risk assessments can assist management and auditors (internal and external) in satisfying regulatory requirements and complying with professional standards pertaining to their responsibility for fraud risk management. For example, in the United States, Public Company Accounting Oversight Board Auditing Standard No. 5, "An Audit of Internal Control Over Financial Reporting That Is Integrated with an Audit of Financial

Statements," specifically states that auditors should take into account the results of the fraud risk assessment when planning and performing the audit of internal control over financial reporting.

WHAT MAKES A GOOD FRAUD RISK ASSESSMENT?

A good fraud risk assessment is one that fits within the culture of the organization, is sponsored and supported by the right people, encourages everyone to openly participate, and is generally embraced throughout the business as an important and valuable process. Conversely, a fraud risk assessment that is conducted without these conditions will have inferior results.

The following are key elements to conducting a good fraud risk assessment.

Collaborative Effort of Management and Auditors

As regulations and professional standards indicate, both management and auditors have a responsibility for fraud risk management. However, each of these parties has unique knowledge and perspective of the fraud risks faced by the organization. Management has intricate familiarity of day-to-day business operations, responsibility for assessing business risks and implementing organizational controls, authority to adjust operations, influence over the organization's culture and ethical atmosphere, and control over the organization's resources (e.g., people and systems). Auditors, conversely, are trained in risk identification and assessment, and have expertise in evaluating internal controls, which is critical to the fraud risk assessment process. Consequently, the fraud risk assessment is most effective when management and auditors share ownership of the process and accountability for its success.

The Right Sponsor

Having the right sponsor for a fraud risk assessment is extremely important in ensuring its success and effectiveness. The sponsor must be senior enough in the organization to command the respect of the employees and elicit full cooperation in the process. The sponsor also must be someone who is committed to learning the truth about where the company's fraud vulnerabilities are; he must be a truth seeker—not someone who is prone to rationalization or denial. In the ideal situation, the sponsor would be an independent board director or audit committee member; however, a chief executive officer or other internal senior leader can be equally effective.

Organizational culture plays a key role in influencing the entity's vulnerability to fraud. If the company's culture is shaped by a strong and domineering leader, obtaining candid participation from participants might be difficult with that leader as sponsor of the fraud risk assessment. Ponder the effectiveness of a fraud risk assessment of Tyco International that is sponsored by Dennis Kozlowski or an assessment of Enron sponsored by Kenneth Lay or Jeffrey Skilling; either would be worthless.

The right sponsor is someone who is willing to hear the good, the bad, and the ugly. For example, assume that a fraud risk assessment reveals that one of the greatest fraud risks facing the organization is bribery/corruption based on the close relationship between one of the key business leaders and the company's business partners. For the fraud risk assessment to be effective, the sponsor needs to be independent and open in his evaluation of the situation and, most importantly, appropriate in his response to the identified risks.

Independence and Objectivity of the People Leading and Conducting the Work

A good fraud risk assessment can be effectively conducted either by people inside the organization or using external resources. Either way, it is critical that the people leading and conducting the fraud risk assessment remain independent and objective throughout the assessment process. Additionally, they must be perceived as independent and objective by others.

Those leading and performing the work should be mindful of any personal biases they may have regarding the organization and the people within it and should take steps to reduce or eliminate all biases that may affect the fraud risk assessment process. For example, if an employee on the fraud risk assessment team had a bad past experience with someone in the accounts payable department, he might allow that experience to affect his evaluation of the fraud risks related to that area of the business. To preclude this possibility, someone else should perform the fraud risk assessment work related to the accounts payable department's activities.

Cultural neutrality is an important aspect of independence and objectivity when leading or conducting a fraud risk assessment. Some organizations have very strong corporate cultures that can play a big role in influencing the way the people inside the organization think about fraud risk. If people within the organization are leading and conducting the fraud risk assessment, they must be able to step outside the corporate culture to assess and evaluate the presence and significance of fraud risks in the business.

A Good Working Knowledge of the Business

The individuals leading and conducting the fraud risk assessment need to have a good working knowledge of the business. Every organization is unique; even companies that appear similar have characteristics that differentiate them—and their fraud risks—from their competitors. Some of those differences can be obvious, whereas others are more subtle.

To ensure a good working knowledge of the business, the fraud risk assessor must know, beyond a superficial level, what the business does and how it operates. He must also have an understanding of what makes the organization both similar to and different from other companies in related lines of business.

Obtaining information about broad industry fraud risks from external sources can be helpful. Such sources include industry news; criminal, civil, and regulatory complaints and settlements; and professional organizations, such as the Institute of Internal Auditors, the American Institute of Certified Public Accountants, and the Association of Certified Fraud Examiners.

Access to People at All Levels of the Organization

It is often said that perception is reality. In other words, how an individual perceives a situation is his reality of that situation. In an organization, it is important that the perceptions of people at all levels are included in the fraud risk assessment process.

Leaders of a business or function often have very different perspectives from their subordinates on how something is perceived or executed, but this does not mean that one perspective is right and the other is wrong. What it does mean is that expectations and perceptions within the organization are not aligned, which could increase fraud risk.

Engendered Trust

If management and employees do not trust the people leading and conducting the fraud risk assessment, they will not be open and honest about the realities of the business, its culture, and its vulnerability to fraud. Trust is not something that can be granted by authority; it must be earned through words and actions. As they engage employees throughout the business, those leading and conducting the fraud risk assessment should deliberately and carefully plan the initial contact with an effort to develop a rapport and gain trust.

The Ability to Think the Unthinkable

Most honest people are not naturally inclined to think like a fraudster. In fact, many large-scale frauds that have occurred would have been deemed unthinkable by people closest to the events. A good fraud risk assessment has to allow for the people leading and conducting the assessment to be expansive in their consideration and evaluation of fraud risk. Thoughts of "it couldn't happen here" should not be allowed to moderate the evaluation of fraud risk.

A Plan to Keep It Alive and Relevant

The fraud risk assessment should not be treated as a one-time exercise that is executed, reported on, and then put on a shelf to collect dust. The organization should strive to keep the process alive and relevant through ongoing dialogue, active management of action plans, and development of procedures to ensure that the assessment is maintained on a current basis.

CONSIDERATIONS FOR DEVELOPING AN EFFECTIVE FRAUD RISK ASSESSMENT

A fraud risk assessment is only effective if the organization embraces it and uses the results to monitor, change, or influence the factors that put the company at risk for fraud. To this end, several matters should be considered during the development of the fraud risk assessment.

Packaging It Right

People do not easily relate to or embrace things they don't understand. Every organization has its own vocabulary and preferred methods of communication. The announcement and execution of the fraud risk assessment, including the reporting of the results, will only be effective if completed in the language of the business. For example:

- In a creative organization where decisions are made based on qualitative assessments and instinct, and where the majority of communication is visual, a quantitative approach to assessing fraud risk—one that is driven by numbers and calculations—would most likely be rejected
- In an organization where the business is built and run on quantitative decision-making models, a qualitative approach with no quantitative components would most likely be rejected

The assessor must remain mindful of the language used throughout the fraud risk assessment. Specifically, he should stay away from technical language that won't resonate with the intended audience. For example, many people might not easily relate to or understand the term *cash larceny*. If cash larceny is one of the organization's greatest fraud risks, it might be more effective to explain the concept in layman's terms, describing the risk as "theft of cash."

One Size Does Not Fit All

Do not try to fit a square peg into a round hole; what works in one organization won't necessarily transfer smoothly to another. Recognizing the nuances of the business and tailoring the approach and execution to the specific organization contributes to the success of the fraud risk assessment. While a generic framework or toolset can be a valuable starting point for the development of the fraud risk assessment, it must be adapted to fit the business model, culture, and language of the organization.

Keeping It Simple

The more complicated the fraud risk assessment is, the harder it will be to execute it and use it to drive action. Whether the assessor uses a generic assessment framework or develops one specifically for the organization, he should focus the effort and time on evaluating the areas that are most likely to have fraud risk.

PREPARING THE COMPANY FOR THE FRAUD RISK ASSESSMENT

Properly preparing the company for the fraud risk assessment is critical to the assessment's success. The culture of the organization should influence the approach used in the fraud risk assessment preparation.

Assembling the Right Team to Lead and Conduct the Fraud Risk Assessment

The organization should build a fraud risk assessment team consisting of individuals with diverse knowledge, skills, and perspectives to lead and conduct the assessment. The size of the team will depend on the size of the organization and the methods used to conduct the assessment. The team should have individuals who are credible and who have experience in gathering and eliciting information.

The team members can include internal and external resources such as:

- Accounting and finance personnel who are familiar with the financial reporting processes and internal controls
- Nonfinancial business unit and operations personnel who have knowledge of day-to-day operations, customer and vendor interactions, and issues within the industry
- Risk management personnel who can ensure that the fraud risk assessment process integrates with the organization's enterprise risk management program
- The general counsel or other members of the legal department
- Members of any ethics or compliance functions within the organization
- Internal auditors

- External consultants with fraud and risk expertise
- Any business leader with direct accountability for the effectiveness of the organization's fraud risk management efforts

Determining the Best Techniques to Use in Conducting the Fraud Risk Assessment

There are many ways to gather information during a fraud risk assessment. Picking a method or combination of methods that is culturally right for the organization will help ensure its success. The assessment team should also consider the best ways to gather candid information from people throughout all levels of the organization, starting by understanding what techniques are commonly and effectively used throughout the organization.

Interviews Interviews can be an effective way to conduct a candid one-on-one conversation, but their usefulness depends on how willing people in the organization are to be open and honest in a direct dialogue with the interviewer. The assessor must consider whether interviews are commonly and effectively used in the organization to gather and elicit information. He should also speak with individuals who have previously conducted interviews with employees to glean lessons learned. For each potential interviewee, the assessor should gauge the willingness of the interviewee to be open and honest—some people, for example, may be good interview candidates, whereas others may need to be engaged through a different approach.

Focus Groups Focus groups enable the assessor to observe the interactions of employees as they discuss a question or issue. Some topics may lend themselves to being discussed in an open forum in which people feel comfortable among their colleagues. Additionally, when discussing tough or thorny issues in a group, an anonymous, real-time voting tool can be an effective way of opening up a dialogue among the participants.

The success of a focus group is highly dependent on the skill of the facilitator. If focus groups are used as part of the fraud risk assessment, they should be led by an experienced facilitator with whom the group can relate, and whom they trust. Getting a group to open up and talk honestly can be very difficult. An experienced facilitator can read the group and use targeted techniques (for example, group icebreakers) to make the session a success.

Surveys Surveys can be anonymous or directly attributable to individuals. Sometimes people share more openly when they feel protected behind a computer or paper questionnaire. In an organization where the culture is not one in which people open up and talk freely, an anonymous survey can be an effective way to get feedback. However, employees can be skeptical about the true anonymity of a survey, especially in organizations that use surveys to solicit feedback anonymously but send follow-up e-mails to individual delinquent respondents. If the assessor determines that an anonymous survey is an appropriate technique to use in the fraud risk assessment, he should clearly and explicitly explain to employees how anonymity will be maintained.

Anonymous Feedback Mechanisms In some organizations, anonymous suggestion boxes or similar mechanisms are used to encourage and solicit frequent employee feedback. In these companies, information pertaining to the fraud risk assessment can be requested in the same way. Additionally, use of an anonymous feedback mechanism can be effective in an environment where people are less likely to be open and honest through other methods and techniques.

One approach to effectively using the anonymous feedback technique involves establishing a question of the day that is prominently displayed above a collection box. An example of such a question is: "If you thought fraud were occurring in the company, would you come forward? Why or why not?" Another approach involves using a table lineup of five to ten opaque boxes, each with a statement posted above it. Employees are provided with poker chips in two different colors and told that one color indicates "I agree" and the other indicates "I disagree." Employees are then encouraged to respond to each statement by putting a corresponding chip in each box to indicate their response.

Obtaining the Sponsor's Agreement on the Work to Be Performed

Before the fraud risk assessment procedures begin, the sponsor and the assessment team need to agree on:

- The scope of work that will be performed
- The methods that will be used (e.g., surveys, interviews, focus groups, or anonymous feedback mechanisms)
- The individuals who will participate in the chosen methods
- The content of the chosen methods
- The form of output for the assessment

Educating the Organization and Openly Promoting the Process

The fraud risk assessment process should be visible and communicated throughout the business. Employees will be more inclined to participate in the process if they understand its purpose and the expected outcomes.

Sponsors should be strongly encouraged to openly promote the process. The more personalized the communication from the sponsor, the more effective it will be in encouraging employees to participate. Whether through a video, town hall meeting, or companywide e-mail, the communication should be aimed at eliminating any reluctance employees have about participating in the fraud risk assessment process.

EXECUTING THE FRAUD RISK ASSESSMENT

Fraud risk assessments can be executed in many ways. To ensure the assessment's success, the approach should be structured, rational, and tailored to the organization. When conducting a fraud risk assessment, it is helpful to use a framework for performing, evaluating, and reporting the results of the work. Fraud risk can be analyzed and reported both qualitatively and quantitatively using a consistent framework.

The sample framework discussed below is based on information contained in *Managing the Business Risk of Fraud: A Practical Guide*, sponsored by the Institute of Internal Auditors, the American Institute of Certified Public Accountants, and the Association of Certified Fraud Examiners.[1] This framework illustrates a comprehensive approach to applying the elements of a fraud risk assessment.

	Like-lihood	Signifi-cance	People and/or Departments	Existing Antifraud Controls	Controls' Effectiveness Assessment	Residual Risks	Fraud Risk Response
Financial Reporting							
Misappropriation of Assets							
Corruption							
Other Risks							

EXHIBIT 13-1   Sample Fraud Risk Assessment Framework

Using this framework, the fraud risk assessment team incorporates the following fraud risk assessment approach:

1. Identify potential inherent fraud risks
2. Assess the likelihood of occurrence of the identified fraud risks
3. Assess the significance to the organization of the fraud risks
4. Evaluate which people and departments are most likely to commit fraud and identify the methods they are likely to use
5. Identify and map existing preventive and detective controls to the relevant fraud risks
6. Evaluate whether the identified controls are operating effectively and efficiently
7. Identify and evaluate residual fraud risks resulting from ineffective or nonexistent controls

The table in Exhibit 13-1 provides a visual representation of the steps involved in this framework and can be filled in as the fraud risk assessment is performed.[2]

Identifying Potential Inherent Fraud Risks

One of the first steps in a fraud risk assessment involves identifying potential fraud risks inherent to the organization. The fraud risk assessment team should brainstorm to identify the fraud risks that could apply to the organization. Brainstorming should include discussions regarding the following factors.

Incentives, Pressures, and Opportunities to Commit Fraud   When assessing the potential incentives, pressures, and opportunities to commit fraud, the fraud risk assessment team should evaluate:

- Opportunities to commit fraud that arise from a person's position (i.e., given his responsibilities and authority)

- Incentive programs and how they may affect employees' behavior when conducting business or applying professional judgment
- Pressures on individuals to achieve performance or other targets and how such pressures might influence employees' behavior
- Opportunities to commit fraud that arise from weak internal controls, such as a lack of segregation of duties
- Highly complex business transactions and how they might be used to conceal fraudulent acts
- Opportunities for collusion (intrinsic to schemes such as bribery or kickbacks)

Risk of Management's Override of Controls   When considering the potential for management's override of controls, the fraud risk assessment team should keep in mind that:

- Management within the organization generally knows the controls and standard operating procedures that are in place to prevent fraud
- Individuals who are intent on committing fraud might use their knowledge of the organization's controls to do so in a manner that will conceal their actions

Population of Fraud Risks   The fraud risk identification process requires an understanding of the universe of fraud risks and the subset of risks that apply to a particular organization. It includes gathering information about the business itself, including its business processes, industry, and operating environment, as well as all associated potential fraud risks. Such information can be obtained from external sources—such as industry news outlets; criminal, civil, and regulatory complaints and settlements; and professional organizations and associations—and from internal sources by interviewing and brainstorming with personnel, reviewing complaints on the whistleblower hotline, and performing analytical procedures.

Fraud risks can be classified according to the three major categories of occupational fraud: fraudulent financial reporting, asset misappropriation, and corruption.

Fraudulent Financial Reporting   Potential fraudulent financial reporting risks include:

- Inappropriately reported revenues, expenses, or both
- Inappropriately reflected balance sheet amounts, including reserves
- Inappropriately improved or masked disclosures
- Concealed misappropriation of assets
- Concealed unauthorized receipts, expenditures, or both
- Concealed unauthorized acquisition, use, or disposition of assets

Asset Misappropriations   Potential asset misappropriation risks include misappropriation of:

- Tangible assets
- Intangible assets
- Proprietary business opportunities

Corruption   Potential corruption risks include:

- Payment of bribes or gratuities to companies, private individuals, or public officials
- Receipt of bribes, kickbacks, or gratuities
- Aiding and abetting of fraud by outside parties, such as customers or vendors

Certain other types of risks that can affect or be affected by each of the major areas of fraud risks include regulatory and legal misconduct, reputation risk, and risk to information technology.

Regulatory and Legal Misconduct   Regulatory and legal misconduct includes a wide range of risks, such as conflicts of interest, insider trading, theft of competitor trade secrets, anticompetitive practices, environmental violations, and trade and customs regulations in areas of import and export. Depending on the particular organization and the nature of its business, some or all of these risks may be applicable and should be considered in the fraud risk assessment process.

Reputation Risk   Reputation risk must be considered as part of the organization's risk assessment process because fraudulent acts can damage an organization's reputation with customers, suppliers, capital markets, and others. For example, fraud leading to a financial restatement can damage an organization's reputation in capital markets, which can increase the organization's cost of borrowing and depress its market capitalization.

Risk to Information Technology   Information technology (IT) is a critical component of fraud risk assessment. Organizations rely on IT to conduct business, communicate, and process financial information. A poorly designed or inadequately controlled IT environment can expose an organization to threats to data integrity, threats from malicious security system crackers, and theft of financial and sensitive business information. Whether in the form of hacking, economic espionage, Web defacement, sabotage of data, viruses, or unauthorized access to data, IT fraud risks can result in significant financial and information losses.

Assessing the Likelihood of Occurrence of the Identified Fraud Risks

Assessing the likelihood of each potential fraud risk is a subjective process that enables the organization to manage its fraud risks and apply preventive and detective controls rationally. The fraud risk assessment team should first consider fraud risks to the organization on an inherent basis, without consideration of known controls. By approaching the assessment in this manner, the team will be better able to consider all relevant fraud risks and then evaluate and design controls to address those risks.

The likelihood of occurrence of each fraud risk can be classified as *remote, reasonably possible*, or *probable*. The fraud risk assessment team should consider the following in assessing the likelihood of occurrence of each fraud risk:

- Past instances of the particular fraud at the organization
- Prevalence of the fraud risk in the organization's industry
- Internal control environment of the organization
- Resources available to address fraud
- Support of fraud prevention efforts by management

- Ethical standards of the organization
- Number of individual transactions involved
- Complexity of the fraud risk
- Number of people involved in reviewing or approving a relevant process
- Unexplained losses
- Complaints by customers or vendors
- Information from fraud surveys such as the ACFE's *Report to the Nations on Occupational Fraud & Abuse*

Assessing the Significance to the Organization of the Fraud Risks

The fraud risk assessment team should consider qualitative and quantitative factors when assessing the significance of identified fraud risks to the organization. For example, a particular fraud risk that might only pose an immaterial direct financial risk to the organization but that could greatly impact its reputation would be deemed a significant risk to the organization.

The significance of each potential fraud can be classified as *immaterial, significant,* or *material*. In assessing the significance of each fraud risk, the fraud risk assessment team should consider the following factors:

- Financial statement and monetary significance
- Financial condition of the organization
- Value of the threatened assets
- Criticality of the threatened assets to the organization
- Revenue generated by the threatened assets
- Significance to the organization's operations, brand value, and reputation
- Criminal, civil, and regulatory liabilities

Evaluating Which People and Departments Are Most Likely to Commit Fraud, and Identifying the Methods They Are Likely to Use

In identifying potential fraud risks, the risk assessment team will have evaluated the incentives and pressures on individuals and departments to commit fraud. The team should use the information gained in that process to identify the individuals and departments most likely to commit fraud and the methods they are likely to use. This knowledge will assist the organization in tailoring its fraud risk response, including establishing appropriate segregation of duties, proper review and approval chains of authority, and proactive fraud auditing procedures.

Identifying and Mapping Existing Preventive and Detective Controls to the Relevant Fraud Risks

After identifying and assessing fraud risks for likelihood of occurrence and for significance, the fraud risk assessment team should identify and map existing preventive and detective controls to the relevant fraud risks.

Preventive Controls   Preventive controls, which are intended to prevent fraud before it occurs, include:

- Bringing awareness to personnel throughout the organization of the fraud risk management program in place
- Performing background checks on employees
- Hiring competent personnel and providing them with antifraud training
- Conducting exit interviews
- Implementing policies and procedures
- Segregating duties
- Ensuring proper alignment between an individual's authority and his level of responsibility
- Reviewing third-party and related-party transactions

Detective Controls   Detective controls, which are intended to detect fraud if it does occur, include:

- Establishing and marketing the presence of a confidential reporting system, such as a whistleblower hotline
- Implementing proactive controls for the fraud detection process, such as reconciliations, independent reviews, physical inspections/counts, analysis, and audits
- Implementing proactive fraud detection procedures, such as data analysis and continuous auditing techniques
- Performing surprise audits

Evaluating Whether the Identified Controls Are Operating Effectively and Efficiently

The fraud risk assessment team must ensure that there are adequate controls in place, that the controls are mitigating fraud risk as intended, and that the benefit of the controls exceeds the cost. Such an assessment requires:

- Review of the accounting policies and procedures in place
- Consideration of the risk of management's override of controls
- Interviews with management and employees
- Observation of control activities
- Sample testing of controls compliance
- Review of previous audit reports
- Review of previous reports on fraud incidents, shrinkage, and unexplained shortages

Identifying and Evaluating Residual Fraud Risks Resulting from Ineffective or Nonexistent Controls

Consideration of the internal control structure might reveal certain residual fraud risks, including management's override of established controls that have not been adequately mitigated due to:

- Lack of appropriate prevention and detection controls
- Noncompliance with established prevention and control measures

These residual fraud risks should be evaluated by the fraud risk assessment team in the development of the fraud risk response for likelihood and significance of occurrence.

ADDRESSING THE IDENTIFIED FRAUD RISKS

Establishing an Acceptable Level of Risk

Because it is neither practical nor cost-effective for an organization to eliminate all fraud risk, management must establish an acceptable level of fraud risk based on the business objectives and risk tolerance of the organization. In responding to fraud risks identified during the fraud risk assessment, management must determine how the fraud risks affect business objectives and, using cost/benefit analysis, decide where to best allocate resources for fraud prevention and detection.

Responding to Residual Fraud Risks

Regardless of the framework used to conduct the fraud risk assessment, management will need to address the identified risks to ensure that the organization is within its established tolerance level for fraud risk. Larry Cook, CFE, principal author of the ACFE Fraud Risk Assessment Tool (located in Appendix C), suggests that management can use one, or a combination, of the following approaches to respond to the organization's residual fraud risks:

- Avoid the risk
- Transfer the risk
- Mitigate the risk
- Assume the risk[3]

Avoid the Risk   Management may decide to avoid the risk by eliminating an asset or exiting an activity if the control measures required to protect the organization against an identified threat are too expensive. For example, a multinational conglomerate might choose not to conduct business in countries with a very poor ranking on the Transparency International Corruption Perception Index. This approach requires the fraud risk assessment team to complete a cost-benefit analysis of the value of the asset or activity to the organization compared to the cost of implementing measures to protect the asset or activity.

Transfer the Risk   Management may transfer some or all of the risk by purchasing fidelity insurance or a fidelity bond. For example, a financial institution, as part of its vendor management program, might require its outside systems analysts to have in place third-party fidelity coverage before allowing them to do work for the financial institution. The cost to the organization is the premium paid for the insurance or bond. The covered risk of loss is then transferred to the insurance company.

Mitigate the Risk Management can mitigate the risk by implementing appropriate countermeasures, such as prevention and detection controls. An example of this is an accounting system in which managers responsible for authorizing or reviewing transactions are provided with read-only access, thus restricting them from entering data or reconciling accounts. The fraud risk assessment team should evaluate each countermeasure to determine whether it is cost-effective and reasonable given the probability of occurrence and impact of loss.

Assume the Risk Management may choose to assume the risk if it determines that the probability of occurrence and impact of loss are low. Management may decide that it is more cost-effective to assume the risk than it is to eliminate the asset or exit the activity, buy insurance to transfer the risk, or implement countermeasures to mitigate the risk.

Combination Approach Management may also elect a combination of these approaches. For example, if the probability of occurrence and impact of loss are high, management may decide to transfer part of the risk through the purchase of insurance, as well as to implement preventive and detective controls to mitigate the risk.

REPORTING THE RESULTS OF THE FRAUD RISK ASSESSMENT

The success of the fraud risk assessment process hinges on how effectively the results are reported and what the organization then does with those results. A poorly communicated report can undermine the entire process and bring all established momentum to a halt. The report should be delivered in the style most suited to the language of the business.

Considerations When Reporting the Assessment Results

To maximize the effectiveness of the fraud risk assessment process, the team should remember several key points when developing the report of the results.

Report Objective—Not Subjective—Results Much instinct and judgment goes into performing the fraud risk assessment. When reporting the results of the assessment, the team must stick to the facts and keep all opinions and biases out of the report. A report that is peppered with the assessment team's subjective perspective will dilute, and potentially undermine, the results of the work.

Keep It Simple The assessment results should be reported in a way that is easy to understand and that resonates with management. The reader of the report should be able to quickly view and comprehend the results. A simple one-page visual can sometimes have the greatest effect.

Focus on What Really Matters Less is often more when it comes to reporting the results of the fraud risk assessment. The team should take care not to turn the report into a laundry list of things that management will have to sort through and prioritize. Instead, the report should be presented in a way that focuses on what really matters, clearly highlighting those points that are most important and that will make the most impact on the organization's fraud risk management efforts.

Identify Actions That Are Clear and Measurable The report should include key recommendations for action that are clear and measurable and that will decrease fraud risks. The actions should be presented in a way that makes apparent exactly what needs to be done. The report should not include recommendations that are vague or that wouldn't reduce the risk of fraud. Additionally, management and those affected by the suggested actions should have vetted and agreed to the recommendations.

MAKING AN IMPACT WITH THE FRAUD RISK ASSESSMENT

To make the most of the fraud risk assessment process, management should not see the final report as the end of the process. The true value of a fraud risk assessment lies in how effectively and extensively management uses the results in its ongoing antifraud efforts.

Beginning a Dialogue across the Company

The results of the initial fraud risk assessment can be used to begin a dialogue across the company that promotes awareness, education, and action planning aimed at reducing the risk of fraud. Engaging in an active dialogue is an effective way to further establish boundaries of acceptable and unacceptable behavior. Open communication about fraud risks also increases the chance that employees will come forward if they believe they have witnessed potential fraud.

Looking for Fraud in High-Risk Areas

An internal audit or investigative team within the organization can use the results of the fraud risk assessment to identify high-risk processes or activities and unusual transactions that might indicate fraud. This practice can also provide some reassurance if the subsequent search for fraud reveals that, despite the assessed risk, fraud does not appear to be occurring at that point in time. Management should remember, however, that just because there is no evidence that fraud is occurring in the present, the risk that it could occur is not eliminated.

Holding Responsible Parties Accountable for Progress

It is often said that what gets measured gets done. To effectively reduce identified fraud risk, management must hold employees accountable for driving results. The organization should track and measure progress against agreed-upon action plans. Publicly celebrating successes can be as effective, or even more effective, at encouraging the right behaviors as at providing negative consequences for failing to deliver results.

Keeping the Assessment Alive and Relevant

Because there are so many factors that can affect an organization's vulnerability to fraud risk, management must ensure that the fraud risk assessment stays current and relevant. Someone within the organization should be assigned ownership of the fraud risk assessment process. That person or team should build processes to ensure that all changes in the business model, company operating environment, and personnel are considered relative to their impact on the company's risk of fraud.

THE FRAUD RISK ASSESSMENT AND THE AUDIT PROCESS

The fraud risk assessment should play a significant role in informing and influencing the audit process. Although auditors should always be on guard for indicators of fraud risk, the results of the fraud risk assessment can help them design audit programs and procedures in a way that enables them to look for fraud in known areas of high risk.

In the course of their work, auditors should validate that the organization is appropriately managing the moderate to high fraud risks identified in the fraud risk assessment by:

- Identifying and mapping the existing preventive and detective controls that pertain to the moderate to high fraud risks identified in the fraud risk assessment
- Designing and performing tests to evaluate whether the identified controls are operating effectively and efficiently
- Identifying within the moderate to high fraud risk areas whether there is a moderate to high risk of management override of internal controls
- Developing and delivering reports that incorporate the results of their validation and testing of the fraud risk controls

The template in Exhibit 13-2 can be used by auditors to evaluate how effectively the moderate to high fraud risks are being managed by the business:

Identified Fraud Risks	Existing Preventive Controls	Existing Detective Controls	Are Controls Effective and Efficient?	Is There a Risk of Management Override?	Is the Fraud Risk Effectively Managed?

EXHIBIT 13-2   Template for Evaluating Management of Fraud Risks

Fraud Risk Assessment Tool

The ACFE's Fraud Risk Assessment Tool, located in Appendix C, can be used to identify an organization's vulnerabilities to fraud, either during the audit process or as a standalone assessment. The Fraud Risk Assessment Tool consists of fifteen modules, each containing a series of questions designed to help organizations focus on specific areas of risk.

SUMMARY

Stakeholders expect management to be prudent when it comes to protecting a business. Since no company is immune to fraud risk, all companies' antifraud programs should include ongoing, continuous fraud risk assessments to proactively identify and address vulnerabilities to internal and external fraud. The fraud risk assessment process begins with the identification and prioritization of fraud risks, but evolves as the results of that identification and prioritization drive education, communication, organizational alignment, and action around effectively managing fraud risk and identifying new fraud risks as they emerge.

A good fraud risk assessment is dependent upon several factors, including the right sponsor, collaboration between management and auditors, the independence and objectivity of those leading and conducting the work, and the assessors' solid working knowledge of the business. Customization, simplicity, and proper packaging are also critical to the effectiveness of the fraud risk assessment. In order to properly prepare for a fraud risk assessment, management must assemble the right team to lead and conduct the assessment, determine the best techniques to use in conducting the assessment, obtain the sponsor's agreement on the work to be performed, educate the employees, and openly promote the process.

A company may find it useful to incorporate its fraud risk assessment strategy into a framework—a helpful tool for performing, evaluating, and reporting the results of the fraud risk assessment. Using one sample framework, the fraud risk assessment team begins with a list of identified fraud risks, which are assessed for relative likelihood and significance of occurrence. Next, the risks are mapped to people and departments impacted and to relevant controls. Subsequently, the relevant controls are evaluated for design effectiveness and are tested to validate their operating effectiveness. Lastly, residual risks are identified and a fraud risk response is developed to address them. In responding to a residual fraud risk, management may choose to avoid, transfer, mitigate, or assume the risk, or some combination thereof. Management's response will depend on factors that include the likelihood and significance of the risk and the cost-effectiveness of the approach.

The success of the fraud risk assessment hinges on management's effectiveness in reporting the results of the assessment and using them in its ongoing antifraud efforts. Management's report should be objective, simple, and focused on important areas, and should include key recommendations for action. By sharing the results of the assessment with auditors, management can assist the auditors in designing audit programs and procedures that detect fraud in high-risk areas. To ensure continued success in reducing fraud risk, management should use the results of the assessment to promote open communication throughout the company about fraud risk, identify high-risk areas, and hold responsible parties accountable for progress.

ESSENTIAL TERMS

Fraud risk   The vulnerability that an organization has to those capable of overcoming the three elements of the fraud triangle: motive, opportunity, and rationalization.

Preventive controls   Manual or automated processes designed to stop an undesirable event from occurring.

Detective controls   Manual or automated processes designed to identify an undesirable event that has already occurred.

Fraud risk assessment   A process aimed at proactively identifying and addressing an organization's vulnerabilities to internal and external fraud.

Fraud risk assessment framework   A tool used in performing, evaluating, and reporting the results of a fraud risk assessment that enables fraud risk to be analyzed and reported both qualitatively and quantitatively.

Inherent fraud risks   Fraud risks that a company faces in the absence of any attempts—such as internal controls—to mitigate them.

Residual fraud risks   Fraud risks that remain after attempts to mitigate them, usually as the result of ineffective or nonexistent controls.

REVIEW QUESTIONS

13-1 (Learning objective 13-1) What are four factors that influence the level of fraud risk faced by an organization?

13-2 (Learning objective 13-2) What is the difference between preventive controls and detective controls?

13-3 (Learning objective 13-3) What is the objective of a fraud risk assessment?

13-4 (Learning objective 13-4) What can an effective fraud risk assessment help management to accomplish?

13-5 (Learning objective 13-5) What characteristics constitute a good fraud risk assessment?

13-6 (Learning objective 13-6) What are three considerations for developing an effective fraud risk assessment?

13-7 (Learning objective 13-7) What can management do to prepare a company for a fraud risk assessment?

13-8 (Learning objective 13-8) What steps are involved in conducting a fraud risk assessment using the sample framework discussed in the chapter?

13-9 (Learning objective 13-9) Describe four approaches for responding to an organization's residual fraud risks.

13-10 (Learning objective 13-10) What are four important considerations to keep in mind when reporting the fraud risk assessment results?

13-11 (Learning objective 13-11) What actions can management take to make the most impact with the fraud risk assessment?

13-12 (Learning objective 13-12) How can a fraud risk assessment inform and influence the audit process?

DISCUSSION ISSUES

13-1 (Learning objective 13-1) How is fraud risk influenced by a company's internal control? How is fraud risk influenced by a company's ethics, values, and expectations?

13-2 (Learning objective 13-6) Why is it important that management and auditors collaborate on a fraud risk assessment?

13-3 (Learning objective 13-6) What qualities and characteristics should be considered when choosing a sponsor for a fraud risk assessment?

13-4 (Learning objective 13-6) Green is an internal auditor and the lead on the company's fraud risk assessment. In the past, he and Blue, an accounts receivable clerk, have had several heated disagreements over accounting procedures. What risk would Green be taking by having Blue perform the fraud risk assessment work related to the accounts receivable department's activities? How might this risk be best addressed?

13-5 (Learning objective 13-7) Who should be included on a fraud risk assessment team?

13-6 (Learning objective 13-8) What topics should be discussed in indentifying fraud risks that could apply to the organization?

13-7 (Learning objective 13-8) What risks related to each of the three primary categories of fraud should the fraud risk assessment team consider?

13-8 (Learning objective 13-8) What risks should the fraud risk assessment team consider in addition to the specific risks related to each of the three primary categories of fraud?

13-9 (Learning objective 13-9) When might an organization choose to avoid a risk rather than assuming, transferring, or mitigating it?

ENDNOTES

1. Institute of Internal Auditors, the American Institute of Certified Public Accountants, and the Association of Certified Fraud Examiners, *Managing the Business Risk of Fraud: A Practical Guide*.
2. Institute of Internal Auditors, the American Institute of Certified Public Accountants, and the Association of Certified Fraud Examiners, pg. 21.
3. Larry E. Cook, "Risky Business: Conducting the Internal Fraud Risk Assessment," *Fraud Magazine*, March/April 2005, Austin, TX: ACFE.

CHAPTER 14

CONDUCTING INVESTIGATIONS AND WRITING REPORTS

LEARNING OBJECTIVES

14-1 Understand the circumstances that may necessitate an internal investigation

14-2 Identify who should be part of a fraud examination team

14-3 Define evidence

14-4 Be familiar with several evidence-gathering techniques

14-5 Understand the considerations and concerns related to preserving documentary evidence

14-6 Understand the importance of and methods for organizing documentary evidence

14-7 Identify several sources of evidence and the types of information each can provide

14-8 Be familiar with the standard format and requirements for a professional investigation report

WHEN IS AN INVESTIGATION NECESSARY?

The need for an internal investigation can arise in a number of circumstances. Obviously, such an examination may be necessary to determine the source of losses caused by occupational fraud. A thorough investigation in these circumstances can help a company reduce its losses, identify the perpetrator, gather evidence for a criminal prosecution or civil trial, and recapture some or all of the amount stolen. It can also shed light on weaknesses in the company's control structure, thereby helping to shore up the company's internal defenses against future employee misconduct.

In addition to preventing losses resulting from fraud, an organization or its officers may have legal duties to investigate alleged misconduct. Certain federal statutes, such as the Foreign Corrupt Practices Act, are specifically aimed at detecting wrongful conduct and require that companies report specific instances of misconduct. Obviously, to make an accurate report of misconduct, the company will need to conduct an investigation into alleged wrongdoing. Regulatory agencies such as the Securities and Exchange Commission require accurate financial reporting by the companies they oversee, and they have the power to impose penalties for reports that are inaccurate or that omit facts that could affect the accuracy of the reported information. An investigation can ensure that all relevant facts are known and reported.

Officers and directors of companies are also bound by duties of loyalty and reasonable care in overseeing the operations of their companies. This means they must act in the best interests of the company and take reasonable steps to prevent harm that the company might suffer as a result of employee misconduct. The failure to investigate reliable allegations of misconduct can amount to a violation of these duties, thereby subjecting the director or officer to civil liability for any damages that the company incurs as a result of the failure to investigate.

In many situations, companies must also conduct an internal investigation before they can dismiss an employee who has committed fraud or otherwise violated company rules and policies. A thoroughly documented investigation will help insulate the company from charges that it discriminated against the employee or otherwise wrongfully terminated him.

Additionally, when an organization might be liable for the conduct of one of its employees, an internal investigation can help mitigate the company's liability by cutting off the wrongful conduct before it is allowed to grow, and by demonstrating that the company has an effective program to detect and prevent criminal misconduct by its employees—a factor that provides for the diminishment of fines under the Organizational Sentencing Guidelines (discussed in more detail in Chapter 16).

A company's managers may find that the best way to fulfill these legal duties and requirements is to conduct an internal investigation of known or suspected misconduct. Put another way, by failing to adequately investigate an allegation of employee fraud, a company may be failing to comply with the law. However, the decision to investigate is often based on very specific facts, and whether an investigation is compelled by some other legal duty or requirement is best determined by the company's lawyer or lawyers, in consultation with senior management and after considering all relevant facts.

PLANNING THE INVESTIGATION

Once the decision has been made to pursue an investigation, the focus shifts. The question is no longer *whether* the company should investigate the matter, but rather *how* the company can carry out the investigation in the most efficient, effective manner. The answer to this primary question requires answering two secondary questions:

- Who will be involved in the investigation?
- What will be the investigative strategy?

Selecting the Investigation Team

Internal investigations of fraudulent activity usually require a cooperative effort among different disciplines. Auditors, fraud examiners, line managers, attorneys, security personnel, and others are all frequently associated with fraud examinations. When choosing an investigation team, it is critical to identify those who can legitimately assist in the investigation and who have a genuine interest in the outcome of the examination. These persons should be included on the investigative team, and all other personnel should be segregated. There are a number of reasons for this. First, the more people involved in the investigation, the greater the chance that one of those persons may be somehow implicated in the fraud itself, or that one of those persons might leak confidential information about the investigation. Second, the persons involved in the investigation team may have to testify in legal proceedings, or the documents they generate may be subject to discovery, if the investigation leads to civil litigation or criminal prosecution. By limiting the number of investigators, the company can limit its exposure to discovery. In addition, any internal investigation, by its nature, can lead to harsh allegations against one or more suspects. This in turn can lead to charges of defamation and invasion of privacy, among others. These charges will be bolstered if it is found that the company spread information about the suspects to people who did not have a legitimate interest in that information. Therefore, by limiting the size of the investigation team, the company can limit its exposure to certain accusations.

None of this is meant to imply that the company should exclude otherwise necessary individuals from the fraud examination team simply out of fear of potentially harmful legal repercussions. On the contrary: the primary goal should be to resolve the allegations of fraud as thoroughly and efficiently as possible, and that requires that all necessary persons be involved in the effort. However, companies should guard against including extraneous personnel who add no real value to the team.

A typical investigation team might include the following types of professionals:

- Certified fraud examiners
- Legal counsel
- Internal auditors
- Security personnel
- IT and computer forensics experts
- Human resources personnel
- A management representative
- Outside consultants

Certified Fraud Examiners   A CFE is trained to conduct a complex fraud examination from inception to conclusion. Fraud examinations frequently present special problems because they require an understanding of complex financial transactions as well as traditional investigative techniques. Security personnel might be well versed in investigative techniques, such as interviewing witnesses and collecting and preserving evidence for trial, but they may not know how to spot a fraudulent transaction on the company's books. Auditors and accountants, on the other hand, may recognize a fraud scheme but may not have the training to conduct other aspects of an investigation. A CFE has training in all aspects of a fraud examination and therefore can serve as a valuable "hinge" to the investigation team, tying together the financial examination and more traditional investigative techniques.

Legal Counsel   It is crucial to have counsel involved in and, in most cases, "directing" the investigation, at least as far as the legal aspects are concerned. An internal investigation can be a veritable hornet's nest of legal questions: Should the company report the results of the investigation, and to whom? How can the company preserve the confidentiality of the investigation? How should the investigation be conducted so as to avoid lawsuits? What areas can the company search, and what information can be gathered without violating an employee's rights? When and how can an employee be fired for wrongful conduct? These are just some of the issues that investigators will face. The investigation team must have legal counsel on hand to sort out these questions, lest the company risk exposing itself to greater danger than the threat it is investigating. In addition, by having an attorney directing the investigation, the company may be able to protect the confidentiality of its investigation under the attorney-client privilege and the work product doctrine.

Internal Auditors Internal auditors are often used to review internal documentary evidence, evaluate tips or complaints, schedule losses, and provide assistance in technical areas of the company's operations. As was pointed out earlier, auditors are frequently the people who detect financial anomalies that lead to fraud investigations. They are expected to be able to identify fraud indicators and notify management if an investigation is required, and they are charged with assessing the probable level of complicity within the organization and with helping design procedural methods to identify the perpetrators as well as the extent of the fraud.

Security Personnel Security department investigators are often assigned the "field work" stage of the investigation, including interviewing outside witnesses and obtaining public records and other documents from third parties. It is crucial that their work be integrated with the financial side of the investigation so that the team does not devolve into two de facto investigations, one for "financials" and one for "field work." The process works best when all aspects of the investigation are coordinated and focused on the same goal.

IT and Computer Forensics Experts If fraud occurs, it is virtually certain that a computer will have been involved at some point. A computer may have been used to create false documents or alter legitimate documents, and the perpetrators may have used e-mail to communicate. The information technology (IT) department may need to be part of an investigation to safeguard data until it can be analyzed. IT personnel can also help identify what data is available and where it is located.

Computer forensics professionals should be used to capture and analyze digital data. Because electronic data can be easily altered, only trained professionals should be used to secure such data so that it can be analyzed more thoroughly without disturbing the original files.

Human Resources Personnel The human resources department should be consulted to ensure that the laws governing the rights of employees in the workplace are not violated. Such involvement will lessen the possibility of a wrongful discharge suit or other civil action by the employee. Advice from a human resources specialist might also be needed, although normally this person would not directly participate in the investigation.

Management Representative A representative of management or, in significant cases, the audit committee of the board of directors, should be kept informed of the progress of the investigation and should be available to lend necessary assistance. A sensitive internal investigation has virtually no hope of success without strong management support.

Outside Consultants In some cases, particularly those in which the suspect employee is especially powerful or popular, it might be useful to employ outside specialists who are relatively immune from company politics or threats of reprisals. Such experts might also have greater experience and investigative contacts than insiders. In addition, some investigatory procedures, such as forensic document analysis, require a high level of proficiency and expertise and should therefore only be undertaken by professionals specifically trained in that field.

DEVELOPING EVIDENCE

Once it has been determined that an investigation is warranted, the fraud examiner will need to take steps to prove or disprove the allegation. This involves undertaking procedures designed to collect and develop evidence. Evidence is anything perceivable by the five senses, including any proof, such as testimony of witnesses, records, documents, facts, data, or tangible objects, that is legally presented at trial to prove a contention and to induce a belief in the minds of a jury.

In addition to interviewing witnesses (discussed in Chapter 15) and using public records (discussed later in this chapter), investigating a case and obtaining evidence may involve the following:

- Covert operations
- Surveillance
- Informants
- "Dumpster-diving"
- Subpoenas
- Search warrants
- Voluntary consent

Covert Operations

Covert operations may be used to obtain evidence regarding the allegation. In some cases, they are the only way to prove a fraud, and thus must be carried out with the highest degree of planning and skill. In a covert operation, the investigator assumes the identity of another person—either real or fictitious—to gather evidence. The length of the operation might vary depending on the type of case and what evidence is needed. A written plan detailing specific objectives, time frames, and approvals should be developed prior to undertaking an undercover operation.

The courts have deemed covert operations as an acceptable method of developing information, provided there is sufficient probable cause that a crime has been committed. Entrapment issues, however, are a concern that must be dealt with in covert operations conducted by law enforcement. In private corporations, entrapment is generally not an issue, but consultation with legal counsel is strongly advised prior to conducting an undercover operation.

Pretexting Covert operations may occasionally involve *pretexting*, which is the practice of obtaining information through some sort of falsehood or deception. The practice is not always illegal, but it should be used with extreme caution. For example, if a fraud examiner is trying to locate a witness or a suspect, she might call the person's relative and pretend to be an old high school friend who is looking for a phone number. Although this type of pretexting generally is not illegal, it is illegal to obtain certain types of information, such as phone records and financial records, through any type of falsehood. Additionally, investigators should never impersonate a member of law enforcement, and they should never impersonate an actual person (particularly the individual being investigated). To do so may lead to charges of identity theft.

The Hewlett-Packard (HP) pretexting scandal provides an excellent example of what can happen when an internal investigation is not properly conducted. The HP scandal began in 2005, when officials at HP initiated a secret internal investigation to discover the source of board room leaks. To uncover the source, HP's chairman hired a team of investigators to procure the private phone records of HP's board members through pretexting. Through such efforts, the investigation uncovered the source, and at a board meeting in May of 2006, HP's chairman informed the board of the investigation scheme and identified the source of the leaks. After the board asked the offender to resign, a fellow HP director resigned in protest of the pretexting methods used during the investigation. Although HP's chairman was confident that pretexting was permissible, she could not foresee the disastrous fallout from the investigation. In 2006, the investigators hired by HP were charged with identity theft, conspiracy, and wire fraud, and investigations into the company's practices were undertaken by the California attorney general's office, the U.S. Attorney in San Francisco, the FBI, the FCC, and the Securities and Exchange Commission. Ultimately, HP paid $14.5 million to the state of California, and the chairman was removed from her position. In response to the scandal, the U.S. Congress passed the Telephone Records and Privacy Protection Act of 2006, which makes it an offense to obtain confidential phone records by pretending to be someone else.

Before engaging in any type of pretexting activity, investigators should consult with an attorney to determine whether the information sought is protected by state or federal law as well as whether the planned impersonation method is legally acceptable.

Surveillance

Surveillance, the secretive and continuous observance of a suspect's activities, is another investigative technique frequently used in developing evidence. A surveillance initiative may be undertaken to obtain probable cause for search warrants, develop other investigative leads, identify co-conspirators, gather intelligence, or locate people and things.

Informants

Informants are individuals who have specific knowledge of a criminal activity. They are used extensively by law enforcement, and can also be used successfully in private investigations if handled properly. Although informants can be extremely helpful in fraud investigations, the fraud examiner should be cautious in all interactions with informants. Because the reasons informants supply information vary—and can include revenge, financial reward, or clearing their consciences—informants may not be trustworthy. Thus, the examiner should always document all contact with informants to help guard against subsequent problems.

"Dumpster-Diving"

On occasion, an investigator might find it necessary to sift through a suspect's trash to obtain evidence and leads. Important documents and information concerning illegal activity might be found in the perpetrator's own garbage. The courts have upheld that investigators may sift through trash without a search warrant, provided that the trash has left the suspect's possession. At that point, there is no longer the reasonable expectation of privacy; thus it is fair game.

Subpoenas

If evidence is held by other parties or is in uncontrolled locations, specific legal action is required before attempting to obtain it. This usually takes the form of a subpoena or other order from the court to produce the documents and records (including electronic records). A *subpoena duces tecum* calls for the production of documents and records. Other forms of court orders can be used to obtain witness evidence and statements. Subpoenas are only available as part of an existing legal action, such as a grand jury investigation, pending criminal charges, or a civil suit. Thus, if no legal action has been initiated, obtaining documents by subpoena is not possible.

Search Warrants

There may be occasions when a fraud examiner will be called upon to assist law enforcement or will request the assistance of law enforcement in a particular investigation. If there is probable cause to believe that certain records are being used or have been used in the commission of a crime, the law enforcement officer will prepare an affidavit for a *search warrant*, which will detail the legal reasoning behind the request for the warrant. Only a judge can issue a search warrant, and only law enforcement can seek and serve a search warrant. Obtaining as much intelligence as possible regarding the location of the potential evidence is very desirable before writing the search warrant affidavit. Therefore, law enforcement personnel will often need guidance from the fraud examiner as they conduct pre-search preparation.

Voluntary Consent

Documents can be obtained by voluntary consent. This is often the simplest means to obtain documentation, and therefore, it is the preferred method in many fraud examinations. However, certain circumstances, such as hesitancy to release private information, or resistance by those involved in the scheme, may preclude obtaining voluntary consent for access to documents. While consent can generally be either oral or written, if documents are obtained from possible adverse witnesses or the target of the examination, it is recommended that the consent be acknowledged in writing.

PRESERVING DOCUMENTARY EVIDENCE

Even if the investigator is careful to obtain the evidence legally, the case can be lost if the examination team fails to preserve the evidence so that it is accepted by the court. For the evidence to be admissible, basic procedures in its handling must be followed. Evidence submitted must be properly identified, and it must be established that the proper chain of custody was maintained. In addition, proof must be provided that the evidence is relevant and material to the case.

The following general rules should be observed with regard to the collection and handling of documents:

- Obtain original documents when feasible. Make working copies for review; keep the originals segregated.
- Do not touch originals any more than necessary; they might later have to undergo forensic analysis.

- Maintain a good filing system for the documents. This is especially critical when large numbers of documents are obtained. Losing a key document is an unpardonable sin, and may mortally damage the case. Documents can be stamped sequentially for easy reference.

Chain of Custody

From the moment evidence is received, its chain of custody must be maintained for it to be accepted by the court. This means that a record must be made when the item is received or when it leaves the care, custody, or control of the fraud examiner. This is best handled by a memorandum of interview with the custodian of the records when the evidence is received. The memorandum should state:

- What items were received
- When they were received
- From whom they were received
- Where they are maintained

If the item is later turned over to someone else, a record of this should also be made—preferably in memorandum form. All evidence received should be uniquely marked so that it can be identified later. The preferable way is to initial and date the item; however, this can pose problems in the case of original business records furnished voluntarily. For them, a small tick mark or other nondescript identifier can be used. If it is not practical to mark the original document, it should be placed in a sealed envelope, which should be initialed and dated.

Preserving the Document

When initialing a document for future identification, fraud examiners should only do so in a noncritical area and using a different type of writing instrument than was used for the questioned writings on the document. The examiner should never write or make markings on the original document other than his unobtrusive initials for identification. Likewise, a document should not be folded, stapled, paper clipped, crumpled, or altered in any other way that would affect or change it from its original condition. If the document is stored in an envelope, the examiner should be careful not to write on the envelope and cause indentations on the original document inside. Photocopies and laser-printed documents should always be stored in paper folders or envelopes, not transparent plastic envelopes, which can result in the copies' sticking to the plastic and destroying some features of the document.

If fingerprint examinations are anticipated, the examiner should use gloves to handle the documents. Tweezers can also help the examiner avoid leaving fingerprints, but they should be used with caution, because they can leave indentations that might obscure faint indented writings or the identifiable indentations that are sometimes left by photocopy and fax machines. If any known people have inadvertently handled the documents with bare hands, their names should be provided to the fingerprint specialist. It may also be necessary to provide the expert with sets of inked fingerprints of these people for elimination purposes.

ORGANIZING DOCUMENTARY EVIDENCE

Keeping track of the amount of paper generated is one of the biggest obstacles in fraud investigations. It is essential that any documents obtained be properly organized early on in an investigation, and that they be continuously reorganized as the case progresses. Remember—it is usually difficult to ascertain the relevance of the evidence early in the case, so reevaluation throughout the investigation is critical. Good organization in complex cases includes the following:

- Segregating documents by either witness or transaction. Chronological organization is generally the least preferred method.
- Making a "key document" file for easy access to the most relevant documents. The examiner should periodically review the key documents, move the less important documents to backup files, and keep only the most relevant documents in the main file.
- Establishing a database early in the case if there is a large amount of information to process. The database should include, at a minimum, the date of the document, the individual from whom the document was obtained, the date obtained, a brief description, and the subject to whom the document pertains.

Chronologies

A chronology of events should be commenced early in the case in order to establish the chain of events leading to the proof. The chronology might or might not be made a part of the formal investigation report; at a minimum, it can be used for analysis of the case and placed in a working paper binder. Keep the chronology brief and include only information necessary to prove the case. Making the chronology too detailed can defeat its purpose. The chronology should be revised as necessary, adding new information and deleting that which is irrelevant.

To-Do Lists

Another indispensable aid is the "to-do" list. The list, which must be updated frequently, should be kept in a manner that allows it to be easily modified and used as a cumulative record of investigation tasks. In a very complex case, the list can be broken into long- and short-term objectives: that which must be done eventually (e.g., prove elements of a particular count) and that which should be done tomorrow (e.g., conduct an interview or draft a subpoena). No matter how organized an examiner might be, some list of this nature must be kept, lest important points be forgotten during the lengthy investigation.

Using Computer Software to Organize Documents and Other Data

Computers are one of the most valuable tools for fraud investigators. In complex fraud cases, the amount of information to be examined can be enormous. Performed manually, an investigation of a complicated fraud scheme could become overwhelming, requiring so much time and effort that it might cease to be cost-effective. Use of a computer database, however, enables investigators to easily store and access pertinent information about the case and the documents that have been assembled. Special software can also be used to sort, chart, and graph the information in the database, making it easier to analyze relationships and identify anomalies. The following are a few of the software programs commonly used for case management and reporting:

- i2 Analyst's Notebook
- CaseMap by CaseSoft
- NetMap by Alta Analytics
- MAGNUM Case Management Software
- Watson and PowerCase from XANALYS

SOURCES OF INFORMATION

A vast variety of information sources is available to the fraud examiner to assist in:

- Locating individuals or verifying their identity
- Researching assets or financial positions
- Documenting lifestyles and background information
- Discovering banking/creditor relationships
- Identifying business affiliations/associates
- Uncovering litigation history

In-House Sources

Some of the most useful information comes from within a subject's employing organization. If an investigator can gain access to a company's records, he can learn a great deal about an individual by examining routine in-house information on file. In-house sources include:

- Personnel files
- Internal phone records and voice mail
- Computer files and records
- Physical files and records
- Timesheets
- Financial records
- Prior audit or investigative files
- Corporate policies and procedures
- Company communications to employees
- Access codes and user identification codes
- Security videos

Public Information

Of all the information available, public records can be one of the most encompassing, challenging, and rewarding sources for an investigator. Public records are those records that a governmental unit is required by law to keep or those that are necessary for a governmental unit to keep in order to discharge its duties imposed by law.

Many types of public records contain similar information about individuals or entities. Yet each agency or governmental unit is responsible for quite different functions that may require them to maintain very unique information. The investigator should be prepared to consult a variety of public records in order to gather the information necessary.

Local or County Records The great majority of an individual's civil records can be found at the county courthouse in the jurisdiction where the subject does business or resides.

Voter Registration Records In order to vote, citizens must register in their respective precincts by filling out a form detailing their name, address, date of birth, Social Security number, and signature. Voter registration records are routinely verified by the county, and old addresses are deleted as new ones appear.

Marriage License Records Marriage license information includes the couple's married names, the maiden name of the female, the addresses of the individuals, proof of the couple's identities (driver's license numbers or passports), and both parties' dates of birth.

Real Property Records When an individual purchases real estate, he becomes a taxpayer and a registrant in several county records. Each real estate transaction will list a deed verifying the transfer of the property. If the individual either buys or sells a house or piece of property, or if his real property becomes subject to a state or federal lien, the transaction will be reflected in the county real property indexes. Additionally, if improvements are made to the property (e.g., adding a new room or installing a pool), a mechanic's lien or other notice may be on file in the county property records.

A search of these records will reveal:

- Residency and addresses of buyer and seller (referred to respectively as grantor and grantee)
- Price of the property
- Mortgage company and amount originally financed
- Real estate ownership
- Who financed the transaction, if applicable
- Title companies involved
- Improvements to the property and the names and addresses of the contractors

Property Tax Records Most counties charge landowners with property taxes for upkeep of local their schools, courthouses, police forces, and so forth. Property tax records can provide the fraud examiner with an idea of the estimated value, for tax purposes, of the property listed; of the identity of the owner of a vacant piece of land or a piece of property, if ownership is unknown; and of the name of the last person to pay taxes on the property.

When searching real property and tax records, the examiner should always look for other names shown on the documents. Frequently, the name of the attorney or notary public who verified the documents is listed, providing another potential source of further information.

Health and Fire Departments   Most county health or fire departments conduct routine inspections of businesses for health and safety code or fire code violations. These inspectors may have valuable information about the business and its operations, employees, and owners.

Sheriff/County Prosecutor   The county sheriff or the county prosecutor may maintain general incident files related to the businesses within the county. These incident files can provide leads on reports or contacts with the managers or owners of the business or on third parties who have made complaints against the subject.

County Fire Marshal   The county fire marshal should have a record of any fires that have occurred at specific properties. These records may contain information about a property's insurer, as well as information about any previously conducted investigations.

Utility Company Records   Many utility companies are nonprofit corporations or municipalities. Although the recent trend has been to restrict access to utility company records, some companies still make their records available to the public. Utility records may contain the phone number of the customer, even if that number is unlisted.

Permits   If a business or individual constructs a new building or makes improvements to an existing building, there should be a building permit on file with the local building authority. In addition, before most businesses can open their doors, the city or county may require that they possess certain permits. The local fire department may require permits ensuring that the business complies with the fire code. The city health department will require permits for restaurants or other businesses that serve food. Planning and zoning departments enforce regulations regarding the types and locations of businesses.

State Records
Business Filings   To open a bank account or to conduct business in a name other than one's own, the law requires certain documents to be filed. These documents can include articles of incorporation, foreign corporation registration, and fictitious name or doing business as (DBA) registration.

Articles of Incorporation Corporations are formed by filing articles of incorporation with the secretary of state (or state corporation bureau or corporate registry office) in the state where the company does business. These corporate records are public records and will include:

- Corporate name
- Ownership information
- Stock value
- Initial shareholders
- Names of the directors and officers
- Registered agent
- Location of the principal office
- Date of incorporation
- Standing/status

This information will permit the investigator to review a corporate structure, identify the registered agent, and trace incorporation dates. The records will often include limited partnership information as well.

Foreign Corporation Registration Some states also require foreign corporations (i.e., corporations that were incorporated in another state) that conduct business transactions in the state to register with the state corporation office. The application is typically filed with the secretary of state and must include the date of incorporation, the principal office, the address of the registered agent, and the names of the officers and directors.

Fictitious Names/Doing Business as Registration A fictitious name or doing business as (DBA) situation occurs when a business owner operates a company under a name that is different from his legal name. DBA information for sole proprietorships or partnerships is typically filed at the county level, though some states require filing at the state level as well. Most states also require limited partnerships, trusts, and joint ventures to file DBA information at the state or county level. DBA filings will provide insight into the true business venture behind the name. Very similar to corporate filings with the Secretary of State, these records will allow an investigator to identify the type of business entity, the date the business was started, and the owners/principals of the business.

Uniform Commercial Code Filings A search of Uniform Commercial Code (UCC) filings can help identify personal property that an individual or business has financed. UCC statements are documents filed by lenders with the secretary of state or with the county level unit to perfect their security interests in financed personal property. Banks, finance companies, and other lenders will generate records or filings of loans granted to individuals and businesses and collateralized by specific assets, such as household furniture, appliances, boats and yachts, automobiles, aircraft, and business equipment.

UCC filings can also disclose when and where a person obtained a personal loan, the type of property that he pledged to the lender to secure the loan, and the current address of the debtor. These documents are great sources for reviewing itemized lists of personal property held by the debtor.

Additionally, UCC filings can help fraud investigators uncover hidden ownership or relationships between parties by providing the names of all listed debtors and their addresses. The examiner may find information linking individuals to the companies they own or discover information about a company's subsidiaries, branch offices, or parent company.

UCC statements can be readily retrieved from the secretary of state's office, through service companies, or through online public records services.

Employee/Labor Records Some states' labor departments require the filing of periodic lists of employees, revealing their names, Social Security numbers, and salaries. These filings can help a fraud examiner track a subject's employment and income. In addition, by examining previous filings, an investigator can identify former employees of the company.

Workers' Compensation Information Because workers' compensation is a state program, these records are held at the state level. Records of workers' compensation claims are available in most states and are normally maintained for seven years, but public access to these records varies from state to state. There are two types of documents relating to workers' compensation cases: (1) injury reports and (2) court-contested claims. The reports commonly show the date of the incident, the amount of time lost, the employer at the time of the incident, the type of injury, the body part affected, and the job-related disability. To obtain workers' compensation information, the requesting party must have the subject's name and Social Security number. Many states also require some type of authorization from the subject before disclosure.

State Tax Filings   The revenue departments of some states require certain businesses to obtain tax permits, such as resale licenses or retail sales tax permits. Although tax returns are generally not available to the public, information regarding applications for and issuance of tax permits often is.

Additionally, law enforcement officials may be able to access corporate, business, and personal state tax information, which may unwittingly reveal hidden assets or investments. Tax returns may also disclose the identity of the accountant or attorney preparing the return.

When examining a state tax return, loans to or from officers, stockholders, or related entities should be examined closely. Any mortgages, notes, and bonds shown as liabilities on a corporate return should be investigated. Interest payments and interest income are also very important. Interest income may be shown from a bank that was previously unknown to the investigator.

Professional Associations and Licensing Boards   Many state and local agencies or bodies maintain records identifying individuals who hold special licenses or memberships. These can include:

- Medical practitioners, such as doctors, dentists, and nurses
- Attorneys
- Certified public accountants
- Real estate licensees
- Notaries
- Law enforcement personnel
- Firefighters
- Security guards
- Stockbrokers
- Teachers
- Insurance agents
- Private investigators
- Bail bond agents
- Travel agents
- Barbers, cosmetologists, and massage therapists
- Contractors, engineers, electricians, and architects

The licenses and applications granted by the state may be public record. Some applications contain no more than a name and address, but other applications contain lengthy personal information, such as previous residential addresses, previous employers, education and training, and financial statements.

The state regulatory or licensing agency may also have the authority to suspend or revoke the licenses necessary for a business to operate.

The Courts Each year, a great deal of litigation occurs, and many people are subjected to judicial action. Researching civil and criminal suits can provide invaluable information to assist in:

- Locating individuals
- Identifying pending actions
- Uncovering closed cases
- Determining marital status
- Tracing sources of funds (e.g., probate)
- Identifying financial conditions (e.g., bankruptcy)
- Discovering litigation history
- Uncovering outstanding judgments

A wealth of information is available from reviewing court files. Often, civil or criminal actions are not readily known and the researcher must be able to identify the jurisdiction, county, or court involved. Most of the papers filed in civil suits are accessible as public records; however criminal and juvenile actions may not be open to review. Additionally, different case types are filed at different levels and in different courts. Therefore, to uncover the information desired, the investigator may be required to check several types of courts at several different levels.

Litigation History Court clerks maintain files on all active and closed lawsuits in their jurisdictions. Information regarding these suits is public record and can be searched by scanning the indexes for the subject's name as plaintiff or defendant.

Based on court issues and the financial nature of the claim, different levels of courts may have jurisdiction over a given case. To determine a full picture of the litigation history against a company or individual, the fraud examiner should search each of the following courts:

- State courts
    - State trial courts of general jurisdiction (criminal/civil)
    - State intermediate appellate courts (criminal/civil)
    - Highest state courts (criminal/civil)
    - Probate courts (estate administration)
    - Family courts (matters concerning adoption, annulments, divorce, alimony, custody, child support, etc.)
    - Traffic courts (minor traffic law violations)
    - Juvenile courts (cases involving delinquent children under a certain age)
    - Small claims courts (civil suits of a relatively low dollar amount)
    - Municipal court (offenses against city ordinances)

- Federal courts
    - U.S. district courts (criminal/civil)
    - U.S. circuit courts of appeal (criminal/civil)
    - U.S. Supreme Court (criminal/civil)

- Bankruptcy courts (federal)
- U.S. Tax Court (cases arising over alleged tax deficiencies)
- U.S. Court of International Trade (cases involving tariffs and international trade disputes)

Divorce Records If the subject of the investigation is in the process of becoming, or has been, divorced, the fraud examiner may wish to search for the opposing spouse. Divorce record searches will return marriage partner names and addresses, location of marriage, divorce filing date, and file number. Moreover, court documents from a divorce case frequently contain the subject's financial inventory, which is submitted at the time of the divorce or separation, as well as the partition of assets to each party in the settlement.

Personal Injury Suit Records Documents in a personal injury suit will frequently contain an accident report, injury history, statements of the involved parties, and information about the financial settlement of the case.

Financial Suit Records Reviewing documents filed in a financial suit will disclose the subject's debtors and creditors, and will present an outside view of an individual's business history or ability to perform.

Bankruptcy Records Bankruptcy documents are usually located in the federal bankruptcy court for the district where the debtor resided or had his principal place of business. When checking bankruptcy court records, the fraud examiner should check not only the individual or business being investigated, but also any related businesses, principals, employees, or relatives.

The Bankruptcy Code (§107) specifically provides that all documents filed with federal bankruptcy courts are public record and can be examined by anyone without charge. A bankruptcy case file may include the case number; the debtor's name(s), Social Security number, and address; the filing date, the bankruptcy chapter designation; and the case closure date. It may also include transcripts of depositions or interviews. If fraud was suspected, the trustee may have conducted a fraud investigation; thus, investigators may wish to check with the trustee to find out whether any such investigations were undertaken.

Probate Records Probate records are documents filed to show the dispersal of assets after a subject's death. The probate court conducts an investigation to verify any debts owed by the individual's estate and sees to the distribution of assets according to the deceased's will (or, if there is no will, by state law) after all debts are paid. Information about the debts left in an individual's estate will give the investigator the names of persons having an interest in the deceased's estate, as well as the subject's financial position at the time of death. Likewise, the dispersal of assets will reveal the names and addresses of heirs to the deceased and provide some indication of the value of the property willed to them.

The Internet The Internet is often the first place fraud examiners turn for information. It is an amazing research tool, but investigators should remember that much of the information on public websites is questionable. Fraud examiners should not rely on information gleaned from public pages without verifying the authenticity and accuracy of the information.

Search engines like Google and Yahoo provide a convenient way to access the wealth of information available on the Internet. In addition, there are many other ways for fraud examiners to find information online. A list of specific helpful Internet resources is included in Appendix A.

Commercial Online Services A commercial online service may be the best and most efficient way to conduct public records searches, as it provides access to a wide range of data in a single place. There are several companies that provide varying levels of public record information to subscribers. The information is stored on a central database that a subscriber can access from his computer. Some companies provide information that is actually retrieved in hard copy and mailed or faxed to the subscriber, even though the request was made through the online service.

While convenient, the use of commercial public record services comes with an important caveat for investigators to keep in mind: Online records companies have to get their information from somewhere. If the information in the source's records is incorrect, the report received from the database company will also be incorrect. Therefore, it is essential to remember that accessing information online is never a full substitute for actual examination of the public records themselves.

Directories Directories are specialized websites that collect the names of numerous other related websites, allowing users to browse through a listing of possible sites to visit. Directories contain direct links to pages that have a common interest. Some all-inclusive directories cover a plethora of different topics, and others are more focused on particular subjects or disciplines (e.g., accounting and auditing directories that fraud examiners may find very useful).

Blogs A blog is a user-created website consisting of diary-like entries. Although there are many different types of blogs, ranging from community and corporate blogs to blogs focusing on a particular subject, the most relevant type for fraud examiners is the personal blog—an ongoing commentary written by one person.

Reviewing an individual's blog can reveal information that may be relevant to an investigation. For example, with information obtained from a personal blog, the investigator may be able to establish a timeline of the individual's activities or gain insight into the subject's thoughts and mindset, which can be used in the interviewing process.

Blogs, unlike social networks, are generally open to everyone; furthermore, many blogs can easily be searched, often using traditional search engines. Google Blog Search, for example, uses Google search technology to search blogs. In addition to traditional search engines, blogs can be searched via specialized blog-search sites, such as Technorati and IceRocket.

Social Networking Sites Social networking sites are specialized websites that help users develop and maintain their relationships more easily. Essentially, social networking sites take traditional networking activities online. With these sites, users can, generally without charge, log onto one of the services, create an account, provide specific details about their life—such as schools attended, past and present employers, hobbies, sports, and interests—and become networked to other individuals that share similar backgrounds or interests. Once users become connected to other members, they can view the activity on each other's pages.

User pages on social networking sites contain valuable information. People regularly post many personal details on their social networking pages, including information about their professional profile, academic history, business connections, personal affiliations, hobbies, favorite sports teams, opinions, work schedule, height, weight, gender, travel schedule, intellectual property, political and charitable causes, updates on family events, drug or alcohol habits, illnesses, and so on. They may also post photos and videos, which can help investigators track changes in physical appearance and location.

Social networking sites can be searched like traditional websites; much of the information available on social networking sites can be found using traditional search engines. However, there is an ever-growing number of specialized resources that an examiner can also use to search these sites. For example, each social network has a search engine for locating members. Users can use these engines to search for members by name, phone number, or e-mail address. In general, users can search for members without logging in, and searches can usually be done anonymously. If, however, a member's profile is private, the researcher will only see a snapshot of the member's information. For example, to view a member's profile in Facebook or LinkedIn, the researcher must connect with the other member.

In addition to traditional search engines and search engines within social networking sites, social network search engines are also available and may provide better results. These search engines use social networks to order, prioritize, or refine search results. Some popular social networking search engines include Spokeo, Yoname, and FriendFeed.

REPORT WRITING

Fraud examinations conclude with reporting the investigation results. In general, this communication takes the form of a formal written report that includes information pertinent to the examination engagement. Such a report is normally used for internal reporting purposes but may also be used for complaints to police services or claims to insurance companies. It is important to note that the topic of writing reports is broad and detailed; many of the finer points of report writing are beyond the scope of this textbook. However, this section is included to provide a general overview of the culmination of the investigation techniques discussed throughout this text.

Purpose of the Report

According to anthropologists, some of the earliest forms of writing were actually drawings recording ceremonial dances. These drawings were made to record specific movements so that others could repeat those that were thought to please the gods. While technology has advanced since those early days, and we no longer write on cave walls or do ceremonial dances to please the gods, we still need to record our specific activities and findings to comply with policies and procedures and, in some cases, to satisfy the courts.

The records or reports stemming from an investigation must be accurate and understandable so that others may know what transpired without having to speak to the report's author. In other words, the report must speak for itself. An important point to remember is that an investigation is often judged not by what was "uncovered," but by the way in which the information is presented. As such, a good investigation report:

- *Conveys evidence:* The written report communicates all evidence necessary for thorough and proper evaluation of the case.
- *Adds credibility:* Because the written report is completed in a timely manner, it adds credibility to the investigation and can be used to corroborate earlier facts.

- *Accomplishes objectives of case:* Knowing that a written report must be issued after the examination is completed, the report forces the examiner to consider his actions beforehand.

Know the Reader

As with any written document, it is important to identify the reader of the internal report. Internally, this may include the board of directors, corporate executives, internal auditors, and in-house legal counsel.

Each of the readers might have different expectations as to the information he expects to see in a report. For instance, the board of directors might only wish to know that an investigation was conducted and what the outcome was (such as the termination and prosecution of the offending employee). An internal auditor would likely be more interested in whether internal controls were overridden, and how. In-house legal counsel might wonder whether proper procedures were followed in the investigation and consequent employee termination. Ultimately, these internal readers will determine what information is included in the report.

Along with the expected internal readers, others who are external to the company might gain access to the internal investigation report. Some of these readers may be given the report voluntarily, and others may gain access to it through other means, including the courts. These external readers could include:

- External auditors
- Outside legal counsel (including those retained by employees who might be the subject of the internal investigation)
- Law enforcement agencies
- Government attorneys or prosecutors
- Other government agencies (e.g., employment or human rights commissions)
- Insurance companies

It is important to remember that while not all investigation reports end up being scrutinized by lawyers and/or used in a civil or criminal trial, they should all be written as if they will be. For this reason, the following points should be followed:

- State only the facts. Do not guess or make assumptions in the report. If information is unknown, that fact should be clearly stated.
- Do not make errors. Minor typographical and other errors might make the report appear unprofessional and could be embarrassing, especially in court. In addition to using a spellchecker, it might be worthwhile to obtain the services of an independent proofreader.
- Do have a follow-up section. In some cases, information or documentation important to the investigation might not be available to the investigator. This should be listed in a separate section.

Format

Using a template or standard report format will reduce the amount of time spent writing a report while ensuring that all pertinent information is included. Nevertheless, some situations might require a customized report format—but even then the basic format outlined below should be followed:

- Author/date
- Summary
- Introduction/purpose
- Body
- Results
- Follow-up/recommendations

These section names are not mandatory and can be changed to suit the report writer's preferences; but as a general rule, all of the information in these sections should be included somewhere in the report.

Summary   This section is intended to give very basic information. It should set out the main points of the report in a few sentences and should include the subject, basis, findings, and outcome of the investigation.

EXAMPLE

This report deals with an internal investigation conducted at the Rockside Industries' Wayside Plant based on an anonymous tip that an employee was submitting false expense claims. The investigation determined that $105,375.89 in false invoices had been submitted for reimbursement through the purchasing department. The director of purchasing and a senior buyer were terminated.

Introduction   This section provides more detail on what the report is about and prepares the reader for what is to come—that is, the body of the report. Unless there is a separate section, this is where the purpose of the report will be explained, along with any required background information.

EXAMPLE

This report documents the results of an internal investigation into the unauthorized use of purchase cards at the Rockside Industries' Wayside plant. It is intended for use by Rockside Industries in its civil action for recovery of misappropriated funds and for making a complaint to police.

On May 10, 2010, the security department received an anonymous tip on the fraud hotline advising that an invoice for the purchase of a computer backup power supply (UPS) was false and that the actual purchase was for a portable DVD player.

Investigation determined that there was no original invoice for the transaction on file; instead, the file contained a photocopy of the invoice. The purchase was made with a corporate purchase card issued to Randall Trait, a senior buyer at Rockside's Wayside plant. It had been approved by Robert Morton, the purchasing director. The vendor, ABLE Tech, was contacted, and it confirmed that the invoice number on the file copy matched an invoice it had for the sale of a portable DVD player.

The Wayside plant has a physical asset database in which all nondisposable items having a purchase price of $200 or more are recorded. Each item is assigned a unique ID number and barcode label, which are used to track the item. This database is maintained by the purchasing director. There was no record of the UPS in the physical assets database, and no ID number had been issued for any similar item in the past six months.

An on-site visit was made to ABLE Tech, which has been an approved vendor since June 12, 2005. The manager, Charles Front, advised that in the past six months, the same individual, whom he knew as Randy Trait, had made three other purchases that Charles had considered to be somewhat odd in that Randy asked that the items be held for pickup by him rather than be delivered to the plant. He provided copies of these invoices, which showed the purchase of a notebook computer, an LCD computer screen, and a digital camcorder.

When these invoices were compared with the plant purchasing records, it was found that the files contained only copies, rather than original invoices, for all three purchases. Each of the file copies reflected the same invoice number, date, and amount as the original invoice, but differed as to what was purchased. All three purchases had been made using the same purchase card as the portable DVD player and had been approved by the director of purchasing, Robert Morton.

Based on this initial information, a complete review was conducted of all purchases made on the card issued to Randall Trait, the senior buyer, for the past eighteen months, the period of time he had been employed by Rockside.

Body This part of the report identifies the employee(s) and other individuals implicated or involved in the matter. This includes any background information that might have been obtained about the employee or other parties.

EXAMPLE

Subject Employee #1

Robert Morton

Position: Rockside Industries Director of Purchasing

Work Location: Wayside Plant

Employment Dates: March 19, 1995 to May 21, 2010

Subject Employee #2

Randall Trait

Position: Senior Buyer

Work Location: Wayside Plant

Employment Dates: November 2, 2008 to May 21, 2010

Nonsubject Employee #1

Phil Brothers

Position: Shipper-Receiver

Work Location: Wayside Plant

Employment Dates: April 11, 1997 to Current

Nonsubject Employee #2

Stanley Lampen

Position: Senior Buyer

Work Location: Wayside Plant

Employment Dates: February 28, 1997–October 15, 2008

Noncompany Witness #1

Charles Front

Owner/Manager ABLE Tech

Approved Vendor Since June 12, 2005

The body of the report also details the methods used to investigate the matter, including any document reviews, interviews, and other procedures such as video surveillance. If necessary, background information can be provided on the department or process involved in the investigation. For example, in an accounts payable fraud, the document flow might be described or set out in a graphic to assist the reader in understanding how the process works.

EXAMPLE

The Wayside Plant Purchasing Department consists of a senior buyer, two junior buyers, and an administrative assistant. These individuals are responsible for all Wayside plant purchases not related to travel/entertainment expenses.

The director of purchasing also works out of the Wayside plant; he is responsible for supervising the purchasing departments of the eight plants located across North America.

Purchase cards are used for individual items with a value of $1,000 or less and purchases of multiple items with a total value of $5,000 or less (before taxes). All other purchases are invoiced and are paid for using corporate checks.

Procedures

1. A purchase requisition form is prepared by an employee and forwarded to the buyer.
2. The buyer sources goods and makes the purchase.
3. The buyer enters the purchase into the ATAC purchasing system.
4. The goods are shipped to the plant and received in the shipping-receiving department.
5. The shipping-receiving department enters the receipt into the ATAC system.
6. The accounts payable department receives notice of the purchase through the ATAC system and the purchase card online statement. Notice of delivery of the goods is also received through the ATAC system.
7. The purchasing director receives and approves a monthly report from the accounts payable department detailing all purchases made on purchase cards.

Results   This section will vary widely depending on the nature of the investigation and the information collected. An investigation that involves only one incident may be explained in a sentence or two. In more complicated or extensive investigations, the narrative may be supplemented by spreadsheets or graphics.

EXAMPLE

A review was conducted of all purchases made with the purchase card issued to Randall Trait, senior buyer, since he commenced employment with Rockside Industries on November 2, 2008.

This review identified forty-seven transactions, totaling $39,864.36, that had altered documentation supporting the transaction. Each purchase had been made following the proper procedures, except that instead of being shipped to the shipping-receiving department, the purchases were picked up at source by Randall Trait. The purchases were entered into the ATAC system as being received using the employee number of Phil Brothers, a shipping-receiving department employee. Brothers was unable to verify whether he made any of the entries, but attendance records confirmed that on seven of the days on which shipments were entered into the ATAC system, Brothers was listed as being absent from work.

These forty-seven transactions are contained in the spreadsheet at Tab 1.

The documentation for each of the transactions is located in Tabs 13–59:

1. Invoice from the accounts payable file
2. Invoice from the approved vendor
3. ATAC system printout showing the purchase being made
4. ATAC system printout showing the purchase being received
5. Monthly report from accounts payable signed by Robert Morton

(Note: No purchase requisition forms were located for any of the forty-seven transactions.)

In addition, the review uncovered an additional 113 transactions, totaling $63,511.53, that also had altered documentation. These transactions were made using a second purchase card that had originally been issued to Stanley Lampen, the buyer whom Randall Trait had replaced. This card had never been canceled or reissued to another employee when Lampen left Rockside's employment. These 113 transactions are contained in the spreadsheet at Tab 2. The documentation for each of the transactions is located in Tabs 60–172:

1. Invoice from the Accounts Payable file
2. Invoice from the approved vendor
3. ATAC system printout showing the purchase being made
4. ATAC system printout showing the purchase being received
5. Monthly report from Accounts Payable signed by Robert Morton

(Note: No purchase requisitions forms were located for any of the 113 transactions.)

In interviews conducted by corporate security, Robert Morton and Randall Trait admitted to making fraudulent purchases using the two purchase cards. Both denied that there were any transactions other than those identified in this report.

Morton admitted that he came up with the idea when Stanley Lampen left the company and his purchase card was never canceled. When Morton obtained a new purchase card for Trait, he also kept Lampen's old card.

Both Morton and Trait admitted that they were childhood friends, and confirmed that it was Morton who had contacted Trait when the buyer's position had opened up. They both also admitted that they had devised the scheme to help out Morton when he got divorced and was having financial difficulties.

When presenting information in spreadsheet form, it might be useful to prepare several versions with the data sorted in different ways—for example, by transaction date or amount. If there are several different types of transactions, they may be grouped by type in this manner as well. To supplement the spreadsheet, a written description of a representative sample of the transactions can be given. Generally, it is not necessary to give a written description of each individual transaction, particularly when they are essentially the same except for time, date, and amount.

Follow-Up/Recommendations This section identifies any investigation procedures that remain outstanding, usually because they are outside the mandate of the investigator. These might include the recovery of property that is in the hands of third parties or collection of information held by vendors/suppliers.

It is also the appropriate place to identify and make any recommendations related to procedures and controls.

EXAMPLE

1. *Purchase requisition forms:* These forms are currently prepared by hand and sent to the buyer making the purchase. After the purchase is made, they are kept by the buyer. Recommendation: A copy of the form should be sent to the accounts payable department, which should keep a copy and send a copy back to the employee requesting the purchase. This would allow for independent confirmation that the employee had actually requested the purchase.

2. *Receiving goods:* All shipments received by the shipping-receiving department are entered into the ATAC system using the employee number of the shipper-receiver. This number is known to numerous employees outside of this department. This was done to allow temporary employees to enter shipments into ATAC. In addition, these entries can be made from any computer terminal in the Wayside plant, not only the shipping-receiving terminal.

   Recommendation: All goods received should be entered into the ATAC using the shipping-receiving department only. Passwords should be required to prevent unauthorized employees from making entries.

Opinions or Conclusions in Report

Other than opinions on technical matters, no opinions of any kind should be included in the written report. If conclusions are not self-evident, then the examiner has usually not completed a good report. In particular, opinions should not be given regarding the guilt or innocence of any person or party.

SUMMARY

The need for an internal investigation can arise in a number of circumstances, including determining the source of and losses from an alleged fraud, complying with federal statutes, fulfilling the professional duties of loyalty and reasonable care, ensuring against allegations of wrongful termination, and mitigating the company's liability related to employee misconduct.

When planning a fraud examination, it is important to consider how the company can carry out the investigation in the most efficient, effective manner. The investigation team should be limited to only those persons who are vital to the fraud examination process, and may consist of certified fraud examiners, legal counsel, auditors, security personnel, IT and computer forensics experts, human resources personnel, management representatives, and outside consultants.

The purpose of the investigation process is to gather evidence to prove or disprove the allegations of fraud. As part of the engagement, the fraud examiner may utilize a variety of investigative techniques such as undertaking covert and surveillance operations, using informants, "dumpster-diving," acquiring subpoenas and search warrants, and obtaining voluntary consent.

Once evidence has been gathered, the investigator must take care to properly preserve the evidence to ensure its admissibility in a court of law. This involves making a formal record of the chain of custody and protecting the physical state and attributes of the evidence. Organization of the evidence is also key. Several computer software programs are available to aid fraud examiners in case management and reporting.

A large number of resources exist to assist investigators in gathering evidence. In-house sources, such as personnel files, phone records, computer and physical files, financial records, access codes and user identification codes, and security videos, are especially useful if the fraud examiner can obtain access to them. Additionally, much information about individuals and businesses can be found in public records.

Fraud examinations generally conclude with a formal written report of the investigation results. A good investigation report must be accurate and understandable so that others may know what transpired without having to speak to the report's author. It should also convey evidence, add credibility to the investigation, and accomplish the objectives of the case. To ensure the report appears professional and achieves its purpose, the investigator must identify the expected reader, include all significant information, and avoid stating any opinions in the report.

ESSENTIAL TERMS

Duty of loyalty The requirement that an employee/agent must act solely in the best interest of the employer/principal, free of any self-dealing, conflicts of interest, or other abuse of the principal for personal advantage.

Duty of reasonable care The expectation that a corporate officer, director, or high-level employee, as well as other people in a fiduciary relationship, will conduct business affairs prudently with the skill and attention normally exercised by people in similar positions.

Certified fraud examiner (CFE) A professional who is trained to conduct complex fraud examinations from inception to conclusion. A CFE has training in all aspects of fraud examination, including identifying fraudulent transactions, obtaining evidence, and interviewing witnesses.

Attorney–client privilege The privilege that precludes disclosure of communications between an attorney and client, but only if the client (1) retained the attorney, (2) did so to obtain legal advice, (3) thereafter communicated with the attorney on a confidential basis, and (4) has not waived the privilege.

Evidence Anything perceivable by the five senses, and any proof such as testimony of witnesses, records, documents, facts, data, or tangible objects legally presented at trial to prove a contention and induce a belief in the minds of a jury.

Covert operations An investigatory procedure in which the investigator assumes a fictitious identity in order to gather evidence.

Surveillance An evidence gathering technique involving the secretive and continuous observance of a suspect's activities.

Subpoena duces tecum A legal order requiring the production of documents.

Search warrant A legal order issued by a judge upon presentation of probable cause to believe the items being sought have been used in the commission of a crime.

Chain of custody Refers to who has had possession of an object and what he has done with it. The chain of custody must be preserved or else the item cannot be used at trial.

REVIEW QUESTIONS

14-1 (Learning objective 14-1) What are some of the reasons a fraud examination should be commenced?

14-2 (Learning objective 14-2) Who are some of the professionals who should be included on a typical fraud examination team?

14-3 (Learning objective 14-2) Under what circumstances might the fraud examination team include outside consultants?

14-4 (Learning objective 14-3) What is evidence? What types of things can be considered evidence?

14-5 (Learning objective 14-4) What are some of examples of evidence-gathering techniques that might be utilized in a fraud examination?

14-6 (Learning objective 14-5) When handling documentary evidence, what types of precautions should a fraud examiner take?

14-7 (Learning objective 14-7) What types of information can be obtained by examining internal documentation?

14-8 (Learning objective 14-8) What are three characteristics/objectives of a good investigation report?

14-9 (Learning objective 14-8) What are five sections that should be included in a standard investigation report? What information is found in each of these sections?

DISCUSSION ISSUES

14-1   (Learning objective 14-2) Who should be responsible for directing an internal fraud investigation? Why?

14-2   (Learning objectives 14-2, 14-6, and 14-7) How can computers and technology help in investigating a fraud? What kinds of challenges can the involvement of technology present to a case?

14-3   (Learning objective 14-4) Jim Block, CFE, is investigating Randy Smith for his role in a potential kickback scheme. Gathering evidence about Randy's financial activity has been difficult. While on a stakeout at Randy's home, Jim sees Randy's wife take out the garbage and place it on the curb. Jim steals the trash bag, sorts through its contents, and discovers multiple bank statements that provide details about some of Randy's illicit financial transactions. Is Jim's acquirement of the bank statements legal even though there was no search warrant?

14-4   (Learning objective 14-6) What are some considerations a fraud examiner should keep in mind when organizing documentary evidence? Which method of evidence organization is preferred?

14-5   (Learning objective 14-7) An investigator is looking for information about some vacant land that may be owned by a suspect in a fraud case. What source or sources of public records would be a good place to find this information?

14-6   (Learning objective 14-8) When reporting the results of an investigation, why is it important that fraud examiners not express opinions in their professional report?

CHAPTER 15

INTERVIEWING WITNESSES

LEARNING OBJECTIVES

After studying this chapter, you should be able to

15-1 List the five types of interview questions

15-2 Understand how to ask introductory questions

15-3 Explain how to construct informational questions

15-4 Understand the differences between open, closed, and leading questions

15-5 Explain how to close an interview

15-6 Define and explain the purpose of assessment questions

15-7 List some nonverbal clues to deception

15-8 List some verbal clues to deception

15-9 Discuss the methodology of admission-seeking questions

15-10 List the elements of a signed statement

OVERVIEW

In the fraud examination field, there is nothing more important to the successful resolution of a case than the ability to conduct a thorough interview of subjects and witnesses. While accountants and auditors routinely ask questions, the queries rarely confront a subject of wrongdoing. For example, if we return to the fictional case from Chapter 1 of Linda Reed Collins, who is suspected of taking kickbacks in return for awarding business, fraud examination methodology requires us to resolve the allegation from inception to disposition. That means interviewing a number of potential witnesses: her coworkers, subordinates, superiors, associates, and other vendors. And, finally, it means interviewing Collins herself, provided we still have sufficient predication to indicate that she has committed fraud against her employer.

But regardless of whom we interview about what subject, there are five general types of questions that we can ask: introductory, informational, assessment, closing, and admission-seeking. In routine interview situations, where the object is to gather information from neutral or corroborative witnesses, only three of the five types of questions will normally be asked: introductory, informational, and closing. If you have reasonable cause to believe the respondent is not being truthful, assessment questions can be asked. Finally, if you decide with reasonable cause that the respondent is responsible for misdeeds, admission-seeking questions can be posed.

Introductory Questions

Introductory questions serve four primary purposes: to provide an introduction, to establish a rapport between you and the subject, to establish the theme of the interview, and to observe the subject's reactions.

Provide the Introduction   You should indicate your name and company, but avoid using titles. As a general proposition, the more informal the interview, the more relaxed the respondent. This leads to better communication. You should also shake hands with the subject. Making physical contact helps break down psychological barriers to communication. Be cautioned against invading the respondent's personal space, however—doing so might make the person uncomfortable. You generally should remain at a distance of four to six feet.

One of the goals is to create a comfortable climate for the subject, one that will encourage open communication. Once the respondent is seated, it is a good idea to ask the subject whether he would like something to drink, whether he needs to take off a coat or jacket, and so forth. It is best to take care of these matters before beginning the interview, so that delays and interruptions can be avoided.

Establish Rapport   Some common ground must be established before questioning begins. This is usually accomplished by engaging in small talk for a few minutes. The small talk should not be overdone, but should be used as a means to break the ice and establish a flow of communication between you and the subject.

Establish the Interview Theme   The interview theme might be related only indirectly to the actual purpose of the interview. The goal of the theme is to get the respondent to "buy in" to assisting in the interview. The theme for the interview should be one that is logical for the respondent to accept and easy to explain. Normally, the more general, the better. One of the most effective interview themes is that you are seeking the subject's help. Nearly all human beings get satisfaction from helping others. Throughout the interview, it is important to include the subject as part of the process as opposed to making him feel like a target of the inquiry. During this phase of the interview, the respondent must not feel threatened in any way.

Observe Reactions   You must be skilled in interpreting the respondent's reactions to questions. The majority of communication between individuals is nonspoken; the subject will provide clues about what he knows—consciously or subconsciously—with his body language, tone of voice, and attitude. You must, therefore, systematically observe the various responses the subject gives during the course of the conversation.

This is done by first posing nonsensitive questions while establishing rapport. By observing the subject's reactions to these kinds of questions, you can establish a baseline for the subject's verbal and nonverbal behavior. Later, when more sensitive questions are asked, you will observe the respondent's reactions. If the respondent's verbal and nonverbal behavior significantly changes as particular questions are posed, you must attempt to determine why. (For a more detailed discussion, see the "Physiology of Deception" section later in this chapter.)

General Rules for the Introductory Phase of the Interview

Don't Interview More Than One Person at a Time   One of the basic rules is to question only one person at a time. The testimony of one respondent will invariably influence the testimony of another. There are few hard-and-fast rules to interviewing, but this is one of them.

Privacy   Another basic rule is to conduct interviews under conditions of privacy. The interview is best conducted out of the sight and sound of friends, relatives, and fellow employees. People are very reluctant to furnish sensitive information within earshot of others.

Ask Nonsensitive Questions   Sensitive questions should be scrupulously avoided until well into the interview. Even then, such questions should be asked only after careful deliberation and planning. During the introductory phase, emotive words of all types generally should be avoided. Such words normally put people on the defensive, making them more reluctant to answer and to cooperate.

EXAMPLE

Instead of	Use
Investigation	*Inquiry*
Audit	*Review*
Interview	*Ask a few questions*
Embezzlement/theft	*Shortage or paperwork problems*

Get a Commitment for Assistance   It is critical to obtain a commitment for assistance from the subject. The commitment must consist of some positive action on the part of the subject; remaining silent or simply nodding the head is not sufficient. You should ask for the commitment before the interview commences, and should encourage the subject to voice a positive, audible "yes" when asked whether he will help. If you encounter silence the first time you ask for assistance, the question should be repeated in a slightly different way until the respondent verbalizes the commitment.

Make a Transitional Statement   Once you have gotten a commitment for assistance, you must describe the purpose of the interview in more detail. This is done using a transitional statement, which sets forth a legitimate basis for the questioning and explains to the subject how he fits into the inquiry. After making the transitional statement, you should seek a second commitment for assistance. Assume, for example, that we are interviewing Linda Reed Collins for the first time. If we don't know for sure that she has done anything wrong, we don't want to put her off; to do so would impede the information-gathering process. After you have introduced yourself and asked Ms. Collins for assistance, here is a way you might make a transitional statement:

EXAMPLE

Interviewer: "It's pretty routine, really. I'm gathering some information about the purchasing function and how it is supposed to work. It would be helpful to me if I could start by asking you to basically tell me about your job. Okay?"

Seek Continuous Agreement   Throughout the interview process—from the introduction to the close—you should attempt to phrase questions so that they can be answered "yes." It is easier for people to reply in the affirmative than the negative.

Do Not Promise Confidentiality   Some subjects may be hesitant to speak to you for fear that the information they share will not be kept confidential. The subject may request a promise of confidentiality for any statements he makes. When this happens, you should inform the subject that all information that is gathered will be provided to individuals who have a "need to know."

You should not make any promise to the subject that the matters he discusses will be confidential. Any information gathered in an interview belongs to the client or employer, not you. You do not have the right to limit the use of the information or to decide how the information will be used. Therefore, to promise the subject that the information will be kept confidential is misleading to the subject, and may taint subsequent use of the information.

Negotiations   In some situations, a subject may attempt to negotiate with you, offering information in exchange for something from the company or the client. If this happens, you should keep the discussion open and listen to what the subject may want. However, unless you are authorized to do so, you should not represent to the subject any "quid pro quo" with respect to cooperation. You should tell the subject that any information he provides will be conveyed to the appropriate individual, and will be taken into account. To negotiate with a subject is to lose control of the interview and investigation.

Discussing the Source of Allegations   In the event that you are following up on a complaint or allegation, you should not discuss either the fact that there is an allegation or the source of the information. It is not your role to provide information. If Collins, for example, asks where the complaint or information originated, you should advise her that as a matter of policy, the basis for any inquiry is not discussed.

Informational Questions

Once the proper format for the interview has been set, you should turn to the fact-gathering portion. Informational questions should be nonconfrontational and nonthreatening, and should be asked for the purpose of gathering unbiased factual information. The great majority of your questions will fall into this category.

There are essentially three types of questions that can be asked: *open, closed*, and *leading*. These types of questions are discussed in more detail below. Each is used in a logical sequence to maximize the development of information. If you have reason to believe that the respondent is being untruthful, assessment questions can be posed; otherwise, the interview is brought to a logical close at the end of the informational phase.

Open Questions   Open questions are those that are worded in a way that makes it difficult to simply answer them using "yes" or "no." The typical open question calls for a monologue response, and can be answered in several different ways. During the information phase of the interview, you should endeavor to ask primarily open questions, in order to stimulate conversation and allow the subject to convey as much information as possible. An open question does not restrict the subject's response. Thus, instead of asking, "You are in charge of purchasing, aren't you?", which directs the subject's response to one particular area, you might ask, "Would you tell me about your job?" The latter example allows for a broad response during which more information will be conveyed. Later, you can go back and draw out more information about a particular topic.

Closed Questions   Closed questions are those that limit the possible responses by requiring a precise answer, usually "yes" or "no." ("Did you approve this vendor?" or "On what day of the week did it happen?") Closed questions are used to deal with specifics, such as amounts, dates, and times. Generally, closed questions should be avoided in the informational part of the interview. However, they are used extensively in the closing phase.

Leading Questions Leading questions contain the answer as a part of the question. They are usually used to confirm facts that are already known. An example of a leading question is, "There haven't been any changes in the operation since last year, have there?" This type of question gives the subject much less room to maneuver than the open question "What changes have been made in the operation since last year?" or the closed question "Have there been any changes in the operation since last year?"

Notice how the leading question directs the subject to answer in a particular way: that there have not been any changes. It implies that you already know the answer, and asks the subject to confirm what is already known. The open question allows more latitude, allowing the subject to make any comments he wants about changes in the operation. The closed question narrows the subject's options a bit, but still allows the subject to confirm or deny that changes have been made. Leading questions can be particularly effective in obtaining confessions or getting subjects to make unpleasant admissions.

Question Sequences As a general rule, questioning should proceed from the general to the specific: that is, it is best to gather general information before seeking details. A variation is to "reach backward" with the questions, by beginning with known information and working toward unknown areas. An efficient method of doing this is to recount the known information and then frame the next question as a logical continuation of the facts previously related.

Informational Question Techniques Below are some suggestions for improving the quality of the interview during the information-gathering phase:

- Begin by asking questions that are not likely to cause the respondent to become defensive or hostile.
- Ask the questions in a manner that will develop the facts in the order of their occurrence, or in some other systematic order.
- Ask only one question at a time, and frame the question so that only one answer is required.
- Ask straightforward and frank questions. Generally avoid shrewd approaches.
- Keep interruptions to a minimum, and do not stop the subject's narrative without good reason.
- Give the respondent ample time to answer; don't rush.
- Try to help the respondent remember, but do not suggest answers—and be careful not to imply any particular answer through your facial expressions, gestures, methods of asking questions, or types of questions asked.
- Repeat or rephrase questions, if necessary, to get the desired facts.
- Be sure you understand the answers; if they are not perfectly clear, have the subject interpret them at that time instead of waiting to do so until later.
- Give the subject an opportunity to qualify her answers.
- Separate facts from inferences.
- Have the subject give comparisons by percentages, fractions, estimates of time and distance, and other such methods to ensure accuracy.
- After the respondent has given a narrative account, ask follow-up questions about every key issue that has been discussed.

- Upon conclusion of the direct questioning, ask the respondent to summarize the information given; then, summarize the facts, and have the respondent verify that these conclusions are correct.

Methodology   In order to begin the informational phase of the interview, you must first make a transition out of the introductory phase. The transition is a signal that you and the subject are going to begin discussing the substantive issues that are the purpose of the interview. The transition usually is accomplished by asking the subject a nonthreatening question about herself or her duties. It often begins with a restatement of the purpose of the interview: "As I said, I am gathering information about the company's operations. Can you tell me about what you do on a day-to-day basis?"

Begin with Background Questions   Assuming that the subject does not have a problem answering the transitional question, you should proceed with a series of easy, open questions designed to follow up on the subject's answer and to expand on the information already provided. Questions like "How long have you been working here?" or "What do you like best about your job?" or "What do your responsibilities involve?" are good examples of background questions that will help you get a better understanding of what the subject does and what information he might possess.

Observe Verbal and Nonverbal Behavior   During the period when the respondent is talking, you should discreetly observe the person's verbal and nonverbal behavior; this will help you calibrate the subject's mannerisms. Later, when more sensitive questions are posed, you can look for deviations in the subject's behavior that might indicate discomfort or deception.

Ask Nonleading (Open) Questions   You should use open questioning techniques almost exclusively during the informational phase of the interview. The questions should not be accusatory. Once the respondent has answered open questions, you can go back and review the facts in greater detail. If the subject's answers are inconsistent, you should try to clarify them. But you should not challenge the honesty or integrity of the respondent at this stage of the interview; doing so can cause the subject to become defensive, and reluctant to provide information.

Approach Sensitive Questions Carefully   Words such as "routine questions" can be used to play down the significance of the inquiry. It is important for information-gathering purposes that you not react excessively to the respondent's statements. You should not express shock, disgust, or similar emotions during the interview. Every answer the subject gives should be treated evenly.

Dealing with Difficult People   You invariably will encounter some people who choose to be difficult during an interview. There are five commonsense steps to take with such people:

Do Not React   A subject might be belligerent or try to antagonize you, often for no apparent reason. There are three natural reactions for you in this situation: to strike back, to give in, or to terminate the interview. None of these tactics is satisfactory, as none leads to a productive interview. Instead, consciously ensure that you do not react to anger with hostility.

Disarm the Person   A common mistake is to try to reason with an unreceptive person. Instead, you should attempt to disarm the hostile person—the best tactic is surprise. If the subject is stonewalling, he expects you to apply pressure; if attacking, he expects you to resist. To disarm the subject, listen, acknowledge the point, and agree in whatever ways you can.

Change Tactics   In some situations, changing tactics to reduce hostility might be the only viable option. This means casting what the subject says in a form that directs attention back to the problem, and to the interests of both sides. An effective technique when faced with a hostile subject is to ask what he would do to solve the problem.

Volatile Interviews   A volatile interview is one that has the potential to bring about strong emotional reactions in the respondent. A typical scenario for a volatile interview occurs when you interview close friends or relatives of a suspect. Some individuals, by nature, are resentful of authority figures such as fraud examiners and law enforcement officers. It is important for you to know how to approach a volatile interview.

There should be two interviewers involved in potentially volatile situations. This procedure provides psychological strength for you. Additionally, the second person can serve as a witness in the event that the subject later makes allegations of improper conduct.

Potentially volatile interviews should be conducted on a surprise basis, meaning that the subject should be given little or no advance notice of the interview. If the interview is not conducted by surprise, you run the risk of the respondent not showing up, showing up with a witness, or being present with counsel.

In a potentially volatile interview, the order of questions should be out of sequence. This is to keep the volatile respondent from knowing the exact nature of the inquiry, and where it is leading. Although you will endeavor to obtain information regarding who, what, why, when, where, and how, the order of the questioning will vary from that of other interviews. This is especially important in situations where the respondent might be attempting to protect herself.

The hypothetical question generally is considered to be less threatening, and is therefore ideally suited for the potentially volatile interview. For example, in an interview of Smith regarding Jones, rather than saying, "Did Ms. Jones do it?" ask, "Is there any reason why Ms. Jones might have done it?"

Closing Questions

In routine interviews, certain questions are asked at closing for the purposes of reconfirming the facts, obtaining previously undiscovered information, seeking new evidence, and maintaining goodwill.

Reconfirming Facts   It is not unusual for the interviewer to have misunderstood or misinterpreted statements made by the subject. Therefore, you should go over key facts to make certain that they have been understood. You should not attempt to revisit all the information that the subject has provided. This is wasteful, unnecessary, and may engender frustration or resentment in the subject. Instead, identify the most relevant facts that the subject provided, and go over each of them in summary form.

It is a good technique to pose leading questions at this phase of the interview. This allows you to state what you understood the subject to have said, and gives the subject a chance to confirm or deny your interpretation—"You knew Ms. Jones had some financial problems, is that right?"

Gathering Additional Facts The closing phase also can be used to obtain previously unknown facts. It provides the subject further opportunity to say whatever he wants about the matter at hand. You should make it a point to ask the subject whether he knows of any other documents or witnesses that would be helpful to the investigation. This information is not always volunteered. The theme of the closing phase should be to provide the subject with an opportunity to furnish any relevant facts or opinions that might have been overlooked.

To obtain additional facts, you can simply ask the subject whether there is anything else he would like to say. This gives the (correct) impression that you are interested in all relevant information, regardless of which side it favors. It can be helpful to involve the respondent in solving the case—"If you were trying to resolve this issue, what would you do?"

Concluding the Interview At the conclusion of an interview, it is a good idea to ask respondents whether they believe they have been treated fairly. This is particularly important at the conclusion of an admission-seeking interview, or when the subject has been uncooperative. You generally should ask the question as if it were perfunctory—"Ms. Collins, this is just a standard question: Do you feel that I have treated you fairly in this interview?"

Before concluding, you should always ask the subject whether he has anything else to say. This gives the subject one final chance to add information. You should ask for permission to call the subject if you have any additional questions. This leaves the door open to additional cooperation. It is a good idea to give the subject a business card or a telephone number, and to invite a call if he remembers anything else that might be relevant. Finally, you should shake hands with the subject and thank her for her time and information.

Assessment Questions

The purpose of assessment questions is to establish the credibility of the respondent. Assessment questions are used only when you consider previous statements by the respondent to be inconsistent because of possible deception. By observing the verbal and nonverbal responses of the respondent to these questions, you can assess the respondent's credibility with some degree of accuracy. That assessment will form the basis of your decision about whether to pose admission-seeking questions to obtain a legal admission of wrongdoing.

If the subject has answered all informational questions about the event and you have reason to believe the subject is being deceptive, a theme must be established to justify additional questions. This theme can ordinarily be put forth by saying, "I have a few additional questions." You should not indicate in any way that these questions are for a different purpose than seeking information.

Norming or Calibrating Norming or calibrating is the process of observing behavior before critical questions are asked, rather than during questioning. Norming should be a routine part of all interviews. People who are being truthful will answer questions one way; those who are being untruthful will generally answer them differently. Assessment questions ask the subject to agree with matters that go against the principles of most honest people. In other words, dishonest people are likely to agree with many of the statements, whereas honest people won't. Assessment questions are designed primarily to get a verbal or nonverbal reaction from the respondent. You will then carefully assess that reaction.

Physiology of Deception It is said that everyone lies, and does so for one of two reasons: to receive rewards or to avoid punishment. In most people, lying produces stress. The human body will attempt to relieve this stress (even in practiced liars) through verbal and nonverbal clues. A practiced interviewer will be able to draw, from a subject's behavior, inferences about the honesty of his statements.

Conclusions concerning behavior must be tempered by a number of factors. The physical environment in which the interview is conducted can affect behavior. If the respondent is comfortable, fewer behavior quirks might be exhibited. The more intelligent the respondent, the more reliable verbal and nonverbal clues will be. If the respondent is biased toward you, or vice versa, this will affect behavior. People who are mentally unstable, or are under the influence of drugs, will be unsuitable to interview. Behavior symptoms of juveniles generally are unreliable. Ethnic and economic factors should be carefully noted. Some cultures, for example, discourage looking directly at someone. Other cultures use certain body language that might be misinterpreted. Because pathological liars often are familiar with advanced interview techniques, they are less likely to furnish observable behavioral clues. You must take all relevant factors into account before drawing any conclusions about the meaning of the verbal and nonverbal signals that a subject demonstrates.

Verbal Clues to Deception

Changes in Speech Patterns Deceptive people often speed up or slow down their speech, or speak louder than usual. There might be a change in voice pitch; as a person becomes tense, the vocal chords constrict. Deceptive people also have a tendency to cough or clear their throats during times of deception.

Repetition of the Question Liars frequently repeat the question asked of them in order to gain more time to think about how to respond to it. The deceptive individual will say, "What was that again?" or use similar language.

Comments Regarding the Interview Deceptive people often comment on the physical environment of the interview room, complaining that it is too hot, too cold, and so on. As they come under increasing stress, they may frequently ask how much longer the interview will take.

Selective Memory In some cases, a deceptive person will have a fine memory for insignificant events, but will claim to be unable to remember important facts.

Making Excuses Dishonest people frequently make excuses about things that look bad for them, such as, "I'm always nervous; don't pay any attention to that."

Oaths On frequent occasions, dishonest people will attempt to add credibility to their lies by use of emphasis. Expressions such as "I swear to God," "Honestly," "Frankly," or "To tell the truth" are frequently used.

Character Testimony A liar often will request that you, "Check with my wife" or "Talk to my minister" in an attempt to add credibility to a false statement.

Answering with a Question Rather than denying allegations outright, a deceptive person frequently answers with a question such as, "Why would I do something like that?" As a variation, the deceptive person sometimes will question the interview procedure, asking, "Why are you picking on me?"

Overuse of Respect   Some deceptive people go out of their way to be respectful and friendly. When accused of wrongdoing, it is unnatural for a person to react in a friendly and respectful manner.

Increasingly Weaker Denials   When an honest person is accused of something he did not do, that person is likely to become angry or forceful in making the denial. The more the person is accused, the more forceful the denial becomes. The dishonest person, on the other hand, is likely to make a weak denial. Upon repeated accusations, the dishonest person's denials become weaker, to the point that the person becomes silent.

Failure to Deny   Honest people are more likely than dishonest people to deny an event directly. An honest person might offer a simple and clear "no" while a dishonest person will qualify the denial: "No, I did not take a kickback on June 27." Other qualifying denial phrases include, "To the best of my memory" and "As far as I recall," or similar language.

Avoidance of Emotive Words   A liar often will avoid emotionally provocative terms such as "steal," "lie," and "crime." Instead, the dishonest person frequently prefers "soft" words such as "borrow" and, referring to a deed in question, "it."

Refusal to Implicate Other Suspects   Both the honest respondent and the liar will have a natural reluctance to name others involved in misdeeds. However, the liar frequently will refuse to implicate possible suspects, no matter how much pressure is applied by you. This is because the culpable person does not want the circle of suspicion to be narrowed.

Tolerant Attitudes   Dishonest people typically have tolerant attitudes toward illegal or unethical conduct. In an internal theft case you might ask, "What should happen to this person when he is caught?" The honest person usually will say, "They should be fired/prosecuted." The dishonest individual, on the other hand, is much more likely to reply, "How should I know?" or "Maybe it is a good employee who got into problems. Perhaps the person should be given a second chance."

Reluctance to Terminate Interview   Dishonest people generally will be more reluctant than honest ones to terminate the interview. The dishonest individual wants to convince you that he is not responsible, so that the investigation will not continue. The honest person, on the other hand, generally has no such reluctance.

Feigned Unconcern   The dishonest person often will try to appear casual and unconcerned, and might react to questions with nervous or false laughter, or with feeble attempts at humor. The honest person, on the other hand, typically will be very concerned at being suspected of wrongdoing, and will treat your questions seriously.

Nonverbal Clues

Full-Body Motions   When asked sensitive or emotive questions, the dishonest person typically will change his posture completely—as if moving away from you. The honest person frequently will lean forward toward you when questions are serious.

Anatomical Physical Responses   Anatomical physical responses are those involuntary reactions by the body to fright such as increased heart rate, shallow or labored breathing, or excessive perspiration. These reactions are typical of dishonest people accused of wrongdoing.

Illustrators   Illustrators are the motions made, primarily with the hands, to demonstrate points when talking. During nonthreatening questions, the illustrators will be used at one rate. During threatening questions, the use of illustrators might increase or decrease.

Hands over the Mouth   Frequently, dishonest people will cover the mouth with the hand or fingers during deception. This reaction goes back to childhood, when many children cover their mouths when telling a lie. It is done, subconsciously, to conceal the statement.

Manipulators   Manipulators are motions such as picking lint from clothing, playing with objects (such as pencils), or holding one's hands while talking. Manipulators are displacement activities, done to reduce nervousness.

Fleeing Positions   During the interview, dishonest people often will posture themselves in a "fleeing position." While the head and trunk might be facing you, the feet and lower portion of the body might be pointing toward the door in an unconscious effort to flee from you.

Crossing the Arms   Crossing one's arms over the middle zones of the body is a classic defensive reaction to difficult or uncomfortable questions. A variation is crossing the feet under the chair and locking them. These crossing motions occur mostly when a person is being deceptive.

Reaction to Evidence   While trying to be outwardly unconcerned, the guilty person will have a keen interest in implicating evidence. The dishonest person often will look at documents presented by you, attempt to be casual about observing them, and then shove them away, as though wanting nothing to do with the evidence.

Fake Smiles   Genuine smiles usually involve the whole mouth; false ones are confined to the upper half. People involved in deception tend to smirk rather than to smile.

Typical Attitudes Displayed by Respondents

Truthful	*Untruthful*
Calm	Impatient
Relaxed	Tense
Cooperative	Defensive
Concerned	Outwardly unconcerned
Sincere	Overly friendly, polite
Inflexible	Defeated
Cordial	Surly

Methodology   Assessment questions should proceed logically from least to most sensitive. In most examples, the basis for the question should be explained before the question is asked. The following questions illustrate the pattern that an interviewer might take in questioning a witness when he has some reason to believe that the respondent, a company employee, has knowledge of a suspected fraud.

EXAMPLE

Interviewer: *"The company is particularly concerned about fraud and abuse. There are laws in effect that will cost the company millions if abuses go on and we don't try to find them. Do you know some of the laws I am talking about?"*

EXPLANATION

Most individuals will not know about the laws concerning corporate sentencing guidelines, and will therefore answer "no." The purpose of this question is to get the respondent to understand the serious nature of fraud and abuse.

EXAMPLE

Interviewer: *"Congress passed a law that can levy fines of more than $200 million against companies that don't try to clean their own houses. And $200 million is a lot of money, so you can understand why the company's concerned, can't you?"*

EXPLANATION

The majority of people will say "yes" to this question. In the event of a "no" answer, you should explain the issue fully and thereafter attempt to get the respondent's agreement. If agreement is not forthcoming, you should assess why not.

EXAMPLE

Interviewer: *"Of course, they are not talking about a loyal employee who gets in a bind. They're talking more about senior management. Have you ever read in the newspapers about what kind of people engage in company misdeeds?"*

EXPLANATION

Most people read the newspapers and are at least generally familiar with the problem of fraud and abuse. Agreement by the respondent is expected to this question.

EXAMPLE

Interviewer: *"Most of them aren't criminals at all. A lot of times, they're just trying to save their jobs, or just trying to get by because the company is so cheap that they won't pay people what they are worth. Do you know what I mean?"*

EXPLANATION

Although the honest person and the dishonest person will both probably answer "yes" to this question, the honest individual is less likely to accept the premise that these people are not wrongdoers. Many honest people will reply to the effect that, while they might understand the motivation, that does not justify stealing.

EXAMPLE

Interviewer: "Why do you think someone around here might be justified in making a secret arrangement with one of the company's vendors?"

EXPLANATION

Because fraud perpetrators frequently justify their acts, the dishonest individual is more likely than the honest person to attempt a justification, such as, "Everyone does it" or "The company should treat people better if they don't want things like this to happen."

The honest person, however, is much less likely to offer a justification.

EXAMPLE

Interviewer: "How do you think we should deal with someone who got in a bind and did something wrong in the eyes of the company?"

EXPLANATION

Similar to other questions in this series, the honest person tends to want to punish the criminal, while the culpable individual will typically avoid suggesting a strong punishment, for example: "How should I know? It's not up to me" or, "If he was a good employee, maybe we should give him another chance."

EXAMPLE

Interviewer: "Do you think someone in your department might have done something wrong because they thought they were justified?"

EXPLANATION

Most people—honest or dishonest—will answer "no" to this question. However, when you get a "yes," the culpable person is more likely to do so without elaborating. The honest person, if answering "yes," will most likely provide details.

EXAMPLE

Interviewer: "Have you ever felt yourself—even though you didn't go through with it—justified in taking advantage of your position?"

EXPLANATION

Again, most people, both honest and dishonest, will answer this question "no." However, the dishonest person is more likely to acknowledge having at least "thought" of doing it.

EXAMPLE

Interviewer: "Who in your department do you feel would think they were justified in doing something against the company?"

EXPLANATION

The dishonest person will not likely furnish an answer to this question, frequently saying something to the effect that anyone could have a justification. Dishonest individuals will be reluctant to provide any answer that narrows the list of possible suspects. The honest individual, however, is more likely to name names—albeit reluctantly.

EXAMPLE

Interviewer: *"Do you believe that most people will tell their manager if they believed a colleague was doing something wrong, like committing fraud against the company?"*

EXPLANATION

The honest person is much more likely to report a misdeed herself, and is more likely to respond "yes" to this question. The dishonest person, on the other hand, is more likely to say "no." When pressed for an explanation, this person might qualify the "no" by adding that the information would be ignored or that it would not be believed.

EXAMPLE

Interviewer: *"Is there any reason why someone who works with you would say they thought you might feel justified in doing something wrong?"*

EXPLANATION

This is a hypothetical question designed to place the thought in the mind of a wrongdoer that someone has named him as a suspect. The honest person typically will say "no." The dishonest person is more likely to try to explain by saying something like, "I know there are people around here that don't like me."

EXAMPLE

Interviewer: *"What would concern you most if you did something wrong and it was found out?"*

EXPLANATION

The dishonest person is likely to accept the proposition of having done something wrong, and to focus on possible repercussions, for example: "I wouldn't want to go to jail." The honest person, on the other hand, is more likely to reject the notion of having committed a crime. If the honest person does address her concerns about being caught in an illegal act, her concerns will usually be along the lines of disappointing friends or family; the dishonest person is more likely to discuss punitive measures.

Admission-Seeking Questions

Admission-seeking interviews are reserved specifically for individuals whose culpability is reasonably certain. They are posed in a precise order designed to (1) clear an innocent person or (2) encourage the culpable person to confess. Admission-seeking questions have at least three purposes. The first is to distinguish the innocent from the culpable. A culpable individual frequently will confess during the admission-seeking phase of an interview, while an innocent person will not do so unless threats or coercion are used. In some instances, the only way to differentiate the culpable from the innocent is to seek an admission of guilt.

The second purpose is to obtain a valid confession. Confessions, under the law, must be voluntarily given and obtained. The importance of a valid and binding confession to wrongdoing cannot be overstated.

The third purpose of the admission-seeking phase is to obtain from the confessor a written statement acknowledging the facts. Although oral confessions are legally as binding as written ones, written statements have greater credibility. They also discourage a person from later attempting to recant.

Presence of Outsiders   It is usually not necessary to inform the subject that he is entitled to have an attorney or other representative present. However, there are cases in which an employee may have the right to have a union representative or even a coworker present. Check with your lawyer if in doubt. Of course, even if the person has a right to have an attorney or other representative present, you should make it clear that the representative will be an observer only; representatives (even attorneys) should not ask questions or object.

Other than the subject and two investigators, no other observers should be permitted in the admission-seeking interview if at all possible. Having others in the room may present legal problems in "broadcasting" the allegation to a third party. Also, it is very difficult to obtain a confession with witnesses present. You should therefore consider whether the case can be proven without the admission-seeking interview.

Miranda Warnings   As a general rule, private employers conducting an internal investigation are not required to give Miranda warnings; however, there are exceptions to the rule. See your attorney for details.

Theme Development   People will confess to wrongdoing when they perceive that the benefits of confession outweigh the penalties. A good interviewer, through the application of sophisticated techniques, will be able to convince the respondent that the confession is in his best interest.

You must offer a morally acceptable reason for the confessor's behavior. You should not imply that the subject is a bad person, and you should never express disgust, outrage, or moral condemnation about the confessor's actions. Culpable people will almost never confess under these conditions. You must be firm, but you must also project compassion, understanding, and sympathy in order to obtain a confession. The goal is to maximize sympathy and minimize the perception of moral wrongdoing.

It is important that you convey absolute confidence in the premise of the admission you seek from the subject—even if you are not fully convinced. People generally will not confess if they believe the accuser has doubts about their guilt. You should make the accusation in the form of a statement of fact; the subject's guilt should already be assumed in the form of the question. Instead of asking, "Did you do it?", ask, "Why did you do it?"

Remember that the first purpose of an admission-seeking question is to distinguish an innocent person from a culpable one. An innocent person generally will not accept the premise that he is responsible. The guilty person, on the other hand, knows he has committed the act, and is not shocked by the premise. The objection, if the person offers one, is more likely to focus on excuses for the conduct rather than outright denial of the conduct.

Obviously, there is a danger during this phase that you will accuse an innocent person of a crime. This is regrettable, but there are some circumstances in which the only way to distinguish the innocent from the culpable is through the use of accusations. You must be careful, however, about opening up yourself or your company to legal liability for the accusation. In general, there is nothing illegal about accusing an innocent person of misdeeds as long as

- The accuser has reasonable suspicion or predication to believe that the accused has committed an offense
- The accusation is made under conditions of privacy
- The accuser does not take any action likely to make an innocent person confess
- The accusation is conducted under reasonable conditions

Steps in the Admission-Seeking Interview

Direct Accusation   During the admission-seeking interview, you must at some point make a direct accusation of the subject. The accusation should not be made in the form of a question, but rather as a statement. Emotive words such as *steal, fraud*, and *crime* should be avoided during the accusatory process. The accusation should be phrased as though the accused's guilt has already been established. Instead of saying, "We have reason to believe that you . . . ", you should say, "Our investigation has clearly established that you . . . ." The first statement leaves some ambiguity as to whether the accused really committed the act; the second affirmatively states that the accused committed the act.

Observe Reaction   When accused of wrongdoing, the typical culpable person will react with silence. If the accused does deny culpability, those denials usually will be weak. In some cases, the accused will almost mumble the denial. It is common for the culpable individual to avoid outright denials. Instead, that person will give reasons why he could not have committed the act in question. The innocent person sometimes will react with genuine shock at being accused. It is not at all unusual for an innocent person, wrongfully accused, to react with anger. As opposed to the culpable person, the innocent person will usually strongly deny carrying out the act or acts in question.

Repeat Accusation   If the accused does not strenuously object after the accusation is made, it should be repeated with the same degree of conviction and strength.

Interrupt Denials   Both the truthful and untruthful person normally will object to the accusation and attempt to deny it. A culpable person is more likely than an innocent one to stop short of an outright denial ("I didn't do it"), and more apt to furnish you with explanations of why he is not, and could not be, the responsible party. In instances in which you are convinced of the individual's guilt, it is very important that the denial be interrupted; an innocent person is unlikely to allow you to prevail in stopping the denial, and it becomes extremely difficult for the accused to change a denial once it has been uttered. If the subject denies the accusation and later admits it, he is admitting to lying. This is very hard to do. Therefore, your job is to prevent an outright denial, thereby making it easier for the subject to eventually confess to the act.

Both the innocent and the guilty person will make an outright denial if forced to do so. Accordingly, you should not solicit a denial at this stage of the admission-seeking interview. Instead of asking, "Did you do this?", which gives the subject a chance to say "no," you should phrase the accusation as though the subject's wrongdoing has already been determined: "Why did you do this?"

Delays One of the most effective techniques for stopping or interrupting a denial is through the use of a delaying tactic. You should not argue with the accused, but rather attempt to delay the outright denial—"I hear what you are saying, but let me finish first. Then you can talk." The innocent person usually will not allow you to continue to develop the theme.

Interruptions Occasionally, it might be necessary to repeatedly interrupt the accused's attempted denial. Because this stage is crucial, you should be prepared to increase the tone of the interruptions to the point at which the accused is prepared to say: "If you keep interrupting, I am going to have to terminate this conversation." The culpable individual will find this threatening, since he wants to know the extent of incriminating evidence in your possession.

Reasoning If the above techniques are unsuccessful, you might attempt to reason with the accused and employ some of the tactics normally used for diffusing alibis (see subsequent discussion). In this technique, the accused is presented with evidence implicating him in the crime. You should not disclose all the facts of the case, but rather small portions here and there.

Establish Rationalization Assuming the subject does not confess to the misconduct when faced with direct accusations, you should proceed to establishing a morally acceptable rationalization that will allow the accused to square the misdeed with her conscience. It is not necessary that the rationalization be related to the underlying causes of the misconduct. It is acceptable for the accused to explain away the moral consequences of the action by seizing on any plausible explanation other than being a "bad person."

If the accused does not seem to relate to one theme, go on to another, and another, until one seems to fit. Thereafter, that theme should be developed fully. Note that the rationalization explains away the moral—though not the legal—consequences of the misdeed. Be cautioned: Do not make any statements leading the accused to believe that he will be excused from legal liability as a result of his cooperation.

Rather than being confrontational, constantly seek agreement from the accused. The goal is to remain in control of the interview while still appearing compassionate and understanding. Again, no matter what conduct the accused has supposedly committed, do not express shock, outrage, or condemnation.

Unfair Treatment Probably the most common explanation for criminal activity in general, and occupational fraud in particular, is in the accused's attempt to achieve equity. As discussed in Chapter 1, studies have shown that counterproductive employee behavior—including stealing—is often motivated by job dissatisfaction. Employees, and others, feel that "striking back" is important to their self-esteem. The sensitive interviewer can capitalize on these feelings by suggesting to the accused that he is a victim: "If you had been fairly treated, this wouldn't have happened, would it?"

Inadequate Recognition Some employees might feel that their efforts have gone completely without notice by the company. As with similar themes, you should be empathetic: "It looks to me that you have given a lot more to this company than they have recognized. Isn't that right?"

Financial Problems Occupational criminals, especially executives and upper management, frequently engage in fraud to conceal a problematic financial condition—either personal or business. You can exploit this theme by expressing sympathy and understanding for the subject's financial problems, as well as understanding for the misconduct: "I know a lot of your investments have taken a beating. I don't know how you managed to keep everything afloat as well as you did. You just did this to stay alive financially, didn't you?"

Aberration of Conduct Many fraudsters believe that their conduct constitutes an aberration in their lives—that it is not representative of their true character. You might establish this theme by agreeing that the misconduct was an aberration: "I know this is totally out of character for you. I know that this would never have happened if something weren't going on in your life. Isn't that right?"

Family Problems Some people commit fraud because of family problems—financial woes caused by divorce, an unfaithful spouse, or demanding children. Men especially—who have been socially conditioned to tie their masculinity to earning power—might hold the notion that wealth connotes family respect. For their part, women have been found to commit white-collar crime in the name of their responsibility to the needs of their husbands and children. The skillful interviewer can convert this motive to his advantage: "I know you have had some family problems. I know your divorce has been difficult for you. And I know how it is when these problems occur. You would have never done this if it hadn't been for the family problems, isn't that right?"

Accuser's Actions You should not disclose the accuser's identity if it is not already known. But in cases where the accuser's identity is known to the accused, it can be helpful to blame the accuser for the problem. Or, the problem can be blamed on the company: "I really blame a large part of this on the company. If some of the things that went on around this company were known, it would make what you've done seem pretty small in comparison, wouldn't it?"

Stress, Drugs, Alcohol Employees sometimes will turn to drugs or alcohol to reduce stress. In some instances, the stress itself will lead to aberrant behavior in a few individuals. A rationalization established by you could play on the subject's substance abuse: "You're one of the most respected people in this company. I know you have been under tremendous pressure to succeed. Too much pressure, really. That's behind what happened, isn't it?"

Revenge Similar to other themes, revenge can be effectively developed as a justification for the subject's misconduct. In this technique, you attempt to blame the offense on the accused's feeling that he needed to "get back" at someone or something: "Linda, what has happened is out of character for you. I think you were trying to get back at your supervisor because he passed you over for a raise. I would probably feel the same. That's what happened, isn't it?"

Depersonalizing the Victim In cases involving employee theft, an effective technique is to depersonalize the victim. The accused is better able to cope with the moral dilemma of her actions if the victim is a faceless corporation or agency: "It's not like what you've done has really hurt one person. Maybe you thought of it this way: 'At most, I've cost each shareholder a few cents.' Is that the way it was?"

Minor Moral Infraction In many cases you can reduce the accused's perception of the moral seriousness of the matter. This is not to be confused with the legal seriousness. Fraud examiners and interviewers should be careful to avoid making statements that could be construed as relieving legal responsibility. Instead, you should play down the moral seriousness of the misconduct. One effective way is through comparisons: "This problem we have doesn't mean you're 'Jack the Ripper.' When you compare what you've done to things other people do, this situation seems pretty insignificant, doesn't it?"

Altruism In many cases, the moral seriousness of the matter can be reduced by claiming the subject acted for the benefit of others. This especially is true if the accused views herself as a caring person: "I know you didn't do this for yourself. I have looked into this matter carefully, and I think you did this to help your husband, didn't you?"

Genuine Need In some cases, employee fraud is predicated by genuine financial need. For example, the accused might be paying for the medical care of sick parents or a child. In those cases, the following techniques might be effective: "You're like everyone else: You have to put food on the table. But in your position, it is very difficult to ask for help. You genuinely needed to do this to survive, didn't you?"

Diffuse Alibis Even if the accused is presented with an appropriate rationalization, it is likely that he will continue to deny culpability. When you are successful in stopping denials, the accused will frequently present one or more reasons why he could not have committed the act in question. You must quickly and decisively diffuse these alibis by convincing the accused of the weight of the evidence. Alibis generally can be diffused using one of the following methods.

Display Physical Evidence It is common for most culpable people to overestimate the amount of physical evidence that you possess. You should try to reinforce this notion through the way the evidence is presented to the accused. The physical evidence—in fraud matters, usually documents—generally should be displayed one piece at a time, in reverse order of importance. In this way, the full extent of the evidence is not immediately known by the accused. When the accused no longer denies culpability, you should stop displaying evidence.

Each time a document or piece of evidence is displayed, you should note its significance. During this phase, the accused is still trying to come to grips with being caught; thus, you should expect that the accused will attempt to lie. As with denials, you should interrupt the expression of alibis and other falsehoods before they are fully articulated. Once the alibis are diffused, you should return to the theme being developed.

Discuss Witnesses Another technique for diffusing alibis is to discuss the testimony of witnesses. The objective is to give enough information about what other people would say without providing too much. Ideally, your statement will create the impression in the mind of the accused that many people are in a position to contradict her story.

Again: Be cautioned about furnishing enough information to the accused to enable her to identify the witnesses. This might place the witness in a difficult position, and the accused could contact the witness in an effort to influence testimony. The accused could take reprisals against potential witnesses, though such cases are rare.

Discuss Deceptions The final technique is to discuss the accused's deceptions. The purpose is to appeal to the person's logic, not to scold or degrade. This technique is sometimes the only one available if physical evidence is lacking. As with other interview situations, the word "lying" should be avoided.

Present Alternative After the accused's alibis have been diffused, he normally will become quiet and withdrawn. Some people in this situation might cry. (If so, be comforting. Do not discourage the accused from showing emotion.) In this stage the accused is deliberating whether to confess. At this point you should present an alternative question to the accused. The alternative question forces the accused to make one of two choices. One alternative allows the accused a morally acceptable reason for the misdeed; the other paints the accused in a negative light. Regardless of which answer the accused chooses, he is acknowledging guilt: "Did you plan this deliberately, or did it just happen?" or "Did you just want extra money, or did you do this because you had financial problems?"

Benchmark Admission Either way the accused answers the alternative question, he has made a culpable statement, or *benchmark admission*. Once the benchmark admission is made, the subject has made a subconscious decision to confess. The questions above are structured so that the negative alternative is presented first, followed by the positive alternative. In this way, the accused has only to nod or say "yes" for the benchmark admission to be made. The accused might also answer in the negative: "I didn't do it deliberately."

In the cases where the accused answers the alternative question in the negative, you should press further for a positive admission: "Then you did it to take care of your financial problems?"

Should the accused still not respond to the alternative question with a benchmark admission, you should repeat the questions or variations thereof until the benchmark admission is made. It is important that you get a response that is tantamount to a commitment to confess. The questions for the benchmark admission should be constructed as leading questions, so that they can be answered "yes" or "no," rather than requiring any sort of explanation; that will come later.

Reinforce Rationalization Once the benchmark admission has been made, you should reinforce the confessor's decision by returning to the theme for the rationalization. This will help the confessor feel comfortable and will let the person know that you do not look down on her. After reinforcing the subject's rationalization, you should make the transition into the verbal confession, in which the details of the offense will be obtained.

Verbal Confession The transition to the verbal confession is made when the accused furnishes the first detailed information about the offense. Thereafter, it is your job to probe gently for additional details—preferably those that would be known only to the perpetrator. As with any interview, there are three general approaches to obtaining the verbal confession: chronologically, by transaction, or by event. The approach to be taken should be governed by the circumstances of the case.

During the admission-seeking interview, it is best to first confirm the general details of the offense. For example, you will want the accused's estimates of the amounts involved, other parties to the offense, and the location of physical evidence. After these basic facts are confirmed, you can then return to the specifics, in chronological order. It is imperative that you obtain an early admission that the accused knew the conduct in question was wrong. This confirms the essential element of intent.

Because of the nature of the psychology of confessions, most confessors will lie about one or more aspects of the offense despite confirming overall guilt. When this happens during the verbal confession, you should make a mental note of the discrepancy and proceed as if the falsehood had been accepted as truthful.

Such discrepancies should be saved until all other relevant facts have been provided by the accused. If the discrepancies are material to the offense, you should either resolve them at the end of the verbal confession or wait and correct them in the written confession. If they are immaterial to the offense, the information can be omitted from the written confession altogether.

You should focus on obtaining the following items of information during the verbal confession:

- Confirmation that the accused knew that the conduct was wrong
- Facts known only to the perpetrator
- Estimated numbers of instances or amounts
- A motive for the offense
- When the misconduct began
- When/whether the misconduct was terminated
- Others who were involved
- Physical evidence
- Disposition of proceeds
- Location of assets
- Specifics of each offense

Confirmation That the Accused Knew That the Conduct Was Wrong
Intent is an essential element in all criminal and civil actions involving fraud. Not only must the confessor have committed the act, but he must also have intended to commit it: "As I understand it, you did this, and you knew it was wrong, but you didn't really mean to hurt the company, is that right?" (Note that the question is phrased so that the confessor acknowledges intent, but "didn't mean *to hurt anyone.*" Make sure the question is not phrased so that the confessor falsely says that he "didn't mean *to do it.*")

Facts Known Only to the Perpetrator
Once the intent question has been solved, the questioning turns to those facts known only to the person who committed the crime. These facts include—at minimum—the accused's estimates of the number of instances of wrongful conduct, as well as of the total amount of money involved. It is best to use open questions here to force the subject to provide as much information about the offense as possible.

Estimated Numbers of Instances/Amounts
In fraud matters in particular, it is common for the accused to underestimate the amount of funds involved as well as the number of instances. This is probably because of a natural tendency of the human mind to block out unpleasant matters. You should take the figures provided by the confessor with a grain of salt. If the accused's response is "I don't know," start with high amounts and gradually work down.

A Motive for the Offense
Motive is an important element of establishing the offense. The motive might be the same as the theme you developed earlier—or it might not. The most common response when a subject is asked about his motive is "I don't know." You should probe for additional information, but if it is not forthcoming, attribute

the motive to the theme developed earlier. The motive should be established along the lines below.

When the Misconduct Began   You will need to determine the approximate date and time that the offense started: "I am sure you remember the first time this happened." Once the subject has admitted to remembering the first instance (which will usually play into the motive), you should simply ask him to "tell me about it." This is phrased as an open question to get the subject to provide as much information as possible.

When/Whether the Misconduct Was Terminated   In fraud matters, especially occupational fraud, the offenses usually are ongoing. That is, the fraudster seldom stops before he is discovered. If appropriate, you should seek the date the offense terminated.

Others Who Were Involved   Most frauds are solo ventures—committed without the aid of an accomplice. However, you should still seek to determine whether other parties were involved. It is best to use soft language: "Who else knew about this besides you?"

By asking who else "knew," you are, in effect, not only asking for the names of possible conspirators, but also about others who might have known what was going on but failed to report it. This question should be leading: not "Did someone else know?", but rather "Who else knew?"

Physical Evidence   Physical evidence—regardless of how limited it might be—should be obtained from the confessor. In many instances, illicit income from fraud is deposited directly in the perpetrator's bank accounts. You should ask the confessor to surrender banking records voluntarily for review. It is recommended that you obtain a separate written authorization, or that language be added to the confession noting the voluntary surrender of banking information. The first method is generally preferable. If other relevant records can be obtained only by the confessor's consent, permission to review those records should also be sought during the oral confession.

Disposition of Proceeds   If it has not come out earlier, you should find out what, in general, happened to any illicit income derived from the misdeeds. It is typical for the money to have been used for frivolous or ostentatious purposes. It is important, however, that the interviewer cast the confessor's actions in a more positive light.

Location of Assets   In appropriate situations, you will want to find out whether there are residual assets that the confessor can use to reduce losses. Rather than asking the accused, "Is there anything left?" the question should be phrased, "What's left?"

Specifics of Each Offense   Once the major hurdles have been overcome, return to the specifics of each offense. Generally, it is best to start with the first instance and work forward chronologically.

Because this portion of the interview is information-seeking in nature, use open questions. It is best to seek the independent recollections of the confessor first before displaying physical evidence. If the confessor cannot independently recall something, documents can be used to refresh her recollection. It is generally best to resolve all issues relating to a particular offense before proceeding to the next offense.

Taking a Signed Statement   At the conclusion of the admission-seeking interview, it is best to obtain a written confession from the subject, if possible. As was discussed earlier, a written statement has greater credibility than an oral confession, and discourages a culpable person from later attempting to recant. The information to be included in the signed statement is essentially the same as that which you should obtain in an oral confession. There are, however, a few extra inclusions that should be made in a written confession.

Voluntary Confessions   The general law of confessions requires that confessions be obtained, and made, completely voluntarily. The statement should contain language expressly stating that the confession is being made voluntarily.

Intent   There is no such thing as an accidental fraud or crime. Both require as part of the elements of proof the fact that the confessor knew the conduct was wrong and intended to commit the act. This can best be accomplished by using precise language in the statement that clearly describes the act (e.g., "I wrongfully took assets from the company that weren't mine" versus "I borrowed money from the company without telling anyone").

As a general rule, strong, emotive words, such as "lie" and "steal," should be avoided, lest the confessor balk at signing the statement. Yet the wording must still be precise:

EXAMPLE

Instead of	*Use*
Lie	*I knew the statement was untrue.*
Steal	*I wrongfully took the property of _____ for my own benefit.*
Embezzle	*I wrongfully took _____ 's property, which had been entrusted to me, and used it for my own benefit.*
Fraud	*I knowingly told _____ an untrue statement and he/she/they relied on it.*

Approximate Dates of Offense   Unless the exact dates of the offense are known, the word "approximately" must precede any dates of the offense. If the confessor is unsure about the dates, language to that effect should be included.

Approximate Amounts of Losses   Include the approximate losses, making sure they are labeled as such. It is satisfactory to state a range ("probably not less than _____ or more than _____ ").

Approximate Number of Instances   Ranges also are satisfactory for the number of instances. The number is important because it helps establish intent by showing a repeated pattern of activity.

Willingness to Cooperate   It makes it easier for the confessor when he perceives that the statement includes language portraying her in a more favorable light. The confessor can convert that natural tendency by emphasizing cooperation and willingness to make amends: "I am willing to cooperate in helping undo what I have done. I promise that I will try to repay whatever damages I caused by my actions."

Excuse Clause   The confessor's moral excuse should be mentioned. You should make sure that the confessor's excuse does not diminish her legal responsibility for the actions. Instead of using language such as "I didn't mean to do this"—which implies lack of intent—focus on an excuse that provides only a moral explanation for the misconduct: "I wouldn't have done this if it had not been for pressing financial problems. I didn't mean to hurt anyone."

Have the Confessor Read the Statement   The confessor must acknowledge that he read the statement, and should initial all the pages of the statement. It might be advisable to insert intentional errors in the statement so that the confessor will notice them. The errors are crossed out, the correct information is inserted, and the confessor is asked to initial the changes. Whether this step is advisable depends on the likelihood that the confessor will attempt to retract the statement or claim that it was not read.

Truthfulness of Statement   The written statement should state specifically that it is true. However, the language also should allow for mistakes. Typical language reads, "This statement is true and complete to the best of my current recollection."

Preparing a Signed Statement   There is no legal requirement that a statement must be in the handwriting or wording of the subject. In fact, it is generally not a good idea to let a confessor draft the statement. Instead, you should prepare the statement for the confessor to sign.

The confessor should read and sign the statement without undue delay. Instead of asking the confessor to sign the statement, say, "Please sign here." Although it is not legally required, it is still a good idea to have two people witness the signing of a statement.

There should not be more than one written statement for each offense. If facts are inadvertently omitted, they can later be added to the original statement as an addendum. For legal purposes, you should prepare separate statements for unrelated offenses, in the event the target is tried separately for each offense.

You should preserve all notes taken during an interview, especially those concerning a confession. Having access to pertinent notes can aid in a cross-examination regarding the validity of a signed statement. Stenographic notes, if any, also should be preserved. Once a confession has been obtained, you should substantiate it through additional investigation, if necessary.

Here is a sample of the way the confession of Linda Reed Collins might be worded:

St. Augustine, Florida

May 1, 2010

I, Linda Reed Collins, furnish the following free and voluntary statement to Loren D. Bridges and Tonya Vincent of Bailey Books, Incorporated. No threats or promises of any kind have been used to induce this statement.

I am senior purchasing agent for Bailey Books, Incorporated, and have been employed by Bailey Books, Incorporated, since 2005. My job is to oversee the purchase of merchandise and other supplies for Bailey Books, Incorporated. As part of my job, I am to ensure that Bailey Books, Incorporated, receives the highest-quality products available at the lowest possible cost.

Commencing in approximately February 2008, and continuing through the current time, I have accepted money from James Nagel, sales representative for Orion Corporation, St. Augustine, Florida. Mr. Nagel offered me money to ensure that his company received preferential treatment in supplying Bailey Books, Incorporated, with stationery and paper products.

On those occasions on which I accepted money, I was aware that Bailey Books, Incorporated, was not obtaining the best product available at the lowest possible price. The price charged for products delivered during the time I accepted money was substantially higher than market value.

On two occasions in April 2009, I authorized the payment of invoices of $102,136 and $95,637, respectively; these invoices were paid without the receipt of any merchandise. Nagel and I subsequently split the proceeds of these invoices equally between us.

I estimate that I have received in excess of $150,000 in connection with Mr. Nagel. I am not sure that anyone at Orion Corporation knew of our arrangement. No one at Bailey Books, Incorporated, had knowledge of, or participated in, my scheme.

I am aware that my conduct is illegal, and that it violated the policies of Bailey Books, Incorporated. I participated in this scheme because my husband and I were having severe financial problems tied to his business. My husband is not aware of this matter. I am truly sorry for my conduct, and I promise to repay any resulting damages.

I have read this statement, consisting of this page. I now sign my name below to affirm that this statement is true and correct to the best of my current knowledge.

Linda Reed Collins

Signature

Witnesses:

Loren D. Bridges

Tonya Vincent

SUMMARY

Nothing is more important to the successful resolution of fraud allegations than the ability to conduct penetrating and legally binding interviews of witnesses and suspects. Regardless of the type of interview being conducted or who is being interviewed, there are five types of questions that can be asked.

Introductory questions set the tone of the interview, and provide a way for an interviewer to introduce the subject matter being discussed. Informational questions are at the heart of the interview. If you have no reason to believe that the witness is providing false information, and if the person being interviewed is not suspected of wrongdoing, closing questions are asked in order to close the interview. Should the

purpose of the interview be to obtain a legally admissible confession of guilt, you will ask assessment questions rather than close the interview; these questions are designed to give you an idea of whether the subject is prone to telling the truth. Admission-seeking questions are constructed in a certain order to improve the likelihood that a subject will confess to wrongdoing.

Because lying does not come naturally to most people, they give off both verbal and nonverbal clues to deception. You must be alert to these clues during the interview. If a subject confesses to wrongdoing during the interview, you should reduce the verbal confession to writing.

ESSENTIAL TERMS

Norming or calibrating The process of observing behavior before critical questions are asked, with the purpose of helping to assess the subject's verbal and nonverbal reactions to threatening questions.

Oaths Certain phrases used frequently by liars to add weight to their false testimony. Examples include "honestly," "frankly," "to tell the truth," and "I swear to God."

Character testimony An attempt by a witness to add credibility to a lie by requesting that you "check with my minister" or "ask my wife."

Illustrators Motions made, primarily by the hands, to demonstrate points when talking. The use of illustrators is usually altered during deception.

Anatomical physical responses The body's involuntary reactions to fright; they include increased heart rate, shallow or labored breathing, and excessive perspiration. These reactions are typical of dishonesty.

Manipulators Motions made by individuals such as picking lint from clothing, playing with objects (such as pencils), or holding one's hands while talking. Manipulators are displacement activities, ways of reducing nervousness.

Fleeing position A posture adopted by an individual under stress during an interview. The head is facing the interviewer, while the feet and legs are pointed toward the door in an unconscious effort to flee the interview.

Benchmark admission A small admission made to wrongdoing that signals a subject's willingness to confess. It is made as a result to an alternative question posed by the interviewer that gives the subject two ways to answer, either of which is an admission of culpability: "Did you just want extra money, or did you do this because you had financial problems?"

Excuse clause A clause inserted in a signed statement that encourages the confessor to sign the statement. It offers a moral, not legal, excuse for the wrongdoing: "I wouldn't have done this if it had not been for pressing financial problems. I didn't mean to hurt anyone."

REVIEW QUESTIONS

15-1 (Learning objective 15-1) What are the five types of interview questions?

15-2 (Learning objective 15-2) What four steps are involved in introductory questions?

15-3 (Learning objective 15-3) What topics should be covered during informational questioning?

15-4 (Learning objective 15-4) When should open questions be used?

15-5 (Learning objective 15-4) When should closed questions be used?

15-6 (Learning objective 15-4) When should leading questions be used?

15-7 (Learning objective 15-5) What are the purposes of closing questions?

15-8 (Learning objective 15-6) What is the purpose of assessment questions, and when are they asked?

15-9 (Learning objective 15-7) What are some nonverbal clues to deception?

15-10 (Learning objective 15-8) What are some of the verbal clues to deception?

15-11 (Learning objective 15-9) What are the steps used in admission-seeking questions?

15-12 (Learning objective 15-10) What are the key elements of a signed statement?

DISCUSSION ISSUES

15-1 (Learning objective 15-1) Why are all five types of interview questions not used in all interviews?

15-2 (Learning objective 15-2) Why are introductory questions so important to an interview's success?

15-3 (Learning objective 15-3) If the witness becomes difficult during the informational phase of an interview, how should this be handled?

15-4 (Learning objective 15-4) Why does the interviewer not use closed or leading questions during the information-gathering phase of the interview?

15-5 (Learning objective 15-5) Why is establishing goodwill with the witness important during the closing phase of the interview?

15-6 (Learning objective 15-6) What is the theory behind how assessment questions work?

15-7 (Learning objectives 15-7 and 15-8) What is the connection between calibrating a witness and verbal and nonverbal clues to deception?

15-8 (Learning objective 15-9) Why are admission-seeking questions asked in a specific order?

15-9 (Learning objective 15-10) Why is the excuse clause used when preparing a signed statement?

CHAPTER 16

OCCUPATIONAL FRAUD AND ABUSE: THE BIG PICTURE

LEARNING OBJECTIVES

After studying this chapter, you should be able to

16-1 Understand and describe abusive conduct

16-2 Determine why attempting to achieve perfection in the workplace is not desirable

16-3 Explain the obstacles to accurately measuring the level of occupational fraud and abuse in organizations

16-4 Determine why greed is an inadequate explanation for occupational fraud and abuse

16-5 Explain the concept of "wages in kind"

16-6 Compare and contrast fraud prevention and fraud deterrence

16-7 Explain the significance of the "perception of detection"

16-8 Identify some of the factors related to increasing the perception of detection

16-9 Explain the relevance of adequate reporting programs to fraud deterrence

16-10 Understand the implications of the Corporate Sentencing Guidelines

16-11 Understand ethics and ethical theory

DEFINING ABUSIVE CONDUCT

The cases we have seen on the preceding pages were, by and large, on the extreme edge of abusive conduct by employees. In short, this data is merely the tip of the iceberg. How deep and massive that iceberg is varies from one organization to another, depending on a complex set of business and human factors.

The depth of the iceberg is also measured by what is defined as abusive conduct. Obviously, the more rules within the organization, the more likely employees are to run afoul of them. A study by Richard Hollinger and John Clark revealed that almost *nine out of ten employees* admitted to committing abusive conduct at some level.[1] Part of that abuse is owing to the diverse nature of individuals. Tom R. Tyler, in his book *Why People Obey the Law*, concluded overwhelmingly that individuals obey only laws they believe in. If a rule makes no sense to employees, they will make their own.[2]

Let me illustrate the point with another personal experience from the FBI. The FBI did a thorough background investigation before they hired me. They investigate each and every agent prospect. When you are hired, it doesn't mean you're perfect—just that they have put you through every wringer they can think of, looking for any imperfection that may surface to disqualify you.

Of those who survive that process, only a tiny percentage are actually hired and put through training school—as I was. From day one, the agents were held to impossibly high standards. To illustrate the mentality at the time, consider what our esteemed instructor told his class of thirty-five eager, bright-eyed trainees. "The FBI doesn't have any ordinary agents. Every single one of them is above average or better," the instructor bragged. One of the trainees sitting toward the back of the class—a mathematical type of guy—raised his hand. "Excuse me," the trainee questioned, "I don't think it is possible for every FBI agent to be above average. By definition, to be above average, there must be an average, and a below average. So not every agent can be above average—it's statistically impossible." The trainee spoke to the instructor with respect but conviction.

The classroom was silent, and every eye went to the front of the room, where the instructor was carefully formulating his response. "Look, Mister," said the instructor. "If J. Edgar Hoover himself said every agent is above average, that's statistical enough for me." And he meant it.

When we graduated from training class and went into the field, the rookie agents had to come to the real world. In the real world, we all got paid 25 percent extra for all the overtime we typically incurred. But the record-keeping requirements were so ridiculous that no one—outside the clerks in Washington—paid any attention to the myriad forms we all had to fill out every month to get paid.

The ridiculous part of the record-keeping, as far as the rank-and-file agent was concerned, was that there was no carryover for overtime accumulated from one period to the next. For example, if you put in 50 percent overtime in pay period 14, you still got paid 25 percent. But if you only put in 10 percent overtime in pay period 15, your overtime would be cut to 10 percent because you could not use the overtime you burned in period 14. But the kicker was that during the course of the year, all the agents would put in at least 25 percent overtime; many ran much higher.

As a result, virtually everyone I knew in the field at that time simply claimed 25 percent each pay period, regardless of the actual time they put in. And we had to certify, under oath, that we had worked that specific amount of overtime—no more, no less. Our agency could not pay us more than 25 percent, so they didn't "officially" want us to put in more time, because government regulations would have required them to pay compensatory time off. So none of us took seriously the certification that bore our signatures. A sworn false statement under oath to the government—which we regularly signed on our forms—warned us all of the criminal penalties involved. Each and every one of us would sign such a form twenty-six times a year—just to get our paychecks. I commented on the irony of it all to a salty old FBI agent one day when both of us were at the sign-in register. "Joe," he said, "welcome to the real world. Here is the way it works: If you've told many lies, you can't get in the FBI. But once you're hired, you have to tell a few just to stay in. And that's all because of these ridiculous regulations."

What is the moral to this story—other than my admitting that during my professional career I have had my own personal experiences with occupational fraud and abuse? There are two morals, in my view. The first is that we cannot eliminate this problem in the workforce without eliminating people. The human race is notoriously subject to periodic fits of bad judgment. Anyone in fraud detection or deterrence who is aiming for perfection from the workforce will not only be disappointed, he will also find that such attitudes invariably increase the problem.

That paradox is the second moral to the story: to quote my longtime colleague Dr. Steve Albrecht, "If you set standards too high, you may be inadvertently giving an employee two choices in his mind—to fail or to lie." Your job in establishing antifraud standards, then, is to make them clear and reasonable. More on that later.

MEASURING THE LEVEL OF OCCUPATIONAL FRAUD AND ABUSE

Since the goal of the antifraud professional is to reduce the losses from these offenses, measuring progress in the traditional sense might be difficult. We have clearly established the reasons why—we only know about the frauds that are discovered.

As we discussed in the introduction to this book, the certified fraud examiners who participated in the *2009 Global Fraud Survey* estimated that the typical organization loses about 5 percent of its gross revenues to all forms of fraud and abuse in the workplace. Considering everything we know, it may be the best number we can use for the present. It at least gives organizations a rough measure of their potential exposure. Whether that exposure is ever discovered is a different matter. We have seen examples of occupational fraud in this book that have gone undetected for years. Except for a fluke of circumstance, many of them could still be thriving today. That, of course, is the most troublesome aspect of many occupational fraud schemes: The longer they go, the more expensive they become. People who start committing fraud will generally continue unless there is a compelling reason to quit.

On an organizational basis, one good indicator of the real risks of fraud is what has happened in the past. Surprisingly few organizations—especially the smaller ones—make any effort to gather historical, fraud-related data: How many offenses occur, what are the losses from each, and what patterns emerge, if any? But remember, this data will not tell you the size of the iceberg, only the size of the tip. Most important, though, gathering historical fraud information will tell you whether the iceberg is growing or melting.

The Human Factor

The diverse case studies in this book have one common element. That is, of course, the human failings that led trusted people to violate that trust. Were these employees, from those in the mailroom to those in the boardroom, all simply greedy? Were they all simply liars? Did they always have defective morals that just surfaced when their honesty was tested? Or were they mistreated, underpaid, and only taking what they considered to be "rightfully" theirs?

The answer, of course, is that it depends. Crime is a complex tapestry of motive and opportunity. The Sultan of Brunei, one of the world's richest men, may have unlimited opportunity to defraud people. But does he have the motive? Contrarily, the minimum-wage cashier may be very motivated to steal in order to keep his lights turned on. But if he is constantly aware that his cash drawer may be counted by surprise, he may not perceive the opportunity to do so. In any antifraud effort, we must always keep in mind that no one factor alone will deter occupational fraud; we must attack the problem on several fronts.

Greed Michael Douglas uttered the now-famous line from the movie, *Wall Street:* "Greed is good." While some may debate whether that is true, there is little debate that greed is certainly a factor in occupational fraud. Indeed, students of this subject are most likely to describe embezzlers and their ilk by that one single word: *greedy*.

The problem with that definition of a fraud motivator is that it is subjective, and begs for the response, "Greedy? Compared to what?" Most of us consider ourselves greedy to some extent; it is, after all, a very human trait. But there are many greedy people who do not steal, lie, and cheat to get what they want. And how can we measure the amount of greed in any way that will become a predictor of behavior? In sum, there is little we can say about greed as a motive that will help us detect or deter occupational fraud.

Wages in Kind In nearly all the case studies in this book, one common thread prevails: Those who chose to commit fraud against their employers felt justified in doing so. A perfect example is the case of Bob Walker, the cashier who began stealing to get even with his employer. Walker had been demoted from a management position to head cashier at his store, a move that included a $300 cut to his monthly pay. Feeling morally justified in his theft, Walker went on to process over $10,000 in false refunds—much more than what his demotion cost him in lost wages.

For the purpose of detecting and deterring occupational fraud, it does not matter whether the employee is *actually* justified, but simply whether he *perceives* that he is. Your prevention efforts must begin with education of employees and staff, attacking this misperception on all fronts—the morality, legality, and negative consequences of committing occupational fraud and abuse.

Employers must also understand the concept of *wages in kind*. I can remember a perfect illustration from my days as an antifraud consultant in the 1980s. A local banker heard me give a speech on fraud prevention, and he later called me. "We have a hell of a time with teller thefts," he confidentially admitted. "I would like to hire you to evaluate the problem and give us some solutions."

I spent several days in the bank, going over the accounting procedures, the history of teller thefts, the personnel policies, and the internal controls. I also interviewed bank supervisors, head tellers, and the rank-and-file. The interviews were particularly revealing.

When it came time to give my report, the banker requested that I meet with his entire board to deliver my conclusions orally and respond to questions. I tried to be as diplomatic as I could, but when the veneer was stripped away, it wasn't a pretty picture. The reason the bank was having problems with teller thefts was because they (1) had inadequate personnel screening procedures, (2) had no antifraud training whatsoever, (3) paid inadequate wages to persons entrusted with drawers full of money, and (4) were perceived by the employees as cheap and condescending. When I finished my presentation to the board, I asked for questions. The silence was deafening. After I stood there for what seemed like eternity, my banker colleague meekly thanked me for my suggestions and told me they would call. They didn't.

Employers must be educated in the concept of wages in kind. There are three basics that are absolutely necessary to minimizing (not eliminating) occupational fraud and abuse. First, hire the right people. Second, treat them well. Third, don't subject them to unreasonable expectations.

Unreasonable Expectations If you have carefully evaluated the case studies in this book, you should have empathy with at least some of the situations that led to an employee deciding to commit fraud. Ernie Philips's situation, for example, reads like the scenario for a *Movie-of-the-Week*. While trying to support a wife and six adopted children, Philips was forced to undergo several back operations that kept him away from work. He then became addicted to the pills that he was given to alleviate the pain from those operations. His CPA practice was on the verge of folding, and he suffered from depression, as well as from chronic anxiety. Under such dire circumstances, how many of us might resort to forging checks in order to get by?

In my view, employers sometimes have unreasonable expectations of their employees that may contribute to occupational fraud and abuse. First, employers frequently expect their employees to be honest in all situations. That belies the human condition. According to Patterson and Kim in *The Day America Told the Truth*, a full 91 percent of people surveyed admitted to lying on a regular basis. Thankfully, most of these lies have nothing to do with fraud. But it must be remembered that though not all liars are fraudsters, all fraudsters are liars. Our approach to deterrence therefore must be not to eliminate lying (something that can't be done), but to keep lies from turning into frauds.

It is easy to see how anyone can confuse the two concepts of lying and fraud. When we lie to our family, our coworkers, our superiors, and our customers, these are typically deceptions motivated by the human desire to tell people what they want to hear—"My, you look nice today!" So keep your eye on the ball: We want to deter fraud specifically; we don't have quite the time to reform humanity, no matter how lofty a goal that is. And deterring fraud requires some understanding.

UNDERSTANDING FRAUD DETERRENCE

Deterrence and prevention are not the same thing, although we frequently use the terms interchangeably. Prevention, in the sense of crime, involves removing the root causes of the problem. In this case, to prevent fraud, we would have to eliminate the motivation to commit it, such as the societal injustices that lead to crime. We as fraud examiners must leave that task to the social scientists. Instead, we concentrate on *deterrence*, the modification of behavior through the perception of negative sanctions.

Fraud offenders are much easier to deter than run-of-the-mill street criminals. Much violent crime is committed in the heat of the moment, and criminologists agree that such crimes are very difficult to stop in advance. But fraud offenders are very deliberate people, as you have seen in this book. At each stage of the offense, they carefully weigh—consciously or subconsciously—the individual risks and rewards of their behaviors. For that reason, their conduct is easier to modify.

The Impact of Controls

Throughout this book, you have witnessed situations that could have been prevented by the most basic control procedure: separating the money from the record-keeping function. Having said that, it is likely that we accountants and auditors ask controls to do too much. After all, many internal controls have nothing to do with fraud. And still others are only indirectly related. My view is that internal controls are only part of the answer to fraud deterrence. However, some do not share that view. They argue that if the proper controls are in place, occupational fraud is almost impossible to commit without being detected.

The Perception of Detection

As alluded to throughout these pages, the deterrence of occupational fraud and abuse begins in the employee's mind. The perception of detection axiom is as follows:

> *Employees who perceive that they will be caught engaging in occupational fraud and abuse are less likely to commit it.*

The logic is hard to dispute. Exactly how much deterrent effect this concept provides is dependent on a number of factors, both internal and external. But as you can see, internal controls can have a deterrent effect only when the employee perceives that such a control exists and is for the purpose of uncovering fraud. "Hidden" controls have no deterrent effect. Conversely, controls that are not even in place—but are perceived to be—will have the same deterrent value.

How does an entity raise the perception of detection? That, of course, varies from organization to organization. But the first step is to bring occupational fraud and abuse out of the closet and deal with the issue in an open forum. Companies and agencies must be cautioned that increasing the perception of detection, if not handled correctly, will smack of "Big Brother" and can cause more problems than it solves. But organizations can take at least six positive steps to increase the perception of detection.

Employee Education   Unless the vast majority of employees are in favor of reducing occupational fraud and abuse, any proactive fraud deterrence program is destined for failure. It is therefore necessary that the entire workforce be enlisted in this effort. Organizations should provide at least some basic antifraud training at the time workers are hired. In this fashion, the employees become the eyes and ears of the organization, and are more likely to report possible fraudulent activity.

Education of employees should be factual rather than accusatory. Point out that fraud—in any form—is eventually very unhealthy for the organization and the people who work there. Fraud and abuse cost raises, jobs, benefits, morale, and profits, as well as the integrity of those who perpetrate them. The fraud-educated workforce is the fraud examiner's best weapon—by far.

Proactive Fraud Policies   When I ask most people how to deter fraud, they typically say something like this: "In order to prevent fraud, we must prosecute more people. That will send a message." There are at least three flaws in this well-meaning argument. First, there is nothing proactive about prosecuting people. As some in Texas would say, it is like closing the barn door after the cows have escaped. Second, whether it really sends much of a message is debatable. This concept is called "general deterrence" by criminologists. As logical as the idea sounds on its face, there is no data—out of scores of studies—that shows it actually works.

Without getting into the intricacies of criminological thought, punishment is believed by many experts to be of little value in deterring crime because the possibilities of being punished are too remote in the mind of the potential perpetrator. Think about it for a second. If you were debating whether to commit a crime (of any kind) the first question that comes into your mind is: "Will I be caught?" not "What is the punishment if I am caught?" If you answer yes to the first question, you are very unlikely to commit the offense. That makes the punishment moot, no matter how severe it is.

The foregoing is not to say that crime should not be punished. Quite the opposite—it is something that must be done in a civilized society. But remember that the primary benefit of any type of punishment is society's retribution for the act, not that punishment will deter others.

A Higher Stance   Proactive fraud policies begin simply with a higher stance by management, auditors, and fraud examiners. That means, as previously stated, bringing fraud out of the closet. At every phase of a routine audit or management review, the subject of fraud and abuse should be brought up in a nonaccusatory manner. People should be asked to share their knowledge and suspicions, if any. They should be asked about possible control and administrative weaknesses that might contribute to fraud. What we are trying to accomplish through this method is to make people subtly aware that if they commit illegal acts, others will be looking over their shoulders.

A higher stance also means making sure that "hidden" controls don't remain that way. Auditors may have a peculiar image to the uninformed. Employees know auditors are there, but they are not quite sure what the auditors actually do. While this attitude can obviously bring benefits if you are trying to conduct your activities in secret, it is counterproductive in proactive fraud deterrence. You must let employees know that you are looking.

Increased Use of Analytical Review   If an employee embezzles $100,000 from a Fortune 500 corporation, it will not cause even a blip in the financial statements. And in large audits, the chance of discovering a bogus invoice is remote at best. That is because of the sampling techniques used by auditors—they look at a relatively small number of transactions in total.

But as you can see from the cases in this book, the real risks are in asset misappropriations in small businesses. These, of course, can be—and frequently are—very material to the bottom line. And the smaller businesses are those that benefit the most from the increased use of analytical review. Throughout this book we have presented dozens of proactive computer-aided audit tests that are specifically tailored to the various forms of occupational fraud that we have discussed. These audit tests were accumulated and organized by Richard B. Lanza in his publication *Proactively Detecting Occupational Fraud Using Computer Audit Reports*,[3] and they have been reprinted here with his permission. These tests should be a part of any organization's proactive fraud program.

Surprise Audits Where Feasible   The story of Bill Gurado best illustrates the concept of the perception of detection in audits. As you recall, Barry Ecker, the auditor, was simply joking when he told Gurado that an audit was imminent. Based on that false information, Gurado confessed that he had been stealing from his branch. The reason? Gurado was convinced his unlawful conduct was about to be discovered.

The threat of surprise audits, especially in businesses that are currency-intensive, may be a powerful deterrent to occupational fraud and abuse. In case after case, all too many fraud perpetrators were aware that audits were coming, so they had time to alter, destroy, and misplace records and other evidence of their offenses. Obviously, surprise audits are more difficult to plan and execute than a normal audit, which is announced in advance. But considering the impact of the perception of detection, surprise audits may certainly be worth the trouble.

Adequate Reporting Programs   As many of the cases in this book illustrate, adequate reporting programs are vital to serious efforts to detect and deter occupational fraud and abuse. In situation after situation we encountered, employees suspected that illegal activity was taking place, but they had no way to report this information without fear of being "dragged into" the investigation.

Reporting programs should emphasize at least six points: (1) fraud, waste, and abuse occur at some level in nearly every organization; (2) this conduct costs jobs, raises, and profits; (3) the organization actively encourages employees to come forward with information; (4) there are no penalties for furnishing good-faith information; (5) there is an exact method for reporting, such as a telephone number or address; (6) a report of suspicious activity does not have to be made by the employee to his immediate supervisor.

A hotline is considered by most professionals to be the cornerstone of an employee reporting program. According to some studies, about 5 percent of hotline calls are actually developed into solid cases. But in many instances, these schemes would not have been discovered by any other method. And as the data from our *2009 Global Fraud Survey* shows, tips from various sources (employees, vendors, customers, and anonymous) are the most common means by which occupational fraud is detected.

Hotlines also help to increase the perception of detection. An employee who is aware that his nefarious activities might be reported by a coworker will be less likely to engage in such conduct. One final advantage of a hotline is that it helps corporations comply in part with the federal Corporate Sentencing Guidelines.

THE CORPORATE SENTENCING GUIDELINES

The Federal Sentencing Guidelines were one of the most dramatic changes in U.S. criminal law. Not only do the Sentencing Guidelines seek to make punishments more uniform, but they also dramatically increase the severity with which convicted defendants are punished. Additionally, the Sentencing Guidelines can mitigate potentially devastating penalties for any entity convicted of a crime that has an effective compliance program in place.

Definition of Corporate Sentencing

Responding to concerns over the wide disparity in federal sentencing, Congress passed the Sentencing Reform Act in 1984. As part of the broader Comprehensive Crime Control Act of 1984, the Sentencing Report Act established the United States Sentencing Commission (USSC), which was charged with promulgating guidelines governing criminal sentencing in federal courts. Once established, the USSC began studying sentences for individuals, and after three years of study, the USSC submitted the draft guidelines for comment and congressional approval. The Federal Sentencing Guidelines for individuals became effective on November 1, 1987.

Shortly after the guidelines became effective, the USSC began studying sanctions for organizations, even though it had no clear direction to do so. Four years later, the USSC submitted its Proposed Guidelines for Sentencing Organizations for congressional approval, and on November 1, 1991, these guidelines became effective. The underlying philosophy of the Guidelines for Organizations has been characterized as a "carrot-and-stick" approach to criminal sentencing. That is, if the organization prevents or discloses certain conduct, its punishment will be reduced.

Specifically, the organizational sentencing guidelines offer a reduced sentence to a convicted organization if it had an effective compliance program in place at the time of the offense. Thus, if an organization had implemented and maintained such a program, the judge overseeing the case would consider the organization's acts of due diligence in trying to prevent the illegal conduct when deciding whether to mitigate the entity's punishment.

For nearly twenty-five years, the Sentencing Guidelines were mandatory in application; however, as a result of the Supreme Court's 2005 decision in *United States v. Booker*, the Guidelines are now considered advisory only. Thus, judges must consider the Sentencing Guidelines when sentencing convicted organizations, but they are not required to issue sentences within the range set forth by the Guidelines. However, sentencing judges are still required to examine the adequacy of the entity's compliance program according to the Guidelines.

Vicarious or Imputed Liability

Unlike individuals, corporations can be held legally responsible for the criminal acts of their employees if those acts are done in the course and scope of their employment and for the ostensible purpose of benefiting the corporation. The corporation will be held criminally responsible even if those in management had no knowledge or participation in the underlying criminal events and even if there were specific policies or instructions prohibiting the activity undertaken by the employees. In fact, a corporation can be held criminally responsible for the collective knowledge of several of its employees even if no single employee intended to commit an offense. Thus, the combination of vicarious or imputed corporate criminal liability and the Sentencing Guidelines for Organizations creates an extraordinary risk for corporations today.

Requirements

The Sentencing Guidelines encourage organizations to exercise due diligence in seeking to prevent and detect criminal conduct by their officers, directors, employees, and agents. At minimum, the following seven steps are required by the Sentencing Guidelines for due diligence:

1. Have policies defining standards and procedures to be followed by the organization's agents and employees
2. Assign specific high-level personnel who have ultimate responsibility to ensure compliance
3. Use due care not to delegate significant discretionary authority to people who the organization knew or should have known had a propensity to engage in illegal activities
4. Communicate standards and procedures to all agents and employees and require participation in training programs
5. Take reasonable steps to achieve compliance—for example, by use of monitoring and auditing systems and by having, and publicizing, a reporting system by which employees can report criminal conduct without fear of retribution (hotline or ombudsman program)
6. Consistently enforce standards through appropriate discipline, ranging from dismissal to reprimand
7. After detection of an offense, take all reasonable steps to appropriately respond to this offense and to prevent further similar offenses—including modifying its program and appropriately disciplining those who were responsible for the offense and those who failed to detect it

The Sentencing Guidelines provide for both criminal and civil sanctions. The maximum fines may reach up to $290 million, and the corporation can be placed on probation for up to five years.

THE ETHICAL CONNECTION

Wheelwright defined ethics as follows:

That branch of philosophy which is the systematic study of reflective choice, of the standards of right and wrong by which a person is to be guided, and of the goods toward which it may ultimately be directed.[4]

More generally, moralists believe that ethical behavior is that which produces the greatest good, and that which conforms to moral rules and principles. Although ethics is often used interchangeably with morality and legality, the terms are not precisely the same. Ethics is much more of a personal decision. In theory, ethics is how you react to temptation when no one is looking.

Fundamentally, there are two schools of ethical thought. The first, adhering to the "imperative principle," advocates that there are concrete ethical principles that cannot be violated. The second, adhering to "situational ethics" or the "utilitarian principle," generally advocates that each situation must be evaluated on its own—in essence, that the end can justify the means. Probably the majority of people in modern-day society follow situational ethics. But regardless of one's particular ethical philosophy, the sticky problems exist in defining what constitutes the "greatest good." It is certainly easy to see how the CEO of a corporation that employs thousands of individuals would rationalize that committing financial statement fraud will help save jobs, thus justifying his conduct to himself as the "greatest good."

Similarly, an employee can perceive that a major corporation having lots of money will never miss the amount he so desperately needs to keep afloat financially. This was demonstrated in the story of Larry Gunter and Larry Spelber, two employees who saw the opportunity to finance their entire educations by taking six small boxes of computer chips from their employer's warehouse. In a building filled to the brim with computer chips, who would miss six boxes?

And it is no surprise that some of the biggest crooks view themselves inwardly as very ethical; to this day, it is doubtful that Charles Keating views himself as more than a victim of circumstance, regardless of the fact that little old ladies across America have lost every dime they owned.

So the reality is that for most, the "greatest good" invariably turns out to be what is the good for the individual making the ethical decision. Is it coincidence? Probably not; ancient and modern philosophers usually subscribe to one of three schools of thought about the essence of people: (1) humans as good, (2) humans as evil, or (3) humans as calculating. In the latter estimation, people will always consistently seek pleasure and/or avoid pain. This is a lesson most of us learn very young.

Behaviorists tell us that the vast majority of our personality has been formed by the age of three. A large part of our personality relates to the values we have, which are instilled in us by our parents and mentors. Without being a cynic (which I admit to), it is highly unlikely that ethical policies—no matter how strong they are—will seriously deter those sufficiently motivated to engage in occupational fraud and abuse.

There is no ethical policy stronger than the leadership provided by the head of the organization. Modeling of behavior occurs with strong influences such as the boss. Indeed, the Treadway Commission specifically commented on the importance of the "tone at the top." Unfortunately, the formal ethics policies in place right now are thought to exist mostly in large organizations. In the small business—which is much more vulnerable to going broke from asset misappropriations—few of the bosses victimized seem to realize the importance of their own personal example.

When employees hear their leaders telling the customer what he wants to hear, when the small business boss fudges on the myriad taxes he must pay, when the chief executive officer lies to the vendors about when they will be paid, nothing good can possibly result. So setting an example is the *real* ethical connection.

Having said that, formal ethics policies are recommended for all organizations, regardless of their size. They certainly don't do any harm, and they just may provide some deterrence. But almost as important is that having an ethics policy makes enforcement of conduct generally easier to legally justify. A sample Code of Business Ethics and Conduct from the ACFE *Fraud Examiner's Manual* is in the appendix to this book. Feel free to use the example to develop your own ethics policy. Three things are important regardless of what form your policy finally takes: (1) Set out specific conduct that violates the policy, (2) state that dishonest acts will be punished, and (3) provide information on your organization's mechanism for reporting unethical conduct.

Although some professionals will disagree, I think it is a terrible idea to lace an ethics policy with draconian statements such as "All violators will be prosecuted to the maximum extent allowed by law." First, even to many honest people, such a statement smacks of a veiled threat. Second, the victim of fraud does not decide criminal prosecution; this decision is made by the state. As a practical matter, your organization has little control, and it is unlikely that many first-time offenders will get more than a probated sentence.

Finally, your organization's ethical policy, whatever it is, can be only as good as the reinforcement it gets. A company that provides just one training program on ethics, never to mention the subject again, cannot expect results, however marginal. So training must be continuous, and it must be positive in tone. Don't preach; instead, keep emphasizing the simple message: fraud, waste, and abuse are eventually bad for the organization, as well as for everyone in it.

CONCLUDING THOUGHTS

Within the pages of this book, many details of occupational fraud and abuse have been revealed. But those searching for a "magic bullet" to detect these offenses are doubtless still looking. Indeed, the dream of many in the accounting community is to develop new audit techniques that will quickly and easily point the finger of suspicion. To those innocent souls I wish good luck. Regardless of the ability of computers to automate a great deal of drudgery, there are no new audit techniques, and there haven't been any for the last several centuries.

Another factor makes the detection of occupational fraud and abuse difficult. Fraud is one of the few crimes whose clues are not unique to commission of the offense. For example, clues in a bank robbery case would be the witnesses who saw the robber, the records reflecting the loss, the security cameras, and such. By contrast, the indicators of a bank embezzlement can be internal control weaknesses, missing or incomplete documents, and figures that don't add up. The problem, of course, is that none of these latter clues is conclusive evidence of fraud; red flags could just as easily turn out to be red herrings.

I am confident that this book will help you detect and deter fraud. But detection can be almost impossible when committed by someone clever, and motivated, enough to hide his tracks. For those of us who are fraud examiners, that fact is sometimes hard to swallow. If you are the best fraud examiner in the world, you will detect some cases and resolve them. But you'll never get them all, no matter how hard you try.

In putting forward your best efforts to detect fraud, you'll sometimes be tempted to try too hard. You will weigh in your mind whether you should take an unauthorized look at the suspect's bank account; you'll wrestle with the dilemma of whether to secretly check the fraudster's credit records. Don't do it.

Overreaching an investigation or fraud examination is the quickest way to ruin it. Not only will you be unsuccessful in proving your case, you will subject yourself to possible criminal and civil penalties. If you get to a point in a fraud examination when you don't know what to do, stop. Resolve all doubt in favor of your suspect, or check with counsel on the next step.

In a perfect world, we would probably abandon our efforts to detect fraud and concentrate exclusively on deterrence. As we all know, prevention of any problem—from cancer to crime—is usually cheaper and more effective than the aftermath. In the area of occupational fraud, for reasons we have discussed extensively in this book, deterrence can work better than for nearly every other type of crime.

Deterrence, as we have explicitly stated, is much more than internal control. And we accountants concentrate primarily on those controls to deter fraud. As history has witnessed, it is an inadequate effort. For a number of years I have advocated the concept of the *Model Organizational Fraud Deterrence Program*. Under the program, we in the audit community would invest the resources to find out what works in organizations that don't have much of a problem with occupational fraud and abuse. What works will be a combination of both accounting and nonaccounting factors. We know some of the factors already, but we need to know more. From new research, we would then develop a complete checklist of the model organization, and use that checklist to audit against. Then the external auditor would attest to the organization's compliance with the model, not to whether the auditor has uncovered material fraud. The latter approach, adopted by the accounting community now, is bound to drive up the cost of the audit and the price of litigation.

So the bad news is that we cannot audit ourselves out of the occupational fraud and abuse problem. But the good news is that there are a multitude of new approaches we can try. Some of them are in this book—which is but a beginning.

SUMMARY

Abusive conduct, which includes fraud, is difficult to define and quantify. This conduct will exist at some level in all organizations. Setting standards of conduct too high can cause employees to fail or to cheat. The level of occupational fraud and abuse is difficult, if not impossible, to accurately measure. Crime is a complex formula that involves not only opportunity, but motives. Greed alone is an inadequate explanation for fraud because it is a natural human trait that exists, to varying degrees, in everyone, and because it cannot be quantified.

"Wages in kind" are taken when employees, who feel mistreated or underpaid, attempt to make up the difference through fraudulent and abusive conduct. Fraud prevention implies removing the root causes of fraud, such as economic conditions. Deterrence is the modification of behavior through the threat of negative sanctions. Controls, per se, don't deter fraud; it is the perception in the mind of the potential perpetrator that his conduct will be detected that provides the deterring effect.

The U.S. Corporate Sentencing Guidelines hold the company liable for the criminal conduct of its employees, and recommend stiff sanctions unless the company has actively tried to prevent fraud from occurring.

The "tone at the top" provides a stronger message to employees than any written ethics policy. History has clearly demonstrated that auditing alone will not deter fraud; new approaches must be considered.

ESSENTIAL TERMS

Abusive conduct Counterproductive, fraudulent, or other activities of employees that are detrimental to the organization.

Wages in kind The actions taken by employees to right what they perceive as workplace wrongs through counterproductive behavior, including fraud and abuse.

Fraud prevention Removing the root causes of fraudulent behavior, such as economic deprivation and social injustices.

Fraud deterrence Discouraging fraudulent activities through the threat of negative sanctions.

Perception of detection The likelihood, as perceived by an employee, that his fraudulent conduct will be discovered.

Corporate Sentencing Guidelines A U.S. federal law passed in 1991 that provides recommended sanctions for organizations that have engaged in criminal conduct. The sanctions can be mitigated if the organization can prove that it complied with one or more of seven steps designed to prevent or deter fraud.

Vicarious or imputed liability A legal theory that holds the organization liable for the criminal conduct of its employees.

Imperative ethical principle The belief that concrete ethical principles exist that must not be violated (e.g., the end does not justify the means).

Utilitarian ethical principle The belief that each behavior should be evaluated on its own merits (e.g., the end justifies the means).

REVIEW QUESTIONS

16-1 (Learning objective 16-1) What is "abusive conduct"?

16-2 (Learning objective 16-2) Why is attempting to achieve perfection in the workplace not desirable?

16-3 (Learning objective 16-3) Why is it difficult or impossible to measure the actual level of occupational fraud and abuse within organizations?

16-4 (Learning objective 16-4) Why is greed an inadequate explanation as the motive for occupational fraud?

16-5 (Learning objective 16-5) What is meant by "wages in kind"?

16-6 (Learning objective 16-6) What is the difference between fraud prevention and fraud deterrence?

16-7 (Learning objective 16-7) What is the significance of the "perception of detection"?

16-8 (Learning objective 16-8) What are some of the factors that may help increase the perception of detection?

16-9 (Learning objective 16-9) Why are adequate reporting programs so important to fraud deterrence?

16-10 (Learning objective 16-10) What are the key elements of the Corporate Sentencing Guidelines?

16-11 (Learning objective 16-11) What is ethics?

DISCUSSION ISSUES

16-1 (Learning objective 16-1) Why do employees engage in abusive conduct against organizations?

16-2 (Learning objective 16-2) How are employees likely to react to unreasonably restrictive rules in the workplace?

16-3 (Learning objective 16-3) What are some of the ways an organization might improve measurement of the level of occupational fraud and abuse?

16-4 (Learning objective 16-4) Since everyone is greedy to some extent, why do only some individuals engage in fraudulent activity?

16-5 (Learning objective 16-5) What actions might an organization take to prevent the taking of "wages in kind"?

16-6 (Learning objective 16-6) Why should fraud examiners seek to deter fraud rather than prevent it?

16-7 (Learning objectives 16-7 and 16-8) How do internal controls impact the "perception of detection"?

16-8 (Learning objective 16-9) What is the most essential element of an adequate reporting program? Why?

16-9 (Learning objective 16-10) What basic procedures should an organization follow in order to fulfill its due diligence responsibility as it relates to the Corporate Sentencing Guidelines?

16-10 (Learning objective 16-11) What is meant by "tone at the top"?

ENDNOTES

1. Richard C. Hollinger and John P. Clark, *Theft by Employees* (Lexington: Lexington Books, 1983).
2. Tom R. Tyler, *Why People Obey the Law* (New Haven: Yale University Press, 1990).
3. Richard B. Lanza, CPA, PMP, *Proactively Detecting Occupational Fraud Using Computer Audit Reports* (Institute of Internal Auditors Research Foundation, 2003), pp. 41–44.
4. Association of Certified Fraud Examiners, *Fraud Examiners' Manual* (Austin: ACFE, 2010).

ONLINE SOURCES OF INFORMATION

COMMERCIAL ONLINE SERVICES

LexisNexis

In one form or another, LexisNexis has been in the information business for nearly thirty years. It prides itself on being "the company that invented electronic information research." Users can obtain access to public records, media publications, and court cases and records. www.lexisnexis.com

USDatalink

The USDatalink investigative database cannot retrieve information as quickly as some of the other databases on the market, but USDatalink is the only company that relies entirely on manual searches for its information. Unlike other public records search services, USDatalink sends its researchers to county courthouses to look up requested information, rather than relying on the electronic (and possibly faulty) information that other online investigative databases use. If a fraud examiner has the time to wait for an answer to his inquiry, USDatalink might be the most reliable option. The database also has media resources. www.usdatalink.com

infoUSA.com

infoUSA.com users have access to information about 14.5 million U.S. and 1.6 million Canadian businesses, 2 million executives and professionals, and 204 million U.S. consumers. Among the facts available through the service are sales volume, corporate linkage, contact names and titles, company history, credit ratings, and any headlines involving the business. Searches are versatile and can be performed according to business size, location, length of time in operation, gender or race of owners, and industry. www.infousa.com

D&B

The variety of information available through D&B (formerly Dun & Bradstreet) is impressive. D&B is probably one of the most comprehensive and diverse sources available, with facts on more than 52 million companies in more than 200 countries. International business information is searchable as well. D&B is renowned for products like *America's Corporate Families* and *Industry Norms and Key Business Ratios*. Information can be purchased on CD-ROM or via the company website. www.dnb.com

DCS Information Systems

Founded in 1967, DCS Information Systems is an established source for reliable investigative information. Its AmeriFind online resource system product is separated into three areas:

- PrimeData, which provides banking and finance information

- QuickFind, which serves general investigations, security, and fraud detection and prevention
- FraudTracer, which serves insurance fraud investigations and claims

www.dcs-amerifind.com

Merlin Information Services

Merlin Information Systems provides access to public records and other databases for use in locating individuals, searching for assets, running background checks, and performing investigative work. Records are available by CD-ROM as well as online. Merlin is also an excellent source for industry links. www.merlindata.com

SEARCH ENGINES

Search engines are online tools that allow users to type in keywords describing the subject in which they are interested. The search engine then scours the pages of the Internet and attempts to locate pages that may contain pertinent information. There are several prominent search engines on the Internet, and each works slightly differently.

Google

Google is the most used search engine in the United States and features many advanced search capabilities. Individual Web pages are ranked by the engine's software according to how often the page is linked to by others, determining the page's perceived "importance" by the number of links and the identity of the linking page. www.google.com

Bing

Bing is an Internet search engine created by Microsoft. Bing automatically groups search results in different categories, depending on the type of search conducted. www.bing.com

Altavista

Altavista is a detail-oriented search engine. Because it reads through the individual text of every page it encounters as it crawls the Internet, Altavista is very useful for finding random information. www.altavista.com

Yahoo!

Yahoo! is a multifaceted website equipped with an excellent search engine. Yahoo!'s filters will return far fewer pages than Altavista, concentrating on ten to twenty pages that will likely be of interest. Therefore, Yahoo! should not be used to look for hard-to-find information, but it is a good source for locating information that the user knows is out there. www.yahoo.com

Meta-search Engines

Meta-search engines send user requests to several other search engines and display the results:

- Metacrawler (www.metacrawler.com) uses meta-search technology to search the Internet's top search engines, including Google, Yahoo! Search, Bing, Ask.com, and more.

- Dogpile (www.dogpile.com) sends search terms to a customizable list of search engines, directories, and specialty search sites and then displays the results from each search engine individually.

- Mamma (www.mamma.com) is a "smart" meta-search engine, meaning that every time a user types in a query, Mamma simultaneously searches a variety of engines, directories, and deep content sites; properly formats the words and syntax for each; compiles their results in a virtual database; eliminates duplicates; and displays them in a uniform manner by relevance.

- SurfWax (www.surfwax.com) is a meta-search engine that provides a single interface to a number of search engines.

SOCIAL NETWORKING SITES

Social networking sites are specialized websites that build on the concept of the traditional social networks by which individuals connect and build relationships with other people.

- Facebook (www.facebook.com) provides a forum for its users to add friends; post messages, photos, and videos; and join networks.

- Twitter (www.twitter.com) enables its users to send and read short, text-based messages (140 characters or less).

- MySpace (www.myspace.com) allows its users to establish a free profile within the MySpace network to interact with friends, family, and colleagues. The site allows members to share photos, updates, and interests with a community of millions.

- LinkedIn (www.linkedin.com) is a professional networking site through which members can establish and build a network of work-related connections.

- Bebo (www.bebo.com) provides an online community that allows its users to meet, communicate, and share photos, music, and other types of files.

- Orkut (www.orkut.com) is designed to help users meet new friends and maintain existing relationships. Although Orkut is less popular in the United States than Facebook and MySpace, it is one of the most visited sites in India and Brazil.

- hi5 (http://hi5.com) aims for an international audience with a localized interface that is available in many languages.

Social Networking Search Engines

There is an ever-growing number of Internet resources for searching social-networking sites. These resources use social networks to order, prioritize, or refine search results.

- Icerocket (www.icerocket.com) specializes in real-time search technology and allows users to search blogs, the news, and popular social networking sites like Twitter and MySpace.

- Spokeo (www.spokeo.com) gathers information about people by searching for their e-mail addresses on various social networking sites.

- Yoname (www.yoname.com) gathers information about people across social networks, blogs, Flickr, and other sites.

- Technorati (http://technorati.com) allows users to search sites like YouTube, MySpace, Blog, and Xanga.

- FriendFeed (www.friendfeed.com) consolidates updates from social networking sites, social bookmarking sites, blogs, and other types of RSS feeds.
- Zoominfo (www.zoominfo.com) finds information about people, companies, and jobs.
- Delver.com (www.delver.com) displays search results prioritized by the searcher's social network and community.
- Lococitato (www.lococitato.com) provides online tools to visually map, search, and record social networks.

PUBLIC RECORDS

Court Information

- PACER (http://pacer.psc.uscourts.gov) provides access to civil and criminal cases from U.S. District Courts, including a national search of all available courts, as well as access to U.S. Bankruptcy and Appellate Courts.
- The U.S. Tax Court (www.ustaxcourt.gov) is an invaluable source for personal financial information, including, on occasion, tax returns and bank account information.
- The National Center for State Courts (www.ncsc.org) provides links to federal, state, local, and international courts.
- Crimetime Publishing (www.crimetime.com) provides links to many civil and criminal courts.
- Courtlink (www.lexisnexis.com/coutlink/online) provides access to the calendar of proceedings of a lawsuit (docket) and the documents filed during the course of that suit. This site also offers information on strategic profiles, alerts of new cases being filed, tracking of ongoing cases, and document retrieval.

Criminal Records

- The Federal Bureau of Prisons' Inmate Locater (www.bop.gov/iloc2/LocateInmate .jsp) allows investigators to determine whether an individual has been incarcerated in a federal prison from 1982 to present. (Archived information on anyone incarcerated prior to 1982 can be obtained by writing the Federal Bureau of Prisons.) This site also lists telephone numbers for each state's Department of Corrections that will provide similar information.
- The Sex Offenders Registry (www.fbi.gov/hq/cid/cac/states.htm) provides links to state sex offender registries.
- The GA Public Records Services (GAPRS) (www.gaprs.biz) can run an on-site criminal record search in any county in the United States. GAPRS provides affordable search services for employment screening, corporate due diligence, fraud investigations, private investigations, and tenant screenings. Average cost (per county): $8.
- Statewide Criminal Record Searches can be conducted through the Federal Bureau of Prisons' website (www.bop.gov), GAPRS (www.gaprs.biz), LexisNexis (www.lexisnexis.com), and Searchsystems.net (www.searchsystems.net).

Personal Identification Information

- The Social Security Administration's Master Death Index (http://ssdi.rootsweb .ancestry.com) is searchable by name, Social Security number, last known address, or dates of birth and death, and lists the names of people who have died and for whom death claims have been filed.

- Anybirthday.com (www.anybirthday.com), a site that has collected approximately 140 million birthdays from public records, can be a useful resource for finding or verifying personal identification information.

- The Selective Service System website (www.sss.gov) is another important resource for verifying personal data; it requires name, date of birth, and Social Security number.

- Ancestry.com (www.ancestry.com) provides access to a wide array of vital records, Social Security death records, and other information.

Locating Individuals

- Yahoo! People Search (http://people.yahoo.com) enables searches by phone number, address, and e-mail address, as well as reverse phone number searches.

- Infospace (www.infospace.com) is an online service that provides residential and business phone numbers and addresses. It also contains directories of e-mail addresses and fax numbers and allows for reverse address and phone searches.

- Switchboard.com (www.switchboard.com) and 411.com (www.411.com) are two sites for conducting residential searches.

- DCS Information Systems (www.dcsinfosys.com) allows searches by first name, age range, and other identifiers.

- Missingmoney.com (www.missingmoney.com) provides access to a national database of state unclaimed property records.

Enforcement Actions

- The List of Parties Excluded from Federal Procurement and Nonprocurement Programs (www.epls.gov), provided by the General Service Administration (GSA), lists parties that are excluded from receiving federal contracts, certain subcontracts, and certain federal financial and nonfinancial assistance and benefits.

- The Bureau of Industry and Security's List of Denied Persons (www.bis.doc.gov/ dpl/default.shtm) provides a list of parties who have been denied export privileges by the U.S. Department of Commerce.

- The Directorate of Defense Trade Controls website (www.pmdtc.state.gov) contains information on compliance with laws and regulations pertaining to defense trade controls.

- The Inspectors General website (www.ignet.gov) provides reports and information collected from inspectors general from fifty-nine federal agencies.

- The Office of Thrift Supervision (OTS) Prohibition Orders Database (www.ots.treas.gov/?p=EnforcementSearch) contains a list of OTS enforcement orders prohibiting the named institution-affiliated parties from participating in the affairs of insured depository institutions, certain other federally chartered institutions, and federal depository institution regulations.

- The SEC Enforcement Actions database (www.sec/gov/divisions/enforce.shtml) allows users to search SEC records to determine whether a company or an individual has been the subject of any SEC enforcement actions.
- LexisNexis CourtLink (http://courtlinklearning.lexisnexis.com) specializes in searching the records of federal agencies. It also retrieves court documents nationwide and files Freedom of Information Act requests.
- The World Bank Listing of Ineligible Firms (www.worldbank.org) provides a list of companies found to have violated the fraud and corruption provisions of the World Bank's Procurement Guidelines or Consultants Guidelines.

Additional Government Resources

- The Federal Deposit Insurance Corporation (FDIC) website (www.fdic.gov) provides searchable databases that allow users to find institutions and their branches to determine their status as insured depository institutions, their financial condition, and their condition relative to other institutions. This database may also contain other financial and nonfinancial information about individual financial institutions.
- The 10K Wizard (www.10Kwizard.com) provides free, real-time online access and full-text search of the SEC's EDGAR system, thus providing the public a real-time link to SEC's filings.
- Fedworld (www.fedworld.gov) provides access to thousands of U.S. government sites.
- USA.gov (www.usa.gov) is the most comprehensive collection of U.S. government websites. Administered by the U.S. General Services Administration's Office of Citizen Services and Communications, this site makes it easy for the public to get U.S. government information and services online.
- PoliticalMoneyLine (www.tray.com) provides information concerning political contributions to federal candidates (and some candidates for statewide offices as well).
- The Center for Responsive Politics (www.opensecrets.org) allows users to track federal campaign contributions and lobbying activity.

Freedom of Information Act (FOIA)

- The Reporters' Committee for Freedom of the Press (www.rcfp.org) provides information about federal and state FOIA laws, the use of hidden cameras, and a state-by-state listing of laws regarding the legality of taping telephone conversations.
- The Department of Justice (www.justice.gov) houses the Office of Information and Privacy, which administers the FOIA.

Sites with Extensive Public Record Links

- KnowX (http://knowx.com) offers public records searches in various categories, including asset searches, adverse filings, property valuation, and people- and business-locator tools. Users can also verify licenses, conduct background checks, and look up a company's history.
- BRB Publishing (www.brbpub.com) provides links to a variety of public record resources and has a database of public record retrievers.

- Investigative Reporters and Editors (www.ire.org) offers a database library containing government data on a variety of subjects.

- Docusearch (www.docusearch.com) provides links to state resources.

- Refdesk (www.refdesk.com) indexes and provides reviews for thousands of current Internet-based reference resources.

- Hoover's (www.hoovers.com) provides comprehensive, up-to-date business information for professionals who need intelligence on U.S. and global companies, industries, and professionals.

- Fuld and Company (www.fuld.com) provides access to a large collection of corporate information.

- Corporate Information (www.corporateinformation.com) provides corporate information on the leading companies in fifty-nine countries. The site also offers extensive analysis reports available for subscription.

- AutotrackXP (www.atxp.choicepoint.com) allows users to browse and search through billions of current and historical records on individuals and businesses.

- Dialog.com (www.dialog.com) offers more than 1,200 databases and contains nearly 2 billion records, including references and abstracts of published literature; statistical tables; the full text of selected articles; and directory, business, and financial data.

NEWS SEARCHES

As sources of information go, few can match the detail and depth of valuable facts that are found in daily newspapers. Fortunately for the investigator, many of the nation's major newspapers are available online for free. Most newspaper sites will execute archive searches on behalf of the user. However, although articles from newspaper archives are often free of change, some sites do charge the user to search the newspaper's archives.

- LexisNexis (www.lexisnexis.com) is a legal and business information database that provides subscribers with daily newspapers for either a flat fee or a per-use fee.

- Factiva (www.factiva.com) is a database tailored for business or financial news searches, maintaining a catalog of more than 20,000 of the world's leading news and business sources from 159 countries.

- Highbeam Research (www.highbeam.com) maintains an extensive archive, updated daily, of more than 60 million documents from leading publications, going back as far as twenty years. Searchable sources include newspapers, magazines, journals, transcripts, books, dictionaries, and almanacs.

- Findarticles (www.findarticles.com) provides free access to articles previously published in more than 3,000 magazines, journals, and other sources.

- Newslink (www.newslink.org) provides links to newspapers, magazines, radio/TV websites, and other resources.

- Northern Light (www.northernlight.com) provides free news searches for the previous two weeks. Northern Light indexes Web pages and searches through pay-per-view articles not generally available to the public.

OTHER SOURCES OF INFORMATION

University Libraries

Another key source of information on the Internet is the vast number of university library archives. The majority of online libraries allow users to search or browse an online catalog of publications and articles available within the library stacks.

State Government Listings

All states have websites available to the public, but some are more useful than others. Most of the sites have links to a state's insurance department and then to its fraud bureau's site. The sites might also have information concerning legislation that could be of importance to the fraud examiner.

Maps

If a fraud examiner has an address and wishes to view a map of the location, there are several services (e.g., Google Maps, Yahoo! Maps, and MapQuest) that allow users to enter an address and view a map of the area. Most of these sites also give directions to get to the address and provide information about the surrounding area. Additionally, some sites provide satellite images of the location, allowing investigators to zoom in on an aerial photograph of the site.

International Websites

Some investigations reach to locations outside of the country, and websites for other countries may be of use to the investigator. Search engines that are specific to a country can cut research time considerably. In addition, the government and law enforcement sites for other countries are also particularly useful, and some of their links back to websites in the United States are very complete.

SAMPLE CODE OF BUSINESS ETHICS AND CONDUCT

INTRODUCTION

This section reaffirms the importance of high standards of business conduct. Adherence to this Code of Business Ethics and Conduct by all employees is the only sure way we can merit the confidence and support of the public.

Many of us came from a culture that provided answers or direction for almost every situation possible. Managing our business was not so complex; the dilemmas we faced were—for the most part—simple, making our choices relatively easy. But we would probably all agree that managing in today's environment is not so simple.

This code has been prepared as a working guide and not as a technical legal document. Thus, emphasis is on brevity and readability rather than on providing an all-inclusive answer to specific questions. For example, the term *employee* is used in its broadest sense and refers to every officer and employee of the company and its subsidiaries. The word *law* refers to laws, regulations, orders, and so forth.

In observance of this code, as in other business conduct, there is no substitute for common sense. Each employee should apply this code with common sense and the attitude of seeking full compliance with the letter and spirit of the rules presented.

It is incumbent on you, as an employee of the company, to perform satisfactorily and to follow our policies and comply with our rules as they are issued or modified from time to time.

These policies and rules are necessary to effectively manage the business and meet the ever-changing needs of the marketplace. Good performance and compliance with business rules lead to success. Both are crucial since our ability to provide you with career opportunities depends totally on our success in the marketplace. Nonetheless, changes in our economy, our markets, and our technology are inevitable. Indeed, career opportunities will vary between the individual companies. For these reasons, we cannot contract or even imply that your employment will continue for any particular period of time. You may terminate your employment at any time, with or without cause, and we reserve that same right. This relationship may not be modified, except in writing signed by an appropriate representative of the company.

This Code of Business Ethics and Conduct is a general guide to acceptable and appropriate behavior at the company, and you are expected to comply with its contents; however, it does not contain all of the detailed information you will need during the course of your employment. Nothing contained in this code or in other communications creates or implies an employment contract or term of employment. Additionally, we are committed to reviewing our policies continually. Thus, this code might be modified or revised from time to time.

You should familiarize yourself with this code so that you might readily identify any proposal or act that would constitute a violation. Each employee is responsible for his actions. Violations can result in disciplinary action, including dismissal and criminal prosecution. However, no reprisal will be made against an employee who in good faith reports a violation or suspected violation.

The absence of a specific guideline practice or instruction covering a particular situation does not relieve an employee from exercising the highest ethical standards applicable to the circumstances.

If any employee has doubts regarding a questionable situation that might arise, the employee should immediately consult his immediate supervisor or a higher-level employee.

Competition and Antitrust

Fair Competition   The company supports competition based on quality, service, and price. We will conduct our affairs honestly, directly, and fairly. To comply with the antitrust laws and our policy of fair competition, employees:

- Must never discuss with competitors any matter directly involved in competition between ourselves and the competitor (e.g., sales price, marketing strategies, market shares, and sales policies)
- Must never agree with a competitor to restrict competition by fixing prices or allocating markets, or by other means
- Must not arbitrarily refuse to deal with or purchase goods and services from others simply because they are competitors in other respects
- Must not require others to buy from us before we will buy from them
- Must not require customers to take from us a service they don't want before permitting them to get one they do want
- Must never engage in industrial espionage or commercial bribery
- Must be accurate and truthful in all dealings with customers, and must be careful to accurately represent the quality, features, and availability of company products and services

Compliance with Laws and Regulatory Orders   The applicable laws and regulatory orders of every jurisdiction in which the company operates must be followed. Each employee is charged with the responsibility of acquiring sufficient knowledge of the laws and orders relating to his duties in order to recognize potential dangers and to know when to seek legal advice.

In particular, when dealing with public officials, employees must adhere to the highest ethical standards of business conduct. When we seek the resolution of regulatory or political issues affecting the company's interests, we must do so solely on the basis of the merits and pursuant to proper procedures in dealing with such officials. Employees may not offer, provide, or solicit, directly or indirectly, any special treatment or favor in return for anything of economic value or for the promise or expectation of future value or gain. In addition, there shall be no entertaining of employees of the U.S. government.

Foreign Corrupt Practices Act   No employee will engage in activity that might involve the employee or the company in a violation of the Foreign Corrupt Practices

Act of 1977. The Foreign Corrupt Practices Act requires that the company's books and records accurately and fairly reflect all transactions, that we maintain a system of internal controls, that transactions conform to management's authorizations, and that the accounting records are accurate. No employee will falsely report transactions or fail to report the existence of false transactions in the accounting records. Employees certifying the correctness of records, including vouchers or bills, should have reasonable knowledge that the information is correct and proper.

Under the Act it is also a federal crime for any U.S. business enterprise to offer a gift, payment, or bribe, or anything else of value, whether directly or indirectly, to any foreign official, foreign political party or party official, or candidate for foreign political office for the purpose of influencing an official act or decision, or seeking influence with a foreign government in order to obtain, retain, or direct business to the company or to any person. Even if the payment is legal in the host country, it is forbidden by the Act and violates U.S. law.

CONFLICTS OF INTEREST

Several situations that could give rise to a conflict of interest. The most common are accepting gifts from suppliers, employment by another company, ownership of a significant part of another company or business, close or family relationships with outside suppliers, and communications with competitors. A potential conflict of interest exists for employees who make decisions in their jobs that would allow them to give preference or favor to a customer in exchange for anything of personal benefit to themselves or their friends and families. Such situations could interfere with an employee's ability to make judgments solely in the company's best interest.

Gifts and Entertainment

Definition of Gifts "Gifts" are items and services of value that are given to any outside parties, excluding the following:

- Normal business entertainment items such as meals and beverages
- Items of minimal value, given in connection with sales campaigns and promotions, employee services, or safety or retirement awards
- Contributions or donations to recognized charitable and nonprofit organizations
- Items or services with a total value under $100 per year

Definition of Supplier "Supplier" includes not only vendors providing services and material to the company, but also consultants, financial institutions, advisors, and any person or institution who does business with the company.

Gifts No employee or member of his immediate family shall solicit or accept from an actual or prospective customer or supplier any compensation, advance loans (except from established financial institutions on the same basis as other customers), gifts, entertainment, or other favors that are of more than token value or that the employee would not normally be in a position to reciprocate under normal expense account procedures.

Under no circumstances may a gift or entertainment be accepted that would influence the employee's judgment. In particular, employees must avoid any interest in or benefit from any supplier that could reasonably cause them to favor that supplier over others. It is a violation of the code for any employee to solicit or encourage a supplier to give any item or service to the employee, regardless of its value. Our suppliers will retain their confidence in the objectivity and integrity of our company only if each employee strictly observes this guideline.

Reporting Gifts   An employee who receives, or whose family member receives, an unsolicited gift prohibited by these guidelines, should report it to his supervisor and either return it to the person making the gift or, in the case of perishable gift, give it to a nonprofit charitable organization.

Discounts   An employee might accept discounts on a personal purchase of the supplier's or customer's products only if such discounts do not affect the company's purchase price and are generally offered to others having a similar business relationship with the supplier or customer.

Business Meetings   Entertainment and services offered by a supplier or customer might be accepted by an employee when they are associated with a business meeting and the supplier or customer provides them to others as a normal part of its business. Examples of such entertainment and services are transportation to and from the supplier's or customer's place of business, hospitality suites, golf outings, lodging at the supplier's or customer's place of business, and business lunches and dinners for business visitors to the supplier's or customer's location. The services should generally be of the type normally used by the company's employees and allowable under the applicable company's expense account.

Outside Employment

Employees must not be employed outside the company (1) in any business that competes with or provides services to the company or its subsidiaries, (2) in a manner that would affect their objectivity in carrying out their company responsibilities, or (3) where the outside employment would conflict with scheduled hours, including overtime, or the performance of the company assignments. Employees must not use company time, materials, information, or other assets in connection with outside employment.

Relationships with Suppliers and Customers

Business transactions must be entered into solely for the best interests of the company. No employee can, directly or indirectly, benefit from his position as an employee or from any sale, purchase, or other activity of the company. Employees should avoid situations involving a conflict or the appearance of conflict between duty to the company and self-interest.

No employee who deals with individuals or organizations doing or seeking to do business with the company, or who makes recommendations with respect to such dealings, should:

- Serve as an officer, director, employee, or consultant
- Own a substantial interest in any competitor of the company, or any organization doing or seeking to do business with the company (*Substantial interest* means

an economic interest that might influence or reasonably be thought to influence judgment or action, but shall not include an investment representing less than 1 percent of a class of outstanding securities of a publicly held corporation.)

In addition, no employee who deals with individuals or organizations doing or seeking to do business with the company, or who makes recommendations with respect to such dealings, may:

1. Have any other direct or indirect personal interest in any business transactions with the company (other than customary employee purchases of company products and services as consumers and transactions where the interest arises solely by reason of the employee relationship or that of a holder of securities)

2. Provide telecommunications or information service or equipment, either directly or as a reseller, in a manner that would place the objectivity or integrity of the company in question

Our policy is that employees will not do business on behalf of the company with a close personal friend or relative; however, recognizing that these transactions do occur, such transactions must be reported on the Conflict of Interest Questionnaire.

This policy applies to the members of the immediate family of each employee, which normally includes the spouse, children, children's spouses, parents, siblings, and the parents and siblings of the spouse.

Employment of Relatives

Relatives of employees will not be employed on a permanent or temporary basis by the company in such a way that the relative directly reports to the employee or the employee exercises any direct influence with respect to the relative's hiring, placement, promotions, evaluations, or pay.

Confidential Information and Privacy of Communications

Confidential Information   Confidential information includes all information, whether technical, business, financial, or otherwise, concerning the company that the company treats as confidential or secret or that is not available or is not made available publicly. It also includes any private information of or relating to customer records, fellow employees, other persons or other companies, and national security information that is obtained by virtue of the employee's position.

Company policy and various laws protect the integrity of the company's confidential information, which must not be divulged except in strict accordance with established company policies and procedures. The obligation not to divulge confidential company information is in effect even though material might not be specifically identified as confidential; this obligation exists during and continues after employment with the company.

A few examples of prohibited conduct are (1) selling or otherwise using, divulging, or transmitting confidential company information, (2) using confidential company information to knowingly convert a company business opportunity for personal use, (3) using confidential company information to acquire real estate that the employee knows is of interest to the company, (4) using, divulging, or transmitting confidential company information in the course of outside employment or other relationship or any succeeding employment or other relationship at any time, (5) trading in the company stocks, or the stocks of any company, based on information that has not been disclosed to the public, or divulging such information to others so that they might trade in such stock (insider trading is prohibited by company policy and federal and state law).

Employees shall not seek out, accept, or use any confidential company information of or from a competitor of the company. In particular, should we hire an employee who previously worked for a competitor, we must neither accept nor solicit confidential information concerning that competitor from our employee.

Classified National Security Information Only employees with proper government clearance and a need to know have access to classified national security information. Government regulations, outlined in company instructions, for safeguarding must be followed. Disclosing such information, without authorization, even after leaving employment, is a violation of law and of this code. Adverse information about employees having government clearance must be reported to the security or legal department representatives having responsibility for clearances.

COMPANY ASSETS

Cash and Bank Accounts

All cash and bank account transactions must be handled so as to avoid any question or suspicion of impropriety. All cash transactions must be recorded in the company's books of account.

All accounts of company funds, except authorized imprest funds, shall be established and maintained in the name of the company or one of its subsidiaries and may be opened or closed only on the authority of the company's Board of Directors. Imprest funds must be maintained in the name of the custodian; the custodian is wholly responsible for these funds. All cash received shall be promptly recorded and deposited in a company or subsidiary bank account. No funds shall be maintained in the form of cash, except authorized petty cash, and no company shall maintain an anonymous (numbered) account at any bank. Because payments into numbered bank accounts by the company may leave the company open to suspicion of participation in a possibly improper transaction, no disbursements of any nature may be made into numbered bank accounts or other accounts not clearly identified to the company as to their ownership.

No payments can be made in cash (currency) other than regular, approved cash payrolls and normal disbursements from petty cash supported by signed receipts or other appropriate documentation. Further, corporate checks shall not be written to "cash," "bearer," or similar designations.

Company Assets and Transactions

Compliance with prescribed accounting procedures is required at all times. Employees having control over company assets and transactions are expected to handle them with the strictest integrity and to ensure that all transactions are executed in accordance with management's authorization. All transactions shall be accurately and fairly recorded in reasonable detail in the company's accounting records.

Employees are personally accountable for company funds over which they have control. Employees who spend company funds should ensure that the company receives good value in return and must maintain accurate records of such expenditures. Employees who approve or certify the correctness of a bill or voucher should know that the purchase and amount are proper and correct. Obtaining or creating "false" invoices or other misleading documentation, or the invention or use of fictitious sales, purchases, services, loan entities, or other financial arrangements, is prohibited.

Employees must pay for personal telephone calls and use, except to the extent that specifically defined benefit programs or allowances provide otherwise.

Expense Reimbursement

Expense actually incurred by an employee in performing company business must be documented on expense reports in accordance with company procedures. In preparing expense reports, employees should review these procedures for the documentation that must be submitted in order to be reimbursed for business expenses.

Company Credit Cards

Company credit cards are provided to employees for convenience in conducting company business. No personal expenses can be charged on company credit cards except as specifically authorized by company procedures. Any charged personal expenses must be paid promptly by the employee. Company credit cards should not be used to avoid preparing documentation for direct payment to vendors. Where allowed by local law, charges on company credit cards for which a properly approved expense report has not been received at the time of an employee's termination of employment might be deducted from the employee's last paycheck. The company will pursue repayment by the employee of any amounts it has to pay on the employee's behalf.

Software and Computers

Computerized information and computer software appear intangible, but they are valuable assets of the company and must be protected from misuse, theft, fraud, loss, and unauthorized use or disposal, just as any other company property.

Use of mainframe computers must be customer service- or job-related. Employees cannot access company records of any kind for their personal use. Misappropriation of computer space, time, or software includes, but is not limited to, using a computer to create or run unauthorized jobs, operating a computer in an unauthorized mode, or intentionally causing any kind of operational failure.

Personal computers can be used for company-sanctioned education programs as well as personal use incidental to company business use with the permission of your supervisor. However, personal use cannot be allowed for personal financial gain.

It is also understood that personal computers will occasionally be used at home with the permission of your supervisor.

POLITICAL CONTRIBUTIONS

Federal law and many state laws prohibit contributions by corporations to political parties or candidates. This includes, in addition to direct cash contributions, the donation of property or services and the purchases of tickets to fundraising events. Employees can make direct contributions of their own money, but such contributions are not reimbursable. In addition, employees can make contributions to a company-sponsored Political Action Committee.

Where corporate political contributions are legal in connection with state, local, or foreign elections, such contribution shall be made only from funds allocated for that purpose, and with the written approval of the president of the company making the contribution. The amounts of contributions made shall be subject to intercompany allocation.

It is improper for an employee to use his position within the company to solicit political contributions from another employee for the purpose of supporting a political candidate or influencing legislation. It is also improper for an employee to make a political contribution in the name of the company.

EMPLOYEE CONDUCT

Conduct on Company Business

Dishonest or illegal activities on company premises or while on company business will not be condoned and can result in disciplinary action, including dismissal and criminal prosecution. The following illustrates activities that are against company policy, and that will not be tolerated on company premises, in company vehicles, or while engaged in company business:

1. Consumption and storage of alcoholic beverages, except where legally licensed or authorized by an officer of the company
2. The use of non-physician prescribed controlled substances, such as drugs or alcohol as well as the unlawful manufacture, distribution, dispensation, possession, transfer, sale, purchase, or use of a controlled substance
3. Driving vehicles or operating company equipment while under the influence of alcohol or controlled substances
4. Illegal betting or gambling
5. Carrying weapons of any sort on company premises, in company vehicles, or while on company business, regardless of whether an employee possesses the legally required permits or licenses

The company reserves the right to inspect any property that might be used by employees for the storage of their personal effects. This includes desks, lockers, and vehicles owned by the company. It is a violation of company policy to store any contraband, illegal drugs, toxic materials, or weapons on company property.

Reporting Violations

All employees are responsible for compliance with these rules, standards, and principles. In the area of ethics, legality, and propriety, each employee has an obligation to the company that transcends normal reporting relationships. Employees should be alert to possible violations of the code anywhere in the company and are encouraged to report such violations promptly. Reports should be made to the employee's supervisor, to the appropriate security, audit, or legal department personnel, or elsewhere, as the circumstances dictate.

Employees will also be expected to cooperate in an investigation of violations. In addition, any employee who has been convicted of a felony, whether related to these rules or not, should also report that fact.

All cases of questionable activity involving the code or other potentially improper actions will be reviewed for appropriate action, discipline, or corrective steps. Whenever possible, the company will keep confidential the identity of employees about or against whom allegations of violations are brought, unless or until it has been determined that a violation has occurred. Similarly, whenever possible, the company will keep confidential the identity of anyone reporting a possible violation. Reprisal against any employee who has, in good faith, reported a violation or suspected violation is strictly prohibited.

All employees are required to notify the company within five days of any conviction of any criminal statute violation occurring on the job. In addition, any employee who has been convicted of a felony, whether related to these rules or not, should report that fact.

Discipline

Violation of this code can result in serious consequences for the company and its image, its credibility, and the confidence of its customers, and can include substantial fines and restrictions on future operations as well as the possibility of fines and prison sentences for individual employees. Therefore, it is necessary that the company ensure that no violations occur. Employees should recognize that it is in their best interest—as well as the company's—to follow this code carefully.

The amount of any money involved in a violation may be immaterial in assessing the seriousness of a violation since, in some cases, heavy penalties may be assessed against the company for a violation involving a relatively small amount of money, or no money.

Disciplinary action should be coordinated with the appropriate human resources representatives. The overall seriousness of the matter will be considered in setting the disciplinary action to be taken against an individual employee. Such action, which might be reviewed with the appropriate human resources organization, might include:

- Reprimand
- Probation
- Suspension
- Salary or wage reduction
- Demotion
- A combination of the above
- Dismissal

In addition, individual cases might involve:

- Reimbursement of losses or damages
- Referral for criminal prosecution or civil action
- Both of the above

Disciplinary action might also be taken against supervisors or executives who condone, permit, or have knowledge of illegal or unethical conduct by those reporting to them and who do not take corrective action. Disciplinary action might also be taken against employees who make false statements in connection with investigations of violations of this code.

The disciplinary action appropriate to a given matter will be determined by the company in its sole discretion. The listing of possible actions is merely informative and does not bind the company to follow any particular disciplinary steps, process, or procedure.

The company's rules and regulations regarding proper employee conduct will not be waived in any respect. Violation is cause for disciplinary action, including dismissal. All employees will be held to the standards of conduct described in this booklet.

The company never has authorized, and never will authorize, any employee to commit an act that violates this code, or to direct a subordinate to do so. Thus no such act is justifiable as having been directed by someone in higher management.

COMPLIANCE LETTER AND CONFLICT OF INTEREST QUESTIONNAIRE

Annually, all officers of the company will represent in writing that there are no violations of this code known to the officer after the exercise of reasonable diligence or, if such violations have been committed, will disclose such violations in a format to be specified.

Annually, each employee will review the Code of Business Ethics and Conduct, sign the code's Acknowledgment form, and complete and sign the Conflict of Interest Questionnaire. If the employee's circumstances change at any time, a new Conflict of Interest Questionnaire or letter of explanation must be requested and completed.

The Code of Business Ethics and Conduct Acknowledgment form should be signed and given to your supervisor for inclusion in your personnel file.

COMPANY NAME, INC.
Conflict of Interest Questionnaire

Managerial employees are being asked to complete this Conflict of Interest Questionnaire. COMPANY NAME, Inc., and its subsidiaries are committed to providing a workplace where employees can and do act responsibly and ethically. The COMPANY NAME, Inc., Code of Business Ethics and Conduct sets out specific standards of conduct which should govern our behavior toward our fellow employees, suppliers, and customers. Please answer each of the following questions and, if necessary, provide an explanation. *For any "yes" response, please explain in the extra space provided on the last page.*

Conflict of Interest

1. During fiscal year _____, did you, or anyone you are aware of, receive from any person or company doing business with your employer any loan, gift, trip, gratuity, or other payment that did or could cause prejudice toward or obligation to the giver, or that could be perceived by others as creating an obligation to the giver? *(Note: Each item, or the total of items, from a single vendor with a value of more than $50.00 must be reported, except that you do not need to report loans made by financial institutions on normal and customary terms, common stock dividends, or insurance policy payments.)*

   ❑ Yes   ❑ No

2. In fiscal year _____, did you, or anyone you are aware of, participate in or influence any transaction between your employer and another entity in which they or any member of their family had a direct or indirect financial interest?

   ❑ Yes   ❑ No

3. In fiscal year _____, did you, or anyone you are aware of, have a material financial interest in or hold a position of influence with any business that furnishes goods or services to your employer? *(Note: Someone who has a "material financial interest" is someone who by virtue of his stock ownership or monetary interest in a company is able to direct or to influence business decisions, or a commissioned sales representative; a "position of influence" is an influential position such as a sole proprietor, partner, member of a board of directors, executive, or manager.)*

   ❑ Yes   ❑ No

4. For fiscal year _____, did you, or anyone you are aware of, use company assets or other resources (including funds, equipment, supplies, or personnel) for purposes other than company business or company-sponsored activities?

   ❑ Yes   ❑ No

5. During fiscal year _____, did you, or anyone you are aware of, receive gifts or entertainment from individuals or organizations having dealings with the Company, including but not necessarily limited to loans, any form of cash gratuities, private or personal discounts not sanctioned by the Company, or remuneration or service related to illegal activities?

   ❑ Yes   ❑ No

6. During fiscal year _____, did you, or anyone you are aware of, accept any consideration or special favors from suppliers or potential suppliers that in fact or appearance could be deemed a bribe, kickback, or reward given to influence business judgment?

  ❑ Yes　　❑ No

7. During fiscal year _____, were you, or anyone you are aware of, involved in a conflict of interest?

  ❑ Yes　　❑ No

8. I have read the attached Conflict of Interest Policy Statement set forth in the COMPANY NAME, Inc., [and Subsidiaries] Code of Business Ethics and Conduct. Accordingly, I have listed below all relationships and outside activities that require disclosure under the policy. I have also listed names, addresses, and the nature of the relationships of all persons or entities doing business with my employer from whom I or any member of my immediate family have received, directly or indirectly, cash or a gift of more than nominal value ($50.00) during the fiscal year ended _____, _____. *(If there are no persons or entities to be listed, so indicate by writing "NONE" in the first space provided below.)*

Name of Person/Entity	Nature of Relationship/Outside Activity

Political

9. In fiscal year _____, did you, or anyone you are aware of, receive any payments from your employer for the purpose of making a contribution to any political party, candidate, or election committee?

  ❑ Yes　　❑ No

Securities Trading

10. Did you, or anyone you are aware of, buy or sell stock based on confidential information, or communicate confidential information to influence COMPANY NAME, Inc., stock transactions?

  ❑ Yes　　❑ No

Financial Integrity

11. Are you aware of any entries made in the books and records of your employer in fiscal year _____ that you believe to be false or intentionally misleading?

  ❑ Yes　　❑ No

12. Are you aware of any assets, liabilities, or transactions that you believe were improperly omitted from the books of your company in fiscal year _____?

❑ Yes   ❑ No

13. In fiscal year _____, are you aware of anyone's having sought to influence any governmental official (including foreign officials) or governmental employee, or individual doing business with your company, by offering money, goods, or services in return for some special consideration?

❑ Yes   ❑ No

Other

14. Are you aware of any incident involving your employer that you feel constituted noncompliance with laws, regulations, policies, guidelines, procedures, or ethical principles, other than those matters referred to in other questions or incidents that have already been reported? *(Note: If you prefer to report an incident or violation anonymously, please answer this question and contact a member of the Ethics Committee or call the Confidential Ethics Hotline.)*

❑ Yes   ❑ No

15. Please provide any explanations for "yes" responses.

_____

_____

_____

_____

_____

_____

_____

_____

16. In the space below, please provide any suggestions you may have for improving the Code of Business Ethics and Conduct and Compliance Program.

_____

_____

_____

_____

Printed Name

_____

Signature

_____

Date

COMPANY NAME, INC., AND SUBSIDIARIES

Employee	Company/Subsidiary	Location

Code of Business Ethics and Conduct Employee Certification

I have read the COMPANY NAME, Inc., and Subsidiaries Code of Business Ethics and Conduct.

☐ I understand that the standards and policies in that Code of Business Ethics and Conduct represent the policies of COMPANY NAME, Inc., and its subsidiaries and that violating those standards and policies, or any legal and regulatory requirements applicable to my job, may result in penalties set forth in the Code of Business Ethics and Conduct or other appropriate sanction.

☐ I understand that there are several sources within the company, including the Ethics Committee, that I can consult if I have questions concerning the meaning or application of the Code of Business Ethics and Conduct or relevant legal and regulatory requirements.

☐ I understand that it is my responsibility to disclose to an ethics officer, a member of the COMPANY NAME, Inc., Operations Audit Department, a member of the Ethics Committee, or the Company's Ethics Hotline any situation that might reasonably appear to be a violation of the Code of Business Ethics and Conduct.

☐ I have read the attached Conflict of Interest Policy Statement that is set forth in the COMPANY NAME, Inc., and Subsidiaries Code of Business Ethics and Conduct. Accordingly, I have listed below all relationships and outside activities that require disclosure under the policy. I have also listed names, addresses, and the nature of the relationships of all persons or entities doing business with my employer from whom I or any member of my immediate family have received, directly or indirectly, cash or a gift of more than nominal value ($50.00) during the fiscal year ended _____, _____. *(If there are no persons or entities to be listed, so indicate by writing "NONE" in the first space provided below.)*

Name of Person/Entity	Address	Nature of Business/Relationship

☐ I am not aware of any exceptions to standards and policies in the Code of Business Ethics and Conduct except the following. *(If none, so indicate by writing "NONE".)*

_____

_____

_____

Signature of Employee   **Date**

FRAUD RISK ASSESSMENT TOOL

INTRODUCTION

The ACFE's Fraud Risk Assessment Tool can be used by fraud examiners to identify their clients' or employers' vulnerabilities to fraud.

The Fraud Risk Assessment Tool consists of fifteen modules, each containing a series of questions designed to help organizations focus on areas of risk. The fraud professional and the client or employer should begin the risk assessment process by working together to answer the questions in each module. It is important that the client or employer select people within the organization who have extensive knowledge of company operations, such as managers and internal auditors, to work with the fraud professional. Upon completing all the questions, the fraud professional should review the results of the assessment with the client or employer in order to:

- Identify the potential inherent fraud risks
- Assess the likelihood and significance of occurrence of the identified fraud risks
- Evaluate which people and departments are most likely to commit fraud, and identify the methods they are likely to use
- Identify and map existing preventive and detective controls to the relevant fraud risks
- Evaluate whether the identified controls are operating effectively and efficiently
- Identify and evaluate residual fraud risks resulting from ineffective or nonexistent controls
- Respond to residual fraud risks

The Fraud Risk Assessment Tool may reveal certain residual fraud risks that have not been adequately mitigated as a result of the lack of, or noncompliance with, appropriate preventive and detective controls. The fraud professional should work with the client to develop mitigation strategies for any residual risks with an unacceptably high likelihood or significance of occurrence. Responses should be evaluated in terms of their costs versus benefits and in light of the organization's level of risk tolerance.

Be aware, however, that this assessment only provides a snapshot of a particular point in time. The dynamic nature of organizations requires routine monitoring and updating of financial risk assessment processes in order for them to remain effective.

MODULE 1: EMPLOYEE ASSESSMENT

The employee assessment questions are designed to assess the probability of a fraudulent event occurring within the organization based on:

- Internal controls
- Internal control environment
- Resources available to prevent, detect, and deter fraud

1. *Are employees provided formal written job descriptions?*
   In addition to clarifying the things for which employees are responsible, job descriptions signify the things for which employees are not responsible. Employees who perform duties outside of their job descriptions represent a significant red flag.

2. *Are employees provided with an organizational chart that shows lines of responsibility?*
   Organizational charts provide employees with a snapshot of an organization's division of work, levels of management, and reporting relationships.

3. *Does the company have written accounting policies and procedures?*
   Accounting policies and procedures, including those related to fraud, should be documented, implemented, and communicated to employees.

4. *Is there a formal policy covering approval authority for financial transactions, such as for purchasing or travel?*
   In order to safeguard assets and financial reporting, companies should develop and implement policies for determining how financial transactions are initiated, authorized, recorded, and reviewed.

5. *Does the company have an ethics statement?*
   The company should implement a formal ethics statement that (1) defines conduct that is unethical, (2) states that unethical acts will be punished, and (3) provides information on reporting unethical conduct.

6. *Does senior management exhibit and encourage ethical behavior?*
   Senior management sets the tone for ethical conduct throughout the organization. The tone should signal that fraud will not be tolerated.

7. *Does the company have written fraud policies and procedures?*
   The company should document and implement fraud policies and procedures that describe (1) fraudulent conduct, (2) punishment for engaging in fraudulent conduct, and (3) how to report fraudulent conduct.

8. *Is a senior member of management responsible for compliance with fraud policies?*
   The responsibility for compliance with fraud and ethics policies should be assigned to a senior member of management.

9. *Does the organization educate employees about the importance of ethics and antifraud programs?*
   All employees should receive training on the ethics and antifraud policies of the company. The employees should sign an acknowledgment that they have received the training and understand the policies.

10. *Does the organization provide an anonymous way to report suspected violations of the ethics and antifraud programs?*
    Organizations should provide employees, vendors, and customers with a confidential system for reporting suspected violations of the ethics and antifraud policies.

11. *Are fraud incidents promptly and thoroughly investigated?*
    Promptly and thoroughly investigating all reported incidents of fraud can minimize losses.

12. *Does the company maintain a record of fraud incidents?*
    A formal record of all reported incidents of fraud, including documentation of investigative activities and final disposition of each incident, should be maintained.

13. *Does the company conduct pre-employment background checks?*
Before offering employment to an applicant, a company should conduct a pre-employment background check.

14. *Does the company have a loss prevention function?*
Responsible personnel should be trained to perform loss prevention functions.

15. *Does the company have an internal audit function?*
Internal audits that focus on high-risk areas for fraud can identify new vulnerabilities, measure the effectiveness of internal controls, and signal that fraud prevention is a high priority for the company.

16. *Are the duties related to authorization, custody of assets, and recording or reporting of transactions segregated?*
The company should segregate the duties related to authorization, custody of assets, and recording or reporting of transactions.

17. *Is compliance with internal controls audited periodically?*
Periodic audits of compliance with internal controls send the message to employees that the company is proactive in its antifraud efforts.

18. *Do employees feel they are treated and compensated fairly?*
Management should establish appropriate lines of communication with employees (such as surveys, exit interviews, and open-door policies) to assess their attitudes toward the organization.

19. *Do any employees have large personal debts or credit problems?*
Employees who have large personal debts or credit problems are a red flag for potential fraud and should be monitored by management.

20. *Do any employees appear to be spending far more than they are earning?*
Management should be observant of signs of employees who are spending far more than they are earning. It is common for employees who steal to use the proceeds for lifestyle improvements, including expensive cars and extravagant vacations.

21. *Do any employees gamble excessively?*
Employees who gamble excessively pose a potential fraud risk to the company and should be monitored by management. Employee assistance programs can be made available to help employees with gambling addictions.

22. *Do any employees use alcohol or drugs excessively?*
Employees who use alcohol or drugs excessively pose a potential fraud risk to the company and should be monitored by management. Employee assistance programs can be made available to help employees with alcohol or drug addictions.

23. *Do any employees resent their superiors?*
Employees who resent their superiors should be monitored by management, as they pose a potential fraud risk to the company.

24. *Do any employees have a close association with vendors or competitors?*
Employees who have a close relationship with a vendor or competitor should be monitored for potential conflict of interest.

25. *Do any employees have outside business interests that might conflict with their duties at the company?*
Employees should be required to provide annual financial disclosures that list outside business interests. Outside interests that conflict with the organization's interests should be prohibited.

26. *Is the company experiencing high employee turnover?*
High employee turnover, especially in areas particularly vulnerable to fraud, is a warning sign of fraud that should be investigated.

27. *Are employees required to take annual vacations?*
Requiring employees to take annual vacations can aid an employer in detecting an ongoing fraud scheme because the employer is more likely to discover a perpetrator running such a scheme when the perpetrator is removed from the scene.

28. *Is the company dominated by a small group of individuals?*
If control is centered in the hands of a few key employees, those individuals should be under heightened security for compliance with internal controls and other policies and procedures.

29. *Does the company have unrealistic productivity measurements and expectations?*
Unrealistic productivity measurements and expectations can place undue pressure on employees and result in employees committing fraudulent acts in order to meet them.

30. *Does management fail to give employees positive feedback and recognition for job performance?*
Providing positive feedback and recognition to employees helps reduce the likelihood of internal fraud and theft through boosting morale. Employees who feel positive about an organization are less likely to commit fraud against that organization.

31. *Are employees afraid to deliver bad news to supervisors or management?*
Management should promote a culture in which employees aren't afraid to deliver bad news. After all, the sooner management receives the bad news, the sooner it can respond.

32. *Is there a lack of communication between employees and management?*
Management can improve communication with employees by creating an atmosphere that encourages open communication. Employees should feel safe in sharing any thoughts, comments, complaints, or suggestions.

33. *Is there a lack of clear organizational responsibilities in the company?*
A lack of clear organizational responsibilities can lead to confusion and frustration for employees. Organizational charts and job descriptions can be used to clarify organizational responsibilities.

34. *Does management not seem to care about or reward appropriate employee behavior?*
Management that does not seem to care about or reward appropriate employee behavior can contribute to low employee morale, and to increased risk of fraud against the company by employees.

MODULE 2: MANAGEMENT/KEY EMPLOYEE ASSESSMENT

The management/key employee assessment questions are designed to assess the probability of a fraudulent event occurring within the organization based on:

- Internal controls
- Internal control environment
- Resources available to prevent, detect, and deter fraud

1. *Is the board of directors composed of mainly officers of the company or related individuals?*
   The board of directors should include independent board members who are not associated with or employed by the company. In theory, independent directors are not subject to the same pressures as management and therefore are more likely to act in the best interests of shareholders.

2. *Is there an independent audit committee?*
   Independent audit committee members who have financial and accounting expertise can be instrumental in preventing and detecting financial fraud.

3. *Has there been high turnover of managers and members of the board of directors?*
   Management should investigate the reasons for high turnover and implement measures to reduce it.

4. *Have an unusually high number of key employees left the company recently?*
   Management should investigate the reasons for their departure and implement measures to reduce turnover.

5. *Is the company involved in any litigation?*
   Management should determine the reason for the litigation, monitor the filings, and take corrective action where necessary.

6. *Does the company have offshore activities or bank accounts?*
   Management should determine the reason for the offshore activities and accounts, ascertain compliance with U.S. laws, and monitor activity closely.

7. *Do any of the senior managers have offshore bank accounts or business interests?*
   The organization should require senior managers to file annual financial disclosure reports and explain the purpose of any offshore bank accounts or business interests.

8. *Are any key employees experiencing financial pressures, such as those caused by debt, gambling, medical bills, or divorce?*
   Key employees who are experiencing financial pressures represent a potential fraud risk to the company and should be monitored by management. Employee assistance programs can be made available to help employees with alcohol, drug, and other problems.

9. *Do any key employees appear to be living beyond their means?*
   Management should be observant of signs of employees' spending far more than they are earning. It is common for employees who steal to use the proceeds for lifestyle improvements, including expensive cars, extravagant vacations, or expensive clothing.

10. *Do any key employees have civil judgments or bankruptcies on record?*
    Key employees who have civil judgments or bankruptcies on record represent a potential fraud risk to the company and should be monitored by management.

11. *Do any key employees have a criminal conviction?*
    Key employees who have known criminal convictions should be subjected to increased review by management for compliance with internal controls and other policies and procedures.

12. *Do one or two key employees appear to dominate the company?*
    If control is centered in the hands of one or two key employees, those individuals should be under heightened scrutiny for compliance with internal controls and other policies and procedures.

13. *Do any key employees have friends or relatives reporting directly to them?*
Organizations should prohibit key employees from having friends or relatives report directly to them.

14. *Do any of the key employees appear to have a close association with a vendor?*
Key employees who have a close association with a vendor should be monitored for potential conflict of interest.

15. *Do any key employees have outside business interests that might conflict with their duties at the company?*
Key employees should be required to provide annual financial disclosures that list outside business interests. Interests that conflict with the organization's interests should be prohibited.

16. *Do any key employees own a portion of any company that does business with this company?*
Organizations should require key employees to disclose any potential conflicts of interest and should closely monitor any such conflicts of interest.

17. *Has any key employee failed to take vacation?*
Requiring key employees to take annual vacations can aid an employer in detecting an ongoing fraud scheme, because the employer is more likely to discover a perpetrator running such a scheme when the perpetrator is removed from the scene.

18. *Do any key employees have a significant amount of their net worth invested in the company?*
Management should subject key employees with a significant amount of their net worth invested in the company to increased review for compliance with internal controls, especially those controls related to financial reporting.

19. *Does the company have unexpectedly high debts?*
Management should determine the reason for debt levels and monitor internal controls for financial reporting.

20. *Is key employee compensation primarily based on company performance?*
Organizations should monitor employees whose compensation is based primarily on company performance for compliance with internal controls, especially controls related to financial reporting.

21. *Is there an incentive to use inappropriate means to minimize earnings for tax reasons?*
Companies should remove any incentive to use inappropriate means to manipulate financial information.

22. *Is there excessive pressure to increase the company's stock price?*
Excessive pressure to increase the company's stock price can result in management manipulating financial results in order to meet expectations.

23. *Has the company recently experienced large operating or investment losses?*
Large operating or investment losses can place undue pressure on management to manipulate results in order to cover up the losses.

24. *Does the organization have sufficient working capital?*
Insufficient working capital can place undue pressure on management to manipulate financial results.

25. *Does the organization have sufficient credit?*
A lack of sufficient credit can place undue pressure on management to manipulate financial results in order to obtain credit.

26. *Is the organization under pressure to report favorable earnings?*
    Excessive pressure to report favorable earnings can result in management committing fraudulent acts in order to meet expectations.

27. *Does the company depend heavily on only a limited number of products or customers?*
    Dependence on only a limited number of products or customers places a company at greater risk for fraudulent acts to occur.

28. *Has the company experienced difficulty in collecting receivables?*
    Cash flow problems, which are a warning sign of possible fraud, can arise when a company experiences difficulty in collecting receivables.

29. *Has the company recently expanded rapidly into new business or product lines?*
    Rapid expansion into new business or product lines can place tremendous financial pressure on a company.

30. *Has the company experienced a reduction in sales volume?*
    A reduction in sales volume can place undue pressure on management to manipulate financial results.

31. *Does the company have strong competitors who are outperforming the company?*
    Strong competition can place a company at greater risk for fraudulent acts to occur.

32. *Is the company under pressure to sell or merge with another company?*
    Situational pressures that may lead to fraudulent acts can arise when a company is under pressure to sell or merge with another company.

33. *Does the company change auditors often?*
    A frequent change in auditors is a red flag of fraud.

34. *Does the company delay or avoid supplying auditors with the information necessary to complete the audits?*
    Delaying or avoiding supplying auditors with the information necessary to complete audits is an indicator of fraudulent activity.

35. *Does the company have problems with regulatory agencies?*
    The company should determine the reasons for the problems with regulatory agencies and implement measures to encourage compliance with regulations.

36. *Does the company have poor accounting records?*
    The company should implement proper accounting records.

37. *Does the accounting department appear to be inadequately staffed?*
    The accounting department should be adequately staffed to allow for proper segregation of duties.

38. *Does the organization fail to disclose questionable or unusual accounting practices?*
    Questionable or unusual accounting practices should be disclosed.

39. *Does the company have a number of large year-end or unusual transactions?*
    Large year-end or unusual transactions should be investigated.

40. *Does the organization lack an adequate internal audit staff?*
    The internal audit department should be adequately staffed.

41. *Does the organization lack an internal control system, or does it fail to enforce the existing internal controls?*
    Organizations should establish and enforce an internal control system.

MODULE 3: PHYSICAL CONTROLS TO DETER EMPLOYEE THEFT AND FRAUD

The physical controls assessment questions are designed to assess the probability of a fraudulent event occurring within the organization based on:

- Physical controls in place to control access to accounting records and information
- Physical controls in place to protect the assets of the organization

1. *Does the organization conduct pre-employment background checks to identify previous dishonest or unethical behavior?*
   Before offering employment to an applicant, a company should conduct a pre-employment background check.

2. *Are there policies and procedures that address dishonest or unethical behavior?*
   The company should document and implement policies and procedures that describe (1) unethical conduct, (2) punishment for engaging in unethical conduct, and (3) how to report unethical conduct.

3. *Does management support the ethics and antifraud policies?*
   Senior management sets the tone for ethical conduct throughout the organization. The tone should signal that fraud will not be tolerated.

4. *Does the organization educate employees about the importance of ethics and antifraud programs?*
   All employees should receive training on the ethics and antifraud policies of the company. The employees should sign an acknowledgment that they have received the training and understand the policies.

5. *Does the organization provide an anonymous way to report suspected violations of the ethics and antifraud policies?*
   Organizations should provide a system for anonymous reporting of suspected violations of the ethics and antifraud policies.

6. *Does the organization restrict access to areas containing sensitive documents (such as invoices, receipts, journals, ledgers, and checks) and maintain a system for providing an audit trail of access?*
   Access to areas containing sensitive documents should be restricted to those individuals who need the information to carry out their jobs. Also, an audit trail of access should be maintained.

7. *Does the organization restrict access to computer systems with sensitive documents (such as accounting software, inventory, and payroll) and create a system to provide an audit trail of access?*
   Access to computer systems should be restricted to those individuals who need the information to carry out their jobs. Also, an audit trail of access should be maintained.

8. *Does the organization restrict access to areas with high-value assets, such as shipping, receiving, storerooms, and cash?*
   Organizations should restrict access to areas with high-value assets and should maintain a log of persons accessing such areas.

9. *Does the organization use CCTV and recording equipment to monitor entries, exits, areas with sensitive or high value assets, and sales areas?*
   Entries, exits, areas with sensitive or high value assets, and sales areas can be monitored using CCTV and recording equipment.

10. *Does the organization conduct random, unannounced audits of inventory, cash, expense, purchasing, billing, and other accounts by internal or external auditors?*
Random, unannounced audits help prevent fraud perpetrators from having time to alter, destroy, and misplace records and other evidence of their offenses.

11. *Does the organization use professional loss prevention or security personnel to monitor physical controls?*
Professional loss prevention or security personnel can be used to monitor physical controls.

12. *Does the organization promptly investigate incidents of suspected or reported fraud?*
Promptly investigating incidents of suspected or reported fraud can minimize losses.

MODULE 4: SKIMMING SCHEMES

Skimming schemes include:

- Collecting cash, but not recording the sale
- Collecting cash, keeping a portion of the cash, and underreporting the sale amount
- Collecting a customer's payment, but not crediting the amount to the customer's account
- Collecting cash and holding it in a personal interest-bearing account before depositing it into the company account

1. *Is there periodic analytical review of sales accounts using vertical, horizontal, and ratio analysis?*
Periodic analytical review of sales accounts using vertical, horizontal, and ratio analysis can highlight discrepancies that point to skimming.

2. *Is there periodic review of the inventory and receiving records using statistical sampling?*
Periodic review of the inventory and receiving records using statistical sampling can highlight discrepancies that point to skimming.

3. *Is there periodic review of the inventory and receiving records using trend analysis?*
Periodic review of the inventory and receiving records using trend analysis can highlight discrepancies that point to skimming.

4. *Is there periodic review of the inventory and receiving records using physical inventory counts?*
Periodic review of the inventory and receiving records using physical inventory counts can highlight discrepancies that point to skimming.

5. *Is there periodic review of the inventory and receiving records using verification of shipping and requisition documents?*
Periodic review of the inventory and receiving records using verification of shipping and requisition documents can highlight discrepancies that point to skimming.

6. *Is there periodic review of inventory accounts for write-offs?*
Inventory accounts should be reviewed periodically for write-offs.

7. *Is there periodic review of accounts receivable and allowance for uncollectible accounts to look for write-offs of accounts receivable?*
Accounts receivable and allowance for uncollectible accounts should be reviewed periodically for write-offs of accounts receivable.

8. *Is there periodic review of cash accounts for irregular entries?*
Cash accounts should be reviewed periodically for irregular entries.

9. *Is the company mail opened by someone other than bookkeepers, cashiers, or other accounting employees who make journal entries?*
Company mail should be opened by someone other than bookkeepers, cashiers, or other accounting employees who make journal entries.

10. *Do vouchers for credit and sales receipts contain serial numbers?*
Vouchers for credit and sales receipts should contain serial numbers.

11. *Is the accounts receivable bookkeeper restricted from preparing the bank deposit?*
The accounts receivable bookkeeper should be restricted from preparing the bank deposit.

12. *Is the accounts receivable bookkeeper restricted from collecting cash from customers?*
The accounts receivable bookkeeper should be restricted from collecting cash from customers.

13. *Is the accounts receivable bookkeeper restricted from access to the cash receipts?*
The accounts receivable bookkeeper should be restricted from access to the cash receipts.

14. *Is the cashier restricted from accessing accounts receivable records?*
The cashier should be restricted from accessing accounts receivable records.

15. *Is the cashier restricted from accessing bank and customer statements?*
The cashier should be restricted from accessing bank and customer statements.

16. *Are the responsibilities for general ledger entry, cash receipt entry, and accounts receivable billing each assigned to a separate employee?*
Having different employees perform these tasks helps minimize the potential for the concealment of theft.

17. *Does the employee who opens incoming checks place restrictive endorsements on all checks received?*
The employee who opens incoming checks should immediately stamp all incoming checks with the company's restrictive endorsement to protect against unintended parties cashing the checks.

18. *Does the person who opens the mail prepare a list of all checks and cash received?*
A list of all checks and cash received should be prepared and reconciled daily against the bank deposit receipt and the cash receipts report.

19. *Does the person who opens the mail deliver all checks and cash to the person responsible for the daily bank deposit?*
The person who opens the mail should deliver all checks and cash to the person responsible for the daily bank deposit.

20. *Does an employee perform an independent verification of the bank deposit ticket to the remittance list generated by the employee who opened the mail?*
An employee should perform an independent verification of the bank deposit ticket to the remittance list generated by the employee who opened the mail.

21. *Does the company use a lockbox service for cash receipts?*
Lockboxes decrease the potential for fraud and error by reducing employee handling of each transaction.

22. *Does the company have a safe with restricted access?*
A safe can be used to physically secure excess cash on hand. Access to the safe should be restricted and an access log should be maintained.

23. *Is cash deposited daily?*
Daily bank deposits should be made so that excess cash does not remain on the premises.

24. *Are there prenumbered cash receipts for cash sales?*
Prenumbered cash receipts should be used for cash sales.

25. *Are employees who handle cash bonded?*
Employees who handle cash should be bonded in order to protect against theft.

26. *Is there a written policy and procedure for turning over delinquent accounts for collection?*
The company should document and implement policies and procedures for turning over delinquent accounts for collection.

27. *Is the person who handles customer complaints independent of the cashier or accounts receivable function?*
The person who handles customer complaints should be independent of the cashier or accounts receivable function.

28. *Is physical access to the accounting system restricted to only authorized persons?*
Physical access to the accounting system should be restricted to those who require it to perform their job functions.

MODULE 5: CASH LARCENY SCHEMES

Cash larceny schemes include:

- Stealing cash at the point of sale or register
- Stealing cash receipts posted to sales and receivable journals
- Stealing cash from bank deposits

1. *Are cash register tape totals reconciled to the amount in the cash drawer?*
Cash register tape totals should be reconciled to the amount in the cash drawer. Any discrepancies should be investigated.

2. *Is an employee other than the register worker responsible for preparing register count sheets and agreeing them to register totals?*
An employee other than the register worker should be responsible for preparing register count sheets and agreeing them to register tape totals.

3. *Is access to registers or the cash box closely monitored? Are access codes kept secure?*
Access to registers or the cash box should be closely monitored and access codes should be kept secure.

4. *Are customer complaints regarding short change or improper posting handled by someone other than the employee who receives the cash?*
Customer complaints regarding short change or improper posting should be handled by someone other than the employee who receives the cash.

5. *Are register workers properly supervised?*
Register workers should be properly supervised by on-duty supervisors or CCTV recording of register activity.

6. *Are CCTV cameras and digital recorders used to monitor register areas?*
CCTV cameras and digital recorders can be used to monitor register areas.

7. *Is each receivable transaction reviewed for legitimacy and supporting documentation?*
Receivable transactions should be reviewed for legitimacy and supporting documentation.

8. *Is an independent listing of cash receipts prepared before the receipts are submitted to the cashier or accounts receivable bookkeeper?*
An independent listing of cash receipts should be prepared before the receipts are submitted to the cashier or accounts receivable bookkeeper.

9. *Does a person independent of the cash receipts and accounts receivable functions compare entries to the cash receipts journals with the bank deposit slips and bank deposit statements?*
Companies should assign a person independent of the cash receipts and accounts receivable functions to compare entries to the cash receipts journals with the bank deposit slips and bank deposit statements.

10. *Are the cash receipts, cash counts, bank deposits, deposit receipt reconciliations, bank reconciliations, posting of deposits, and cash disbursements duties segregated?*
The primary way to prevent cash larceny is to segregate duties.

11. *Does an employee other than the cashier or accounts receivable bookkeeper make the daily bank deposit?*
Having an employee other than the cashier or accounts receivable bookkeeper make the daily bank deposit is an important segregation of duties that can help to prevent cash larceny.

12. *Is job or assignment rotation mandatory for employees who handle cash receipts and accounting duties?*
Many internal fraud schemes are continuous in nature and require ongoing efforts by the employee to conceal defalcations. By establishing mandatory job or assignment rotation, the concealment element is interrupted.

13. *Are vacations mandatory for employees who handle cash receipts and who are entrusted with accounting duties?*
Many internal fraud schemes are continuous in nature and require ongoing efforts by the employee to conceal defalcations. By establishing mandatory vacations, the concealment element is interrupted.

14. *Are surprise cash counts conducted?*
Surprise cash counts help prevent fraud perpetrators from having time to alter, destroy, and misplace records and other evidence of their offenses.

15. *Are journal entries made to the cash accounts reviewed and analyzed on a regular basis?*

Journal entries made to the cash accounts should be reviewed and analyzed on a regular basis.

16. *Does the company use a point of sale (POS) system?*
A POS system will allow the organization to gather sales information in a comprehensive and timely format.

17. *Does the POS system track perpetual inventory?*
The POS system should be configured to track perpetual inventory.

18. *Does the POS system track exceptions, such as voids, refunds, no sales, overages, and shortages?*
The POS system should be configured to track exceptions, such as voids, refunds, no sales, overages, and shortages.

19. *Are register exception reports reviewed on a regular basis?*
Register exception reports should be reviewed on a regular basis by management.

20. *Are all employees except managers prohibited from making changes to the POS system?*
All employees, except for managers, should be prohibited from making changes to the POS system.

21. *Is access to the accounts receivable subledger and the general ledger restricted to authorized employees? Does access leave an audit trail?*
Access to the accounts receivable subledger and general ledger should be restricted to authorized employees. An audit trail of who accessed the ledgers, including time and date of access, should be kept.

MODULE 6: CHECK TAMPERING SCHEMES

- Forged maker schemes involve forging an authorized signature on a company check.
- Forged endorsement schemes consist of forging the signature endorsement of an intended recipient of a company check.
- Altered payee schemes involve changing the payee designation on the check to the perpetrator or an accomplice.
- Authorized maker schemes occur when employees who have signature authority write fraudulent checks for their own benefit.

1. *Are unused checks stored in a secure container with limited access?*
Blank checks, which can be used for forgery, should be stored in a secure area such as a safe or vault. Security to this area should be restricted to authorized personnel.

2. *Are unused checks from accounts that have been closed promptly destroyed?*
Companies should promptly destroy all unused checks from accounts that have been closed.

3. *Are electronic payments used when possible in order to limit the number of paper checks issued?*
Companies can minimize the possibility of check tampering and theft by using electronic payment services to handle large vendor and financing payments.

4. *Are printed and signed checks mailed immediately after signing?*
Printed and signed checks should be mailed immediately after signing.

5. *Are new checks purchased from reputable check vendors?*
All new checks should be purchased from reputable, well-established check producers.

6. *Do company checks contain security features to ensure their integrity?*
Companies can reduce their exposure to physical check tampering by using checks containing security features, such as high-resolution microprinting, security inks, and ultraviolet ink.

7. *Has the company notified its bank to not accept checks over a predetermined maximum amount?*
Companies should work in a cooperative effort with banks to prevent check fraud, establishing maximum dollar amounts above which the company's bank will not accept checks drawn against the account.

8. *Has the company established positive pay controls with its bank by supplying the bank with a daily list of checks issued and authorized for payment?*
One method for a company to help prevent check fraud is to establish positive pay controls by supplying its banks with a daily list of checks issued and authorized for payment.

9. *Is the employee who prepares the check prohibited from signing the check?*
Check preparation should not be performed by a signatory on the account.

10. *Are detailed comparisons made between the payees on the checks and the payees listed in the cash disbursements journal?*
Companies should perform detailed comparisons of the payees on the checks and the payees listed in the cash disbursements journal.

11. *Are employees responsible for handling and coding checks periodically rotated?*
Periodic rotation of personnel responsible for handling and coding checks can be an effective check disbursement control.

12. *Are bank reconciliations completed immediately after bank statements are received?*
Companies should complete bank reconciliations immediately after bank statements are received. The Uniform Commercial Code states that discrepancies must be presented to the bank within thirty days of receipt of the bank statement in order to hold the bank liable.

13. *Are bank statements and account reconciliations independently audited to confirm accuracy?*
Bank statements and account reconciliations should be independently audited for accuracy.

14. *Are cancelled checks independently reviewed for alterations and forgeries?*
Cancelled checks should be independently reviewed for alterations and forgeries.

15. *Are checks for a material amount matched to the supporting documentation?*
Checks for material amounts should be matched to the supporting documentation.

16. *Are voided checks examined for irregularities and to ensure they haven't been processed?*
The list of voided checks should be verified against physical copies of the checks. Bank statements should be reviewed to ensure that voided checks have not been processed.

17. *Are missing checks recorded and stop payments issued?*
Missing checks may indicate lax control over the physical safekeeping of checks. Stop payments should be issued for all missing checks.

18. *Do questionable payees or payee addresses trigger review of the corresponding check and support documentation?*
Questionable payees or payee addresses should trigger a review of the corresponding check and support documentation.

19. *With the exception of payroll, are checks issued to employees reviewed for irregularities?*
Checks payable to employees, with the exception of regular payroll checks, should be closely scrutinized for schemes such as conflicts of interest, fictitious vendors, or duplicate expense reimbursements.

20. *Are two signatures required for check issuance?*
Requiring dual signatures on checks can reduce the risk of check fraud.

21. *Are all company payments made by check or other recordable payment device?*
Making payments by check or other recordable payment device can reduce the risk of disbursement frauds.

22. *Are handwritten checks prohibited?*
Handwritten checks are especially vulnerable to check fraud and should be prohibited.

MODULE 7: CASH REGISTER SCHEMES

- False refund schemes occur when an employee (1) issues a refund for fictitious merchandise and keeps the money or (2) overstates the amount of merchandise returned and skims the excess money.
- False void schemes occur when a register worker retains a customer receipt, processes a fictitious voided sale, and keeps the money.

1. *Are refunds, voids, and discounts evaluated on a routine basis to identify patterns of activity among employees, departments, shifts, merchandise, etc.?*
Companies should routinely evaluate refunds, voids, and discounts to search for patterns of activity that might signal fraud.

2. *Is there a sign posted at the register asking the customer to request and examine a sales receipt?*
Signs asking customers to request and examine sales receipts should be posted at registers.

3. *Are cash disbursements recorded on a prenumbered form and reconciled daily?*
Cash disbursements should be recorded on prenumbered forms and reconciled daily.

4. *Do the cash disbursement forms have an explanation section or code?*
An explanation section or code should be included on cash disbursement forms.

5. *Are customers involved in voided sales and refunds randomly contacted to verify the accuracy of the transaction?*
Customers involved in voided sales and refunds should be randomly contacted to verify the accuracy of the transactions.

6. *Is access to the necessary control keys for refunds and voids restricted to supervisors?*
   Access to the necessary control keys for refunds and voids should be restricted to supervisors.

7. *Do void or refund transactions have to be approved by a supervisor and documented?*
   All void or refund transactions should be approved by a supervisor and documented.

8. *Is documentation of void and refund transactions maintained on file?*
   Documentation of void and refund transactions should be maintained on file.

9. *Is missing or altered register tape thoroughly investigated?*
   Companies should thoroughly investigate any missing or altered register tape.

10. *Are gaps in the register tape investigated?*
    Companies should investigate any gaps in the register tape.

11. *Are multiple voids or refunds for amounts just under any review limit investigated?*
    Multiple voids or refunds for amounts just under review limits should be investigated.

12. *Is an employee other than the register worker responsible for preparing register count sheets and comparing them to register totals?*
    An employee other than the register worker should be responsible for preparing register count sheets and comparing them to register totals.

13. *Are customer complaints regarding payment errors thoroughly investigated?*
    Customer complaints regarding payment errors should be thoroughly investigated.

14. *Does each cashier have a separate access code to the register?*
    Each cashier should be assigned a separate access code to the register.

15. *Does each cashier have a separate cash drawer?*
    Each cashier should have a separate cash drawer.

16. *Is an over and short log kept for each person and/or register?*
    An over and short log should be kept for each person and/or register.

17. *Are over and short incidents thoroughly investigated and monitored?*
    Over and short incidents should be thoroughly investigated and monitored.

18. *Are all "no sale" receipts accounted for and attached to a daily cashier's report?*
    All "no sale" receipts should be accounted for and attached to a daily cashier's report.

19. *Is access to the register area restricted to authorized employees and supervisors?*
    Companies should restrict access to register areas to authorized employees and supervisors.

20. *Are all cashiers periodically integrity shopped?*
    Companies should periodically conduct integrity shopping on all cashiers.

MODULE 8: PURCHASING AND BILLING SCHEMES

- Shell company schemes occur when an employee submits invoices for payment from a fictitious company controlled by the employee.
- Pay-and-return schemes occur when an employee arranges for overpayment of a vendor invoice and pockets the overpayment amount when it is returned to the company.

- Personal purchase schemes occur when an employee submits an invoice for personal purchases to the company for payment, or when an employee uses a company credit card for personal purchases.

1. *Does the organization have a purchasing department?*
   The organization should have a purchasing department that is separate from the payment function.

2. *Is the purchasing department independent of the accounting, receiving, and shipping departments?*
   The purchasing department should be independent of the accounting, receiving, and shipping departments.

3. *Do purchase requisitions require management approval?*
   Management should approve all purchase requisitions.

4. *Do purchase orders specify a description of items, quantities, prices, and dates?*
   Purchase orders should specify a description of items, quantities, prices, and dates.

5. *Are purchase order forms prenumbered and accounted for?*
   Purchase order forms should be prenumbered and accounted for.

6. *Does the company maintain a master vendor file?*
   The company should maintain a master vendor file.

7. *Are competitive bids required for all purchases?*
   Companies should require competitive bids for all purchases.

8. *Does the receiving department prepare receiving reports for all items received?*
   The receiving department should prepare receiving reports for all items received.

9. *Does the receiving department maintain a log of all items received?*
   The receiving department should maintain a log of all items received.

10. *Are copies of receiving reports furnished to the accounting and purchasing departments?*
    Copies of receiving reports should be furnished to the accounting and purchasing departments.

11. *Are purchasing and receiving functions separate from invoice processing, accounts payable, and general ledger functions?*
    Purchasing and receiving functions should be segregated from invoice processing, accounts payable, and general ledger functions.

12. *Are vendor invoices, receiving reports, and purchase orders matched before the related liability is recorded?*
    Companies should match vendor invoices, receiving reports, and purchase orders before recording the related liability.

13. *Are purchase orders recorded in a purchase register or voucher register before being processed through cash disbursements?*
    Purchase orders should be recorded in a purchase register or voucher register before being processed through cash disbursements.

14. *Are procedures adequate to ensure that merchandise purchased for direct delivery to the customer is promptly billed to the customer and recorded as both a receivable and a payable?*
    Companies should implement procedures adequate to ensure that merchandise purchased for direct delivery to the customer is promptly billed to the customer and recorded as both a receivable and a payable.

15. *Are records of goods returned to vendors matched to vendor credit memos?*
    Records of goods returned to vendors should be matched to vendor credit memos.

16. *Is the accounts payable ledger or voucher register reconciled monthly to the general ledger control accounts?*
    The accounts payable ledger or voucher register should be reconciled monthly to the general ledger control accounts.

17. *Do write-offs of accounts payable debit balances require approval of a designated manager?*
    Write-offs of accounts payable debit balances should require approval of a designated manager.

18. *Is the master vendor file periodically reviewed for unusual vendors and addresses?*
    The master vendor file should be reviewed periodically for unusual vendors and addresses.

19. *Are vendor purchases analyzed for abnormal levels?*
    Vendor purchases should be analyzed for abnormal levels.

20. *Are control methods in place to check for duplicate invoices and purchase order numbers?*
    Companies should implement control methods to check for duplicate invoices and purchase order numbers.

21. *Are credit card statements reviewed monthly for irregularities?*
    Credit card statements should be reviewed monthly for irregularities.

22. *Are vendors with post office box addresses verified?*
    All vendors with post office box addresses should be verified.

23. *Are voucher payments reviewed regularly for proper documentation?*
    Voucher payments should be reviewed regularly for proper documentation.

24. *Is access to the accounts payable subledger and the general ledger restricted? Does access create an audit trail?*
    Access to the accounts payable subledger and the general ledger should be restricted, and an audit trail should be created.

MODULE 9: PAYROLL SCHEMES

- Ghost employee schemes occur when a person not employed by the company is on the payroll.
- Overpayment schemes occur when a company pays an employee based on falsified hours or rates.
- Commission schemes occur when the amount of sales made or the rate of commission is fraudulently inflated.

1. *Is the employee payroll list reviewed periodically for duplicate or missing Social Security numbers?*
   Organizations should check the employee payroll list periodically for duplicate or missing Social Security numbers that may indicate a ghost employee or overlapping payments to current employees.

2. *Are personnel records maintained independently of payroll and timekeeping functions?*
Personnel records should be maintained independently of payroll and timekeeping functions.

3. *Are references checked on all new hires?*
Organizations should perform reference checks on all new hires.

4. *Are sick leave, vacations, and holidays reviewed for compliance with company policy?*
Sick leave, vacations, and holidays should be reviewed for compliance with company policy.

5. *Are appropriate forms completed and signed by the employee to authorize payroll deductions and withholding exemptions?*
Employees should complete and sign appropriate forms to authorize payroll deductions and withholding exemptions.

6. *Is payroll periodically compared with personnel records for terminations?*
Payroll should periodically be compared with personnel records for terminations to ensure that terminated employees have been removed from the payroll.

7. *Are payroll checks prenumbered and issued in sequential order?*
Payroll checks should be prenumbered and issued in sequential order.

8. *Is the payroll bank account reconciled by an employee who is not involved in preparing payroll checks, does not sign the checks, and does not handle payroll distribution?*
The payroll bank account should be reconciled by an employee who is not involved in preparing payroll checks, does not sign the checks, and does not handle payroll distribution.

9. *Are payroll registers reconciled to general ledger control accounts?*
Payroll registers should be reconciled to general ledger control accounts.

10. *Are cancelled payroll checks examined for alterations and endorsements?*
Cancelled payroll checks should be examined for alterations and endorsements.

11. *Is access restricted to payroll check stock and signature stamps?*
Access to payroll check stock and signature stamps should be restricted.

12. *Are payroll withholdings for taxes, insurance, etc., examined to determine if any employees are not having these items deducted from their paychecks?*
Payroll checks that do not have withholdings for taxes, insurance, etc., should be investigated.

13. *Is the employee payroll list reviewed periodically for duplicate or missing home addresses and telephone numbers?*
The employee payroll list should be reviewed for duplicate or missing home addresses and telephone numbers.

14. *Is the account information for automatically deposited payroll checks reviewed periodically for duplicate entries?*
Account information for automatically deposited payroll checks should be reviewed periodically for duplicate entries.

15. *Is an employee separate from the payroll department assigned to distribute payroll checks?*
An employee separate from the payroll department should be assigned to distribute payroll checks.

16. *Are new employees required to furnish proof of immigration status?*
Companies must require new employees to furnish proof of immigration status.

17. *Does any change to an employee's salary require more than one level of management approval?*
Changes to an employee's salary should require more than one level of management approval.

18. *Does overtime have to be authorized by a supervisor?*
Overtime should be authorized by a supervisor.

19. *Do supervisors verify and sign timecards for each pay period?*
Supervisors should verify and sign time timecards for each pay period.

20. *Are commission expenses compared to sales figures to verify amounts?*
Comparing commission expenses to sales figures to verify amounts is an important control procedure that can help to detect payroll fraud.

21. *Does someone separate from the sales department calculate sales commissions?*
Someone separate from the sales department should calculate sales commissions.

MODULE 10: EXPENSE SCHEMES

- Mischaracterized expense schemes occur when an employee requests reimbursement for a personal expense, claiming the expense to be business related.
- Overstated expense schemes occur when an employee overstates the cost of actual expenses and seeks reimbursement.
- Fictitious expense schemes occur when an employee invents a purchase and seeks reimbursement for it.
- Multiple reimbursement schemes occur when an employee submits a single expense for reimbursement multiple times.

1. *Are the expense accounts reviewed and analyzed periodically using historical comparisons or comparisons with budgeted amounts?*
Companies should periodically review and analyze expense accounts using historical comparisons or comparisons with budgeted amounts.

2. *Do employee expense reimbursement claims receive a detailed review before payment is made?*
Employee expense reimbursement claims should receive a detailed review before payment is made.

3. *Are employees required to submit detailed expense reports?*
Employees should be required to submit detailed expense reports containing receipts, explanations, amounts, etc.

4. *Is a limit placed on expenses such as hotels, meals, and entertainment?*
Companies should place a spending limit on expenses such as hotels, meals, and entertainment.

5. *Are receipts required for all expenses to be reimbursed?*
Companies should require receipts for all expenses to be reimbursed.

6. *Are supervisors required to review and approve all expense reimbursement requests?*
All expense reimbursement requests should be reviewed and approved by supervisors.

7. *Is there a random authentication of expense receipts and expenses claimed?*
A policy requiring the periodic review of expense reports, coupled with examining the appropriate detail, can help deter employees from submitting personal expenses for reimbursement.

MODULE 11: THEFT OF INVENTORY AND EQUIPMENT

- Fake sale schemes occur when an accomplice of an employee "buys" merchandise but the employee does not ring up the sale, allowing the accomplice to take the merchandise without making any payment.

- Purchasing schemes occur when an employee who has purchasing authority uses that authority to purchase and misappropriate merchandise.

- Receiving schemes occur when an employee misappropriates assets purchased by the company as they are received at the company.

- False shipment schemes occur when an employee creates false sales documents and false shipping documents to make it appear that missing inventory was not actually stolen, but rather sold.

- Misuse of company assets occurs when an employee borrows company assets for personal use without authorization.

- Larceny schemes occur when an employee takes inventory from the company premises without attempting to conceal the theft in the accounting records.

1. *Has a recent inventory of company equipment, listing serial numbers and descriptions, been completed?*
Companies should inventory company equipment and maintain a list of the equipment, serial numbers, and descriptions.

2. *Does the company assign an individual from outside of the department to conduct the department's inventory?*
An employee who doesn't work in the department should be assigned to conduct the department's inventory.

3. *Are unexplained entries to the inventory records examined for source documentation?*
Unexplained entries to the inventory records should be examined for source documentation.

4. *Is the company experiencing sizeable inventory increases without comparable sales increases?*
Sizeable inventory increases without comparable sales increases may indicate an inventory overstatement fraud scheme and should be investigated.

5. *Are analytical reviews of beginning inventory, sales, cost of goods sold, and ending inventory conducted periodically to look for unexplained differences?*
Analytical reviews of beginning inventory, sales, cost of goods sold, and ending inventory should be conducted periodically. Any discrepancies should be investigated.

6. *Is there an unusual volume of inventory adjustments, write-offs, or disposals?*
   Any unusual volume of inventory adjustments, write-offs, or disposals should be investigated.

7. *Does the organization have written inventory instructions and orders?*
   Organizations should document and implement inventory instructions and orders.

8. *Does someone independent of the purchasing, receiving, and warehousing functions physically count the inventory?*
   Physical inventory counts should be conducted by someone independent of the purchasing, receiving, and warehousing functions.

9. *Are prenumbered inventory tags used?*
   Prenumbered inventory tags should be used.

10. *Are the inventory tags controlled and accounted for?*
    Inventory tags should be controlled and accounted for.

11. *Do the inventory procedures prevent double counting?*
    Organizations should implement inventory procedures that prevent double counting.

12. *Are inventory counts subject to independent recounts?*
    Inventory counts should be subject to independent recounts.

13. *Is the inventory reasonably identifiable for proper classification in the accounting system, such as description, condition, or stage of completion?*
    The inventory should be reasonably identifiable for proper classification in the accounting system, such as description, condition, or stage of completion.

14. *Are differences between physical counts and inventory records investigated before inventory records are adjusted?*
    Differences between physical counts and inventory records should be investigated before inventory records are adjusted.

15. *Is scrap inventoried, and is scrap disposal accounted for?*
    Scrap should be inventoried, and scrap disposal should be accounted for.

16. *Are the following duties segregated: requisition of inventory, receiving of inventory, disbursement of inventory, writing off of inventory as scrap, and receipt of proceeds from the sale of scrap inventory?*
    The following duties should be segregated: requisition of inventory, receiving of inventory, disbursement of inventory, writing off of inventory as scrap, and receipt of proceeds from the sale of scrap inventory.

17. *Is a receiving report prepared for all purchased goods?*
    A receiving report should be prepared for all purchased goods.

18. *Are copies of receiving reports sent directly to the purchasing and accounting departments?*
    Copies of receiving reports should be sent directly to the purchasing and accounting departments.

19. *Is the receiving department provided with a copy of the purchase order on all items to be received?*
    The receiving department should be provided with a copy of the purchase order on all items to be received.

20. *Are partial shipments annotated on purchase orders or attached as separate sheets?*
Partial shipments should be annotated on purchase orders or attached as separate sheets.

21. *Are overage, shortage, and damage reports completed and sent to the purchasing and accounting departments?*
Overage, shortage, and damage reports should be completed and sent to the purchasing and accounting departments.

22. *Are quantities of materials received counted and compared to purchase orders?*
Quantities of materials received should be counted and compared to purchase orders.

23. *Is there a written policy allowing management to inspect all desks, file cabinets, and other containers on company property?*
Companies should document and implement a written policy allowing management to inspect all desks, file cabinets, and other containers on company property.

24. *Is there an equipment removal authorization policy requiring written management approval to remove any company equipment from the company premises?*
Companies should document and implement an equipment removal authorization policy requiring written management approval to remove any company equipment from the company premises.

25. *Is there a policy requiring the inspection of packages, boxes, and other containers before they leave the company premises?*
Companies should document and implement a policy requiring the inspection of packages, boxes, and other containers before they leave the company premises.

26. *Is the removal of trash and trash receptacles periodically monitored?*
Companies should periodically monitor the removal of trash and trash receptacles.

27. *Are the shipping and receiving areas adequately supervised to prevent theft?*
Shipping and receiving areas should be adequately supervised to prevent theft.

28. *Are high-value items stored in secure or continuously monitored areas?*
High-value items should be stored in secure or continuously monitored areas.

29. *Is the shipping function separate from the purchasing and inventory functions?*
The shipping function should be separate from the purchasing and inventory functions.

30. *Are shipping documents prenumbered and accounted for?*
Shipping documents should be prenumbered and accounted for.

31. *Are shipping orders matched with sales orders and contracts?*
Shipping orders should be matched with sales orders and contracts to prevent inventory and vendor schemes.

32. *Are shipments of goods required to have authorized sales orders and contracts prior to shipping?*
Shipments of goods should be required to have authorized sales orders and sales contracts prior to shipping.

33. *Are shipping documents forwarded directly to the accounting department for recording inventory reduction and cost of sales?*
Shipping documents should be forwarded directly to the accounting department for recording inventory reduction and cost of sales.

MODULE 12: THEFT OF PROPRIETARY INFORMATION

- Theft of proprietary information involves theft or disclosure of confidential or trade secret information for financial gain.

1. *Are there policies and procedures addressing the identification, classification, and handling of proprietary information?*
The company should implement policies and procedures addressing the identification, classification, and handling of proprietary information.

2. *Are employees who have access to proprietary information required to sign nondisclosure agreements?*
Employees who have access to proprietary information should be required to sign nondisclosure agreements.

3. *Are employees who have access to proprietary information required to sign noncompete agreements to prevent them from working for competitors within a stated period of time and location?*
Employees who have access to proprietary information should be required to sign noncompete agreements to prevent them from working for competitors within a stated period of time.

4. *Are employees provided with training to make them aware of proprietary information, their responsibility to protect the information, and the company policies and procedures relating to proprietary information?*
Employees should be provided with training to make them aware of proprietary information, their responsibility to protect proprietary information, and company policies and procedures relating to proprietary information.

5. *Is there an established procedure to identify what information should be classified as sensitive, and for how long?*
Companies should implement a procedure to identify what information should be classified as sensitive, and for how long.

6. *Are sensitive documents properly classified and marked as confidential?*
Sensitive documents should be properly classified and marked as confidential.

7. *Is sensitive information properly secured when not being used?*
Sensitive information should be properly secured when not being used.

8. *Is access to sensitive information physically controlled and accounted for?*
Access to sensitive information should be physically controlled and accounted for.

9. *Is sensitive information promptly destroyed when it is no longer needed?*
Organizations should promptly destroy sensitive information when it is no longer needed.

10. *Are compromises to the security of proprietary information promptly investigated to determine the source?*
Companies should promptly investigate any compromises to the security of proprietary information to determine the source.

11. *Are employees required to use screensaver and/or server passwords to protect unattended computer systems?*
Employees should be required to use screensaver and/or server passwords to protect unattended computer systems.

12. *Are confidential documents shredded when discarded?*
Confidential documents should be shredded when discarded.

MODULE 13: CORRUPTION

- Bribery schemes involve the offering, giving, receiving, or soliciting of a thing of value to influence a business decision.

- Kickback schemes occur when vendors make undisclosed payments to employees of purchasing companies in order to enlist the employees in overbilling schemes.

- Bid-rigging schemes occur when an employee fraudulently assists a vendor in winning a contract through the competitive bidding process.

- Economic extortion schemes occur when an employee demands payment from a vendor for decisions made in the vendor's favor. Refusal to pay the extorter results in harm to the vendor.

- Illegal gratuities schemes involve giving or receiving something of value to reward a business decision.

1. *Is there a company policy that addresses the receipt of gifts, discounts, and services offered by a supplier or customer?*
Organizations should implement a policy that addresses the receipt of gifts, discounts, and services offered by a supplier or customer.

2. *Is there an established bidding policy?*
Organizations should establish a bidding policy.

3. *Are purchases reviewed to detect out of line costs?*
Organizations should review purchases for costs that are out of line.

4. *Are purchases reviewed to identify favored vendors?*
Purchases should be reviewed to identify favored vendors.

5. *Are purchases reviewed to identify excessive amounts?*
Purchases should be reviewed and any excessive amounts should be investigated.

6. *Are prebid solicitation documents reviewed for any restrictions on competition?*
Prebid solicitation documents should be reviewed for any restrictions on competition.

7. *Are bid solicitation packages numbered and controlled?*
Bid solicitation packages should be numbered and controlled.

8. *Is communication between bidders and purchasing employees restricted?*
Companies should restrict and monitor communication between bidders and purchasing employees.

9. *Are the bids received kept confidential?*
All bids received should be kept confidential.

10. *Are bidders' qualifications verified?*
Companies should verify bidders' qualifications.

11. *Are contracts awarded based on predetermined criteria?*
Companies should establish predetermined criteria upon which to award contracts.

12. *Are purchasing account assignments rotated?*
Periodic rotation of purchasing account assignments can be an effective corruption control.

13. *Are vendors surveyed periodically regarding company purchasing practices?*
Organizations should periodically survey vendors regarding company purchasing practices.

MODULE 14: CONFLICTS OF INTEREST

- Purchase schemes involve the overbilling of a company for goods or services by a vendor in which an employee has an undisclosed ownership or financial interest.

- Sales schemes involve the underselling of company goods by an employee to a company in which the employee maintains a hidden interest.

1. *Are there periodic comparisons of vendor information with employee information, such as addresses and telephone numbers?*
Organizations should conduct periodic comparisons of vendor information with employee information, such as addresses and telephone numbers.

2. *Are vendors who employ former company employees under increased scrutiny?*
Vendors who employ former company employees should be under increased scrutiny for potential conflicts of interest.

3. *Does the organization have a reporting procedure for personnel to report their concerns about vendors receiving favored treatment?*
Organizations should provide personnel with a confidential system for reporting concerns about vendors receiving favored treatment.

4. *Are employees required to complete an annual disclosure document that includes business ownership, income, and investment information?*
Employees should be required to provide annual disclosures that list business ownership, income, and investment information.

5. *Does the organization require vendors to sign an agreement allowing vendor audits?*
Organizations should require vendors to sign an agreement allowing vendor audits.

6. *Are vendor audits conducted by someone independent of the purchase, sales, billing, and receiving departments?*
Vendor audits should be conducted by someone independent of the purchase, sales, billing, and receiving departments.

MODULE 15: FRAUDULENT FINANCIAL REPORTS

- Fictitious revenue schemes involve recording fictitious revenue from the sale of goods or services.

- Improper timing schemes involve recording revenues or expenses in improper accounting periods.

- Understating liabilities schemes involve concealing or understating liabilities and expenses, capitalizing expenses, or expensing capital expenses.
- Improper disclosure schemes involve the improper disclosure of material information, such as contingent liabilities, significant events, management fraud, related-party transactions, or accounting changes.
- Improper asset valuation schemes involve the improper valuation of inventory, accounts receivable, fixed assets, intangibles, or other assets.

1. *Are the organization's accounting records in proper form?*
   Organizations should maintain accounting records in proper form.

2. *Does the organization employ an adequate number of accounting employees?*
   The accounting department should be adequately staffed to allow for proper segregation of duties.

3. *Does the organization have an effective internal audit staff?*
   An effective internal audit staff can focus on high-risk areas for fraud and can identify new vulnerabilities, measure the effectiveness of internal controls, and signal that fraud prevention is a high priority for the company.

4. *Are proper internal controls established and maintained?*
   Organizations should establish and enforce an internal control system.

5. *Does the organization embrace the concept of internal controls?*
   Embracing the concept of internal controls requires that senior managers and employees understand why internal controls are important and what adopting such measures means to them.

6. *Are senior managers visible in their support of internal controls?*
   Senior managers should be visible in their support of internal controls.

7. *Are the organization's financial goals and objectives realistic?*
   Unrealistic financial goals and objectives can result in managers and employees committing fraudulent acts in order to meet them.

8. *Does the organization consistently achieve its financial goals and objectives?*
   Any failure to meet financial goals and objectives should be researched.

9. *Is the organization's reported financial performance stable or increasing?*
   Management should investigate any unstable or decreasing financial performance.

10. *Does the company have stable relationships with its banks?*
    The company should strive to have stable relationships with its banks.

11. *Are there unrealistic changes or increases in financial statement account balances?*
    Management should determine the reasons for any unrealistic changes or increases in financial statement account balances.

12. *Are the account balances realistic in light of the nature, age, and size of the company?*
    Management should investigate any unrealistic account balances.

13. *Do actual physical assets exist in the amounts and values indicated on the financial statements?*
    An inventory of physical assets should be conducted to verify that the physical assets exist in the amounts and values indicated on the financial statements.

14. *Have there been significant changes in the nature of the organization's revenues or expenses?*

The organization should determine the reasons for any significant changes in the nature of its revenues or expenses.

15. *Do one or a few large transactions account for a significant portion of any account balance or amount?*

    Situations in which one or a few large transactions account for a significant portion of any account balance or amount should be researched.

16. *Are there significant transactions that occur near the end of a period that positively impact results of operations, especially transactions that are unusual or highly complex?*

    Any significant transactions that occur near the end of a period and positively impact results of operations should be scrutinized for legitimacy, especially if the transactions are unusual or highly complex.

17. *Are financial results fairly consistent across periods?*

    The company should be able to explain any variances in financial results across periods.

18. *Is there an inability to generate cash flows from operations while experiencing earnings growth?*

    Any inability to generate cash flows from operations while experiencing earnings growth should be investigated.

19. *Is there significant pressure to obtain additional capital necessary to stay competitive?*

    Insufficient working capital can place undue pressure on management to manipulate financial results.

20. *Are reported assets, liabilities, revenues, or expenses based on significant estimates that involve unusually subjective judgments or uncertainties?*

    Significant estimates, especially those that involve unusually subjective judgments or uncertainties, should be reviewed for reasonableness.

21. *Are reported assets, liabilities, revenues, or expenses based on significant estimates that are subject to potential significant change in the near term in a manner that may have a financially disruptive effect on the organization?*

    Significant estimates that are subject to potential significant change in the near term in a manner that may have a financially disruptive effect on the organization should be scrutinized.

22. *Is the company experiencing unusually rapid growth or profitability, especially when compared with that of other companies in the same industry?*

    Unusually rapid growth or profitability, especially when compared with that of other companies in the same industry, is a red flag of fraud and should be investigated.

23. *Is the organization highly vulnerable to changes in interest rates?*

    The organization should increase review of its financial reporting during periods of high vulnerability.

24. *Are there unrealistically aggressive sales or profitability incentive programs?*

    Unrealistically aggressive sales or profitability incentive programs can place undue pressure on employees and can result in employees committing fraudulent acts in order to meet them.

25. *Is there a threat of imminent bankruptcy, foreclosure, or hostile takeover?*
   A threat of imminent bankruptcy, foreclosure, or hostile takeover places a company at increased risk for fraudulent activity to occur.

26. *Is there a high possibility of adverse consequences on significant pending transactions, such as business combinations or contract awards, if poor financial results are reported?*
   A high possibility of adverse consequences on significant pending transactions, such as business combinations or contract awards, if poor financial results are reported can place extreme pressure on management to manipulate results.

27. *Is there a poor or deteriorating financial position when management has personally guaranteed significant debts of the entity?*
   The existence of a poor or deteriorating financial position when management has personally guaranteed significant debts of the entity can result in management committing fraudulent acts in order to protect itself from financial harm.

28. *Does the firm continuously operate on a crisis basis or without a careful budgeting and planning process?*
   A careful budgeting and planning process can help a firm to monitor progress toward its goals, control spending, and predict cash flow and profit.

29. *Does the organization have difficulty collecting receivables or have other cash flow problems?*
   Management should determine the reasons for any collection or cash flow problems.

30. *Is the organization dependent on one or two key products or services, especially products or services that can become quickly obsolete?*
   Dependence on one or two key products can place tremendous pressure on a company, exposing it to increased risk of fraud.

31. *Do the footnotes contain information about complex issues?*
   Any complex issues should be explained in the footnotes.

32. *Are there adequate disclosures in the financials and footnotes?*
   Generally accepted accounting principles concerning disclosures require that financial statements (1) include all relevant and material information in the financials or footnotes and (2) not be misleading.

BIBLIOGRAPHY

Albrecht, W. Steve and David J. Searcy. "Top 10 Reasons Why Fraud Is Increasing in the U.S." *Strategic Finance*, May 2001.

Albrecht, W. Steve, Keith R. Howe, and Marshall B. Romney. *Deterring Fraud: The Internal Auditor's Perspective*. Altamonte Springs, FL: The Institute of Internal Auditors Research Foundation, 1984.

Albrecht, W. Steve, Gerald W. Wernz, and Timothy L. Williams. *Fraud: Bringing Light to the Dark Side of Business*. New York: Irwin Professional Publishing, 1995.

Albrecht, W. Steve., Conan C. Albrecht, Chad O. Albrecht, and Mark F. Zimbelman. *Fraud Examination*, 3rd ed. Mason, OH: South-Western, 2009.

Albrecht, W. Steve, Marshal B. Romney, David J. Cherrington, I. Reed Payne, and Allan J. Roe. *How to Detect and Prevent Business Fraud*. Englewood Cliffs, NJ: Prentice-Hall, Inc., 1982.

American Accounting Association. *Accounting Education,* Vol. 18, Number 2. Sarasota, FL: American Accounting Association, 2003.

American Accounting Association. *Accounting Horizons*, Vol. 7, Number 4. Sarasota, FL: American Accounting Association, 2003.

American Accounting Association. *Auditing: A Journal of Practice & Theory*, Vol. 22, Number 2. Sarasota, FL: American Accounting Association, 2003.

American Institute of Certified Public Accountants, Inc. *Statements on Auditing Standards*.

_____. "Responsibilities and Functions of the Independent Auditor," SAS 1 (AU 110).

_____. "Illegal Acts by Clients," SAS 54 (AU 317).

_____. "Auditing Accounting Estimates," SAS 57 (AU 342).

_____. "Special Reports," SAS 62 (AU 623).

_____. "Compliance Auditing Considerations in Audits of Governmental Entities and Recipients of Governmental Financial Assistance," SAS 74 (AU 801).

_____. "Communications Between Predecessor and Successor Auditors," SAS 84 (AU 315).

_____. "Consideration of Fraud in a Financial Statement Audit," SAS 99 (AU 316).

_____. "Planning and Supervision," SAS 108 (AU 311).

_____. "The Auditor's Communication With Those Charged With Governance," SAS 114 (AU 380).

Androphy, Joel M. *White Collar Crime*. New York: McGraw-Hill, 1992.

Antle, Rick and Stanley J. Garstka. *Financial Accounting*. Cincinnati, OH: South-Western, 2002.

Arens, Alvin A., Randal J. Elder, and Mark S. Beasley. *Essential Auditing and Assurance Services: An Integrated Approach*. Upper Saddle River, NJ: Prentice Hall, 2003.

Associated Press. "Software Executive Pleads Guilty to Stock Fraud." *USA Today*. January 31, 1997.

Association of Certified Fraud Examiners. *2010 ACFE Report to the Nations on Occupational Fraud and Abuse*. ACFE, 2010, Austin, TX.

Association of Certified Fraud Examiners. *Fraud Examiners' Manual*. ACFE, 2010, Austin, TX.

Association of Certified Fraud Examiners, *Report to the Nation on Occupational Fraud and Abuse*. Austin, TX: ACFE, 1996.

Banks, David G. "Vendor Fraud: Finding Deals Gone Awry." *The White Paper*, Vol. 16, No. 5. September/October 2002.

Beasley, M. S., J. V. Carcello, and D. R. Hermanson. *Fraudulent Financial Reporting: 1987–1997: An Analysis of U.S. Public Companies*. Committee of Sponsoring Organizations (COSO), 1999.

Beasley, M. S., J. V. Carcello, D. R. Hermanson, and T. L. Neal. *Fraudulent Financial Reporting 1998–2007: An Analysis of U.S. Public Companies*. The Committee of Sponsoring Organizations of the Treadway Commission (COSO), 1999.

Beckett, Paul. "SEC, Publisher of On-Line Newsletter Settle Fraud Case Involving the Internet." *Wall Street Journal*, February 26, 1997.

Bintliff, Russell L. *White Collar Crime Detection and Prevention*. Englewood Cliffs, NJ: Prentice Hall, 1993.

Binstein, Michael and Charles Bowden. *Trust Me: Charles Keating and the Missing Millions*. New York: Random House, 1993.

Biegelman, Martin T. "Designing a Robust Fraud Prevention Program, Part One." *The White Paper*, Vol. 18, No. 1. January/February 2004.

Biegelman, Martin T. "Sarbanes–Oxley Act: Stopping U.S. Corporate Crooks from Cooking the Books." *The White Paper*, Vol. 17, No. 2. March/April 2003.

Bishop, Toby J. F. and Joseph T. Wells, CFE, CPA. "Breaking Tradition in the Auditing Profession." *The White Paper*, Vol. 17, No. 5. September/October 2003.

Black, Henry Campbell. *Black's Law Dictionary*, 5th ed. St. Paul, MN: West Publishing Co., 1979.

Bliven, Bruce. "The Tempest Over Teapot." *American Heritage*. September/October, 1995.

Blount, Ernest C. *Occupational Crime: Deterrence, Investigation, and Reporting in Compliance with Federal Guidelines*. Boca Raton: CRC Press, 2003.

Bologna, Jack. *Corporate Fraud: The Basics of Prevention and Detection*. Boston: Butterworth-Heinemann, 1984.

Bologna, Jack and Robert J. Lindquist. *Fraud Auditing and Forensic Accounting*. New York: John Wiley & Sons, 1987.

Bologna, Jack. *Handbook on Corporate Fraud*. Boston: Butterworth-Heinemann, 1993.

Bonner, S. E., Z. V. Palmrose, and S. M. Young. "Fraud Type and Auditor Litigation: An Analysis of SEC Accounting and Auditing Enforcement Releases," *The Accounting Review*, Vol. 73. October 1998.

Brian, Brad D. and Barry F. McNeil. *Internal Corporate Investigations*, 2nd ed. Chicago: ABA Publishing, 2003.

Brickner, Daniel R. SAS 99: "Another Implement for the Fraud Examiner's Toolbox." *The White Paper*, Vol. 17, No. 3. May/June 2003.

Caplan, Gerald M. *ABSCAM Ethics: Moral Issues & Deception in Law Enforcement*. Cambridge, MA: Ballinger, 1983.

Carozza, Dick. "Accounting Students Must Have Armor of Fraud Examination." *The White Paper*, Vol. 16, No. 1. January/February 2002.

Clarke, Michael. *Business Crime: Its Nature and Control*. New York: St. Martin's Press, 1990.

Clarkson, Kenneth W., Roger LeRoy Miller, and Gaylord A. Jentz. *West's Business Law: Text & Cases*, 3rd ed. St. Paul, MN: West Publishing Company, 1986.

Clinard, Marshall B., and Peter C. Yeager. *Corporate Crime*. New York: Macmillan Publishing Co., Inc., 1980.

Coderre, David G. *Computer-Aided Fraud Prevention & Detection: A Step-by-Step Guide*. Hoboken, NJ: John Wiley & Sons, 2009.

Comer, Michael J. *Corporate Fraud*. Aldershot: Network Security Management Ltd., 1998.

Comer, Michael J. *Investigating Corporate Fraud*. Aldershot: Gower Publishing Limited, 2003.

Cook, Larry E. "Risky Business: Conducting the Internal Fraud Risk Assessment." *Fraud Magazine*, March/April 2005.

Cotton, David L. "Fixing CPA Ethics Can Be an Inside Job." *Washington Post*, October 20, 2002.

Cressey, Donald R. *Other People's Money*. Montclair NJ: Patterson Smith, 1953.

Davia, Howard R., Patrick C. Coggins, John C. Wideman, and Joseph T. Kastantin. *Accountant's Guide to Fraud Detection and Control*, 2nd ed. New York: John Wiley & Sons, 2000.

Davis, Robert C., Arthur J. Lurigio, and Wesley G. Skogan, eds. *Victims of Crime*, 2nd ed. Thousand Oaks, CA: Sage Publications, 1997.

Dean, Bruce A. "Wrap It Up: Packing Your Case for Prosecution." *The White Paper*, Vol. 16, No. 1. January/February 2002.

Department of the Treasury: Internal Revenue Service. *Financial Investigations: A Financial Approach to Detecting and Resolving Crimes*. Washington, DC: U.S. Government Printing Office, 1993.

Dirks, Raymond L. and Leonard Gross. *The Great Wall Street Scandal*. New York: McGraw-Hill Book Company, 1974.

Drake, John D. *The Effective Interviewer: A Guide for Managers*. New York: AMACOM, 1989.

Ermann, M. David and Richard J. Lundman. *Corporate Deviance*. New York: Holt, Rhinehart and Winston, 1982.

Farrell, Barbara R. and Patricia Healy. "White Collar Crime: A Profile of the Perpetrator and an Evaluation of the Responsibilities for Prevention and Detection." *Journal of Forensic Accounting*, Vol. 1, 2000.

Financial Accounting Standards Board. *Accounting Standards Codification* (ASC). Financial Accounting Foundation, Norwalk, CT.

———. ASC Topic 225, "Income Statement."

———. ASC Topic 250, "Accounting Changes and Error Corrections."

———. ASC Topic 350, "Intangibles—Goodwill and Other."

———. ASC Topic 450, "Contingencies."

———. ASC Topic 605, "Revenue Recognition."

———. ASC Topic 730, "Research and Development."

———. ASC Topic 820, "Fair Value Measurements and Disclosures."

Financial Accounting Standards Board. *Concepts Statements*. Financial Accounting Foundation, Norwalk, CT.

———. "Qualitative Characteristics of Accounting Information," Concepts Statement No. 2.

———. "Recognition and Measurement in Financial Statements of Business Enterprises," Concepts Statement No. 5.

_____. "Elements of Financial Statements," Concepts Statement No. 6.

Flesher, Dale L., Paul J. Miranti and Gary John Previts. "The First Century of the CPA." *Journal of Accountancy*, October 1996.

Fusaro, Peter C. and Ross M. Miller. *What Went Wrong at Enron*. Hoboken, NJ: John Wiley & Sons, 2002.

Fridson, Martin S. *Financial Statement Analysis*. New York: John Wiley & Sons, 1991.

Gardner, Dale R. "Teapot Dome: Civil Legal Cases that Closed the Scandal." *Journal of the West*, October 1989.

Gaughan, Patrick A. *Measuring Business Interruption Losses and Other Commercial Damages*. Hoboken, NJ: John Wiley & Sons, 2004.

Geis, Gilbert. *On White-Collar Crime*. Lexington, MA: Lexington Books, 1982.

Geis, Gilbert and Robert F. Meier. *White-Collar Crime: Offenses in Business, Politics, and the Professions*, rev. ed. New York: The Free Press, Macmillan, 1977.

Georgiades, George. *Audit Procedures*. New York: Harcourt Brace Professional Publishing, 1995.

Green, Scott. *Manager's Guide to the Sarbanes-Oxley Act: Improving Internal Controls to Prevent Fraud*. Hoboken, NJ: John Wiley & Sons, 2004.

Greene, Craig L. "Audit Those Vendors." *The White Paper*, Vol. 17, No. 3. May/June 2003.

Greene, Craig L. "When Employees Count Too Much." *The White Paper*, Vol. 16, No. 6. November/December 2002.

Hall, Jerome. *Theft, Law and Society*, 2nd ed. Indianapolis: Bobbs-Merrill, 1952.

Hayes, Read. *Retail Security and Loss Prevention*. Stoneham, MA: Butterworth-Heinemann, 1991.

Hetherington, Cynthia, and Michael L. Sankey. *The Manual to Online Public Records*. Tempe, AZ: BRB Publications, Inc., 2008.

Hubbard, Thomas D. and Johnny R. Johnson. *Auditing*, 4th ed. Houston, TX: Dame Publications, Inc., 1991.

Hylas, R.E. and R.H. Ashton. "Audit Detection of Financial Statement Errors", *The Accounting Review*. Vol. LVII, No. 4.

Inbau, Fred E., John E. Reid, and Joseph P. Buckley. *Criminal Interrogation and Confessions*. Baltimore, MD: Williams & Wilkins, 1986.

Ingram, Donna. "Revenue Inflation and Deflation." *The White Paper*, Vol. 16, No. 6. November/December 2002.

Inkeles, Alex. *National Character: A Psycho-Social Perspective*. New Brunswick, NJ: Transaction Publishers, 1997.

Institute of Internal Auditors. *International Professional Practices Framework*. 2009.

Institute of Internal Auditors, the American Institute of Certified Public Accountants, and the Association of Certified Fraud Examiners. *Managing the Business Risk of Fraud: A Practical Guide*. 2008.

Kant, Immanuel. *Lectures on Ethics*. New York: Harper & Row, 1963.

Ketz, J. Edward. *Hidden Financial Risks: Understanding Off-Balance Sheet Accounting*. Hoboken, NJ: John Wiley & Sons, 2003.

Kimmel, Paul D., Jerry J. Weygandt, and Donald E. Kieso. *Financial Accounting: Tools for Business Decision Making*, 3rd ed. New York: John Wiley & Sons, 2004.

Koletar, Joseph W. *Fraud Exposed: What You Don't Know Could Cost Your Company Millions*. Hoboken, NJ: John Wiley & Sons, 2003.

Langsted, Lars B., Peter Garde, and Vagn Greve. *Criminal Law Denmark*, 2nd ed. Copenhagen: DJOF Publishing, 2004.

Lanza, Richard B. *Proactively Detecting Occupational Fraud Using Computer Audit Reports*. Altamonte Springs, FL: IIA Research Foundation, 2003.

Lundelius Jr., Charles R. *Financial Reporting Fraud: A Practical Guide to Detection and Internal Control*. New York: AICPA, 2003.

Mancino, Jane. "The Auditor and Fraud." *Journal of Accountancy*. April 1997.

Marcella, Albert J., William J. Sampias, and James K. Kincaid. *The Hunt for Fraud: Prevention and Detection Techniques*. Altamonte Springs, FL: Institute of Internal Auditors, 1994.

Marshall, David H. and Wayne W. McManus. *Accounting: What the Numbers Mean*, 3rd ed. Chicago: Irwin, 1996.

Mee, Charles L. Jr. *The Ohio Gang: The World of Warren G. Harding*. New York: M. Evans and Company, 1981.

Merriam-Webster's Collegiate Dictionary, 11th ed. Springfield, MA: Merriam-Webster, 2008.

Mill, John Stuart. *Utilitarianism*. Indianapolis, IN: The Bobbs-Merrill Company, Inc., 1957.

Miller, Norman C. *The Great Salad Oil Swindle*. Baltimore, MD: Penguin Books, 1965.

Moritz, Scott. "Don't Get Burned by Smiling CEO Candidates." *The White Paper*, Vol. 16, No. 5. September/October 2002.

Nash, Jay Robert. *Hustlers & Con Men: An Anecdotal History of the Confidence Man and His Games*. New York: Lippincott, 1976.

National Commission on Fraudulent Financial Reporting. *Report of the National Commission on Fraudulent Financial Reporting*. New York: American Institute of Certified Public Accountants, October 1987.

Noonan, John T. Jr. *Bribes*. New York: Macmillan, 1984.

O'Brien, Keith. *Cut Your Losses!* Bellingham, WA: International Self-Press Ltd., 1996.

O'Gara, John D. *Corporate Fraud: Case Studies in Detection and Prevention*. Hoboken, NJ: John Wiley & Sons, 2004.

Patterson, James and Peter Kim. *The Day America Told the Truth*. New York: Prentice Hall Publishing, 1991.

Rabon, Don. *Investigative Discourse Analysis*. Durham, NC: Carolina Academic Press, 1994.

Rakoff, Hon. Jed S., Linda R. Blumkin, and Richard A. Sauber. *Corporate Sentencing Guidelines: Compliance and Mitigation*. New York: Law Journal Press, 2002.

Ramos, Michael J. *How to Comply with Sarbanes–Oxley Section 404: Assessing the Effectiveness of Internal Control*. Hoboken, NJ: John Wiley & Sons, 2004.

Rezaee, Zabiollah. *Financial Statement Fraud: Prevention and Detection*. New York: John Wiley & Sons, 2002.

Robertson, Jack C. *Auditing*, 6th ed. Homewood, IL: BPI Irwin, 1990.

Robertson, Jack C. *Auditing*, 7th ed. Boston: BPI Irwin, 1991.

Robertson, Jack C. *Fraud Examination for Managers and Auditors*. Austin, TX: Association of Certified Fraud Examiners, 1996.

Romney, Marshall B., W. Steve Albrecht, and D. J. Cherrington. "Red-flagging the White-Collar Criminal," *Management Accounting*, March 1980.

Sarnoff, Susan K. *Paying for Crime*. Westport, CT: Praeger, 1996.

Seidler, Lee J., Fredrick Andrews, and Marc J. Epstein. *The Equity Funding Papers: The Anatomy of a Fraud*. New York: John Wiley & Sons, 1997.

Sharp, Kathleen. *In Good Faith*. New York: St. Martin's Press, 1995.

Siegel, Larry J. *Criminology*, 3rd ed. New York: West Publishing Company, 1989.

Siegel, Larry J. Criminology, 4th ed. New York: West Publishing Company, 1992.

Silverstone, Howard and Michael Sheetz. *Forensic Accounting and Fraud Investigation for Non-Experts*. Hoboken, NJ: John Wiley & Sons, 2004.

Snyder, Neil H., O. Whitfield, William J. Kehoe, James T. McIntyre, Jr., and Karen E. Blair. *Reducing Employee Theft: A Guide to Financial and Organizational Controls*. New York: Quorum Books, 1991.

Summerford, Ralph Q. and Robin E. Taylor. "Avoiding Embezzlement Embarrassment (and Worse)." *The White Paper*, Vol. 17, No. 6. November/December 2003.

Sutherland, Edwin H. *White-Collar Crime*. New York: Dryden Press, 1949.

Thomas, William C. "The Rise and Fall of Enron." *Journal of Accountancy*, April 2002.

Thornhill, William T. *Forensic Accounting: How to Investigate Financial Fraud*. Burr Ridge, IL: Irwin Professional Publishing, 1995.

Tyler, Tom R. *Why People Obey the Law*. New Haven, CT: Yale University Press, 1990.

United States Central Intelligence Agency. *The World Factbook*. https://www.cia.gov/library/publications/the-world-factbook/

United States General Accounting Office. *Financial Statement Restatements: Trends, Market Impacts, Regulatory Responses, and Remaining Challenges*. GAO-03-138, 2002. http://www.gao.gov/new.items/03138.pdf

Van Drunen, Guido. "Traveling the World in Style on the Company's Nickel." *The White Paper*, Vol. 16, No. 1. January/February 2002.

Vaughan, Diane. *Controlling Unlawful Organizational Behavior*. Chicago: The University of Chicago Press, 1983.

Watson, Douglas M. "Whom Do You Trust Doing Business and Deterring Fraud in a Global e-Marketplace." *The White Paper*, Vol. 16, No. 2. March/April 2002.

Wells, Joseph T. CFE, CPA (ed.). *Computer Fraud Casebook: The Bytes That Bite*. Hoboken, NJ: John Wiley & Sons, 2009.

———. November 2001. "A Fish Story—Or Not?" *Journal of Accountancy*.

———. January 1993. "Accountancy and White-Collar Crime." *The Annals of the American Academy of Political and Social Science*.

———. July 2001. ". . . And Nothing but the Truth: Uncovering Fraudulent Disclosures." *Journal of Accountancy*.

———. January 2002. ". . . And One for Me." *Journal of Accountancy*.

———. July 2002. "Billing Schemes, Part 1: Shell Companies that Don't Deliver." *Journal of Accountancy*.

———. August 2002. "Billing Schemes, Part 2: Pass-Throughs." *Journal of Accountancy*.

———. September 2002. "Billing Schemes, Part 3: Pay-and-Return Invoicing." *Journal of Accountancy*.

———. October 2002. "Billing Schemes, Part 4: Personal Purchases." *Journal of Accountancy*.

———. August 1996. "Collaring Crime at Work." *Certified Accountant*.

———. June 2002. "Control Cash-Register Thievery." *Journal of Accountancy*.

Wells, Joseph T. CFE, CPA. *Corporate Fraud Handbook*, 2nd ed. Hoboken, NJ: John Wiley & Sons, 2007.

———. April 2003. "Corruption: Causes and Cures." *Journal of Accountancy*.

———. December 2001. "Enemies Within." *Journal of Accountancy*.

Wells, Joseph T., CFE, CPA. "Follow Fraud to the Likely Perp." *Journal of Accountancy*, March 2001.

———. November 2003. "Follow the Greenback Road." *Journal of Accountancy*.

———. August 1992. "Fraud Assessment Questioning." *Internal Auditor*.

Wells, Joseph T. CFE, CPA (Ed.) *Fraud Casebook: Lessons from the Bad Side of Business*. Hoboken, NJ: John Wiley & Sons, 2007.

———. 1992. *Fraud Examination: Investigative and Audit Procedures*. New York: Quorum Books.

———. July 1992. "Getting a Handle on a Hostile Interview." *Security Management*.

———. June 2001. "Ghost Goods: How to Spot Phantom Inventory". *Journal of Accountancy*.

———. August 2001. ". . . Irrational Ratios." *Journal of Accountancy*.

———. December 2002. "Keep Ghosts Off the Payroll." *Journal of Accountancy*.

———. June 2003. "Lambs to Slaughter." *Internal Auditor*.

———. February 2002. "Lapping It Up." *Journal of Accountancy*.

———. May 2002. "Let Them Know Someone's Watching," *Journal of Accountancy*.

———. June 2003. "Money Laundering: Ring Around the Collar." *Journal of Accountancy*.

———. April, 2002. "Occupational Fraud: The Audit as Deterrent." *Journal of Accountancy*.

———. March 2003. "Protect Small Business." *Journal of Accountancy*.

———. December 2003. "Rules for the Written Record." *Journal of Accountancy*.

———. August 2003. "Sherlock Holmes, CPA, Part 1." *Journal of Accountancy*.

———. September 2003. "Sherlock Holmes, CPA, Part 2." *Journal of Accountancy*.

———. February 1990. "Six Common Myths About Fraud." *Journal of Accountancy*.

———. December 16, 2002. "So, You Want to Be a Fraud Examiner." *Accounting Today*.

———. Spring 2003. Vol. 2, No. 1. "Sons of Enron." *MWorld*.

———. November 2002. "Ten Steps Into a Top-Notch Interview." *Journal of Accountancy*.

———. October 1994. "The Billion Dollar Paper Clip." *Internal Auditor*.

———. October 2003. "The Fraud Examiners." *Journal of Accountancy*.

———. February 2003. "The Padding that Hurts." *Journal of Accountancy*.

———. Vol. 17, No. 2. March/April 2003. "The Rewards of Dishonesty." *The White Paper*.

———. May 2003. "The World's Dumbest Fraudsters." *Journal of Accountancy*.

———. May 2001. "Timing Is of the Essence." *Journal of Accountancy*.

———. September 2001. "Why Ask You Ask." *Journal of Accountancy*.

———. February 2001. "Why Employees Commit Fraud." *Journal of Accountancy*.

Wells, Joseph T., CFE, CPA., Tedd A. Avey, BComm, CA, G. Jack Bologna, JD, CFE, BBA, and Robert J. Lindquist, CFE, FCA. *The Accountant's Handbook of Fraud and Commercial Crime*. Toronto: Canadian Institute of Chartered Accountants, 1992.

Welsch, Glenn A., D. Paul Newman, and Charles T. Zlatkovich. *Intermediate Accounting*, 7th ed. Homewood, IL: Irwin, 1986.

Wojcik, Lawrence A. "Sensational Cases and the Mundane—Lessons to be Learned." *The First Annual Conference on Fraud*. The American Institute of Certified Public Accountants, NY 1996.

Zack, Gerard M. *Fraud and Abuse in Nonprofit Organizations: A Guide to Prevention and Detection*. Hoboken, NJ: John Wiley & Sons, 2003.

INDEX